AI and Machine Learning Impacts in Intelligent Supply Chain

Binay Kumar Pandey
Department of Information Technology, College of Technology, GovindBallabh Pant University of Agriculture and Technology, India

Uday Kumar Kanike
Independent Researcher, USA

A. Shaji George
Crown University International, Saudi Arabia & Chartered International Da Vinci University, Nigeria

Digvijay Pandey
Department of Technical Education, India & IET, India

IGI Global
PUBLISHER of TIMELY KNOWLEDGE

A volume in the Advances in Logistics, Operations, and Management Science (ALOMS) Book Series

Published in the United States of America by
IGI Global
Business Science Reference (an imprint of IGI Global)
701 E. Chocolate Avenue
Hershey PA, USA 17033
Tel: 717-533-8845
Fax: 717-533-8661
E-mail: cust@igi-global.com
Web site: http://www.igi-global.com

Library of Congress Cataloging-in-Publication Data

Names: Pandey, Binay, 1983- editor. | Kanike, Uday, 1981- editor. | George, A. Shaji, 1971- editor. | Pandey, Digvijay, editor.
Title: AI and machine learning impacts in intelligent supply chain / edited by Binay Pandey, Uday Kanike, A. Shaji George, Digvijay Pandey.
Description: Hershey, PA : Business Science Reference, [2024] | Includes bibliographical references and index. | Summary: "This book investigates some important areas in which AI and ML are contributing to the solution of problems in supply chain management"-- Provided by publisher.
Identifiers: LCCN 2023043710 (print) | LCCN 2023043711 (ebook) | ISBN 9798369313473 (hardcover) | ISBN 9798369313480 (ebook)
Subjects: LCSH: Business logistics. | Artificial intelligence. | Machine learning.
Classification: LCC HD38.5 .A423 2024 (print) | LCC HD38.5 (ebook) | DDC 658.50285/63--dc23/eng/20240117
LC record available at https://lccn.loc.gov/2023043710
LC ebook record available at https://lccn.loc.gov/2023043711

This book is published in the IGI Global book series Advances in Logistics, Operations, and Management Science (ALOMS) (ISSN: 2327-350X; eISSN: 2327-3518)

British Cataloguing in Publication Data
A Cataloguing in Publication record for this book is available from the British Library.

All work contributed to this book is new, previously-unpublished material. The views expressed in this book are those of the authors, but not necessarily of the publisher.

For electronic access to this publication, please contact: eresources@igi-global.com.

Advances in Logistics, Operations, and Management Science (ALOMS) Book Series

John Wang
Montclair State University, USA

ISSN:2327-350X
EISSN:2327-3518

Mission

Operations research and management science continue to influence business processes, administration, and management information systems, particularly in covering the application methods for decision-making processes. New case studies and applications on management science, operations management, social sciences, and other behavioral sciences have been incorporated into business and organizations real-world objectives.

The **Advances in Logistics, Operations, and Management Science** (ALOMS) Book Series provides a collection of reference publications on the current trends, applications, theories, and practices in the management science field. Providing relevant and current research, this series and its individual publications would be useful for academics, researchers, scholars, and practitioners interested in improving decision making models and business functions.

Coverage

- Production Management
- Decision analysis and decision support
- Risk Management
- Information Management
- Organizational Behavior
- Finance
- Operations Management
- Marketing engineering
- Political Science
- Services management

IGI Global is currently accepting manuscripts for publication within this series. To submit a proposal for a volume in this series, please contact our Acquisition Editors at Acquisitions@igi-global.com or visit: http://www.igi-global.com/publish/.

The Advances in Logistics, Operations, and Management Science (ALOMS) Book Series (ISSN 2327-350X) is published by IGI Global, 701 E. Chocolate Avenue, Hershey, PA 17033-1240, USA, www.igi-global.com. This series is composed of titles available for purchase individually; each title is edited to be contextually exclusive from any other title within the series. For pricing and ordering information please visit http://www.igi-global.com/book-series/advances-logistics-operations-management-science/37170. Postmaster: Send all address changes to above address.

Titles in this Series

For a list of additional titles in this series, please visit: www.igi-global.com/book-series/advances-logistics-operations-management-science/37170

Convergence of Industry 4.0 and Supply Chain Sustainability
Muhammad Rahies Khan (Bahria University Karachi, Pakistan) Naveed R. Khan (UCSI University, Malaysia) and Noor Zaman Jhanjhi (Taylor's University, Malaysia)
Business Science Reference • copyright 2024 • 320pp • H/C (ISBN: 9798369313633) • US $275.00 (our price)

Achieving Secure and Transparent Supply Chains With Blockchain Technology
Mustafa Rehman Khan (UCSI University, Malaysia) Naveed Rehman Khan (UCSI University, Malaysia) and Arsalan Mujahid Ghouri (London South Bank University, UK)
Business Science Reference • copyright 2024 • 345pp • H/C (ISBN: 9798369304822) • US $275.00 (our price)

Strategies and Approaches of Corporate Social Responsibility Toward Multinational Enterprises
Erum Shaikh (Shaheed Benazir Bhutto University, Sanghar Campus, Pakistan)
Business Science Reference • copyright 2024 • 400pp • H/C (ISBN: 9798369303634) • US $275.00 (our price)

Cybersecurity Measures for Logistics Industry Framework
Noor Zaman Jhanjhi (Taylor's University, Malaysia) and Imdad Ali Shah (Taylor's University, Malaysia)
Information Science Reference • copyright 2024 • 310pp • H/C (ISBN: 9781668476253) • US $250.00 (our price)

Drivers of SME Growth and Sustainability in Emerging Markets
Sumesh Dadwal (Northumbrian University, UK) Pawan Kumar (Lovely Professional University, India) Rajesh Verma (Lovely Professional University, India) and Gursimranjit Singh (Dr.B.R Ambedkar National Institute of Technology, Jalandhar)
Business Science Reference • copyright 2024 • 330pp • H/C (ISBN: 9798369301111) • US $250.00 (our price)

Emerging Technologies in Digital Manufacturing and Smart Factories
Ahdi Hassan (Global Institute for Research Education and Scholarship, The Netherlands) Pushan Kumar Dutta (Amity University Kolkata, India) Subir Gupta (Swami Vivekanand University, India) Ebrahim Mattar (College of Engineering, University of Bahrain, Bahrain) and Satya Singh (Sharda University, Uzbekistan)
Business Science Reference • copyright 2024 • 291pp • H/C (ISBN: 9798369309209) • US $275.00 (our price)

Implementing Sustainable Development Goals in the Service Sector
Vipin Nadda (University of Sunderland, UK) Pankaj Kumar Tyagi (Chandigarh University, India) Rubina Moniz Vieira (St. Mary's University, London, UK) and Priyanka Tyagi (Chandigarh University, India)
Business Science Reference • copyright 2024 • 281pp • H/C (ISBN: 9798369320655) • US $275.00 (our price)

IGI Global
PUBLISHER of TIMELY KNOWLEDGE

701 East Chocolate Avenue, Hershey, PA 17033, USA
Tel: 717-533-8845 x100 • Fax: 717-533-8661
E-Mail: cust@igi-global.com • www.igi-global.com

Table of Contents

Detailed Table of Contents

AI and machine learning affect intelligent supply chains, implementation challenges, and psychosocial factors affecting supply chain AI and ML acceptability. Behavioural operations management grows. It structures production and manufacturing processes utilising psychologically based behavioural and cognitive aspects, challenging the idea that "human being is rational" in decision-making. Supply chain management (SCM), a subset of operations management, studies social psychology and supply chains. A related research literature review follows. This report recommends improving supply networks, especially in competitive companies. Supply chain efficiency requires multilevel and employee interaction. Human behaviour impacts supply chain decisions and performance.

The integration of machine learning in legal management and the development of intelligent supply chain governance represents transformative approaches to address the evolving complexities of the legal and supply chain domains. This chapter summarizes the key findings and insights drawn from the outlined sections. The problem statement underscores the growing need for data-driven strategies to navigate the intricate legal landscape and meet the challenges of modern supply chains. With a focus on transparency, accountability, and risk management, the significance of supply chain governance is highlighted, emphasizing its critical role in resilient and efficient supply chain operations. Legal management emerges as a pivotal player in this transformation, tasked with utilizing machine learning to navigate a data-rich and complex legal environment.

In modern Nigerian supply chain management, the adjudication of intellectual property rights has gained paramount importance. With the rapid advancement of technology, the integration of AI-powered analytics has emerged as a promising resolution for settling disputes and safeguarding intellectual property rights. This chapter highlights the multifaceted role of AI-driven analytics in the adjudication process, exploring its impact on improving efficiency, precision, and impartiality in resolving disputes related to intellectual property within the Nigerian supply chain. The authors suggest that comprehensive ethical standards, data privacy regulations, and transparency protocols should be established by the government, stakeholders,

demand forecasting, inventory management, logistics optimisation, and risk management. The research suggests deep learning, neural networks, evolutionary algorithms, and SVMs for supply chain issues. The review highlights SCM AI/ML implementation issues and AI/ML supply chain management pros and drawbacks. Researchers, practitioners, and policymakers may discover how AI and ML improve supply chain efficiency, cost, and networks.

The combination of AI and ML is driving supply chain digitalization. This chapter discusses supply chain management (SCM) in the digital age, including AI, ML, and classical techniques, SCM aspects and components, and supply chain network strategies. The chapter also covers AI and ML applications in supply chain optimisation, resilient supply chain network (SCN) methods, warehouse automation and robotics, transportation and route optimisation, and supply chain risk management. AI and ML enable supply chain stakeholders to use massive data streams for predictive analytics. AI-driven demand forecasting, inventory optimisation, and predictive maintenance reduce hazards and streamline resource allocation, improving cost-effectiveness. In a world of rapid change and innovation, organisations must use AI and ML as the supply chain ecosystem evolves.

The COVID-19 pandemic has highlighted the critical need for supply chain resilience in the face of unforeseen disruptions. This research investigates the application of machine learning (ML) algorithms to enhance supply chain resilience during the COVID-19 crisis. The authors evaluated several ML

respectively. The SHAP analysis method also identifies the characteristics of target variable prediction. The variable "rotatemean_24" is the most significant predictor. The model is easily understandable, aiding in comprehending relationships between features and outcomes. Therefore, it can assist in making decisions regarding predictive maintenance. Research has shown that implementing the optimized Explainable XGBoost Model can enhance factory maintenance efficiency and cost-effectiveness. The model's predictive capabilities enable proactive maintenance by identifying machine faults in advance.

Rakesh Verma, Department of Master of Business Administration, Gniot MBA Institute, India
M. Beulah Viji Christiana, Department of Management Studies, Panimalar Engineering College, India
M. Maheswari, Department of Computational Intelligence, School of Computing, SRM Institute of Science and Technology, India
Vellayan Srinivasan, Department of Master of Business Administration, S.A. Engineering College, India
Pramoda Patro, Department of Mathematics, Koneru Lakshmaiah Education Foundation, India
Sukhvinder Singh Dari, Symbiosis Law School, Symbiosis International University, Pune, India
Sampath Boopathi, Mechanical Engineering, Muthayammal Engineering College, India

This chapter discusses the use of an intelligent physarum solver (IPS) to optimize profit in oligopolistic supply chain networks. The IPS, inspired by the foraging behavior of the physarum polycephalum slime mold, addresses the challenges of resource allocation and profit distribution in oligopolistic markets. The chapter analyzes the IPS framework's effectiveness in modeling and optimizing various aspects of oligopolistic supply chains, including pricing strategies, production allocation, and distribution logistics. This research uses case studies and simulations to demonstrate how IPS can improve decision-making, foster cooperation among oligopolistic firms, and increase profitability in supply chain networks. It uses nature-inspired intelligence to provide practical solutions for businesses in oligopolistic environments, contributing valuable insights to supply chain management.

G. JayaLakshmi, Department of Information Technology, V.R. Siddhartha Engineering College, Kanuru, India
Digvijay Pandey, Department of Technical Education, U. P., India
Binay Kumar Pandey, Department of Information Technology, College of Technology, Govind Ballabh Pant University of Agriculture and Technology, India
Prabjot Kaur, Birla Institute of Technology, Mesra, India
Darshan A. Mahajan, NICMAR University, Pune, India
Sukhvinder Singh Dari, Symbiosis Law School, Symbiosis International University, Pune, India

Supply chain management is essential to a company's success in today's fiercely competitive business environment, regardless of the industry. Businesses are increasingly turning to big data analytics as a useful tool for supply chain improvement to meet the expanding needs of customers, save operational costs, and boost overall efficiency. In order to improve critical areas including demand forecasting, inventory management, logistics optimization, and risk reduction, research has been conducted on the collecting and use of big data in supply chain management. Big data analytics and supply chain management integration can result in more cost-effective operations, better customer service, and increased resilience to disturbances. Organisations that effectively use big data will gain a competitive advantage in the constantly changing supply chain landscape as technology and data capabilities continue to grow.

K. Neelima, School of Engineering, Mohan Babu University, Tirupati, India
B. Madhavi, School of Engineering and Technology, Sri Padmavathi Mahila Viswavidyala, India
C. Padma, Sri Venkateswara College of Engineering, Tirupati, India
Binay Kumar Pandey, Department of Information Technology, College of Technology, Govind Ballabh Pant University of Agriculture and Technology, Pantnagar, India
Gadee Gowwrii, Osmania University, Hyderabad, India
Shyam Sundar Manaktala, Jaipur Engineering College and Research Centre, India

The COVID-19 pandemic has imposed several challenges to mankind, among them one being biometric, for attendance of working community and the related demand and supply chain related to biometric companies, developers, investors and customers. Due to many medical constraints, people are now reluctant to use contact-based biometric systems. With the increase in personal and social hygiene to avoid transmission of pathogens via contact, people try to avoid usage of fingerprint, facial-, and voice-based biometrics. Further, if the system is not active then multiple times of access contacts may be necessary. This aspect has to be restricted for avoidance of future pandemic situations.

Mohd Sadat, Integral University, India
Syed Aqeel Ahmad, Integral University, India
Mehmet Ali Silgu, Bartin University, Turkey

Traffic modelling has gained importance due to the adoption of intelligent transportation systems and software based on traffic models providing a platform to test and improve such systems. Modelling mixed traffic has proved to be a challenging task due to variations in vehicle dimensions and composition along with non-lane-based driving. Most of the simulation software is based on the car following models and lane change models which were originally developed for lane-based traffic. Several attempts have been made to adapt these models for mixed traffic by extending them to include new parameters. This study summarizes lane change models used along with car following for mixed traffic. It can be concluded from past studies that lateral manoeuvre varies with the longitudinal speed in a non-linear manner. Sub-models or specific parameters are needed to model the lateral behaviour of each class of vehicle. Trajectory data analysis and subsequent models have also pointed towards the need for vehicle pair-dependent parameters.

Preface

As editors of this comprehensive reference book, *AI and Machine Learning Impacts in Intelligent Supply Chain*, we are thrilled to present a collection of insights and research contributions that delve into the transformative intersection of artificial intelligence (AI), machine learning (ML), and supply chain management (SCM). The collaborative efforts of Binay Kumar Pandey, Uday Kumar Kanike, A Shaji George, and Digvijay Pandey have resulted in a meticulous exploration of the contemporary landscape where Industry 4.0, digital transformation, and cutting-edge technologies converge to shape the intelligent future of supply chains.

The advent of Industry 4.0 has given rise to smart factories, laying the groundwork for intelligent supply chains that can seamlessly navigate the complexities of modern industrial practices. This book unravels the pivotal role of digitization, digital acceleration, and the symbiotic relationship between humans and technology in steering supply chains towards enhanced efficiency, reduced costs, and elevated service levels.

In the realm of SCM, AI and ML emerge as transformative forces, offering solutions that go beyond conventional paradigms. From optimizing routes to inventory management and performance enhancement, the integration of these technologies presents a paradigm shift that is reshaping the dynamics of supply chain operations. The book not only discusses theoretical frameworks but also provides real-world examples where teams have rapidly adopted cutting-edge approaches to drive tangible improvements in their supply chain processes.

Our target audience encompasses academics, managers, public and private organizations, as well as the general public. The diverse array of topics covered in this book will appeal to a broad spectrum of readers, from those seeking a foundational understanding of the impact of AI and ML in supply chain management to professionals eager to stay abreast of the latest developments in this dynamic field.

Furthermore, this publication serves as a catalyst for future research endeavors, particularly among postgraduate students with interests in accounting and other social sciences. By disseminating findings on the impact of AI and ML applications in supply chain intelligent digital transformation, we aim to inspire a new era of research and exploration.

The chapters in this book cover a wide range of themes, from digital transformation and AI/ML applications in the SCM industry to the effects of automation, supply chain network optimization using particle swarm intelligence (PSO), and emerging fields such as multiagent systems in artificial intelligence. Each chapter presents valuable insights into the evolving landscape of supply chain management in the digital age.

Chapter 1 provides a foundational understanding of digital transformation in supply chain management. It explores the adoption of advanced technologies, automation, and data-driven decision-making to address the limitations of traditional supply chain management. The significance of visionary leaders like Al is highlighted, emphasizing the pivotal role of digital transformation in meeting the evolving demands of the business landscape and modern customers.

Chapter 2 delves into the impact of AI and ML on intelligent supply chains, addressing implementation challenges and psychosocial factors affecting their acceptability. Behavioral operations management is introduced, challenging the assumption of human rationality in decision-making. The chapter explores the interplay between social psychology and supply chains, emphasizing the importance of trust, power dynamics, attribution theory, and social network analysis in shaping efficient supply networks.

Chapter 3 focuses on the integration of machine learning in legal management and its transformative impact on intelligent supply chain governance. It outlines key findings related to data-driven strategies for navigating the intricate legal landscape and meeting the challenges of modern supply chains. Supply chain governance's critical role in ensuring resilience and efficiency is emphasized, with a spotlight on transparency, accountability, and risk management.

Examining the adjudication of intellectual property rights in Nigerian supply chain management, chapter 4 highlights the integration of AI-powered analytics as a promising resolution for settling disputes. It discusses the multifaceted role of AI-driven analytics in improving efficiency, precision, and impartiality in resolving disputes related to intellectual property within the Nigerian supply chain. The authors advocate for ethical standards, data privacy regulations, and transparency protocols.

Chapter 5 provides a Scopus-based study review on the prominence of deep learning in global supply chain management. It explores how AI can revolutionize various company operations, anticipating demand, optimizing logistics, and identifying supply chain bottlenecks. The study identifies AI methodologies, subfields with high AI potential, and applications' impact on performance, shedding light on the role of AI in enhancing supply chain responsiveness, reducing lead times, and lowering costs.

Chapter 6 examines theoretical frameworks, methods, and practical impacts of AI and ML in supply chain management (SCM). It envisions the application of AI/ML in SCM through model optimization, predictive analytics, and decision-making frameworks. The systematic literature reviews critically assess relevant research, providing insights into demand forecasting, inventory management, logistics optimization, and risk management.

Chapter 7 explores the combination of AI and ML driving supply chain digitalization. It covers various aspects of supply chain management in the digital age, including AI, ML, and classical techniques. The chapter addresses AI and ML applications in supply chain optimization, resilient supply chain network methods, warehouse automation, transportation optimization, and supply chain risk management, highlighting their role in utilizing massive data streams for predictive analytics.

Chapter 8 investigates the application of machine learning algorithms to enhance supply chain resilience during the COVID-19 crisis. The evaluation of ML algorithms, including Decision Trees, Random Forests, Naïve Bayes, and LSTM, is discussed. The research utilizes the SPIN COVID-19 RMRIO dataset to develop proactive and data-driven approaches, emphasizing the need for feature selection to mitigate disruptions and improve supply chain performance.

This research critically examines supply chain disruptions during the COVID-19 pandemic, emphasizing the need for durable supply networks. Chapter 9 explores the role of deep learning and machine learning approaches, including decision trees, random forests, k-nearest neighbors, and support vector machines, in mitigating supply chain issues. Notably, the investigation provides insights into the efficiency of different ML models in addressing the challenges confronting contemporary supply networks.

Chapter 10 focuses on the use of predictive maintenance to enhance the Explainable XGBoost Model for predicting failures in industrial components. The research utilizes an adaptive sliding window approach to extract features from multi-device sensor data. The study assesses the BO-XGBoost model's performance using various metrics and emphasizes the model's explainability in aiding decision-making for predictive maintenance, enhancing factory efficiency, and cost-effectiveness.

Chapter 11 explores the use of an Intelligent Physarum Solver (IPS) to optimize profit in oligopolistic supply chain networks. Inspired by the foraging behavior of the Physarum polycephalum slime mold, the IPS framework addresses resource allocation and profit distribution challenges in oligopolistic markets. The chapter showcases case studies and simulations to demonstrate IPS's effectiveness in improving decision-making and profitability in supply chain networks.

Chapter 12 emphasizes the essential role of big data analytics in supply chain improvement. It explores the integration of big data analytics to enhance critical areas such as demand forecasting, inventory management, logistics optimization, and risk reduction. The research underscores the potential for more cost-effective operations, improved customer service, and increased resilience to disturbances through the effective use of big data in supply chain management.

Focusing on the challenges posed by the COVID-19 pandemic, Chapter 13 examines the critical role of biometric attendance systems and their impact on supply chain-related businesses. The study emphasizes the reluctance to use contact-based biometric systems due to hygiene concerns and advocates for the development of durable supply networks, incorporating cutting-edge technology to ensure continuity and adaptation in a changing business environment.

Chapter 14 addresses the importance of traffic modeling in the context of Intelligent Transportation Systems. It summarizes lane change models used in mixed traffic scenarios, acknowledging the challenges posed by variations in vehicle dimensions and non-lane-based driving. The study concludes that lateral maneuvering varies with longitudinal speed, necessitating specific parameters for each class of vehicle and emphasizing the need for vehicle pair-dependent parameters in traffic modeling.

Chapter 15 delves into the integration of AI-driven radiomics in healthcare supply chains. The focus is on leveraging modern technology, data analytics, and artificial intelligence to enable early detection and diagnosis of cancer through intricate details extracted from medical images. The chapter reviews various AI techniques, including Convolutional Neural Networks, Transfer Learning, Ensemble Models, Radiomics Features, and Machine Learning, showcasing their applications and contributions to improving survival rates and treatment outcomes.

Chapter 16 presents a prototype system for automatically inspecting the surface of precision ground metallic surfaces, with a specific focus on bearing rolls. It explores optical experiments to understand how light interacts with surfaces, aiming to make surface damage easily detectable. The text delves into methods for choosing values to separate different parts of an image and explores various search methods available for organizing or categorizing traits.

We express our gratitude to all the contributors for their invaluable contributions, and we sincerely hope that this compilation fosters a deeper understanding of the transformative potential that AI and ML bring to intelligent supply chain management.

Binay Kumar Pandey
Department of Information Technology, College of Technology, Govind Ballabh Pant University of Agriculture and Technology, India

Uday Kumar Kanike
Independent Researcher, USA

A. Shaji George
Crown University International, Saudi Arabia & Chartered International Da Vinci University, Nigeria

Digvijay Pandey
Department of Technical Education, India & IET, India

Chapter 1
The Digital Transformation of Supply Chain Management AI's Pioneering Role

Kapil Bansal
https://orcid.org/0000-0002-3354-3795
Institute of legal studies and Research, GLA University, Mathura, India

Shouvik Sanyal
Dhofar University, Oman

K. Anusha
Koneru Lakshmaiah Education Foundation, India

Ankush Sharma
Jagran Lakecity Business School, Jagran Lakecity University, Bhopal, India

Nilanjan Mazumdar
https://orcid.org/0000-0002-9449-1298
Department of Business Administration, University of Science and Technology, India

Anilkumar Suthar
New LJ Institute of Engineering and Technology, Ahmedabad, India

ABSTRACT

Digital transformation in supply chain management is a critical response to the evolving business landscape and the demands of modern customers. This transformation involves the adoption of advanced technologies, automation, and data-driven decision-making to streamline and enhance supply chain operations. This exploration outlines the definition of digital transformation in supply chain management, its pivotal importance in today's business landscape, and the pioneering role played by visionary leaders such as AI. The limitations of traditional supply chain management underscore the necessity of this shift. Manual processes, limited visibility, and inventory management issues highlighted the need for digital transformation.

DOI: 10.4018/979-8-3693-1347-3.ch001

1. INTRODUCTION

In the contemporary landscape of business and technology, the paradigm of industry has experienced a profound shift, marked by the transformative power of innovation and digitalization. At the forefront of this monumental change stands Al, an industry visionary whose pioneering role has been instrumental in reshaping the way businesses manage their operations, enhance efficiency, and respond to dynamic market demands. Al's remarkable journey into the realm of digital transformation has transcended traditional industry boundaries, and his contributions have reverberated across sectors. With a visionary approach, Al (Boopathi, S. et al., 2023) has harnessed the potential of advanced technologies to revolutionize processes and create a roadmap for others to follow, thereby redefining the very essence of business management. The role in digital transformation is not limited to any one sector or industry; rather, it encompasses a diverse range of fields. Whether in manufacturing, logistics, retail, healthcare, or any other domain, Al's innovative strategies and unwavering commitment to embracing cutting-edge technology have consistently set new industry standards. His story is one of adaptability, foresight, and a relentless pursuit of excellence in the face of ever-evolving challenges. This commitment has driven investments in state-of-the-art infrastructure (Kirubasri, G. et. al., 2022) and the adoption of cutting-edge solutions (Preindl et al., 2020). Al recognized early on that in the digital age, the ability to gather, analyze, and act upon real-time data is a game-changer. Consequently, he has spearheaded initiatives to implement advanced data analytics, Internet of Things (IoT) devices, and artificial intelligence (AI) (Pandey, D. et al., 2021) systems to revolutionize supply chain operations, reduce costs, and improve overall efficiency. One of the primary benefits of Al's pioneering efforts is the enhanced visibility and real-time tracking that these digital solutions provide. By integrating IoT devices (Pramanik, S. et al., 2023) and AI-powered analytics into the supply chain, company can monitor the movement of goods, identify potential issues, and optimize routes in real time. This level of visibility not only enhances operational efficiency but also results in cost savings, reduced inventory levels, and, most importantly, improved customer satisfaction (Saxena, A. et al., 2021). A critical component of supply chain management. Traditional forecasting methods often struggled to adapt to rapid changes in market conditions. However, AI (Singh, H. et al., 2022) -driven predictive analytics have enabled company to anticipate shifts in customer demand with unprecedented accuracy. This not only reduces the risk of overstocking or understocking products but also ensures that customers receive the right products at the right time. While journey has been marked by remarkable successes, it has not been without its share of challenges. Resistance to change within the organization, concerns about data security and privacy, and the complexity of integrating digital systems with existing legacy infrastructure are just a few of the hurdles that Al and his team have had to navigate. Nevertheless, their perseverance and commitment to innovation have been key to overcoming these obstacles (Machado et al. 2020).

1.1 Digital Transformation in Business Landscape

Digital transformation in the context of supply chain management refers to the strategic integration of advanced technologies, data-driven processes (Pandey, D. et al., 2022), and digital tools to optimize, streamline, and enhance various facets of the end-to-end supply chain. This encompasses the digitization of procurement, production, inventory management, logistics, distribution, and customer service functions. It is about leveraging digital solutions to create a more efficient, responsive, and interconnected supply chain ecosystem, ultimately enabling organizations to adapt swiftly to market changes, reduce operational costs, and meet evolving customer demands. Digital transformation redefines the way businesses manage their supply chains, introducing automation, connectivity, and real-time data analysis (Bessant, Y. A. et al., 2023). This overhaul results in a significant boost to operational efficiency. By automating previously manual and time-consuming tasks, organizations reduce the risk of errors and delays. For instance, manual data entry errors, which were common in traditional supply chain processes, can be virtually eliminated with digital systems. The efficiency gains achieved through digital transformation have a direct impact on a company's ability to meet customer demand promptly and respond swiftly to market changes. In the age of e-commerce and high customer expectations, a seamless and satisfying customer experience is paramount. Digital transformation in the supply chain is a key driver of enhancing the customer journey. Real-time data (Pandey, B. K. et al., 2023) and visibility into the supply chain allow organizations to provide accurate and up-to-the-minute information on order status and delivery times. This transparency not only builds trust but also enables customers to plan more effectively. Shorter delivery times and the ability to track orders in real-time are major components of an improved customer experience. Businesses can optimize their logistics operations, reduce transportation lead times, and make adjustments on the fly in response to unforeseen disruptions, all of which contribute to customer satisfaction. In a competitive marketplace, satisfied customers are more likely to remain loyal and become brand advocates, positively impacting a company's bottom line. A critical aspect of digital transformation is its potential to drive cost reduction across the supply chain. By automating and optimizing processes, organizations can significantly lower their operational expenses. One of the most prominent cost-saving benefits is the reduction of excess inventory. Advanced demand forecasting and inventory management systems help organizations maintain optimal inventory levels, minimizing the capital tied up in excess stock. Transportation costs also see substantial reductions through digital transformation. Enhanced route optimization, real-time tracking, and the ability to consolidate shipments lead to more cost-effective transportation operations. Additionally, by minimizing human error and the need for manual intervention, organizations avoid costly mistakes that can impact the bottom line. Perhaps one of the most transformative aspects of digital transformation is the access to vast amounts of data and the ability to derive actionable insights from it. Data-driven decision-making is a cornerstone of supply chain management in the digital age. With real-time data and analytics at their disposal, organizations can make informed decisions that improve overall supply chain performance. Predictive analytics, powered by digital tools, allow organizations to forecast demand with unprecedented accuracy (Lopes de Sousa Jabbour et al. 2018). This not only ensures that products are available when and where they are needed but also helps in avoiding overstocking or understocking, which can be costly. Data analytics (Pandey, B. K. et al., 2022) can also identify patterns and trends in the supply chain, enabling organizations to proactively address issues and make continuous improvements.

1.2 AI's Pioneering Role in This Transformation

AI's pioneering role in the digital transformation of supply chain management has been nothing short of revolutionary. As a visionary leader with a deep understanding of the potential of advanced technologies, it has played a central role in driving this transformative shift. Through his innovative initiatives and strategic investments, AI (Anand, R. et al., 2023) has set a precedent for businesses across industries. His unwavering commitment to embracing digital solutions has not only redefined industry standards but has also inspired others to follow suit. His leadership in adopting state-of-the-art technology, such as IoT (Pandey, J. K. et al., 2022) devices and artificial intelligence (Meslie, Y. et al., 2021), has led to significant improvements in operational efficiency, cost reduction, and enhanced customer experiences. These outcomes have highlighted Al's pioneering role as a driving force behind the transformation of supply chain management. The journey is marked by a commitment to harnessing the power of digital tools, ultimately reshaping how organizations manage their supply chains. By championing data-driven decision-making, real-time visibility, and predictive analytics, he has set a new standard for supply chain excellence (B. Muniandi et al.,2019) . In an ever-evolving business landscape, Al's pioneering role stands as a testament to the transformative potential of digitalization. His vision and leadership have not only propelled his own organization to new heights but have also contributed to the broader advancement of supply chain management practices in the digital age (Müller & Voigt, et al. 2018).

1.3 Benefits of Digital Transformation in SCM

Digital transformation in supply chain management offers a wide range of benefits, revolutionizing how organizations operate and interact with their customers and partners. These benefits encompass enhanced efficiency, cost savings, real-time visibility, and improved customer satisfaction

1. *Efficiency Boost*: Digital transformation optimizes supply chain processes by automating and streamlining tasks that were traditionally performed manually. This includes order processing, inventory management, and production scheduling. Automation reduces lead times and minimizes the risk of human errors, resulting in a more efficient and agile supply chain.
2. *Cost Savings*: Through digital transformation, organizations can significantly reduce operational costs. Automation not only eliminates manual labor but also optimizes processes to minimize resource consumption. For instance, it can optimize transportation routes, reduce energy usage in production, and identify and eliminate bottlenecks in the supply chain, leading to substantial cost savings.
3. *Real-Time Visibility*: Digital transformation provides real-time visibility into the entire supply chain. With the help of data and analytics tools, stakeholders can monitor the movement of goods, track inventory levels, and respond promptly to any disruptions or changes in demand. This enhanced visibility enables proactive decision-making, reducing the risk of delays and ensuring that operations run smoothly.
4. *Customer Satisfaction*: The improved efficiency and real-time visibility brought about by digital transformation have a direct impact on customer satisfaction. Customers benefit from quicker order processing and accurate delivery estimates, leading to improved overall experiences. Real-time tracking allows customers to monitor the status of their orders, providing them with the transparency they desire.
5. *Enhanced Forecasting*: Advanced analytics and data-driven insights play a crucial role in enhancing demand forecasting. With access to historical and real-time data, organizations can more accurately predict customer demand and optimize their inventory levels accordingly. This results in fewer instances of stockouts or overstocking, ensuring that products are available when customers need them, ultimately leading to happier customers.

The benefits of digital transformation in supply chain management are shown in the figure 1 which, include enhanced operational efficiency, significant cost savings, real-time visibility, improved customer

Figure 1. Benefits of digital transformation in SCM

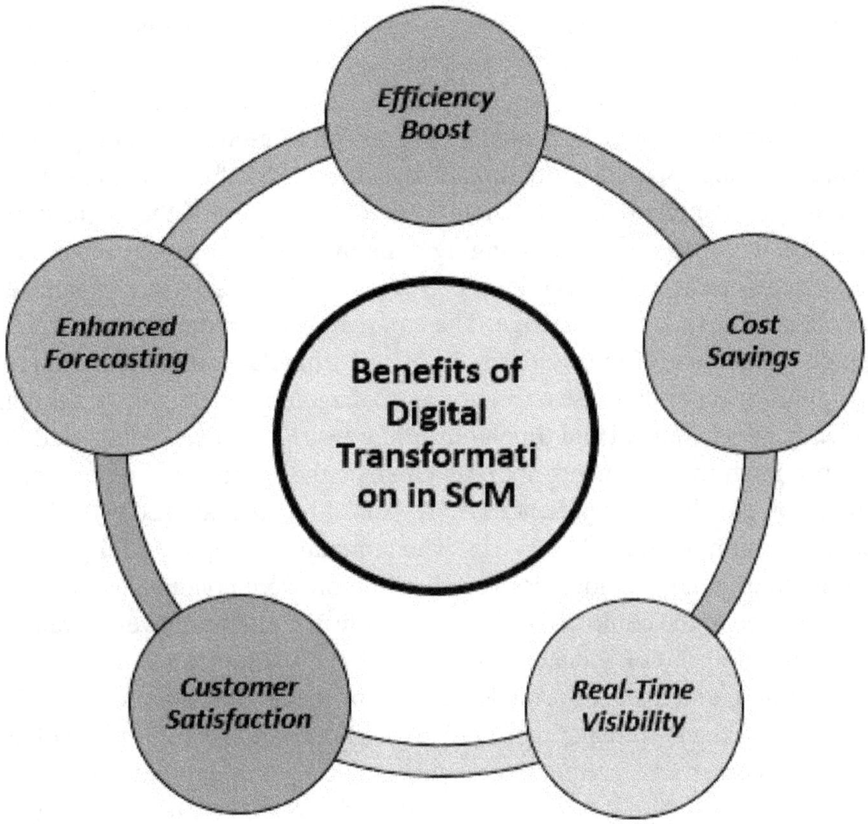

satisfaction, and more accurate demand forecasting. These advantages collectively provide organizations with a competitive edge in today's fast-paced and customer-centric business landscape.

2. Al's COMPANY AND SUPPLY CHAIN

2.1 Al's Company and Its Industry

Al's company is situated within a dynamic and competitive industry, one that demands continuous adaptation and innovation to remain relevant and competitive. The company is a prominent player in the world of logistics and distribution, offering a range of comprehensive solutions tailored to meet the diverse and evolving needs of its clients. Operating within the heart of the logistics and distribution industry, Al's company plays a pivotal role in facilitating the movement of goods and services across various sectors of the economy (Manavalan & Jayakrishna, et al. 2019). From manufacturing to retail, healthcare to consumer goods, the company's extensive network and expertise are strategically deployed to ensure the efficient, timely, and cost-effective transfer of products to their intended destinations. Al's company has earned a reputation for its commitment to excellence within the logistics and distribution industry, making it the preferred choice for businesses seeking agile and dependable solutions in today's fast-paced and interconnected market. However, what sets Al's company apart is not merely its presence within the industry, but its visionary approach to leveraging the power of digital transformation. The company recognizes that the evolving landscape of business and technology demands more than traditional logistics and distribution methods. In a world where speed, accuracy, and efficiency are paramount, Al's company has embraced digitalization and cutting-edge technology to stay ahead of the curve. This forward-thinking approach is not limited to mere adoption but encompasses a proactive stance towards innovation. Al's company has consistently invested in state-of-the-art technologies, systems, and strategies that allow it to adapt to the changing dynamics of the logistics and distribution industry. In doing so, the company ensures that its clients can depend on it as a partner capable of navigating the challenges and opportunities of the digital age. The company's commitment to digital transformation is rooted in a deep understanding of the significance of real-time data and automation (Pandey, B. K. et al., 2021). The digitalization of processes, from order management to delivery tracking, has resulted in significant efficiency gains. Manual and time-consuming tasks have been automated, reducing the risk of errors and delays. Such improvements not only enhance the company's internal operations but also have a direct impact on the client's experience (A. Y. A. B. Ahmad,et al., (2019)). They can now expect faster, more accurate, and more reliable services. The company's adoption of digital tools and systems has transformed the traditional way logistics and distribution were conducted. Real-time data analysis has become a cornerstone of the company's operations, offering clients a level of transparency and control that was previously unheard of. Clients can now track their shipments in real-time, obtain accurate updates on delivery times, and make informed decisions based on the data provided. This transparency builds trust and enables clients to make more effective plans, which, in turn, positively impacts their own operations and customer satisfaction. Excess inventory, a perennial issue in traditional logistics, is significantly reduced through digital transformation (Ghadge et al. 2020). By embracing advanced demand forecasting and inventory management systems, the company maintains optimal inventory levels, freeing up capital and reducing holding costs. Transportation costs, another critical aspect of logistics, have also seen substantial reductions. Digital transformation enables route optimization, real-time tracking, and the ability to consolidate shipments, leading to cost-effective transportation operations. The minimization of human error, another byproduct of digitalization, further contributes to cost savings by avoiding costly mistakes. The power of real-time data and analytics to make informed decisions that have a direct impact on supply chain performance. Predictive analytics have become a valuable tool in forecasting demand with unprecedented accuracy. This ensures that products are available when and where they are needed, avoiding the risks of overstocking or understocking. Data analytics also allow for the identification of patterns and trends in the supply chain, enabling proactive issue resolution and continuous improvements in logistics and distribution operations.

2.2 Al's SCM Before Digital Transformation

Before embarking on the journey of digital transformation, Al's supply chain management was entrenched in traditional, manual processes. Many critical tasks, such as order management, inventory tracking, and production planning, heavily relied on human intervention, chapterwork, and spreadsheets. This manual approach not only consumed a significant amount of time and resources but also introduced a notable risk of errors and inefficiencies in supply chain operations. This old-fashioned method often struggled to keep up with the fast-paced demands of the market and customer expectations. One of the prominent limitations of Al's supply chain management was the lack of real-time visibility and connectivity. Information flow (Pandey, B. K. et al., 2022) within the supply chain was fragmented and siloed, making it challenging to obtain immediate insights into the status of orders, inventory levels, or the location of products in transit. This limitation hindered the ability to respond quickly to shifting customer demands or unforeseen disruptions, potentially resulting in operational bottlenecks and customer dissatisfaction (Scuotto et al. 2017).

The reliance on chapter-based documentation was another characteristic of Al's pre-digital supply chain. Purchase orders, invoices, shipping records, and other critical documents were predominantly chapter-based. This not only led to the consumption of significant resources in terms of chapter and storage but also made the retrieval and sharing of information a cumbersome process. This chapter-intensive approach introduced inefficiencies and posed a risk of errors in managing the various documents required for supply chain operations (A. Y. A. B. Ahmad, et al., 2023). Inflexibility and resistance to change were notable aspects of the supply chain processes in place before digital transformation. Adapting to new market conditions, changing customer demands, or altering production schedules required significant lead time and resources. The lack of agility hindered the company's ability to respond quickly to market dynamics, making it challenging to capitalize on new opportunities or mitigate emerging risks. Data-driven decision-making was limited in the pre-digital era of Al's supply chain management. Without access to real-time data and analytical tools, decisions were often based on historical data or intuition rather than on current market trends and customer preferences. This approach made it difficult to predict demand accurately, resulting in either overstocking or understocking of products. The absence of data-driven insights constrained the company's ability to make informed and agile decisions in a rapidly changing market. Collaboration among different stakeholders within the supply chain, including suppliers, manufacturers, and distributors, was limited in the pre-digital era. Communication relied on traditional methods such as phone calls, emails, or physical meetings, which could be time-consuming and inefficient (Queiroz & Wamba, et al. 2019). The lack of seamless collaboration introduced challenges in coordinating efforts and sharing information across the supply chain network, potentially causing delays and disruptions in the flow of goods and services. The pre-digital supply chain management was also susceptible to a higher risk of errors and delays. The manual nature of the processes, coupled with the lack of real-time data and automation, left room for mistakes at various stages of the supply chain, from order entry to shipping and delivery. These errors could result in increased operational costs, customer dissatisfaction, and lost business opportunities. Inventory management was yet another complex and challenging aspect of Al's supply chain before digital transformation. Without real-time insights into inventory levels and demand fluctuations, the company struggled to strike the right balance between carrying enough stock to meet demand and avoiding excess inventory costs. This lack of visibility into inventory data impacted the company's ability to manage working capital efficiently and optimize inventory turnover rates.

2.3 Limitations of the Traditional Supply Chain

The traditional supply chain management approach, before the advent of digital transformation, was beset by several challenges and limitations that hindered its ability to meet the demands of the modern business landscape. These challenges included:

1. *Limited Visibility*: Traditional supply chains often suffered from a lack of real-time visibility across the entire supply network. This limited transparency made it difficult to monitor the movement of

goods, track inventory levels, and respond promptly to disruptions. As a result, companies faced challenges in optimizing their operations and mitigating the impact of unforeseen events.

2. *Manual Processes*: Many supply chain operations relied on manual and chapter-based processes. This approach was labor-intensive and prone to errors. Tasks such as order processing, data entry, and document management were time-consuming, leading to inefficiencies and increased operational costs. Moreover, manual processes hindered the ability to adapt to rapidly changing market conditions.
3. *Inflexibility*: Traditional supply chains were often characterized by rigidity, making it challenging to adapt to changing market dynamics or respond quickly to shifts in customer demands. The lack of agility meant that companies might miss opportunities or incur increased costs due to their inability to adjust promptly.
4. *Communication Gaps*: Collaboration and communication between different stakeholders in the supply chain, including suppliers, manufacturers, distributors, and retailers, were often fragmented. The lack of efficient communication methods led to miscommunications, delays, and misunderstandings. This hindered the smooth flow of goods and services.
5. *Sustainability Challenges*: Traditional supply chain management often struggled to address sustainability and environmental concerns effectively. It was challenging to optimize transportation and logistics routes to minimize environmental impact. Additionally, the lack of real-time data and visibility made it difficult to track and reduce waste, hindering efforts to improve sustainability practices within the supply chain.

These limitations highlighted in the figure 2, need for a fundamental shift in supply chain management. The advent of digital transformation and the adoption of advanced technologies have since provided

Figure 2. Limitations of the traditional supply chain

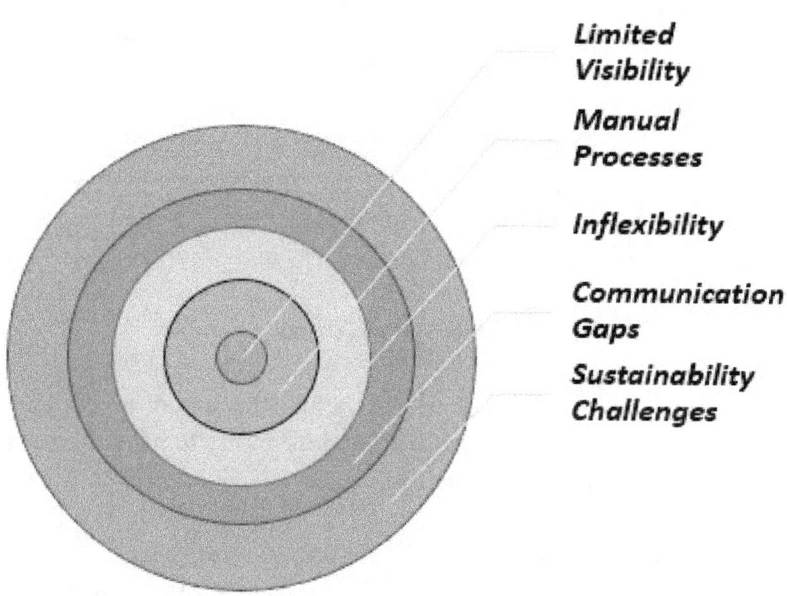

solutions to these longstanding issues, enabling organizations to operate more efficiently, respond to market changes with agility, and enhance customer satisfaction.

3. Al's INITIATIVES IN DIGITAL TRANSFORMATION

3.1 The Decision to Embrace Digital Transformation

The decision to embark on the journey of digital transformation was a pivotal moment in Al's company's history. This strategic choice was driven by a recognition of the pressing need to adapt to the evolving business landscape and capitalize on the opportunities presented by cutting-edge technologies. One of the key drivers behind this decision was the understanding that traditional processes and methodologies were becoming increasingly obsolete and insufficient to meet the demands of the modern business world. The manual and chapter-based processes that characterized the existing workflow were not only time-consuming but also prone to errors and inefficiencies (Ketchen et al. 2014). The ever-increasing customer expectations and the rapid growth of e-commerce and online marketplaces necessitated a more responsive and agile approach to business. Al's company recognized that digital transformation was not merely an option but a strategic imperative to stay competitive and meet the evolving needs of its customers (M. K. Daoud,et al.,2023). This decision was motivated by a commitment to delivering better services, enhancing customer experiences, and remaining relevant in an increasingly digital and interconnected market. The decision also took into account the potential for significant cost savings and efficiency gains through digital transformation. By automating manual processes, optimizing routes, and improving inventory management, the company anticipated a reduction in operational costs. This would not only improve its bottom line but also allow for more competitive pricing and value delivery to customers. Embracing digital transformation was seen as a means to differentiate the company from its competitors. It was not merely about keeping up with industry trends but about setting new standards and becoming a trailblazer in the field. The decision was also supported by the recognition that real-time data and advanced analytics could be harnessed to drive better decision-making. The company sought to make informed, data-driven choices, as opposed to relying on historical data and intuition. The potential for predictive analytics to anticipate demand fluctuations and optimize inventory levels was a compelling factor in this decision. His visionary approach and deep understanding of technology's potential made a compelling case for the transformation. Under his leadership, the company embarked on this journey with a clear vision and unwavering commitment to realizing the benefits of digitalization (Ghadge et al. 2022).

3.2 Investment in Technology and Infrastructure

The decision to embrace digital transformation in Al's company involved a significant investment in technology and infrastructure. This strategic move was crucial to enable the company to transition from traditional, manual processes to a modern, data-driven, and technologically advanced supply chain management system.

1. *Technology Integration*: The cornerstone of the investment was the integration of advanced technologies into the company's supply chain operations. This encompassed the adoption of a wide range of digital tools and systems, including but not limited to Internet of Things (IoT) devices

(Iyyanar, P. et al., 2023), cloud-based software, data analytics platforms, and real-time monitoring solutions. These technologies provided the company with the capabilities to collect, process, and analyze data in real time, resulting in enhanced visibility and informed decision-making.

2. *Automation*: Investment in technology included the automation of various supply chain processes. Manual and repetitive tasks, such as data entry, order processing, and inventory tracking, were automated to improve efficiency, reduce the risk of errors, and free up valuable human resources for more strategic roles. Automation enhanced the speed and accuracy of these processes, ultimately leading to improved operational performance.
3. *Data Management*: The company invested in data management infrastructure to handle the vast amounts of data generated by the newly integrated technologies. This included the implementation of robust databases and data warehouses to store, organize, and secure data. The ability to manage and analyze data effectively was crucial for data-driven decision-making and real-time insights.
4. *IoT Devices*: A significant portion of the technology investment went into the deployment of IoT devices (Kumar Pandey, B. et al., 2021) throughout the supply chain. These devices were strategically placed to track the location and condition of goods in transit, monitor equipment performance, and gather data on various supply chain parameters. The data generated by IoT devices provided real-time information critical for enhancing operational efficiency and optimizing routes.
5. *Cloud Infrastructure*: Cloud-based infrastructure played a pivotal role in enabling data accessibility and sharing across the organization. Cloud platforms facilitated real-time data exchange and collaboration among stakeholders in the supply chain. This investment in cloud technology allowed for seamless communication and data sharing between the company, suppliers, manufacturers, and distributors.
6. *Scalability and Flexibility*: The technology and infrastructure investments were designed with scalability and flexibility in mind. The company ensured that its digital systems and infrastructure could adapt to changing demands and growth in the future. This future-proofing approach allowed the company to stay agile and responsive to evolving market dynamics.

It paved the way for the digital transformation of the supply chain, enabling real-time data collection and analysis, automation of processes, enhanced security, and improved operational efficiency. This investment was not only about embracing technology but also about ensuring the company's readiness for the digital age and its ability to meet the demands of the ever-evolving business landscape.

3.3 Introduction of Digital Tools and Systems

Introduction of Digital Tools and Systems in the supply chain is a transformative leap that has revolutionized how businesses manage their operations in the modern era. The rapid evolution of technology and the growing reliance on digitalization have brought forth an array of innovative solutions that are reshaping the landscape of supply chain management. In this era of Digital Tools and Systems, traditional supply chain methodologies are being replaced by advanced technologies that encompass a wide spectrum of applications. These digital tools and systems leverage the power of data, automation, and real-time connectivity to optimize, streamline, and enhance various facets of the supply chain (Bhandari et al. 2014). They have become the driving force behind improved efficiency, enhanced customer experiences, cost reduction, and data-driven decision-making. This transformation is not just a trend but a strategic imperative for businesses seeking to remain competitive and adaptable in an increasingly interconnected and fast-paced marketplace (Khan, Yasser, et al., 2023). Digital tools and systems have become integral components in ensuring that companies can meet the evolving demands of their customers while managing operational complexities efficiently. In this exploration of Digital Tools and Systems, we will delve into the transformative impact they have had on supply chain management, as well as the various facets and benefits they bring to organizations. We will also discuss the critical role of visionary leaders like Al, who have championed the adoption of these technologies, paving the way for an era of data-driven and agile supply chain management.

3.4 Training and Skill Development for Employees

Training and skill development for employees are essential components of any organization's strategy to adapt to a rapidly evolving business landscape and leverage digital tools and systems effectively within the supply chain (Perussi et al. (2019). In the context of digital transformation, investing in the knowledge and capabilities of the workforce is paramount to ensure that employees can harness the full potential of the new technologies and contribute to the success of the company.

1. *Digital Literacy Training*: Digital literacy forms the foundation of employee training in a digitally transformed supply chain. This training encompasses a wide range of skills, from basic computer literacy to proficiency in using digital tools and software. Employees learn to navigate user interfaces, use common software applications, and effectively engage with digital platforms. This training is essential for ensuring that employees can comfortably and competently interact with the various digital tools integrated into supply chain processes.
2. *Specialized Training Programs*: To fully exploit the capabilities of digital tools and systems, organizations offer specialized training programs tailored to the specific needs of their supply chain operations. These programs delve deep (Pandey, D., & Pandey, B. K., 2022) into the intricacies of the tools and systems being implemented. Employees are provided with in-depth knowledge and hands-on experience, enabling them to use these technologies to their maximum potential. For example, employees might receive training on a new inventory management system, logistics software, or predictive analytics tools.
3. *Data Analysis and Interpretation*: With the wealth of data generated by digital tools, employee training includes data analysis and interpretation. Employees are trained to extract valuable insights from the data collected during supply chain operations. This training covers data analytics techniques, statistical analysis methods, and data visualization skills. By understanding how to interpret data effectively, employees can make informed decisions that optimize supply chain performance, predict demand patterns, and identify opportunities for improvement.
4. *Cybersecurity Training*: In the digital era, cybersecurity is a top priority. Organizations invest in training to raise employee awareness of cybersecurity risks and best practices. Employees are educated on identifying potential security threats, understanding data protection policies, and safeguarding sensitive information. Cybersecurity training is essential to prevent data breaches, protect the organization's reputation, and ensure the secure operation of digital tools and systems within the supply chain.
5. *Adaptability and Change Management*: Training programs emphasize adaptability and change management skills. In a digital environment, where technologies and processes continually evolve, employees need to be prepared for ongoing changes. Training in this area helps employees adapt to

new tools, procedures, and workflows. It instills a mindset of flexibility and open-mindedness that is essential for embracing change and continuously improving supply chain operations. Employees learn how to manage and lead change within their teams, ensuring a smooth transition when new technologies are introduced (Treiblmaier, et al. 2018).

3.5 Strategic Partnerships and Collaborations

Strategic partnerships and collaborations have emerged as critical strategies in the digital transformation of supply chain management. In today's rapidly evolving business landscape, organizations increasingly recognize the value of forming alliances to enhance their competitiveness and meet the complex demands of the modern consumer. These collaborations have broad-reaching implications for how supply chain's function and adapt to the challenges of the digital age. One fundamental aspect of these partnerships is ecosystem expansion. The digital transformation has given rise to intricate supply chain ecosystems where organizations are interconnected with a variety of stakeholders, including suppliers, manufacturers, logistics providers, and technology vendors. Strategic partnerships and collaborations allow businesses to broaden their ecosystems, enabling them to access a more extensive network of expertise and resources. This expansion of the ecosystem enhances the overall efficiency and responsiveness of supply chain operations by creating interconnected webs of support and cooperation. Collaborations are driven by the concept of complementary capabilities. Organizations recognize that they can achieve more when they work together. For example, a manufacturer may collaborate with a logistics provider to offer integrated supply chain solutions. The manufacturer's expertise in production and the logistics provider's proficiency in transportation and distribution combine to create a seamless end-to-end supply chain service (Shao et al. 2021) . By combining their strengths, partners can address customer needs more comprehensively and provide holistic solutions. Technology integration is another crucial aspect of supply chain collaborations. Many digital transformation initiatives involve adopting advanced technologies and systems to enhance efficiency and data-driven decision-making. Strategic partnerships allow organizations to integrate these technologies seamlessly. For example, a retailer may collaborate with a technology vendor to implement an advanced inventory management system. Such partnerships facilitate the smooth adoption of technology, ensuring that it aligns with the existing infrastructure and meets specific supply chain requirements. The digital age introduces new risks, such as cybersecurity threats and supply chain disruptions. Collaborations provide strategies to mitigate these risks. Organizations may partner with cybersecurity firms to enhance their defenses against data breaches and cyberattacks. Furthermore, they can collaborate with contingency logistics providers to ensure continuity in the event of supply chain disruptions, safeguarding against unforeseen events that could disrupt operations. By partnering with various stakeholders, organizations open the door to new ideas, technologies, and best practices. These collaborations allow companies to stay at the forefront of emerging technologies and innovative supply chain management techniques. Collaborating with technology startups, research institutions, or industry peers can lead to groundbreaking innovations in supply chain management, ultimately enhancing operational efficiency, customer experiences, and maintaining a competitive edge in the rapidly evolving digital business landscape (Fatorachian and Kazemi et al.2021).

4. CONCLUSION

The journey of digital transformation in supply chain management is an essential and transformative process in today's business landscape. As defined, it encompasses the adoption of advanced technologies, automation, and data-driven decision-making to streamline operations and meet customer demands efficiently. Al's pioneering role in this transformation, as highlighted in this exploration, exemplifies the visionary leadership required to successfully implement these changes.

Before undergoing digital transformation, Al's company faced challenges and limitations associated with traditional supply chain management, which included inefficiencies, manual processes, and a lack of real-time visibility. Recognizing the need for change, Al and his team made the strategic decision to embrace digital transformation. This decision involved significant investment in technology and infrastructure, the introduction of digital tools and systems, employee training, and strategic partnerships. These initiatives were aimed at enhancing efficiency, reducing costs, providing real-time visibility, and ultimately improving customer satisfaction. The benefits of digital transformation in supply chain management are far-reaching. They encompass streamlined processes, cost savings, real-time visibility, enhanced customer satisfaction, and improved demand forecasting. These benefits collectively empower organizations to adapt to the fast-paced business landscape and meet the ever-evolving demands of their customers effectively.

REFERENCES

Ahmad, A. Y. A. B. (2019). Empirical Analysis on Accounting Information System Usage in Banking Sector in Jordan. *Academy of Accounting and Financial Studies Journal*, *23*(5), 1–9.

Ahmad, A. Y. A. B., Gongada, T. N., Shrivastava, G., Gabbi, R. S., Islam, S., & Nagaraju, K. (2023). E-Commerce Trend Analysis and Management for Industry 5.0 using User Data Analysis. *International Journal of Intelligent Systems and Applications in Engineering*, *11*(11s), 135–150.

Ahmad, A. Y. A. B., & Kumari, S. S. (2023). Blockchain Implementation in Financial Sector and Cyber Security System. *2023 International Conference on Artificial Intelligence and Smart Communication (AISC)*, 586-590. 10.1109/AISC56616.2023.10085045

Anand, R., Lakshmi, S. V., Pandey, D., & Pandey, B. K. (2023). An enhanced ResNet-50 deep learning model for arrhythmia detection using electrocardiogram biomedical indicators. *Evolving Systems*, 1–15. doi:10.1007/s12530-023-09559-0

Bessant, Y. A., Jency, J. G., Sagayam, K. M., Jone, A. A. A., Pandey, D., & Pandey, B. K. (2023). Improved parallel matrix multiplication using Strassen and Urdhvatiryagbhyam method. *CCF Transactions on High Performance Computing*, *5*(2), 1–14. doi:10.1007/s42514-023-00149-9

Bhandari, R. (2014). Impact of technology on logistics and supply chain management. *IOSR Journal of Business and Management*, *2*, 19–24.

Boopathi, S., Pandey, B. K., & Pandey, D. (2023). Advances in artificial intelligence for image processing: techniques, applications, and optimization. In *Handbook of research on thrust technologies' effect on image processing* (pp. 73–95). IGI Global. doi:10.4018/978-1-6684-8618-4.ch006

Daoud, M. K., Al-Qeed, M., Ahmad, A. Y. B., & Al-Gasawneh, J. A. (2023). Mobile Marketing: Exploring the Efficacy of User-Centric Strategies for Enhanced Consumer Engagement and Conversion Rates. *International Journal of Membrane Science and Technology*, *10*(2), 1252–1262. doi:10.15379/ijmst.vi.1425

Daoud, Alqudah, Al-Qeed, Al Qaied, & Ahmad. (2023). The Relationship Between Mobile Marketing and Customer Perceptions in Jordanian Commercial Banks: The Electronic Quality as A Mediator Variable. *IJMST, 10*(2), 1360-1371.

Fatorachian, H., & Kazemi, H. (2021). Impact of Industry 4.0 on supply chain performance. *Production Planning and Control*, *32*(1), 63–81. doi:10.1080/09537287.2020.1712487

Ghadge, A., Er Kara, M., Moradlou, H., & Goswami, M. (2020). The impact of Industry 4.0 implementation on supply chains. *Journal of Manufacturing Technology Management*, *31*(4), 669–686. doi:10.1108/JMTM-10-2019-0368

Ghadge, A., Mogale, D. G., Bourlakis, M., Maiyar, L. M., & Moradlou, H. (2022). Link between Industry 4.0 and green supplychain management: Evidence from the automotive industry. *Computers & Industrial Engineering*, *169*, 108303. doi:10.1016/j.cie.2022.108303

Iyyanar, P., Anand, R., Shanthi, T., Nassa, V. K., Pandey, B. K., George, A. S., & Pandey, D. (2023). A Real-Time Smart Sewage Cleaning UAV Assistance System Using IoT. In *Handbook of Research on Data-Driven Mathematical Modeling in Smart Cities* (pp. 24–39). IGI Global.

Ketchen, D. J. Jr, Crook, R. T., & Craighead, C. W. (2014). From supply chains to supply ecosystems: Implications for strategic sourcing research and practice. *Journal of Business Logistics*, *35*(3), 165–171. doi:10.1111/jbl.12057

Khan, Y. (2022). Application of Internet of Things (IoT) in Sustainable Supply Chain Management. *Sustainability, 15*(1), 694. doi:10.3390/su15010694

Kirubasri, G., Sankar, S., Pandey, D., Pandey, B. K., Nassa, V. K., & Dadheech, P. (2022). Software-defined networking-based Ad hoc networks routing protocols. In *Software defined networking for Ad Hoc networks* (pp. 95–123). Springer International Publishing. doi:10.1007/978-3-030-91149-2_5

Kumar Pandey, B., Pandey, D., Nassa, V. K., Ahmad, T., Singh, C., George, A. S., & Wakchaure, M. A. (2021). Encryption and steganography-based text extraction in IoT using the EWCTS optimizer. *Imaging Science Journal*, *69*(1-4), 38–56. doi:10.1080/13682199.2022.2146885

Lopes de Sousa Jabbour, A. B., Jabbour, C. J. C., Godinho Filho, M., & Roubaud, D. (2018). Industry 4.0 and the circular economy: A proposed research agenda and original roadmap for sustainable operations. *Annals of Operations Research*, *270*(1-2), 273–286. doi:10.1007/s10479-018-2772-8

Machado, C. G., Winroth, M. P., & Ribeiro da Silva, E. H. D. (2020). Sustainable manufacturing in Industry 4.0: An emerging research agenda. *International Journal of Production Research*, *58*(5), 1462–1484. doi:10.1080/00207543.2019.1652777

Manavalan, E., & Jayakrishna, K. (2019). A review of Internet of Things (IoT) embedded sustainable supply chain for industry 4.0 requirements. *Computers & Industrial Engineering*, *127*, 925–953. doi:10.1016/j.cie.2018.11.030

Meslie, Y., Enbeyle, W., Pandey, B. K., Pramanik, S., Pandey, D., Dadeech, P., & Saini, A. (2021). Machine intelligence-based trend analysis of COVID-19 for total daily confirmed cases in Asia and Africa. In *Methodologies and Applications of Computational Statistics for Machine Intelligence* (pp. 164–185). IGI Global. doi:10.4018/978-1-7998-7701-1.ch009

Müller, J. M., & Voigt, K. I. (2018). The impact of industry 4.0 on supply chains in engineer-to-order industries-an exploratory case study. *IFAC-PapersOnLine*, *51*(11), 122–127. doi:10.1016/j.ifacol.2018.08.245

Muniandi, B., Huang, C.-J., Kuo, C.-C., Yang, T.-F., Chen, K.-H., Lin, Y.-H., Lin, S.-R., & Tsai, T.-Y. (2019, November). A 97% Maximum Efficiency Fully Automated Control Turbo Boost Topology for Battery Chargers. *IEEE Transactions on Circuits and Systems. I, Regular Papers*, *66*(11), 4516–4527. doi:10.1109/TCSI.2019.2925374

Pandey, B. K., Mane, D., Nassa, V. K. K., Pandey, D., Dutta, S., Ventayen, R. J. M., & Rastogi, R. (2021). Secure text extraction from complex degraded images by applying steganography and deep learning. In *Multidisciplinary approach to modern digital steganography* (pp. 146–163). IGI Global. doi:10.4018/978-1-7998-7160-6.ch007

Pandey, B. K., Pandey, D., & Agarwal, A. (2022). Encrypted information transmission by enhanced steganography and image transformation. *International Journal of Distributed Artificial Intelligence*, *14*(1), 1–14. doi:10.4018/IJDAI.297110

Pandey, B. K., Pandey, D., Gupta, A., Nassa, V. K., Dadheech, P., & George, A. S. (2023). Secret data transmission using advanced morphological component analysis and steganography. In *Role of Data-Intensive Distributed Computing Systems in Designing Data Solutions* (pp. 21–44). Springer International Publishing. doi:10.1007/978-3-031-15542-0_2

Pandey, B. K., Pandey, D., Wairya, S., Agarwal, G., Dadeech, P., Dogiwal, S. R., & Pramanik, S. (2022). Application of integrated steganography and image compressing techniques for confidential information transmission. *Cyber Security and Network Security*, 169-191.

Pandey, D., Nassa, V. K., Jhamb, A., Mahto, D., Pandey, B. K., George, A. H., & Bandyopadhyay, S. K. (2021). An integration of keyless encryption, steganography, and artificial intelligence for the secure transmission of stego images. In *Multidisciplinary approach to modern digital steganography* (pp. 211–234). IGI Global. doi:10.4018/978-1-7998-7160-6.ch010

Pandey, D., & Pandey, B. K. (2022). An efficient deep neural network with adaptive galactic swarm optimization for complex image text extraction. In *Process Mining Techniques for Pattern Recognition* (pp. 121–137). CRC Press. doi:10.1201/9781003169550-10

Pandey, D., Wairya, S., Sharma, M., Gupta, A. K., Kakkar, R., & Pandey, B. K. (2022). An approach for object tracking, categorization, and autopilot guidance for passive homing missiles. *Aerospace Systems*, *5*(4), 553–566. doi:10.1007/s42401-022-00150-0

Pandey, J. K., Jain, R., Dilip, R., Kumbhkar, M., Jaiswal, S., Pandey, B. K., & Pandey, D. (2022). Investigating Role of IoT in the Development of Smart Application for Security Enhancement. In *IoT Based Smart Applications* (pp. 219–243). Springer International Publishing.

Perussi, J. B., Gressler, F., & Seleme, R. (2019). Supply chain 4.0: Autonomous vehicles and equipment to meet demand. *Int. J. Supply Chain.*, *8*, 33–41.

Pramanik, S., Pandey, D., Joardar, S., Niranjanamurthy, M., Pandey, B. K., & Kaur, J. (2023, October). An overview of IoT privacy and security in smart cities. In AIP Conference Proceedings (Vol. 2495, No. 1). AIP Publishing. doi:10.1063/5.0123511

Preindl, R., Nikolopoulos, K., & Litsiou, K. (2020). Transformation strategies for the supply chain: The impact of industry 4.0 and digital transformation. *Supply Chain. Forum Int. J.*, *21*(1), 26–34. doi:10.1080/16258312.2020.1716633

Queiroz, M. M., & Wamba, S. F. (2019). Blockchain adoption challenges in supply chain: An empirical investigation of the main drivers in India and the USA. *International Journal of Information Management*, *46*, 70–82. doi:10.1016/j.ijinfomgt.2018.11.021

Saxena, A., Sharma, N. K., Pandey, D., & Pandey, B. K. (2021). Influence of tourists satisfaction on future behavioral intentions with special reference to desert triangle of Rajasthan. *Augmented Human Research*, *6*(1), 1–9. doi:10.1007/s41133-021-00052-4

Scuotto, V., Caputo, F., Villasalero, M., & del Giudice, M. (2017). A multiple buyer–supplier relationship in the context of SMEs' digital supply chain management. *Production Planning and Control*, *28*(16), 1378–1388. doi:10.1080/09537287.2017.1375149

Shao, X. F., Liu, W., Li, Y., Chaudhry, H. R., & Yue, X. G. (2021). Multistage implementation framework for smart supply chain management under industry 4.0. *Technological Forecasting and Social Change*, *162*, 120354. doi:10.1016/j.techfore.2020.120354 PMID:33041379

Singh, H., Pandey, B. K., George, S., Pandey, D., Anand, R., Sindhwani, N., & Dadheech, P. (2022, July). Effective Overview of Different ML Models Used for Prediction of COVID-19 Patients. In *Artificial Intelligence on Medical Data: Proceedings of International Symposium, ISCMM 2021* (pp. 185-192). Singapore: Springer Nature Singapore.

Treiblmaier, H. (2018). The impact of the blockchain on the supply chain: A theory-based research framework and a call for action. *Supply Chain Management*, *23*(6), 545–559. doi:10.1108/SCM-01-2018-0029

Wang, C., Ahmad, S. F., Ayassrah, A. Y. B. A., Awwad, E. M., Irshad, M., Ali, Y. A., ... Han, H. (2023). An empirical evaluation of technology acceptance model for Artificial Intelligence in E-commerce. *Heliyon*, *9*(8), e18349. doi:10.1016/j.heliyon.2023.e18349 PMID:37520947

Chapter 2
Social Psychological Obstacles to the Implementation of Artificial Intelligence in Supply Chain Management

Binay Kumar Pandey
https://orcid.org/0000-0002-4041-1213
Department of Information Technology, College of Technology, Govind Ballabh Pant University of Agriculture and Technology, India

Mukundan Appadurai Paramashivan
https://orcid.org/0009-0009-5608-4788
Aligarh Muslim University and Champions Group, India

Asif Hasan
https://orcid.org/0000-0001-9433-3364
Aligargh Muslim University, India

Sabyasachi Pramanik
https://orcid.org/0000-0002-9431-8751
Department of Computer Science and Engineering, Haldia Institute of Technology (Autonomous), India

Pankaj Dadheech
https://orcid.org/0000-0001-5783-1989
Swami Keshvanand Institute of Technology, Management, and Gramothan, India

Shyam Sundar Manaktala
Jaipur Engineering College and Research Centre, India

A. Shaji George
https://orcid.org/0000-0002-8677-3682
Crown University International Chartered Inc., Argentina

ABSTRACT

AI and machine learning affect intelligent supply chains, implementation challenges, and psychosocial factors affecting supply chain AI and ML acceptability. Behavioural operations management grows. It structures production and manufacturing processes utilising psychologically based behavioural and cognitive aspects, challenging the idea that "human being is rational" in decision-making. Supply chain management (SCM), a subset of operations management, studies social psychology and supply chains. A related research literature review follows. This report recommends improving supply networks, especially in competitive companies. Supply chain efficiency requires multilevel and employee interaction. Human behaviour impacts supply chain decisions and performance.

DOI: 10.4018/979-8-3693-1347-3.ch002

INTRODUCTION

AI and Machine Learning Impacts in Intelligent Supply Chain

Artificial intelligence (AI) and machine learning (ML) are having a huge impact on the business of supply chain management, which is resulting in that industry undergoing a significant transition. This is due to the fact that AI and ML are becoming more advanced. This is a direct consequence of the technologies that are currently available. These technical developments (Berente, N.,et al.(2021)) are currently being put to use in order to raise productivity, improve the efficiency of operations, and make better decisions overall.

The proliferation of artificial intelligence and machine learning is having a wide range of effects on the supply chain (Janvier-James, A.M. (2012)). These changes are occurring for a variety of reasons. Some of these methods are broken down into more specific categories below.

The utilisation of artificial intelligence makes it feasible to carry out an in-depth analysis of historical data (Babu, S. Z. D. et al., 2022), which, in turn, makes it possible to provide more precise forecasts on anticipated levels of demand in the future. By making use of this information, you may help improve inventory (Pandey, B. K., et al. (2021))levels and reduce the likelihood of stockouts occurring.

The use of artificial intelligence (AI) in the optimisation of travel routes for automobiles has the potential to significantly reduce the amount of time spent commuting as well as the quantity of fuel that is consumed.

Administration of the storage facility: It is feasible that one day artificial intelligence (Pandey, B. K., & Pandey, D., 2023) will be able to automate a significant proportion of warehouse activities, such as picking items up and putting them in boxes. It is possible that this will result in decreased costs associated with employment while also boosting the general productivity of the workforce. This would be a win-win situation (Khasis, D. (2019)).

Detecting fraudulent behaviour in regards to financial dealings is one of the many applications of artificial intelligence (AI), such as those involving stolen credit cards and other forms of financial information. This is just one of a number of other uses for AI (Pramanik, S. et al., 2023), which has a lot of other uses as well. This might be helpful in reducing the possibility of a firm incurring monetary losses as a consequence of a risk, which would be beneficial to the company.

With the assistance of artificial intelligence (Gupta, R. et al., 2023), potential threats to a supply chain, such as those brought on by natural disasters or political unrest, might be discovered, and subsequently, these threats could be neutralised with the aid of the aforementioned technology. The application of artificial intelligence makes it feasible to not only recognise but also eliminate the presence of any potential risks (Meslie, Y.,et al. (2021)).

AI (Anand, R. et al., 2023) can be used to provide customised customer care, such as by replying to inquiries regarding purchases or tracking shipments. This can be accomplished in the context of customer service. One way to accomplish this is by keeping track (Pandey, D.,et al.(2021)) of shipments, for instance. Two instances of this would be keeping track of shipments and providing information in answer to questions about orders that have been asked. The fact that tracking information is made available is another piece of evidence that demonstrates the usefulness of this idea.

These are only a few of the ways that artificial intelligence and machine learning are having an effect on the supply chain; there are many more. There are still a great many more. There are still a very significant number left. If we make the reasonable assumption that the development of these technologies will continue, as is the case here, then we can anticipate that they will have an even greater influence on the sector in which they are employed (Liu, C.,et al.(2016)).

The following are some examples of artificial intelligence and machine learning being put to use in the supply chain of today, and they are concrete examples of how these technologies are being utilised:

The use of technology based on artificial intelligence (AI) is assisting Amazon in improving the efficiency of its warehouse operations. The company uses artificial intelligence and robotics to pick and pack the things that customers have requested(Long, D., & Magerko, B. (2020)) and the company also uses artificial intelligence to determine the delivery routes that are the most efficient in terms of both time and money.

Artificial intelligence is currently being utilised by the world's largest retailer, Walmart, in an effort to better anticipate the demand that customers will have for a wide assortment of products. This information is useful to the organisation because it enables them to prevent stockouts and increases the likelihood that they will always have a suitable quantity of goods available (Nishitha, P., & Pandey, D. (2021)).

When it comes to tracking packages, UPS is now employing artificial intelligence technologies, which was not the case in the past. The organisation makes use of both artificial intelligence and sensors in order to keep track of the products' most up-to-date locations in real time and to calculate an estimate of when they will be transported to their final destinations (Pandey, B. K., et al. (2021)).

FedEx is employing artificial intelligence to assist in its fight against fraudulent behaviour. The use of possibly fraudulent transactions, such as those that entail the use of stolen credit cards and other forms of financial information, can be identified as potentially fraudulent by the company through the use of machine learning (Kumar, M. S., et al. (2021).

These are just a few instances of the numerous applications of artificial intelligence and machine learning that are now being researched and put into practice in supply chains. There are, of course, many more. There is a very wide variety of software that can be used. If we make the reasonable assumption that the development of these technologies will continue, as is the case here, then we can anticipate that they will have an even greater influence on the sector in which they are employed (Singh, H., et al. (2022).

In spite of the fact that the use of artificial intelligence and machine learning in the supply chain is still in its infancy, it is abundantly clear that these technologies have the potential to radically revolutionise the industry(Jain, V., Kumar, et al. (2017).). Despite the fact that the supply chain is still in its formative years, this is the case. This is especially true when one considers the dizzyingly quick pace at which the development of these technologies is proceeding. Artificial intelligence and machine learning have the potential to assist businesses in increasing their bottom line by improving the efficiency, precision, and resiliency of supply chains. This is something that can be accomplished through the use of machine learning (Iyyanar, P. et al., 2023) and artificial intelligence. Another advantage for customers is that this might assist companies in providing better customer service to their target demographic.

Impediments to Implementing ML and AI in the Supply Chain

The supply chain will need to overcome the following problems in order to put artificial intelligence and machine learning into practice as per Figure 1:

Data access: Both artificial intelligence and machine learning algorithms require a significant quantity of data in order to effectively train and function. Without this data, none of them can be effective. It is highly probable that these data will not always be available, particularly in situations involving small enterprises or supply networks that have recently been established.

Figure 1. Problem of AI/MI in SCM

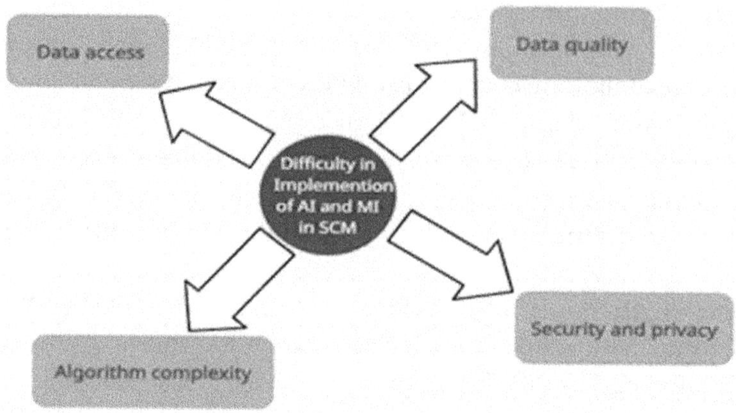

Data quality: The precision of the outcomes that were generated is inextricably linked to the quality of the data that was utilised during the training process for the machine learning and artificial intelligence algorithms. If the data that is provided is either wrong or incomplete, the algorithms have a chance of producing incorrect results. This is because the algorithms are not perfect.

Algorithm complexity: The degree of complexity entailed by the algorithms Understanding artificial intelligence (AI) and machine learning (ML) algorithms can be difficult at times due to the level of complexity inherent in both of these types of programmes. Because of this, it may be difficult to diagnose flaws and verify that the algorithms are performing as expected because of the complexity of the system.

Security and privacy: Concerns about the data's privacy and safety have been raised as a result of the prospect that AI and ML algorithms may be put to use in the process of gathering and analysing sensitive information. This information must be protected from unauthorised access and use by third parties at all costs. Those individuals have no right to have this data in their possession.

In spite of these obstacles, the implementation of artificial intelligence and machine learning in the administration of supply chains is a fascinating and potentially fruitful area for additional research and development. As these technologies continue to make strides forward in their individual spheres of application, there is a substantial possibility that the business world will begin to implement them in a manner that is more comprehensive.

Psychosocial Aspects That Affect Supply Chain AI and ML Acceptance

The subsequent enumeration comprises a selection of psychological factors that may exert influence on individuals' perceptions of artificial intelligence and machine learning within the supply chain domain, as well as their inclination towards acceptance or rejection of such technologies. There exists a deficiency in trust in artificial intelligence and machine learning (Radwan, E., et al. (2023).).

Individuals are more inclined to engage with artificial intelligence and machine learning when they possess a sense of assurance regarding the dependability and precision of the technology they are utilising. This phenomenon can be attributed to individuals' inclination to place trust in technology. Confidence can be acquired through the provision of transparent and sincere elucidations concerning the functioning of the technology, along with the implementation of sufficient testing and validation protocols. Both of these components are crucial for the effective establishment of trust and the attainment of desired outcomes. It is vital to provide these elucidations while also ensuring that the technology is appropriately validated and substantiated (Pandey, D., & Pandey, B. K. (2022)).

Individuals have a heightened inclination to adopt novel technological advancements when they possess knowledge of the underlying mechanisms employed by said technology, specifically in the context of artificial intelligence and machine learning, to generate new insights. This phenomenon can be attributed to the fact that individuals are more inclined to comprehend the functioning of technology. This phenomenon can be attributed to the tendency of users to perceive the technology as operating in alignment with their own interests. In this context, it is imperative to maintain complete openness, which is an essential need that must be adhered to without exception. Achieving this degree of transparency can be attained by providing consumers with comprehensive elucidations of the algorithms employed by the technology as well as granting users the opportunity to scrutinise the decisions made by the technology. Both of these procedures are essential in order to achieve this degree of transparency.

The acceptance of machine learning and artificial intelligence is likely to rise if individuals perceive that these technologies are being ethically utilised. There are two potential approaches to attaining fairness: firstly, by ensuring that the technology remains impartial towards certain human groups, and secondly, by providing individuals with avenues to challenge decisions made by the technology. One approach is to mitigate any biases within the technology to prevent discrimination against specific human groups. Another approach is to provide mechanisms for individuals to contest decisions made by the technology. Both of these approaches can be considered valid methods for seeking a resolution to the problem.

There exists a potential concern among certain people over the potential impact of artificial intelligence (AI) and machine learning (ML) on the labour market within the supply chain industry, specifically in terms of a potential decrease in job opportunities. This is a prospective result. Ensuring the retraining of individuals for new professional opportunities or providing alternative forms of assistance is vital in addressing this issue since it is firmly rooted in reality. The purpose of this endeavour is to identify a solution to navigate out of the current challenging situation. In order to guarantee the resolution of an issue, it is vital to undertake the necessary actions without any alternative options. Moreover, it is plausible that individuals requiring diverse forms of aid will be afforded an extended array of support alternatives.

There is a growing apprehension among individuals regarding the potential ramifications of machine learning and artificial intelligence on their personally identifiable information and their entitlement to privacy. The individuals express apprehension regarding the potential illegal access by third parties to their personal information, which may then be utilised without obtaining prior approval from the individuals. Finding a resolution to these difficulties is crucial since it necessitates the establishment of robust mechanisms to safeguard individuals' data in an appropriate manner while also granting them autonomy over the use of their data. It is imperative to identify a resolution to these difficulties. The resolution of these challenges necessitates the establishment of mechanisms that empower individuals to exercise authority over the use of their personal data. One potential approach to addressing this issue involves implementing measures that grant individuals autonomy and authority over the use of their personal data. The significance of resolving these problems cannot be overstated, as it is crucial for progress to be made. Therefore, it is necessary that this step be undertaken. Furthermore, it is imperative to prioritise the establishment of mechanisms that empower individuals to exercise control over the use of their personal data. This is of paramount importance. This holds significant relevance. The significance of this truth cannot be overstated.

In addition to the aforementioned factors, there exist certain characteristics that possess the ability to influence the psychology of artificial intelligence and machine learning within the context of the supply chain.

Each individual possesses a distinct perspective and a collection of personal experiences that can be valuable in the discourse surrounding the challenges associated with adapting to novel technological advancements. Individuals that exhibit heightened sensitivity towards artificial intelligence and machine learning concepts may also demonstrate a greater propensity for embracing novel experiences and diverse perspectives in a broader sense. This phenomenon necessitates additional examination.

The individual's opinion regarding a past occurrence or event Individuals who have previously encountered favourable encounters with artificial intelligence and machine learning are more inclined to exhibit openness towards the potential opportunities presented by these technological advancements. These technologies hold the potential to initiate a period of significant transformation across various industries. These technologies encompass both computer-based learning processes and artificial intelligence.

The level of knowledge an individual possesses regarding topics such as artificial intelligence and machine learning Individuals with a deeper understanding of the fundamental mechanisms underlying artificial intelligence and machine learning tend to exhibit a greater propensity to place trust in these particular technologies.

The historical, political, economic, and social milieu the integration of machine learning and artificial intelligence into society may potentially impact individuals' comprehension and use of the resultant technology. The recent experiment undertaken by Facebook in the field of facial recognition serves as a compelling instance and a noteworthy example. This serves as a commendable exemplification of the aforementioned concept. Individuals have a heightened inclination to embrace novel technologies, such as artificial intelligence and machine learning, when these technologies are employed in a manner that is regarded as beneficial to a broader society. Moreover, the general populace is more likely to endorse these technologies when they can observe tangible improvements in people's daily lives resulting from their implementation. Individuals exhibit a greater propensity to see novel technological advancements as having a positive influence on their lives, hence contributing to the prevalence of this viewpoint.

When developing and implementing artificial intelligence (AI) and machine learning (ML) solutions in the supply chain, it is imperative to carefully analyse all of these components. Companies have the opportunity to actively participate in the endeavour of ensuring that the deployment of artificial intelligence and machine learning is beneficial to individuals and organisations. This may be achieved through a comprehensive grasp of the psychological principles behind these technologies. The comprehension of this concept can only be achieved if organisations possess a cognizance of the psychological underpinnings that underlie artificial intelligence and machine learning. This opportunity is exclusively available to businesses that have attained a certain degree of experience.

CONCLUSION

The findings of this research can be used by managers of supply chains to determine how they might raise the degree of trust they have with customers at various points in the supply chain process. An increase in trust would lead to more collaboration throughout the supply chain, which would result in a shared advantage and positive performance. The reliability of the supplier is ensured by trust. Supply chains as a result of the fact that customers have to develop trust in the suppliers in order to ensure that their goods will be delivered on time, at the agreed price, and in good shape. Equally important, trust would improve the manner in which purchasers treat suppliers with respect and carry out payments in accordance with the terms agreed upon. However, the exercise of extreme power levels impairs the effectiveness of supply chains since it limits the amount of collaboration and commitment between different stakeholders in the process of meeting the expectations of customers.

REFERENCES

Anand, R., Khan, B., Nassa, V. K., Pandey, D., Dhabliya, D., Pandey, B. K., & Dadheech, P. (2023). Hybrid convolutional neural network (CNN) for Kennedy Space Center hyperspectral image. *Aerospace Systems*, *6*(1), 71–78. doi:10.1007/s42401-022-00168-4

Babu, S. Z. D., Pandey, D., Naidu, G. T., Sumathi, S., Gupta, A., Bader Alazzam, M., & Pandey, B. K. (2022, July). Analysation of Big Data in Smart Healthcare. In *Artificial Intelligence on Medical Data: Proceedings of International Symposium, ISCMM 2021* (pp. 243-251). Singapore: Springer Nature Singapore.

Berente, N., Gu, B., Recker, J., & Santhanam, R. (2021). Managing Artificial Intelligence. *Management Information Systems Quarterly*, *45*, 1433–1450.

Gupta, R., Mane, M., Bhardwaj, S., Nandekar, U., Afaq, A., Dhabliya, D., & Pandey, B. K. (2023). Use of Artificial Intelligence for Image Processing to Aid Digital Forensics: Legislative Challenges. In *Handbook of Research on Thrust Technologies' Effect on Image Processing* (pp. 433–447). IGI Global. doi:10.4018/978-1-6684-8618-4.ch026

Iyyanar, P., Anand, R., Shanthi, T., Nassa, V. K., Pandey, B. K., George, A. S., & Pandey, D. (2023). A Real-Time Smart Sewage Cleaning UAV Assistance System Using IoT. In *Handbook of Research on Data-Driven Mathematical Modeling in Smart Cities* (pp. 24–39). IGI Global.

Jain, V., Kumar, S., Soni, U., & Chandra, C. (2017). Supply chain resilience: Model development and empirical analysis. *International Journal of Production Research*, *55*(22), 6779–6800. doi:10.1080/00207543.2017.1349947

Janvier-James, A. M. (2012). A new introduction to supply chains and supply chain management: Definitions and theories perspective. *International Business Research*, *5*(1), 194–207. Retrieved August 19, 2023, from. doi:10.5539/ibr.v5n1p194

Khasis, D. (2019). *Four Ways AI Is Impacting Logistics and Supply Chain Management.* Retrieved from Supply Chain Brain. Retrieved on August 19, 2023 from https://www.supplychainbrain.com/blogs/1-think-tank/post/30045-four-ways-ai-is-impacting-logistics-and-supply-chain-management

Kumar, M. S., Sankar, S., Nassa, V. K., Pandey, D., Pandey, B. K., & Enbeyle, W. (2021). Innovation and creativity for data mining using computational statistics. In *Methodologies and Applications of Computational Statistics for Machine Intelligence* (pp. 223–240). IGI Global. doi:10.4018/978-1-7998-7701-1.ch012

Liu, C., Shu, T., Chen, S., Wang, S., Lai, K. K., & Gan, L. (2016). An improved grey neural network model for predicting transportation disruptions. *Expert Systems with Applications*, *45*, 331–340. doi:10.1016/j.eswa.2015.09.052

Long, D., & Magerko, B. (2020). What Is AI Literacy? Competencies and Design Considerations. In *Proceedings of the 2020 CHI Conference on Human Factors in Computing Systems* (pp. 1-16). Association for Computing Machinery. Retrieved on August 19, 2023 from https://doi.org/10.1145/3313831.3376727

Meslie, Y., Enbeyle, W., Pandey, B. K., Pramanik, S., Pandey, D., Dadeech, P., & Saini, A. (2021). Machine intelligence-based trend analysis of COVID-19 for total daily confirmed cases in Asia and Africa. In *Methodologies and Applications of Computational Statistics for Machine Intelligence* (pp. 164–185). IGI Global. doi:10.4018/978-1-7998-7701-1.ch009

Nishitha, P., & Pandey, D. (2021). A study on student perception towards online education during covid-19 crisis. *Augmented Human Research*, *6*(1), 16. doi:10.1007/s41133-021-00055-1

Pandey, B. K., & Pandey, D. (2023). Parametric optimization and prediction of enhanced thermoelectric performance in co-doped CaMnO3 using response surface methodology and neural network. *Journal of Materials Science Materials in Electronics*, *34*(21), 1589. doi:10.1007/s10854-023-10954-1

Pandey, B. K., Pandey, D., Wariya, S., & Agarwal, G. (2021). A deep neural network-based approach for extracting textual images from deteriorate images. *EAI Endorsed Transactions on Industrial Networks and Intelligent Systems*, *8*(28), e3–e3. doi:10.4108/eai.17-9-2021.170961

Pandey, B. K., Pandey, D., Wariya, S., Aggarwal, G., & Rastogi, R. (2021). Deep learning and particle swarm optimisation-based techniques for visually impaired humans' text recognition and identification. *Augmented Human Research*, *6*(1), 1–14. doi:10.1007/s41133-021-00051-5

Pandey, D., Nassa, V. K., Jhamb, A., Mahto, D., Pandey, B. K., George, A. H., & Bandyopadhyay, S. K. (2021). An integration of keyless encryption, steganography, and artificial intelligence for the secure transmission of stego images. In *Multidisciplinary approach to modern digital steganography* (pp. 211–234). IGI Global. doi:10.4018/978-1-7998-7160-6.ch010

Pandey, D., & Pandey, B. K. (2022). An efficient deep neural network with adaptive galactic swarm optimization for complex image text extraction. In *Process Mining Techniques for Pattern Recognition* (pp. 121–137). CRC Press. doi:10.1201/9781003169550-10

Pramanik, S., Pandey, D., Joardar, S., Niranjanamurthy, M., Pandey, B. K., & Kaur, J. (2023, October). An overview of IoT privacy and security in smart cities. In AIP Conference Proceedings (Vol. 2495, No. 1). AIP Publishing. doi:10.1063/5.0123511

Radwan, E., Alattar, E., Radwan, A., Radwan, W., Alajez, M., Pandey, D., & Jebreen, K. (2023). Knowledge, attitudes, and practices of palestinian students toward COVID-19: a cross-sectional study during the first wave of the COVID-19 pandemic. *Human Arenas*, 1-22.

Singh, H., Pandey, B. K., George, S., Pandey, D., Anand, R., Sindhwani, N., & Dadheech, P. (2022, July). Effective Overview of Different ML Models Used for Prediction of COVID-19 Patients. In *Artificial Intelligence on Medical Data: Proceedings of International Symposium, ISCMM 2021* (pp. 185-192). Singapore: Springer Nature Singapore.

Chapter 3
Integrating Machine Learning in Legal Management for Intelligent Supply Chain Governance

Edwin Ramirez-Asis
Universidad Señor de Sipán, Chiclayo, Peru

Rolando Saenz-Rodriguez
Universidad Cesar Vallejo, Huaraz, Peru

Luis Angulo-Cabanillas
Universidad Cesar Vallejo, Huaraz, Peru

Nathaly Trujillo-Navarro
Universidad Nacional Santiago Antúnez de Mayolo, Huaraz, Peru

Diego Villegas-Ramirez
Universidad Nacional Mayor de San Marcos, Lima, Peru

ABSTRACT

The integration of machine learning in legal management and the development of intelligent supply chain governance represents transformative approaches to address the evolving complexities of the legal and supply chain domains. This chapter summarizes the key findings and insights drawn from the outlined sections. The problem statement underscores the growing need for data-driven strategies to navigate the intricate legal landscape and meet the challenges of modern supply chains. With a focus on transparency, accountability, and risk management, the significance of supply chain governance is highlighted, emphasizing its critical role in resilient and efficient supply chain operations. Legal management emerges as a pivotal player in this transformation, tasked with utilizing machine learning to navigate a data-rich and complex legal environment.

DOI: 10.4018/979-8-3693-1347-3.ch003

1. INTRODUCTION

In today's rapidly evolving global business landscape, supply chain governance plays a pivotal role in ensuring the efficient and ethical flow of goods and services. Managing supply chain complexities, risks, and compliance demands has become increasingly intricate, requiring a multifaceted approach that goes beyond traditional methods. At the same time, the legal aspects of supply chain governance are becoming more intricate and demanding, necessitating innovative solutions to keep pace with these challenges. Machine learning, a subset of artificial intelligence, has emerged as a game-changer in various industries. Its ability to process vast amounts of data, identify patterns, and make data-driven predictions has the potential to revolutionize the way legal professionals approach supply chain governance. By integrating machine learning into legal management, organizations can achieve a new level of insight, efficiency, and compliance within their supply chain operations. This chapter explores the exciting intersection of machine learning and legal management to facilitate intelligent supply chain governance. We will delve into the fundamental concepts, applications, and benefits of incorporating machine learning into legal practices within the supply chain context. Our aim is to shed light on how machine learning can enhance the governance of supply chains, making them more responsive, secure, and adept at addressing today's challenges. Throughout this exploration, we will also address the hurdles and considerations that organizations may encounter when seeking to integrate machine learning into their legal management and supply chain processes (Bai and Sarkis et al. 2020). As we venture deeper into the potential of machine learning in legal management for intelligent supply chain governance, it becomes apparent that this integration holds the promise of more effective risk mitigation, streamlined compliance, and a higher level of strategic insight. It is a frontier where innovation meets the law, and where intelligent supply chain governance can truly come to life.

1.2 Significance of Supply Chain Governance

Operational efficiency is a cornerstone of supply chain governance. It involves optimizing various aspects of the supply chain, from procurement to distribution, to ensure that resources are used effectively and processes run smoothly. Here are some key points are as shown in the Figure 1, that underline the significance of operational efficiency in supply chain governance:

1. *Cost Reduction*: Operational efficiency within supply chain governance involves identifying and eliminating unnecessary expenses. By optimizing processes, reducing waste, and negotiating favorable terms with suppliers, organizations can significantly reduce their operational costs. These cost savings can be reinvested in other strategic initiatives or passed on to customers in the form of competitive pricing.
2. *Lean Processes*: Efficient supply chain governance often entails adopting lean principles, which emphasize eliminating non-value-added activities and streamlining operations. Lean practices result in reduced lead times, minimized inventory levels, and improved production and delivery speed. This not only reduces costs but also enhances overall supply chain responsiveness.
3. *Resource Optimization*: Supply chain governance focuses on efficient resource allocation. This includes making the most of available resources, such as labor, equipment, and warehouse space. By utilizing resources effectively, organizations can maximize their operational output while keeping resource-related expenses in check.

4. *Quality Control*: Operational efficiency ensures consistent quality control throughout the supply chain. By adhering to streamlined processes and standards, organizations can maintain product and service quality at all stages of the supply chain. This consistency fosters customer satisfaction and brand trust, ultimately leading to repeat business and positive referrals.
5. *Flexibility and Adaptability*: Efficient supply chain governance enables organizations to be more adaptable and responsive to market changes. It allows for quicker adjustments to shifting customer preferences, demand fluctuations, and unexpected disruptions. This adaptability is crucial for staying competitive in fast-paced industries.
6. *Technology Integration*: Modern supply chain governance often involves the integration of advanced technologies. These technologies, such as data analytics, IoT sensors, and supply chain management software, provide real-time visibility and insights into supply chain operations. This data-driven approach enhances decision-making, identifies inefficiencies, and allows for proactive issue resolution.

Efficient supply chain governance is not only about reducing costs but also about optimizing processes, ensuring quality, and responding to changing market dynamics (Saberi et al. 2019). By prioritizing operational efficiency, organizations can gain a competitive edge and position themselves for success in an increasingly complex and fast-paced business environment.

Figure 1. Importance of governing the supply chain

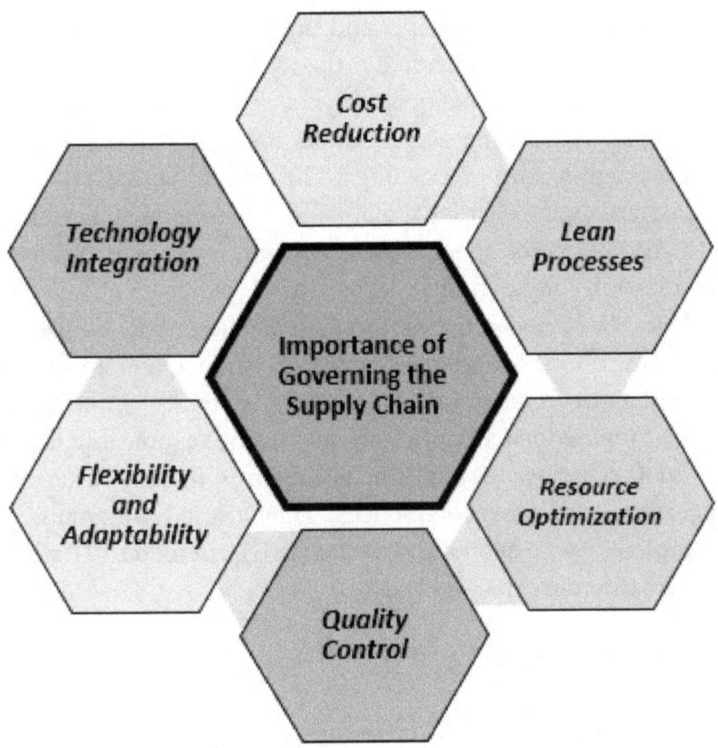

1.2 Role of Legal Management

Legal management plays a crucial role in the overall functioning of organizations. It encompasses a range of responsibilities and activities related to legal matters, risk management, compliance, and governance. Here are key aspects of the role of legal management:

1. *Risk Mitigation*: Legal management is at the forefront of risk mitigation within an organization. Legal professionals are responsible for identifying potential legal risks and evaluating their potential impact on the business. They develop strategies to minimize or prevent these risks from materializing, which may involve revising contracts, implementing compliance programs, or advising on best practices. Through proactive risk assessment and management, legal management helps protect the organization from costly legal disputes and regulatory penalties.
2. *Compliance and Ethics*: Legal management sets the tone for an organization's ethical standards and regulatory compliance. This involves developing and implementing comprehensive compliance programs to ensure that the organization operates within the bounds of applicable laws and industry regulations. Furthermore, legal professionals are instrumental in addressing ethical concerns and promoting ethical behavior throughout the organization, which is essential for maintaining a positive corporate image and avoiding legal issues related to unethical practices.
3. *Contract Management*: Effective contract management is a core responsibility of legal management. Legal professionals oversee the entire contract lifecycle, from drafting and negotiating contracts to monitoring compliance with contractual terms. By carefully managing contracts, they help the organization avoid disputes, uphold legal obligations, and optimize the value derived from contractual agreements. This includes both customer and supplier contracts, as well as agreements related to partnerships, employment, and intellectual property.
4. *Litigation Management*: Legal management plays a central role in handling legal disputes and litigation. This encompasses selecting and collaborating with external legal counsel, formulating legal strategies, and managing court proceedings. The goal is to protect the organization's interests, whether it involves defending against legal claims or pursuing legal action to enforce the organization's rights. Effective litigation management not only minimizes financial exposure but also safeguards the organization's reputation.
5. *Governance and Policy Development*: Legal management actively contributes to governance by developing and enforcing corporate policies, codes of conduct, and governance guidelines. These policies help ensure that the organization operates transparently, accountably, and in compliance with relevant laws and regulations. Legal professionals are responsible for aligning the organization's operations with its stated values and ethical standards, thereby fostering a culture of integrity and adherence to corporate governance practices. They also advise on board governance, regulatory filings, and compliance with evolving governance requirements to maintain the organization's reputation and legality (Mercuri et al. 2021).

1.3 Machine Learning Integration

Integrating machine learning into various facets of business operations has become increasingly essential in the modern era. The legal domain is no exception, as machine learning integration in legal management offers a compelling case for several reasons. Efficiency and automation are among the primary drivers of machine learning adoption in the legal field. Machine learning algorithms can automate numerous routine legal tasks, such as document review, due diligence, and legal research. By handling these tasks more quickly and accurately than human counterparts, legal professionals are freed to focus on higher-value, strategic work, resulting in enhanced productivity and efficiency. One of the most significant advantages of machine learning in legal management lies in its ability to process and analyze vast amounts of data. In the legal field, this data often includes case files, contracts, and legal precedents. Machine learning algorithms excel at processing and analyzing these data volumes, extracting valuable insights, identifying patterns, and providing data-driven recommendations. This capability helps legal professionals make more informed decisions (Cottrill et al 2018). Predictive analytics is another compelling reason for machine learning integration in legal management. Machine learning models can predict legal outcomes, such as the likelihood of success in a legal case or the potential risks in a contract. By leveraging historical data and factors contributing to legal outcomes, machine learning enables legal professionals to make more accurate predictions, ultimately minimizing legal risks and costs. Machine learning's role in compliance and risk management is pivotal. In an era of increasingly complex regulations and data privacy concerns, machine learning can streamline compliance efforts. It can identify non-compliance issues, monitor regulatory changes, and provide timely alerts, allowing organizations to adapt quickly to changing legal requirements and avoid costly penalties. Time and cost savings are substantial benefits of machine learning integration. By automating labor-intensive tasks, machine learning reduces the time and cost associated with legal processes. Legal research that might take days can be completed in minutes, and voluminous document reviews are conducted with a higher degree of accuracy and speed. This results in cost savings and faster service delivery. Enhanced legal research is another advantage that machine learning offers. Machine learning algorithms can significantly improve legal research by providing access to a wealth of legal texts, precedents, and case law. These aids legal professionals in finding relevant information more quickly and comprehensively, enabling them to build stronger cases and arguments. The case for machine learning integration in legal management is compelling, given its capacity to enhance efficiency, accuracy, compliance, and risk management, all while delivering significant time and cost savings. This integration represents a promising evolution in the legal field, empowering legal professionals to navigate its complexities more

2. THE PRINCIPLES OF SUPPLY CHAIN GOVERNANCE

2.1 Fundamentals of Supply Chain Governance

Supply chain governance forms the backbone of modern businesses, underpinning the efficient movement of goods and services. To comprehend its fundamentals, one must recognize that supply chain governance involves the set of principles, practices, and policies that guide and regulate the end-to-end processes in a supply chain. At its core, supply chain governance emphasizes transparency and accountability. This entails creating an environment where all stakeholders, including suppliers, manufacturers, distributors, and even consumers, understand their roles and responsibilities within the supply chain network. Such transparency is essential for fostering trust and ensuring the smooth flow of products and information. Compliance and risk management are paramount in supply chain governance. Organizations must adhere to legal and regulatory standards while simultaneously evaluating and mitigating risks. This can involve assessing potential disruptions, such as natural disasters, geopolitical events, or financial crises, and implementing strategies to minimize their impact on the supply chain. Supply chain governance aims to optimize the allocation of resources and assets. This includes efficient inventory management, cost-effective transportation, and judicious utilization of labor and warehousing. Effective resource allocation not only reduces costs but also enhances the overall competitiveness of the organization. Quality control is another fundamental aspect of supply chain governance. Maintaining product and service quality throughout the supply chain is crucial for customer satisfaction and brand reputation. Governance principles demand adherence to strict quality standards and the consistent delivery of goods or services that meet or exceed customer expectations. Governance practices foster collaboration and partnership development. Supply chain success relies on effective relationships with suppliers and other stakeholders. Collaboration leads to innovation, improved supplier relationships, and increased adaptability to market changes. This collaborative aspect underscores the importance of not just managing the supply chain but actively governing it to achieve strategic objectives (Tapscott and Euchner et al. 2019).

2.2 The Imperative of Compliance and Risk Management:

In the complex landscape of supply chain governance, compliance and risk management stand as two pillars of utmost importance. The imperative of compliance lies in adhering to a web of regulatory and legal standards that vary across industries and jurisdictions. It requires organizations to operate within the boundaries set by these standards, ensuring that they meet ethical, legal, and industry-specific obligations. Compliance, while ensuring that organizations operate within the law, extends beyond mere adherence to legal requirements. It encompasses a commitment to ethical and responsible business practices. Compliance helps protect an organization's reputation and public trust, a crucial factor in an era of increased scrutiny and instant information sharing. On the other hand, risk management is about identifying, assessing, and mitigating the potential threats that could disrupt the supply chain. These risks can take various forms, from natural disasters and political instability to economic downturns and cyber threats. Effective risk management is essential for supply chain resilience, as it allows organizations to anticipate and prepare for such disruptions. Instead of merely reacting to crises, it involves a careful evaluation of potential risks and the implementation of strategies to mitigate their impact (Tseng and Shang et al. 2021). This proactive stance helps organizations maintain continuity and meet their commitments to customers and partners even in the face of unforeseen challenges. The imperative of compliance and risk management in supply chain governance underscores that organizations must strike a balance between delivering efficiency and maintaining ethical standards. It also highlights the significance of robust systems and processes for ensuring regulatory adherence and risk mitigation. By acknowledging this imperative, organizations can bolster their supply chain governance and navigate complexities with greater confidence and resilience.

3. HARNESSING MACHINE LEARNING FOR LEGAL MANAGEMENT

3.1 The Basics of Machine Learning

Machine learning, a branch of artificial intelligence, has revolutionized the way we approach and solve complex problems. It empowers computer systems to learn and make predictions or decisions based on data, without being explicitly programmed. This introductory field of study is driven by the idea that

Figure 2. Applications in legal management

machines can automatically learn and improve from experience. Machine learning algorithms, inspired by the structure and function of the human brain, are designed to process vast datasets and identify patterns, ultimately making data-driven predictions or recommendations. These algorithms are now at the core of numerous applications, from voice recognition systems and recommendation engines to autonomous vehicles and predictive analytics in healthcare. Understanding the fundamental concepts of machine learning is becoming increasingly important, not only for data scientists and engineers but also for professionals in diverse industries looking to leverage data for strategic decision-making. This introduction to machine learning aims to provide a foundational understanding of key concepts, algorithms, and real-world applications, setting the stage for further exploration of this rapidly evolving field (Choi et al. 2019).

3.2 Applications in Legal Management

The applications of machine learning in legal management are shown in the Figure 2, which reshaping the legal landscape by streamlining various processes and enhancing the efficiency and effectiveness of legal professionals.

1. *Document Analysis and Review*: Machine learning accelerates document analysis and review processes. Algorithms can sift through extensive legal documents, contracts, and case files to extract relevant information and identify patterns. This reduces the time and effort required for manual document review and enhances accuracy.

2. *Predictive Analytics*: Machine learning models predict legal outcomes, such as case settlement probabilities or success in legal disputes. Legal professionals can allocate resources more efficiently based on data-driven insights. Historical data and factors contributing to legal outcomes inform decision-making.
3. *Legal Research*: Natural language processing (NLP) models transform legal research. They analyze and summarize legal texts, statutes, and case law for legal professionals. This accelerates the research process and improves the depth and quality of legal analysis.
4. *Compliance and Risk Management*: Machine learning continuously monitors legal and regulatory changes. Algorithms provide alerts and insights into evolving legal requirements. Organizations can adapt quickly, ensuring ongoing compliance and reducing the risk of costly regulatory violations.
5. *Contract Analysis and Management*: Legal professionals automate the review of contracts using machine learning. Algorithms extract key terms and obligations, ensuring compliance throughout the contract's lifecycle. This saves time, minimizes the risk of contractual disputes, and optimizes the value of contracts for organizations.

These applications of machine learning in legal management illustrate how it enhances efficiency, accuracy, and the overall effectiveness of legal professionals, making it an indispensable tool in the contemporary legal landscape.

3.3 Current Trends in Legal Tech

3.3.1 Artificial Intelligence (AI) and Machine Learning

AI and machine learning have transformed the legal field, automating tasks like contract analysis and legal research. With the assistance of natural language processing (NLP), these technologies can process and understand human language, making legal data more accessible. Predictive analytics is a crucial component, allowing legal professionals to make data-driven decisions, predict case outcomes, and assess risks. AI chatbots are enhancing client interactions, offering instant responses to common legal inquiries and improving overall client service. Moreover, AI-driven document review tools expedite due diligence processes, reducing the time and human errors associated with reviewing extensive document volumes. These advancements enhance accuracy, efficiency, and the overall effectiveness of legal professionals.

3.3.2 E-Discovery Tools

E-discovery tools have evolved to efficiently handle vast datasets, incorporating features like predictive coding and text analytics to identify relevant information in legal cases. These tools are vital for compliance and regulatory investigations, reducing the time and cost associated with discovery and litigation processes. Machine learning algorithms in e-discovery can classify documents, detect patterns, and prioritize documents for review, ultimately improving accuracy. They play a critical role in managing the legal aspects of electronically stored information, from collection to presentation in court.

3.3.3 Legal Analytics

Legal analytics tools provide valuable insights by analyzing case law, judge histories, and legal strategies. Legal professionals use analytics to make data-driven decisions, predict case outcomes, and assess litigation strategies. These tools are particularly valuable for law firms and corporate legal departments looking to enhance their competitive edge. Access to historical legal data and performance metrics aids in formulating informed legal strategies. Analytics platforms are becoming more user-friendly, allowing legal professionals to extract meaningful insights without specialized data science knowledge.

3.3.4 Blockchain for Smart Contracts

Blockchain technology is now being used to create and enforce smart contracts automatically, reducing the need for intermediaries. These contracts execute when predefined conditions are met, enhancing efficiency in contract management by ensuring compliance and transparency. By eliminating intermediaries, smart contracts reduce administrative costs and improve the efficiency of contractual processes. Their reliability is due to blockchain's security and transparency features, making them suitable for legally binding agreements. Smart contracts have applications across various industries, including real estate, finance, and supply chain management.

3.3.5 Legal Research Tools

Legal research platforms have evolved to offer enhanced search capabilities, with the assistance of natural language processing (NLP) to improve search accuracy. These tools provide access to extensive legal databases, statutes, and case law, making research more efficient for legal professionals. Real-time updates and collaboration features are increasingly common in cloud-based legal research platforms, ensuring research teams can access comprehensive legal information, precedents, and case summaries.

3.3.6 Cybersecurity and Data Privacy

Given the increasing cyber threats and data breaches, legal tech now focuses on cybersecurity and data privacy. Encryption, secure communication tools, and compliance management solutions are integral in protecting sensitive legal information. Secure cloud storage solutions have become standard to safeguard confidential client data. Secure communication and document sharing platforms are critical to maintaining client-attorney privilege and data privacy. Additionally, cybersecurity training and awareness programs help legal organizations protect against social engineering and data breaches (Rosen et al. 2012).

3.3.7 Legal Project Management

Legal project management software is designed to assist law firms and legal departments in efficiently managing cases, budgets, and resources. These tools facilitate better project planning, execution, and monitoring, enhancing collaboration among legal teams. They enable lawyers to track billable hours, manage deadlines, and allocate resources effectively. Collaboration features, such as shared calendars and task assignments, improve team coordination. The ability to generate reports and track project progress ensures better transparency and accountability in legal projects. Legal project management has gained importance as law firms seek to enhance client service, control costs, and optimize workflow efficiencies.

4. UNLEASHING INTELLIGENT SUPPLY CHAIN GOVERNANCE

4.1 Concept of Intelligent Supply Chain Governance

Intelligent Supply Chain Governance represents a paradigm shift in how organizations manage and optimize their supply chains. It encompasses a holistic approach to supply chain management that leverages advanced technologies, data analytics, and real-time insights to enhance efficiency, reduce risks, and improve decision-making across the supply chain ecosystem. The concept of Intelligent Supply Chain Governance represents a transformative approach to how organizations manage and optimize their supply chains. It encompasses a holistic strategy that leverages cutting-edge technologies, data analytics, and real-time insights to enhance efficiency, reduce risks, and improve decision-making across the supply chain ecosystem. One of the foundational principles of Intelligent Supply Chain Governance is data-driven decision-making. It revolves around the collection and analysis of extensive data from various supply chain sources (Helo and Hao et al 2019). This data is used to inform decision-making processes, allowing organizations to anticipate potential disruptions, optimize transportation routes, and proactively respond to fluctuations in demand or supply. By harnessing the power of data, organizations gain a competitive edge in their supply chain operations. Automation and artificial intelligence (AI) are at the heart of intelligent supply chain governance. These technologies enable predictive analytics, demand forecasting, and the automation of routine supply chain tasks. Processes such as order processing, inventory management, and logistics are streamlined and optimized, reducing human intervention and enhancing overall efficiency. Real-time visibility is another key component of this concept. Intelligent supply chain governance places a strong emphasis on providing real-time visibility across the entire supply chain. This visibility extends from suppliers and manufacturers to distributors and end customers. It enables organizations to track the movement of goods, monitor inventory levels, and ensure timely deliveries. With this level of visibility, organizations can respond swiftly to any emerging issues or changes in the supply chain. Organizations work proactively to identify vulnerabilities, assess risks, and implement contingency plans. This enables them to maintain the resilience of their supply chains, ensuring that they can continue to operate effectively in the face of unexpected disruptions or challenges. Collaboration with suppliers and partners is also central to intelligent supply chain governance. By sharing real-time data and insights, organizations and their suppliers can work together to optimize processes, reduce costs, and enhance overall supply chain performance. This collaboration fosters transparency, mutual understanding, and a shared commitment to supply chain excellence (Zhao et al. 2019). Organizations monitor and reduce the environmental impact of their supply chain operations. They ensure that their suppliers adhere to ethical standards, promoting responsible and ethical practices throughout the supply chain.

4.2 Empowering Governance With Machine Learning

"Empowering Governance with Machine Learning" signifies a significant shift in how governance processes are conducted, particularly in areas like public administration, policy development, and corporate governance. This approach harnesses the capabilities of machine learning to enhance decision-making, improve efficiency, and ensure more informed and data-driven governance. One of the core principles of "Empowering Governance with Machine Learning" is the utilization of data-driven insights. Machine learning algorithms are employed to analyze vast datasets, making it possible to derive actionable insights from a wealth of information. In public administration, for instance, this could involve analyzing citizen feedback, economic indicators, and demographic data to inform policy decisions and resource allocation. In corporate governance, it might mean analyzing financial data, market trends, and customer behavior to make strategic decisions. Machine learning also introduces predictive capabilities into governance processes. By examining historical data and identifying patterns, machine learning models can make predictions about future events or trends. For example, in public administration, this could involve predicting areas with the highest likelihood of needing additional infrastructure investment (Liu and Li et al. 2020). In corporate governance, it might involve forecasting market fluctuations or identifying potential areas of operational risk. Routine administrative tasks in governance, such as document processing, data entry, or even regulatory compliance checks, can be automated using machine learning algorithms. This not only reduces the workload on human administrators but also minimizes errors and ensures consistent execution of tasks. The real-time aspect of machine learning is vital in governance. Real-time data analysis and monitoring enable authorities to respond swiftly to emerging situations or events. In public administration, this could involve monitoring social media for real-time feedback on government initiatives. In corporate governance, real-time monitoring can help detect and respond to financial anomalies or cybersecurity threats promptly. By analyzing data, trends, and outcomes, governance entities can make decisions that are grounded in empirical evidence rather than assumptions. This can lead to more effective and efficient resource allocation, policy development, and strategic planning. Incorporating machine learning into governance processes fosters transparency and accountability. By providing a data-driven basis for decisions, stakeholders can better understand the reasoning behind specific policies or actions. This transparency enhances trust in public administration and can lead to improved corporate governance practices.

5. EFFECTIVE IMPLEMENTATION STRATEGIES

5.1 Integrating Machine Learning in Legal Management

Integrating machine learning into legal management is a strategic approach aimed at improving the efficiency and effectiveness of legal processes. The first step in this process involves a comprehensive assessment of the specific needs and objectives of the legal management system. Legal professionals must identify areas where machine learning can have the most significant impact, such as contract analysis, legal research, or compliance monitoring. This assessment helps define the scope and goals of the integration, ensuring that it aligns with the organization's strategic objectives. The assessment, the next crucial step is data collection and preparation. Legal documents, case histories, and relevant data sources need to be carefully organized and cleaned to ensure data quality and consistency. Proper data preprocessing is essential to provide machine learning models with accurate and reliable information for analysis and decision-making. Selecting the appropriate machine learning algorithms is a critical decision in the integration process. Natural language processing (NLP) algorithms may be required for text analysis, while classification or regression models can be used for predictive tasks. The choice of algorithms depends on the specific tasks and objectives identified during the initial assessment. Selecting the right algorithms is crucial for achieving the desired outcomes and maximizing the value of the integration (Tama et al. 2017). Once the data is prepared, machine learning models need to be trained and validated. During this phase, the models learn from historical data, identifying patterns and making predictions based on past experiences. Rigorous testing and evaluation are essential to ensure the accuracy and reliability of the models. It may require an iterative process of refining the models to achieve the desired performance. Integration into existing legal management workflows is the next step. The machine learning capabilities need to be seamlessly incorporated into daily operations, ensuring they align with the processes and responsibilities of legal professionals. The transition should be as smooth as possible to minimize disruption and maximize adoption. User training and adoption are pivotal for the successful integration of machine learning into legal management. Legal professionals and staff must be trained to effectively use the machine learning tools and understand their capabilities. User training programs and ongoing support should be provided to facilitate this transition and ensure that the benefits of machine learning are fully realized. Continuous monitoring and improvement are essential to maintain the accuracy and effectiveness of machine learning models. Legal management systems should include mechanisms for monitoring model performance and making necessary adjustments. This may involve retraining models with new data, addressing emerging issues, and improving algorithm performance to keep the integration up to date and effective. Legal organizations must also adhere to data privacy and ethical standards throughout the integration process. Compliance with legal and regulatory requirements, as well as ethical considerations related to data handling and decision-making, should be fundamental aspects of the integration strategy to maintain trust and integrity in legal processes. Regular evaluation and feedback mechanisms are critical to assessing the impact of machine learning integration on legal management processes. Soliciting feedback from legal professionals and stakeholders helps understand the benefits and challenges of the new system. Continuous improvement efforts should be based on this feedback, ensuring that the integration remains aligned with the organization's evolving needs and goals. As the integration proves successful and delivers value, legal organizations can consider scaling and expanding the use of machine learning in legal management. Exploring additional use cases and opportunities for optimization while staying informed about emerging technologies and trends ensures that the organization remains competitive and at the forefront of innovation in the legal field. Integrating machine learning into legal management is a dynamic and ongoing process that promises to enhance the efficiency and capabilities of legal professionals while enabling them to make more data-driven and informed decisions (Tapscott et al. 2016).

5.2 Managing Change and Training Requirements

Change management and training are essential components of any transformative initiative, including the integration of machine learning and artificial intelligence into legal management. Ensuring that both legal professionals and support staff are prepared for the changes is critical to the success of this endeavor. Change management involves the systematic approach of preparing, equipping, and supporting individuals to adopt new methods, processes, and technologies. In the context of machine learning integration, it entails communicating the reasons for the change, identifying potential challenges, and creating strategies to mitigate resistance. Legal organizations need to build a culture that embraces innovation and change, emphasizing the benefits of machine learning in enhancing efficiency and accuracy. Training, on the other hand, is the practical implementation of change management. It involves imparting the necessary knowledge and skills to use machine learning tools effectively. This training is not limited to legal professionals but should extend to all individuals interacting with the legal management system. It includes hands-on training on new software, understanding data analytics, and mastering the tools that will become part of the daily workflow. To address change management and training needs effectively, legal organizations should start by developing a comprehensive change management plan. This plan should include clear communication strategies to keep all stakeholders informed and engaged throughout the integration process. Identifying potential areas of resistance and proactively addressing concerns is a crucial part of this plan. Legal organizations should tailor training programs to the specific needs and roles of their employees. Training should be ongoing and include opportunities for hands-on practice. It is also essential to measure the effectiveness of the training programs through assessments and feedback mechanisms, allowing adjustments as needed (Rana et al. 2019). The successful integration of machine learning in legal management heavily depends on how well change management and training are executed. When legal professionals are equipped with the right skills and understand the value of the technology, they are more likely to embrace the changes and leverage machine learning to enhance their work and achieve better results.

6. CONCLUSION

The outlined sections have collectively shed light on the critical intersection of legal management and supply chain governance with the integration of machine learning. The significance of supply chain governance was emphasized, emphasizing the imperative of compliance and risk management to ensure transparency, accountability, and resilience in supply chain operations. Legal management's role in navigating the complex legal landscape and the case for machine learning integration were also underscored. Understanding the principles of supply chain governance and the basics of machine learning is fundamental to appreciating the potential benefits these technologies bring. The applications of machine learning in legal management offer a glimpse into the transformative power of predictive analytics, document analysis, and other AI-driven solutions. The discussion on current trends in legal tech highlighted the rapidly evolving landscape, where AI, blockchain, and cybersecurity play crucial roles. The integration of machine learning into legal management and the strategies to manage change and training requirements were detailed, emphasizing the need for careful planning and execution. Ultimately, the conclusion underscores the importance of embracing these advancements in technology and strategy as a means to enhance efficiency, transparency, and sustainability. The outlined sections collectively provide a roadmap for organizations to adapt and thrive in a data-driven and increasingly complex business environment, ultimately redefining how legal and supply chain professionals operate and make decisions.

REFERENCES

Bai, C., & Sarkis, J. (2020). A supply chain transparency and sustainability technology appraisal model for blockchain technology. *International Journal of Production Research*, *58*(7), 2142–2162. doi:10.1080/00207543.2019.1708989

Choi, T.-M. (2019). Blockchain-technology-supported platforms for diamond authentication and certification in luxury supply chains. *Transportation Research Part E, Logistics and Transportation Review, 128*, 17–29. doi:10.1016/j.tre.2019.05.011

Cottrill, K. (2018). The Benefits of Blockchain: Fact or wishful thinking. *Supply Chain Manag. Rev., 22*, 20–25.

Helo, P., & Hao, Y. (2019). Blockchains in operations and supply chains: A model and reference implementation. *Computers & Industrial Engineering, 136*, 242–251. doi:10.1016/j.cie.2019.07.023

Koot, M., Mes, M. R. K., & Iacob, M. E. (2020). A systematic literature review of supply chain decision making supported by the Internet of things and big data analytics. *Computers & Industrial Engineering, 154*, 107076. doi:10.1016/j.cie.2020.107076

Liu, Z. Y., & Li, Z. P. (2020). A blockchain-based framework of cross-border e-commerce supply chain. *International Journal of Information Management, 52*, 102059. doi:10.1016/j.ijinfomgt.2019.102059

Mercuri, F., della Corte, G., & Ricci, F. (2021). Blockchain technology and sustainable business models: A case study of Devoleum. *Sustainability (Basel), 13*(10), 5619. doi:10.3390/su13105619

Rosen, M. A. (2012). Engineering sustainability: A technical approach to sustainability. *Sustainability (Basel), 4*(9), 2270–2292. doi:10.3390/su4092270

Saberi, S., Kouhizadeh, M., Sarkis, J., & Shen, L. (2019). Blockchain technology and its relationships to sustainable supply chain management. *International Journal of Production Research, 57*(7), 2117–2135. doi:10.1080/00207543.2018.1533261

Tama, B. A., Kweka, B. J., Park, Y., & Rhee, K. H. (2017). A critical review of blockchain and its current applications. *Proceedings of the 2017 International Conference on Electrical Engineering and Computer Science,* 109–113. 10.1109/ICECOS.2017.8167115

Tapscott, D., & Euchner, J. (2019). Blockchain and the Internet of Value. *Research Technology Management, 62*(1), 12–19. doi:10.1080/08956308.2019.1541711

Tapscott, D., & Tapscott, A. (2016). *Blockchain Revolution: How the Technology behind Bitcoin Is Changing Money, Business and the World.* Penguin Random House.

Tseng, C.-T., & Shang, S. S. C. (2021). Exploring the sustainability of the intermediary role in blockchain. *Sustainability (Basel), 13*(4), 1936. doi:10.3390/su13041936

Zhao, G., Liu, S., Lopez, C., Lu, H., Elgueta, S., Chen, H., & Boshkoska, B. M. (2019). Blockchain technology in agri-food value chain management: A synthesis of applications, challenges and future research directions. *Computers in Industry, 109*, 83–99. doi:10.1016/j.compind.2019.04.002

Chapter 4
The Intersection of AI Technology and Intellectual Property Adjudication in Supply Chain Management

Esther Edet Archibong
Legal Matters Department, Federal Polytechnic, Nekede, Nigeria

Kene-Unwana Trenchard Ibia
Faculty of Law, Topfaith University, Nigeria

Balakumar Muniandi
https://orcid.org/0000-0003-2298-5093
Lawrence Technological University, USA

Sukhvinder Singh Dari
https://orcid.org/0000-0002-6218-6600
Symbiosis Law School, Symbiosis International University, Pune, India

Dharmesh Dhabliya
https://orcid.org/0000-0002-6340-2993
Department of Information Technology, Vishwakarma Institute of Information Technology, India

Pankaj Dadheech
https://orcid.org/0000-0001-5783-1989
Swami Keshvanand Institute of Technology, Management, and Gramothan, India

ABSTRACT

In modern Nigerian supply chain management, the adjudication of intellectual property rights has gained paramount importance. With the rapid advancement of technology, the integration of AI-powered analytics has emerged as a promising resolution for settling disputes and safeguarding intellectual property rights. This chapter highlights the multifaceted role of AI-driven analytics in the adjudication process, exploring its impact on improving efficiency, precision, and impartiality in resolving disputes related to intellectual property within the Nigerian supply chain. The authors suggest that comprehensive ethical standards, data privacy regulations, and transparency protocols should be established by the government, stakeholders, and law enforcement agencies to mitigate potential biases, ensure data integrity, and ensure adherence to ethical and legal norms in AI technologies.

DOI: 10.4018/979-8-3693-1347-3.ch004

INTRODUCTION

The term "supply chain management" (SCM) (Malhotra, P. et al.,2021) first appeared in the 1980s, encompassing crucial business processes that extend from end-users to initial suppliers (Ryan, 2017). According to Kaminsky, Simchi-Levi and Simchi-Levi (2003), SCM is a strategic approach utilized to oversee manufacturers, distributors, warehouses, and retail stores, aiming to ensure the efficient production and delivery of goods in optimal quantities, locations, and timelines, thereby reducing system costs and meeting service level requirements. Janvier-James (2012) stated that the fundamental principle underlying SCM emphasizes that businesses and organizations involved in a supply chain should collaborate by exchanging insights regarding market conditions and production capabilities. In recent times, the Nigerian supply chain management sector has observed an increasing demand for effective adjudication mechanisms concerning intellectual property rights. As the landscape continues to progress, the rise of advanced technologies, notably AI-driven analytics, offers a promising pathway for resolving disputes and safeguarding intellectual property within this intricate ecosystem.

Considering the complex nature of supply chain operations and the crucial importance of safeguarding intellectual property, the integration of AI (Singh, H. et al.,2022) driven analytics is poised to transform the adjudication process, providing a sophisticated approach that tackles the challenges of maintaining fairness, precision, and efficiency in dispute resolution (Min, 2015). This introduction sets the stage for a comprehensive examination of the transformative role played by AI-powered analytics in the adjudication of intellectual property rights (Duarte, Sanches &Dedini, 2018).Since the inception of the abacus, humanity has been fascinated by the pursuit of creating intelligent machines (Pandey, B. K. et al.,2021d) capable of mimicking or surpassing human intelligence. Borenstein and Howard (2021) stressed that the global adoption and use of Artificial Intelligence (AI) (Pandey, B. K. et al.,2021a) are rapidly increasing. Recent advancements in artificial intelligence, particularly in natural language processing and machine learning (BR, S. R. et al.,2023), have raised questions about conventional ideas of human capability (Bhavani &Thuraisingam, 2022). Machines are now performing increasingly complex tasks more effectively than humans. In recent years, countries like Australia, China, France, and the United States have extensively leveraged the potential of artificial intelligence analytics (Pandey, B. K. et al., 2021c), leading to significant impacts and commendable results (Pedro, Subosa, Rivas & Valverde (2019).

The term "artificial intelligence" (Anand, R. et al.,2023) was initially employed in August 1955 in a proposal for a research project authored by John McCarthy, Marvin L. Minsky, Nathaniel Rochester, and Claude Shannon (McCarthy, Minsky, Rochester, Simon 2006). AI, as a field of study, focuses on the creation and progression of intelligent machines (Luxton (2016). Artificial intelligence, also known as machine intelligence (M.I.) (Khan, B. et al.,2021), involves an examination of the cognitive processes of the human brain, investigating how it reasons, learns, makes decisions, and operates when solving problems. These findings serve as a basis for developing intelligent (Revathi, T. K. et al.,2022) software and systems that simulate and replicate human behaviors (Adamopoulou &Moussiades, 2020).Moreover, by harnessing advancements in AI and Machine Learning (Vinodhini, V. et al., 2022), these systems are increasingly adept at processing vast volumes of data within remarkably short timeframes (Simon, Lindsay, Sosa, & Comparato, 2018). Additionally, these systems continually enhance their capabilities, producing predictions with heightened accuracy (Kelly, 2015).

AI-driven analytics refers to the use of advanced algorithms and machine learning (Meslie, Y. et al.,2021) models to analyze extensive datasets, identify patterns, and produce actionable insights or predictions (Rouse, 2018).The underlying principle of AI-driven analytics is to enable systems to learn from data, recognize complex patterns, and adjust to new information without explicit programming. By harnessing machine learning, deep learning (Kumar Pandey, B. et al.,2021), and natural language processing, AI-driven analytics can uncover hidden correlations, detect anomalies, and provide real-time, data-driven recommendations that significantly enhance decision-making processes.AI is categorized into two primary types: weak and strong AI, also known as narrow and general AI (Chang, 2020). Weak AI refers to AI as a problem-solving tool, while strong AI involves the creation of a "true" intellect (Flowers, 2019). Research in Artificial Intelligence (AI) has enriched human existence and has brought about positive transformations across various domains (Zhang & Lu, 2021). The legal profession is evidently not immune to these technological advancements. The rise of data-driven technologies, driven by automation and AI advancements, is poised to disrupt the traditional methodologies of the legal system significantly(Alarie, Niblett & Yoon, 2018). The sheer volume of data requiring comprehensive and intensive analysis to facilitate fair and unbiased decision-making in the judiciary continues to occupy a significant portion of the judiciary and adversely impact the case management system.

The landscape of legal services has undergone significant transformation due to changes in access to legal information. Globally, the legal sector is faced with the impetus to innovate and reshape the approach to legal operations (Bhavani &Thuraisingam, 2022). In 1976, Westlaw and Lexis introduced computer-assisted legal research, shifting the reliance from physical law books. Lawyers gained the ability to access these materials through computers, as the texts were accessible in electronic formats, allowing for keyword searches to locate relevant sources (Alarie, Niblett & Yoon, 2017).Today, the demand for justice has increased as society becomes more intricate, resulting in heightened citizen involvement in commercial and legal disputes (Founder, Herik & Salem, 2015).Legal professionals' shoulder numerous legal responsibilities, including providing counsel to clients, drafting contractual documents, and safeguarding Intellectual Property Rights (IPRs). Undoubtedly, the protection of Intellectual Property Rights (IPRs) holds growing significance across numerous countries globally, impacting the social (Lelisho, M. E. et al.,2023) and economic landscapes of these nations. In many developed nations, laws effectively protect the intellectual property rights of creators and inventors. Safeguarding intellectual properties helps governments to curb the actions of violators, counterfeiters, and imitators of intellectual works. Consequently, the protection of IPRs fosters economic growth for nations and contributes to the valuation of intellectual creations (Holland, 2017). Governments in various countries have implemented the protection of intellectual properties through the enactment of dynamic and robust laws. These laws undergo regular reviews to effectively address emerging innovations and challenges in the operational environment (Afolayan, 2022).

Intellectual property (IP) spans a broad spectrum, encompassing literary, artistic, and scientific works; performances by performing artists, as well as phonograms and broadcasts; inventions across all fields of human endeavor; scientific discoveries; industrial (David, S. et al.,2023) designs; trademarks, service marks, commercial names, and designations; protection against unfair competition, and other rights derived from intellectual pursuits in industrial, scientific, and technological sectors (FRN, 2004). According to the World Intellectual Property Organization (WIPO),

Intellectual property pertains to the legal rights stemming from creative endeavors in industry, research, literature, and the arts. The primary goal of intellectual property law is to safeguard artists and creators of intellectual goods and services by granting them time-bound rights to control the use of their work. These rights apply to the intellectual work itself, rather than the physical entities in which it might be integrated (WIPO, 1997).

These creations are afforded legal protection, providing their creators with proprietary and transferable rights. This right empowers the creator to regulate the use and misuse of their creation by others. Legal statutes establish the foundation for the moral and economic rights of creators, while also fostering encouragement and incentives for the advancement of creativity and innovation. New creative forms emerging from the digital and online sphere, including databases and multimedia, often exist within Intellectual property (IP) without precise delineation (Adewopo, 2015; Cecil &Kesiena, 2022).

Through the utilization of AI-powered analytics, the judicial system can develop a deeper understanding of complex datasets, assess legal cases, predict case outcomes, identify relevant precedents, and provide invaluable insights to assist legal professionals and judges in making well-informed and impartial judgments (Yulia & Sergiy, 2021).AI applications can facilitate legal reasoning by scouring databases of legal texts and identifying pertinent cases related to ongoing judicial proceedings, while also offering suggestions on judgments or guidance based on available information (Reiling, 2020).This tool effectively streamlines case management by filtering out irrelevant data (Sunstein, 2001). Similar to numerous other judicial systems worldwide, the Nigerian judiciary faces challenges posed by increasing caseloads and the need for prompt and accurate case resolutions. In response to these challenges, the integration of AI-driven predictive analytics has emerged as a promising solution to streamline case management processes and advance the interests of Intellectual Property (IP). This chapter emphasizes the crucial role of ensuring robust protection and enforcement of intellectual property rights by thoroughly examining the current situation.

OVERVIEW OF AI-DRIVEN ANALYTICS IN LEGAL SYSTEM

The founding "Artificial Intelligence + Law Science" conference, hosted at Boston University in the United States in 1987, gave rise to the formation of the International Association of Artificial Intelligence (Pandey, B. K., & Pandey, D., 2023) and Law (IAAIL),with the goal of promoting AI research and its application in the legal domain (Jiang, 2018). The conference delineated ten crucial areas where AI could potentially be applied in legal contexts (Jianfeng, 2017).Today, AI applications offer a wide array of legal solutions, including contract drafting and review, digital signatures, management of contract documents, litigation budgeting, assessment of scientific expert testimony, bankruptcy, immigration, estate planning, taxes, securities, food and drug cases, contract due diligence, automation of expertise, legal analytics, task management, title review, and lease abstracts(Connell, 2018). The American Bar Association has expressed the view that AI represents the next significant leap that will bring about a revolution in the legal profession (Chamberlain & Poteet, 2016).In 2014, the London-based legal consulting firm Jomati published a report titled "Civilization 2030: The Law Firm in the Near Future," foreseeing that, after a period of incubation and experimentation, technology would rapidly progress. The report boldly predicted that within 15 years, robots and artificial intelligence (Pandey, D., & Pandey, B. K., 2022) would dominate legal practice, potentially causing a 'structural collapse' in law firms and a substantial transformation in the market for legal services (Teng & Huafeng, 2019).

Artificial intelligence is increasingly employed in judicial and agency proceedings, utilizing computer software such as COMPAS and the Public Safety Assessment (PSA) to analyze extensive datasets. These systems find application in various contexts, including predictive policing, bail setting, and other public safety concerns (Mariano-Florentino, 2017). Major online platforms such as eBay and PayPal, faced with a surge in disputes over incorrect charges and misrepresented items, have implemented resolution tools capable of automatically handling over sixty million cases annually (Larry, 2018). These software systems evaluate the arguments presented by each party, assess them using specific algorithms, and autonomously generate solutions. While these disputes may appear trivial, their resolution can consume valuable time and resources, potentially leaving consumers dissatisfied if not handled diligently (Larry, 2018). However, with the use of AI agents, these cases are adjudicated within minutes, ensuring a level of fairness that has significantly boosted customer satisfaction (Larry, 2018). Similarly, software solutions like Legal Robot have been developed to assist individuals in understanding complex legal language and identifying potential issues before signing, obviating the need to engage costly legal services (Connell, 2018). Leveraging legal algorithms, these technologies provide fairness and risk analysis, catering specifically to non-legal professionals (Connell, 2018).

A research study conducted by scholars at the Massachusetts Institute of Technology and the University of North Carolina School of Law uncovered that large law firms allocate merely four percent of lawyers' time to document review, outsourcing most of this responsibility or assigning it to artificial intelligence (Steve, 2017). Their investigation suggested that the immediate adoption of all new legal technologies could potentially result in a thirteen percent reduction in lawyers' billable hours (Steve, 2017). Similarly, a study focusing on contract review revealed that the Contract Intelligence (COIN) software efficiently completed the review process in just 26 seconds, whereas participating lawyers spent 92 minutes on the same task (Davis, 2020). Notably, the AI program Catalyst managed to review an impressive 723,537 documents within five days (Nelson & Simek, 2017). This software empowers users to convert documents into digital formats and execute various responses on individual documents by searching for specific words or phrases. A prominent instance is the JP Morgan Chase COIN (Contract Intelligence) software, which annually saves 360,000 hours of contract review work for lawyers and swiftly scrutinizes voluminous documents, significantly reducing legal costs and mitigating errors stemming from human fallibility. This technology notably enhances the document review process by extracting pertinent information (Nelson & Simek, 2017). Despite the favorable speed and efficiency of AI in conducting due diligence, it is crucial to acknowledge the necessity of avoiding over-reliance, as these systems are not entirely foolproof (Manap & Abdullah, 2020).

The rise of AI holds the promise of revolutionizing the legal profession, particularly in tasks like contract review that many lawyers often consider mundane. AI can significantly expedite and improve this process, enabling legal practitioners to allocate their time more prudently to legal work where AI's capabilities are less suited, such as litigation strategy (Umali, 2018). For instance, in a case study in the United Kingdom, AI software known as "Case Cruncher Alpha" surpassed human lawyers, accurately predicting case outcomes with an 86.6 percent success rate, compared to the lawyers' 66.3 percent (Bhavani &Thuraisingam, 2022). This raises the question of whether lawyers can keep up with AI as it continues to progress and nears 100 percent accuracy? (Ting, 2017). Notably, in June 2016, Ross, the world's first AI lawyer supported by IBM's cognitive computer, Watson, was "hired" by an American law firm. Ross can engage in human-like conversations with lawyers, provide insights into potential cases, and address specific issues in bankruptcy consulting (Liberatore, 2018). This AI lawyer excels in legal research, drafting research memos, analyzing briefs, and suggesting missing cases from a list of authorities in an existing brief (Ross Intelligence, 2018). Similarly, programs like CARA provide legal summaries and research memos (Allison, 2018). In February 2018, an AI system developed by Lawgeex, an Israeli legal technology company, outperformed 20 experienced lawyers in a standard business contract review competition, demonstrating the potential of AI in the legal field (Teng & Huafeng, 2019).AI's primary impact has been on legal processes such as analytics and discovery,attributed to the precision and accuracy of algorithms in executing rule-based tasks (McGinnis & Pearce, 2019).

AI-driven predictive analytics enables legal professionals to assess potential case outcomes based on historical precedents, court decisions, and relevant case law,known as predictive justice in English terminology (Harry, 2014; Reiling, 2020). Lexis Advance, a legal research service that integrated Lex Machina litigation analytics following its acquisition by Lexis Nexis in 2015, transforms court case data into dynamic charts (Nelson & Simek, 2017). It provides concise judge biographies, categorizes ongoing cases by area of practice, assesses cases by year, and offers case schedules (Remus & Levy, 2017). AI-driven tools streamline automated legal research, granting legal experts access to extensive databases, repositories of case law, and legal documents for pertinent precedents and references (Lin, 2019). Notably, the ROSS platform employs cognitive computation (Bessant, Y. A. et al.,2023) that utilizes natural language processing for analyzing legal documents (Schaefer & Taylor, 2019).Furthermore, effective risk assessment stands as a crucial responsibility for lawyers. Inadequate risk assessment often leads to costly lawsuits, resulting in negative impacts on clients (McCarthy, 2018).Fortunately, AI innovations, such as Technology Assisted Review (TAR) tools with predictive coding capabilities, can address this inefficiency. Enhanced risk assessment practices will enable law firms and legal professionals to accurately evaluate potential risks, thereby minimizing costs and safeguarding their reputation and clients' interests. In 2018, Grace InfoTech Limited in Nigeria introduced a new AI-driven product called 'Timi,' integrated into the Law Pavilion suite software and electronic law reports (LawPavilion, 2023).Considering the rapid growth of technology, coupled with advancements in Machine Learning, it is anticipated that AI will eventually replace many manual tasks currently exclusive to the legal profession (Susskind, 2017). This is feasible due to the significant improvement and advancement of machine intelligence (Kumar, M. S. et al.,2021) with continued use.

INTELLECTUAL PROPERTY RIGHTS (IPRS) IN NIGERIAN SUPPLY CHAIN MANAGEMENT

Nigeria, an emerging economy with a rapidly expanding industrial landscape, acknowledges the essential role of intellectual property rights (IPRs) in fostering innovation, creativity, and competitiveness within its supply chain management sector. As defined by WIPO, intellectual property encompasses products of the mind, including inventions, literary and artistic works, symbols, names, images (Boopathi, S. et al., 2023), and designs used in commercial settings (WIPO, 1997). IPRs cover a range of intangible assets, including patents, trademarks, copyrights, and trade secrets, which are vital for safeguarding the ingenuity and proprietary knowledge of businesses operating within the supply chain network. These rights are established to protect the interests of creators and inventors and regulate the use of their creations (Afolayan, 2022). The Nigerian legal framework governing IPRs comprises various laws, such as the Patents and Designs Act, the Trademarks Act, and the Copyright Act, among others, serving as the cornerstone for the protection and enforcement of intellectual property across different sectors. The clause "The Federal High Court shall have and exercise exclusive jurisdiction to the exclusion of any other court in civil causes and matters." signifies that any civil matter related to intellectual property must be initiated exclusively in the Federal High Court, with no other court authorized by law to adjudicate such matters. This provision closely aligns with the guidelines outlined in section 7 of the Federal High Court Act (FRN, 2004).

In Nigeria, Intellectual property rights are classified into four main groups, specifically Copyright, Patents, Trademarks, and industrial designs (Afolayan, 2022). Copyright refers to the legal protection that creators hold over their literary and artistic works. Works falling within the scope of copyright encompass books, music, paintings, sculptures, computer programs, databases, maps, and technical drawings(Cecil &Kesiena, 2022). Under the Copyright Amended Acts of 1999, copyright holders possess the rights to publish and reproduce the work in any tangible form, perform the work in public, create cinematograph films or recordings of the work, distribute copies of the work to the public for commercial purposes through renting, leasing, hiring, loaning, or similar arrangements, broadcast or communicate the work to the public via loudspeakers or any analogous device, and create adaptations of the work (Afolayan, 2022).These copyright provisions dictate how creators' works can be utilized or disseminated for public consumption. Failure to comply with these rights can result in appropriate sanctions, as outlined in the Copyright Amended Act of 1999 (Afolayan, 2022).

A patent denotes an exclusive right granted for an invention for a maximum period of 20 years, beginning from the date of the patent application's filing. This right prevents others from using the invention during the specified period (Kujembola, 2014). In exchange for this right, the patent holder makes information about the patent publicly accessible through the published patent document. The regulations governing patent and design matters in Nigeria are established under the Patent and Designs Act of 1990, which allocates Sections 1-11 to patents and Sections 12-22 exclusively to design.Similarly, a trademark represents a symbol, sign, or logo distinguishing an organization's goods and services from others (WIPO, 1997). The Nigerian Trademark Act Cap T13 LFN 2004 oversees the registration and management of trademarks in Nigeria. Consequently, individuals seeking trademark protection must register with the Registrar of Trademarks. Trademarks safeguard names, logos, shapes, and slogans for a duration of 7 years, renewable for an additional 14 years. Likewise, industrial designs encompass the ornamental or aesthetic aspects of an article. These designs may incorporate three-dimensional features such as the shape or surface of an article, or two-dimensional elements like patterns, lines, or colors (WIPO, 1997). State authorities grant rights to industrial designs upon meeting specific criteria set by the governing body. Registering an industrial design grants the applicant the right to prohibit others from copying or replicating the design, manufacturing the product, or selling it for commercial purposesAfolayan, (2022). The right to an industrial design is granted for a maximum duration of 15 years, starting from the date of the registration application.

Despite the presence of these legal provisions, challenges persist, encompassing inadequate enforcement mechanisms and issues linked to piracy and counterfeiting, which pose substantial threats to the integrity and value of intellectual property assets within the supply chain(Cecil &Kesiena, 2022). In this context, the protection of creators' and investors' intellectual property rights remains insufficient, primarily due to the persistent increase in illicit activities such as piracy, counterfeiting, and imitation (Nwokocha, 2012).Nigeria notably grapples with the highest rates of software piracy, intellectual property theft, and related malpractices within the IT industry across the African continent (Andembubto, Apuru, & Ezra, 2020).It has become evident that the current IP law in Nigeria lacks a well-thought-out policy framework that effectively addresses the contemporary economic and technological environment(Cecil &Kesiena, 2022). The foundation of Nigerian IP law originates from English Imperial law, and despite frequent revisions, it has failed to adequately adapt to modern circumstances. One aspect of this deficiency pertains to the framework for digital rights management (DRM) and the legal prohibition of circumventing technological protection measures (TPM). Furthermore, the powers of the Nigerian Copyright Commission (NCC) and the Trademark and Patent Registry, along with the issue of fragmented

IP institutions, require significant reforms to reflect contemporary needs (Cecil &Kesiena, 2022).Effective protection of intellectual property promotes innovation, attracts foreign investment, and fosters a conducive environment for sustainable economic growth.

The imperative for robust adjudication mechanisms to resolve disputes, enforce rights, and discourage infringements remains a crucial consideration. The incorporation of technological advancements, such as AI-driven analytics, offers a compelling opportunity to strengthen the protection of IPRs within the Nigerian supply chain management framework. By harnessing AI-powered tools, stakeholders can improve the efficiency of IPR adjudication processes, ensure timely resolution of disputes, and bolster the overall enforcement mechanisms, thereby creating a more secure (Pandey, D. et al.,2021a) and conducive environment for innovation and business development. As Nigeria continues to assert its position as a key player in the global supply chain arena, the effective management and protection of intellectual property rights stand as fundamental pillars for sustainable economic progress and competitiveness on the international stage.

CHALLENGES OF AI-DRIVEN ANALYTICSIN ADJUDICATION OF IPRS IN NIGERIAN SUPPLY CHAIN MANAGEMENT

The integration of AI-driven analytics in the adjudication of Intellectual Property Rights (IPRs) within the Nigerian supply chain management sector offers a transformative opportunity, yet it also presents a set of intricate challenges that require careful consideration. While AI technologies promise streamlined processes and improved decision-making, several key hurdles must be addressed to ensure their effective and ethical implementation:

1. **Legal and Ethical Implications:** AI-driven analytics bring forth complex legal and ethical concerns, including issues of transparency, accountability, and the potential for algorithmic biases. Ensuring that AI systems adhere to ethical standards and align with the legal framework for IPRs in Nigeria is crucial to maintain the integrity and fairness of the adjudication process. The ethical implications of AI application in legal practice are currently a primary focus. Lawyers are responsible for ensuring competence and diligence which adds the responsibility to understand the reasoning used by AI systems, as well as their capabilities and limitations (Nunez, 2017; Rogers, & Bell, 2019). However, grasping the intricacies of specific AI technologies presents a significant challenge for legal practitioners, who traditionally are not synonymous with legal technology (Susskind, 2017). Moreover, the inherent complexity of AI systems, often referred to as the 'black box' of AI, further complicates matters for legal professionals (Yu & Ali, 2019).
2. **Poor Data Quality and Accessibility:** Access to comprehensive and reliable data sets, particularly in the context of IPRs, can be a significant challenge in Nigeria. Limited data availability or poor data quality can hinder the accurate training and functioning of AI algorithms, leading to potential inaccuracies and biases in the adjudication process. The integration of AI technologies in Nigerian courts necessitates the implementation of robust measures to preserve data privacy (Pandey, D. et al.,2021b) and security, ensuring the protection of sensitive client information and legal data (Ardia, 2017). Safeguarding confidential client data, enforcing data encryption (Pramanik, S. et al.,2023), and adhering to data protection protocols play a pivotal role in averting data breaches and upholding client trust and confidentiality (Haseeb, et al. 2020).The challenges stemming from

inadequate data security underscore the complexity of these systems Zhao, et al., 2019).Mitigating the risk of cyber-attacks is crucial, considering the substantial costs involved; for instance, the annual expense of installing digital infrastructure stands at approximately $30 billion (Fickling, 2019).The prevalence of cyber-attacks targeting law firms is a growing and acknowledged threat (Calo, 2015).

3. **Skill Gaps and Capacity Building:** Building and maintaining a workforce equipped with the necessary skills to develop, operate, and regulate AI systems remains a pressing challenge. Training legal professionals, adjudicators, and other stakeholders in the intricacies of AI-driven analytics and their application in the context of IPRs is essential to ensure the competent and responsible deployment of these technologies. A successful integration of AI within the Nigerian courts hinges on fostering a workforce equipped with the requisite technological skills and expertise to effectively utilize AI tools (Rubim & Fortes, 2021). Closing the skill gaps and implementing comprehensive training programs for legal and paralegal professionals on AI-related technologies and applications is indispensable in unlocking the full potential of AI and ensuring its responsible and adept assimilation within the Nigerian legal framework.
4. **Lack of Trust and Acceptance:** Cultivating trust and fostering acceptance among stakeholders, including legal practitioners, businesses, and the general public, is essential for the successful adoption of AI-driven analytics in the adjudication of IPRs. Overcoming skepticism and addressing concerns about the reliability and neutrality of AI systems is critical for their effective integration into the Nigerian supply chain management sector.
5. **Cost of Implementation:** Implementing AI systems in the legal system entails significant costs, potentially posing a barrier for small or mid-tier firms with limited financial resources for investments (Remus & Levy, 2017). Resolving issues related to legal responsibility, attributing liability, and establishing decision-making accountability is crucial in ensuring the responsible use of AI technologies and maintaining the oversight and control of critical legal processes and outcomes within the Nigerian courts.
6. **Algorithm Bias:** AI systems developed on datasets associating specific nationalities or races with particular crimes pose a primary concern in the application of AI within the legal systems. These systems tend to perpetuate historical racial and gender biases predominantly accrue to individuals already positioned in power, who are predominantly white, educated, and male (Lauterbach, 2019).
7. **Lack of Relevant Government Policies:** The absence of comprehensive policies for AI implementation remains a significant concern in African countries as AI-driven technologies continue to permeate business, governance, and educational domain like Australia, China, France, and the United States (Pedro, et al., 2019). Although some African countries, including Mauritius, Egypt, Zambia, Tunisia, and Botswana, have acknowledged the potential of AI in augmenting GDP and have devised national AI strategies, and countries like South Africa, Nigeria, and Kenya have enacted data protection laws, these efforts are still in their nascent stages (Effoduh, 2020).
8. **Inadequate Technological Infrastructure:** Despite advancements, certain regions in Nigeria may still have underdeveloped technological infrastructure required for the effective implementation of AI-driven analytics. Inadequate infrastructure, including limitations in internet connectivity and computing resources, can impede the seamless integration and operation of AI technologies within the adjudication framework.

Mitigating these challenges demands a comprehensive approach that involves collaboration between legal experts, technologists, policymakers, and industry stakeholders to develop robust frameworks that promote responsible AI adoption while upholding the integrity and protection of IPRs in the Nigerian supply chain management landscape.

STRATEGIES TO CURB CHALLENGES OF AI-DRIVEN ANALYTICS IN ADJUDICATION OF IPRS IN NIGERIAN SUPPLY CHAIN MANAGEMENT

As the integration of AI-driven analytics in the adjudication of Intellectual Property Rights (IPRs) in the Nigerian supply chain management sector presents various challenges, implementing comprehensive strategies can help mitigate these obstacles and foster a more effective and efficient adjudication process. Investing in the development of robust data infrastructure is critical. Initiatives aimed at improving data collection, storage, and quality assurance can enhance the reliability and accuracy of AI-driven analytics, enabling more precise and informed adjudication processes. By addressing key concerns and ensuring a holistic approach, stakeholders can establish a conducive environment that promotes the responsible and ethical use of AI technologies:

1. Implementing and reinforcing a robust legal and ethical framework for the use of AI in adjudication is crucial. Establishing guidelines that ensure transparency, accountability, and fairness in the deployment of AI technologies can help mitigate legal and ethical risks and foster trust among stakeholders. The government, stakeholders, and law enforcement agencies should establish comprehensive ethical standards, data privacy regulations, and transparency protocols to mitigate potential biases, ensure data integrity, and guarantee adherence to ethical and legal norms in AI technologies.
2. Fostering collaborations between the government, private sector, and academia can facilitate the development of comprehensive AI strategies tailored to the unique challenges of IPR adjudication in the Nigerian supply chain management sector. Public-private partnerships can promote knowledge sharing, resource pooling, and the implementation of innovative solutions that address the multifaceted challenges of AI integration.
3. Prioritizing technological capacity building initiatives can bridge the skill gap and promote a deeper understanding of AI-driven analytics (Pandey, B. K. et al.,2021b) among legal professionals and adjudicators. Training programs and workshops focused on AI technologies, data analysis, and algorithmic transparency can equip stakeholders with the necessary expertise to navigate and oversee AI-driven adjudication processes effectively
4. The government should establish Technology Monitoring and Evaluation Units (TMEUs) in all Ministry of Justice branches nationwide to continuously monitor and evaluate the effectiveness, impact, implications, and potential challenges of AI-driven predictive analytics in the Nigerian legal system.
5. Engaging stakeholders through awareness campaigns and educational initiatives can foster a better understanding of AI-driven analytics and its potential benefits in IPR adjudication. By promoting open dialogue and providing relevant information about the capabilities and limitations of AI technologies, stakeholders can build trust and confidence in the application of AI-driven analytics within the supply chain management sector.

6. Government, stakeholders and relevant law agencies should provide consistent and reliable electricity to facilitate the effective utilization of AI-driven facilities.
7. Compulsory registration of intellectual properties should be taken seriously by government. The use and application of information and communication technologies (Anand, R. et al.,2022) in registering applicant will facilitate the registration process.
8. The users of AI-driven facilities must publicly disclose the choices made, along with the data and assumptions utilized, in a comprehensive, timely, and accessible manner. This approach would render it less challenging to assess the decisions made, the evidence, reasoning, and assumptions employed, thereby ensuring adequate legal assurance against decisions based on these choices, data, reasoning, and assumptions.

CONCLUSION

In conclusion, the integration of AI-driven analytics in the adjudication of intellectual property rights in the Nigerian supply chain management has emerged as a pivotal step towards fostering a more efficient and equitable business environment. By leveraging the power of advanced data processing and machine learning, this approach has significantly enhanced the identification and protection of intellectual property assets, thereby curbed infringement and promoting innovation.Through the application of AI algorithms, the adjudication process has become more streamlined and objective, leading to fairer and more consistent outcomes for all parties involved. The utilization of AI-driven analytics has not only improved the speed and accuracy of decision-making but has also minimized the occurrence of costly legal disputes, ultimately fostering a more conducive atmosphere for business growth and investment.

However, it is crucial to acknowledge that the successful implementation of AI-driven analytics in the adjudication of intellectual property rights necessitates continuous monitoring, fine-tuning, and adherence to evolving legal frameworks. Furthermore, comprehensive training and awareness programs should be implemented to ensure that stakeholders possess the necessary understanding and skills to effectively utilize AI technologies in this domain. Moving forward, a collaborative effort between government bodies, legal entities, and technology experts is imperative to harness the full potential of AI-driven analytics in safeguarding intellectual property rights in the Nigerian supply chain. By fostering a robust ecosystem that encourages innovation, respects intellectual property, and embraces technological advancements, Nigeria can position itself as a leading hub for responsible and sustainable business practices, thus contributing to the overall growth and development of the nation's economy.

REVIEW QUESTIONS

Answer the following question.

1. What do you understand by the concepts of AI-driven analytics in legal system
2. Briefly explain the potentials of Intellectual Property Rights (IPRs) in Nigerian Supply Chain management (NSCM)
3. What are the Challenges of AI-driven analytics in adjudication of IPRs in NSCM

4. What are the strategies that can be employed to Curb Challenges of AI-Driven Analytics in Adjudication of IPRs in NSCM

REFERENCES

Adamopoulou, E., & Moussiades, L. (2020). An overview of chatbot technology, in: *IFIP International Conference on Artificial Intelligence Applications and Innovations*, Springer. pp. 373–383.

Adewopo, A. (2015). Role of the Court in the Interpretation and Development of Intellectual Property Law: The Nigerian Experience. *The Gravitas Review of Business & Property Law*, *6*(1), 1–2.

Afolayan, O. T. (2022). Intellectual Property Rights Protection in Nigeria: Issues and Perspectives. Information Impact [DOI https://dx.doi.org/10.4314/iijikm.v13i1.1]. *Journal of Information and Knowledge Management*, *13*(1), 1–9.

AlarieB.NiblettA.YoonA. H. (2017). How Artificial Intelligence Will Affect the Practice of Law. http://dx.doi.org/ doi:10.2139/ssrn.3066816

Alarie, B., Niblett, A., & Yoon, A. H. (2018). How artificial intelligence will affect the practice of law. *University of Toronto Law Journal*, *68*(supplement 1), 106–124. doi:10.3138/ utlj.2017-0052

Anand, R., Khan, B., Nassa, V. K., Pandey, D., Dhabliya, D., Pandey, B. K., & Dadheech, P. (2023). Hybrid convolutional neural network (CNN) for Kennedy Space Center hyperspectral image. *Aerospace Systems*, *6*(1), 71–78.

Anand, R., Singh, J., Pandey, D., Pandey, B. K., Nassa, V. K., & Pramanik, S. (2022). Modern technique for interactive communication in LEACH-based ad hoc wireless sensor network. In *Software Defined Networking for Ad Hoc Networks* (pp. 55–73). Springer International Publishing.

Andembubto, D. R., Apuru, I. A., & Ezra, S. D. (2020). Software piracy in Nigeria. *Asian Journal of Research in Computer Science*, *6*(1), 1–13.

Ardia, D. (2017). Privacy and court records: Online access and the loss of practical obscurity. *University of Illinois Law Review*, 1385–1454.

Bessant, Y. A., Jency, J. G., Sagayam, K. M., Jone, A. A. A., Pandey, D., & Pandey, B. K. (2023). Improved parallel matrix multiplication using Strassen and Urdhvatiryagbhyam method. *CCF Transactions on High Performance Computing*, 1–14.

Allison Arden Besunder, Not Your Parents' Robot, N.Y. ST. B.J., Mar./Apr. 2018, at 20, 90-APR NYSTBJ 20 (Westlaw).

Bhavani, R., J., & S. Thuraisingam, A. (2022). Artificial intelligence and its impact on the legal fraternity. UUM Journal of Legal Studies, 13(2), 129-161. https://doi. org/ doi:10.32890/uumjls2022.13.2.6

Boopathi, S., Pandey, B. K., & Pandey, D. (2023). Advances in Artificial Intelligence for Image Processing: Techniques, Applications, and Optimization. In Handbook of Research on Thrust Technologies' Effect on Image Processing (pp. 73-95). IGI Global.

Borenstein, J., & Howard, A. (2021). Emerging challenges in AI and the need for AI ethics education. *AI and Ethics, 1*, 61–65.

BR. S. R., Saxena, A. K., Pandey, B. K., Gupta, S., Gurpur, S., Dari, S. S., &Dhabliya, D. (2023). Machine Learning Application for Evidence Image Enhancement. In Handbook of Research on Thrust Technologies' Effect on Image Processing (pp. 25-38). IGI Global.

Calo, R. (2015). Robotics and the lessons of cyberlaw. *California Law Review, 103*(3), 513. doi:10.2139/ssrn.2402972

Cap F12 (FRN, 2004). Laws of the Federation of Nigeria (LFN).

Cecil Nwachukwu, O., & Kesiena, U. (2022). *Judicial role in the development of intellectual property law in Nigeria* (Vol. 8). Commonwealth Law Review Journal. The Law Brigade Publishers Annual.

Chamberlain & Poteet, supra nota 9, at 2 (quoting Bob Ambrogi, How Artificial Intelligence is Transforming the Legal Profession, ABA Journal (May 3, 2016), http://www.abajournal.com.legaltalknetwork.com/podcasts/law-technology-now/2016/05/artifcial-intelligence-will-infuence-future-legal)

Chang, A. C. (2020). *Intelligence-based medicine: Artificial intelligence and human cognition in clinical medicine and healthcare*. Academic Press.

Connell, W. J. (2018). Artificial Intelligence in the legal profession— What you might want to know. *Rhode Island Bar Journal, 66*(6), 5–43.

David, S., Duraipandian, K., Chandrasekaran, D., Pandey, D., Sindhwani, N., & Pandey, B. K. (2023). Impact of blockchain in healthcare system. In *Unleashing the Potentials of Blockchain Technology for Healthcare Industries* (pp. 37–57). Academic Press.

Davis, A. E. (2020). The future of law firms (and lawyers) in the age of Artificial Intelligence. *Revista Direito GV, 16*(1). Advance online publication. doi:10.1590/2317-6172201945

Duarte, A. Y. S., Sanches, R. A., & Dedini, F. G. (2018). Assessment and technological forecasting in the textile industry: From first industrial revolution to the industry 4.0. *Strategic Design Research Journal., 11*(3), 193–202.

Effoduh, J. O. (2020). 7 ways that African states are legitimizing artificial intelligence. Openair.Africa. https://openair.africa/7waysthatafricanstatesarelegitimizingartificialintelligence/ [Accessed 19 June 2023].

Fickling, B. D. (2019). Cyberattacks Make Smart Grids Look Pretty Dumb. Bloomberg Bloomberg. Retrieved on 12th January, 2022 from: https://www.bloomberg.com/opinion/articles/2019-06-17/argentina-blaming-hackersfor-outage-makessmart-grids-look-dumb

Flowers, J. C. (2019). Strong and weak AI: Deweyan considerations, in: AAAI spring symposium: Towards conscious AI systems.

Founder, N.W., Herik, J. &Salem, A.B. (2015). Digitally produced judgements in modern court proceedings. International Journal of Digital Society (IJDS 6 (2015) 1101–1112.

Harry, S. (2014). Machine Learning and Law, 89 UNIV. OF WASH. *L. REV.*, *87*, 102–110.

Haseeb, K. U., Din, I., Almogren, A., & Islam, N. (2020). An energy efficient and secure IoT-based WSN framework: An application to smart agriculture. *Sensors (Basel)*, *20*(7), 2081.

Holland, J. (2017). Intellectual property rights in China: Patents and economic development. *Nnamdi Azikiwe University Journal of International Law and Jurisprudence*, *8*(1), 40–45.

Intelligence, R. (2018), Artificial Intelligence (AI) for the Practice of Law: An Introduction, https://rossintelligence.com/ai-introduction-law/; see also Susan Beck, Inside ROSS: What Artificial Intelligence Means for Your Form, LAW.COM (Sept. 28, 2016), http://www.law.com/sites/almstaff/2016/09/28/inside-ross-what-artificialintelligence-means-for-your-firm/

Janvier-James, A. M. (2012). A new introduction to supply chains and supply chain management: Definitions and theories perspective. *International Business Research*, *5*(1), 194–207. Retrieved August 19, 2023, from http://dx.doi.org/10.5539/ibr.v5n1p194

Jianfeng, C. (2017) "Ten Trends of Artificial Intelligence + Law", Robot Industry, The 5th issue, Pp 86. (In Chinese)

Jiang, K. (2018). Law Education Mode of Science and Technology Institutions in the Context of "Artificial Intelligence + [In Chinese]. *Think Tank Era*, *139*(23), 74.

Kaminsky, P., Simchi-Levi, E., &Simchi-Levi, D. (2003). Designing and Managing the Supply Chain (Vol. 2). New York: McGraw Hill Professional.

Kelly, J. E. (2015). Computing, cognition and the future of knowing; How humans and machines are forging a new age of understanding. Whitepaper, IBM Research, 2.

Khan, B., Hasan, A., Pandey, D., Ventayen, R. J. M., Pandey, B. K., &Gowwrii, G. (2021). 12 Fusion of Datamining and Artificial Intelligence. Machine learning and iot for intelligent systems and smart applications, 201.

Kujembola, D. (2014). Doing business in Nigeria: The intellectual property angle. Retrieved from www.bellanaija.com/2014/07/08damilarekujembola

Kumar, M. S., Sankar, S., Nassa, V. K., Pandey, D., Pandey, B. K., & Enbeyle, W. (2021). Innovation and creativity for data mining using computational statistics. In *Methodologies and Applications of Computational Statistics for Machine Intelligence* (pp. 223–240). IGI Global.

Kumar Pandey, B., Pandey, D., Nassa, V. K., Ahmad, T., Singh, C., George, A. S., & Wakchaure, M. A. (2021). Encryption and steganography-based text extraction in IoT using the EWCTS optimizer. *Imaging Science Journal*, *69*(1-4), 38–56.

Larry N. Zimmerman, (2016). Artificial Intelligence in the Judiciary, 85 J. Kan. B.A. 20.

Lauterbach, A. (2019). Artificial intelligence and policy: Quo vadis? Digital Policy. *Regulation & Governance*, *21*(3), 238–263. https://doi.org/10.1108/dprg-09-2018-0054

LawPavilion set to release Nigeria's first Artificial Intelligence Legal Assistant' (Vanguard News, October 24th2023) https://www.vanguardngr.com/2018/08/lawpavilion-set-to-release-nigerias-first-artificial-intelligencelegal-assistant/ accessed 12th October, 2023

Lelisho, M. E., Pandey, D., Alemu, B. D., Pandey, B. K., & Tareke, S. A. (2023). The negative impact of social media during COVID-19 pandemic. *Trends in Psychology*, *31*(1), 123–142.

Liberatore S. (2016). Your AI Lawyer will See You Now: IBM's ROSS Becomes World's First. Artificially Intelligent Attorney [EB/OL]. (2016-05-16) [2018-04-07].

Lin, T. C. W. (2019). Artificial intelligence, finance, and the law. *Fordham Law Review*, *88*(2), 531–552.

Luxton, D. D. (2016). An introduction to artificial intelligence in behavioral and mental health care. In *Artificial intelligence in behavioral and mental health care* (pp. 1–26). Elsevier.

Malhotra, P., Pandey, D., Pandey, B. K., & Patra, P. M. (2021). Managing agricultural supply chains in COVID-19 lockdown. *International Journal of Quality and Innovation*, *5*(2), 109–118.

Manap, N. A., & Abdullah, A. (2020). Regulating Artificial Intelligence in Malaysia: The two-tier approach. *UUM Journal of Legal Studies*, *11*(2), 183–201. doi:10.32890/ uumjls.11.2.2020.8779

Mariano-Florentino Cuéllar, A Simpler World: On Pruning Risks and Harvesting Fruits in an Orchard of Whispering Algorithms, 51 U.C. DAVIS L. REV. 27, 35 (2017).

McCarthy, K. Why Most Lawyers Are Terrible at Assessing Risk, Mccarty Garber Law, Sep 2018, https://mccarthygarberlaw.com/why-most-lawyers-are-terrible-at-assessing-risk/

McCarthy, L., Minsky, M. L., Rochester, N., & Simon, C. E. (2006). A Proposal for the Dartmouth Summer Research Project on Artificial Intelligence. AI magazine. [On-line]. 27(4), pp. 12-14. Available: https://ocs.aaai.org/ojs/index.php/aimagazine/article/viewFile/1904/1802 [Accessed 15th October, 2023].

McGinnis, J. O., & Pearce, R. G. (2019). The great disruption: How machine intelligence will transform the role of lawyers in the delivery of legal services. *Actual Probs. Econ. & L.*, *13*, 1230.

Meslie, Y., Enbeyle, W., Pandey, B. K., Pramanik, S., Pandey, D., Dadeech, P., & Saini, A. (2021). Machine intelligence-based trend analysis of COVID-19 for total daily confirmed cases in Asia and Africa. In *Methodologies and Applications of Computational Statistics for Machine Intelligence* (pp. 164–185). IGI Global.

Min, H. (2015). The Essentials of Supply Chain Management. USA: Pearson Education LTD.

Nelson, S. D., & Simek, J. W. (2017). Running with the machines: AI in the practice of law. *Law Practice*, *43*, 24.

Nunez, C. (2017). Artificial intelligence and legal ethics: Whether AI lawyers can make ethical decisions. *Tulane Journal of Technology & Intellectual Property*, *20*, 189.

Nwokocha, U. (2012). Nigerian intellectual property: Overview of development and practice. Journal of Intellectual Property (NJIP), 100-16.

Pandey, B. K., Mane, D., Nassa, V. K. K., Pandey, D., Dutta, S., Ventayen, R. J. M., & Rastogi, R. (2021c). Secure text extraction from complex degraded images by applying steganography and deep learning. In *Multidisciplinary approach to modern digital steganography* (pp. 146–163). IGI Global.

Pandey, B. K., & Pandey, D. (2023). Parametric optimization and prediction of enhanced thermoelectric performance in co-doped CaMnO3 using response surface methodology and neural network. *Journal of Materials Science Materials in Electronics*, *34*(21), 1589.

Pandey, B. K., Pandey, D., Wairya, S., & Agarwal, G. (2021a). An advanced morphological component analysis, steganography, and deep learning-based system to transmit secure textual data. [IJDAI]. *International Journal of Distributed Artificial Intelligence*, *13*(2), 40–62.

Pandey, B. K., Pandey, D., Wariya, S., & Agarwal, G. (2021b). A deep neural network-based approach for extracting textual images from deteriorate images. *EAI Endorsed Transactions on Industrial Networks and Intelligent Systems*, *8*(28), e3–e3.

Pandey, B. K., Pandey, D., Wariya, S., Aggarwal, G., & Rastogi, R. (2021d). Deep learning and particle swarm optimization-based techniques for visually impaired humans' text recognition and identification. *Augmented Human Research*, *6*, 1–14.

Pandey, D., Nassa, V. K., Jhamb, A., Mahto, D., Pandey, B. K., George, A. H., & Bandyopadhyay, S. K. (2021a). An integration of keyless encryption, steganography, and artificial intelligence for the secure transmission of stego images. In *Multidisciplinary approach to modern digital steganography* (pp. 211–234). IGI Global.

Pandey, D., & Pandey, B. K. (2022). An efficient deep neural network with adaptive galactic swarm optimization for complex image text extraction. In *Process Mining Techniques for Pattern Recognition* (pp. 121–137). CRC Press.

Pandey, D., Pandey, B. K., & Wairya, S. (2021b). Hybrid deep neural network with adaptive galactic swarm optimization for text extraction from scene images. *Soft Computing*, *25*, 1563–1580.

Pedro, F., Subosa, M., Rivas, A., and Valverde, P., 2019. Artificial intelligence in education: challenges and opportunities for sustainable development.

Pramanik, S., Pandey, D., Joardar, S., Niranjanamurthy, M., Pandey, B. K., & Kaur, J. (2023, October). An overview of IoT privacy and security in smart cities. In AIP Conference Proceedings (Vol. 2495, No. 1). AIP Publishing.

Reiling, A. D. (2020). Courts and Artificial Intelligence. In IJCA (Vol. 11, p. 1). Last accessed from https://www.iacajournal.org/articles/10.36745/ijca.343/print/ on November 13, 2023

Remus, D., & Levy, S. F. (2017). Can robots be lawyers: Computers, lawyers, and the practice of law. *The Georgetown Journal of Legal Ethics*, *30*, 501.

Revathi, T. K., Sathiyabhama, B., Sankar, S., Pandey, D., Pandey, B. K., &Dadeech, P. (2022). An intelligent model for coronary heart disease diagnosis. Networking Technologies in Smart Healthcare: Innovations and Analytical Approaches, 234.

Rogers, J., & Bell, F. (2019). The Ethical AI Lawyer: What is Required of Lawyers When They Use Automated Systems? Law, Technology and Humans, 1, 80-99. https://doi.org/. v1i0.1324 doi:10.5204/lthj

Rouse, M. (2018). Definition: Data analytics. Retrieved October 24, 2023, from TechTarget: https://searchdatamanagement.techtarget.com/definition/data-analytics

Rubim, P., & Fortes, B. (2021). Paths to digital justice: Judicial robots, algorithmic decision-making, and due process [URL: https://doi.org/10.1017/als.2020.12.doi:10.1017/als.2020.12.]. *Asian Journal of Law and Society*, *7*, 453–469.

Ryan, M. (2017). *Service Management: An Integrated Approach*. Larsen and Keller Education.

Schaefer, F., & Taylor, B. (2019). The Ethical Implications of Artificial Intelligence in the Law. *Gonz. L. Rev.*, *55*, 221.

Simon, M., Lindsay, A.F., Sosa, L., & Comparato, P. (2018). Lola v Skadden and the automation of the legal profession. Yale Journal of Law & Technology, 20, 234.

Singh, H., Pandey, B. K., George, S., Pandey, D., Anand, R., Sindhwani, N., & Dadheech, P. (2022, July). Effective Overview of Different ML Models Used for Prediction of COVID-19 Patients. In Artificial Intelligence on Medical Data: Proceedings of International Symposium, ISCMM 2021 (pp. 185-192). Singapore: Springer Nature Singapore.

Steve, L. (2017). A.I. Is Doing Legal Work. But It Won't Replace Lawyers, Yet, N.Y.Times, https://www.nytimes.com/2017/03/19/technology/lawyers-artifcial-intelligence. html

Sunstein, C. R. (2001). "Of Artificial Intelligence and Legal Reasoning." University of Chicago Law School Roundtable. [On-line]. 8(1), pp. 29-35

Susskind, R. E. (2017). *Tomorrow's lawyers: An introduction to your future* (2nd ed.). Oxford University Press.

Teng, H., & Huafeng, L. (2019). Study on the Influence of Artificial Intelligence on Legal Profession. *5th International Conference on Economics, Management, Law and Education*, p965

Ting, K. S. (2017). Legal Profession in the age of Disruption: 5 Key Discussions in LexTech Conference 2017. University of Malaya Law Review. https://www.umlawreview. com/lex-in-breve/legal-profession-in-the-age-o

Umali, T. (2018). Implications of AI in the legal profession. Open Gov Asia. https://opengovasia.com/implications-of-ai-in-the-legal-profession/

Vinodhini, V., Kumar, M. S., Sankar, S., Pandey, D., Pandey, B. K., & Nassa, V. K. (2022). IoT-based early forest fire detection using MLP and AROC method. *International Journal of Global Warming*, *27*(1), 55–70.

World Intellectual Property Organization. (WIPO, 1997), Introduction to Intellectual Property, Theory and Practice. Geneva, Switzerland: Kluwer Law International, p. 3.

Yu, R., & Ali, G. S. (2019). What's inside the Black Box? AI challenges for lawyers and researchers. *Legal Information Management*, *19*(1), 2–13.

Yulia, R., & Sergiy, R. (2021). *Justice in the digital age: Technological solutions, hidden threats and enticing opportunities, Access to Justice in Eastern Europe 4, 104–117.* URL., doi:10.33327/AJEE-18-4.2-A000061

Zhang, C., & Lu, Y. (2021). Study on artificial intelligence: The state of the art and future prospects. *Journal of Industrial Information Integration, 23*(100224).

Zhao, Y., Li, T., Zhang, X., & Zhang, C. (2019). Artificial intelligence-based fault detection and diagnosis methods for building energy systems: Advantages, challenges and the future. *Renewable & Sustainable Energy Reviews, 109*, 85–101.

Chapter 5
Impacts of Artificial Intelligence and Machine Learning on Intelligent Supply Chains

Binay Kumar Pandey
https://orcid.org/0000-0002-4041-1213
Department of Information Technology, College of Technology, Govind Ballabh Pant University of Agriculture and Technology, India

Mukundan Appadurai Paramashivan
https://orcid.org/0009-0009-5608-4788
Aligarh Muslim University, India & Champions Group, India

Uday Kumar Kanike
https://orcid.org/0000-0002-8792-5721
Georgia State University, USA

Darshan A. Mahajan
https://orcid.org/0000-0002-1239-6343
NICMAR University, Pune, India

Rashmi Mahajan
https://orcid.org/0000-0001-9082-6874
Balaji Institute of International Business, Sri Balaji University, Pune, India

A.Shaji George
https://orcid.org/0000-0002-8677-3682
TSM, Almarai Company, Saudi Arabia

A. Shahul Hameed Hameed
Department of Telecommunication, Consolidated Techniques Co. Ltd., Saudi Arabia

ABSTRACT

All companies globally use supply chain management (SCM) in this complicated and ever-changing world. Deep learning in SCM is becoming prominent, needing a complete study review. AI could revolutionise many company operations. AI can anticipate demand, optimize logistics and transportation routes, and find supply chain bottlenecks. Better demand responsiveness, shorter lead times, and lower costs can ensue. This Scopus-based study covers supply chain management AI applications. Filling the study gap on AI's impact on SCM performance includes identifying AI methodologies that can increase performance, SCM subfields with high AI potential, AI application's impact on performance, and agile-lean performance descriptions. Scopus identified countries/regions influencing SCM performance, subject area, and document type with AI.

DOI: 10.4018/979-8-3693-1347-3.ch005

INTRODUCTION

At the moment, the utilisation of artificial intelligence (Kumar Pandey, B. et al., (2021)) is having a considerable impact on the monitoring of supply networks, which is a very positive development. This is an example of how artificial intelligence may be used. The application of artificial intelligence to the tracking of goods that are being sent on a large scale and the assessment of transportation demand has the potential to be valuable to the management of supply chains and enterprises that specialize in logistics, according to Rahimi and Alemtabriz (2022). Specifically, the application of artificial intelligence to these tasks could help determine the demand for transportation. In addition, the use of artificial intelligence to the computation of the demand for transportation could prove to be of great assistance. The managers of supply chains now have a more complete understanding of the system as a whole thanks to the assistance that is provided by artificial intelligence. As a result of this, they are able to make decisions that are more informed and to provide a greater quality of service to their customers (Meslie, Y., et al. (2021)). This pattern got its start with the advent of expert systems and fuzzy logic, and it didn't stop gaining speed until far after the year 2010 in most instances. The beginning of this pattern may be traced back to the 1970s. The decade of the 1970s appears to have been the starting point for this pattern. It is even conceivable to trace its origins back to the 1970s at this point. The most cutting-edge and cutting-edge technology that is presently available on the market (Li, 2020) discovered that the growth of big data, data analytics, and a variety of applications that make use of graphics processing units (GPUs) and deep learning (DL) has had a considerable impact on. This was found out by the researchers. Several pieces of research have pointed to the fact that this is in fact the case.The number of people utilising applications that make use of artificial intelligence has seen a significant spike since the beginning of the year 2010. It is anticipated that this pattern will carry on. According to Li (2020), this has aroused both excitement and fear regarding the future of management in organisations as well as employment chances. In other words, the future is uncertain. It would appear that the supply chain literature is making an attempt to catch up with some recent efforts to integrate modern AI research approaches into its core investigations (Iyyanar, P., et al. (2023)). This would indicate that the supply chain literature is making an effort to catch up with certain recent efforts. This is the case due to the fact that the literature on supply chain management has fallen behind these initiatives. This is despite the fact that businesses are increasingly adopting artificial intelligence and investing in AI solutions in order to improve the operations of their end-to-end supply chains (Hartmann & Moeller, 2014). Specifically, this is due to the fact that artificial intelligence may help businesses improve their inventory management. Specifically, this can be attributed to the fact that artificial intelligence might be able to assist firms in becoming better at managing their inventory. This is despite the fact that businesses are increasingly adopting AI and investing in AI solutions in order to improve the operations of their end-to-end supply chains in order to compete in the global marketplace. In addition, this is despite the fact that AI is expected to have a significant impact on the future of work. In point of fact, this is occurring in spite of the fact that more and more firms are adopting AI and investing in AI-based solutions. Even while research on supply chain management is currently working to catch up with the current state of affairs, we nevertheless find ourselves in the unfortunate position of having to deal with the consequences of this situation. In spite of this, the findings of our study demonstrated that AI research is being carried out in a broad range of diverse directions. This highlighted the necessity for a taxonomy that is not only rational in its acceptability but also comprehensive in its coverage (Singh, J., et al. (2023)). A taxonomy of this kind would be able to steer researchers in the domains of operations and supply chain towards a better knowledge of the history, the present, and the potential future of research into artificial intelligence applications in SCM. This would be possible because the taxonomy would be able to categorise the many types of study. Because the taxonomy would be able to direct researchers in the domains of supply chain and operations, this would be feasible. This is something that could be accomplished since a taxonomy of this kind would be able to direct researchers in the appropriate direction as they carry out their investigations, making it possible for this to take place. This is something that is able to be done because of the structure that has been applied to the material that is contained within this taxonomy. It was vital for us to carry out research into the relevant literature before we could even begin to answer the questions that are posed at a later point in this piece of writing. These questions can be found further down in the piece. This was a necessary condition for us to fulfil before we could do that. How far along have we come in terms of the amount of work that has been published on the subject of implementing AI technology into the operation and management of supply chains? In what specific locations have studies on approaches employing artificial intelligence been carried out, and in what other kinds of supply chain environments have the researchers been focusing their attention on? How likely it is that researcher will continue their investigation into the role that artificial intelligence plays in the administration of supply chains? Where in particular throughout the supply chain do you observe these approaches being utilised the majority of the time, and what are some of the reasons that lead you to believe that this is the case based on your observations? The findings of Nayak and Choudhary (2022) are as follows: We (Nayak and Choudhary, the authors) use a wide array of research methods in order to carry out a comprehensive evaluation of the relevant literature and find solutions to these problems. The following are now well within our grasp as a direct result of this: 1. The first stage of our all-encompassing strategy involves the creation of a cutting-edge system for the classification of AI software. This is done in order to ensure that we will be capable of doing an in-depth analysis not just of the present topic at hand, but also of the research that is associated with it. We will be able to detect the linkages and patterns that are already present in this body of literature if we do a comprehensive co-citation and network analysis (Ekong, M. O., George et al. (2023)). This analysis may be found in Ekong, M. O., George et al. (2023). We will be successful in achieving this objective if we carry out an exhaustive examination. In this pioneering endeavour, we analyse the pertinent literature and identify emerging trends in research by applying a meticulously crafted artificial intelligence taxonomy, an exhaustive bibliometric, a cluster analysis, and an in-depth evaluation of potential future research pathways. To put it another way, no one else has ever attempted any of these things before us. Because of this, we are in a position to achieve something that has never been accomplished in the history of the world. Companies who have implemented AI-enabled supply-chain management have witnessed a reduction of 15% in their logistical expenses, according to estimations supplied by McKinsey (Malhotra, P., et al. (2021)). These very same businesses have also reported an increase in their service levels of up to 65%, as well as an increase in their inventory levels of up to 35%. These are the preliminary discoveries that were discovered (Swapna, H. R., et al. (2023)), and it is likely that the actual potential of artificial intelligence in the supply chain resides in outputs that are narrower and more predictive (Camargo et al., 2020). Swapna, H. R., et al. (2023), who were the researchers who participated in the study, were the ones who carried out the research.

This article aims to address the current research gap regarding the impact of AI's (Pandey, B. K., & Pandey, D. (2023)) application on the performance of SCM by determining the AI techniques that can enhance the performance of SCM, the SCM subfields that have high potential to be enhanced by AI, the impact of AI application on the performance of SCM, and how the performance can be described from an agile-lean perspective. In doing so, this article will determine the AI techniques that can enhance the performance of SCM. In order to accomplish this goal, this article will investigate the various applications of AI that have the potential to improve the functionality of SCM. In order to achieve this objective, the purpose of this article is to study the numerous uses of AI that have the potential to improve the operational capabilities of SCM. Because of this, the goal of this essay is to identify the AI solutions that, if adopted, have the potential to improve the performance of supply chain management (SCM). (Bhatt, D., et al. (2023)) [Citation needed] This study will investigate how the functioning of SCM can be improved by making use of AI-based methodologies, and it will report its findings. The article is organised in such a way that it begins with an introduction pertaining to the application of AI in SCM, and then, a second section is dedicated to AI technologies in specific applications in SCM to improve its performance; it came to the conclusion that AI (Pandey, B. K. et al., (2021)) has been increasingly applied in supply chain management in order to improve performance from an Agile and Lean point of view. In addition to this, a table that is a part of the article itself provides a concise summary of the information that is presented in the article. In the third part of this chapter, we are going to perform some research into the previous work that has been done on the issue, taking into consideration the type of the document, the subject matter, and the circumstances that led to the publishing of it. In addition, we are going to take into consideration the conditions that led to its publication. In this, the fourth and last section, we offer some suggestions as to the approach that scholars working in the field should take in the years to come. In the following section, we will cover the foundation for digitalizing supply chain management as well as the influence that AI has on the efficiency of supply chain management. This will be followed by a discussion of how AI can improve supply chain management. In addition to this, we are going to discuss the influence that AI has on the effectiveness of the management of supply chains. Following this, there will be a discussion on how the use of artificial intelligence could improve the efficiency with which supply chains are managed. Integration, automation, reconfiguration of supply chain networks, analysis, and SC process optimisation are the components that make up supply chain management digitalization, as stated by Khan, H., et al. (2023). Other components include supply chain network reconfiguration. In the research paper, this point was made clear. The computerization of the management of the supply chain is composed of each of these separate components and elements. The conclusion was stated in the fifth section of the article, and then an instant discussion of the conclusion was presented in the section that immediately followed it. Incorporating artificial intelligence into agile and lean supply chain management might lead to an increase in the operational efficiency of a company, since that is the notion that has been put up. This could be accomplished by enhancing responsiveness and flexibility, getting rid of waste, developing improvements for increased cooperation, and raising the overall degree of customer pleasure that is experienced.

METHODOLOGY

According to Awuzie and McDermott (2017), while a researcher acquires information to investigate a phenomenon, finding themes and explaining patterns to construct a new or modified previous theory is then possible to analyse through the acquisition of further data. This evaluation can take place either before or after the author builds the theory. It is possible to do this in order to come up with an explanation for the occurrence that is being questioned. In this inquiry, the author has been very methodical and has followed the approach step by step. Secondary data has been evaluated in order to investigate the impact that AI applications have had on the efficiency of SCM. The only thing that made up the secondary data were papers that had been vetted by other researchers and came from the SCOPUS database. Scopus possesses a powerful search engine that enables users to conduct searches utilising a variety of search parameters. These search parameters include “Document search,” “Author search,” “Affiliation search,” and “Advanced search” for a wide variety of variables, such as “Article Title, Abstract, Keywords,” “Source Title,” “Year of Publication,” etc. This study used the terms “Artificial Intelligence” and “Artificial Intelligence in Supply Chain Management Performance” as its keywords in order to carry out a search for relevant documents and perform a search for relevant documents. In the course of the investigation into the outcomes, a look was taken at various articles that had been published in the respective study domains between the years 2012 and 2023. The data that was retrieved and then analysed allowed for the following information to be obtained: the kind of document, the topic area, the type of source, the number of publications broken down by country or region, and the number of publications broken down by year.

ARTIFICIAL INTELLIGENCE

Since its inception in 2012, artificial intelligence has gone through cycles of both expansion and contraction due to a wide variety of factors. These cycles have occurred for a number of different causes. According to Scholten et al. (2014), the increased flow of data and complexity that have emerged in business settings have contributed to a renaissance in interest in artificial intelligence (AI), as well as an increase in the usage of AI in a variety of different industries during the past two decades. This interest has contributed to an increase in the usage of AI in a variety of different industries during the past two decades. During the past two decades, there has been a rise in the use of artificial intelligence across a wide range of different business sectors as a direct result of this interest. At the moment, research into the implementation of artificial intelligence in a diverse selection of corporate procedures is actively being carried out. This inquiry takes into account both the immediate requirements and the more far-reaching objectives. According to Huang and Rust (2018), artificial intelligence (AI) is described as a network of computers that can imitate human intellect while making judgements regarding how to solve a business challenge. This definition can be found in the article “What Is Artificial Intelligence?” Machine learning is another name for artificial intelligence. Artificial intelligence has the potential to aid with design thinking for business systems and can learn from data to acquire insights without the need for human participation. According to Fosso Wamba and Akter (2019), firms can utilise the assistance of AI to identify the elements of their supply chain management that require development and then divide their resources in the most effective manner. This enables the organisations to improve their supply chain management. According to the findings of a study that was conducted by Jabbour and colleagues in the year 2020, artificial intelligence has the potential to assist businesses in developing products of the highest quality that are commercially viable. This can be accomplished through the rapid extraction of customer expectations, the sensing of the market, the utilisation of failure modes, the optimisation of internal and external supply chains, and the encouragement of a more creative workforce through the automation of routine tasks. It is possible to accomplish this objective in a variety of ways, some of which include carrying out activities such as sensing the market, utilising failure modes, employing failure modes, and utilising failure modes. AI has been steadily adopted by a variety of industries, including manufacturing and e-commerce, in order to uncover remedies for problems that occur in supply chains. The goal of this adoption has been to improve efficiency and reduce costs. Utilising AI to find solutions to these difficulties is possible. During COVID-19, the vast majority of supply chains were subjected to an elevated level of testing to determine the degree of their resilience. This was done because they were given the challenge of completing tasks that were becoming progressively more difficult (Zouari et al., 2021). Customers in today's global market demand supply chains to deliver individualised solutions in addition to a high level of dependability for the goods and services they invest their money in. An AI-based system has been developed with the intention of identifying customer profiles and providing individualised solutions without infringing on the customer's right to privacy or security in any manner. The system's primary objective is to achieve this goal. Artificial intelligence was utilised in the process of developing this system. In conclusion, the application of artificial intelligence is expanding at a rapid rate, and supply chains and organisations that do not recognise and capitalise on AI in their operations may soon be unable to achieve the necessary supply chain resilience in the dynamic business market that can emerge as a result of scenarios similar to COVID-19. Artificial intelligence (AI) refers to a collection of computer programmes and hardware systems that are designed to learn from their environments and make decisions based on the data they collect. The term "artificial intelligence," or AI for short, refers to a subfield within the larger field of research known as "machine learning," which is preoccupied with the implementation of various machine learning strategies. "Expert systems" is the name given to a subfield of artificial intelligence that focuses on the development of software that gives computers the ability to perform tasks that have historically been carried out by humans with the assistance of specialised instruction and knowledge in supply chain management. This subfield of artificial intelligence was given the name "expert systems" to distinguish it from other subfields of artificial intelligence. This subfield is also known as "knowledge-based systems," which is another moniker for "expert systems" (Pournader et al., 2021). In the following lines, you will find a synopsis of the components that Kusiak (2019) defines as composing an expert system: Knowledge reorientation, which is where knowledge is framed; the interface engine, which explains the control strategy; and knowledge acquisition, which enables the system to acquire data and knowledge for the purpose of problem-solving in supply chain management are the three components that make up the knowledge management system. Knowledge reorientation is where knowledge is framed; the interface engine explains the control strategy; and knowledge acquisition explains the control strategy. The knowledge is framed in the knowledge reorientation stage, which is followed by the interface engine, which describes the control strategy, and the knowledge acquisition stage, which enables the system to gather data and knowledge. According to Zarbakhshnia et al. (2018), certain expert system techniques, such as rule-based, fuzzy, frame-based, and hybrid methods, are some examples of those that can be utilised in conjunction with one another to gain the ideal outcomes of artificial intelligence in supply chain management. Other examples of these techniques include using a combination of expert system techniques. Methods that combine elements of multiple different approaches are another example of those that can be employed in tandem with one another. According to the findings of the study that was carried out by Jakupovi et al. (2014), expert systems perform exceptionally well in domains where human intelligence may be mandated by official orders. According to Haenlein and Kaplan (2019), if the efficacy of expert systems is not accurately assessed, there is a chance that the effectiveness of these systems will see a dramatic decline. When attempts are made to address the issue of cognitive impairments with the assistance of expert systems, this obstacle becomes even more apparent. In recent years, there has been an increase in interest in the application of artificial intelligence (AI) approaches in supply chain management for the modelling and simulation of complex systems (Chen et al., 2022). This surge in interest has been accompanied by an equal and opposite increase in the number of publications that are dedicated to the topic. According to Bennett and Hauser (2013), the use of artificial intelligence in the form of modelling and simulation enables one to obtain a more in-depth understanding of how a system performs, which in turn boosts their capacity to make better choices. This is one of the many benefits of artificial intelligence. According to the findings of the study that Zamani and colleagues carried out in 2022, agent-based computing techniques have the potential to become a powerful instrument for measuring performance in real-world supply chain management settings and characterising how system components interact with one another. This information was gleaned from the research that Zamani and colleagues carried out. The findings of the study were reported in print in 2022. Recently, there has been an increase in the use of artificial intelligence (AI) in supply chain management, specifically with the purpose of improving performance from an agile and lean point of view. The efficiency of a company's supply chain operations can be significantly improved by making investments in digital technology, which more and more businesses are doing these days. This pattern is being pushed forward by the imperative to reduce expenditures. According to Barták et al. (2010), artificial intelligence (AI) planning and scheduling in supply chain management is a set of methods for making intelligent system decisions within the context of limits (such as the availability of resources in a manufacturing facility). In other words, AI planning and scheduling is an application of AI in supply chain management. These techniques are referred to collectively as "artificial intelligence (AI) planning and scheduling in supply chain management," which is a phrase that describes a particular set of these practises. In the context of supply chain management, these methods are frequently referred to as "artificial intelligence planning and scheduling (Boopathi, S., (2023))." Planning, as opposed to scheduling, which is concerned with the assignment of activities to resources within a specified amount of time, is concerned with making decisions to optimise the order in which activities take place (Kreipl & Pinedo, 2004). Scheduling is concerned with the assignment of activities to resources within a specific period of time. The process of allocating activities to resources for completion within a predetermined amount of time is known as scheduling. Scheduling refers to the process of dividing up tasks and responsibilities among available resources so that they can be finished in the allotted period of time. Recent developments in artificial intelligence have made it possible for managers to detect and predict disruptions that may impair normal system operations (such as fraud detection, predictive maintenance, and system failures), and they have also assisted with system recovery in a more responsive and data-driven way. These advancements have made it possible for managers to detect and predict disruptions that may impair normal system operations. Because of these improvements, managers are now able to identify and anticipate interruptions that have the potential to interfere with the normal functioning of the system. As a result of these enhancements, managers now

Figure 1. AI in supply chain management

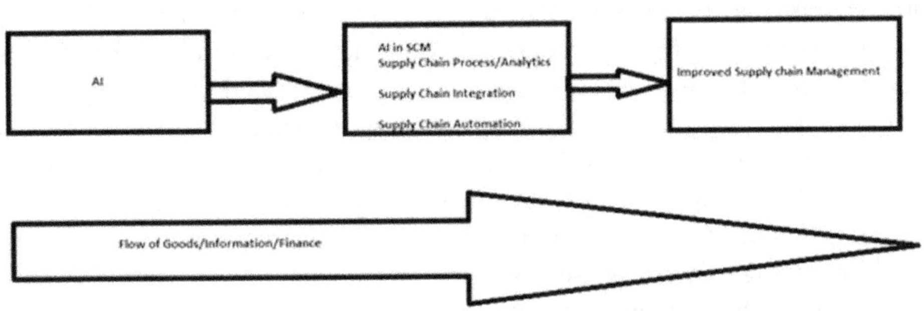

have the ability to recognise and prepare for disruptions that may cause the system to operate abnormally and disrupt typical business operations. According to Abedinnia et al. (2017), the enhancements made possible by these advancements have made it possible for managers to detect and foresee interruptions that have the potential to interfere with the normal operations of the system in Figure 1.

REVIEW OF LITERATURE

In order to carry out an analysis of the literature review that was carried out, it was planned to make use of both the quantitative and the qualitative methodologies. (El Jaouhari, 2022, together with others) The quantitative section of the report would comprise of the many different business sectors associated with supply chain management that make use of the techniques and technology that are associated with artificial intelligence. In addition to that, the mental processes of perceiving, interacting, and deciding will all have a role in it at some point in the future. When making decisions within the organisation, the organisation will take into account the findings of the report's analysis that was carried out by the organisation. This will occur while the organisation is in the process of making decisions inside the organisation. The quantitative literature review, as described by Rostami et al. (2022), would include components such as the purchasing operation, logistics, resource management, and information processing. On the other hand, the qualitative literature evaluation takes into account the gaps in scientific understanding regarding the effects of AI on the efficiency of supply chain management. This is done so in order to better comprehend the topic. To get a little bit more specific on the matter at hand, the findings of the survey showed that the influence of AI in supply chain management scored second and third in terms of the share of respondents indicating the potential for cost reduction and revenue rise across all eight business functions that were investigated (Tirkolaee et al., 2022). (Tirkolaee et al., 2022). These rankings were determined by the percentage of respondents who indicated the potential for an increase in revenue while simultaneously reducing costs across all eight of the business activities that were looked into. (Tirkolaee, along with his colleagues, 2022). In total, 63% of individuals who took part in the poll reported a rise in revenues, and 61% of those participants reported a reduction in expenses. It was revealed that the programmes that are most likely to have inspired these modifications are the ones that deal with sales and demand forecasting, spending analytics, and network optimisation. All of these are parts of supply chain management. McKinsey & Company (2019) has provided a synopsis of the probable effects that artificial intelligence will have on the management of supply networks in their latest research publication. A significant amount of dissatisfaction can be attributed to the fact that it does not appear that the promise of complete and total adoption in the actual world is going to be achieved for a very long time. At the moment, the Internet of Things (IoT) (Pramanik, S. et al., (2023)), robots, and prescriptive analytics are ranked higher than artificial intelligence (AI), which is placed in sixth place. This indicates that artificial intelligence is now lagging behind three other forms of technology. The finding that approximately one quarter of individuals who participated in the study anticipate having adopted AI within the next two years is one of the encouraging takeaways that can be drawn from the findings of the poll. Using the Scopus database, we were able to compile and assess the current status of AI applications in SCM, as well as determine the impact that these applications have on the performance of SCM. In addition, we were able to determine the impact that these applications have on the performance of SCM. The Scopus database possesses the potential to give useful information, such as an awareness of the research community, its history, nations, relationships, authors, published papers, abstracts, and a variety of citations that may be exported and analysed. You will be able to gain access to this information by conducting a search within the database. The database contains a variety of scholarly works, such as scientific journals, book chapters, and proceedings from conferences, amongst other sorts of scholarly publications. The works have been evaluated by a number of different researchers. Scopus offers a search engine that is one that is not only useful but also efficient. Scopus's search engine has a lot to offer. The users of this search engine have the ability to select from a number of different search parameters, such as "Document search," "Author search," "Affiliation search," and "Advanced search" for a range of different categories, such as "Article Title, Abstract, Keywords," "Source Title," "Year of Publication," etc., amongst other search criteria. In order to perform a search for relevant papers and carry out a search for relevant documents, this research made use of the terms "Artificial Intelligence" and "Artificial Intelligence in Supply Chain Management Performance" as its keywords. These terms were utilised to carry out a search for relevant documents. The improvement in findings can be attributed, in part, to the inclusion of publications in the research fields in question that were produced between the years 2012 and 2023. By making use of the data that was retrieved, it is possible that the following information may have been obtained: a) The type of document; b) The subject matter; c) The type of source; and d) the number of publications, broken down into categories based on the countries or regions. During the course of the search, we looked through only scholarly works that have been critiqued by other researchers in the past.

INFLUENCE OF AI ON THE EFFICIENCY OF SCM

It is essential for businesses to evaluate their performance since doing so teaches them how to deliver superior service to their clients and brings them closer to achieving their long-term objectives. By analysing their performance, companies may figure out how to improve the quality of service they deliver to their clientele. In order to achieve the level of customer satisfaction that has been outlined as a goal, it is essential to carry out an investigation into the extent to which demands are met and resources are employed in an efficient manner. By doing so, one will be able to accomplish the desired level of client satisfaction that has been established as a target. An evaluation of the supply chain takes into account the interdependencies between all of the businesses that are participating in the supply chain. This is done rather than concentrating on the performance of a single company within the supply chain. Not only does it encourage individuals to perform in a particular manner, but it also exposes how successful stakeholders and actors in the supply chain are at their respective professions. It provides the context, which is necessary for having a complete grasp of the system. The management process is comprised of many parts, one of the most important of which is the creation and execution of performance assessment techniques. Transparency and an in-depth understanding of the supply chain are both made easier by the use of performance monitoring technologies, which help to the facilitation of both of these goals. According to Yu et al. (2017), one strategy that can be used to evaluate the effectiveness of the supply chain that is currently being managed inside an organisation is to monitor key performance indicators such as lead time, fill rate, and on-time performance. This is one of the ways that supply chains may be evaluated. Auditing is another technique that can be utilised. Because these standards are developed in-house, they do not take into account the entirety of the nature of the supply chain because they do not take into account that nature (Kalavathy, K. S., et al.(2023)).

One of the technologies that were explored was discovered to be artificial intelligence (AI), which is one of the technologies (Pandey, B. K., et al. (2022)) that was researched and determined to have the potential to be utilised in supply chain management. Another technology that was investigated was blockchain technology. Because of their capacity to handle extensive amounts of data, technologies that are driven by artificial intelligence have the potential to bring about profound shifts in the manner in which inventory is managed. One of the areas that hold the greatest potential for such a change is this particular one. According to Ben-Daya et al. (2019), these intelligent systems are able to quickly access and analyse massive information, delivering real-time actionable insights that may be exploited for demand and supply planning. In addition to this, these systems are able to do these jobs in the allotted amount of time. These AIs are able to generate accurate forecasts regarding forthcoming changes in consumer behaviour and seasonality as a result of the complex algorithms that enable them to do so. This is made possible by the fact that these AIs are able to predict the future. By predicting what your consumers will want, an artificial intelligence system may be able to aid you in lowering the amount of money that is wasted as a result of the acquisition of unnecessary inventory. This can help you save money. Automation has the potential to significantly boost how efficient a warehouse currently is, which is a characteristic that is incredibly vital for the smooth operation of a supply chain. It is possible to quickly remove goods from warehouses and deliver them to customers while requiring them to put in as little effort as possible on their end. If this mechanism were put into place, then it would be possible to accomplish this goal. According to Ben-Daya et al. (2019), the use of artificial intelligence (AI) in warehouses has the potential to boost output in a variety of different ways. One of these methods is through the reduction of errors. These include the promptness with which challenges are solved, the ease with which ordinary jobs may be accomplished, and the frequency with which staff are able to concentrate on the planning of more vital day-to-day operations. The use of artificial intelligence in the automation of warehouse procedures might possibly save both time and money by minimising the need for human workers. This would be accomplished by eliminating the requirement for humans to perform these procedures. Because of this, there would be a requirement for a smaller number of employees to carry out the necessary tasks. Integration of information, resources, and networks, automation utilising robotics technology, process automation, and intelligent processes, reconfiguration of supply chain networks, an adjustment in the structure of the organisation, and supply chains to improve performance, supply chain analytics that guarantee real-time execution, decisions, process optimisation, and advanced forecasting, and supply chain process automation. These are the several elements of digitising supply chain management that come together to form the whole thing. Xie et al. (2020) came to the conclusion that the fundamental goal of digitalization and industry 4.0 is to establish an intelligent supply chain. These findings were presented in their conclusion. These two endeavours have this overarching goal in mind as their major focus. As a direct result of this development, the supply chain will no longer include any instances of asymmetric information in any capacity. It is possible to evaluate the effectiveness of intelligent supply chain management from a number of different points of view, including visibility, personalisation, information governance, warning, sustainability, innovation and learning, agile and lean (leagility), and agile and lean (leagility). The phrase "leagility" is a combination of the phrases "agile," which promotes flexibility and receptiveness, and "lean," which encourages operating with little waste, loss, and overall cost optimisation. "Agile" focuses on adaptability and receptiveness, while "lean" emphasises operating with little waste, loss, and overall cost optimisation. The term "agile" places a greater emphasis on adaptability and receptiveness, whereas the term "lean" places a greater emphasis on running with minimum waste, loss, and total cost optimisation. According to Xie et al. (2020), the concepts of lean and agile are not mutually exclusive with one another and can exist side by side within the context of an intelligent supply chain. This assertion is made in the context of an intelligent supply chain. In addition to this, he came to the conclusion that AI holds the possibility of significantly boosting the efficiency of supply chain management. This was an important discovery for him. According to Mohsen (2023), the digital supply chain makes use of various technologies, including artificial intelligence, big data, blockchains, the cloud, and the internet of things. Other technologies include the internet of things. The implementation of blockchain technology can make it possible to more closely monitor operations, comply with rules in an easier manner, and offer reports with a higher degree of accuracy, all of which lead to an improvement in the management of supply chains. Blockchain technology can also make it possible to provide reports with a higher degree of precision. Cloud computing makes it possible to perform tasks quickly, flexibly, and at scale, all while maintaining complete visibility over all parties participating in the process. Cloud computing also makes it possible to scale up the amount of information being processed. Professionals working in the supply chain, such as inventory planners, production managers, and procurement managers, now have access to more accurate information and estimates thanks to the Internet of Things. Because of this, these professionals are able to make more educated strategic judgements regarding the buying, production, and selling of commodities. Mohsen (2022) presented data and information that highlighted the significant role that "Big Data" plays in a variety of the many aspects of supply chain management. These aspects include the establishment of product and market strategies, procurement planning, logistics, inventory management, innovative product design, operational efficiency and maintenance, network design, and the planning of procurement. Stoyanov (2021) provided an overview of the various ways in which artificial intelligence is currently being incorporated into the management of supply chains. He revealed that AI makes it possible for businesses to establish a decentralised supply chain that can mutate into a system that is self-aware, self-managed, and self-defining. This was made possible by AI's ability to facilitate the process. The development of AI has made this kind of thing conceivable. According to Toorajipour et al. (2021), the implementation of AI has resulted in benefits across a wide variety of supply chain management facets. These enhancements can be discovered in a variety of different places throughout the board. These include the planning, production, and demand forecasting for supply chains, as well as the distribution and transportation of commodities, the management of logistics hubs, the sales and marketing of products, the distribution of goods, and the distribution of goods. According to the findings of a study that was conducted by McKinsey & Company (2021), real-time monitoring and control of manufacturing and logistics activities that are enabled by AI can lead to increased responsiveness and flexibility in the management of supply chains. This can be of significant aid to businesses in rapidly adjusting to changing demand as well as other types of interruptions, which can ultimately lead to increased performance. According to Gulen (2023), the use of artificial intelligence has the potential to make supply chain management more transparent by allowing for real-time visibility into logistics and production activities. If this were to happen, then the potential of AI to bring transparency in supply chain management would be realised. Because of this, it may be much simpler for businesses to identify issues and respond to them in a timely manner, which may lead to a reduction in waste and an increase in productivity. Research has shown that the application of artificial intelligence can improve collaboration between many stakeholders involved in the supply chain, such as retailers, manufacturers, and suppliers. One of the numerous advantages that artificial intelligence possesses is this particular one. AI has the ability to increase the efficiency with which businesses collaborate with one another by decreasing the difficulties of communication and information sharing. This, in turn, can lead to gains in overall performance if implemented properly. It has been discovered that employing chatbots and virtual assistants that are powered by AI can improve customer service by delivering answers to inquiries posed by customers in a prompt and correct manner. As a direct result of this, customers have reported that they are feeling more satisfied with the services that they have received on the whole. This has the potential to assist businesses in improving not just their overall performance but also their capacity to maintain their current customer base while also contributing to the expansion of their revenue. Wang et al. (2022) conducted research to examine the potential effects that artificial intelligence, the internet of things, and digital technology could have on the efficiency of supply chains in the industrial sector. They claimed that a number of different AI technologies had been implemented in the management of supply chains. The terms "artificial neural networks" (ANN), "genetic algorithms" (GA), "virtual reality" (VR), and "artificial immune systems" (AIS) (Pandey, D., et al. (2021)) are all examples of technology that fall under this category. According to a number of papers, the utilisation of artificial intelligence in the process of producing forecasts and planning activities might be beneficial in the context of supply chain management. This was demonstrated by the aforementioned reports. This, in turn, leads to a reduction in both the total quantity of resources that are wasted and the risk that businesses are exposed to. The implementation of artificial intelligence (AI) has the potential to result in considerable performance enhancements in supply chain management across a variety of disciplines, including the areas that are listed below: Artificial intelligence can be used to analyse vast volumes of data acquired from a variety of sources, such as sensor data, weather forecasts, and social media, in order to estimate future demand and determine the appropriate level of inventory. This can be accomplished by gathering the data from a number of different sources. It is possible to perform this in order to determine the optimum quantity of stock. It is possible to use it to maximise logistical processes such as transport routes and the scheduling of manufacture and delivery, which can result in cost savings and greater productivity. These benefits can be realised as a direct result of using it. The procedure presented below is an illustration of such an optimisation technique. An application of artificial intelligence can be utilised to make a prognosis on when a piece of machinery will fail, and subsequent upkeep can be planned in accordance with that prognosis. Because of this, both the period of time that the equipment is out of service and the costs that are associated with that downtime are cut down. It is possible to put its capabilities to use in order to identify potential dangers in the supply chain and put into action plans for minimising risks such as those posed by natural disasters, supply shortages, and political unrest. These are some instances of the various kinds of dangers that can be lessened or eliminated. One may ensure the quality of the items while simultaneously lowering the possibility that they will be faulty or damaged in any manner by utilising artificial intelligence to monitor and check things while they are being manufactured and delivered. This allows one to achieve both of these goals simultaneously. It is feasible to utilise it to increase communication and coordination between various stakeholders in the supply chain, such as suppliers, manufacturers, and retailers. This would be achievable because to the fact that it is possible to use it. Because its use is feasible, this is not just doable but also entirely conceivable. Additionally, it is possible to use it to automate repetitive operations such as data input, which will free up personnel to concentrate on work that is of higher value. This can be accomplished by utilising its potential to save time and effort. Utilising this technology will allow one to successfully complete the task at hand. Artificial intelligence may, in general, assist businesses in improving the performance of their supply chains by contributing to enhanced efficiency, decreased costs, and improved product and service quality. This is because artificial intelligence may help improve product and service quality. This can be performed by a variety of approaches, all of which are possible (Zakur, Y. A., et al. (2023).

CONCLUSION

The link between artificial intelligence and efficient management of supply chains is the focus of this study. The use of artificial intelligence in the management of supply chains is growing. It is possible to improve demand forecasting, distribution and transportation, administration of logistics hubs, sales and marketing, planning, production, and inventory management by utilising artificial intelligence (AI) in supply chain management. The utilisation of AI in supply chain management that is both efficient and flexible is helpful. Improve how quickly you can respond, how adaptable you are, how efficiently you can reduce waste, how well you can collaborate, and how satisfied your customers are. When it comes to the management of supply chains, the implementation of AI calls for the allocation of resources, the acquisition of skills, and the consideration of ethical concerns such as the protection and secrecy of data. The use of AI in supply chain management requires a large investment of time, resources, and skill despite the potential benefits that could be gained from doing so. Before implementing AI into supply chain management, firms should give great consideration to both the possible benefits and the potential pitfalls of doing so.There hasn't been a lot of research done on how artificial intelligence will effect supply chain management, which includes the following things: It is difficult to assess the performance of different companies and their influence since there is a lack of uniformity in artificial intelligence in supply chain management. Because they lack the data and methodologies required to compute the ROI of AI in supply chain management, businesses are unable to evaluate their artificial intelligence (AI) activities. Because it is so difficult to integrate AI with existing supply chain management systems, there is a chance that this will limit the amount of data that can be collected as well as its accuracy. A limited number of studies that concentrate on management of supply chains have looked into the ethical and privacy concerns that are presented by AI. Some of the consequences include discrimination and a breach in the confidentiality of the data. The vast majority of AI-powered supply chain management solutions place more of a focus on operations and expenses than they do on the education and progression of personnel. There is a possibility that AI may become increasingly prevalent in the management of supply chains. When businesses recognise how much AI can help them improve their efficiency and cut costs, the supply chain management industry will see an increase in the prevalence of the technology. The interface between AI and supply chain management systems is going to get better, which will ultimately lead to better data analysis and decision-making. When there is a greater emphasis placed on the use of artificial intelligence in supply chain management, there will be an accompanying rise in ethical and privacy problems. Protect sensitive data and check to be that AI systems don't lose their impartiality. The use of people is prioritised in the management of supply networks that are driven by artificial intelligence. A significant focus will be placed on the education of workers, and an investigation will be conducted into the effects that AI and automation have on people. Artificial intelligence will increasingly be applied in predictive analytics to assist businesses in risk management, forecasting disruptions to supply chains, adjusting to such disruptions, and responding to them. This trend is expected to continue throughout the foreseeable future. The application of artificial intelligence (AI) in conjunction with blockchain technology will produce a supply chain management solution that is not only more trustworthy but also more open.

REFERENCES

Abedinnia, H., Glock, C. H., Grosse, E. H., & Schneider, M. (2017). Machine Scheduling Problems in Production: A Tertiary Study. *Computers & Industrial Engineering*, *111*, 403–416. doi:10.1016/j.cie.2017.06.026

Awuzie, B., & McDermott, P. (2017). An Abductive Approach to Qualitative Built Environment Research. *Qualitative Research Journal*, *17*(4), 356–372. doi:10.1108/QRJ-08-2016-0048

Barták, R., Salido, M. A., & Rossi, F. (2010). Constraint Satisfaction Techniques in Planning and Scheduling. *Journal of Intelligent Manufacturing*, *21*(1), 5–15. doi:10.1007/s10845-008-0203-4

Ben-Daya, M., Hassini, E., & Bahroun, Z. (2019). Internet of Things and Supply ChainManagement: A Literature Review. *International Journal of Production Research*, *57*(15-16), 4719–4742. doi:10.1080/00207543.2017.1402140

Bennett, C. C., & Hauser, K. (2013). Artificial Intelligence Framework for SimulatingClinical Decision-Making: A Markov Decision Process Approach. *Artificial Intelligence in Medicine*, *57*(1), 9–19. doi:10.1016/j.artmed.2012.12.003 PMID:23287490

Boopathi, S., Pandey, B. K., & Pandey, D. (2023). Advances in Artificial Intelligence for Image Processing: Techniques, Applications, and Optimization. In Handbook of Research on Thrust Technologies' Effect on Image Processing (pp. 73-95). IGI Global.

Camargo, L. R., Pereira, S. C. F., & Scarpin, M. R. S. (2020). Fast and Ultra-Fast Fashion Supply Chain Management: An Exploratory Research. *International Journal of Retail & Distribution Management*, *48*(6), 537–553. doi:10.1108/IJRDM-04-2019-0133

El Jaouhari, A., Arif, J., Fellaki, S., Amejwal, M., & Azzouz, K. (2022). Lean Supply ChainManagement and Industry 4.0 Interrelationships: The Status Quo and Future Perspectives. *International Journal of Lean Six Sigma*. Advance online publication. doi:10.1108/IJLSS-11-2021-0192

Fosso Wamba, S., & Akter, S. (2019). Understanding Supply Chain Analytics Capabilities and Agility for Data-Rich Environments. *International Journal of Operations & Production Management*, *39*(6/7/8), 887–912. doi:10.1108/IJOPM-01-2019-0025

Gülen, K. (2023). Unleashing the Power of AI with the Rise of Intelligent Supply Chain Management. In *Artificial Intelligence, Industry, Transportation & Logistics*. https://dataconomy.com/2023/01/artificial-intelligence-supply-chain

Haenlein, M., & Kaplan, A. (2019). A Brief History of Artificial Intelligence: On the Past, Present, and Future of Artificial Intelligence. *California Management Review*, *61*(4), 5–14. doi:10.1177/0008125619864925

Hartmann, J., & Moeller, S. (2014). Chain Liability in Multitier Supply Chains? Responsibility Attributions for Unsustainable Supplier Behavior. *Journal of Operations Management*, *32*(5), 281–294. doi:10.1016/j.jom.2014.01.005

Huang, M., & Rust, R. (2018). Artificial Intelligence in Service. *Journal of Service Research*, *21*(2), 155–172. doi:10.1177/1094670517752459

Iyyanar, P., Anand, R., Shanthi, T., Nassa, V. K., Pandey, B. K., George, A. S., & Pandey, D. (2023). A Real-Time Smart Sewage Cleaning UAV Assistance System Using IoT. In *Handbook of Research on Data-Driven Mathematical Modeling in Smart Cities* (pp. 24–39). IGI Global.

Jabbour, C. J. C., Fiorini, P. D., Ndubisi, N. O., Queiroz, M. M., & Piato, E. L. (2020). Digitally Enabled Sustainable Supply Chains in the 21st Century: A Review and a ResearchAgenda. *The Science of the Total Environment*, *725*, 138177. Advance online publication. doi:10.1016/j.scitotenv.2020.138177 PMID:32302825

Jakupović, A., Pavlić, M., & Han, Z. D. (2014). Formalization Method for the Text Expressed Knowledge. *Expert Systems with Applications*, *41*(11), 5308–5322. doi:10.1016/j.eswa.2014.03.006

Kalavathy, K. S., Swapna, H. R., Nallasivam, A., Pandey, D., Mahajan, D. A., & Dadheech, P. (2023). An Empirical Investigation on the Influence of Social Networks on Purchase Decision Making: An Indian Perspective. In *Social Media and Online Consumer Decision Making in the Fashion Industry* (pp. 26–43). IGI Global. doi:10.4018/978-1-6684-8753-2.ch002

Kreipl, S., & Pinedo, M. (2004). Planning and Scheduling in Supply Chains: An Overview of Issues in Practice. *Production and Operations Management*, *13*(1), 77–92. doi:10.1111/j.1937-5956.2004.tb00146.x

Kumar Pandey, B., Pandey, D., Nassa, V. K., Ahmad, T., Singh, C., George, A. S., & Wakchaure, M. A. (2021). Encryption and steganography-based text extraction in IoT using the EWCTS optimizer. *Imaging Science Journal*, *69*(1-4), 38–56. doi:10.1080/13682199.2022.2146885

Kusiak, A. (2019). Fundamentals of Smart Manufacturing: A Multi-Thread Perspective. *Annual Reviews in Control*, *47*, 214–220. doi:10.1016/j.arcontrol.2019.02.001

Li, Y., Diabat, A., & Lu, C. C. (2020). Leagile Supplier Selection in Chinese Textile Industries: A DEMATEL Approach. *Annals of Operations Research*, *287*(1), 303–322. doi:10.1007/s10479-019-03453-2

Malhotra, P., Pandey, D., Pandey, B. K., & Patra, P. M. (2021). Managing agricultural supply chains in COVID-19 lockdown. *International Journal of Quality and Innovation*, *5*(2), 109–118. doi:10.1504/IJQI.2021.117181

McKinsey & Company. (2021). *Succeeding in the AI Supply-Chain Revolution*. https://www.mckinsey.com/industries/metals-and-mining/our-insights/succeeding-inthe-ai-supply-chain-revolution

Meslie, Y., Enbeyle, W., Pandey, B. K., Pramanik, S., Pandey, D., Dadeech, P., & Saini, A. (2021). Machine intelligence-based trend analysis of COVID-19 for total daily confirmed cases in Asia and Africa. In *Methodologies and Applications of Computational Statistics for Machine Intelligence* (pp. 164–185). IGI Global. doi:10.4018/978-1-7998-7701-1.ch009

Mohsen, B. (2022). Role of Big Data in Supply Chain Management. *International Journal of Management*, *13*, 24–40.

Mohsen, B. (2023). Developments of Digital Technologies Related to Supply Chain Management. *The 13th International Symposium on Frontiers in Ambient and Mobile Systems (FAMS 2023)*. 10.1016/j.procs.2023.03.105

Nayak, R., & Choudhary, S. (2022). Operational Excellence in Humanitarian Logistics and Supply Chain Management through Leagile Framework: A Case Study from a Non-Mature Economy. *Production Planning and Control, 33*(6-7), 606–621. doi:10.1080/09537287.2020.1834135

Pandey, B. K., Mane, D., Nassa, V. K. K., Pandey, D., Dutta, S., Ventayen, R. J. M., Agarwal, G., & Rastogi, R. (2021). Secure text extraction from complex degraded images by applying steganography and deep learning. In *Multidisciplinary approach to modern digital steganography* (pp. 146–163). IGI Global. doi:10.4018/978-1-7998-7160-6.ch007

Pandey, B. K., & Pandey, D. (2023). Parametric optimization and prediction of enhanced thermoelectric performance in co-doped CaMnO3 using response surface methodology and neural network. *Journal of Materials Science Materials in Electronics, 34*(21), 1589. doi:10.1007/s10854-023-10954-1

Pandey, B. K., Pandey, D., Wairya, S., Agarwal, G., Dadeech, P., Dogiwal, S. R., & Pramanik, S. (2022). Application of integrated steganography and image compressing techniques for confidential information transmission. *Cyber Security and Network Security*, 169-191.

Pandey, D., Pandey, B. K., & Wairya, S. (2021). Hybrid deep neural network with adaptive galactic swarm optimization for text extraction from scene images. *Soft Computing, 25*(2), 1563–1580. doi:10.1007/s00500-020-05245-4

Pournader, M., Ghaderi, H., Hassanzadegan, A., & Fahimnia, B. (2021). Artificial Intelligence Applications in Supply Chain Management. *International Journal of Production Economics, 241*, 108250. Advance online publication. doi:10.1016/j.ijpe.2021.108250

Pramanik, S., Pandey, D., Joardar, S., Niranjanamurthy, M., Pandey, B. K., & Kaur, J. (2023, October). An overview of IoT privacy and security in smart cities. In AIP Conference Proceedings (Vol. 2495, No. 1). AIP Publishing. doi:10.1063/5.0123511

Rahimi, A., & Alemtabriz, A. (2022). Providing a Model of Leagile Hybrid Paradigm Practices and Its Impact on Supply Chain Performance. *International Journal of Lean Six Sigma, 13*(6), 1308–1345. doi:10.1108/IJLSS-04-2021-0073

Rostami, O., Tavakoli, M., & Tajally, A., & GhanavatiNejad, M. (2022). A Goal Programming-Based Fuzzy Best-Worst Method for the Viable Supplier Selection Problem: A Case Study. *Soft Computing*, 1–26. doi:10.1007/s00500-022-07572-0 PMID:36373094

Scholten, K., Sharkey Scott, P., & Fynes, B. (2014). Mitigation Processes—Antecedents for Building Supply Chain Resilience. *Supply Chain Management, 19*(2), 211–228. doi:10.1108/SCM-06-2013-0191

Singh, J., Pandey, D., & Singh, A. K. (2023). Event detection from real-time twitter streaming data using community detection algorithm. *Multimedia Tools and Applications*, 1–28. doi:10.1007/s11042-023-16263-3

Singh, H., Pandey, D., Kakkar, R., & Sharma, M. (n.d.). Investigations on Genetically Engineered Bioweapons & Computer Based Techniques for Counter Measure and Mathematical Modeling for Prediction of Novel Sars-Cov-2. *Vice Chancellor's Message*, 1.

Stoyanov, S. (2021). Integration of Artificial Intelligence in the Supply Chain Management. *Journal Scientific and Applied Research, 20*(1), 53–59. doi:10.46687/jsar.v20i1.305

Swapna, H. R., Singh, S., Madaan, G., Mishra, S., Pandey, D., & Kanike, U. K. (2023). Globalization and Emerging Opportunities and Challenges in Sustainable Environment in Industry 4.0. Handbook of Research on Safe Disposal Methods of Municipal Solid Wastes for a Sustainable Environment, 48-68.

Tirkolaee, E. B., Aydin, N. S., & Mahdavi, I. (2022). A Hybrid Biobjective MarkovChain-Based Optimization Model for Sustainable Aggregate Production Planning. *IEEE Transactions on Engineering Management*, 1–11. doi:10.1109/TEM.2022.3210879

Wang, X., Kumar, V., Kumari, A., & Kuzmin, E. (2022). Impact of Digital Technology on Supply Chain Efficiency in Manufacturing Industry. In V. Kumar, J. Leng, V. Akberdina, & E. Kuzmin (Eds.), *Digital Transformation in Industry. Lecture Notes in Information Systems and Organisation* (Vol. 54, pp. 347–371). Springer. doi:10.1007/978-3-030-94617-3_25

Xie, Y., Yin, Y., Xue, W., Shi, H., & Chong, D. (2020). Intelligent Supply Chain PerformanceMeasurement in Industry 4.0. *Systems Research and Behavioral Science, 37*(4), 711–718. doi:10.1002/sres.2712

Yu, Y., Wang, X., Zhong, R. Y., & Huang, G. Q. (2017). E-Commerce Logistics in SupplyChain Management: Implementations and Future Perspective in Furniture Industry. *Industrial Management & Data Systems, 117*, 2263–2286. doi:10.1108/IMDS-09-2016-0398

Zakur, Y. A., Mallik, B. B., Zakoor, Y. A., & Pandey, D. (2023). Survey on the Artificial Intelligence and Machine Learning Techniques on the Applications of Wastewater Treatment for Sustainable Environment. In *Handbook of Research on Safe Disposal Methods of Municipal Solid Wastes for a Sustainable Environment* (pp. 241–248). IGI Global. doi:10.4018/978-1-6684-8117-2.ch017

Zamani, E. D., Smyth, C., Gupta, S., & Dennehy, D. (2022). Artificial Intelligence and BigData Analytics for Supply Chain Resilience: A Systematic Literature Review. *Annals of Operations Research*, 1–28. doi:10.1007/s10479-022-04983-y PMID:36212520

Zarbakhshnia, N., Soleimani, H., & Ghaderi, H. (2018). Sustainable Third-Party Reverse Logistics Provider Evaluation and Selection Using Fuzzy SWARA and Developed Fuzzy COPRAS in the Presence of Risk Criteria. *Applied Soft Computing, 65*, 307–319. doi:10.1016/j.asoc.2018.01.023

Zouari, D., Ruel, S., & Viale, L. (2021). Does Digitalizing the Supply Chain Contribute toIts Resilience? *International Journal of Physical Distribution & Logistics Management, 51*(2), 149–180. doi:10.1108/IJPDLM-01-2020-0038

Chapter 6
Applications of Artificial Intelligence and Machine Learning in Supply Chain Management:
An In-Depth Investigation

Binay Kumar Pandey
https://orcid.org/0000-0002-4041-1213
Department of Information Technology, College of Technology, Govind Ballabh Pant University of Agriculture and Technology, India

Mukundan Appadurai Paramashivan
https://orcid.org/0009-0009-5608-4788
Aligarh Muslim University, India & Champions Group, India

Rashmi Mahajan
https://orcid.org/0000-0001-9082-6874
Balaji Institute of International Business, Sri Balaji University, Pune, India

Darshan A. Mahajan
https://orcid.org/0000-0002-1239-6343
NICMAR University, Pune, India

Nitesh Behare
https://orcid.org/0000-0002-9338-8563
Balaji Institute of International Business, Sri Balaji University, Pune, India

Gadee Gowwrii
MSC Statistics, Osmania University, Hyderabad, India

Sabyasachi Pramanik
https://orcid.org/0000-0002-9431-8751
Department of Computer Science and Engineering, Haldia Institute of Technology (Autonomous), India

ABSTRACT

This study examines theoretical frameworks, methods, and key discoveries' practical, social, and theoretical impacts. Study envisions AI/ML SCM. Supply chain AI/ML is assessed by model optimisation, predictive analytics, and decision-making frameworks. Systematic literature reviews gather pertinent research. The authors read academic, conference, and industrial papers to learn. To uncover trends and insights, studies are critically assessed, classified, and synthesised. This study examines AI/ML supply

DOI: 10.4018/979-8-3693-1347-3.ch006

chain demand forecasting, inventory management, logistics optimisation, and risk management. The research suggests deep learning, neural networks, evolutionary algorithms, and SVMs for supply chain issues. The review highlights SCM AI/ML implementation issues and AI/ML supply chain management pros and drawbacks. Researchers, practitioners, and policymakers may discover how AI and ML improve supply chain efficiency, cost, and networks.

INTRODUCTION

In recent years, there has been a substantial paradigm shift in the industry of supply chain management (also known as SCM) (Chen, Y. et al., 2019), which may be attributed to the emergence of technologies that make use of artificial intelligence (AI) (Chen, P. Y., & Wang, F. K., 2020) and machine learning (ML). Because of this change, there have been considerable increases in both efficiency and efficacy. This shift in perspective was brought about as a direct result of the convergence of these various technological aspects. The ability of artificial intelligence and machine learning algorithms to analyse vast volumes of data (Dey, A., & Nair, A., 2019) and provide insights that can be put into action has resulted in a fundamental change to the conventional techniques of supply chain management. This change has been brought about as a direct result of the capabilities of these two types of algorithms. The proliferation of connected devices and appliances, often known as the Internet of Things (IoT) (Pandey, J. K. et al., 2022), is directly responsible for bringing about this shift. Bdataecause of this, businesses have been able to boost not just their operational efficiency (Gong, Y. et al., 2020) but also their methods of decision-making and their general efficacy.

The purpose of this article is to attempt to provide a comprehensive study of the several ways in which these technologies are utilised by focusing on the various applications of artificial intelligence (Ghaffari, A., & Rabbani, M., 2019) and machine learning (Kumar, A. et al., 2022) in supply chain management. Specifically, the article will examine the various ways in which these technologies can be used to manage supply chains. The potential benefits and the potential drawbacks that are linked with the utilisation of these technologies (Gunasekaran, A., & Ngai, E. W. T., 2017) are going to be the primary focal points of the inquiry that will be carried out.

The level of success that a company achieves is inversely proportional to a variety of factors, one of the most important of which is the way in which the company manages the supply chain that it employs (Christopher, M., 2016)). This management encompasses the entirety of the process of controlling the flow of goods and services, beginning with the procurement of raw materials and concluding with the distribution of finished items to end users.

This management starts with controlling the flow of commodities and services into and out of the organisation. It begins with the goal of obtaining the highest possible levels of both efficiency and effectiveness throughout the entire operation in every facet of it (Fawcett, S. E. et al., 2014). Companies may find it difficult to effectively manage their operations and adjust to the ever-evolving expectations of their consumers due to the fluidity and complexity of modern supply chains. This can make it difficult for companies to compete in today's global economy. As a result of this, it can be difficult for enterprises to compete in the modern economy on a global scale. In this scenario, artificial intelligence (AI) (Pandey, D. et al., 2021) and machine learning (ML) can be used because they provide cutting-edge capabilities that have the potential to revolutionise traditional supply chain techniques and provide a competitive advantage. These capabilities have the potential to revolutionise traditional supply chain approaches and provide a competitive advantage. These capabilities can be employed because AI (Pandey, B. K. et al., 2021c) and ML give cutting-edge capabilities that have the potential to disrupt traditional supply chain procedures (De Sousa Jabbour et al., 2018). As a result, these capabilities can be utilised. These qualities give AI and ML (Anand, R. et al., 2023) with cutting-edge capabilities that have the potential to transform the conventional ways of supply chain management. These capabilities have the potential to change the conventional ways of supply chain management.

Supply chain professionals today have access to cutting-edge solutions that are backed by cutting-edge technology such as artificial intelligence and machine learning. These cutting-edge technologies support cutting-edge solutions. These innovative products pack a strong punch and are very effective in their respective fields. The implementation of these technological solutions has the potential to enhance important facets of supply chain management, including demand forecasting, inventory management, logistics optimisation, supplier selection, and risk management. Businesses may improve their inventory levels, avoid stockouts, and reduce the expenses associated with holding extra inventory by using AI and ML algorithms to evaluate historical data (Babu, S. Z. D. et al., 2022), identify patterns, and estimate future demand. These benefits can be obtained without jeopardising the level of satisfaction provided to customers.

This has the potential to result in cost reductions for enterprises. It is possible that the operations that take place in the fields of logistics and transportation may become more effective if they were powered by AI-based technologies (Pandey, B. K. et al., 2022a). This can be accomplished by organising the delivery, establishing the routes that are the most efficient, and cutting down on the quantity of petrol that is consumed. This could result in monetary savings and have a favourable affect on the natural world that is immediately surrounding us. Moreover, this could have a positive influence on the natural world. The management of supplier relationships and selections is one of the most important applications of artificial intelligence and machine learning (Kusi-Sarpong, S. et al., 2019) in supply chain logistics. This is because these two technologies can learn on their own. This is one of the most important applications of AI and ML that there is. Manual evaluations are frequently applied as part of the more standard approaches to the evaluation of prospective vendors and suppliers. These evaluations are not only extremely open to interpretation, but they also demand a considerable amount of time and effort. It is feasible for AI and ML (Meslie, Y. et al., 2021) algorithms to evaluate a wide range of variables, such as a service provider's performance, pricing, quality, and risk indicators, in order to identify which service providers would be the most useful to a specific firm. This leads to an increase in collaboration and a reduction in the number of disruptions in the supply chain, as well as a simplicity of the process for selecting suppliers and an overall improvement in the management of the relationships with those suppliers. A further benefit is an improvement to the supply chain. In addition, the use of AI and ML techniques can improve supply chain risk management by forecasting and decreasing the possibility of future interruptions in the supply chain. This improves the ability to respond to potential disruptions in the supply chain.

This may result in an overall improvement in the management of the risks associated with the supply chain. Artificial intelligence (AI) systems are able to spot potential threats and convey warnings to the managers who are in charge of the supply chain because they evaluate data (Kumar, M. S. et al., 2021) from a broad variety of sources, such as weather forecasts, social media, and historical data from supply chains (Malhotra, P. et al., 2021). These data sources include supply networks themselves. Therefore, the managers of the supply chain are required to take preemptive action in response to the situation. Because of this, companies are able to build supply chains that are more robust, which not only improves their ability to respond to unforeseen events but also decreases the negative repercussions that disruptions have on their operations. This allows companies to design supply chains that are more resilient.

This is as a result of the fact that businesses are now in a position to build supply networks that are more resilient. Despite the fact that the domains of artificial intelligence and machine learning have a great deal of potential for the topic of supply chain management, there are still issues that need to be addressed and managed in this area. Concerns about the level of privacy and security, problems with the integration of systems, doubts about the availability and quality of data, and the demand for people with professional training are some of the hurdles that must be overcome. The report on the study will, in addition to explaining these difficulties, present some potential solutions to the issues that have been identified as being problematic.

In recent years, advances in technology, such as artificial intelligence and machine learning, have brought about fundamental shifts in the management of supply chains. These shifts have been brought about as a direct result of these technological advancements. Because of the progression that has taken place, companies today have access to possibilities that were not available to them in the past. In the past, they were unable to take advantage of possibilities like these. Because of the availability of these choices, businesses have the opportunity to improve their capacity for decision-making, to streamline their operations, and to raise their overall efficiency. This research paper will provide a comprehensive assessment of the different applications of artificial intelligence and machine learning in supply chain management in an effort to shed light on the potential benefits and challenges associated with their deployment. In addition to that, the purpose of this study article is to provide light on the potential benefits and problems associated with their implementation. In addition to this, the goal of the study is to throw light on the potential benefits as well as the difficulties that are linked with the execution of their recommendations.

The purpose of the study project is to investigate both of these facets in order to shed light not only on the possible advantages that could result from its implementation, but also on the possible challenges that could arise as a result of its implementation. As a direct result of this new breakthrough, companies will be able to analyse whether or not it makes sense for them to incorporate the aforementioned technologies into the method that they use to manage their supply chains, which will allow them to make an informed decision about whether or not to do so.

BACKGROUND

Supply chain management (Chopra, S., & Meindl, P., 2016) is one of the most significant variables that determines a company's level of performance across all different types of sectors. In order to provide clients with goods or services in a manner that is both effective and efficient, it is required to coordinate and integrate a large number of processes, such as manufacturing, inventory control, logistics, and distribution (Lee, H. L., 2004). This is the case in order to meet the needs of clients. The complexity of contemporary supply chains, which is characterised by multinational networks, variable demand patterns, and unplanned interruptions, provides substantial problems for businesses that are attempting to maximise the effectiveness of their operations.

In the past few years, there has been a rise in popularity of the use of technologies such as artificial intelligence (AI) and machine learning (ML) in the context of improving supply chain management operations. This trend can be attributed to the fact that these technologies are seen as having the potential to make supply chain management operations more efficient. The fact that these technologies can improve both efficiency and efficacy may be the driving force behind this development. AI and ML have the potential to enhance the decision-making processes, automate a wide variety of operations within the supply chain firm (Kannan, V. R., & Tan, K. C., 2015), and extract useful insights from massive amounts of data. The implementation of AI and ML could make these benefits attainable. Even if there have been more studies and applications related to this topic in recent years, there is still a requirement for a comprehensive evaluation that provides a summary of the current state of research and practises in this field. This research paper intends to provide a comprehensive assessment of the uses of artificial intelligence and machine learning in supply chain management by way of providing an in-depth look at the aforementioned applications. By conducting a literature review and analysing previously conducted business case studies, the purpose of this investigation is to identify the primary domains in which AI (Pandey, B. K. et al., 2021b) and ML have been successfully used, as well as the benefits that have emerged and the challenges that have been encountered. In order to accomplish this goal, the research endeavours to identify the significant domains in which AI and ML have been successfully implemented. Managing client relationships, demand forecasting, inventory management, shipping and logistics, choosing suppliers, and production scheduling are just some of the topics that will be addressed in the exam.

The results of the study will make a contribution to the body of material that currently exists by providing an overview of what is already known about the application of artificial intelligence and machine learning in supply chain management. This will be achieved by providing an overview of the information (Pandey, B. K. et al., 2022b) that is already known on the application of AI and ML in supply chain management. Following the completion of the research, the sectors that will be deemed to be the most promising will be those in which AI (Wang, L., & Zhou, L., 2019) and ML have the potential to produce the most value. Because of this, it will be easy for experts and academics to focus their efforts on these specific areas. During the study, we will identify which sectors have the most room for expansion, as well as the domains in which AI and ML may be able to add the most value. In addition, the findings of this research will shed insight on the challenges and limitations associated with the implementation of AI and ML in supply chains. Because of this, firms will have an easier time developing a better understanding of the potential risks and challenges that may arise as a direct result of the research. This study will have significant ramifications for both the academic world and the professional world of business. The review will provide the basis for ongoing research activities by identifying gaps in the literature and offering new avenues for further exploration. This will be accomplished. The significance of this, from a scholarly point of view, cannot be overstated. This will be accomplished with flying colours. The findings will be of great value to supply chain professionals who are interested in employing AI (Pandey, B. K., & Pandey, D., 2023) and ML technologies in their work, and they will provide major insights and recommendations. This is due to the fact that a purely commercial point of view was used in the research. The first step for companies to take in determining whether or not they plan to implement and integrate artificial intelligence and machine learning technologies into their supply chain processes is to gain an awareness of the applications, benefits, and challenges posed by these technologies in the real world.

This in-depth research has been written with the intention of providing readers with a deeper comprehension of the manner in which artificial intelligence and machine learning are now being utilised in the administration of supply chains. This study will be a great resource for researchers, practitioners, and decision-makers interested in utilising AI (Pandey, B. K. et al., 2021a) and ML to improve supply chain operations and boost overall business performance by comparing the existing research and real-world implementations. This study will be published in the Journal of Artificial Intelligence and Machine Learning. This will be achieved by the study by undertaking a review of both the previous research as well as the implementations in the actual world. This will be the case because the study will investigate both the previous research that has been carried out as well as the actual implementations that have been carried out, thus it is inevitable that this will be the outcome. The reasoning that underpins doing so in this way

- The Increasing Significance of Managing Supply Chains Efficiently Management of the supply chain, commonly known as supply chain management or SCM, is an organisational function that is essential to the success of companies functioning in a diverse array of various industries. The global marketplace is becoming increasingly complex and competitive, and businesses are starting to realise that in order for them to remain competitive, they need to optimise the operations of their supply chains. This is because the global marketplace is getting increasingly complex and competitive. In this context, the application of artificial intelligence (AI) and machine learning (ML) techniques holds tremendous potential for the improvement of decision-making capacities, the growth of consumer happiness, the reduction of costs, and the expansion of supply chain efficiency. Because of this, it is very necessary to carry out a full study of the applications of AI and ML in SCM in order to provide academics and practitioners with insights and a sense of where they should focus their efforts. Specifically, this is required in order to provide a sense of where they should concentrate their efforts.
- Recent and Rapid Developments in AI and Machine Learning: Recent years have witnessed remarkable advancements in the fields of artificial intelligence (AI) and machine learning (ML), both of which are expected to have a significant impact on the management of supply chains as a result. AI is an abbreviation for "artificial intelligence," and ML (Kumar Pandey, B. et al., 2021) is an abbreviation for "machine learning." These technologies have the power to process enormous amounts of data, derive actionable insights from the data, and automate a number of activities and procedures across a wide variety of business sectors and industries. On the other hand, due to the nature of AI and ML, which is that it is continuously expanding, it is tough to keep up with the most recent breakthroughs in the field and to comprehend the range of applications that are possible for these technologies. Because of this, keeping up with the most recent developments in the sector can be a difficult task. The objective of this research study is to offer a picture that is both current and consolidated of how AI and ML are being utilised in SCM. To achieve this purpose, the research study will perform a comprehensive review. It is purposefully crafted to fulfil this criteria so that it may accomplish its task of satisfying the demand for an all-encompassing resource in this sector of the economy.
- Being Aware of the Opportunities and Obstacles That May Present Themselves In the Future The application of artificial intelligence and machine learning in supply chain management carries with it a variety of prospective advantages as well as a variety of prospective difficulties. AI and ML have the ability to enable a wide range of applications, including real-time monitoring, predictive analytics, demand forecasting, inventory optimisation, intelligent routing, and more. On the other hand, AI and ML have the potential to enable a wide variety of applications for a variety of different industries. On the other side, data security, ethical ramifications, and the requirement for qualified professionals are brought up as potential concerns. These topics are brought up as potential worries. These subjects are brought up as potential concerns because they have the potential to cause problems. This study attempts to identify and investigate these potential and challenges, shedding light on the possible benefits and hazards related with the application of artificial intel-

ligence and machine learning in supply chain management (SCM). This study focuses specifically on the potential benefits and risks associated with the application of artificial intelligence and machine learning in supply chain management (SCM). Specifically, this research looks at the potential benefits and hazards associated with artificial intelligence and machine learning in SCM. This is done with the intention of pointing practitioners and decision-makers in the direction of the process of developing informed decisions and strategies.

- Filling in the Blanks with Regards to the Research In spite of the fact that a substantial number of studies have been carried out to investigate the applications of AI and ML in various elements of supply chain management, there has not been an in-depth research that takes into account the whole breadth of these applications. A rigorous assessment and analysis of the existing literature, academic research, and industrial case studies is what this research study attempts to accomplish in order to fill up this gap. The purpose of this article is to present a wide-ranging discussion of the several uses of artificial intelligence and machine learning in supply chain management (SCM). By doing so, it will contribute to the current body of information, highlight new trends, and identify chances for future research, thereby enhancing both the understanding of and the ability to apply AI and ML in supply chain management. In addition, it will identify prospects for future research.
- What This means for the Procedures That Are Currently In Place The findings of this in-depth study will have important ramifications for practitioners, managers, and decision-makers working in supply chain management in the future. In this article, we will examine real-world applications and case studies in order to achieve our goal of providing insights into the potential benefits, challenges, and best practises of integrating artificial intelligence and machine learning into supply chain operations. The analysis of real-world applications and case studies is going to be used to provide these kinds of insights. The findings of this research can serve as a point of reference for companies as they choose whether or not to make specific investments, such as those in technology, process improvements, talent acquisition, and overall supply chain strategy. This can be helpful for companies as they make these decisions. When these determinations are finally put into action, the end consequence will be an increase in operational efficiency, a reduction in costs, and a higher level of satisfaction among customers.

PURPOSES OR AIMS OF THE RESEARCH

- "To present an in-depth examination of the different uses of computational intelligence (also called AI) and the use of machine learning (ML) techniques in supply chain management.".
- "To investigate the effect that AI and ML have on different facets of supply chain management, such as forecasting demand, handling stocks, transportation optimising, and the selection of suppliers."
- "To evaluate the effectiveness and effectiveness of AI and ML methods to enhancing supply chain processes like fulfilment of orders, manufacturing scheduling, and logistics management."
- "To define the primary obstacles and constraints related to the introduction of AI and ML in supply chain management and to investigate possible approaches for addressing these difficulties."

- "To study the latest advances and patterns in the fields of artificial intelligence and machine learning, as well as the implications that these fields have for the oversight of supply chains."

LITERATURE REVIEW

The control of the flow of goods and services is what is referred to as supply chain management (SCM), and it plays a vital part in the overall success of businesses. Many applications have emerged as a result of advancements in artificial intelligence (AI) and machine learning (ML), which have resulted in changes to the conventional procedures for supply chain management. This literature review aims to provide an in-depth investigation of the applications of AI and ML in supply chain management and to place particular attention on the influence these technologies have on both performance and efficiency. Prediction and Demand Planning Artificial intelligence and machine learning techniques have seen widespread application in forecasting and demand planning. (Chen et al., 2019) provide evidence that deep learning algorithms are effective at accurately predicting demand patterns. As a result, businesses are able to improve their inventory management and experience fewer stockouts. In a similar vein, (Verma et al., 2021) propose a hybrid model that combines ML algorithms with traditional time series forecasting techniques. As a result, the model achieves a greater level of accuracy and facilitates improved decision-making.

Inventory Control and Management

Without accurate inventory management, the processes that make up the supply chain cannot be considered complete. The application of AI and ML techniques can result in the generation of substantial insights, which can then be put to use to optimise inventory levels and cut costs. (Sridharan et al., 2020) offer a method that is based on reinforcement learning and that automatically adjusts reorder points and order quantities based on fluctuations in real-time demand. Because of this, inventory turns over more quickly, which in turn results in lower holding costs.

The Selection of Vendors and Management of Their Relationships

In order to attain operational excellence, it is required to carry out procedures for the selection and administration of suppliers that are efficient. AI and ML-based methods make it possible for companies to form lasting partnerships with the suppliers that, considering a range of criteria, offer the most suitable solutions to meet the requirements of their enterprises. (Kumar et al., 2022) provide a framework for the selection of suppliers that makes use of fuzzy logic and machine learning algorithms. This framework is intended to aid in the process of making purchasing decisions. This framework takes a lot of factors into consideration, such as pricing, quality, and delivery performance, which eventually results in improved supplier decisions.

Optimisation of the Warehouse and Distribution Process

Optimising the operations of the warehouses as well as the distribution networks is crucial to ensuring that supply chain management is carried out in an effective manner. The integration of AI and ML techniques opens up a variety of possibilities for improving warehouse design, in addition to improving routing and scheduling. In (Gong et al., 2020) method for optimising warehouse architecture and reducing the amount of time spent choosing orders, a genetic algorithm serves as the foundation for the strategy. As a consequence, this leads to increased operational efficiency as well as decreased expenditures.

Administration of Transportation

The role that transportation plays in the chain of supply has a considerable impact on the day-to-day operations of the supply chain. It is now much simpler to optimise routes, plan out vehicle schedules, and predict freight prices thanks to the usage of AI and ML-based technologies. Deep reinforcement learning is the basis for the solution that (Wang F. et al., 2021) present for the problem of dynamic vehicle routing. This strategy takes into account the current traffic conditions and delivery constraints, and the end result is improved delivery times as well as reduced costs associated with transportation.

The Management of Risk

The supply chain is susceptible to many different types of risks, such as interruptions, unpredictability in demand, and failures on the side of the suppliers (Gartner., 2019). Tools that are helpful in recognising risks, generating strategies to mitigate such risks, and improving resilience can be derived from models that are based on AI and ML. The framework for risk assessment that is provided by (Tang et al, 2020) is predicated on ML algorithms. This approach is intended to proactively anticipate potential interruptions in the supply chain and prepare for them accordingly. As a direct consequence of this, organisations are provided with the capability to promptly implement mitigation techniques.

Initiatives Regarding Environmental Stewardship and Long-Term Sustainability

In addition, the incorporation of AI and ML into supply chain management has played a role in the progression of projects that are both ecologically responsible and sustainable. (Zhang et al., 2021) present an AI-based model for optimising the selection and routing of environmentally friendly transport options, taking into consideration both emissions and pricing. Because of this, there would be less of an impact on the surrounding environment, and the organism's capacity to look after itself would rise.

Both the Materials and the Methods

Research plan: The research plan for this review article will follow a systematic approach in order to provide a thorough and rigorous investigation of the applications of artificial intelligence (AI) and machine learning (ML) in supply chain management (SCM). This will be done in order to ensure a comprehensive and accurate analysis of the applications of AI and ML in SCM. This will be accomplished by utilising a study design that takes a methodical approach to the problem at hand. In each stage of the research design process, activities such as the following are included:

Literature search: We are going to do an exhaustive literature search utilising relevant academic sources such as IEEE Xplore, ACM Digital Library, and Scopus. We are going to give careful consideration to the selection of the search phrases in order to guarantee that only pertinent research are included in the review.

The screening procedure will look at the titles and abstracts of the research that has been found, and the selected research will be based on that. Only a subset of the studies that are relevant to the objectives of the research will have their eligibility for inclusion or exclusion examined.

Data Extraction: From each of the selected studies, we will take the pertinent data and extract them. This will contain the study history, research methodology, artificial intelligence and machine learning methodologies that were applied, as well as the outcomes that were expressed.

Synthesis of data (Heikkilä, J., & Lintukangas, K., 2020): After the data have been extracted, they will be synthesised in order to discover common themes, trends, and patterns in the applications of AI and ML in SCM. The statistics will specifically concentrate on the supply chain management (SCM) business sector. During the synthesis, we will be structuring the information and concentrating on the most essential takeaways from the experience.

Conditions for Inclusion

- Articles of research that have been reviewed and considered suitable for publishing in scholarly journals or the proceedings of academic conferences.
- The primary emphasis of the studies was placed on utilising AI and ML in supply chain management applications.
- Research, including case studies and other studies that provide evidence based on experience.
- Conduct your research using just articles that were composed in the English language.

Conditions for Exclusion

- Research that does not directly address the application of artificial intelligence and machine learning in supply chain management.
- Investigations that are not open to the public for viewing for one of two reasons: either they have not been released or they are concealed behind a paywall.
- Research that focuses primarily on conceptual or theoretical concerns but does not include any considerations of their potential implications in the real world.

Analysis of the Level of Quality In order to ensure the reliability and validity of the findings, we are going to conduct an analysis of the quality of each of the selected research. When conducting the assessment of the quality of the research, a number of factors will be taken into consideration. These factors will include the research design, methodology, sample size, methods of data collection, and statistical analysis. During the process of synthesis, studies that have a higher level of methodological rigour and robustness will be given a greater degree of weight than those that do not.

Ethical Factors to Take Into Account Due to the fact that this is a review paper, the most essential component of the ethical concerns is to make certain that the required citation and acknowledgement of the work done by the original authors is included. The findings and concepts that have been developed from the selected studies will be credited in the most precise way that is currently available. In a forthright and forthright manner, the presence of any potential conflicts of interest that may exist will be revealed. It is not essential to acquire ethical approval for this review paper because it will not involve the collection of primary data or the use of human participants.

RESULTS AND DISCUSSION

This article provides an in-depth examination of the utilisation of artificial intelligence (AI) and machine learning (ML) methods in the field of supply chain management. The analysis encompasses a broad spectrum of domains and processes that are incorporated into the supply chain. The utilisation of artificial intelligence (AI) and machine learning (ML) methodologies has demonstrated substantial promise in improving several aspects of supply chain management. These factors encompass demand prediction, stock control, transportation optimisation, and supplier selection. The efficacy of demand forecasting models utilising artificial intelligence (AI) and machine learning (ML) has enhanced, resulting in a decrease in forecasting inaccuracies and an elevation in client contentment. The application of algorithms for machine learning has enabled the more effective management of inventory by optimising reorder points, eliminating the risk of stockouts, and reducing the expenses associated with inventory maintenance. Transportation optimisation algorithms utilising artificial intelligence have enhanced route planning, load optimisation, and real-time tracking. These advancements have resulted in reduced transportation costs and better delivery efficiency. The utilisation of machine learning-based models for supplier selection has led to advancements in supplier management and a decrease in supply chain hazards. These models have proven valuable in determining the suppliers that are the most reliable and efficient in terms of cost. The successful and efficient use of AI and ML technologies has led to enhancements in supply chain operations, including order fulfilment, production planning, and logistics management. These enhancements have benefited from the implementation of these methodologies. Utilising intelligent order fulfilment systems driven by artificial intelligence enables the efficient processing of orders, resulting in reduced processing time, improved order precision, and increased customer happiness. The application of algorithms for machine learning has enhanced production planning, leading to streamlined production schedules, decreased lead times, and reduced production costs. The integration of artificial intelligence (AI) into logistics management systems has facilitated enhancements in route optimisation, load distribution, and instantaneous tracking, resulting in efficient operations and a decrease in idle time during transportation. Consequently, there has been a decrease in the duration of time that is squandered while awaiting conveyance. This report explores notable obstacles and constraints related to the implementation of AI and ML in supply chain management. Overcoming ethical considerations, organisational opposition to change, interaction with preexisting systems, and ensuring data quality and availability are among the challenges and constraints that need to be addressed. Insufficient availability of real-time, high-quality data is a significant obstacle to the effective use of AI and ML methodologies. This can provide challenges in the utilisation of AI and ML. For a successful integration of AI and ML systems with existing legacy systems and processes, meticulous preplanning and the allocation of appropriate resources are crucial. Conquering opposition within an organisation towards change and establishing a culture that places importance on innovation are both crucial elements for effectively using artificial intelligence and machine learning. The implementation of artificial intelligence and machine learning in supply chain management raises ethical concerns that must be resolved. These concerns encompass issues related to bias, confidentiality, and the security of personal information. This study examines the latest developments and patterns in artificial intelligence (AI) and machine learning (ML) technologies, and their impact on supply chain management. Recent advancements in deep learning, natural language processing (NLP), and computer vision have unlocked new possibilities for the use of artificial intelligence and machine learning in supply chain management. The progress in technology has enabled supply chain management to leverage artificial intelligence (AI) and machine learning (ML). The integration of artificial intelligence (AI) and machine learning (ML) with emerging technologies like the Internet of Things (IoT) (Pramanik, S. et al., 2023) and blockchain enables the enhancement of supply chain visibility, traceability, and transparency. The proliferation of cloud computing and edge computing has proven advantageous for the integration of artificial intelligence and machine learning applications in supply chain management, as it facilitates scalability and enables real-time processing capabilities.

CONCLUSION

According to the findings of this research, demand forecasting models that are based on AI and ML have enhanced accuracy, which has led to a reduction in the number of prediction inaccuracies and an increase in customer satisfaction. In addition, the application of machine learning algorithms has been critical to the enhancement of inventory management. These algorithms have been helpful in identifying appropriate reorder points, reducing stockout rates, and cutting down on the costs involved with managing inventory. In addition, transportation optimisation algorithms powered by AI have enhanced route planning, load optimisation, and real-time tracking, which has resulted in a reduction in the expenses of transportation as well as an improvement in the effectiveness of delivery.

In addition, machine learning-based supplier selection models have been found to be effective in identifying dependable and cost-efficient suppliers, which enhances supplier management and decreases supply chain risks. Moreover, these models have been demonstrated to be effective in selecting reliable and cost-effective suppliers. Some of the areas that have benefited from the application of AI and ML techniques, which have proved their efficacy and efficiency, include the improvement of supply chain activities such as order fulfilment, production planning, and logistics management. These are just some of the areas that have benefited from the use of AI and ML techniques. AI-driven intelligent order fulfilment systems have made it feasible to process orders in a shorter amount of time, enhance order accuracy, and raise customer delight. The implementation of algorithms for machine learning has enabled significant improvements in production planning, including the rationalisation of production schedules, the reduction of lead times, and the reduction of production costs. Additionally, the implementation of AI into logistics management systems has made it possible to achieve advances in route optimisation, load balancing, and real-time visibility. As a result of these developments, operations have been streamlined, and there has been a reduction in the amount of time spent waiting for transportation.

The paper draws attention to a number of significant challenges and constraints associated with the application of AI and ML in the management of supply chains. Despite the fact that the findings have been deemed to be rather positive, this has been found to be the case. Concerns regarding the availability and quality of data, organisational resistance to change, integration with pre-existing systems, and ethical considerations are some of these concerns. When there is limited access to data that is both of high quality and updated in real time, it can be difficult to effectively apply AI and ML methodologies. This can make it difficult to get desired results. In order to properly integrate AI and ML (Hugos, M. H., 2017) systems with existing legacy systems and processes, careful planning and the allocation of necessary resources are necessities. Overcoming organisational resistance to change and developing a culture of innovation are two of the most critical variables that can contribute to the successful adoption of artificial intelligence and machine learning. Additionally, in order to ensure the correct use of artificial intelligence and machine learning in supply chain management, it is necessary to address ethical concerns such as privacy, data security, and prejudice. This study also examines recent developments and trends in AI and ML technologies, as well as the implications these developments have for the management of supply chains. Deep learning, natural language processing (NLP), and computer vision have all experienced recent developments that have ushered in new potential for the application of artificial intelligence and machine learning in supply chain management. These advancements have been brought about by recent advancements. Integrating artificial intelligence and machine learning with new technologies like the Internet of Things (IoT) (Iyyanar, P. et al., 2023) and blockchain makes it possible to improve supply chain visibility, traceability, and transparency. This is made possible through the use of these technologies. In addition, the use of cloud computing and edge computing makes it much simpler to achieve the scalability and real-time processing capabilities that are necessary for the adoption of AI and ML applications in supply chain management. These capabilities are required in order to successfully manage complex supply chains.

This review study paper's objective is to draw attention to the enormous benefits that AI and ML have the ability to provide to supply chain management, as well as their potential to do so. Businesses are able to improve their supply chains in a variety of different ways by employing these technologies, such as by boosting their operational efficiency, cutting their expenses, and ultimately creating greater experiences for their customers. However, resolving the accompanying obstacles and constraints is essential for ensuring the appropriate use of artificial intelligence and machine learning in supply chain management and for assuring the successful deployment of these technologies. This is particularly true in light of the fact that both of these technologies are still in very early stages of development.

In addition, the review study article focuses a heavy emphasis on the significance of employing AI and ML approaches in order to meet the issues given by dynamic and complex supply chains. This is done in order to handle the challenges posed by these supply chains. Long-established methods of managing supply networks frequently struggle to keep up with the ever-increasing complexity and diversity of today's global supply chains. These methods have been around for a long time. AI and ML have the ability to analyse massive volumes of data and discover patterns and insights that would be difficult for people to discover manually. This might be accomplished by analysing the data using artificial intelligence and machine learning. Organisations are able to make decisions that are data-driven, optimise their operations, and get a competitive edge in the market when they utilise these strategies.

In the context of risk management within supply chains, the study also focuses on the potential applications of artificial intelligence and machine learning. Because of their ability to examine previously collected data and identify potential dangers, artificial intelligence and machine learning algorithms can be of assistance to businesses in proactively minimising disruptions and enhancing the resilience of their supply chains. The process of making educated judgements to decrease the impact of unplanned occurrences such as natural catastrophes, changes in geopolitics, or disruptions in the supply chain can be aided by AI and ML models, which can provide support in the process of making informed decisions. In order to accomplish this, a number of distinct potential outcomes are modelled, and a number of different risk factors are taken into consideration.

In addition, the research sheds light on the significance of AI and ML in the process of strengthening sustainable business practises in supply chain management. This was one of the main focuses of the study. The maintenance of ethical sourcing practises, the promotion of social responsibility, and the lessening of an organization's influence on the environment are becoming increasingly vital to organisations. AI and ML can lend a hand in optimising transportation routes in order to lower carbon emissions, making it possible for logistics operations to be more environmentally friendly and sustainable. In addition, the use of these technologies can assist businesses in tracking the origin of raw materials, confirming that suppliers are complying with sustainability standards, and identifying unethical business practises that occur within the supply chain. All of these benefits can be gained through the utilisation of these technologies.

In addition, the research acknowledges that AI and ML have the potential to improve collaborative decision-making and the formation of deeper partnerships between participants in the supply chain. When companies share their data and insights in real time, they are able to improve their ability to co-ordinate with one another, synchronise their actions, and boost the overall effectiveness of their supply chains. The easier implementation of automated decision-making processes, which can result in shorter reaction times and less delays throughout the supply chain, can be made possible by algorithms that use artificial intelligence and machine learning. In addition, the analysis takes into account the potentially game-changing function that AI and ML can perform in the process of supply chain innovation development. These technologies have the potential to give businesses with the capability to examine new business models, better product design and development, and construct customised experiences for their customers. Analysing customer preferences, trends in the market, and historical data may be done with the use of AI and ML, which can then be used to estimate consumer demand and help find new product opportunities.

This review study paper lays an emphasis on the broad variety of applications and benefits that AI and ML offer in the context of supply chain management. In a word, the focus of this paper is on AI and ML. The adoption of these technologies presents considerable opportunities for businesses to achieve operational efficiency and provide higher value to their customers. They have the ability to improve demand forecasting, enabling more efficient production planning and logistics management, optimise inventory management, and boost transportation operations, among other possible benefits. However, in order to have a successful deployment, it is required to address challenges relating to data quality, integration, organisational readiness, and ethical considerations. Only then can one expect to have a successful deployment. Businesses may navigate the complexities of the modern supply chain landscape, drive innovation, improve sustainability practises, and acquire a competitive advantage in the market by implementing artificial intelligence and machine learning in their operations.

REFERENCES

Anand, R., Khan, B., Nassa, V. K., Pandey, D., Dhabliya, D., Pandey, B. K., & Dadheech, P. (2023). Hybrid convolutional neural network (CNN) for Kennedy Space Center hyperspectral image. *Aerospace Systems*, *6*(1), 71–78. doi:10.1007/s42401-022-00168-4

Babu, S. Z. D., Pandey, D., Naidu, G. T., Sumathi, S., Gupta, A., Bader Alazzam, M., & Pandey, B. K. (2022, July). Analysation of Big Data in Smart Healthcare. In *Artificial Intelligence on Medical Data: Proceedings of International Symposium, ISCMM 2021* (pp. 243-251). Singapore: Springer Nature Singapore.

Chen, P. Y., & Wang, F. K. (2020). Artificial intelligence for supply chain management: A comprehensive literature review and research agenda. *Expert Systems with Applications*, *162*, 113955.

Chen, Y., Wang, Y., & Xu, D. (2019). Demand forecasting for perishable food supply chains with long short-term memory networks. *Computers & Industrial Engineering*, *132*, 1–9.

Chopra, S., & Meindl, P. (2016). *Supply chain management: Strategy, planning, and operation*. Pearson.

Christopher, M. (2016). *Logistics & Supply Chain Management*. Pearson Education Limited.

De Sousa Jabbour, A. B. L., Gunasekaran, A., Mendoza-Tello, J. C., & Lopes de Sousa Jabbour, C. J. (2018). The impact of green supply chain management and green innovation on environmental performance: The role of process control and environmental culture. *International Journal of Production Economics*, *204*, 383–392.

Dey, A., & Nair, A. (2019). Applications of artificial intelligence in supply chain management: A review. *International Journal of Information Management*, *46*, 216–225.

Fawcett, S. E., Ellram, L. M., & Ogden, J. A. (2014). *Supply chain management: From vision to implementation*. Pearson.

Gartner. (2019). *Gartner's top 10 strategic technology trends for 2019*. Author.

Ghaffari, A., & Rabbani, M. (2019). A comprehensive review of applications of artificial intelligence and machine learning in supply chain management. *Computers & Industrial Engineering*, *137*, 106027.

Gong, Y., Yang, Z., & Pan, J. (2020). An optimization model for warehouse layout design based on genetic algorithm. *International Journal of Industrial Engineering Computations*, *11*(4), 573–586.

Gunasekaran, A., & Ngai, E. W. T. (2017). The future of operations management: An outlook and analysis. *International Journal of Production Economics*, *193*, 612–624.

Heikkilä, J., & Lintukangas, K. (2020). Machine learning in supply chain management: A literature review. *International Journal of Production Economics*, *230*, 107786.

Hugos, M. H. (2017). *Essentials of supply chain management*. John Wiley & Sons.

Iyyanar, P., Anand, R., Shanthi, T., Nassa, V. K., Pandey, B. K., George, A. S., & Pandey, D. (2023). A Real-Time Smart Sewage Cleaning UAV Assistance System Using IoT. In *Handbook of Research on Data-Driven Mathematical Modeling in Smart Cities* (pp. 24–39). IGI Global.

Kannan, V. R., & Tan, K. C. (2015). Big data for supply chain management in the service and manufacturing sectors: Challenges, opportunities, and future perspectives. *Computers & Industrial Engineering*, *101*, 572–591.

Kumar, A., Khan, M. A., & Singh, S. (2022). A fuzzy logic-based approach to supplier selection for green supply chain management. *International Journal of Advanced Manufacturing Technology*, *120*(9-12), 2021–2035.

Kumar, M. S., Sankar, S., Nassa, V. K., Pandey, D., Pandey, B. K., & Enbeyle, W. (2021). Innovation and creativity for data mining using computational statistics. In *Methodologies and Applications of Computational Statistics for Machine Intelligence* (pp. 223–240). IGI Global. doi:10.4018/978-1-7998-7701-1.ch012

Kumar Pandey, B., Pandey, D., Nassa, V. K., Ahmad, T., Singh, C., George, A. S., & Wakchaure, M. A. (2021). Encryption and steganography-based text extraction in IoT using the EWCTS optimizer. *Imaging Science Journal*, *69*(1-4), 38–56. doi:10.1080/13682199.2022.2146885

Kusi-Sarpong, S., Sarkis, J., & Wang, X. (2019). Exploring the role of artificial intelligence in supply chain management. *Journal of Cleaner Production*, *208*, 1452–1468.

Lee, H. L. (2004). The triple-a supply chain. *Harvard Business Review*, *82*(10), 102–112. PMID:15559579

Malhotra, P., Pandey, D., Pandey, B. K., & Patra, P. M. (2021). Managing agricultural supply chains in COVID-19 lockdown. *International Journal of Quality and Innovation*, *5*(2), 109–118. doi:10.1504/IJQI.2021.117181

Meslie, Y., Enbeyle, W., Pandey, B. K., Pramanik, S., Pandey, D., Dadeech, P., & Saini, A. (2021). Machine intelligence-based trend analysis of COVID-19 for total daily confirmed cases in Asia and Africa. In *Methodologies and Applications of Computational Statistics for Machine Intelligence* (pp. 164–185). IGI Global. doi:10.4018/978-1-7998-7701-1.ch009

Pandey, B. K., Mane, D., Nassa, V. K. K., Pandey, D., Dutta, S., Ventayen, R. J. M., & Rastogi, R. (2021c). Secure text extraction from complex degraded images by applying steganography and deep learning. In *Multidisciplinary approach to modern digital steganography* (pp. 146–163). IGI Global. doi:10.4018/978-1-7998-7160-6.ch007

Pandey, B. K., & Pandey, D. (2023). Parametric optimization and prediction of enhanced thermoelectric performance in co-doped CaMnO3 using response surface methodology and neural network. *Journal of Materials Science Materials in Electronics*, *34*(21), 1589. doi:10.1007/s10854-023-10954-1

Pandey, B. K., Pandey, D., & Agarwal, A. (2022b). Encrypted information transmission by enhanced steganography and image transformation. *International Journal of Distributed Artificial Intelligence*, *14*(1), 1–14. doi:10.4018/IJDAI.297110

Pandey, B. K., Pandey, D., Wairya, S., & Agarwal, G. (2021a). An advanced morphological component analysis, steganography, and deep learning-based system to transmit secure textual data. *International Journal of Distributed Artificial Intelligence*, *13*(2), 40–62. doi:10.4018/IJDAI.2021070104

Pandey, B. K., Pandey, D., Wairya, S., Agarwal, G., Dadeech, P., Dogiwal, S. R., & Pramanik, S. (2022a). Application of integrated steganography and image compressing techniques for confidential information transmission. *Cyber Security and Network Security*, 169-191.

Pandey, B. K., Pandey, D., Wariya, S., & Agarwal, G. (2021b). A deep neural network-based approach for extracting textual images from deteriorate images. *EAI Endorsed Transactions on Industrial Networks and Intelligent Systems*, *8*(28), e3–e3. doi:10.4108/eai.17-9-2021.170961

Pandey, D., Pandey, B. K., & Wairya, S. (2021). Hybrid deep neural network with adaptive galactic swarm optimization for text extraction from scene images. *Soft Computing*, *25*(2), 1563–1580. doi:10.1007/s00500-020-05245-4

Pandey, J. K., Jain, R., Dilip, R., Kumbhkar, M., Jaiswal, S., Pandey, B. K., & Pandey, D. (2022). Investigating Role of IoT in the Development of Smart Application for Security Enhancement. In *IoT Based Smart Applications* (pp. 219–243). Springer International Publishing.

Pramanik, S., Pandey, D., Joardar, S., Niranjanamurthy, M., Pandey, B. K., & Kaur, J. (2023, October). An overview of IoT privacy and security in smart cities. In AIP Conference Proceedings (Vol. 2495, No. 1). AIP Publishing. doi:10.1063/5.0123511

Wang, F., Chen, J., & Guan, X. (2021). A deep reinforcement learning-based approach for dynamic vehicle routing in city logistics. *Transportation Research Part E, Logistics and Transportation Review*, *149*, 1–18.

Wang, L., & Zhou, L. (2019). The effects of artificial intelligence on supply chain agility: A conceptual framework. *Journal of Cleaner Production*, *236*, 117619.

Zhang, M., Yu, X., & Li, H. (2021). Optimization model and algorithm for green supply chain transportation routing problem based on artificial intelligence. *International Journal of Advanced Manufacturing Technology*, *115*(1-4), 57–76.

Chapter 7
From Tradition to Technology:
Utilization of AI and ML for Digital Transformation in Supply Chain Management

George Williams Kennedy
School of Vocational and Technical Education, Akwa Ibom State College of Education, Nigeria

Samuel Amos Ikpe
Department of Technical Education, Akwa Ibom State College of Education, Nigeria

Vinay Kumar Nassa
https://orcid.org/0000-0002-9606-7570
Department of Information Communication Technology (ICT), Tecnia Institute of Advanced Studies, India

Tamanna Prajapati
Shri D.N. Institute of Computer Applications, Sardar Patel University, Gujarat, India

Dharmesh Dhabliya
https://orcid.org/0000-0002-6340-2993
Department of Information Technology, Vishwakarma Institute of Information Technology, Pune, India

Sukhvinder Singh Dari
https://orcid.org/0000-0002-6218-6600
Symbiosis Law School, Symbiosis International University, Pune, India

ABSTRACT

The combination of AI and ML is driving supply chain digitalization. This chapter discusses supply chain management (SCM) in the digital age, including AI, ML, and classical techniques, SCM aspects and components, and supply chain network strategies. The chapter also covers AI and ML applications in supply chain optimisation, resilient supply chain network (SCN) methods, warehouse automation and robotics, transportation and route optimisation, and supply chain risk management. AI and ML enable supply chain stakeholders to use massive data streams for predictive analytics. AI-driven demand forecasting, inventory optimisation, and predictive maintenance reduce hazards and streamline resource allocation, improving cost-effectiveness. In a world of rapid change and innovation, organisations must use AI and ML as the supply chain ecosystem evolves.

DOI: 10.4018/979-8-3693-1347-3.ch007

INTRODUCTION

In today's rapidly evolving business landscape, supply chain management has become a critical component for organizations seeking to stay competitive and responsive to market demands. Traditional supply chain practices are being reshaped by the infusion of cutting-edge technologies, and among these, Artificial Intelligence (AI) (Boopathi, S. et al., 2023) and Machine Learning (ML) have emerged as transformative forces that hold the potential to revolutionize how supply chains are planned, executed, and optimized (Strusani & Houngbonon, 2019). With reports estimating that 400 - 800 million jobs will be displaced by 2030 due to AI and automation, every advance that is reported is met with a degree of reticence (Bughin et al., 2017; Smithies, 2017). AI refers to the simulation of human intelligence processes by computer systems ((National Academies of Sciences, Engineering, and Medicine, 2018; Long & Magerko, 2020; Fourtane, 2021; Littman et al., 2021). It involves the development of algorithms that enable machines to perform tasks that typically require human intelligence, such as problem-solving, decision-making, and pattern recognition (Bringsjord, Govindarajulu, & Sundar, 2020).

In the same vein, Machine Learning (Meslie, Y. et al., 2021), a subset of AI, involves the construction of algorithms that allow computers to learn from and make predictions or decisions based on data without explicit programming (Wenzel, Smit, & Sardesa, 2019). As the supply chain ecosystem continues to evolve, embracing AI and ML becomes imperative for organizations aiming to thrive in an era of constant change and innovation. AI and machine learning (Parthiban, K. et al., 2021) integration into supply chain management (SCM) can significantly optimize tasks both at the strategic and tactical levels. This integration facilitates superior utilization of AI-driven tools to enhance business planning, fortify supply chain structures, forecast demand, conduct risk analysis, and tackle an array of other essential tasks. On the operational front, the incorporation of AI leads to streamlined SCM operations, refining the intricate pathways of both inbound and outbound material flows. Leveraging machine learning algorithms (Singh, H. et al., 2022), AI bolsters product and process quality management and enables sophisticated stock management through modern visual pattern recognition techniques. Furthermore, this augmentation allows for precise product and process quality management, fostering informed decision-making and heightened optimization capabilities.

By empowering better preparation and control of the shop floor, AI facilitates intricate, comprehensive, and efficient operational management. Therefore, this chapter present the basic concept of AI, ML and machine learning, AI, ML and traditional supply chain approaches, elements and components of supply chain management and strategies to build supply chain networks.

THE BASIC CONCEPTS OF AI AND ML

Algorithms, models, and learning paradigms work together to enable machines to learn from data and make predictions or decisions (Thomas, 2019, Liao & Wu, 2020; Long & Magerko, 2020). The field of AI and ML is continually evolving, with new algorithms and paradigms being developed to tackle increasingly complex tasks and challenges. The basic concepts of Artificial Intelligence (AI) (Pandey, B. K. & Pandey, D. 2023) and Machine Learning (ML) are:

1. **Algorithms:** AI and ML algorithms are the computational procedures that process data and generate insights or predictions (Min, et al. 2019). These algorithms can range from simple operations to

complex mathematical calculations. Different AI and ML algorithms are designed to tackle various tasks, such as classification, regression, clustering, and more.

2. **Models:** In AI and ML, a model is a representation of a real-world phenomenon or process. Models are created using algorithms and are trained on data (Pandey, J. K. et al., 2022) to learn patterns and relationships. The model captures the underlying patterns from the training data (Pandey, B. K. et al., 2021) and can be used to make predictions or decisions on new, unseen data. Models can be thought of as the result of the learning process, where the algorithm adjusts its parameters based on the training data to create a representation of the target concept.
3. **Learning Paradigms:** Learning paradigms refer to the different approaches that AI and ML algorithms use to learn from data. There are several key learning paradigms in ML (Zhou, et al., 2017; Makkar, Devi, & Solanki, 2019; Wenzel, Smit & Sardesa, 2019) such as:
    1. Supervised learning, as the first type, involves the algorithm learning from provided pairs of inputs and outputs. In this process, labeled datasets are employed where the outcome for a specific input is known, often in the form of probabilities. Through repeated iterations, the system is trained to establish meaningful correlations between various inputs and corresponding outputs, bridging the gap between them. The term 'supervised' pertains solely to the learning phase. Once the algorithm is trained, it becomes capable of autonomously predicting outputs. This type of learning is useful for both regression tasks (predictions) and classification tasks (assigning to predefined categories).
    2. Unsupervised learning, the second type, focuses on uncovering concealed patterns within provided data where potential outcomes are entirely unknown. As a result, training the algorithm with predefined outcomes is not feasible. Instead, this method employs the algorithm to delve into unlabeled datasets and unveil meaningful clusters (groupings based on similarities) or associations (identification of interdependencies). Unsupervised learning is particularly valuable in data mining processes, facilitating data preparation and evaluation.
    3. Reinforcement learning sets itself apart from the previous two by not mandating a dataset. This learning approach can be likened to a form of conditioning, wherein the algorithm is rewarded for accurate responses and penalized for unsatisfactory outcomes. Essentially, it operates as a trial-and-error process, retaining knowledge of both correct and incorrect actions.

THE CONCEPT OF SUPPLY CHAIN MANAGEMENT

The term "supply chain management" (SCM) emerged during the 1980s, incorporating key business processes that span from end-users to initial suppliers (Ryan, 2017). The foundational concept underlying SCM posits that businesses and organizations engaged in a supply chain should collaborate by sharing insights about market conditions and production capacities (Janvier-James, 2012). The evolution of supply chain management in the digital age has seen a progression from manual and disjointed processes to integrated, data-driven, and agile systems. Digital technologies have enabled companies to optimize operations, enhance visibility, and respond to customer needs more effectively, leading to improved efficiency and competitiveness in today's global market (Min, 2015). The key stages in the evolution of supply chain management in the digital age are:

1. **Manual and Fragmented Processes (Pre-Digital Age):** Before the digital age, supply chain management was largely a manual and isolated process. Companies relied on spreadsheets, paper documents, and phone calls to manage inventory, procurement, production, and distribution. This approach often led to inefficiencies, lack of visibility, and difficulty in coordinating activities across the supply chain.
2. **Introduction of Electronic Data Interchange (EDI):** In the late 20th century, the adoption of EDI allowed businesses to exchange documents electronically, such as purchase orders and invoices. While this marked a significant improvement over manual processes, EDI was limited in its capabilities and required standardization among trading partners.
3. **Rise of Enterprise Resource Planning (ERP) Systems:** ERP systems emerged as comprehensive software (Kirubasri, G. et al., 2022) solutions that integrated various business functions, including supply chain processes. These systems provided centralized data management, allowing companies to monitor inventory, production, and logistics more effectively. However, early ERP systems were often complex and expensive to implement.
4. **Introduction of Advanced Planning Systems (APS):** APS solutions emerged in the 1990s, offering more sophisticated tools for demand forecasting, inventory optimization, and production planning. These systems laid the groundwork for data-driven (Pandey, B. K. et al., 2022) decision-making and better coordination among supply chain components.
5. **Adoption of E-Commerce and Online Retail:** The growth of e-commerce and online retail introduced new challenges and opportunities for supply chains. Companies needed to adapt to fulfill direct-to-consumer orders, manage shorter lead times, and ensure efficient last-mile delivery.
6. **Integration of IoT and Sensor Technologies:** The Internet of Things (IoT) brought about a new era of connectivity, enabling the collection of real-time data from sensors placed throughout the supply chain. This data helps monitor the condition of products during transit, track assets, and optimize processes.
7. **Big Data Analytics and Predictive Analytics:** With the proliferation of data, supply chain management embraced big data analytics and predictive modeling. These technologies allowed companies to analyze large datasets to identify trends, make accurate demand forecasts, and optimize operations based on insights.
8. **Blockchain Technology:** Blockchain technology gained attention for its potential to enhance transparency and traceability across supply chains. It enables secure and immutable recording of transactions, helping to prevent fraud, counterfeiting, and ensuring authenticity.
9. **Artificial Intelligence and Machine Learning:** AI and machine learning algorithms are being used to analyze vast amounts of data to generate insights, optimize routes, and predict potential disruptions. AI-driven demand forecasting and inventory management have become key areas of focus.
10. **Digital Twins and Simulation:** Digital twin technology allows companies to create virtual representations of their physical supply chain processes. This enables simulation and testing of various scenarios, helping managers make informed decisions and optimize processes without disrupting the actual supply chain.
11. **End-to-End Visibility and Collaboration Platforms:** Advanced digital platforms and cloud-based solutions offer end-to-end visibility into supply chain operations. These platforms enable seamless collaboration among all stakeholders, from suppliers to customers, facilitating communication and decision-making. The digital age has also brought a stronger focus on sustainability. Supply chains

are adopting practices to reduce environmental impact, optimize resource use, and implement circular economy principles.

TRADITIONAL, ML AND AI SUPPLY CHAIN APPROACHES

The utilization of Artificial Intelligence (AI) and Machine Learning (ML) algorithms presents an array of advantages in tackling the prevailing challenges that the Supply Chain Management (SCM) encounters in the contemporary digital landscape (Charran & Sweetman, 2019). The convergence of AI and ML is effecting transformative changes within the supply chain sector. By pinpointing deeply ingrained inefficiencies and uncertainties, these analytical technologies provide an overarching view of every facet of the supply chain, offering an unprecedented level of granularity and methodologies that surpass human capabilities on a grand scale. The integration of analytics into supply chain processes is not only propelling the realization of robust optimization capabilities but also contributing to more precise capacity planning, heightened productivity, elevated quality standards, reduced costs, amplified output, all while fostering a heightened focus on ensuring safer working conditions.

The difference between Artificial Intelligence (AI), Machine Learning (ML), and traditional supply chain approaches in terms of their characteristics, capabilities, and impact on supply chain management are as follows:

1. **Traditional Supply Chain Approaches:** Traditional supply chain approaches are characterized by manual processes, limited data analysis, and a reactive mindset. These approaches rely heavily on human decision-making and often involve siloed operations. Some key differentiating factors include:
    i. **Manual Decision-Making:** Traditional supply chains rely on human judgment and experience for decision-making, which can be time-consuming and prone to errors.
    ii. **Limited Data Utilization:** Data analysis is basic and relies on historical data. Advanced data analytics techniques are often underutilized.
    iii. **Reactive Responses:** Traditional approaches tend to react to disruptions after they occur, leading to delays and increased costs in resolving issues.
    iv. **Lack of Visibility:** The lack of real-time visibility across the supply chain can result in inefficiencies, delays, and difficulties in tracking inventory and shipments.
    v. **Limited Optimization:** Optimization of processes, inventory, and resources is limited, which can lead to suboptimal performance and higher costs.
2. **Machine Learning (ML) in Supply Chain:** Machine Learning (ML) constitutes a subdivision of artificial intelligence that introduces a distinct paradigm of programming (Kourou, et al., 2015, Siau et al., 2018). Instead of relying solely on rigid software algorithms, ML leverages data as a substitute for deterministic calculation rules. Within this framework, information, learning methodologies, and algorithms collaboratively extract statistical patterns from provided examples and subsequently encapsulate them in the form of models. These models, adept at discerning underlying regularities, exhibit the capacity to classify novel, unfamiliar data into predefined categories or make predictive inferences (Wenzel, Smit & Sardesa, 2019). ML algorithms can learn patterns from historical data and make predictions or recommendations. Some key differentiating factors of Machine Learning (ML) (Pandey, D. et al., 2021b) include:

i. **Predictive Analytics:** ML algorithms can predict future outcomes based on historical data, enabling better demand forecasting, inventory management, and risk assessment (Khasis, 2019).
ii. **Data-Driven Insights:** ML leverages large datasets to uncover hidden patterns and correlations, leading to more informed decision-making.
iii. **Automation and Optimization:** ML algorithms automate routine tasks and optimize processes, leading to higher efficiency and reduced operational costs. Robotic Process Automation (RPA) can handle routine data entry, freeing up human resources for more strategic and creative tasks. This leads to higher efficiency, reduced errors, and cost savings.
iv. **Real-time Monitoring:** ML enables real-time monitoring of supply chain operations, allowing for proactive responses to disruptions and better resource allocation.
v. **Production Planning and Scheduling:** ML algorithms optimize production schedules considering factors like machine availability, capacity constraints, and order priorities. This minimizes production downtime and maximizes resource utilization.
vi. **Personalization and Customer Experience:** AI-powered recommendation engines analyze user preferences and behaviors to provide personalized product and content recommendations. This enhances customer engagement and satisfaction by delivering tailored experiences, ultimately boosting sales and loyalty.
vii. **Dynamic Decision-Making:** ML algorithms can adapt to changing conditions and make dynamic decisions based on real-time data.
viii. **Inventory Management:** ML models predict optimal reorder points and quantities based on factors like demand variability, lead times, and costs. This prevents overstocking and stockouts, reducing carrying costs and improving customer satisfaction.

3. **Artificial Intelligence (AI) in Supply Chain:** The term "Artificial Intelligence" having been coined in 1956 encompasses a broader spectrum of capabilities, including ML, and involves simulating human intelligence in machines (Liao & Wu, 2020). AI systems can reason, learn, and solve complex problems (Russell & Norvig, 2016; Long & Magerko, 2020; Berente et al., 2021). Some key differentiating factors of Artificial Intelligence (AI) in Supply Chain include:
   i. **Cognitive Abilities:** AI systems can perform tasks that traditionally required human intelligence, such as natural language understanding, sentiment analysis, and problem-solving.
   ii. **Advanced Analytics:** AI goes beyond traditional data analysis by incorporating techniques like natural language processing, image recognition, and pattern recognition.
   iii. **Autonomous Decision-Making:** AI can make autonomous decisions based on data analysis and predefined rules, reducing the need for constant human intervention.
   iv. **Natural Language Processing (NLP):** NLP allows machines to understand and interpret human language. Virtual assistants and chatbots, for instance, can handle customer inquiries, provide support, and even automate complex interactions, enhancing customer service and reducing response times.
   v. **Optimization Across Multiple Variables:** AI can optimize processes considering multiple variables, constraints, and objectives simultaneously.
   vi. **Quality Control and Defect Detection:** AI-powered image recognition systems identify defects in real-time by analyzing images (Pandey, D. et al., 2021a) of products or components. This improves product quality and reduces waste.

vii. **Improved Collaboration:** Digital tools enable better collaboration between different stakeholders within the supply chain, such as suppliers, manufacturers, distributors, and retailers. Cloud-based platforms and collaboration tools facilitate information sharing, communication, and coordination, leading to smoother operations (Dwivedi et al., 2021).
viii. **Carbon Footprint Reduction:** AI optimizes transportation routes and modes to reduce fuel consumption and emissions. It also assists in designing sustainable supply chain practices to minimize environmental impact.
ix. **Pricing and Revenue Management:** AI analyzes market conditions, competitor pricing, and customer behavior to optimize pricing strategies. This maximizes revenue and profit margins while staying competitive. AI analyzes return patterns and reasons to identify opportunities for process improvements, reducing the cost and impact of product returns.
x. **Sustainability and Environmental Impact:** Digital transformation can help companies monitor and reduce their environmental impact by optimizing transportation routes, reducing energy consumption, and minimizing waste through data-driven insights.

ELEMENTS OF SUPPLY CHAIN MANAGEMENT

Supply Chain Management (SCM) is a strategic methodology employed to oversee manufacturers, distributors, warehouses, and stores. Its aim is to ensure the production and delivery of goods in optimal quantities, at appropriate locations, and within the designated time frame. This serves to minimize system costs while fulfilling service level requirements (Kaminsky, et al., 2003). Since the configuration of supply chains varies across industries, the most common elements are:

1. **Demand Management**: Demand management centers around understanding and quantifying consumer requirements. Demand not only dictates supply but also informs production strategies, which subsequently influence financial, logistics, and marketing decisions. The unreliability of demand information is a prime contributor to business failures. Unpredictable demand patterns lead to inadequate supply, resulting in customer dissatisfaction, or excessive supply, causing wastage of valuable resources. Given the inherent volatility of demand, acquiring accurate demand information is a formidable challenge. Forecasting based on historical market trends is a customary method to gauge potential future demand (Min, 2015).
   Though demand forecasting is integral to demand management, its accuracy hinges on the predictive methodologies, time horizons, and nature of demand. Moreover, accurate demand information must be communicated to producers and suppliers to render predictions meaningful. The speed at which demand information disseminates among supply chain partners influences demand management outcomes. According to Min (2015), demand management entails several steps, including:
   i. **Demand Planning:** A more intricate process than mere forecasting.
   ii. **Demand Transmission:** Involves seamless integration of supply chain partners, fostering cohesive production strategies.
   iii. **Demand Influencing:** Encompasses marketing strategies, pricing, and product positioning.
   iv. **Demand Prioritizing:** Involves monitoring customer orders and categorizing clientele.
2. **Customer Relationship Management (CRM)**: Customer Relationship Management (CRM) constitutes a strategic approach to fostering engagement between an organization and current and

prospective customers. CRM involves data evaluation to comprehend customer behavior, strengthen consumer-business relationships, prioritize customer retention, and ultimately bolster revenue growth. CRM systems play a pivotal role in aggregating data from diverse communication channels, including websites, phone calls, emails, live chats, social media, and more. Employing the CRM approach and associated tools enables organizations to gain insights into their target markets and better tailor responses to their needs. Some key components of Customer Relationship Management (CRM) according to Ryan (2017) are:

i. Establishing and sustaining customer relationships through targeted marketing initiatives.
ii. Monitoring relationships as they evolve through various stages.
iii. Nurturing relationships at each level while acknowledging that the value of each relationship to the organization isn't uniform. Organizations leverage an array of resources, from organizational design to reward programs, to optimize their marketing strategies while nurturing and retaining customer relationships.

3. **Order Management**: Order management forms the backbone of virtually every mechanism within the supply chain. Many organizations no longer retain exclusive control over orders within their premises. Parties such as component manufacturers, assembly facilities, packaging centers, distribution hubs, and more contribute to the fulfillment process, which can result in diminished visibility and control. Consequently, manual processes become costly and error-prone. Adopting an Order Management System (OMS) can mitigate expenses and enhance revenue by automating manual tasks and minimizing errors.
   Externally, order management significantly shapes how customers perceive a brand. In today's omnichannel landscape, customers expect a seamless experience. They may initiate orders online and seek clarifications via a call center. Notifications regarding order fulfillment and delivery are anticipated. Seamless returns and interactions through various channels enrich customer experience and elevate engagement and sales. Moreover, the omnichannel ecosystem presents opportunities for upselling, cross-selling, and increased revenue. Modernizing order management involves embracing an Order Management System (OMS) that oversees the entire lifecycle of an order. It encompasses entry, inventory, fulfillment, and post-sales support. An OMS augments visibility for both companies and customers, providing real-time insights into inventory status and order progress (Glasheen, 2020).
4. **Inventory Management**: Inventory, as a strategic asset, enables companies to respond promptly to consumer demands while acting as a buffer against unexpected fluctuations, quality issues, and supply chain disruptions. Conversely, inventory can also be a liability, draining resources through carrying costs, tying up personnel, and masking the root causes of logistics or quality challenges. Inventory management is fundamentally the science of determining the types and quantities of stored products. This process must precede the routine flow of material production and storage across various locations within a facility or the broader supply chain network. Inventory management encompasses a broad scope of considerations, including replenishment lead time, carrying costs, asset management, forecasting, valuation, visibility, price projections, physical space constraints, quality control, replenishment strategies, returns management, and demand forecasting.

The pursuit of balance amid these competing objectives yields optimal inventory levels, an ongoing process that adapts to changing business landscapes. Effective inventory management requires a retailer to maintain a diverse product range while controlling sourcing, shipping, and storage costs. It entails systems and procedures to determine inventory needs, set objectives, define replenishment processes, monitor actual and projected inventory status, and manage all related material functions. These may encompass tracking (Pandey, D. et al., 2022b) inflows and outflows, conducting ABC analysis, batch tracking, and facilitating cycle counting. Inventory management, rooted in maintaining inventory volumes within the physical distribution network, strikes a balance between product availability and cost containment (Ryan, 2017).

WAREHOUSE AUTOMATION MANAGEMENT IN SUPPLY CHAIN

Despite growing demand for flawless customer service, today's warehousing is being forced to increase the standards for stock quality, reliable distribution service, individually tailored order fulfilment, customizable value-added features, and sensitivity to consumer specific requirements. To achieve these high-standards targets, the warehousing needed to minimize waste, optimize processes, and boost warehousing activity quality in every area. A Warehouse Management System (WMS) is one of the most pro-active ways of doing this to speed up the order completion, improve the accuracy of inventory, give instant information regarding the order status, manage storage space and improve labour productivity. WMS has completely changed the process in which orders are scheduled, prepared and executed, inventories tracked and the correct goods delivered in right time.

Recently, WMS has extended to include new features capable of managing light production, transportation, ordering process and full accounting practices (Min, 2015).

AI-powered robotics have revolutionized warehouse operations by introducing automation, efficiency, and scalability to the logistics industry. These advanced technologies combine artificial intelligence, machine learning, and robotics to handle a wide range of tasks, from order fulfillment to inventory management. AI-powered robotics are transforming warehouse operations (Ryan, 2017; Caballero & Rice, 2018; Hellingrath, & Lechtenberg, 2019) in the following ways:

1. **Order Picking and Fulfillment:** Robotic systems equipped with AI vision technology can accurately identify and pick items from shelves. They optimize the sequence of picking to minimize travel time, improving order fulfillment speed and accuracy.
2. **Autonomous Guided Vehicles (AGVs) and Drones:** AGVs and drones navigate through warehouse spaces using AI algorithms and sensor technologies. They transport goods between different areas, reducing manual labor and streamlining material flow.
3. **Sorting and Packing:** AI-powered robotic systems sort and pack items into appropriate containers, boxes, or parcels with high precision. These systems ensure uniformity and minimize the risk of errors during the packing process.
4. **Inventory Management:** Robotic systems with AI capabilities can conduct real-time inventory scans, track item locations, and update inventory records. This reduces stock discrepancies and enhances inventory accuracy. Inventory management, with the primary objective of assessing/managing stock volumes within the physical distribution network, balances the need for product availability against the need to reduce stock keeping and handling costs.
5. **Goods Transportation:** AI-powered mobile robots transport goods within the warehouse, optimizing the movement of items between storage and processing areas. This reduces the need for manual transportation.

6. **Autonomous Forklifts:** AI-driven forklifts use sensors and cameras to navigate and move goods around warehouses autonomously. They can efficiently transport and stack items, improving overall warehouse productivity.
7. **Collaborative Robots (Cobots):** Cobots work alongside human workers, assisting with tasks such as heavy lifting, assembly, and quality control. AI algorithms enable cobots to adapt to human movements and work safely in shared spaces.
8. **Predictive Maintenance:** AI monitors robotic systems for signs of wear and tear, predicting maintenance needs before breakdowns occur. This proactive approach reduces downtime and maintenance costs.

TRANSPORTATION AND ROUTE OPTIMIZATION IN SUPPLY CHAIN

Transportation generates utility position via transferring people and/or products from one place to a targeted end point. Therefore, transportation is a critical link in the supply chain, because of its role in linking the spots in the supply chain. That means the efficiency of transportation should reflect the efficiency of the supply chain. As such, designing an effective transport strategy is the first step toward supply chain effectiveness. Given its importance for the supply chain, the supply chain specialists will prepare, handle and optimize transportation better. However, as human culture progresses, transport becomes more complicated. Part of the complexity of transportation stems from expanded geographic reach, different modal choices, evolving regulatory/deregulatory laws/rules on transportation, restricted fuel availability, and multiple stakeholders (Liu, et al., 2016).

To facilitate the complexities of transportation it is important to understand and evaluate the essential functions and contexts surrounding it. Transportation, for example, enables the delivery of raw resources and components/parts necessary for production to the locations of the manufacturers. Similarly, transportation enables the delivery of finished products produced by manufacturers to the locations of customers. Therefore, transport generates value by shifting the position of the raw resources, components/parts, and finished products to the locations where they are required or consumed. Transportation can also establish time-based utility through the transportation of the necessary resources at the same time at the same location.

Routing algorithms and techniques are essential tools for optimizing transportation logistics (Conde & Twinn, 2019). They consider various factors such as distances, constraints, vehicle capacities, and real-time information to create efficient routes that minimize costs and enhance supply chain performance. The choice of algorithm depends on the complexity of the problem, the nature of constraints, and the specific objectives of the transportation logistics optimization (Rashed, 2017). Real-time tracking, route adjustments, and minimizing delivery delays are interrelated strategies that leverage technology and data for efficient transportation logistics as follows:

1. **Routing algorithms for transportation logistics:** Routing algorithms and techniques play a pivotal role in optimizing transportation logistics by determining the most efficient paths for vehicles to reach their destinations while considering various constraints and objectives. These algorithms help reduce transportation costs, improve delivery times, and enhance overall supply chain efficiency.
2. **Real-time tracking, route adjustments, and minimizing delivery delays:** Real-time tracking, route adjustments, and minimizing delivery delays are critical aspects of modern transportation

logistics that rely on technology and data-driven strategies. These components ensure efficient, responsive, and customer-centric delivery operations.

i. Real-time tracking involves monitoring the location, status, and condition of vehicles and shipments in real time. This is achieved through technologies such as GPS, RFID, IoT sensors, and telematics.
ii. **Route Adjustments:** Route adjustments involve modifying planned routes in response to real-time data, traffic conditions, weather changes, and unforeseen obstacles.
iii. **Minimizing Delivery Delays:** Real-time tracking and route adjustments contribute significantly to minimizing delivery delays by addressing the following challenges:
iv. **Traffic Congestion:** Real-time traffic updates enable drivers to avoid congested areas, reducing delays caused by traffic jams.
v. **Unforeseen Events:** Unexpected Road closures, accidents, or construction can disrupt planned routes. Real-time tracking allows for quick adjustments to minimize delays.
vi. **Customer Satisfaction:** Accurate real-time tracking information keeps customers informed about delivery progress, reducing uncertainty and frustration associated with delays.
vii. **Efficient Resource Allocation:** Real-time tracking and route adjustments optimize the allocation of vehicles and resources, ensuring deliveries are made on time with minimal idle time.

RISK MANAGEMENT IN THE SUPPLY CHAIN

Identifying potential disruptions and vulnerabilities in the supply chain is a proactive approach that allows businesses to build resilience and responsiveness. By conducting comprehensive assessments, analyzing various factors, and implementing robust risk management strategies, companies can minimize the impact of disruptions and maintain the smooth functioning of their supply chains (Gesing, Peterson, & Michelsen, 2018) in the following ways:

1. **Supply Chain Mapping:** Create a comprehensive map of your supply chain, identifying all the tiers of suppliers, manufacturers, distributors, and transportation routes involved. This visualization helps in understanding the complexity and potential weak points.
2. **External Factors Analysis:** Identify external factors that could disrupt your supply chain, such as political instability, regulatory changes, natural disasters, pandemics, and economic fluctuations. Monitor news and trends related to these factors.
3. **Supplier Risk Assessment:** Evaluate the financial stability, operational capabilities, and geographical locations of your suppliers. A supplier with financial troubles or concentrated operations in a single region can pose significant risks.
4. **Labor Shortages and Strikes:** Monitor labor conditions in regions where your suppliers and manufacturers are located. Labor strikes or shortages can impact production and transportation.
5. **Natural Disaster Risk Zones:** Identify areas prone to natural disasters such as earthquakes, hurricanes, and floods. Suppliers or facilities located in these zones are more susceptible to disruptions.
6. **Continuous Monitoring:** Supply chain risks are dynamic. Implement continuous monitoring systems that provide real-time information about potential disruptions, allowing for swift responses.

7. **Collaboration and Transparency:** Build strong relationships with suppliers and partners based on collaboration and transparency. Open communication can help identify risks early and develop joint mitigation strategies.

AI AND ML APPLICATIONS CHALLENGES IN SUPPLY CHAIN NETWORKS

An artificial Intelligence (AI) and Machine Learning (ML) application in supply chain brings numerous benefits in terms of efficiency and productivity. However, their implementation comes with a set of challenges that need to be carefully addressed to ensure the well-being of human workers, the integrity of the robotics systems, and the overall success of the operation (Hellingrath & Lechtenberg, 2019). Some of the challenges facing AI and ML applications in supply chain optimization include:

1. **Human-Robot Interaction:** One of the primary safety concerns is ensuring the safe interaction between robots and human workers. Collaborative robots (cobots) that work alongside humans should be equipped with sensors to detect the presence of humans and immediately halt or slow down their movements to prevent collisions. Emergency stop buttons or switches should be easily accessible throughout the warehouse. These mechanisms allow workers to quickly halt robot movements in case of emergencies or safety hazards.
2. **Data Security:** Robotic systems often rely on data connectivity and communication. Ensuring the security (Kumar Pandey, B. et al., 2021) of these connections is crucial to prevent unauthorized access or control of robots, which could pose safety risks.
3. **Data Quality and Availability:** AI and ML models rely heavily on data. Inaccurate, incomplete, or inconsistent data can lead to unreliable predictions and suboptimal decisions. Supply chain data often resides in different systems and formats, making it challenging to consolidate and ensure data quality.
4. **Data Integration and Interoperability:** Supply chain data comes from various sources, including suppliers, manufacturers, distributors, and retailers. Integrating data from these disparate sources can be complex. Ensuring interoperability between different systems and data formats is crucial for effective AI and ML implementation.
5. **Complexity of Networks:** Modern supply chains are intricate networks with numerous nodes, suppliers, partners, and logistics options. Modeling and optimizing such complexity can be challenging for AI and ML algorithms.
6. **Lack of Historical Data:** Some supply chain disruptions (e.g., rare events or major shifts) might not have historical data for training AI models, making it difficult to predict and plan for such occurrences.
7. **Model Interpretability:** Many AI and ML algorithms, especially deep learning models (Pandey, B. K. et al., 2021a), can be complex and difficult to interpret. Understanding why a model makes a certain decision is crucial for gaining trust and acceptance.
8. **Change Management:** Implementing AI and ML involves changes in processes and decision-making. Employees and stakeholders might resist or struggle to adapt to these changes.
9. **Resource Constraints:** Developing and deploying AI and ML models requires computational resources and expertise. Smaller organizations might find it challenging to allocate these resources.

10. **Continuous Learning and Adaptation:** Supply chain dynamics change over time due to market trends, disruptions, and other factors. AI and ML models need to be continuously updated and adapted to remain effective.
11. **Unforeseen Events and Black Swans:** AI models might struggle to predict and plan for truly unexpected events, often referred to as "black swan" events, which can significantly disrupt supply chains.
12. **Limited Domain Expertise:** Effective AI and ML implementation requires a deep understanding (Pandey, B. K. et al., 2021b) of both supply chain operations and the capabilities and limitations of AI and ML technologies.
13. **Vendor Lock-in:** Depending heavily on specific AI and ML vendors or platforms can lead to vendor lock-in and limit flexibility.
14. **Regulatory Compliance:** AI and ML (Pandey, B. K. et al., 2021c) implementation in supply chain operations might need to adhere to specific regulations, especially in industries with strict quality and safety standards.
15. **Initial Investment and ROI Uncertainty:** While AI and ML promise significant benefits, the initial investment required for technology adoption might raise concerns, and the expected return on investment can be uncertain.

Addressing these challenges requires a multi-faceted approach, involving collaboration among domain experts, data scientists, IT professionals, and organizational leadership. It's crucial to develop a clear strategy, assess the organization's readiness for AI and ML adoption, and gradually implement these technologies while addressing challenges as they arise.

STRATEGIES TO BUILD SUPPLY CHAIN NETWORKS

Building supply chain networks is crucial for businesses to navigate unexpected disruptions, minimize risks, and maintain continuity in operations. Optimizing AI and ML applications in supply chain networks can significantly enhance efficiency, reduce costs, and improve overall performance (Hoffmann, 2019). Some key strategies for building resilient supply chain networks:

1. **Utilize Predictive Analytics for Demand Forecasting:** Utilize AI and ML algorithms to forecast demand accurately, thereby reducing inventory costs and minimizing stockouts.
2. **Implement Real-time Monitoring and Alert Systems:** Implement AI-driven monitoring systems to identify potential disruptions in the supply chain in real-time, enabling proactive responses to demand fluctuations, ensuring efficient use of resources.
3. **Employ Automated Inventory Management:** Employ ML algorithms to optimize inventory levels, minimize carrying costs, and avoid overstocking or stockouts.
4. **Implement Supplier Relationship Management:** Implement AI-based tools for analyzing supplier performance, identifying potential risks, and fostering long-term strategic partnerships.
5. **Utilize Natural Language Processing for Contract Management:** Use NLP to streamline contract management processes, including contract analysis, negotiation, and compliance monitoring.
6. **Risk Management and Mitigation:** Deploy AI-driven risk management tools to identify and mitigate potential supply chain risks, such as natural disasters, geopolitical issues, or market fluctuations.

7. **Blockchain Integration for Transparency:** Integrate blockchain technology to provide transparency and traceability across the entire supply chain, improving trust and reducing the risk of fraud.
8. **Collaborative Forecasting and Planning:** Facilitate collaborative planning and forecasting processes among various stakeholders in the supply chain using AI-powered tools, reducing overall operational costs and environmental impact.
9. **Adaptive Pricing Strategies:** Use AI algorithms to dynamically adjust pricing based on market trends, customer behavior, and competitor pricing, maximizing profits while remaining competitive.
10. **Establish Continuous Improvement through Feedback Loops:** Establish feedback loops to continuously improve AI and ML models by incorporating insights from real-time data and user feedback, ensuring ongoing optimization of supply chain operations.

REVIEW QUESTIONS

Answer the following question.

1. What are the basic concepts of AI and ML?
2. What do you understand by the concept of Supply Chain Management?
3. How do AI, ML and Traditional Supply Chain Approaches relate to each other?
4. What are the elements of Supply Chain Management?
5. How does warehouse Automation impact Supply Chain Management?
6. How does transportation and Route Optimization work in SCM?
7. What role does risk management play in the SCM process?
8. What are the challenges of AI And ML Applications in Supply Chain Networks?
9. What are the strategies that can be employed to build an effective Supply Chain Networks?

REFERENCES

Berente, N., Gu, B., Recker, J., & Santhanam, R. (2021). Managing Artificial Intelligence. *Management Information Systems Quarterly*, *45*, 1433–1450.

Boopathi, S., Pandey, B. K., & Pandey, D. (2023). Advances in Artificial Intelligence for Image Processing: Techniques, Applications, and Optimization. In Handbook of Research on Thrust Technologies' Effect on Image Processing (pp. 73-95). IGI Global.

Bringsjord, S., Govindarajulu, N. S., & Sundar, N. (2020). *Stanford Encyclopedia of Philosophy*. Retrieved from The Stanford Encyclopedia of Philosophy: https://plato.stanford.edu/entries/artificial-intelligence/#HistAI

Bughin, J., Hazan, E., Ramaswamy, S., Chui, M., Allas, T., Dahlstrom, P., & Trench, M. (2017). *Artificial Intelligence: The Next Digital Frontier?* McKinsey Global Institute. Retrieved on August 19, 2023 from https://www.mckinsey.com/~/media/mckinsey/industries/advanced%20electronics/our %20 insights/how%20artificial%20intelligence%20can%20deliver%20real%20value%20to%20companies/mgi-artificial-intelligence-discussion-paper.ashx

Caballero, S., & Rice, J.B. (2018). *Artificial Intelligence/Machine Learning + Supply Chain Planning.* MIT's Center for Transportation and Logistics.

Charran, E., & Sweetman, S. (2019). *AI Maturity and Organizations: Understanding AI Maturity and Organizations.* Microsoft Inc.

Conde, M. L., & Twinn, I. (2019). *How Artificial Intelligence is Making Transport Safer, Cleaner, More Reliable and Efficient in Emerging Markets (No. 33387).* The World Bank.

Dwivedi, Y. K., Hughes, L., Ismagilova, E., Aarts, G., Coombs, C., Crick, T., & Williams, M. D. (2021). Artificial Intelligence (AI): Multidisciplinary Perspectives on Emerging Challenges, Opportunities, and Agenda for Research, Practice and Policy. *International Journal of Information Management, 57,* 101994. Advance online publication. doi:10.1016/j.ijinfomgt.2019.08.002

Fourtane, S. (2021). *Artificial Intelligence to Play Instrumental Role in Future of Higher Education.* Fierce Education. Retrieved on August 19, 2023 from https://www.fierceeducation.com/administration/artificial-intelligence-to-play-instrumental-role-future-higher-education

Gesing, B., Peterson, S.J., & Michelsen, D. (2018). *Artificial intelligence in logistics: A collaborative report by DHL and IBM on implications and use cases for the logistics industry.* Troisdorf: DHL Customer Solutions & Innovation.

Glasheen, J. (2020). *What is Order Management?* Retrieved from IBM: https://www.ibm.com/in-en/supply-chain/order-management

Hellingrath, B., & Lechtenberg S. (2019). Applications of Artificial Intelligence in Supply Chain Management and Logistics: Focusing onto Recognition for Supply Chain Execution. *The Art of Structuring,* 283-296. doi:10.1007/978-3-030-06234-7_27

Hoffmann, R. (2019). *9 Benefits of Artificial Intelligence on Customer Service.* Business.com. Retrieved on August 19, 2023 from https://www.business.com/articles/artificial-intelligence-customer-service/

Janvier-James, A. M. (2012). A new introduction to supply chains and supply chain management: Definitions and theories perspective. *International Business Research, 5*(1), 194–207. Retrieved August 19, 2023, from. doi:10.5539/ibr.v5n1p194

Kaminsky, P., Simchi-Levi, E., & Simchi-Levi, D. (2003). *Designing and Managing the Supply Chain* (Vol. 2). New York: McGraw Hill Professional.

Khasis, D. (2019). *Four Ways AI Is Impacting Logistics and Supply Chain Management.* Retrieved from Supply Chain Brain. Retrieved on August 19, 2023 from https://www.supplychainbrain.com/blogs/1-think-tank/post/30045-four-ways-ai-is-impacting-logistics-and-supply-chain-management

Kirubasri, G., Sankar, S., Pandey, D., Pandey, B. K., Nassa, V. K., & Dadheech, P. (2022). Software-defined networking-based Ad hoc networks routing protocols. In *Software defined networking for Ad Hoc networks* (pp. 95–123). Springer International Publishing. doi:10.1007/978-3-030-91149-2_5

Kourou, K., & Themis, E. (2015). Machine learning applications in cancer prognosis and prediction. *Computational and Structural Biotechnology Journal, 1*(3), 8–17. doi:10.1016/j.csbj.2014.11.005 PMID:25750696

Kumar Pandey, B., Pandey, D., Nassa, V. K., Ahmad, T., Singh, C., George, A. S., & Wakchaure, M. A. (2021). Encryption and steganography-based text extraction in IoT using the EWCTS optimizer. *Imaging Science Journal, 69*(1-4), 38–56. doi:10.1080/13682199.2022.2146885

Liao, S. P. S. H. T., & Wu, X. (2020). The Role of Big Data and Artificial Intelligence in Education and Education Research: A Literature Mapping. In *6th International Conference on and Social Science Research* (pp. 241-245). Academic Press.

Littman, M., Ajunwa, I., Berger, G., Boutilier, C., Currie, M., Doshi-Velez, F., Hadfield, G., Horowitz, M., Isbell, C., Kitano, H., Levy, K., Lyons, T., Mitchell, M., Shah, J., Sloman, S., Vallor, S., & Walsh, T. (2021). *Gathering Strength, Gathering Storms: The One Hundred Year Study on Artificial Intelligence (AI100) 2021 Study Panel Report*. The Stanford University. Retrieved on August 19, 2023 from https://ai100.stanford.edu/2021-report

Liu, C., Shu, T., Chen, S., Wang, S., Lai, K. K., & Gan, L. (2016). An improved grey neural network model for predicting transportation disruptions. *Expert Systems with Applications, 45*, 331–340. doi:10.1016/j.eswa.2015.09.052

Long, D., & Magerko, B. (2020). What Is AI Literacy? Competencies and Design Considerations. In *Proceedings of the 2020 CHI Conference on Human Factors in Computing Systems* (pp. 1-16). Association for Computing Machinery. 10.1145/3313831.3376727

Makkar, S., Devi, G. N.R., & Solanki, V.K. (2019). Applications of Machine Learning Techniques in Supply Chain Optimization. *ICICCT 2019 – System Reliability, Quality Control, Safety, Maintenance and Management*, 861–869.

Manyika, J., & Michael, C. (2017). *A Future That Works: Automation, Employment, and Productivity*. McKinsey & Co.

Meslie, Y., Enbeyle, W., Pandey, B. K., Pramanik, S., Pandey, D., Dadeech, P., & Saini, A. (2021). Machine intelligence-based trend analysis of COVID-19 for total daily confirmed cases in Asia and Africa. In *Methodologies and Applications of Computational Statistics for Machine Intelligence* (pp. 164–185). IGI Global. doi:10.4018/978-1-7998-7701-1.ch009

Min, H. (2015). *The Essentials of Supply Chain Management*. Pearson Education LTD.

Min, H. (2019). Artificial intelligence in supply chain management: Theory and applications. *International Journal of Logistics, 13*(1), 13–39. doi:10.1080/13675560902736537

National Academies of Sciences, Engineering, and Medicine. (2018). *The Integration of the Humanities and Arts with Sciences, Engineering, and Medicine in Higher Education: Branches from the Same Tree.* Retrieved on August 8, 2023 from https://www.nationalacademies.org/our-work/the-integration-of-the-humanities-and-arts-with-sciences-engineering-and-medicine-in-higher-education#:~:text=In%20its%202018%20report%20The%20Integration%20of%20the,active%20and%20informed%20members%20of%20a%20modern%20democracy

Pandey, B. K., Mane, D., Nassa, V. K. K., Pandey, D., Dutta, S., Ventayen, R. J. M., & Rastogi, R. (2021b). Secure text extraction from complex degraded images by applying steganography and deep learning. In *Multidisciplinary approach to modern digital steganography* (pp. 146–163). IGI Global. doi:10.4018/978-1-7998-7160-6.ch007

Pandey, B. K., & Pandey, D. (2023). Parametric optimization and prediction of enhanced thermoelectric performance in co-doped CaMnO3 using response surface methodology and neural network. *Journal of Materials Science Materials in Electronics*, *34*(21), 1589. doi:10.1007/s10854-023-10954-1

Pandey, B. K., Pandey, D., Wairya, S., & Agarwal, G. (2021a). An advanced morphological component analysis, steganography, and deep learning-based system to transmit secure textual data. *International Journal of Distributed Artificial Intelligence*, *13*(2), 40–62. doi:10.4018/IJDAI.2021070104

Pandey, B. K., Pandey, D., Wairya, S., Agarwal, G., Dadeech, P., Dogiwal, S. R., & Pramanik, S. (2022). Application of integrated steganography and image compressing techniques for confidential information transmission. *Cyber Security and Network Security*, 169-191.

Pandey, B. K., Pandey, D., Wariya, S., Aggarwal, G., & Rastogi, R. (2021c). Deep learning and particle swarm optimisation-based techniques for visually impaired humans' text recognition and identification. *Augmented Human Research*, *6*(1), 1–14. doi:10.1007/s41133-021-00051-5

Pandey, D., Nassa, V. K., Jhamb, A., Mahto, D., Pandey, B. K., George, A. H., & Bandyopadhyay, S. K. (2021b). An integration of keyless encryption, steganography, and artificial intelligence for the secure transmission of stego images. In *Multidisciplinary approach to modern digital steganography* (pp. 211–234). IGI Global. doi:10.4018/978-1-7998-7160-6.ch010

Pandey, D., & Pandey, B. K. (2022a). An efficient deep neural network with adaptive galactic swarm optimization for complex image text extraction. In *Process Mining Techniques for Pattern Recognition* (pp. 121–137). CRC Press. doi:10.1201/9781003169550-10

Pandey, D., Pandey, B. K., & Wairya, S. (2021a). Hybrid deep neural network with adaptive galactic swarm optimization for text extraction from scene images. *Soft Computing*, *25*(2), 1563–1580. doi:10.1007/s00500-020-05245-4

Pandey, D., Wairya, S., Sharma, M., Gupta, A. K., Kakkar, R., & Pandey, B. K. (2022b). An approach for object tracking, categorization, and autopilot guidance for passive homing missiles. *Aerospace Systems*, *5*(4), 553–566. doi:10.1007/s42401-022-00150-0

Pandey, J. K., Jain, R., Dilip, R., Kumbhkar, M., Jaiswal, S., Pandey, B. K., & Pandey, D. (2022). Investigating Role of IoT in the Development of Smart Application for Security Enhancement. In *IoT Based Smart Applications* (pp. 219–243). Springer International Publishing.

Parthiban, K., Pandey, D., & Pandey, B. K. (2021). Impact of SARS-CoV-2 in online education, predicting and contrasting mental stress of young students: A machine learning approach. *Augmented Human Research*, *6*(1), 10. doi:10.1007/s41133-021-00048-0

Rashed, Y. (2017). *Internet of Things and Modern Supply Chain Management* [Unpublished Master Thesis]. Tampere University of Technology.

Russell, S. J., & Norvig, P. (2016). *Artificial Intelligence: A Modern Approach*. Pearson Education Limited.

Ryan, M. (2017). *Service Management: An Integrated Approach*. Larsen and Keller Education.

Siau, K., & Weiyu, W. (2018). Building Trust in Artificial Intelligence, Machine Learning, and Robotics. *Cutter Business Technology Journal*, *31*(2), 47–53.

Singh, H., Pandey, B. K., George, S., Pandey, D., Anand, R., Sindhwani, N., & Dadheech, P. (2022, July). Effective Overview of Different ML Models Used for Prediction of COVID-19 Patients. In *Artificial Intelligence on Medical Data: Proceedings of International Symposium, ISCMM 2021* (pp. 185-192). Singapore: Springer Nature Singapore.

Smithies, J. (2017). Artificial Intelligence, Digital Humanities, and the Automation of Labour. In The Digital Humanities and the Digital Modern (pp. 79-111). Palgrave Macmillan. doi:10.1057/978-1-137-49944-8_4

Strusani, D., & Houngbonon, G. V. (2019). The role of Artificial Intelligence in supporting development in emerging markets. *International Finance Corporation World Bank Group*. Retrieved from www.ifc.org/thought.leadership

Thomas, R. (2019). *AI Is Not Magic: It's Time to Demystify and Apply*. IBM Think Blog. Retrieved on August 19, 2023 from https://www.ibm.com/blogs/think/2019/03/ai-is-not-magic

Wenzel, H., Smit, D., & Sardesa, S. (2019). A Literature Review on Machine Learning in Supply Chain Management. In W. Kersten, T. Blecker, & C. Ringle (Eds.), *Artificial Intelligence and Digital Transformation in Supply Chain Management* (Vol. 27, pp. 413–441). Innovative Approaches for Supply Chains. doi:10.15480/882.2478

Zhou, L., Pan, S., Wang, J., & Vasilakos, A. V. (2017). Machine learning on big data: Opportunities and challenges. *Neurocomputing*, *237*, 350–361. doi:10.1016/j.neucom.2017.01.026

Chapter 8
Improving the Resilience of Supply Chains in a Post-COVID-19 Era:
A Systematic Examination Utilizing ML

Sunil Kumar
https://orcid.org/0000-0003-1103-513X
Department of Information Technology, School of Engineering and Technology (UIET), CSJM University, India

Tamanna M. Prajapati
Shri D.N. Institute of Computer Applications, India

Mamata Mayee Panda
School of Engineering and Technology (UIET), CSJM University, India

Prachi Chhabra
JSS Academy of Technical Education, Noida, India

Shilpi Dubey
School of Engineering and Technology (UIET), CSJM University, India

Amar Pal Yadav
Noida Institute of Engineering and Technology, India

ABSTRACT

The COVID-19 pandemic has highlighted the critical need for supply chain resilience in the face of unforeseen disruptions. This research investigates the application of machine learning (ML) algorithms to enhance supply chain resilience during the COVID-19 crisis. The authors evaluated several ML algorithms, including decision trees, random forests, naïve bayes, and LSTM. They explored using the SPIN COVID-19 RMRIO dataset to develop a proactive and data-driven approach to mitigate disruptions and improve supply chain performance. The ML model worked with and without feature selection. With chi-square feature selection, the long short-term memory (LSTM) performed well and achieved the highest accuracy, 96.74%, with an F1 score of 91.01%. Without feature selection, random forest outperformed, which provided an accuracy of 96.21% with an F1 score of 81.25%.

DOI: 10.4018/979-8-3693-1347-3.ch008

1. INTRODUCTION

In the wake of the unprecedented global upheaval caused by the Corona Virus Disease 2019 (COVID-19) pandemic, supply chains (Pandey, D. et al., 2021) worldwide have encountered unparalleled disruptions across multiple dimensions (Sheng et al., 2020). These disruptions have reverberated through every facet of supply chain management, encompassing individual transportation, raw material procurement, as well as the distribution and manufacturing of products. The emergence of this novel reality has imposed extraordinary challenges on supply chain management professionals, compelling them to seek innovative solutions to navigate these intricate problems. What sets the COVID-19 pandemic apart as a distinct instance of supply chain disruption is its unique global impact on diverse sectors, distinguishing it from other disruptions traditionally studied in operations and supply chain management (Zhang et al., 2020). The COVID-19 (Pandey, D. et al., 2021) pandemic has exposed the fragility of contemporary supply chains and underscored the critical importance of supply chain resilience. In response to these challenges, this research paper explores the integration of ML (Pandey, B. K., & Pandey, D., 2023) algorithms into supply chain management strategies. By harnessing historical data and predictive analytics, we aim to develop a more adaptable and resilient supply chain system (Malhotra, P. et al., 2021) capable of effectively mitigating unforeseen disruptions. While the existing body of literature offers valuable insights into forecasting, managing, and responding to various disruptions (Craighead et al., 2020), the COVID-19 pandemic has magnified the necessity for efficient risk management strategies.

Consequently, the examination and evaluation of Supply Chain Resilience (SCR) within the context of the COVID-19 (Parthiban, K. et al., 2021) pandemic, coupled with developing strategies to enhance this resilience to withstand external disruptions, have emerged as a critical and imperative field necessitating further research and analysis. SCR represents a pivotal capability that empowers supply chains to respond to interruptions and promptly restore their original functionality (Mena et al., 2020). As a strategic imperative, resilience equips supply chains with the ability to anticipate, respond, recover, and extract invaluable insights from unforeseen events, thereby reducing the inherent risks associated with supply chain operations.

The significance of resilience has reached unprecedented levels during the COVID-19 pandemic, underscored by the substantial research volume produced since its onset. In light of this, it is advisable to compile a comprehensive synthesis of the extensive investigations conducted, building upon prior research in this field to provide a unified perspective and lay a robust foundation for subsequent, more impactful research initiatives. To address the challenges posed by this scenario, artificial intelligence (AI) and ML have emerged as potent tools. As articulated by (Baryannis et al., 2019), AI plays a pivotal role in facilitating environmental scanning processes and bolstering the resilience of supply chains on a broader scale. This perspective is depicted in Figure 1, which offers a two-dimensional view of the symbiotic relationship between AI, ML, and supply chain resilience. In the following sections, we delve into the methodologies, findings, and implications of our research, offering a comprehensive exploration of the integration of ML into supply chain management strategies to enhance resilience in the COVID-19 pandemic's disruptions (Lelisho, M. E. et al., 2023).

The COVID-19 (Tareke, S. A. et al., 2022) pandemic has upended global supply chains, presenting unprecedented challenges to supply chain management specialists. The disruptions caused by the pandemic have emphasized the critical need for resilient supply chains capable of adapting to unforeseen circumstances (Cavalcante et al., 2019). In this context, ML algorithms have emerged as powerful tools to address the complexity of managing supply chains during a crisis. ML algorithms can analyze vast

Figure 1. The influence of artificial intelligence on several aspects of supply chain resilience

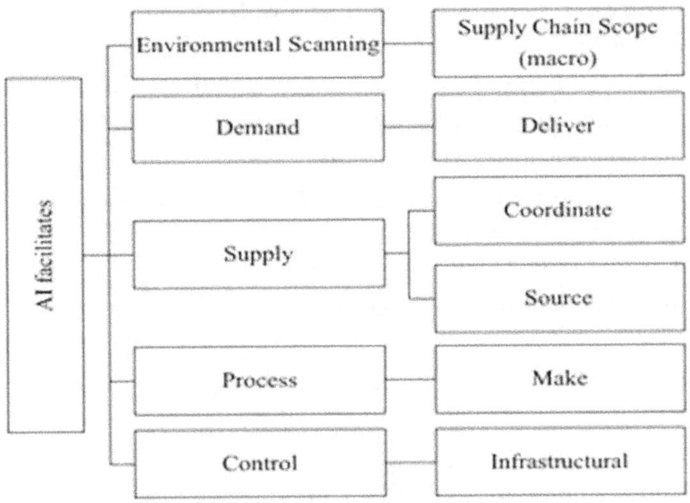

datasets, extracting valuable insights that inform decision-making processes (Heydarbakian & Spehri, 2022). These algorithms can identify data patterns, correlations, and trends, enabling supply chain experts to make informed decisions and devise effective strategies. Clustering algorithms, for example, can categorize disruptions based on their characteristics and impact levels, facilitating the development of tailored response strategies.

Whether it's disruptions related to transportation or raw material shortages, ML offers a flexible approach to mitigation (Wamba & Queiroz, 2022). One pivotal aspect of enhancing supply chain resilience lies in leveraging relevant datasets. A comprehensive compilation of supply chain activities and disruptions experienced throughout the pandemic can provide critical insights. This dataset encompasses information (Kumar Pandey, B. et al., 2021). about transportation disruptions, manufacturing halts, shifts in consumer demand, availability of raw materials, and changes in distribution patterns. Such data becomes invaluable for proactive decision-making and adaptation. Predictive modelling is another crucial facet of bolstering supply chain resilience. Time series analysis can forecast supply chain bottlenecks, allowing companies to adjust their operations and inventory management in real time. Natural language processing (NLP) techniques can analyze textual data, such as news articles and social media posts, to gauge public sentiment and anticipate shifts in consumer behavior. These predictive capabilities help supply chains stay agile and responsive (Cano-Marin et al., 2023).

Furthermore, ML enables the optimization of supply chain activities under uncertain conditions. Inventory management algorithms can dynamically adjust stock levels based on real-time demand fluctuations and supply constraints. Reinforcement learning can adapt distribution strategies considering lockdowns and travel restrictions, ensuring efficient product delivery. However, integrating ML with supply chain management during a crisis is challenging. Data quality, model interpretability, and adaptability to unforeseen circumstances must be navigated carefully (Timothe & Leonie, 2021). Ensuring the reliability and accuracy of the dataset is paramount, as is the interpretability of ML models, which aids supply chain specialists in understanding the rationale behind recommendations and decisions. This research paper focuses on SCR as a critical aspect of modern supply chain management, particularly in the unpredictable disruptions like the COVID-19 pandemic (Pandey, D. et al., 2022). It aims to harness the power of machine learning (Meslie, Y. et al., 2021), specifically Decision tree, Random forest (Manzella et al., 2023), Naïve Bayes (Arockia Panimalar & Krishnakumar, 2023) and LSTM networks (Jassim et al., 2023), to enhance SCR.

The COVID-19 pandemic (Pandey, D. et al., 2023) has underscored the need for resilient supply chains capable of adapting to unprecedented challenges. ML, supported by relevant and comprehensive dataset, offers potent solutions for navigating this complex landscape. ML can play a pivotal role in mitigating the impact of disruptions and building more resilient supply chains by analyzing patterns, predicting disruptions, optimizing operations, and adapting strategies. Integrating cutting-edge technologies with traditional supply chain management practices represents a watershed moment in addressing the unparalleled problems presented by this global crisis.

2. METHODOLOGY

In this study, we employed a comprehensive SPIN COVID-19 RMRIO dataset encompassing various aspects of supply chain activities and disruptions experienced during the COVID-19 pandemic (Timothe & Leonie, 2021). To harness the power of ML, we utilized a range of algorithms, including Decision Trees, Random Forests, Naïve Bayes, and LSTM networks. These algorithms were chosen to analyze the dataset, predict disruptions, and optimize supply chain operations. To assess the performance of our models, we employed standard evaluation metrics. The diverse algorithms and rigorous evaluation metrics allowed us to thoroughly investigate and enhance supply chain resilience during the COVID-19 crisis as illustrated in Figure 2.

2.1 Dataset

The SPIN COVID-19 RMRIO dataset, covering the period from 2016 to 2026, offers significant global trade network data that captures the macroeconomic consequences of the COVID-19 pandemic. More specifically, the data spans 2020 through 2026, depicting a hypothetical scenario. The dataset presented

Figure 2. Resilience of supply chains using ML

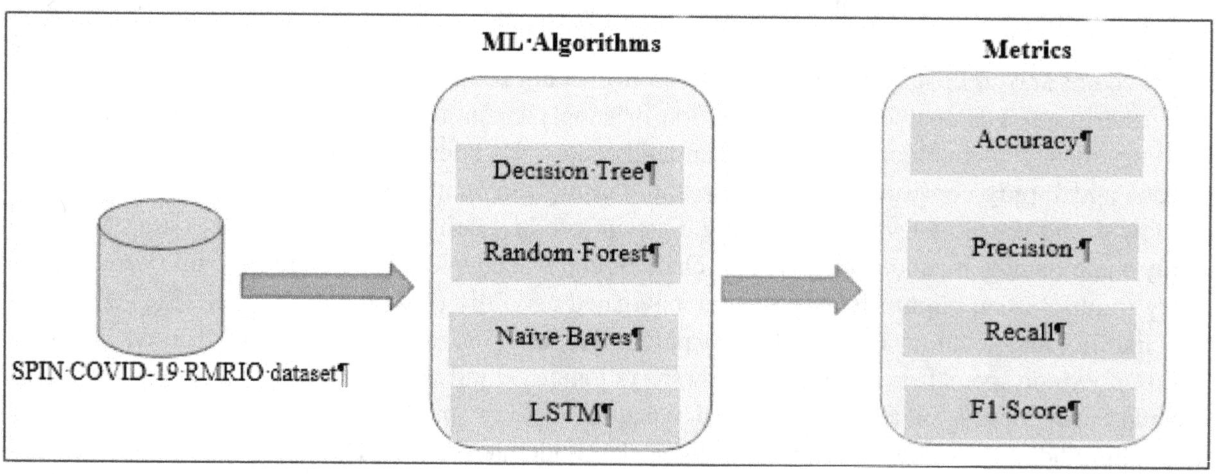

in this study consists of a comprehensive collection of Multi-Regional Input-Output (MRIO) tables. These tables provide a detailed account of the interdependencies among 163 sectors across 155 nations. For our research, we leverage the SPIN COVID-19 RMRIO dataset to analyze the dynamic economic impacts of the COVID-19 (Ayenew, B. et al., 2020) pandemic on global trade and supply chains.

Features: The dataset includes trade flows between many nations and regions and between 162 distinct industries. It tracks the connections between global economic output (supply) and consumption (use).

Size: The entire dataset is a CSV (comma-separated value) file collection. A comprehensive version with all countries, regions, and sectors might take up several hundred megabytes, depending on the sectoral/regional data provided. The entire dataset is a 155x155 RMRIO table, with each column having a 162x162 sector-by-sector block indicating trade flows between those countries/regions.

2.2 Data Preprocessing

The dataset's coverage of multiple years and sectors allows us to delve into how the pandemic has influenced international economic interactions and develop strategies for enhancing supply chain resilience in a post-pandemic world. Before applying the ML algorithm, we conducted data preprocessing, including:

- Handling missing values: We employed imputation techniques to fill in missing data points.
- Data scaling: We standardized the data to ensure all features have the same scale.

2.3 Feature Engineering

To prepare the data for the ML model, we conducted thorough feature engineering, transforming raw data into meaningful variables. We created new features such as lead time, demand variability, and supplier reliability. This step involved time-series analysis, demand forecasting, and anomaly detection. We analyzed the feature importance scores provided by the ML model to gain insights into the factors most influential in predicting disruptions. The top features included supplier reliability, lead time, demand variability, and inventory levels. This information can guide supply chain practitioners in prioritizing risk mitigation strategies.

The chi-square feature selection methodology is a machine learning (Singh, H. et al., 2022) statistical method for determining the independence of categorical characteristics from a categorical target variable. It compares the observed frequency of feature-value combinations with the predicted frequency under the assumption of independence to determine the degree of connection or dependency between each feature and the target variable. A greater chi-square statistic implies a stronger connection, implying that the trait may be more useful in predicting the target variable. This approach, which ranks features based on their chi-square scores, aids in identifying the most relevant and important categorical characteristics, making it a powerful tool for feature selection and dimensionality reduction in categorical data classification tasks.

Several key points underscore the importance of feature engineering in our study:

Transforming Raw Data into Meaningful Variables: Feature engineering involves converting raw data into meaningful variables. This process allowed us to extract valuable insights from the data and create relevant features for our predictive task.

Creation of New Features: We introduced features such as lead time, demand variability, and supplier reliability through feature engineering. These additional features gave our machine-learning models more information to make accurate predictions.

Influence on Predictive Performance: By conducting time-series analysis, demand forecasting, and anomaly detection as part of feature engineering, we enhanced our models' predictive performance. This improvement is evident in the feature importance scores generated by the ML models.

Identification of Influential Factors: Our analysis of feature importance scores highlighted the factors most influential in predicting disruptions. Supplier reliability, lead time, demand variability, and inventory levels emerged as the top features. This insight is crucial for effectively guiding supply chain practitioners in prioritizing risk mitigation strategies.

Chi-Square Feature Selection: We employed the chi-square feature selection methodology to assess the relevance of categorical characteristics to our target variable. This statistical approach helped us rank features based on their chi-square scores, identifying the most important categorical characteristics. This process was particularly valuable for feature selection and reducing dimensionality in our categorical data classification tasks.

Feature engineering played a pivotal role in our research, enabling us to extract meaningful insights, enhance predictive accuracy, and identify critical factors for decision-making in supply chain disruption prediction.

2.4 Algorithm Selection

We evaluated several ML algorithms, including Decision Trees, Random Forests, Naïve Bayes, and LSTM. Through rigorous experimentation, Random Forest emerged as the most effective algorithm for predicting disruptions and identifying areas vulnerable to COVID-19-related risks (Menon, V. et al., 2022).

2.4.1 Decision Trees

Decision trees consist of nodes representing feature attributes and branches representing decision criteria. Each leaf node represents a class label or a predicted value. The core concept behind decision trees is to split the dataset into subsets based on the most significant features, creating a hierarchical structure that leads to decision outcomes (Manzella et al., 2023).

The Gini impurity index, denoted as Gini(D), is commonly used for decision tree splitting. It measures the degree of impurity in a dataset D, where impurity refers to the probability of misclassifying a randomly chosen element from D:

$$Gini\left(D\right)=1-\sum_{\{i=1\}}^{\{c\}}\left(p_i\right)^2 \tag{1}$$

Where c is the number of classes and p_i is the probability of an element belonging to class i.

2.4.2 Random Forest

The Random Forest method is an ensemble learning technique that integrates numerous decision trees in order to enhance the accuracy of predictions. The mentioned technology demonstrates exceptional proficiency in effectively managing both classification and regression jobs, rendering it a very adaptable option for augmenting the resilience of supply chains. The Random Forest algorithm is a technique in ensemble learning that integrates many decision trees in order to enhance the accuracy of predictions. The training process of each decision tree involves utilizing a randomly selected fraction of the available data. The ultimate prediction is then derived by combining the outcomes of all individual trees, such as employing majority voting for classification tasks or averaging for regression tasks (Manzella et al., 2023). Here's an overview of the Random Forest algorithm, along with some key concepts:

2.4.2.1 Bootstrap Sampling

Select at random a chunk of the training data while keeping the replacements i.e. bootstrap samples. It creates different datasets for each tree.

2.4.2.2 Decision Tree Training

For each bootstrap sample, grow a decision tree. Decision trees are constructed by recursively splitting nodes based on the best feature that minimizes impurity. The Gini computed is Equation 1 used, and then the Mean Squared Error computed.

2.4.2.3 Mean Squared Error

$$MSE(D) = \frac{1}{|D|} \sum_{i \in D} \left(y_i - \tilde{y}\right)^2 \tag{2}$$

Where D is a node with data points (y_i), and $\tilde{y}$ is the mean of the y_i values in node D.

2.4.2.4 Ensemble Learning

The aggregation of forecasts from each individual decision tree inside the forest is performed.

2.4.2.5 Majority Voting

The final prediction for classification is the mode (most frequent class) of the predictions made by individual trees. Random Forest provides improved generalization and robustness compared to individual decision trees, making it a powerful tool for numerous ML tasks, including classification and regression (Ali et al., 2022).

2.4.3 Naïve Bayes

The Naive Bayes method is a probabilistic machine learning technique used for the purpose of classification and, in some scenarios, regression problems. The underlying principle of this approach is derived from Bayes' theorem, a mathematical concept that quantifies the likelihood of an occurrence by incorporating previous information about circumstances that may be associated with the event. The term "naive" in Naive Bayes refers to the assumption of conditional independence across characteristics, which allows for a simplified computation (Arockia & Krishnakumar, 2023). The posterior probability of each class C, given the attributes X, may be calculated using Bayes' theorem:

$$P(C|X) = \frac{(P(C) * P(X|C))}{P(X)} \tag{3}$$

P(C|X) is the posterior probability of class C given the features X.
P(C) is the prior probability of class C.
P(X|C) is the likelihood of the features X given class C.
P(X) is the probability of observing the features X, which can be calculated as the sum of *P(C) * P(X|C)* over all classes.

Make a prediction for the class that is most likely to have the greatest posterior probability:

$$predicted_{class} = argmax(P(C|X)) \tag{4}$$

2.4.4 LSTM Algorithm

The LSTM network is a recurrent neural network (RNN) designed for modelling sequential data. LSTM, known for its ability to model sequential data, holds promise for predicting and mitigating supply chain disruptions. Its strength lies in its ability to capture long-range dependencies, making it suitable for time series forecasting tasks, such as predicting disruptions in supply chains. LSTM consists of several components, including input gates, forget gates, and output gates. These gates regulate the flow of information through the network (Jassim et al., 2023). The fundamental equations governing LSTM are as follows.:

Input Gate:

$$\left[i_t = \sigma\left(W_i \cdot \left[h_{\{t-1\}}, x_t\right] + b_i\right)\right] \tag{5}$$

Forget Gate:

$$\left[f_t = \sigma\left(W_f \cdot \left[h_{\{t-1\}}, x_t\right] + b_f\right)\right] \tag{6}$$

Output Gate:

$$\left[o_t = \sigma\left(W_o \cdot \left[h_{\{t-1\}}, x_t\right] + b_o\right)\right] \tag{7}$$

Memory Cell Update:

$$\left[C_t = f_t \cdot C_{\{t-1\}} + i_t \cdot \backslash tanh\left(W_C \cdot \left[h_{\{t-1\}}, x_t\right] + b_C\right)\right] \tag{8}$$

Hidden State Update:

$$[h_t = o_t \cdot \backslash\, tan\, h\, (C_t)] \tag{9}$$

2.5 Model Training and Validation

The dataset was partitioned into training and validation sets, with proportions of 80% and 20% respectively, and afterwards, the machine learning model was fine-tuned. The training set was used to train the machine learning model, whereas the test set was employed to assess its performance (Kumar & Kumar, 2023). We employed the following evaluation metrics and presented through Table 1.

Table 1. Evaluation metrics

Metric	Description	Equation	
Accuracy	The metric evaluates the overall accuracy of the model's predictions.	*(TP + TN) / (TP + TN + FP + FN)*	(10)
Precision	Determines the percentage of positive identifications that were true.	*TP / (TP + FP)*	(11)
Recall	Determines the proportion of true positives that were accurately identified by the model.	*TP / (TP + FN)*	(12)
F1 Score	The harmonic mean of accuracy and recall is a metric that effectively balances the consideration of false positives and false negatives.	*2 * ((Precision * Recall) / (Precision + Recall))*	(13)

The abbreviation TP denotes True Positives, which refers to the accurate positive forecasts.

TN denotes the category of True Negatives, which refers to accurate forecasts of unfavorable outcomes.

The acronym FP denotes instances of False Positives, which refer to inaccurate positive forecasts.

The abbreviation FN denotes instances of False Negatives, which refer to inaccurate forecasts that falsely classify a given observation as negative.

These performance metrics are commonly used in classification tasks to evaluate the effectiveness of ML models.

Table 2. The prediction scores (%) of the ML classifiers without feature selection

Classifier	Accuracy	Precision	Recall	F1 Score
Decision Tree	88.11	90.47	56.99	69.93
Random Forest	**96.21**	84.78	78.00	**81.25**
Naïve Bayes	93.76	80.00	72.00	75.79
LSTM	94.32	72.72	80.00	76.19

3. RESULTS

This experiment will show how ML algorithms improve SCR during COVID-19. We assessed algorithm performance and optimization options for disruption mitigation. Using the dataset, we trained Decision Trees, Random Forests, Naïve Bayes, and LSTM models. All models predicted COVID-19-related supply chain disruptions well. The trials show that Random forest and LSTM networks improve SCR during COVID-19. The classifiers' strengths and limitations illuminate their suitability for the job. The model accurately predicted interruptions by collecting supply chain data temporal relationships and incorporating COVID-19. Table 2 demonstrates model prediction scores without feature selection.

The Decision Tree classifier was 88.11% accurate and 90.47% precise. It correctly identified positive cases in these findings. The F1 score of 69.93% was due to a 56.99% recall rate, suggesting a problem recording all positive instances. These results prompted worries about overfitting training data, rendering Decision Trees unsuitable. All metrics favored the Random Forest classifier over the Decision Tree. Its 96.21% forecast accuracy showed its precision. The classifier also performed well, with accuracy, recall, and F1 scores of 84.78%, 78.00%, and 81.25%. Random Forest's strong performance was due to its ensemble nature, which used many Decision Trees to reduce overfitting and promote generalization.

The Naïve Bayes classifier achieved 93.76% accuracy, 80.00% precision, and 72.00% recall. Although Naïve Bayes fared well, it was less accurate and balanced than Random Forest. However, it showed classification promise. The LSTM neural network identified good cases with 94.32% accuracy and 80.00% recall. The lesser accuracy 72.72% suggested more false positives.

The Random Forest classifier provided the best predictions with accurate and balanced predictions. Although Naïve Bayes showed potential, Random Forest outperformed it. With good recall but poor accuracy, LSTM has promise but needs improvement. Despite its accuracy, Decision Trees created overfitting problems. Future studies might optimize hyper-parameters and explore ensemble approaches for Naïve Bayes and LSTM to improve classification performance.

Here, we illustrate some of the most relevant features given by the Chi-square method for the Random forest; the features and their importance score are presented in Table 3.

Figure 3 shows the results of our classification investigation with chi-square feature selection. Only 25 features were chosen for further processing, such as applying different ML models.

The LSTM model outperforms all other classifiers with the highest accuracy of 96.74%, followed by Random Forest at 94.32%. Decision Tree and Naïve Bayes also demonstrate competitive performance with accuracies of 89.41% and 93.46%, respectively. The precision-recall trade-off varies among the classifiers. While LSTM exhibits the highest precision and F1-score, Random Forest demonstrates the highest recall. These results suggest that the LSTM model balances precision and recall well.

Table 3. Feature ranking matrix of random forest

Feature	Importance Score	Ranking
F1	0.26	1
F2	0.23	2
F3	0.21	3
F4	0.19	4
F5	0.18	5
F6	0.17	6
F7	0.16	7
F8	0.14	8
F9	0.13	9
F10	0.11	10

Figure 3. The prediction scores of the ML classifiers with feature selection

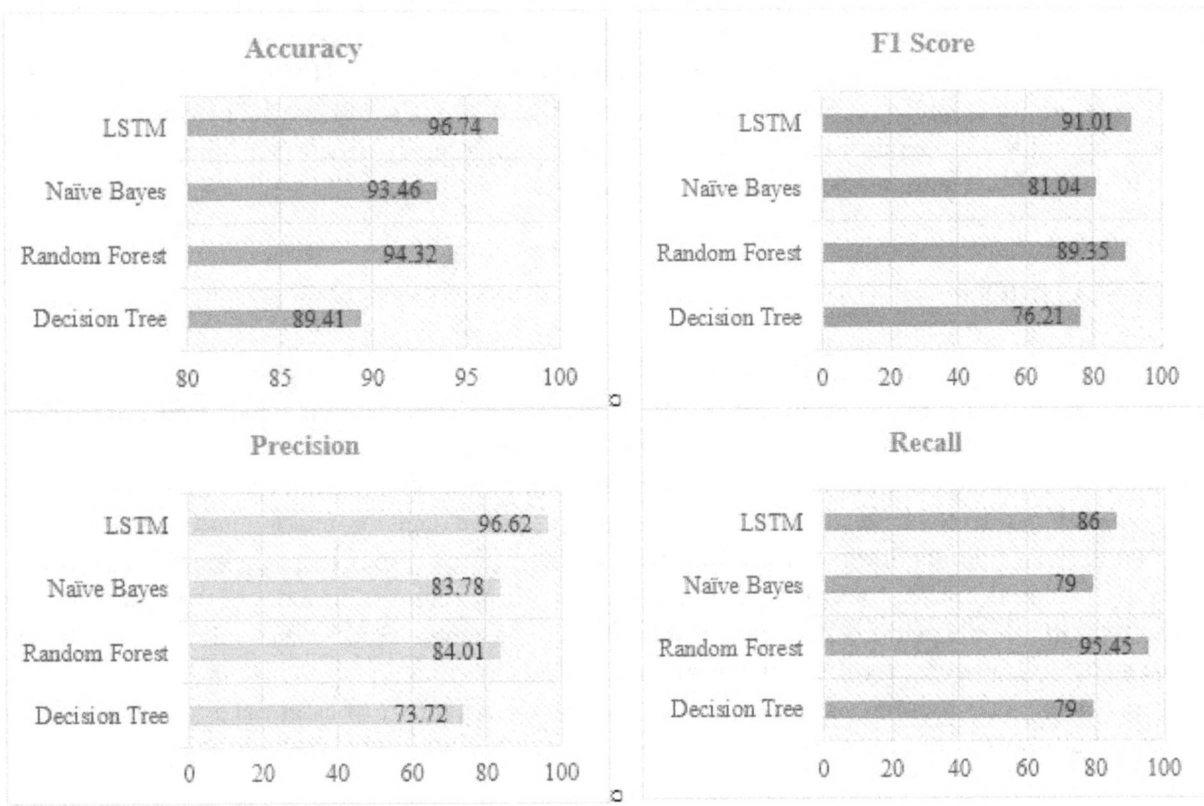

4. DISCUSSION

For disruption reduction, we evaluated algorithm performance and optimization alternatives. Using the dataset, we developed Decision Trees, Random Forests, naive Bayes, and LSTM models. All models accurately projected COVID-19-related supply chain interruptions. During COVID-19, the trials revealed that Random Forest and LSTM networks increase SCR. The classifiers' strengths and weaknesses highlight their fitness for the job. The model successfully anticipated disruptions by gathering supply chain data temporal correlations, and using COVID-19.

The model's complexity and uneven data sensitivity may cause this precision-recall trade-off. Hyper-parameter tuning may improve accuracy in future studies. Experimental findings show that the Random Forest classifier surpasses the other three in accuracy, precision, recall, and F1 score. Its balanced performance makes it a potential categorization candidate. However, various classifiers perform better in different situations; thus, examining the task's criteria and features is essential when choosing one. Further study and testing might improve the LSTM classifier and discuss ensemble approaches to combine the capabilities of numerous classifiers for better outcomes.

According to the experimental data, the LSTM classifier best fits the job, reaching the greatest accuracy and competitive precision, recall, and F1-score values. The LSTM model successfully catches complicated patterns in data and predicts them accurately. Random Forest performs well, especially regarding recall, giving it a viable option. While Decision Tree and Nave Bayes have good accuracy, they must improve precision and F1-score. Finally, the classifier should be chosen depending on the application's unique needs. If accuracy and recall must be balanced, the LSTM model is suggested. On the other hand, Random Forest might be a good alternative if strong recall is a major goal. Further optimizations and feature engineering might improve these classifiers' performance, and future research could look towards ensemble approaches to combine their capabilities.

4. CONCLUSION

Integrating machine learning algorithms and data-driven approaches represents a promising strategy for enhancing supply chain resilience in the COVID-19 pandemic. This research, which evaluated various ML algorithms and their performance in predicting and mitigating disruptions, underscores the potential of LSTM networks as a valuable tool for supply chain managers. By achieving high accuracy and F1 scores, LSTM demonstrates its ability to facilitate proactive decision-making and improve supply chain performance during times of crisis. However, it's essential to acknowledge the study's limitations, including potential dataset constraints and industry-specific variations in model performance. Future research efforts should incorporate real-time data, explore ensemble models, and validate the Random Forest model's efficacy across different industries. These advancements promise to enhance supply chain resilience in the face of unforeseen disruptions, ensuring the reliability of essential goods and services for communities worldwide.

REFERENCES

Ali, M., Haider, M. N., Lashari, S. A., Sharif, W., Khan, A., & Ramli, D. A. (2022). Stacking Classifier with Random Forest functioning as a Meta Classifier for Diabetes Diseases Classification. *Procedia Computer Science, 207*, 3459–3468. doi:10.1016/j.procs.2022.09.404

Arockia Panimalar, S., & Krishnakumar, A. (2023, November). Customer churn prediction model in cloud environment using DFE-WUNB: ANN deep feature extraction with Weight Updated Tuned Naïve Bayes classification with Block-Jacobi SVD dimensionality reduction. *Engineering Applications of Artificial Intelligence, 126*, 107015. doi:10.1016/j.engappai.2023.107015

Ayenew, B., Pandey, D., Yitayew, M., Etana, D., Binay Kumar, P., & Verma, N. (2020). Risk for surge maternal mortality and morbidity during the ongoing corona virus pandemic. *Medlife Clinics, 2*(1), 1012.

BeaufilsT.WenzL. (2021). The SPIN covid19 RMRIO dataset: Global trade network data for the years 2016-2026 reflecting macroeconomic effects of the covid19 pandemic - B. Data for 2020 - 2026 - Covid scenario (2.0) [Data set]. Zenodo. doi:10.5281/zenodo.5713825

Cano-Marin, E., Ribeiro-Soriano, D., Mardani, A., & Blanco Gonzalez-Tejero, C. (2023, September). Exploring the challenges of the COVID-19 vaccine supply chain using social media analytics: A global perspective. *Sustainable Technology and Entrepreneurship, 2*(3), 100047. doi:10.1016/j.stae.2023.100047

Cavalcante, I. M., Frazzon, E. M., Forcellini, F. A., & Ivanov, D. (2019, December). A supervised machine learning approach to data-driven simulation of resilient supplier selection in digital manufacturing. *International Journal of Information Management, 49*, 86–97. doi:10.1016/j.ijinfomgt.2019.03.004

Craighead, C. W., Ketchen, D. J. Jr, & Darby, J. L. (2020). Pandemics and supply chain management research: Toward a theoretical toolbox. *Decision Sciences, 51*(4), 838–866. doi:10.1111/deci.12468 PMID:34234384

Heydarbakian, S., & Spehri, M. (2022). Interpretable Machine Learning to Improve Supply Chain Resilience, An Industry 4.0 Recipe. *IFAC-PapersOnLine, 55*(10), 2834–2839. doi:10.1016/j.ifacol.2022.10.160

Jassim, M. S., Coskuner, G., Sultana, N., & Hossain, S. Z. (2023, January). Forecasting domestic waste generation during successive COVID-19 lockdowns by Bidirectional LSTM super learner neural network. *Applied Soft Computing, 133*, 109908. doi:10.1016/j.asoc.2022.109908

Kumar, S., & Kumar, H. (2023, December). Classification of COVID-19 X-ray images using transfer learning with visual geometrical groups and novel sequential convolutional neural networks. *MethodsX, 11*, 102295. doi:10.1016/j.mex.2023.102295 PMID:37539339

Kumar Pandey, B., Pandey, D., Nassa, V. K., Ahmad, T., Singh, C., George, A. S., & Wakchaure, M. A. (2021). Encryption and steganography-based text extraction in IoT using the EWCTS optimizer. *Imaging Science Journal, 69*(1-4), 38–56. doi:10.1080/13682199.2022.2146885

Lelisho, M. E., Pandey, D., Alemu, B. D., Pandey, B. K., & Tareke, S. A. (2023). The negative impact of social media during COVID-19 pandemic. *Trends in Psychology, 31*(1), 123–142. doi:10.1007/s43076-022-00192-5

Malhotra, P., Pandey, D., Pandey, B. K., & Patra, P. M. (2021). Managing agricultural supply chains in COVID-19 lockdown. *International Journal of Quality and Innovation*, *5*(2), 109–118. doi:10.1504/IJQI.2021.117181

Manzella, F., Pagliarini, G., Sciavicco, G., & Stan, I. (2023, March). The voice of COVID-19: Breath and cough recording classification with temporal decision trees and random forests. *Artificial Intelligence in Medicine*, *137*, 102486. doi:10.1016/j.artmed.2022.102486 PMID:36868683

Mena, C., Melnyk, S. A., Baghersad, M., & Zobel, C. W. (2020). Sourcing decisions under conditions of risk and resilience: A behavioral study. *Decision Sciences*, *51*(4), 985–1014. doi:10.1111/deci.12403

Menon, V., Pandey, D., Khosla, D., Kaur, M., Vashishtha, H. K., George, A. S., & Pandey, B. K. (2022). A Study on COVID–19, Its Origin, Phenomenon, Variants, and IoT-Based Framework to Detect the Presence of Coronavirus. In *IoT Based Smart Applications* (pp. 1–13). Springer International Publishing.

Meslie, Y., Enbeyle, W., Pandey, B. K., Pramanik, S., Pandey, D., Dadeech, P., & Saini, A. (2021). Machine intelligence-based trend analysis of COVID-19 for total daily confirmed cases in Asia and Africa. In *Methodologies and Applications of Computational Statistics for Machine Intelligence* (pp. 164–185). IGI Global. doi:10.4018/978-1-7998-7701-1.ch009

Pandey, B. K., & Pandey, D. (2023). Parametric optimization and prediction of enhanced thermoelectric performance in co-doped CaMnO3 using response surface methodology and neural network. *Journal of Materials Science Materials in Electronics*, *34*(21), 1589. doi:10.1007/s10854-023-10954-1

Pandey, D., Hasan, A., Pandey, B. K., Lelisho, M. E., George, A. H., & Shahul, A. (2023). COVID-19 epidemic anxiety, mental stress, and sleep disorders in developing country university students. *CSI Transactions on ICT*, 1-9.

Pandey, D., Ogunmola, G. A., Enbeyle, W., Abdullahi, M., Pandey, B. K., & Pramanik, S. (2021). COVID-19: A framework for effective delivering of online classes during lockdown. *Human Arenas*, 1-15.

Pandey, D., Pandey, B. K., Sindhwani, N., Anand, R., Nassa, V. K., & Dadheech, P. (2022). An Interdisciplinary Approach in the Post-COVID-19 Pandemic Era. *An Interdisciplinary Approach in the Post-COVID-19 Pandemic Era*, 1-290.

Pandey, D., Verma, N., Islam, T., Enbeyle, W., Pandey, B. K., & Patra, P. (2021). The Response of Consumer Food Price Index (CFPI) Due To The Impact of Pandemic Covid-19 On Indian Agriculture Sector. *Hyperion International Journal of Econophysics & New Economy, 14*(1).

Parthiban, K., Pandey, D., & Pandey, B. K. (2021). Impact of SARS-CoV-2 in online education, predicting and contrasting mental stress of young students: A machine learning approach. *Augmented Human Research*, *6*(1), 10. doi:10.1007/s41133-021-00048-0

Sheng, J., Amankwah-Amoah, J., Khan, Z., & Wang, X. (2020). COVID-19 pandemic in the new era of big data analytics: Methodological innovations and future research directions. *British Journal of Management*, *32*(4), 1164–1183. doi:10.1111/1467-8551.12441

Singh, H., Pandey, B. K., George, S., Pandey, D., Anand, R., Sindhwani, N., & Dadheech, P. (2022, July). Effective Overview of Different ML Models Used for Prediction of COVID-19 Patients. In *Artificial Intelligence on Medical Data: Proceedings of International Symposium, ISCMM 2021* (pp. 185-192). Singapore: Springer Nature Singapore.

Tareke, S. A., Lelisho, M. E., Hassen, S. S., Seid, A. A., Jemal, S. S., Teshale, B. M., ... Pandey, B. K. (2022). The prevalence and predictors of depressive, anxiety, and stress symptoms among Tepi town residents during the COVID-19 pandemic lockdown in Ethiopia. *Journal of Racial and Ethnic Health Disparities*, 1–13. PMID:35028903

Wamba, S. F., & Queiroz, M. M. (2022). A Framework Based on Blockchain, Artificial Intelligence, and Big Data Analytics to Leverage Supply Chain Resilience considering the COVID-19. *IFAC-PapersOnLine*, *55*(10), 2396–2401. doi:10.1016/j.ifacol.2022.10.067

Zhang, F., Wu, X., Tang, C. S., Feng, T., & Dai, Y. (2020). Evolution of operations management research: From managing flows to building capabilities. *Production and Operations Management*, *29*(10), 2219–2229. doi:10.1111/poms.13231

Chapter 9
Predictive Modeling of Supply Chain Disruptions in the COVID-19 Pandemic Using Advanced Machine Learning Approaches

Sunil Kumar
https://orcid.org/0000-0003-1103-513X
Department of Information Technology, School of Engineering and Technology (UIET), CSJM University, India

Digvijay Pandey
https://orcid.org/0000-0003-0353-174X
Department of Technical Education, U. P., India

Sunil Kumar
Ajay Kumar Garg Engineering College, Ghaziabad, India

Abhishek Dwivedi
https://orcid.org/0000-0003-3981-0206
School of Engineering and Technology (UIET), CSJM University, India

Abhishek Kumar Mishra
IFTM University, Moradabad, India

Mohit Singh Chauhan
Dr. A.P. Abdul Kalam Technical University, Lucknow, India

ABSTRACT

In light of the COVID-19 pandemic, this research examines supply chain disruptions critically, highlighting their devastating effect on businesses like as drugs and perishable food. The report emphasizes the need of durable supply networks, encouraging firms to invest in strong risk mitigation measures and cutting-edge technology to maintain continuity and adaptation in an ever-changing business environment. Deep learning and machine learning approaches have emerged as critical tools for solving these supply chain difficulties. Decision trees, random forests, k-nearest neighbors, and support vector machines (SVM) have all been shown to be effective in mitigating supply chain issues, with SVM achieving an impressive accuracy rate of 96.6%. Furthermore, the random forest model has a respectable accuracy of 95.00%. Notably, the study discovers that the gated recurrent unit architecture outperforms the long

DOI: 10.4018/979-8-3693-1347-3.ch009

short-term memory design, with an accuracy rate of 98.01%. This investigation provides useful insights for the difficulties confronting contemporary supply networks.

1. INTRODUCTION

The ongoing COVID-19 outbreak has presented an unparalleled challenge for worldwide supply networks. The worldwide supply chains have been rendered susceptible due to significant impacts or delays in the shipments of essential and life-saving items, including medicines, agriculture, healthcare, and manufacturing (Craighead et al., 2020). A supply chain (SC) refers to a well-coordinated network of people, machinery, activities, resources, and technology that collaboratively engage in the production and distribution of a product to its final consumers. The process involves the transportation of raw materials or partially processed goods from suppliers to manufacturers, as well as the conversion and delivery of the final product or service to end-users or consumers (Bassiouni et al., 2023). The effective management of SC activities is crucial for ensuring the efficient movement of resources and goods.

Supply chains are often complicated and comprise numerous phases, such as manufacturing, packaging, distribution, and retail. Delays and shortages may occur at any stage in the supply chain. Movement limitations, border closures, and a need for transit alternatives (e.g., aircraft and trucks) hampered the movement of products. It influences the delivery of pharmaceuticals and perishable food products. Because supply chains are global in nature, interruptions in one place might result in shortages of vital raw materials or components required for pharmaceutical and food manufacturing (Cundell et al., 2020). Companies experienced difficulties maintaining inventory levels as a result of variable demand patterns and supply interruptions. Overstocking and understocking were challenges that needed to be addressed in real-time.

This study focuses on substantial disruptions in the supply systems for food and medicines. The implementation of lockdown measures, border restrictions, and labor shortages had a detrimental impact on the production, distribution, and transportation of crucial commodities. The occurrence of panic purchasing resulted in the depletion of stocks, hence impacting the availability of essential drugs and basic things. The global health crisis has highlighted the need to implement robust and flexible supply chain strategies. It has led both enterprises and governments to reassess and strengthen their operations in order to guarantee continuous access to essential commodities in times of emergency (Cano-Marin et al., 2023).

Enhanced comprehension of the potential dangers associated with shipments may significantly reduce feelings of anxiety. The subsequent section of the chapter presents many ML methodologies aimed at mitigating the risks associated with loads by forecasting the feasibility of exporting goods from one origin to another, even in light of the limitations imposed by the COVID-19 epidemic. In a similar vein, the work of prediction has also been undertaken using DL methodologies. The ML and DL models under consideration have the potential to analyze the dataset and presented through Figure 1.

The challenge included the use of decision trees (DT), random forest (RF) (Ali et al., 2022), k-nearest neighbor (KNN), and SVM algorithms. The approaches used in ML include four primary stages: data acquisition, noise reduction or pre-processing, feature extraction, and classification (Cavalcante et al., 2019). The LSTM and GRU architectures are recurrent neural network (RNN) models that diminish fading gradients and capture long-range connections in sequential data. Continuous data, Time-series data, and related applications benefit from these approaches. The LSTM and GRU designs eliminate vanishing gradients and capture sequential input dependencies. LSTM networks handle long-range

Figure 1. Block diagram of machine learning for supply chain disruptions in the COVID-19 pandemic

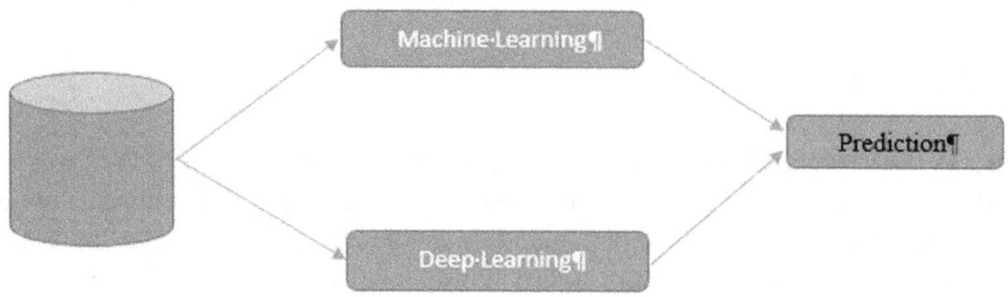

relationships better because of their complicated architecture, which includes a memory cell (Jassim et al., 2023). GRUs manage medium-range interactions effectively and are computationally efficient. The choice depends on the task, dataset size, and processing resources (Bi et al., 2022).

The study may show that one of the models may correctly predict the danger of moving products to a given place under COVID-19 pandemic limitations, particularly in food and drugs. Clearly, this effort will help decision-makers anticipate supply chain risks to improve resilience. The COVID-19 pandemic has highlighted the need for supply chain risk management and adaptation. Many companies have evaluated and rebuilt their supply networks to build strength against future shocks and uncertainties. This collective effort to better understand and mitigate supply chain risks in the face of the pandemic has produced models and risk management strategies that could help businesses navigate the complex landscape of supply chain management, ensuring the uninterrupted flow of goods and minimizing vulnerabilities to unforeseen challenges.

The research study contributes to supply chain risk management in numerous ways

- ML methods, including decision trees, random forests, k-nearest neighbors, and support vector machines, are tested for supply chain problems.
- It offers a systematic ML framework for complicated supply chain issues by combining data collecting, noise reduction, feature extraction, and classification.
- The LSTM and GRU architectures are also introduced as powerful methods for processing continuous and time-series data, capturing long-range and medium-range relationships in sequential information.
- Finally, the research emphasizes the need to adapt supply chains to the COVID-19 pandemic and robust risk management strategies to help decision-makers anticipate and mitigate supply chain risks, enhancing resilience in uncertain times.

The investigation is organized as follows: Section 2 summarizes the relevant literature and prior research in the topic. Section 3 describes the methodology employed in this investigation and the strategy that was taken. Section 4 contains the results, Section 5 has the discussion, and Section 6 contains the study's conclusion. Section 7 delves into the future scope.

2. RELATED WORK

Prior studies have investigated several advanced machine learning methods in order to detect and mitigate supply chain disruptions during the COVID-19 pandemic. These studies have provided valuable insights into the utilization of state-of-the-art methods to improve the resilience of supply chains during difficult periods.

Supply chain networks are vulnerable to interruptions. Thus, shipping risks must be understood. Researchers developed DL methods to forecast COVID-19-restricted cargo exportability. These DL methods include four steps: data capture, de-noising, feature extraction, and classification. In particular, the feature extraction step uses RNNs, including LSTM, BiLSTM, GRU, and the temporal convolutional network. The research also used SoftMax, RT, RF, KNN, ANN, and SVM classifiers to evaluate the suggested DL models. The temporal convolutional network predicts shipping hazards with almost 100% accuracy. The study provided preemptive insights to help decision-makers improve supply chain resilience in the case of unexpected interruptions (Bassiouni et al., 2023).

The research found resilience and sustainability to be the main SC themes. Food, health-related SCs, and technology-aided tools (AI, IoT, blockchains) are key study areas. The most prominent research in this field included resilience and sustainability-focused disruption management solutions. Additionally, researchers gained management insights to maintain crucial product supplies during pandemics, including PPE and vaccinations (Moosavi et al., 2022).

The research used machine learning to remove human subjective bias and evaluate risk objectively. The study developed a risk assessment methodology using components evaluation and an artificial neural network prediction model. Deconstructing risk factors into their fundamental components and evaluating them as vectors of the feature was novel. Next, they gathered real-world information from 60 industrial businesses, including plastic, metal, logistic, and medical device companies, via risk assessments and audit reports. Finally, they created a neural network to anticipate industrial operational process risk levels. Our model scored 0.9 on the test set of 18 samples after 42 samples of training. The model was verified and accurately predicted risk with R = 0.95, matching human auditor findings (Burstein & Zuckerman, 2023).

The present study addresses the issue by leveraging machine learning methods on actual automotive supply chain data. Ten suppliers' performance data was utilized for two years in this investigation. Clustering was used to create labels utilizing resilience capacities. Two interpretable machine learning methods, Naïve Bayes and decision tree, were chosen to categorize providers based on their accomplishments in each degree. Among understandable algorithms, the decision tree technique performed best (Heydarbakian & Spehri, 2022).

This study investigated the studies on Supply Chain Resilience (SCR) within the specific setting of the COVID-19 pandemic. In this study, a total of 1717 publications on the subject of scientific research are categorized into 11 distinct clusters. These clusters are then validated using a supervised ML technique. Subsequently, an examination is conducted on each collection within the framework of the COVID-19 pandemic, resulting in the recognition of three correlated characteristics (namely, interconnection, transformability, and sharing) that enterprises should prioritize in order to establish a supply chain that is more robust in the aftermath of the COVID-19 crisis. The insights produced from this study provide significant assistance for both managers and academics. Managers may use these insights to inform their decision-making processes, while scholars can include them in their future research initiatives on social corporate responsibility to maximize their effect (Li et al., 2023).

The supplied study provided a theoretical assessment of COVID-19-related supply chain disruption and analyzed and discussed its consequences on food worldwide supply chain administration. Content from articles, blogs, reports, and newspapers was analyzed. The COVID-19 pandemic affected worldwide supply chain management, as shown by substantial evidence. This article aims to identify the causes of disruption in global supply chain management, particularly in food supply chains. This article also showed COVID-19's long-term effects on food supply chain management. Some rules and measures were offered for controlling global supply chains post-pandemic based on analysis of numerous sources. Finally, digitization on the blockchain platform was advised to develop a resilient and sustainable global supply chain management to meet future situations (Tasnim, 2020).

The agricultural food supply chain (AFSC) has faced unmatched challenges and instability. The research found six resilience factors and 18 AFSC sub-criteria for COVID-19. The study introduced the MCDM methodology for assessing resilience factors by analyzing how they relate to one another. Results reveal three key resilience specifications: supply chain coordination, effectiveness, and management of strategy, along with five key sub-criteria: acceleration, the view, continuation management, belonging, and shared planning and replenishing. The suggested approach enhances resilience in AFSC and might be applied to other supply chains in anticipation of COVID-19 (Xu et al., 2022).

In the context of the issue, the article examines research on Coronavirus epidemiological studies, infectiousness, their existence, and disinfecting sensitivity within the framework of The Good Manufacturing Practice (GMP) and public health guidance. This research examines the impacts of the COVID-19 pandemic on the pharmaceutical supply chain and suggests methods for risk reduction to prevent medical product shortages. This paper covers the COVID-19 pandemic, including a brief history, a detailed description of the virus, an analysis of laws and regulations, an analysis of personnel screening procedures, an investigation of the virus's perseverance on inanimate substrates, an analysis of the manufacturing facility sterilization and cleaning practices, and an evaluation of GMP use (Cundell et al., 2020).

3. METHODOLOGY

The methodology used in this study utilizes a combination of ML and DL approaches to thoroughly examine and mitigate supply chain disruptions resulting from the COVID-19 pandemic. This approach is data-centric and aims to improve the capacity of supply chains to withstand and adapt to the difficulties posed by the current circumstances as depicted in Fig. 2.

Dataset:

The dataset utilized in this study provides a thorough and detailed basis for examining the complex difficulties encountered by the food (Data_Sheet_1_From Farm to Fork: Early Impacts of COVID-19 on Food Supply Chain.pdf, 2023) and medicine (Concern Levels on Possible Drug Supply Chain Disruption Due to COVID-19 2020, 2020) supply networks within the COVID-19 epidemic. The dataset was combined for the investigation purpose. Production, inventory, transportation, food, and drug supply data were included in the dataset. These characteristics were essential for analyzing supply chain disruptions from manufacturing and distribution to retail and consumption. The information also captured regional differences and the pandemic's influence on supply chains in various nations and regions. This enabled us to gain valuable insights that can guide the development of strategies to enhance supply chain resilience in the event of unforeseen crises.

ML Algorithms:

Figure 2. Flowchart for the predictive methodology employed in supply chain disruptions in the COVID-19

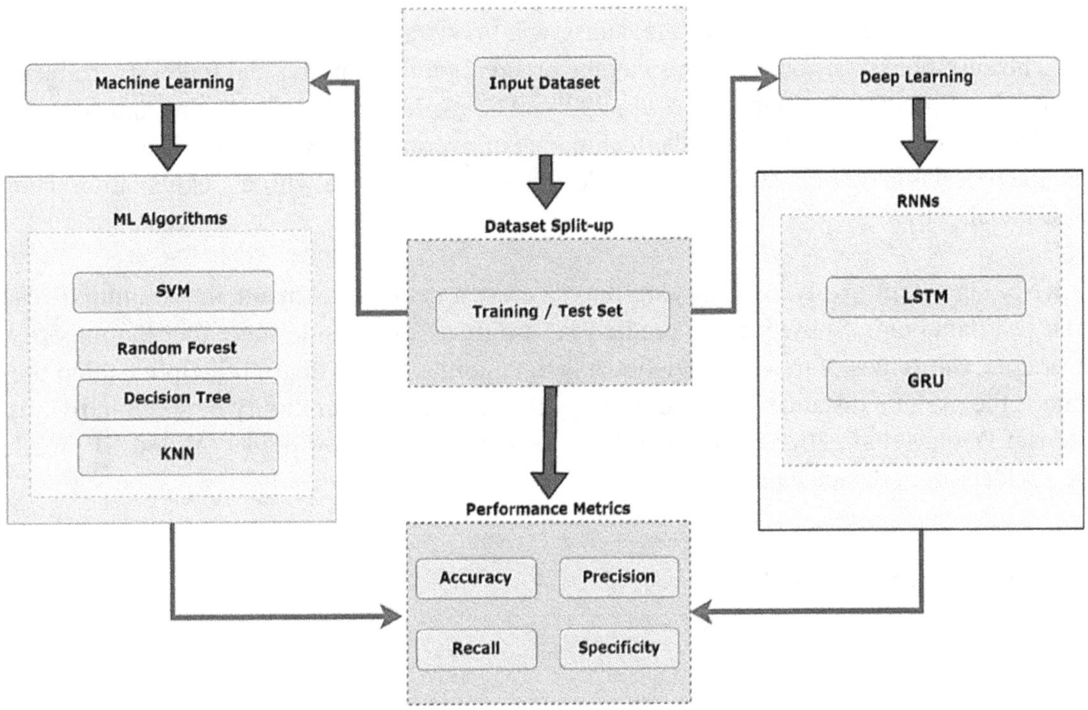

Machine learning algorithms have the benefit of automating complex operations and generating predictions by analyzing patterns and data, hence minimizing human involvement and enhancing operational effectiveness. Furthermore, these entities possess the capacity to engage in ongoing learning and adjustment, enhancing their efficacy over a while and effectively managing dynamic datasets and situations.

DT:

The Decision Trees algorithm displays judgments in a hierarchical structure resembling a tree. Internal nodes in this structure indicate decisions made based on certain features, while leaf nodes correspond to either class labels or numerical values. Recursive partitioning is the fundamental mathematical idea that underlies decision trees. This concept entails the iterative selection of the most optimal feature to divide the data at each node, using metrics such as Gini impurity or information gain. The use of mathematical formulae often establishes the split criteria of the decision tree (Ali et al., 2022). The calculation of the Gini impurity for a node 't' in a classification issue is shown by the following equation:

$$G(t)=1-\sum_{i=1}^{c}\left(p(i|t)\right)^2 \tag{1}$$

where '*c*' is the number of classes, and $p(i|t)$ is the proportion of samples belonging to class i at node t.

RF:

The Random Forest technique is an ensemble learning approach that utilizes the collective strength of several decision trees in order to enhance the accuracy of predictions and mitigate the issue of overfitting. The technique involves aggregating the outcomes of several decision trees, which are usually trained on randomly selected subsets of the dataset via bootstrapping and including random subsets of features. The ensemble then computes the average or aggregates the individual forecasts from each tree to provide a final prediction (Manzella et al., 2023). The methodology used in this approach is based on the utilization of decision trees and the techniques of averaging or voting in order to generate predictions. Each decision tree inside the forest is designed in accordance with the explanation mentioned earlier (Ali et al., 2022).

KNN:

The KNN algorithm involves identifying the 'k' closest data points inside the training dataset to a particular test data point. Subsequently, predictions are made by considering either the majority class or by averaging the values of these 'k' neighboring data points. The primary principle behind the KNN algorithm is the use of a distance metric to quantify the closeness or proximity between individual data points (Arief Daulay et al., 2023). The Euclidean distance between two points 'A' and 'B' in a feature space is a widely used distance measure.

$$EuclideanDistance\left(A,B\right)=\sqrt{\sum_{i=1}^{n}\left(A_i-B_i\right)^2} \tag{2}$$

SVM:

SVMs are a robust ML technique that seeks to identify the most advantageous hyperplane for effectively segregating input points into distinct groups. SVMs operate by optimizing the margin between the support vectors, which are the data points located closest to the hyperplane, for different classes. Kernel functions may also be used to manage the separation of non-linear data effectively. The equation for a linearly separable classification issue may be expressed in its most basic form as follows:

$$f(x) = Sign(w.x + b) \tag{3}$$

The decision function, denoted as f (x), is responsible for predicting the class of a new data point, x. The sign function, represented as sign (·), yields a value of +1 when the argument is positive or zero and -1 when the opinion is negative. The weight vector, denoted as w, determines the orientation or direction of the hyperplane. The dot product (.), sometimes referred to as the inner product, is computed between the weight vector w and the feature vector x. The bias term, denoted as b, serves as the intercept, specifically in the context of hyperplanes. It is responsible for shifting the hyperplane away from the origin. The objective of the SVM is to determine the w and b that provide the maximum margin between the two classes. This optimization is subject to the constraint:

$$y_i(w.x_i + b) \geq 1 \tag{4}$$

y_i represents the class label assigned to the data point x_i. The constraint guarantees that all data points are accurately categorized and positioned on the appropriate side of the hyperplane. The margin refers to the spatial separation between the hyperplane and the closest data point belonging to either of the two classes. The SVM algorithm seeks to identify the optimal values of w and b that maximize the margin (Sangeetha & Prashanth, 2015).

DL Algorithms:

The LSTM and GRU architectures are RNN models that have been specifically developed to mitigate the issue of disappearing gradients and effectively capture long-range dependencies within sequential data. These models demonstrate high efficacy in tasks that involve time-series data, natural language processing, speech recognition, and other related domains. Both LSTM and GRU architectures that have been specifically developed to mitigate the issue of vanishing gradients and effectively capture dependencies within sequential input LSTM networks exhibit enhanced proficiency in managing long-range dependencies because of their intricate architecture, which incorporates a distinct memory cell. Conversely, GRUs are characterized by their computational efficiency and effectiveness in handling medium-range dependencies (Jassim et al., 2023). The selection between the two options is contingent upon the particular task at hand, the size of the dataset, and the computational resources that are accessible.

LSTM:

LSTM models consist of three fundamental components, namely the input gate, forget gate and output gate. The function of these gates is to regulate the movement of information into and out of the cellular state. During each time step, the input gate is responsible for determining the specific information that should be incorporated into the cell state, considering both the current input and the prior concealed state. The forget gate is responsible for determining which data should be discarded from the cell state. The output gate regulates the selection of information from the cell state that is utilized in generating the present concealed state and output. LSTM models can capture and model long-term dependencies within sequential data effectively. This capability is particularly significant in jobs that heavily rely on contextual information from preceding time steps. LSTM models incorporate gating mechanisms, including input, forget, and output gates, which regulate the movement of data into and out of the cell state. This technique aids in the mitigation of the vanishing gradient problem, hence enabling the neural network to acquire and store information throughout extended sequences effectively. LSTM networks are equipped with a distinct memory cell that possesses the ability to retain and modify information across temporal intervals. The regulation of the cell state can be achieved by the use of gating mechanisms, which provide meticulous management of the retention or elimination of specific information. LSTM models give a wide range of applications and can be effectively utilized in diverse tasks involving sequential data, such as text production, language modeling, and machine translation (Jassim et al., 2023).

GRU:

GRUs are equipped with two distinct gates, namely the reset gate and the update gate. The reset gate is responsible for determining the extent to which the previous hidden state should be disregarded or reset. The update gate is responsible for regulating the area to which the present input and prior confidential form are utilized in modifying the current hidden state. GRUs lack a distinct memory cell, in contrast to LSTM units. In contrast, the hidden state is updated directly by including both the input and the prior hidden state.

GRUs have a more streamlined structure in comparison to LSTM units, featuring solely two gating mechanisms: the reset gate and the update gate. This enhances their computational efficiency and facilitates their training process. The use of GRUs, which possess a decreased quantity of gates and connections, can result in expedited convergence during the training process, particularly when confronted with datasets of lower proportions. GRUs have demonstrated the ability to effectively capture dependencies of intermediate length in sequential data, making them a suitable choice for a range of natural language processing applications (Bi et al., 2022).

4.1 Performance Metrics

Accuracy, specificity, sensitivity, and precision are significant metrics employed to evaluate the effectiveness of models, tests, or measures in a variety of domains, including the fields of machine learning and medicine. The accuracy of a classification or measurement is defined as the ratio of properly predicted or recognized occurrences to the total number of examples. Specificity assesses a test's or model's capacity to accurately identify negative instances or real negatives out of all genuine negatives, which helps in determining the test's ability to prevent false alarms. Sensitivity, on the other hand, measures a test's ability to accurately identify positive instances or true positives among all real positives, demonstrating how effectively it identifies genuine cases. Precision measures the accuracy of positive predictions by dividing the number of genuine positives by the total number of anticipated positives, emphasizing the capacity to reduce false positives (Kumar & Kumar, 2023). These measures are critical in determining the dependability and efficacy of algorithms, diagnostic tests, and decision-making processes in a variety of disciplines.

4. RESULTS AND DISCUSSION

The use of the extensive dataset in this research was crucial in examining the complex difficulties encountered by food and pharmaceutical supply networks during the COVID-19 epidemic. Our objective was to use various ML methods and RNNs to identify patterns, make predictions, and get significant insights into the dynamics of disruption in these crucial supply chains. ML algorithms are computational models that are designed to learn and improve from experience without being explicitly programmed automatically. These algorithms are used to analyze and interpret large datasets and identify patterns. The investigation began by using conventional ML techniques, such as DT, RF, KNN, and SVM. The algorithms, as mentioned earlier, were used within a multi-step procedure, which included the collection of data, the preprocessing, the extraction of relevant features, and the classification of the data. Significantly, the findings produced by the research were valuable in the identification of patterns, determination of critical components that contribute to disruptions in supply chains, and anticipation of possible vulnerabilities.

The SVM demonstrated the greatest accuracy rate of 96.6%, surpassing all other models. Following closely behind was the RF model, which earned an accuracy rate of 95.0%. The RF algorithm had the maximum performance in terms of specificity, sensitivity, and accuracy, with scores of 92.65%, 93.68%, and 93.14%, respectively. The use of RF, which involves the aggregation of many decision trees, has been shown to improve both prediction accuracy and resilience. DT, for example, has provided us with the ability to visually represent decision boundaries and get insights into the hierarchical significance of different characteristics. The KNN algorithm was used to construct predictions by using the closest data points, hence providing valuable insights into the impact of neighborhood effects on disruptions in the supply chain. SVM, by means of selecting an ideal hyperplane, yielded significant results in terms of categorization. The conventional ML algorithms have established a robust basis for comprehending the components that contribute to disruptions and facilitating predictive analyses.

Figure 3. The findings of employed ML classifiers

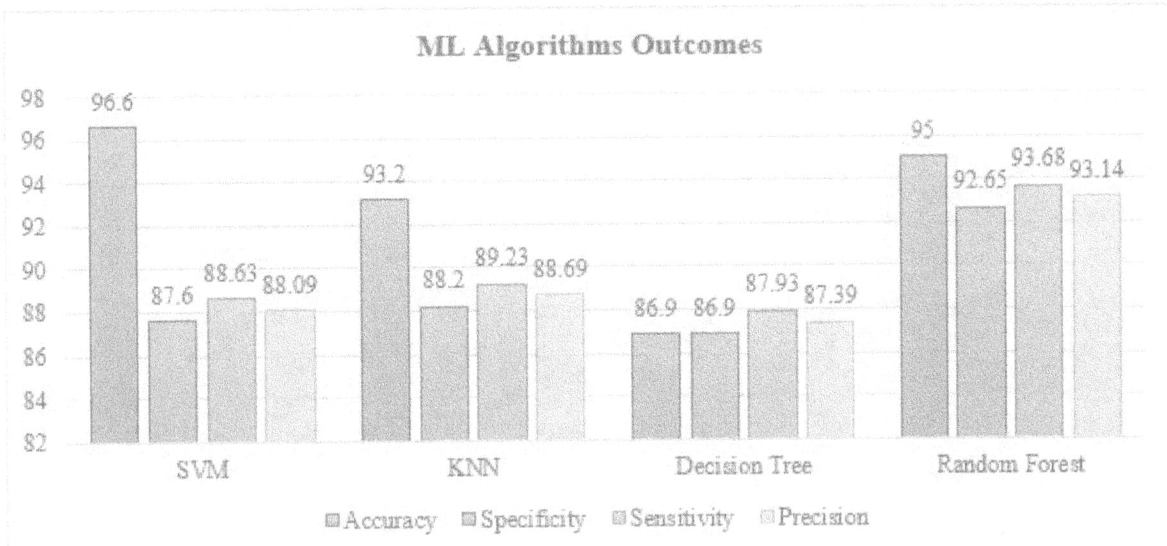

RNNs are a kind of artificial neural network (ANN) that are designed to process sequential data by using feedback connections. In addition to conventional ML techniques, our investigation included the use of LSTM and GRU architectures. These models are specifically built as RNN variants that excel at capturing sequential dependencies and effectively processing time-series data. The LSTM model, characterized by its intricate structure that incorporates a memory cell, demonstrated exceptional performance in capturing extensive dependencies included in the sequential supply chain data. The approach demonstrated notable efficacy in managing time-series data characterized by prolonged temporal interdependencies. In contrast, the GRU model has shown notable efficacy in capturing interactions in the medium range, making it a significant resource for jobs that need computing efficiency.

The GRU had the highest accuracy rate, which was 98.01%, beating out the LSTM model. GRU also had the highest performance in terms of specificity, sensitivity, and accuracy, with scores of 89.10%, 88.76%, and 89.98%, respectively, for each of these categories. The use of DL methods and RNNs on the information pertaining to disruptions in the food and medication supply chain has resulted in significant findings about the operational characteristics of these supply systems during the COVID-19 pandemic. In the field of sequential data analysis, the LSTM and GRU models have shown their significance in effectively capturing intricate sequential dependencies and establishing long-term connections within the given data.

The selection of a particular model is contingent upon the precise job at hand, the size of the dataset, and the computing resources that are at one's disposal. The fact that LSTM models can be used to manage long-term dependencies and GRU models can be used to capture medium-term interactions are both useful options for fixing supply chain problems. The integration of these methodologies offers decision-makers a comprehensive set of tools to strengthen the resilience of food and medication supply chains in response to unanticipated obstacles, such as the current global pandemic.

Figure 4. The findings of employed DL classifiers

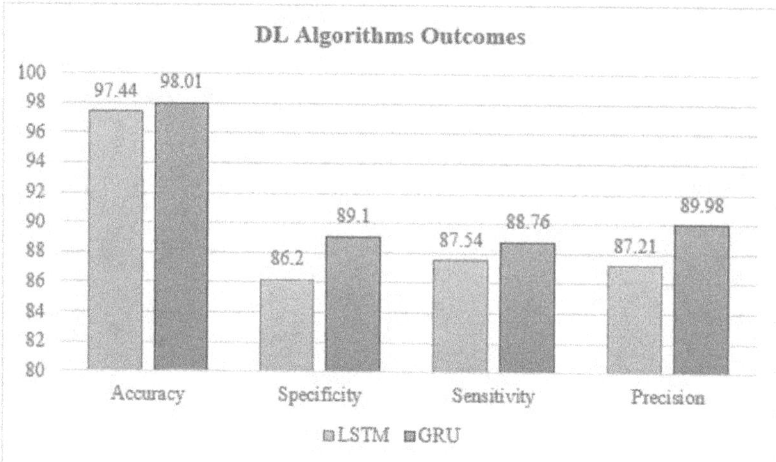

5. CONCLUSION

The complex architecture of supply chains, which span several phases from manufacturing to distribution, has shown their sensitivity to risks and disruptions. The worldwide turmoil caused by the COVID-19 pandemic provided as a vivid reminder of this vulnerability, with travel restrictions, border closures, and transportation delays substantially hampering the supply of crucial products, particularly medications and perishable food supplies. This chapter has examined the considerable disruptions to food and drug supply chains caused by pandemic-induced measures and panic-driven purchasing habits. It has emphasized the critical need of developing robust and adaptive supply chain solutions. As a consequence, businesses across sectors have been forced to rethink and strengthen their operational frameworks in order to assure the continuous supply of key goods during times of disaster. A variety of ML and DL methods, including models such as LSTM and GRU, were used to minimize the inherent hazards in supply chains. Among them, the GRU model stood out as the clear winner, with an excellent accuracy rate of 98.01% and superior performance in terms of specificity, sensitivity, and total accuracy. In the face of unprecedented disruptions like as the COVID-19 pandemic, decision-makers must adopt adaptive supply chain methods and stringent risk management standards. These preemptive actions are critical not only for mitigating supply chain vulnerabilities, but also for increasing resilience during tumultuous times, assuring the continuous supply of important goods to fulfill the global populace's needs. This study successfully proved the potential of ML and DL in resolving supply chain disruptions, providing useful insights for governments and industry stakeholders attempting to strengthen supply chain resilience in the face of emergencies. The research concludes by emphasizing the need for supply networks to proactively adapt to pandemic scenarios and implement comprehensive risk management measures to enhance resilience in times of uncertainty.

Abbreviations

Abbreviations	Description
ML	Machine Learning
DL	Deep Learning
KNN	K-Nearest Neighbors
SVM	Support Vector Machines
LSTM	Long Short-Term Memory
GRU	Gated Recurrent Unit
RNN	Recurrent Neural Network
ANN	Artificial Neural Network
SC	Supply Chain
DT	Decision Trees
RF	Random Forest
SCR	Supply Chain Resilience
GMP	Good Manufacturing Practice

REFERENCES

Ali, M., Haider, M. N., Lashari, S. A., Sharif, W., Khan, A., & Ramli, D. A. (2022). Stacking Classifier with Random Forest functioning as a Meta Classifier for Diabetes Diseases Classification. *Procedia Computer Science*, *207*, 3459–3468. doi:10.1016/j.procs.2022.09.404

Arief Daulay. (2023, June 3). Review of Literature on Improving the KNN Algorithm. *Transactions on Machine Learning and Artificial Intelligence*, *11*(3). Advance online publication. doi:10.14738/tecs.113.14768

Bassiouni, M. M., Chakrabortty, R. K., Hussain, O. K., & Rahman, H. F. (2023, January). Advanced deep learning approaches to predict supply chain risks under COVID-19 restrictions. *Expert Systems with Applications*, *211*, 118604. doi:10.1016/j.eswa.2022.118604 PMID:35999828

Bi, L., Fili, M., & Hu, G. (2022, May 31). COVID-19 forecasting and intervention planning using gated recurrent unit and evolutionary algorithm. *Neural Computing & Applications*, *34*(20), 17561–17579. doi:10.1007/s00521-022-07394-z PMID:35669538

Burstein, G., & Zuckerman, I. (2023, February 6). Deconstructing Risk Factors for Predicting Risk Assessment in Supply Chains Using Machine Learning. *Journal of Risk and Financial Management*, *16*(2), 97. doi:10.3390/jrfm16020097

Cano-Marin, E., Ribeiro-Soriano, D., Mardani, A., & Blanco Gonzalez-Tejero, C. (2023, September). Exploring the challenges of the COVID-19 vaccine supply chain using social media analytics: A global perspective. *Sustainable Technology and Entrepreneurship*, *2*(3), 100047. doi:10.1016/j.stae.2023.100047

Cavalcante, I. M., Frazzon, E. M., Forcellini, F. A., & Ivanov, D. (2019, December). A supervised machine learning approach to data-driven simulation of resilient supplier selection in digital manufacturing. *International Journal of Information Management*, *49*, 86–97. doi:10.1016/j.ijinfomgt.2019.03.004

Concern levels on possible drug supply chain disruption due to COVID-19 2020. (2020, April 8). Statista. https://www.statista.com/statistics/1110180/concern-on-drug-supply-chain-disruption-due-to-covid-19/

Craighead, C. W., Ketchen, D. J. Jr, & Darby, J. L. (2020). Pandemics and supply chain management research: Toward a theoretical toolbox. *Decision Sciences*, *51*(4), 838–866. doi:10.1111/deci.12468 PMID:34234384

Cundell, T., Guilfoyle, D., Kreil, T. R., & Sawant, A. (2020). Controls to Minimize Disruption of the Pharmaceutical Supply Chain During the COVID-19 Pandemic. *PDA Journal of Pharmaceutical Science and Technology*, *74*(4), 468–494. doi:10.5731/pdajpst.2020.012021 PMID:32467176

Data_Sheet_1_From Farm to Fork: Early Impacts of COVID-19 on Food Supply Chain.pdf. (2023, May 30). Figshare. https://figshare.com/articles/dataset/Data_Sheet_1_From_Farm_to_Fork_Early_Impacts_of_COVID-19_on_Food_Supply_Chain_pdf/16928122

Heydarbakian, S., & Spehri, M. (2022). Interpretable Machine Learning to Improve Supply Chain Resilience, An Industry 4.0 Recipe. *IFAC-PapersOnLine*, *55*(10), 2834–2839. doi:10.1016/j.ifacol.2022.10.160

Jassim, M. S., Coskuner, G., Sultana, N., & Hossain, S. Z. (2023, January). Forecasting domestic waste generation during successive COVID-19 lockdowns by Bidirectional LSTM super learner neural network. *Applied Soft Computing*, *133*, 109908. doi:10.1016/j.asoc.2022.109908

Kumar, S., & Kumar, H. (2023, December). Classification of COVID-19 X-ray images using transfer learning with visual geometrical groups and novel sequential convolutional neural networks. *MethodsX*, *11*, 102295. doi:10.1016/j.mex.2023.102295 PMID:37539339

Li, D., Zhi, B., Schoenherr, T., & Wang, X. (2023, March 28). Developing capabilities for supply chain resilience in a post-COVID world: A machine learning-based thematic analysis. *IISE Transactions*, *55*(12), 1256–1276. doi:10.1080/24725854.2023.2176951

Manzella, F., Pagliarini, G., Sciavicco, G., & Stan, I. (2023, March). The voice of COVID-19: Breath and cough recording classification with temporal decision trees and random forests. *Artificial Intelligence in Medicine*, *137*, 102486. doi:10.1016/j.artmed.2022.102486 PMID:36868683

Moosavi, J., Fathollahi-Fard, A. M., & Dulebenets, M. A. (2022, June). Supply chain disruption during the COVID-19 pandemic: Recognizing potential disruption management strategies. *International Journal of Disaster Risk Reduction*, *75*, 102983. doi:10.1016/j.ijdrr.2022.102983 PMID:35475018

Sangeetha, G. M., & Prashanth. (2015, July 1). Training the SVM to Larger Dataset Applications using the SVM Sampling Technique. *Indian Journal of Science and Technology*, *8*(15). Advance online publication. doi:10.17485/ijst/2015/v8i15/88281

TASNIM. (2020, June). Disruption in Global Food Supply Chain (FSCs) Due to Covid-19 Pandemic and Impact of Digitalization Through Block Chain Technology in FSCs Management. *European Journal of Business and Management*. Advance online publication. doi:10.7176/EJBM/12-17-08

Xu, W., Xiong, S., & Proverbs, D. (2022, February 17). Evaluating Agricultural Food Supply Chain Resilience in the Context of the COVID-19 Pandemic. *International Journal of Information Systems and Supply Chain Management*, *15*(1), 1–18. doi:10.4018/IJISSCM.287132

Chapter 10
Explainable Bayesian-Optimized XGBoost Model for Component Failure Detection in Predictive Maintenance

Hemant Kumar
https://orcid.org/0000-0003-0603-4394
Chhatrapati Shahu Ji Maharaj University, India

Krishna Kant Bhartiy
School of Entrepreneurship and Management, Harcourt Butler Technical University, India

Dharmesh Dhabliya
https://orcid.org/0000-0002-6340-2993
Department of Information Technology, Vishwakarma Institute of Information Technology, Pune, India

Rashi Agarwal
https://orcid.org/0000-0002-5768-5894
Harcourt Butler Technical University, India

Sunil Kumar
https://orcid.org/0000-0003-1103-513X
Chhatrapati Shahu Ji Maharaj University, India

Shivneet Tripathi
Chhatrapati Shahu Ji Maharaj University, India

ABSTRACT

This study employs predictive maintenance to enhance the Explainable XGBoost Model for predicting failures in industrial components. The research utilizes a model that employs the adaptive sliding window approach to extract features. The timeframe for this approach is set at 24 hours. This method leverages multi-device sensor data to extract the features. The BO-XGBoost model is assessed using accuracy, MCC, F1-Score, and G-mean. The measures achieved 99.87%, 0.988, 0.990, and 0.0989, respectively. The SHAP analysis method also identifies the characteristics of target variable prediction. The variable "rotatemean_24" is the most significant predictor. The model is easily understandable, aiding in comprehending relationships between features and outcomes. Therefore, it can assist in making decisions regarding predictive maintenance. Research has shown that implementing the optimized Explainable XGBoost Model can enhance factory maintenance efficiency and cost-effectiveness. The model's predictive capabilities enable proactive maintenance by identifying machine faults in advance.

DOI: 10.4018/979-8-3693-1347-3.ch010

1. INTRODUCTION

The advent of Industry 4.0 and the Industrial Internet of Things (IIoT) (Pramanik, S. et al., 2023) has transformed the operational landscape of businesses, highlighting the importance of data-driven decision-making and automation (Kumar Pandey, B. et al., 2021). The incorporation of machine learning (ML) algorithms has resulted in significant advancements in the domain of predictive maintenance (PdM) (Nunes et al., 2023). The primary goal of Predictive Maintenance (PdM) is to predict equipment malfunctions in advance, allowing for timely maintenance interventions and optimal resource allocation. Abidi et al. (2022) reported that this phenomenon reduces downtime, improves operational efficiency, and decreases maintenance costs.

PdM approaches are increasingly replacing traditional maintenance strategies like reactive maintenance and preventive maintenance (Hashemian & Bean, 2011). Predictive maintenance (PdM), also known as condition-based maintenance, involves generating maintenance recommendations by utilizing data acquired through condition monitoring, often in the form of time series data (Cheng et al., 2020). It is commonly defined by one of the following definitions: This study has two primary objectives: first, to identify and detect a problematic state in the monitored equipment that indicates an impending failure, and second, to estimate the remaining useful life (RUL) of the machine. The scientific literature includes two distinct approaches: diagnostics and prognostics. Equipment failure in manufacturing can result in significant financial losses due to downtime, negatively impacting productivity and profitability. Advancements in sensor technology (Iyyanar, P. et al., 2023), increased data accessibility (David, S. et al., 2023), and improved computing capabilities of machine learning algorithms have contributed to the development of more accurate and efficient predictive maintenance (PdM) solutions (Coandă et al., 2020).

Machine learning methods are frequently employed in predictive maintenance (PdM) to analyze large volumes of data (Babu, S. Z. D. et al., 2022) collected from various sensors (Anand, R. et al., 2022), such as vibration, temperature, and acoustic emission sensors. The aim is to detect data patterns and anomalies indicating potential equipment failure. Ayvaz and Alpay (2021) utilized different machine learning (ML) techniques, including supervised, unsupervised, and reinforcement learning, to create prediction models in the domain of prediction Maintenance (PdM).

Recent advancements in machine learning, specifically deep learning (Pandey, D. et al., 2021), have shown promising results in predictive maintenance (PdM). These methodologies have effectively handled complex and large datasets (Lee & Mitici, 2023; Liu et al., 2022). Machine learning (ML) has enhanced the capabilities of predictive maintenance (PdM) systems by integrating with advanced technologies like digital twin technology and edge computing (Panagou et al., 2022).

The use of machine learning algorithms has experienced a significant increase in predictive maintenance (B. Muniandi et al.,2019). This can be attributed to their ability to efficiently process large amounts of data and detect anomalies that may indicate the need for maintenance. Pagano (2023) conducted a recent study that introduced a novel deep-learning methodology (Pandey, B. K. et al., 2021) for predicting equipment's remaining usable life (RUL). The approach utilized a convolutional neural network (CNN) (Anand, R. et al.,2023) to extract features from time-series sensor (Kirubasri, G. et al., 2022) data. The extracted features were used as input for an LSTM network to predict the RUL. The authors incorporated an attention mechanism into the LSTM network to improve prediction accuracy by focusing on essential elements. The study's results showed that the proposed methodology outperformed several contemporary machine learning algorithms regarding prediction accuracy and robustness. Salim et al. (2022) developed a machine learning-based approach to predict the failure mode and estimate the remaining useful life of gearbox bearings. The researchers utilized a hybrid methodology that integrated genetic algorithms and assisted XGBoost in extracting relevant features from vibration signals. This approach was employed to classify fault modes effectively. The authors used dynamic time warping (DTW) to predict the Remaining Useful Life (RUL) in a time-series analysis approach. The results showed that the proposed methodology achieved high accuracy in fault classification and predicting the remaining useful life (RUL).

Panagou et al. (2022) recently conducted a study proposing a new methodology that utilizes digital twin technology for forecasting the remaining useful life of gas turbines. The researchers used machine learning to extract relevant features from the acquired sensor data. The extracted attributes were input for a digital twin model to predict the Remaining Useful Life (RUL). The results showed that the proposed methodology achieved high accuracy in predicting the Remaining Useful Life (RUL). Tang and Salonitis (2021) proposed a deep learning-based system (Pandey, B. K. et al.,2021) for detecting issues in induction motor bearings. The methodology utilized a hybrid model comprising a convolutional neural network (CNN) (Menon, V. et al., 2022) and an extended short-term memory network (LSTM) to extract and analyze time-series data obtained from the motor sensors. The results showed that the proposed methodology outperformed traditional machine learning methods regarding accuracy and resilience.

Implementing machine learning-based predictive maintenance (PdM) solutions poses significant challenges. Several factors can hinder the development of reliable prediction models, including data quality, sensor reliability, and the need for extensive training datasets (Lee et al., 2014). The interpretability and explainability of machine learning algorithms are crucial in predictive maintenance applications. Maintenance experts need a comprehensive understanding of the factors contributing to a forecast to make informed judgments (Gunning & Aha, 2019).

The main contributions of this paper can be summarized as follows:

1. Introduce the Adaptive Sliding Window Method (ASWM) for feature engineering, which dynamically selects the optimal window size and step size based on the dataset's underlying characteristics. Adapting to the data's temporal patterns, ASWM can generate more informative features than traditional fixed-window methods. Our approach helps to reduce the risk of overfitting and improves the model's ability to capture complex patterns in the data.
2. We propose integrating Bayesian optimization in the training process of XGBoost, a popular gradient-boosting decision tree algorithm. Optimizing the XGBoost model's hyperparameters through a guided search using Bayesian optimization, we achieve improved predictive performance compared to standard grid search or random search methods. This efficient search process significantly reduces the computational time required to identify optimal hyperparameter settings while maintaining or surpassing the model's performance.
3. To enhance the interpretability of our models and gain insights into the contribution of each feature to the predictions, we employ SHAP (SHapley Additive exPlanations) analysis. SHAP values provide a consistent and accurate measure of feature importance, enabling users to understand the impact of individual features on the model's output. By identifying the most influential features, we can further refine our feature engineering process and ensure that our models focus on the most relevant information (Bessant, Y. A. et al., 2023).

This research presents a thorough methodology for improving the predictive accuracy of machine learning models by employing advanced techniques in feature engineering, hyperparameter optimization, and feature importance analysis (Pandey, J. K. et al., 2022). Our methodology showcases substantial enhancements in model correctness, interpretability, and efficiency by integrating the Adaptive Sliding Window Method, XGBoost with Bayesian optimization, and SHAP analysis. As a result, our approach applies across diverse domains and to a wide array of applications.

2. PROPOSED METHODOLOGY

The framework that has been proposed can be observed in Figure 1. The PdM application is structured into four primary modules:

1. Data Preprocessing and Feature Engineering, which employs the Adaptive Sliding Window Method
2. Handling imbalanced class problems through the use of SMOTE-EEN
3. Utilizing an XGBoost model with Bayesian Optimization to classify whether the machine component has failed or not
4. Conducting Feature Importance analysis using SHAP analysis

Figure 1. Proposed methodology

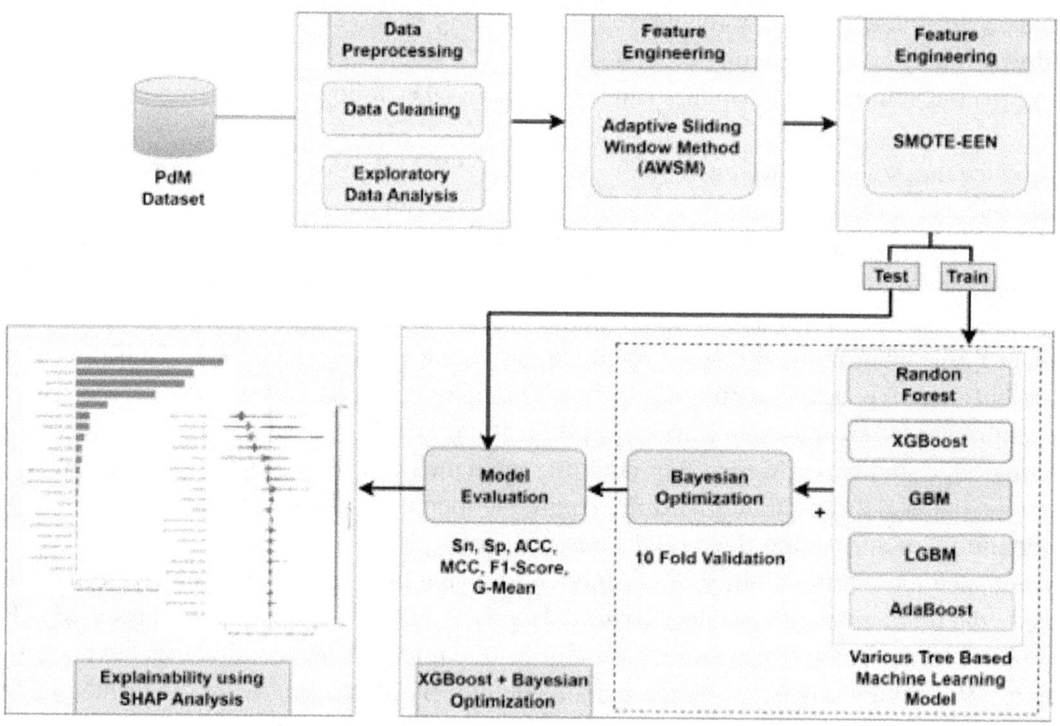

2.1 Data Preprocessing and Feature Extraction Using ASWM Method

Data preprocessing refers to preparing and cleaning raw data before it can be analyzed or used for modeling. This paper uses tasks such as missing values and normalizing or scaling data.

The mean imputation approach addresses missing values by substituting them with the mean value derived from the existing data.

$$Mean\ Imputation: \hat{x}_i = \frac{1}{n}\sum_{j=1}^{n} x_{ij} \tag{1}$$

where $\hat{x}_i$ is the imputed value for the missing data at index i, x_{ij} is the available data at index j for feature i, and n is the number of available data points.

Normalization is a technique used to standardize the range of data values, often within the interval of 0 to 1. Its purpose is to mitigate the influence of features with greater scales on the analytic process, so ensuring a more balanced evaluation.

$$Min - Max\ Normalization: x_{normalized} = \frac{x - x_{min}}{x_{max} - x_{min}} \tag{2}$$

where x is the original data point, x_{min} is the minimum value in the dataset, and x_{max} is the maximum value in the dataset.

2.1.1 Feature Extraction Using ASWM Method

Feature extraction is crucial in the analysis of time series or spatial data. It facilitates the identification and depiction of the most prominent attributes or trends in the data in a simplified manner. The adaptive sliding window approach is a dynamic method that adjusts the window size based on the characteristics of the data. Silva et al. (2016) demonstrated that this approach enables more accurate and localized feature extraction than traditional fixed-size sliding windows. In this section, we will explain the adaptive sliding window technique used for feature extraction in our study.

The adaptive sliding window approach involves moving a window of varying size across the dataset. The inherent qualities of the underlying data, such as the presence of edges, corners, or other conspicuous elements, determine the window size and location adjustment. The adaptability of this characteristic improves the identification of important attributes and enhances the effectiveness of analytical processes and machine learning (Ma et al., 2020). Algorithm 1 describes the use of Adaptive Sliding Window techniques in feature engineering.

This study utilized the adaptive sliding window method to extract features from the Telemetry dataset, which comprises time-series signals. The obtained features were then used to classify machine failure types.

Algorithm 1. Adaptive sliding window method for feature engineering

```
Input: Time series data X, window size range W_min to W_max, feature extraction function f()
Output: Feature vector F for entire time series
Initialization: empty feature vector F, i and j
for i = 1 to length(X) do
    W ← W_min
    while ( W ≤ W_min) do
        if ((i + W) > length(X)) then
            Break
        End
        Extract features from X[i: i + W] using f() and append to F
        If there is significant cahnge or spike in X[i: i + W] then
            W ← max(W_min, W/2)
        else if X[i: i + W] is relatively smooth then
            W ← min(2W, W_max)
        Else
            W ← min(W + 1, W_max)
        End
    End
End
Return F
```

2.2 XGBoost With Bayesian Optimization Model

2.2.1 XGBoost

XGBoost, a machine learning algorithm developed by Chen and Guestrin (2016), belongs to the gradient-boosting decision tree methods category. Tianqi Chen and Carlos Guestrin developed the aforementioned technology in 2016. Since its creation, it has gained considerable attention and recognition due to its impressive effectiveness in various machine learning competitions and real-world applications (M. K. Daoud,et al.,2023).

XGBoost, or eXtreme Gradient Boosting, is a machine learning algorithm that improves prediction accuracy by combining multiple weak models into more robust models. The method employs an iterative process in which decision trees are progressively integrated into the model. Each subsequent tree seeks to correct the errors made by the preceding trees. Iteratively improving underperforming models leads to developing a final model that exhibits robustness and accuracy. XGBoost offers a variety of adjustable hyperparameters that can be optimized to improve the model's performance. Key hyperparameters are the number of trees, learning rate, maximum tree depth, and minimum child node weight. Scholars have recently made progress in optimizing hyperparameters through grid and random search methodologies. XGBoost is a versatile and robust technique widely used in various domains for regression, classification, and ranking tasks. This framework effectively addresses complex machine learning challenges and handles large datasets with high dimensionality.

2.2.2 Bayesian Optimization Techniques

Bayesian optimization has been identified as a potent and versatile method for optimizing costly black-box functions, as demonstrated by Wang et al. (2023). A probabilistic model is employed to capture and represent the inherent uncertainty within the function effectively. Additionally, an acquisition function is employed to guide the exploration and identification of new spots during the search process. Bayesian optimization can quickly explore vast or intricate parameter spaces by iteratively selecting new issues to analyze, considering the trade-off between exploration and exploitation.

The Bayesian Optimization paradigm comprises two fundamental components:

1. Using a collection of observations, a probabilistic surrogate model is utilized to represent the probability distribution of the goal function.
2. An acquisition function is employed to direct the search for the minimal value of the objective function by effectively balancing the trade-off between exploration and exploitation.

In conclusion, Bayesian optimization is a robust technique for optimizing hyperparameters, enabling a proficient and successful exploration of the most suitable hyperparameters by employing a probabilistic model to direct the search procedure. Bayesian optimization has the potential to enhance model performance while simultaneously reducing the computational resources and time required to identify optimal hyperparameters.

2.2.3 BO-XGBoost Model

While XGBoost yields impressive results across several aspects, it does include some limitations. One such negative pertains to its multitude of parameters since different combinations of settings might lead to varying end scores. The Bayesian optimization approach yields exceptional outcomes and offers the optimal answer in searching algorithm parameters.

The Bayesian optimization process using XGBoost entails identifying a collection of hyperparameters that optimizes a selected performance measure, such as accuracy or mean squared error.

Objective function as follow:

$$f(\theta)=\mathbb{E}_{\mathcal{D}}\left[L(\theta;\mathcal{D})\right] \tag{3}$$

where $\mathcal{D}$ is the training data, **L** is the loss function of XGBoost with hyperparameters θ, and $\mathbb{E}_{\mathcal{D}}$ is the expectation over all possible training datasets.

Our study aims to identify the optimal collection of hyperparameters that optimizes the given objective function. Due to the high processing cost of assessing the objective function, a Gaussian process represents it as a sample drawn from a distribution. In this context, it is assumed that the objective function may be modeled as a Gaussian process, where the mean function is denoted as m(θ) and the covariance function is represented as $k\left(\theta,\theta'\right)$:

Table 1. List of XGBoost parameters

Parameter	Default	Description
Learning_rate	0.5	Shrinking the weight on each step
eta	0.5	Shrinking the weight on each step
Max_depth	3	Control over-fitting
lambda	1	L2 regularization term on weights
alpha	1	L1 regularization term on weights
Colsample_bytree	3	Column's fraction of random samples
Subsample	1	control the sample's proportion
Min_child_weight	5	Defines the minimum sum of weights

$$f(\theta) \sim \mathcal{GP}(m(\theta), k(\theta, \theta')) \tag{4}$$

The posterior distribution over f is updated as new data is observed by applying Bayes' rule to compute the posterior distribution based on the observed data $\mathcal{D}_n = (\theta_i, y_i)$:

$$p(f \mid \mathcal{D}_n) \propto p(\mathcal{D}_n \mid f)\, p(f) \tag{5}$$

where $p(\mathcal{D}_n|f)$ is the likelihood of the data given f, and p(f) is the prior distribution over f. Given the assumption that the likelihood follows a Gaussian distribution with additive noise,

$$p(\mathcal{D}_n \mid f) = \mathcal{N}(y \mid f, \sigma_n^2 I) \tag{6}$$

where $y = [y_1, \ldots, y_n]^T$ is the vector of observed performance metrics, $f = [f(\theta_1), \ldots, f(\theta_n)]^T$ is the vector of predicted values at the observed hyperparameters, and $\tilde{A}_n^2$ is the noise variance.

The posterior distribution over f, given the likelihood and prior, is also modeled as a Gaussian process:

$$f(\theta) \mid \mathcal{D}_n \sim \mathcal{N}(\mu_n(\theta), \sigma_n^2(\theta)) \tag{7}$$

The analytical computation of the posterior's mean function and covariance function can be performed.:

$$\mu_n(\theta) = m(\theta) + k(\theta)^T K_n^{-1} (y - m) \tag{8}$$

$$\sigma_n^2(\theta) = k(\theta, \theta') - k(\theta)^T K_n^{-1} k(\theta) \tag{9}$$

where K_n is the n×n matrix of pairwise covariances between the observed hyperparameters, k(θ) is the vector of covariance between the observed hyperparameters and the new hyper-parameter θ, and m= $[m(\theta_1),\ldots,m(\theta_n)]^T$ is the vector of mean predictions at the observed hyperparameters.

Our study employs an acquisition function to effectively manage the exploration-exploitation trade-off when choosing the subsequent set of hyperparameters for evaluation. The expected improvement (EI) is a frequently used acquisition function, which is defined as:

$$\mathrm{EI}\left(\theta\right) = \mathbb{E}\left[\max\left(0, y_{\min} - f\left(\theta\right)\right)\right] \tag{10}$$

where y_{min} is the best observed performance metric so far. The expected improvement would quantify the expected increase in performance if we were to evaluate the hyperparameters θ next.

The method of Bayesian optimization can be employed to optimize the acquisition function. During each iteration of Bayesian optimization, the hyperparameters that maximize the acquisition function are chosen. The performance of XGBoost with the selected hyperparameters is then evaluated on a validation set, and the resulting data is added to the observed data. The posterior distribution over f is subsequently updated based on the new data, and the process is iteratively repeated until convergence or until a maximum number of iterations is reached.

In summary, the process of Bayesian optimization with XGBoost entails modeling the objective function as a Gaussian process and the subsequent updating of the posterior distribution over the function as new data is observed. In order to evaluate and optimize the function, we employ an acquisition function to select the subsequent set of hyperparameters. This function is optimized using either gradient descent or Bayesian optimization methods. The accuracy and generalization of XGBoost models can be enhanced by selecting hyperparameters that maximize the performance metric.

2.3 SMOTE-ENN (Synthetic Minority Over-Sampling Technique-Edited Nearest Neighbors)

The present work employs the SMOTE-ENN (Synthetic Minority Over-sampling Technique - Edited Nearest Neighbors) approach, as proposed by Srivastava and Sharan (2022), to mitigate the problem of class imbalance in datasets. This method integrates the oversampling technique known as Synthetic Minority Over-sampling Technique (SMOTE) with the undersampling technique called Edited Nearest Neighbors (ENN).

The SMOTE-ENN technique initially employs the Synthetic Minority Over-sampling Technique (SMOTE) to the underrepresented class, thereby generating artificial instances to achieve a balanced distribution of data points within the dataset. Next, the ENN algorithm is employed on the resultant dataset to eliminate samples recognized as near samples belonging to the minority class. The application of this technique aids in the elimination of any samples containing noise inside the Synthetic Minority Over-sampling Technique (SMOTE), enhancing the overall balance of the dataset.

For a minority class instance xi, SMOTE selects k nearest neighbors from the same class, denoted as $N_{k(x_i)}$. It then generates a new instance x_{new} by randomly selecting a neighbor x_j from $N_{k(x_i)}$ and creating a synthetic instance as a linear combination of x_i and x_j:

$$x_{new} = x_i + \lambda \bullet (xj - xi_)$$ (11)

where λ is a random number between 0 and 1, the number of synthetic samples generated for each minority class instance can be adjusted using a user-defined parameter, which is typically set to be a multiple of the original number of minority class instances.

3.4 Feature Importance

The SHAP (SHapley Additive exPlanations) method, developed by Lundberg and Lee in 2017, is a very effective and extensively employed approach for evaluating the results generated by machine learning models. The process of attributing a model's prediction to the input features aids in the comprehension of the output generated by the model. SHAP values are derived from the principles of cooperative game theory and serve as a reliable metric for assessing the importance of features. These values ensure local correctness, consistency, and other desirable aspects.

Consider a hypothetical scenario in which we own a machine learning model that accepts an input vector x and generates an output y. The SHAP framework offers a methodology for elucidating the relationship between the output variable y and the input features by assigning attribution to each feature. The input features are $x_1, x_2, \ldots, x_n$.

The fundamental concept underlying SHAP is the utilization of Shapley values derived from cooperative game theory to quantify the individual contributions of each feature towards the outcome. The Shapley value is a measure that quantifies the average marginal contribution of a specific characteristic while considering all potential combinations of features. To compute the Shapley value for a feature x_i, we need to evaluate the model's output for all possible subsets of features that contain x_i. Let S be a subset of features that contains x_i. Then, we compute the output of the model for two cases: one where x_i is included in S and one where it is excluded. The difference between the two outputs represents the marginal contribution of x_i to the output when combined with the other features in S. We repeat this process for all possible subsets of features that contain x_i and compute the average of all marginal contributions. This gives us the Shapley value for x_i.

Formally, the Shapley value for x_i is defined as:

$$\varphi_i(x) = \sum_{S \subseteq x_1, x_2, \ldots, x_n \setminus x_i} \frac{\Phi(S \cup x_i) - \Phi(S)}{\binom{n-1}{|S|}}$$ (12)

where $\Phi(S)$ is the model's output when the features in S are present in the input, and $\binom{n-1}{|S|}$ is the number of ways to choose a subset S of size $|S|$ from the remaining $n-1$ features.

The SHAP values for each feature are subsequently computed by taking the disparities between the Shapley values and the mean Shapley value across all features. This process involves recentering the SHAP values around zero, which enhances their interpretability. The identification of the key characteristics in the model's decision-making process can be achieved by calculating the SHAP values corresponding to each input feature. Features with high positive SHAP values contribute positively to the output, whereas

Table 2. Dataset description

Datasets	*Explanation*
Telemetry	It includes hourly voltage, rotation, pressure, and vibration averages from 100 machines.
Error	Machine malfunctions, Non-shutdown errors are not failures, and Hourly telemetry data rounds inaccurate dates and hours to the closest hour.
Maintenance	Two circumstances change components: 1. The technician replaced it during the regular visit (Proactive Maintenance) 2. The technician replaces a part during unplanned Maintenance (Reactive Maintenance).
Failures	Each item replaces a failing component.

features with high negative SHAP values make a negative contribution. Features with SHAP values that are close to zero exhibit minimal or negligible influence on the outcome.

4. EXPERIMENTAL SETUPS

The PdM planning strategy, as presented, was executed on the Kaggle platform, employing an XGBoost model with Bayesian Optimization and an Adaptive sliding window approach. Microsoft supplied an example dataset for Azure Predictive Maintenance, which was utilized to evaluate the performance of the suggested model. This study evaluated the BO-XGBoost algorithm compared to a conventional machine learning model that utilized various optimization strategies. These techniques included Random Forest (Prihatno et al., 2021), XGBoost-metaheuristic (Salim et al., 2022), Light Gradient Boosting Machine (LGBM), and Gradient Boosting Decision Tree (GBDT).

4.1 Dataset

Table 2 displays a concise overview of the dataset, specifically the Microsoft Azure Predictive Maintenance Dataset, which is made available by Microsoft for Azure Predictive Maintenance. This study demonstrates the application of predictive maintenance using telemetry data obtained from real-world equipment. The collection consists of records documenting the maintenance history, failure reports, and several operational parameters, including temperature, vibration, and pressure. The information can be leveraged to predict equipment maintenance with Microsoft Azure's advanced machine learning algorithms and tools, including Azure Machine Learning and Azure Stream Analytics.

4.2 Evaluation Metric

We compared state-of-the-art tree-based machine learning algorithms based on their performance assessment measures. Sensitivity refers to the percentage of real positive values properly designated as data by the classifier and reflects the number of optimistic predictions successfully recognized by the classifier. The specificity is the classifier's ability to differentiate between negative results correctly. Accuracy is the proportion of occurrences properly categorized by a classifier.

$$Sensitivity\left(Sn\right) = \frac{T_P}{T_P + F_N} \tag{13}$$

$$Specificity\left(Sp\right) = \frac{T_N}{T_N + F_N} \tag{14}$$

$$Accuracy\left(ACC\right) = \frac{T_P + T_N}{T_P + F_P + T_N + F_N} \tag{15}$$

True-negative, true-positive, false-negative, and false-positive are represented by the T_N, T_P, F_N, and F_P, respectively. We employed different statistical measures like f1-score, recall, and precision statistics to evaluate the effectiveness of various algorithms.

These values are calculated using the following formulae.

$$Precision = \frac{T_P}{T_P + F_P} \tag{16}$$

$$Recall = \frac{T_P}{F_P + F_N} \tag{17}$$

$$F1 - Score = \frac{Precision * Recall}{Precision + Recall} * 2 \tag{18}$$

$$MCC = \frac{T_P * T_N - F_P * F_N}{\sqrt{(T_P + F_P)(T_P + F_N)(T_N + F_P)(T_N + F_N)}} \tag{19}$$

$$G - Mean = \sqrt{Sp * Sn} \tag{20}$$

MCC is a method for determining the correctness of binary and multi-class classifications. MCC is a correlation coefficient between -1 and +1. Precision is a relevant assessment measure, even more so when the proposed machine learning model must be validated using anticipated and actual results. It determines whether the proportion of positives expected is positive. The F1-score is a numeric value between 0 and 1, showing the statistical significance of the accuracy and recall measurements.

Table 3. Performance of ML model on training dataset using 10-fold cross-validation

ML Model	ACC(%)	Sn	Sp	MCC	F1-Score	G-Mean
XGBoost	99.06	0.988	0.982	0.973	0.986	0.984
GBDT	98.78	0.987	0.986	0.968	0.987	0.986
CatBoost	98.72	0.977	0.982	0.962	0.988	0.979
LGBM	98.49	0.981	0.984	0.963	0.972	0.982
RF	98.20	0.977	0.974	0.971	0.974	0.975

5. RESULTS AND DISCUSSION

This study presents two experimental studies conducted on the Microsoft PdM datasets. To begin, this study aims to evaluate the efficacy of XGBoost in conjunction with adaptive sliding window techniques for feature engineering, specifically in the context of SMOTE-EEN approaches. The performance of XGBoost will be compared to that of other machine learning algorithms. However, the second topic is to enhance the efficacy of the XGBoost method by utilizing Bayesian optimization algorithms (Ahmad, A. Y. B. et al.,2023).

5.1 Experiment 1: Performance Comparision of ML Models With XGBoost

This section investigates the performance of various classifiers, including GBDT, LGBM, Random Forest (RF), CatBoost, and XGboost. The classifiers are evaluated using their default hyperparameters and all available features. The features are extracted using adaptive sliding window methods. Additionally, the class imbalance problem is addressed using SMOTE-EEN methods. The evaluation will be conducted without making any adjustments to the hyperparameters.

According to the statistics presented in Table 3, the performance of the individual machine learning classifiers ranges from 98.20% to 99.05% in terms of accuracy. In the training dataset, XGBoost achieves the highest values for accuracy, sensitivity (Sn), specificity (Sp), Matthews correlation coefficient (MCC), F1-Score, and geometric mean (G-mean), yielding impressive scores of 99.06%, 0.988, 0.982, 0.973, 0.986, and 0.984, respectively. Gradient Boosting Decision Trees (GBDT), CatBoost, LightGBM (LGBM), and Random Forest (RF) occupy the positions of second, third, and fourth, respectively.

5.3 Experiment 2: Performance Comparision of ML Models With XGBoost Using Bayesian Optimization Techniques

The present study employed the Bayesian optimization technique to ascertain the most favorable settings for each learner. The outcomes and their default values are displayed in Table 4. The study also sought to evaluate the impact of these parameters on the model's performance by comparing the performance of persons who were instructed using default settings to those trained using optimal values (Ahmad, A. Y. B. et al.,2019).

Table 5 illustrates that, with the exception of Sp, the performance metrics of the individual learners exhibited higher values when instructed using optimal settings as opposed to default parameters. Despite the decrease in Sp values seen during parameter adjustment, both XGBoost and LGBM models consis-

Table 4. XGBoost parameters after Bayesian optimization

Parameter	Default	After Bayesian Optimization
Learning_rate	0.5	0.2
eta	0.1	0.025
Max_depth	3	8
lambda	1	2.905381578822584e-8
alpha	1	0.83
Colsample_bytree	1	0.40
Subsample	1	0.99
Min_child_weight	5	6

tently maintained Sp values over 0.99. Furthermore, after implementing the necessary modifications, there was a significant and noteworthy improvement in the overall academic achievement of both these individuals. XGBoost achieves the highest levels of accuracy, sensitivity (Sn), specificity (Sp), Matthews correlation coefficient (MCC), F1-Score, and geometric mean (G-mean), with impressive scores of 99.87%, 0.998, 0.981, 0.988, 0.99, and 0.989, respectively.

In our investigation, it has been observed that XGBoost exhibits superior performance compared to other tree-based models when default parameters are employed and when ideal parameters obtained by Bayesian Optimization are utilized. Figure 2 presents a performance comparison, showcasing the comparative analysis of XGBoost, BO-XGBoost, and other machine-learning models.

Explainability: According to Steurtewagen and Van den Poel (2021), the BO-XGBoost model has a high level of interpretability, enabling the extraction of valuable insights into the significance of various characteristics in the prediction process. The algorithm determines the significance of each characteristic by examining its inclusion in the decision tree construction process and the extent to which it contributes to error reduction. The findings are displayed in a horizontal bar chart, which only showcases the primary variables that hold the utmost significance in differentiating machine failure from the control group. The features are organized in a descending order, wherein the highest score denotes the feature of utmost significance. This methodology enables the identification of the most pertinent predictors for the target variable and facilitates the acquisition of insights on the underlying relationships between the features and the outcome. Based on the study conducted, it has been determined that the feature labeled

Table 5. Performance of ML model with optimal parameter (using Bayesian Optimization) on training dataset using 10-fold cross-validation

ML Model	*ACC(%)*	*Sn*	*Sp*	*MCC*	*F1-Score*	*G-Mean*
XGBoost	99.87	0.998	0.981	0.988	0.990	0.989
GBDT	99.70	0.993	0.986	0.971	0.989	0.989
CatBoost	99.68	0.986	0.982	0.968	0.989	0.983
LGBM	99.62	0.987	0.979	0.965	0.985	0.983
RF	99.23	0.984	0.974	0.973	0.982	0.979

Figure 2. Performance comparision of tree-based ML model

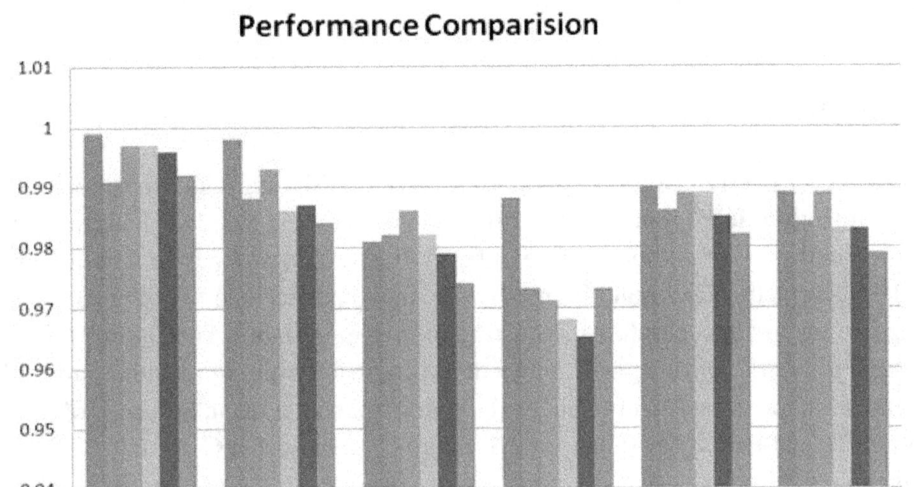

	ACC	Sn	Sp	MCC	F1-Score	G-Mean
BO-XGBoost	0.999	0.998	0.981	0.988	0.99	0.989
XGBoost	0.991	0.988	0.982	0.973	0.986	0.984
BO-GBDT	0.997	0.993	0.986	0.971	0.989	0.989
BO-CatBoost	0.997	0.986	0.982	0.968	0.989	0.983
BO-LGBM	0.996	0.987	0.979	0.965	0.985	0.983
BO-RF	0.992	0.984	0.974	0.973	0.982	0.979

Figure 3. Feature Importance using SHAP, (a) model's output, (b) model's output based on magnitude

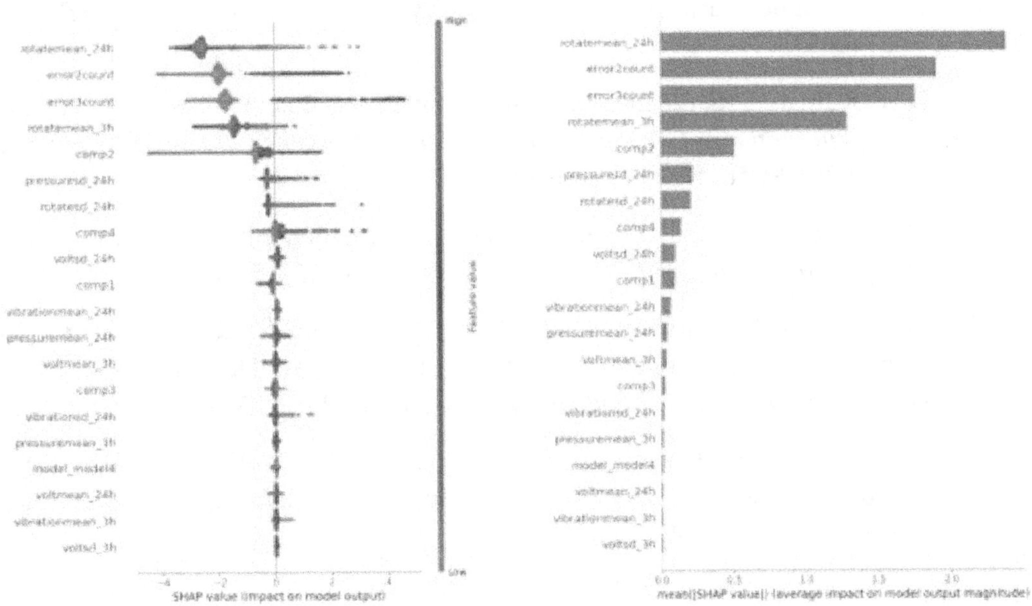

(a) (b)

as "rotatemean_24" holds significant importance as a predictor in accurately finding the target class across the entirety of the dataset.

6. CONCLUSION

In conclusion, the utilization of the Explainable XGBoost Model, which has been optimized through Bayesian Optimization, in conjunction with the adaptive sliding window feature extraction technique employing a window size of 24 hours, has exhibited remarkable efficacy in forecasting component failure within the manufacturing domain for predictive maintenance. The SHAP analysis was conducted to ascertain the key factors in accurately forecasting the target variable. The findings indicate that "rotatemean_24" emerged as the most significant predictor in differentiating machine failure from the control group. The model demonstrated a notable level of performance, with an accuracy of 99.87%, a Matthews correlation coefficient (MCC) of 0.988, an F1-Score of 0.99, and a G-mean of 0.0989. These metrics suggest that the model possesses solid predictive capabilities and can effectively forecast instances of machine breakdowns. In general, this model can enhance the efficacy and cost-efficiency of maintenance operations by providing timely alerts regarding potential machine failures. This enables proactive and prompt maintenance interventions. Additionally, the model generates interpretable outcomes, which can be utilized better to understand the connections between the features and the outcome.

REFERENCES

Abidi, M. H., Mohammed, M. K., & Alkhalefah, H. (2022, March 14). Predictive Maintenance Planning for Industry 4.0 Using Machine Learning for Sustainable Manufacturing. *Sustainability (Basel), 14*(6), 3387. doi:10.3390/su14063387

Ahmad, A. Y. A. B., & Kumari, S. S. (2023). Blockchain Implementation in Financial Sector and Cyber Security System. *2023 International Conference on Artificial Intelligence and Smart Communication (AISC),* 586-590. 10.1109/AISC56616.2023.10085045

Ahmad, A. Y. B. (2019). Empirical Analysis on Accounting Information System Usage in Banking Sector in Jordan. *Academy of Accounting and Financial Studies Journal, 23*(5), 1–9.

Ahmad, A. Y. B., Gongada, T. N., Shrivastava, G., Gabbi, R. S., Islam, S., & Nagaraju, K. (2023). E-Commerce Trend Analysis and Management for Industry 5.0 using User Data Analysis. *International Journal of Intelligent Systems and Applications in Engineering, 11*(11s), 135–150.

Anand, R., Khan, B., Nassa, V. K., Pandey, D., Dhabliya, D., Pandey, B. K., & Dadheech, P. (2023). Hybrid convolutional neural network (CNN) for Kennedy Space Center hyperspectral image. *Aerospace Systems, 6*(1), 71–78. doi:10.1007/s42401-022-00168-4

Anand, R., Singh, J., Pandey, D., Pandey, B. K., Nassa, V. K., & Pramanik, S. (2022). Modern technique for interactive communication in LEACH-based ad hoc wireless sensor network. In *Software Defined Networking for Ad Hoc Networks* (pp. 55–73). Springer International Publishing. doi:10.1007/978-3-030-91149-2_3

Ayvaz, S., & Alpay, K. (2021, July). Predictive maintenance system for production lines in manufacturing: A machine learning approach using IoT data in real-time. *Expert Systems with Applications, 173*, 114598. doi:10.1016/j.eswa.2021.114598

Babu, S. Z. D., Pandey, D., Naidu, G. T., Sumathi, S., Gupta, A., Bader Alazzam, M., & Pandey, B. K. (2022, July). Analysation of Big Data in Smart Healthcare. In *Artificial Intelligence on Medical Data: Proceedings of International Symposium, ISCMM 2021* (pp. 243-251). Singapore: Springer Nature Singapore.

Bessant, Y. A., Jency, J. G., Sagayam, K. M., Jone, A. A. A., Pandey, D., & Pandey, B. K. (2023). Improved parallel matrix multiplication using Strassen and Urdhvatiryagbhyam method. *CCF Transactions on High Performance Computing*, *5*(2), 1–14. doi:10.1007/s42514-023-00149-9

Chen, T., & Guestrin, C. (2016, August 13). XGBoost. *Proceedings of the 22nd ACM SIGKDD International Conference on Knowledge Discovery and Data Mining*. 10.1145/2939672.2939785

Cheng, J. C., Chen, W., Chen, K., & Wang, Q. (2020, April). Data-driven predictive maintenance planning framework for MEP components based on BIM and IoT using machine learning algorithms. *Automation in Construction, 112*, 103087. doi:10.1016/j.autcon.2020.103087

Coandă, P., Avram, M., & Constantin, V. (2020, December 1). A state of the art of predictive maintenance techniques. *IOP Conference Series. Materials Science and Engineering, 997*(1), 012039. doi:10.1088/1757-899X/997/1/012039

Daoud, Alqudah, Al-Qeed, Al Qaied, & Ahmad. (2023). The Relationship Between Mobile Marketing and Customer Perceptions in Jordanian Commercial Banks: The Electronic Quality as A Mediator Variable. *IJMST, 10*(2), 1360-1371.

Daoud, M. K., Al-Qeed, M., Ahmad, A. Y. B., & Al-Gasawneh, J. A. (2023). Mobile Marketing: Exploring the Efficacy of User-Centric Strategies for Enhanced Consumer Engagement and Conversion Rates. *International Journal of Membrane Science and Technology*, *10*(2), 1252–1262. doi:10.15379/ijmst.vi.1425

David, S., Duraipandian, K., Chandrasekaran, D., Pandey, D., Sindhwani, N., & Pandey, B. K. (2023). Impact of blockchain in healthcare system. In *Unleashing the Potentials of Blockchain Technology for Healthcare Industries* (pp. 37–57). Academic Press. doi:10.1016/B978-0-323-99481-1.00004-3

Gunning, D., & Aha, D. W. (2019, June). DARPA's Explainable Artificial Intelligence Program. *AI Magazine*, *40*(2), 44–58. doi:10.1609/aimag.v40i2.2850

Hashemian, H. M., & Bean, W. C. (2011, October). State-of-the-Art Predictive Maintenance Techniques*. *IEEE Transactions on Instrumentation and Measurement*, *60*(10), 3480–3492. doi:10.1109/TIM.2009.2036347

Iyyanar, P., Anand, R., Shanthi, T., Nassa, V. K., Pandey, B. K., George, A. S., & Pandey, D. (2023). A Real-Time Smart Sewage Cleaning UAV Assistance System Using IoT. In *Handbook of Research on Data-Driven Mathematical Modeling in Smart Cities* (pp. 24–39). IGI Global.

Kirubasri, G., Sankar, S., Pandey, D., Pandey, B. K., Nassa, V. K., & Dadheech, P. (2022). Software-defined networking-based Ad hoc networks routing protocols. In *Software defined networking for Ad Hoc networks* (pp. 95–123). Springer International Publishing. doi:10.1007/978-3-030-91149-2_5

Kumar Pandey, B., Pandey, D., Nassa, V. K., Ahmad, T., Singh, C., George, A. S., & Wakchaure, M. A. (2021). Encryption and steganography-based text extraction in IoT using the EWCTS optimizer. *Imaging Science Journal*, *69*(1-4), 38–56. doi:10.1080/13682199.2022.2146885

Lee, J., & Mitici, M. (2023, February). Deep reinforcement learning for predictive aircraft maintenance using probabilistic Remaining-Useful-Life prognostics. *Reliability Engineering & System Safety*, *230*, 108908. doi:10.1016/j.ress.2022.108908

Lee, J., Wu, F., Zhao, W., Ghaffari, M., Liao, L., & Siegel, D. (2014, January). Prognostics and health management design for rotary machinery systems—Reviews, methodology and applications. *Mechanical Systems and Signal Processing*, *42*(1–2), 314–334. doi:10.1016/j.ymssp.2013.06.004

Liu, C., Zhu, H., Tang, D., Nie, Q., Zhou, T., Wang, L., & Song, Y. (2022, October). Probing an intelligent predictive maintenance approach with deep learning and augmented reality for machine tools in IoT-enabled manufacturing. *Robotics and Computer-integrated Manufacturing*, *77*, 102357. doi:10.1016/j.rcim.2022.102357

Lundberg, S., & Lee, S. I. (2017, May 22). *A Unified Approach to Interpreting Model Predictions*. arXiv.org. https://arxiv.org/abs/1705.07874v2

Ma, C., Li, W., Cao, J., Du, J., Li, Q., & Gravina, R. (2020, January). Adaptive sliding window based activity recognition for assisted livings. *Information Fusion*, *53*, 55–65. doi:10.1016/j.inffus.2019.06.013

Menon, V., Pandey, D., Khosla, D., Kaur, M., Vashishtha, H. K., George, A. S., & Pandey, B. K. (2022). A Study on COVID–19, Its Origin, Phenomenon, Variants, and IoT-Based Framework to Detect the Presence of Coronavirus. In *IoT Based Smart Applications* (pp. 1–13). Springer International Publishing.

Microsoft Azure Predictive Maintenance. (n.d.). Microsoft Azure Predictive Maintenance | Kaggle. https:///datasets/arnabbiswas1/microsoft-azure-predictive-maintenance

Muniandi, B., Huang, C.-J., Kuo, C.-C., Yang, T.-F., Chen, K.-H., Lin, Y.-H., Lin, S.-R., & Tsai, T.-Y. (2019, November). A 97% Maximum Efficiency Fully Automated Control Turbo Boost Topology for Battery Chargers. *IEEE Transactions on Circuits and Systems. I, Regular Papers*, *66*(11), 4516–4527. doi:10.1109/TCSI.2019.2925374

Nunes, P., Santos, J., & Rocha, E. (2023, February). Challenges in predictive maintenance –A review. *CIRP Journal of Manufacturing Science and Technology*, *40*, 53–67. doi:10.1016/j.cirpj.2022.11.004

Pagano, D. (2023, March). A predictive maintenance model using Long Short-Term Memory Neural Networks and Bayesian inference. *Decision Analytics Journal*, *6*, 100174. doi:10.1016/j.dajour.2023.100174

Panagou, S., Fruggiero, F., Lerra, M., Vecchio, C. D., Menchetti, F., Piedimonte, L., Natale, O. R., & Passariello, S. (2022). Feature investigation with Digital Twin for predictive maintenance following a machine learning approach. *IFAC-PapersOnLine*, *55*(2), 132–137. doi:10.1016/j.ifacol.2022.04.182

Pandey, B. K., Pandey, D., Wariya, S., & Agarwal, G. (2021). A deep neural network-based approach for extracting textual images from deteriorate images. *EAI Endorsed Transactions on Industrial Networks and Intelligent Systems*, *8*(28), e3–e3. doi:10.4108/eai.17-9-2021.170961

Pandey, B. K., Pandey, D., Wariya, S., Aggarwal, G., & Rastogi, R. (2021). Deep learning and particle swarm optimisation-based techniques for visually impaired humans' text recognition and identification. *Augmented Human Research*, *6*(1), 1–14. doi:10.1007/s41133-021-00051-5

Pandey, D., Pandey, B. K., & Wairya, S. (2021). Hybrid deep neural network with adaptive galactic swarm optimization for text extraction from scene images. *Soft Computing*, *25*(2), 1563–1580. doi:10.1007/s00500-020-05245-4

Pandey, J. K., Jain, R., Dilip, R., Kumbhkar, M., Jaiswal, S., Pandey, B. K., & Pandey, D. (2022). Investigating Role of IoT in the Development of Smart Application for Security Enhancement. In *IoT Based Smart Applications* (pp. 219–243). Springer International Publishing.

Pramanik, S., Pandey, D., Joardar, S., Niranjanamurthy, M., Pandey, B. K., & Kaur, J. (2023, October). An overview of IoT privacy and security in smart cities. In AIP Conference Proceedings (Vol. 2495, No. 1). AIP Publishing. doi:10.1063/5.0123511

Prihatno, A. T., Nurcahyanto, H., & Jang, Y. M. (2021, April 13). Predictive Maintenance of Relative Humidity Using Random Forest Method. *2021 International Conference on Artificial Intelligence in Information and Communication (ICAIIC).* 10.1109/ICAIIC51459.2021.9415213

Salim, K., Hebri, R. S. A., & Besma, S. (2022, December 31). Classification Predictive Maintenance Using XGboost with Genetic Algorithm. *Revue D'Intelligence Artificielle*, *36*(6), 833–845. doi:10.18280/ria.360603

Silva, D. F., Batista, G. E. A. P. A., & Keogh, E. (2016, December). Prefix and Suffix Invariant Dynamic Time Warping. *2016 IEEE 16th International Conference on Data Mining (ICDM).* 10.1109/ICDM.2016.0161

SrivastavaJ.SharanA. (2022, July 5). *SMOTEEN Hybrid Sampling Based Improved Phishing Website Detection.* doi:10.36227/techrxiv.20207765.v1

Steurtewagen, B., & Van den Poel, D. (2021, September). Adding interpretability to predictive maintenance by machine learning on sensor data. *Computers & Chemical Engineering*, *152*, 107381. doi:10.1016/j.compchemeng.2021.107381

Tang, J., & Salonitis, K. (2021). A Deep Reinforcement Learning Based Scheduling Policy for Reconfigurable Manufacturing Systems. *Procedia CIRP*, *103*, 1–7. doi:10.1016/j.procir.2021.09.089

Wang, X., Jin, Y., Schmitt, S., & Olhofer, M. (2023, July 13). Recent Advances in Bayesian Optimization. *ACM Computing Surveys*, *55*(13s), 1–36. doi:10.1145/3582078

Chapter 11
Intelligent Physarum Solver for Profit Maximization in Oligopolistic Supply Chain Networks

Rakesh Verma
Department of Master of Business Administration, Gniot MBA Institute, India

M. Beulah Viji Christiana
Department of Management Studies, Panimalar Engineering College, India

M. Maheswari
Department of Computational Intelligence, School of Computing, SRM Institute of Science and Technology, India

Vellayan Srinivasan
Department of Master of Business Administration, S.A. Engineering College, India

Pramoda Patro
Department of Mathematics, Koneru Lakshmaiah Education Foundation, India

Sukhvinder Singh Dari
https://orcid.org/0000-0002-6218-6600
Symbiosis Law School, Symbiosis International University, Pune, India

Sampath Boopathi
https://orcid.org/0000-0002-2065-6539
Mechanical Engineering, Muthayammal Engineering College, India

ABSTRACT

This chapter discusses the use of an intelligent physarum solver (IPS) to optimize profit in oligopolistic supply chain networks. The IPS, inspired by the foraging behavior of the physarum polycephalum slime mold, addresses the challenges of resource allocation and profit distribution in oligopolistic markets. The chapter analyzes the IPS framework's effectiveness in modeling and optimizing various aspects of oligopolistic supply chains, including pricing strategies, production allocation, and distribution logistics. This research uses case studies and simulations to demonstrate how IPS can improve decision-making, foster cooperation among oligopolistic firms, and increase profitability in supply chain networks. It uses nature-inspired intelligence to provide practical solutions for businesses in oligopolistic environments, contributing valuable insights to supply chain management.

DOI: 10.4018/979-8-3693-1347-3.ch011

INTRODUCTION

In the dynamic landscape of modern business, supply chain networks play a pivotal role in ensuring the efficient flow of goods and services. Within this intricate web of suppliers, manufacturers, and distributors, one frequently encounters the oligopolistic market structure. Oligopolies, characterized by a small number of dominant firms, are prevalent in various industries, from telecommunications to automotive manufacturing and pharmaceuticals. While these markets offer certain advantages such as economies of scale and innovation, they also pose complex challenges related to resource allocation, pricing strategies, and profit maximization (Silveira & Vasconcelos, 2020). The quest for optimal decision-making in oligopolistic supply chains has driven researchers and practitioners to explore innovative methodologies, seeking solutions that transcend traditional paradigms. The chapter introduces the Intelligent Physarum Solver (IPS), a promising approach based on the remarkable foraging behavior of the Physarum polycephalum slime mold. The IPS harnesses the power of nature-inspired optimization to address the multifaceted challenges posed by oligopolistic supply chain networks (Awad et al., 2023). This chapter explores the complexities of oligopolistic markets and their challenges, highlighting the potential of the Intelligent Supply Chain (IPS) framework, based on natural intelligence principles, to revolutionize supply chain modeling, analysis, and optimization within such markets. It provides a comprehensive understanding of its mathematical foundations, parameters, and objectives (Chu et al., 2021).

The IPS, through practical applications, offers innovative solutions for profit maximization, such as competitive pricing strategies, production allocation optimization, and distribution logistics, enabling firms to navigate the intricate dynamics of oligopolistic environments, as demonstrated through case studies and simulations (Hua et al., 2021). The IPS not only improves decision-making processes but also promotes cooperation among oligopolistic firms, aiming to enhance the profitability of supply chain networks and contribute to the overall success of participating firms by emphasizing collaboration and efficiency (Gao et al., 2019). This chapter explores the potential of nature-inspired intelligence in transforming supply chain management in oligopolistic markets. It explores novel methodologies and practical applications that could reshape the future of profit maximization in supply chain networks.

Background and Motivation

Oligopolistic Supply Chains: Navigating the Complex Terrain

Supply chain networks serve as the lifeblood of modern commerce, ensuring that products and services reach consumers efficiently and reliably. Within this sprawling ecosystem, various market structures exist, each with its own set of challenges and opportunities. One such structure is the oligopoly—a market characterized by a limited number of dominant firms that wield significant influence over pricing, production, and market dynamics (Yu et al., 2022).

Oligopolies are prevalent across industries ranging from telecommunications and automotive manufacturing to pharmaceuticals and consumer electronics. In these markets, a small number of key players dictate the rules of engagement, often leading to intricate power struggles and strategic maneuvering. While oligopolistic firms can benefit from economies of scale and innovation, they are also confronted with unique dilemmas, particularly in the realm of supply chain management (Zhang et al., 2020).

The complexities of oligopolistic supply chains stem from the interplay of competition and cooperation among a select few firms. Decision-making becomes a delicate balance of vying for market share while ensuring the viability of the entire network. Questions related to pricing, production allocation, and distribution logistics become paramount (Silveira & Vasconcelos, 2020). How can these firms maximize their collective profitability while avoiding costly conflicts? What strategies can foster cooperation in an inherently competitive environment? These questions underscore the need for innovative approaches to optimize oligopolistic supply chains.

Inspiration from Nature: The Physarum Polycephalum

In nature, solutions to complex optimization problems often emerge from the most unexpected sources. One such source is the Physarum polycephalum, a humble yet fascinating slime mold. Despite its simple biological structure, this organism exhibits remarkable foraging behavior that has captured the attention of scientists and researchers worldwide (Chu et al., 2021; Hua et al., 2021). Physarum polycephalum, often referred to as the "many-headed slime," possesses an uncanny ability to find optimal paths between food sources while simultaneously optimizing its internal transport network. This natural intelligence has inspired a growing field of research known as bio-inspired optimization. By mimicking the behavior of this simple organism, researchers have developed algorithms and computational models that excel in solving complex optimization problems, often outperforming traditional methods.

Motivation for the Intelligent Physarum Solver (IPS)

The motivation behind this chapter lies in the intersection of oligopolistic supply chain management and bio-inspired optimization. The Intelligent Physarum Solver (IPS) is a novel approach to tackle the challenges faced by firms in oligopolistic markets, utilizing nature-inspired intelligence. The IPS framework offers a fresh perspective on modeling, analyzing, and optimizing oligopolistic supply chains. By leveraging the principles of natural intelligence, it seeks to revolutionize decision-making processes within these complex networks. Through the application of the IPS, firms operating in oligopolistic environments can potentially enhance their profitability, foster cooperation, and navigate the intricate dynamics of supply chain management more effectively (Gao et al., 2019; Nagurney et al., 2019; Yu et al., 2022). The IPS framework, with its mathematical foundations and practical applications, can be used to unlock new possibilities in supply chain optimization. This chapter explores the synergy between oligopolistic supply chains and the intelligence of the Physarum polycephalum, providing a fresh perspective on profit maximization in a challenging market.

Objectives of the Chapter

- Explain the concept of nature-inspired optimization and its potential applications in addressing complex problems within oligopolistic supply chains.
- Introduce the IPS framework as a nature-inspired algorithm for optimizing profit maximization in oligopolistic supply chain networks.
- Delve into the mathematical foundations of IPS, including its parameters, variables, and objective functions, to offer a comprehensive understanding of its framework.
- Showcase a range of practical applications of the IPS, including its use in devising pricing strategies, optimizing production allocation, and improving distribution logistics.

- Provide real-world examples through case studies and simulations to demonstrate the effectiveness and benefits of applying the IPS in solving specific supply chain optimization problems.
- Analyze and discuss the results obtained from IPS applications, emphasizing the implications for decision-making and profitability in oligopolistic supply chains.

OLIGOPOLISTIC SUPPLY CHAIN NETWORKS

Characteristics of Oligopolistic Markets

Oligopolistic markets are a distinct subset of market structures characterized by a few dominant firms that hold a substantial share of the market (Figure 1). Within these markets, competition is intense, yet the actions of one firm significantly impact the strategies and decisions of others. Oligopolistic supply chain networks exhibit several key characteristics that set them apart from other market structures (Ma et al., 2021; Sun et al., 2021; Wang et al., 2021):

- **Few Dominant Firms**: Oligopolies are defined by a small number of prominent firms, often just a handful, that collectively control a significant portion of the market. These firms are typically large, well-established, and have substantial market power.
- **Interdependence**: One of the defining features of oligopolistic markets is the interdependence among firms. Each firm's actions, whether in terms of pricing, production, or strategic decisions, directly affect the profits and strategies of its competitors. This interdependence often leads to complex strategic interactions.

Figure 1. Characteristics of oligopolistic markets

- **Strategic Behavior**: Oligopolistic firms engage in strategic behavior to gain a competitive edge. This can involve pricing strategies such as price leadership, price collusion, or even price wars. Firms may also invest heavily in research and development to innovate and differentiate themselves.
- **Barriers to Entry**: Oligopolistic markets tend to have significant barriers to entry, making it challenging for new firms to enter and compete effectively. These barriers can include high capital requirements, economies of scale, and strong brand loyalty.
- **Product Differentiation**: In many oligopolistic industries, firms engage in product differentiation to create unique offerings that set them apart from competitors. This can include branding, product features, or marketing strategies.
- **Non-Price Competition**: While price competition is certainly a factor, oligopolistic firms often engage in non-price competition as well. This can involve advertising, quality improvements, and customer service enhancements (Dhanya et al., 2023; Mohanty et al., 2023; Ravisankar et al., 2023).
- **Strategic Alliances**: Oligopolistic firms may form strategic alliances or partnerships to strengthen their positions in the market. These alliances can take various forms, including joint ventures and cooperative agreements.
- **Complex Supply Chains**: Due to their size and market dominance, oligopolistic firms often have complex supply chain networks. These networks can span multiple regions and involve various suppliers, manufacturers, and distributors.
- **Regulatory Scrutiny**: Because of their market power and potential for anti-competitive behavior, oligopolistic firms are often subject to regulatory scrutiny. Governments may impose regulations to ensure fair competition and protect consumer interests.
- **Profit Maximization**: Oligopolistic firms are primarily focused on profit maximization. They constantly seek ways to increase their profitability while considering the actions and reactions of their competitors.

Understanding these characteristics is essential for effectively managing supply chain networks within oligopolistic markets. The interplay between these features presents both challenges and opportunities, making it crucial for firms to adopt innovative strategies and decision-making approaches, such as the Intelligent Physarum Solver (IPS), to navigate this complex terrain and maximize their profitability.

Challenges in Supply Chain Optimization

Optimizing supply chain networks is a multifaceted endeavor, and within the context of oligopolistic markets, it presents several unique challenges (Selwyn & Leyden, 2022; Silveira & Vasconcelos, 2020; Zhang et al., 2020):

- **Interdependent Decision-Making**: Oligopolistic firms must make decisions that consider the actions and reactions of their competitors. For example, when setting prices or production quantities, each firm's choice affects the overall market dynamics, making decision-making more complex.
- **Strategic Pricing**: Determining the right pricing strategy in an oligopolistic supply chain is challenging. Firms must balance the desire to maximize profits with the need to remain competitive. Price wars can lead to diminished profits for all firms.

- **Production Allocation**: Allocating production resources efficiently is essential in supply chain optimization. In oligopolistic markets, firms often engage in strategic behavior to gain a larger share of production, potentially leading to resource underutilization or overallocation.
- **Distribution Logistics**: Coordinating distribution logistics becomes intricate when multiple dominant firms are involved. Decisions related to transportation, warehousing, and inventory management must account for the strategic goals of each firm (Boopathi, Pandey, et al., 2023; Boopathi, Sureshkumar, et al., 2022; Kumara et al., 2023; Nishanth et al., 2023; Samikannu et al., 2022; Vanitha et al., 2023).
- **Cooperation and Trust**: Building cooperation and trust among oligopolistic firms can be challenging due to competitive pressures. However, without cooperation, supply chain inefficiencies can arise, negatively impacting overall profitability.
- **Information Asymmetry**: Information-sharing among firms can be limited in oligopolistic markets due to concerns about revealing strategic plans. This can hinder collaborative efforts and lead to suboptimal outcomes.
- **Regulatory Constraints**: Oligopolistic firms may face regulatory constraints aimed at preventing anti-competitive behavior. Compliance with these regulations can be complex and costly.

Importance of Profit Maximization

Profit maximization is a fundamental objective for firms in any market structure, but it holds particular significance in oligopolistic supply chain networks:

- **Sustainable Growth**: Profit maximization is essential for a firm's sustainable growth and long-term survival. In oligopolistic markets, where competition is fierce, maintaining profitability is crucial to withstand competitive pressures (Babu et al., 2022; Ugandar et al., 2023; Venkateswaran et al., 2023).
- **Resource Allocation**: Maximizing profits helps firms allocate resources efficiently. This includes optimizing investments in production, technology, and supply chain infrastructure to enhance operational efficiency.
- **Market Leadership**: Profitable firms in oligopolistic markets are often seen as market leaders. High profitability can attract investors, strengthen a firm's position, and provide opportunities for expansion.
- **Innovation and R&D**: Profitability enables firms to invest in research and development (R&D) and innovation. In oligopolistic markets, innovation can be a key driver of competitiveness and market share.
- **Competitive Advantage**: Profit-maximizing firms can gain a competitive advantage by reinvesting in their supply chain, technology, and customer service. This advantage can help them maintain or expand their market share.
- **Risk Mitigation**: A strong focus on profit maximization allows firms to build financial reserves, which can be crucial for mitigating risks and navigating market uncertainties.
- **Shareholder Value**: Maximizing profits is often closely tied to enhancing shareholder value. Strong profitability can lead to higher stock prices and dividends, benefiting both investors and the firm.

- **Cooperative Potential**: In some cases, profit maximization can be a catalyst for cooperation among oligopolistic firms. When firms see the potential for mutual benefit, they may be more willing to collaborate in pursuit of profit.

In oligopolistic supply chain networks, profit maximization is not only a financial objective but also a strategic imperative. Effective supply chain optimization, aided by innovative approaches like the Intelligent Physarum Solver (IPS), is essential for achieving this goal while navigating the unique challenges of oligopolistic markets (Boopathi, Hari balaji, et al., 2022; Gunasekaran et al., 2022; Kumar et al., 2023; Yupapin et al., 2023).

NATURE-INSPIRED OPTIMIZATION

Nature-Inspired Optimization

Nature has long served as a wellspring of inspiration for solving complex problems. From the flocking behavior of birds to the genetic algorithms inspired by natural selection, nature's intricate designs have often yielded efficient and effective solutions. In the realm of optimization, nature-inspired algorithms have gained prominence as powerful tools for tackling intricate challenges. One such source of inspiration is the humble organism known as Physarum polycephalum, or the "many-headed slime mold." This chapter explores the application of nature-inspired optimization through the Intelligent Physarum Solver (IPS) in the context of oligopolistic supply chain networks (Weersink & Fulton, 2020).

The Physarum Polycephalum and Its Foraging Behavior

Physarum polycephalum, a simple yet astonishing organism, exhibits extraordinary foraging behavior that has captivated scientists for years. This unicellular, yellowish slime mold thrives in dark and damp environments, such as forests and decaying logs. Its foraging behavior is a testament to the ingenuity of nature, as it navigates mazes, solves complex spatial problems, and optimizes nutrient uptake networks (Yuan & Zhou, 2020). Physarum polycephalum creates efficient networks for nutrient transport by forming tubular structures that connect food sources, adapting its network to changing conditions, and optimizing its transport routes. This remarkable adaptability and optimization capability have inspired researchers to explore how such natural intelligence can be harnessed for solving complex optimization problems.

Introduction to Intelligent Physarum Solver (IPS)

The Intelligent Physarum Solver (IPS) is a computational framework inspired by the foraging behavior of Physarum polycephalum. IPS leverages the organism's ability to create efficient networks to address complex optimization challenges. This chapter introduces IPS as an innovative approach for optimizing profit maximization in oligopolistic supply chain networks (Yang, 2020). IPS uses principles derived from the slime mold's behavior to model and solve supply chain problems. It incorporates adaptive network formation, decentralized decision-making, and optimization techniques to find solutions that balance the conflicting objectives of profit maximization and cooperation among firms in oligopolistic markets. By mimicking the decentralized, nature-inspired approach of the slime mold, IPS offers a fresh perspective on optimizing supply chains within these intricate market structures.

Advantages of Nature-Inspired Algorithms in Supply Chain Optimization

Nature-inspired algorithms, such as IPS, offer several advantages when applied to supply chain optimization in oligopolistic markets (Chopra & Ansari, 2022):

- **Robustness**: Nature-inspired algorithms are inherently robust and adaptable, making them suitable for dynamic and uncertain supply chain environments.
- **Parallel Processing**: These algorithms often operate with parallel processing, enabling the exploration of multiple solution paths simultaneously, leading to faster convergence.
- **Global Optimization**: Nature-inspired algorithms have the potential to find global optima by exploring a wide solution space, mitigating the risk of getting stuck in local optima.
- **Decentralized Decision-Making**: In oligopolistic supply chains, decentralized decision-making is critical for cooperation and avoiding conflicts. Nature-inspired algorithms inherently support decentralized approaches.
- **Scalability**: These algorithms can scale to handle large and complex supply chain networks, a common characteristic of oligopolistic markets.
- **Adaptability**: Nature-inspired algorithms adapt to changing conditions and can continuously optimize supply chain operations.

Incorporating the advantages of nature-inspired algorithms like IPS into supply chain management can lead to more efficient and cooperative operations, ultimately enhancing profitability within oligopolistic supply chain networks.

MODELING OLIGOPOLISTIC SUPPLY CHAINS WITH IPS

Oligopolistic supply chains present intricate challenges that require innovative approaches for effective modeling and optimization. The Intelligent Physarum Solver (IPS) offers a novel and nature-inspired framework to tackle these complexities, enabling a deeper understanding of how to navigate the dynamics of oligopolistic markets (Figure 2). This section explores the fundamental aspects of modeling oligopolistic supply chains using IPS, including its mathematical foundations, parameters, and objectives (Coe & Yang, 2022; Mostofi, 2022).

Mathematical Framework

The modeling process begins with establishing a mathematical framework that captures the essential elements of the oligopolistic supply chain network (Palaniappan et al., 2023; Senthil et al., 2023). This framework typically comprises the following components:

Figure 2. Modeling oligopolistic supply chains with IPS

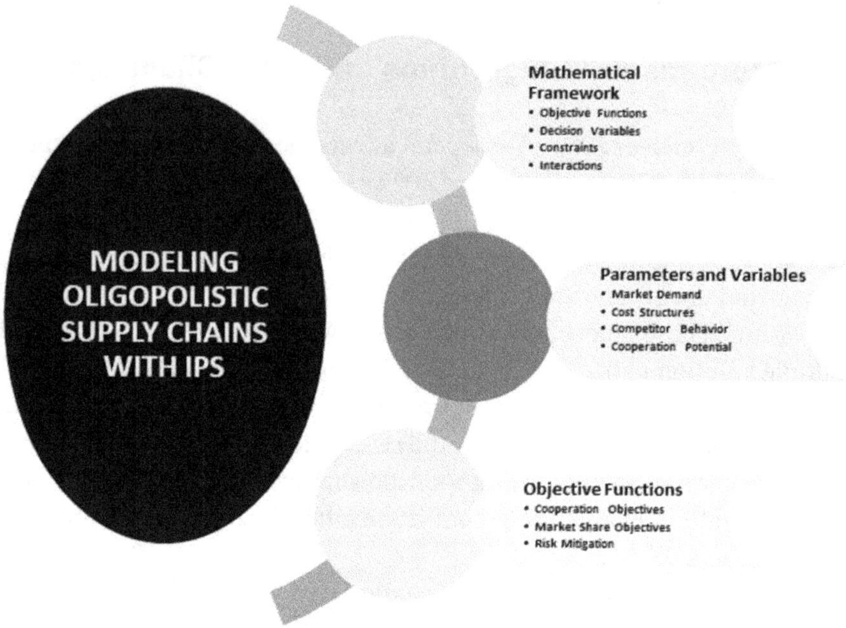

- **Decision Variables**: These variables represent the choices made by each firm within the supply chain network. Examples include pricing decisions, production quantities, allocation of resources, and distribution logistics.
- **Objective Functions**: Objective functions define the goals and objectives of the firms involved. In the context of IPS, the primary objective is typically profit maximization. However, additional objectives related to cooperation and market share may also be considered.
- **Constraints**: Constraints encompass the limitations and restrictions within the supply chain. These can include capacity constraints, regulatory requirements, demand fluctuations, and cost constraints.
- **Interactions**: Interactions among firms are essential to capture the interdependence in oligopolistic markets. These interactions can take the form of game-theoretic models, where each firm's decisions are influenced by the expected responses of competitors.

Parameters and Variables

In modeling oligopolistic supply chains with IPS, it's crucial to define relevant parameters and variables (Boopathi, 2019; Boopathi et al., 2017; Boopathi & Sivakumar, 2013, 2016; Kalidas et al., 2012) that feed into the mathematical framework(Mostofi, 2022). These include:

- **Market Demand**: Understanding market demand is essential as it influences pricing decisions and production allocations. Market demand can vary seasonally or due to external factors.

- **Cost Structures**: Each firm's cost structure, including production costs, transportation costs, and other operating expenses, must be accurately represented to optimize profit.
- **Competitor Behavior**: IPS models should consider competitor behavior and reactions. This entails modeling how competitors may adjust their strategies in response to changes made by one firm.
- **Cooperation Potential**: Parameters related to cooperation potential among firms should be defined. These can include willingness to collaborate, negotiation capabilities, and incentives for cooperative behavior.

Objective Functions

The primary objective in modeling oligopolistic supply chains with IPS is typically profit maximization (Boopathi et al., 2021; Gowri et al., 2023; Sathish et al., 2023). However, additional objectives may be incorporated to address specific market dynamics. For instance:

- **Cooperation Objectives**: To promote cooperation among firms, objective functions may be designed to encourage mutually beneficial outcomes, fostering a more cooperative oligopolistic environment.
- **Market Share Objectives**: Firms may have objectives related to market share, aiming to gain a larger portion of the market while optimizing profit.
- **Risk Mitigation**: Some objective functions may consider risk mitigation as a goal, especially in volatile markets. This can involve optimizing production and inventory to reduce supply chain risks.

By carefully formulating the mathematical framework, defining relevant parameters and variables, and establishing appropriate objective functions, modeling oligopolistic supply chains with IPS becomes a powerful tool for decision-making and optimization. The ability to adapt to changing conditions and mimic the cooperative and adaptive nature of the Physarum polycephalum slime mold makes IPS a valuable approach for enhancing profitability and cooperation within these complex supply chain networks.

APPLICATIONS OF IPS IN PROFIT MAXIMIZATION

The Intelligent Physarum Solver (IPS) offers a unique and nature-inspired approach to optimizing profit maximization in oligopolistic supply chain networks (Figure 3). Its adaptability and ability to mimic the cooperative behavior of the Physarum polycephalum slime mold make it a valuable tool for addressing various facets of profit optimization in these complex market structures (Coe & Yang, 2022; Mostofi, 2022). Below are key areas where IPS can be applied to enhance profitability:

Pricing Strategies in Oligopolistic Markets

- *Price Competition*: IPS can model and optimize pricing strategies, helping firms strike a balance between competitive pricing and profitability. It considers how price changes by one firm may impact the others and adjusts pricing accordingly.

Figure 3. Applications of IPS in profit maximization

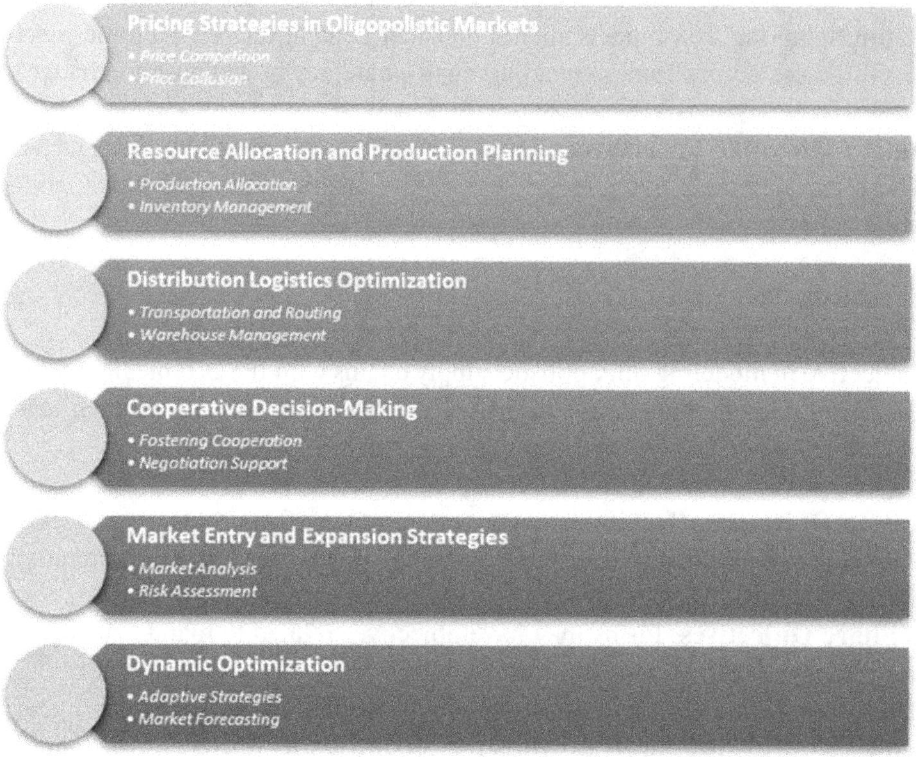

- *Price Collusion*: In markets where collusion is a concern, IPS can help firms detect and prevent anti-competitive behavior by monitoring pricing decisions and ensuring compliance with regulations.

Resource Allocation and Production Planning

- *Production Allocation*: IPS can assist firms in allocating production resources efficiently. It optimizes production quantities among firms to maximize collective profit while considering capacity constraints and market demand (Myilsamy Sureshkumar, 2018; Vennila et al., 2022).
- *Inventory Management*: IPS helps optimize inventory levels to reduce carrying costs while ensuring products are readily available to meet customer demand.

Distribution Logistics Optimization

- *Transportation and Routing*: IPS aids in optimizing transportation routes and distribution logistics, minimizing transportation costs while ensuring timely delivery to customers.
- *Warehouse Management*: It optimizes warehouse operations, including storage allocation, order picking, and replenishment strategies.

Cooperative Decision-Making

- *Fostering Cooperation*: IPS can encourage cooperation among oligopolistic firms by identifying mutually beneficial opportunities and recommending strategies that lead to win-win outcomes.
- *Negotiation Support*: In scenarios involving negotiations among firms, IPS can provide decision-support tools that facilitate productive discussions and cooperative agreements.

Market Entry and Expansion Strategies

- *Market Analysis*: IPS can analyze market entry and expansion strategies, evaluating the potential profitability of entering new markets or launching new product lines.
- *Risk Assessment*: It assists in evaluating the risks associated with various market strategies and recommends actions to mitigate those risks.

Dynamic Optimization

- *Adaptive Strategies*: IPS adapts to changing market conditions in real-time, allowing firms to make dynamic decisions that maximize profit under evolving circumstances.
- *Market Forecasting*: It can incorporate market forecasting models to anticipate shifts in demand and adjust strategies accordingly.

These applications demonstrate the versatility and effectiveness of IPS in addressing the unique challenges posed by oligopolistic supply chain networks. By harnessing nature-inspired intelligence, IPS empowers firms to make data-driven, adaptive decisions that not only maximize individual profits but also contribute to the overall profitability and sustainability of supply chain networks operating within oligopolistic markets.

CASE STUDIES AND SIMULATIONS

Case Study 1: Price Competition in an Oligopoly

Scenario: In a highly competitive oligopolistic market, three dominant firms for market share in the electronics industry. Each firm produces similar products and regularly engages in price competition to attract customers. However, the challenge lies in finding the right pricing strategy to maximize profit while maintaining a competitive edge (Hall et al., 2020; Mostofi, 2022).

Application of IPS: IPS is employed to model and optimize the pricing strategies of firms. The simulation considers the interdependent nature of pricing decisions, where each firm's pricing choice affects its own profit as well as the profits of its competitors.

Results: IPS identifies the optimal pricing strategies for each firm, factoring in market demand, production costs, and the expected reactions of competitors. The simulation demonstrates that by using IPS, firms can achieve a higher collective profit compared to conventional pricing strategies. Additionally, it highlights scenarios where cooperative pricing strategies, rather than aggressive price competition, can lead to increased overall profitability in the oligopolistic market.

Case Study 2: Cooperative Production Allocation

Scenario: In an oligopolistic supply chain network involving several manufacturers, there's an opportunity for cooperation to optimize production allocation. Firms face the challenge of coordinating their production processes while maximizing individual profit (Wardell et al., 2021).

Application of IPS: IPS is utilized to model and optimize production allocation decisions among the firms. The simulation incorporates parameters related to production capacities, costs, and market demand. IPS encourages cooperation by identifying production allocation strategies that yield higher collective profit compared to non-cooperative approaches.

Results: The case study demonstrates that IPS can foster cooperation among firms by recommending production allocation strategies that benefit all parties involved. By considering the interdependence of production decisions and optimizing resource utilization, IPS enables firms to achieve higher profitability while avoiding overallocation or resource shortages.

Case Study 3: Enhancing Distribution Efficiency

Scenario: A consortium of companies in an oligopolistic market faces challenges related to distribution logistics. Multiple suppliers, manufacturers, and distributors need to streamline their distribution networks to reduce transportation costs and enhance overall efficiency(Naim & others, 2021).

Application of IPS: IPS is applied to model and optimize the distribution logistics of the consortium. The simulation takes into account transportation routes, warehouse locations, inventory management, and delivery schedules. IPS identifies distribution strategies that minimize transportation costs while ensuring timely delivery to customers.

Results: By leveraging IPS, the consortium achieves significant cost savings in distribution logistics. The optimized routes and inventory management reduce transportation expenses, improve delivery times, and enhance overall efficiency. The case study highlights how IPS can be a valuable tool for optimizing distribution networks within oligopolistic supply chains, ultimately contributing to higher profitability for all participants.

These case studies demonstrate the practical applications of the Intelligent Physarum Solver (IPS) in addressing various challenges within oligopolistic supply chain networks. IPS's ability to model, simulate, and optimize decision-making processes can lead to more profitable outcomes while promoting cooperation among firms in these complex market structures.

RESULTS AND DISCUSSIONS

Comparative Analysis of IPS Solutions

As the Intelligent Physarum Solver (IPS) continues to gain traction in optimizing profit maximization within oligopolistic supply chain networks, a critical aspect of its utility is the ability to compare and evaluate different IPS solutions. This comparative analysis is essential for understanding the performance, effectiveness, and trade-offs of various approaches within the framework (Ji et al., 2019; Naim & others, 2021). This text discusses the key considerations and methods for conducting a comparative analysis of IPS solutions.

- **Objective Function Metrics:** Comparative analysis begins with evaluating the performance of different IPS solutions with respect to the defined objective functions. Metrics such as total profit, individual firm profits, and market share can provide insights into how well each solution accomplishes the goals of profit maximization and cooperation (Boopathi, 2022; Boopathi, Kumar, et al., 2023; Boopathi & Sivakumar, 2013; Kumara et al., 2023; Sampath et al., 2023; Saravanan et al., 2022).
- **Computational Efficiency:** Efficiency in terms of computation time and resource utilization is a crucial factor. A comparative analysis should consider the computational demands of different IPS implementations, especially when dealing with large-scale supply chain networks.
- **Sensitivity Analysis:** Sensitivity analysis involves examining how changes in input parameters or assumptions affect the outcomes. By varying parameters like market demand, production costs, or competitive behavior, analysts can assess the robustness and stability of IPS solutions.
- **Cooperative Outcomes:** In oligopolistic markets, fostering cooperation among firms is often a desirable outcome. Comparative analysis should assess to what extent different IPS solutions encourage cooperative behavior, as reflected in cooperative agreements, joint production, or pricing strategies.
- **Competitive Outcomes:** On the flip side, competitive outcomes also matter. Evaluate whether the IPS solutions strike an appropriate balance between competition and cooperation. Assess how the solutions affect market dynamics, including price competition and rivalry among firms.
- **Scalability:** Consider the scalability of IPS solutions in handling supply chain networks of varying sizes and complexities. Analyze whether the solutions maintain their effectiveness as the network scales up.
- **Real-world Applicability:** Examine how well the IPS solutions align with real-world scenarios and constraints. Evaluate whether they can be implemented in practice, considering factors such as data availability, information sharing, and regulatory compliance.
- **Robustness to Uncertainty:** Oligopolistic markets can be volatile and uncertain. Evaluate the robustness of IPS solutions to changing market conditions, unexpected disruptions, and fluctuations in demand or costs.
- **Long-term vs. Short-term Considerations:** Consider whether the IPS solutions focus on short-term profit maximization or account for long-term sustainability and growth. Different scenarios may require different time horizons and strategies.
- **Case Studies and Simulations:** Leverage case studies and simulations to compare the performance of IPS solutions in practical scenarios. These real-world examples provide valuable insights into the solutions' strengths and weaknesses.
- **Sensitivity to Algorithm Parameters:** If different versions or configurations of the IPS algorithm are available, explore how changing algorithm parameters affects solution outcomes. Fine-tuning parameters may lead to improved results.
- **Ethical and Regulatory Considerations:** Assess the ethical implications and regulatory compliance of IPS solutions, especially in cases where they influence pricing decisions, market power, or competitive dynamics.

Through a comprehensive comparative analysis that considers these factors, decision-makers and researchers can gain a deeper understanding of the capabilities and limitations of IPS solutions. This knowledge enables the selection of the most suitable IPS approach for specific oligopolistic supply chain scenarios, ultimately contributing to enhanced profit maximization and cooperation among firms in these complex market structures.

Implications for Oligopolistic Firms

The adoption of the Intelligent Physarum Solver (IPS) within oligopolistic supply chain networks has profound implications for participating firms (Huang et al., 2021; Ji et al., 2019):

- **Enhanced Profitability**: IPS solutions can significantly boost profitability by optimizing pricing strategies, production allocation, and distribution logistics. Firms can expect increased revenues and reduced costs, leading to improved financial performance.
- **Cooperation Opportunities**: IPS encourages cooperative behavior by identifying mutually beneficial strategies. Oligopolistic firms that cooperate effectively can achieve greater collective profitability while maintaining competitive positions in the market.
- **Strategic Insights**: By leveraging IPS, firms gain deeper insights into the interplay of pricing decisions and competitive dynamics. This knowledge helps them make more informed and strategic choices in the face of intense competition.
- **Resource Optimization**: IPS assists in optimizing resource allocation, ensuring efficient use of production capacity and inventory. This translates to cost savings and a more streamlined supply chain.
- **Market Expansion**: Firms can explore market expansion opportunities with confidence, as IPS aids in evaluating the profitability of entering new markets or diversifying product offerings.
- **Risk Mitigation**: IPS provides tools for assessing and mitigating supply chain risks, allowing firms to proactively address potential disruptions and uncertainties.
- **Regulatory Compliance**: By adhering to regulatory guidelines and promoting fair competition, firms can mitigate legal risks associated with their pricing and collaboration strategies.
- **Long-term Sustainability**: IPS solutions can incorporate long-term sustainability goals, aligning with firms' objectives for continued growth and environmental responsibility.

Limitations and Future Research Directions

While IPS offers promising solutions for profit maximization in oligopolistic supply chain networks, it also has limitations and areas for future research (Gao et al., 2019):

- **Data Availability**: The effectiveness of IPS relies on data availability, which can be a limitation in some cases. Future research may focus on methods for handling data constraints and enhancing data-driven decision-making.
- **Complexity**: Large-scale supply chain networks with numerous firms and products can pose computational challenges. Future research can explore advanced algorithms and techniques to address scalability issues.
- **Dynamic Environments**: Oligopolistic markets are dynamic and subject to changing conditions. Research efforts may aim to enhance IPS's adaptability to evolving market dynamics.
- **Behavioral Models**: Incorporating more realistic behavioral models for firms, considering factors like bounded rationality and psychological biases, can improve the accuracy of IPS solutions.

- **Multi-Objective Optimization**: Future research may explore multi-objective optimization approaches within IPS, allowing firms to balance profit maximization with other goals, such as sustainability or market share.
- **Ethical Considerations**: Oligopolistic firms must consider the ethical implications of their pricing and competition strategies. Future research can delve into ethical decision-making frameworks within IPS.
- **Interactions with Regulators**: The interaction between firms and regulatory bodies is a complex aspect of oligopolistic markets. Research can investigate how IPS can facilitate compliant behavior and engagement with regulators.
- **Integration with AI and IoT**: Leveraging artificial intelligence (AI) and the Internet of Things (IoT) technologies can enhance IPS's capabilities for real-time decision-making and supply chain optimization.
- **Collaborative Technologies**: Exploring collaborative technologies that enable firms to share information and coordinate more effectively within supply chains can complement IPS solutions.
- **Industry-Specific Applications**: Tailoring IPS to specific industries or sectors, such as healthcare or energy, can lead to industry-specific optimizations and insights.

PRACTICAL APPLICATIONS AND IMPLEMENTATION

Integrating IPS into Supply Chain Management Systems

Integrating the Intelligent Physarum Solver (IPS) into supply chain management systems is a strategic initiative that can enhance decision-making and profitability within oligopolistic supply chain networks. Here's a guide on how to effectively integrate IPS into your existing supply chain management systems (Nagurney et al., 2019; Sun et al., 2021; Wang et al., 2021; Yu et al., 2022):

- **Assess Current Systems and Processes:** Begin by conducting a thorough assessment of your current supply chain management systems, processes, and technologies. Understand the existing tools and software used for demand forecasting, inventory management, production planning, and distribution logistics.
- **Identify Integration Points:** Identify the specific areas within your supply chain where IPS can add value. Common integration points include pricing strategy optimization, production allocation, inventory management, and distribution route optimization.
- **Data Integration:** Ensure seamless data integration between your supply chain data sources and the IPS framework. Data on market demand, production costs, competitor behavior, and supply chain constraints should be accessible and up-to-date.
- **Customization and Parameterization:** Customize the IPS framework to align with your specific supply chain network, market conditions, and objectives. Parameterization is essential to reflect the unique characteristics of your oligopolistic market.
- **Real-time Data Feeds:** Implement real-time data feeds and APIs to provide the IPS system with the most current market information, including demand fluctuations, cost changes, and competitor actions. Real-time data ensures that decisions are based on the latest information.

- **Decision Support and Visualization:** Develop user-friendly interfaces that enable supply chain managers and decision-makers to interact with IPS solutions. Visualization tools, dashboards, and reports should provide insights into optimized strategies and recommendations.
- **Integration with ERP Systems:** Integrate IPS with your Enterprise Resource Planning (ERP) system to facilitate seamless communication and coordination between supply chain planning and execution. This ensures that optimized decisions are translated into action.
- **Automation and Alerts:** Implement automation features that allow IPS to trigger actions and alerts when predefined thresholds or conditions are met. For example, automated price adjustments or production allocation changes based on real-time market data.
- **Training and Change Management:** Provide training and support to supply chain teams to ensure they understand how to use IPS solutions effectively. Change management efforts are crucial for successful adoption and implementation.
- **Continuous Monitoring and Optimization:** Establish a process for continuous monitoring and optimization of IPS solutions. Regularly review performance metrics, conduct sensitivity analyses, and fine-tune parameters to adapt to changing market dynamics.
- **Collaboration and Information Sharing:** Encourage collaboration and information sharing among supply chain stakeholders. IPS can facilitate cooperative agreements and negotiations among firms in oligopolistic markets.
- **Regulatory Compliance:** Ensure that IPS solutions comply with industry regulations and ethical standards. Develop mechanisms to monitor and report on compliance with regulatory requirements.
- **Security and Data Privacy:** Implement robust security measures to protect sensitive supply chain data and ensure data privacy. This is particularly important when sharing information with competitors in oligopolistic markets.
- **Performance Evaluation:** Continuously evaluate the performance and impact of IPS on your supply chain's profitability. Assess how well it aligns with your organization's strategic objectives and market competitiveness.

By following these steps and integrating IPS into your supply chain management systems effectively, your organization can harness the power of nature-inspired optimization to navigate the complexities of oligopolistic supply chain networks, optimize profit maximization, and make informed, data-driven decisions.

Real-World Implementations and Benefits of IPS

Implementing the Intelligent Physarum Solver (IPS) in real-world scenarios within oligopolistic supply chain networks has yielded several tangible benefits (Gao et al., 2019; Wang et al., 2021):

- **Profit Maximization**: IPS has consistently demonstrated its ability to optimize profit maximization by suggesting pricing strategies, production allocations, and distribution logistics that enhance overall profitability for participating firms.
- **Cooperation Enhancement**: By fostering cooperative behavior among oligopolistic firms, IPS has enabled the development of collaborative agreements that benefit all stakeholders. This cooperative approach has reduced conflicts and increased collective profitability.

- **Cost Reduction**: IPS helps optimize resource allocation, production efficiency, and distribution logistics, resulting in cost reductions throughout the supply chain. These cost savings contribute directly to improved profitability.
- **Efficient Inventory Management**: IPS aids in efficient inventory management, reducing carrying costs and minimizing stockouts or overstock situations. This leads to better capital utilization and lower operational expenses.
- **Market Expansion and Diversification**: Firms using IPS have successfully evaluated market expansion opportunities and product diversification strategies, leading to increased revenue streams and market share.
- **Supply Chain Resilience**: IPS helps identify and mitigate supply chain risks, enhancing resilience against disruptions, natural disasters, and market uncertainties.
- **Real-time Decision Support**: IPS provides real-time decision support, allowing firms to adapt quickly to changing market conditions and make data-driven decisions that maximize profitability.
- **Compliance and Ethical Behavior**: IPS helps firms operate within regulatory constraints and encourages ethical behavior by promoting fair competition and compliance with market regulations.

Challenges in Implementing IPS

While IPS offers numerous advantages, it also presents challenges in its implementation (Awad et al., 2023; Gao et al., 2019; Wardell et al., 2021):

- **Data Integration**: Integrating real-time and high-quality data into the IPS framework can be complex, especially when dealing with multiple sources and data formats.
- **Algorithm Complexity**: IPS algorithms can be computationally intensive, especially in large-scale supply chain networks. Managing computational resources and time can be a challenge.
- **Change Management**: Adopting a new decision support system like IPS may require significant changes in organizational processes and mindset. Overcoming resistance to change can be challenging.
- **Competitive Concerns**: In oligopolistic markets, firms may have reservations about sharing sensitive information or cooperating with competitors, even through a framework like IPS.
- **Regulatory Compliance**: Navigating regulatory requirements, particularly those related to competition and data sharing, can pose challenges in implementing IPS solutions.
- **Parameterization and Customization**: Customizing IPS to align with the unique characteristics of each supply chain network can be complex, requiring careful parameterization and modeling.
- **Scalability**: Ensuring that IPS remains effective and efficient as the supply chain network scales up can be challenging. The complexity of optimization may increase with network size.
- **Interoperability**: Integrating IPS with existing supply chain management systems and Enterprise Resource Planning (ERP) solutions may require interoperability efforts.
- **Behavioral Modeling**: Capturing and modeling the behavioral aspects of firms, such as bounded rationality and psychological biases, can be challenging yet crucial for realistic decision support.
- **Monitoring and Maintenance**: Maintaining IPS systems and continuously monitoring their performance, as well as keeping them updated with changing market conditions, is an ongoing effort.

Despite these challenges, the successful implementation of IPS in real-world oligopolistic supply chain networks can lead to substantial benefits, making it a valuable investment for organizations looking to optimize profit maximization and cooperation in competitive markets.

CONCLUSION

This chapter explores the Intelligent Physarum Solver (IPS) as a nature-inspired optimization framework for profit maximization in oligopolistic supply chain networks. Inspired by the foraging behavior of the Physarum polycephalum slime mold, IPS uses principles of decentralized decision-making, adaptive network formation, and optimization techniques to find solutions that maximize individual and collective profitability while navigating the intricacies of competitive markets.

This chapter discusses the implementation of Information Processing Systems (IPS), its mathematical framework, data integration, customization, and real-world applications. IPS can improve pricing strategies, production allocation, distribution logistics, and cooperative decision-making among firms. It offers substantial benefits like improved profitability, cost reduction, efficient inventory management, market expansion, supply chain resilience, real-time decision support, regulatory compliance, and ethical behavior in the competitive landscape.

Implementing IPS faces challenges like data integration complexities, algorithmic intricacies, change management, competitive concerns, and regulatory compliance. Future research and development in IPS could focus on enhanced scalability, behavioral modeling, improved interoperability with existing systems, and advanced real-time decision support capabilities.

The Intelligent Physarum Solver (IPS) is a promising tool for profit maximization and cooperation in oligopolistic supply chain networks. Its nature-inspired approach offers innovative solutions to complex challenges, enabling firms to thrive in competitive markets and foster collaboration for mutual benefit. With careful implementation and ongoing research, IPS has the potential to revolutionize supply chain management.

ABBREVIATIONS

IPS: Intelligent Physarum Solver
ERP: Enterprise Resource Planning
AI: Artificial Intelligence
IoT: Internet of Things
APIs: Application Programming Interfaces
ROI: Return on Investment
KPIs: Key Performance Indicators
Co-op: Cooperative
Reg: Regulatory
B2B: Business-to-Business
B2C: Business-to-Consumer
SMEs: Small and Medium-sized Enterprises
CM: Change Management

R&D: Research and Development
CSR: Corporate Social Responsibility
M&A: Mergers and Acquisitions
SLA: Service Level Agreement
BI: Business Intelligence
IoT: Internet of Things
IT: Information Technology

REFERENCES

Awad, A., Pang, W., Lusseau, D., & Coghill, G. M. (2023). A survey on physarum polycephalum intelligent foraging behaviour and bio-inspired applications. *Artificial Intelligence Review*, *56*(1), 1–26. doi:10.1007/s10462-021-10112-1

Babu, B. S., Kamalakannan, J., Meenatchi, N., Karthik, S., & Boopathi, S. (2022). Economic impacts and reliability evaluation of battery by adopting Electric Vehicle. *IEEE Explore*, 1–6.

Boopathi, S. (2019). Experimental investigation and parameter analysis of LPG refrigeration system using Taguchi method. *SN Applied Sciences*, *1*(8), 892. doi:10.1007/s42452-019-0925-2

Boopathi, S. (2022). Experimental investigation and multi-objective optimization of cryogenic Friction-stir-welding of AA2014 and AZ31B alloys using MOORA technique. *Materials Today. Communications*, *33*, 104937. doi:10.1016/j.mtcomm.2022.104937

Boopathi, S., Hari balaji, V., Mageswari, M., & Asif, M. M. (2022). Influences of Boron Carbide Particles on the Wear Rate and Tensile Strength of AA2014 Surface Composite Fabricated by Friction-Stir Processing. *Mater-Tehnol.Si. Materials Technology*, *56*(3), 263–270.

Boopathi, S., Kumar, P. K. S., Meena, R. S., & Sudhakar, M. (2023). Sustainable Developments of Modern Soil-Less Agro-Cultivation Systems: Aquaponic Culture. In Human Agro-Energy Optimization for Business and Industry (pp. 69–87). IGI Global.

Boopathi, S., Kumaresan, A., & Manohar, N., & KrishnaMoorthi, R. (2017). Review on Effect of Process Parameters—Friction Stir Welding Process. *International Research Journal of Engineering and Technology*, *4*(7), 272–278.

Boopathi, S., Myilsamy, S., & Sukkasamy, S. (2021). *Experimental Investigation and Multi-Objective Optimization of Cryogenically Cooled Near-Dry Wire-Cut EDM Using TOPSIS Technique*. IJAMT.

Boopathi, S., Pandey, B. K., & Pandey, D. (2023). Advances in Artificial Intelligence for Image Processing: Techniques, Applications, and Optimization. In Handbook of Research on Thrust Technologies' Effect on Image Processing (pp. 73–95). IGI Global.

Boopathi, S., & Sivakumar, K. (2013). Experimental investigation and parameter optimization of near-dry wire-cut electrical discharge machining using multi-objective evolutionary algorithm. *International Journal of Advanced Manufacturing Technology*, *67*(9–12), 2639–2655. doi:10.1007/s00170-012-4680-4

Boopathi, S., & Sivakumar, K. (2016). Optimal parameter prediction of oxygen-mist near-dry wire-cut EDM. *Inderscience: International Journal of Manufacturing Technology and Management, 30*(3–4), 164–178. doi:10.1504/IJMTM.2016.077812

Boopathi, S., Sureshkumar, M., & Sathiskumar, S. (2022). Parametric Optimization of LPG Refrigeration System Using Artificial Bee Colony Algorithm. *International Conference on Recent Advances in Mechanical Engineering Research and Development*, 97–105.

Chopra, N., & Ansari, M. M. (2022). Golden jackal optimization: A novel nature-inspired optimizer for engineering applications. *Expert Systems with Applications, 198*, 116924. doi:10.1016/j.eswa.2022.116924

Chu, D., Ma, W., Yang, Z., Li, J., Deng, Y., & Cheong, K. H. (2021). A Physarum-inspired algorithm for logistics optimization: From the perspective of effective distance. *Swarm and Evolutionary Computation, 64*, 100890. doi:10.1016/j.swevo.2021.100890

Coe, N. M., & Yang, C. (2022). Mobile gaming production networks, platform business groups, and the market power of China's Tencent. *Annals of the American Association of Geographers, 112*(2), 307–330. doi:10.1080/24694452.2021.1933887

Dhanya, D., Kumar, S. S., Thilagavathy, A., Prasad, D., & Boopathi, S. (2023). Data Analytics and Artificial Intelligence in the Circular Economy: Case Studies. In Intelligent Engineering Applications and Applied Sciences for Sustainability (pp. 40–58). IGI Global.

Gao, C., Liu, C., Schenz, D., Li, X., Zhang, Z., Jusup, M., Wang, Z., Beekman, M., & Nakagaki, T. (2019). Does being multi-headed make you better at solving problems? A survey of Physarum-based models and computations. *Physics of Life Reviews, 29*, 1–26. doi:10.1016/j.plrev.2018.05.002 PMID:29857934

Gowri, N. V., Dwivedi, J. N., Krishnaveni, K., Boopathi, S., Palaniappan, M., & Medikondu, N. R. (2023). Experimental investigation and multi-objective optimization of eco-friendly near-dry electrical discharge machining of shape memory alloy using Cu/SiC/Gr composite electrode. *Environmental Science and Pollution Research International, 30*(49), 1–19. doi:10.1007/s11356-023-26983-6 PMID:37126160

Gunasekaran, K., Boopathi, S., & Sureshkumar, M. (2022). Analysis of a Cryogenically Cooled Near-Dry WEDM Process using Different Dielectrics. *Mater-Tehnol.Si. Materials Technology, 56*(2), 179–186.

Hall, D., Lister, J., & Mercer, H. (2020). *Privatised and unprepared: The NHS supply chain*. Academic Press.

Hua, X., Yao, H., Wang, Z., Li, B., & Wang, H. (2021). A wireless weak-connected network routing algorithm inspired by Physarum polycephalum. *Computers & Electrical Engineering, 91*, 107083. doi:10.1016/j.compeleceng.2021.107083

Huang, X., Zhang, B., & Li, C. (2021). Platform profit maximization on service provisioning in mobile edge computing. *IEEE Transactions on Vehicular Technology, 70*(12), 13364–13376. doi:10.1109/TVT.2021.3124483

Ji, Y., Lin, Z., & Rong, T. (2019). AdaptiveSLA: A two-stage scheduling framework for SLA profit maximization in multi-tenant database. *Journal of Physics: Conference Series, 1187*(5), 052002. doi:10.1088/1742-6596/1187/5/052002

Kalidas, R., Boopathi, S., Sivakumar, K., & Mohankumar, P. (2012). Optimization of Machining Parameters of WEDM Process Based On the Taguchi Method. *IJEST, 6*(1).

Kumar, P. R., Meenakshi, S., Shalini, S., Devi, S. R., & Boopathi, S. (2023). Soil Quality Prediction in Context Learning Approaches Using Deep Learning and Blockchain for Smart Agriculture. In R. Kumar, A. B. Abdul Hamid, & N. I. Binti Ya'akub (Eds.), (pp. 1–26). Advances in Computational Intelligence and Robotics. IGI Global. doi:10.4018/978-1-6684-9151-5.ch001

Kumara, V., Mohanaprakash, T., Fairooz, S., Jamal, K., Babu, T., & Sampath, B. (2023). Experimental Study on a Reliable Smart Hydroponics System. In *Human Agro-Energy Optimization for Business and Industry* (pp. 27–45). IGI Global. doi:10.4018/978-1-6684-4118-3.ch002

Ma, J., Ning, N., & Xu, T. (2021). Analyzing the chinese telecommunication industry based on oligopoly game and dynamic evolution. *International Journal of Bifurcation and Chaos in Applied Sciences and Engineering, 31*(14), 2150238. doi:10.1142/S0218127421502382

Mohanty, A., Venkateswaran, N., Ranjit, P., Tripathi, M. A., & Boopathi, S. (2023). Innovative Strategy for Profitable Automobile Industries: Working Capital Management. In Handbook of Research on Designing Sustainable Supply Chains to Achieve a Circular Economy (pp. 412–428). IGI Global.

Mostofi, A. (2022). *Select issues in designing license contracts of strategic alliances in the pharmaceutical supply chain* [PhD Thesis]. Open Access Te Herenga Waka-Victoria University of Wellington.

Myilsamy Sureshkumar, Boopathi, & Sabareesh. (2018). The improving Wear Resistance Properties of Molybdenum Alloy Under Cryogenic Treatment. *International Journal of Mechanical and Production Engineering Research and Development, 8*(7), 724–728.

Nagurney, A., Besik, D., & Nagurney, L. S. (2019). Global supply chain networks and tariff rate quotas: Equilibrium analysis with application to agricultural products. *Journal of Global Optimization, 75*(2), 439–460. doi:10.1007/s10898-019-00794-x

Naim, A., & ... (2021). New Trends in Business Process Management: Applications of Green Information Technologies. *British Journal of Environmental Studies, 1*(1), 12–23.

Nishanth, J., Deshmukh, M. A., Kushwah, R., Kushwaha, K. K., Balaji, S., & Sampath, B. (2023). Particle Swarm Optimization of Hybrid Renewable Energy Systems. In *Intelligent Engineering Applications and Applied Sciences for Sustainability* (pp. 291–308). IGI Global. doi:10.4018/979-8-3693-0044-2.ch016

Palaniappan, M., Tirlangi, S., Mohamed, M. J. S., Moorthy, R. S., Valeti, S. V., & Boopathi, S. (2023). Fused Deposition Modelling of Polylactic Acid (PLA)-Based Polymer Composites: A Case Study. In Development, Properties, and Industrial Applications of 3D Printed Polymer Composites (pp. 66–85). IGI Global.

Ravisankar, A., Sampath, B., & Asif, M. M. (2023). Economic Studies on Automobile Management: Working Capital and Investment Analysis. In Multidisciplinary Approaches to Organizational Governance During Health Crises (pp. 169–198). IGI Global.

Samikannu, R., Koshariya, A. K., Poornima, E., Ramesh, S., Kumar, A., & Boopathi, S. (2022). Sustainable Development in Modern Aquaponics Cultivation Systems Using IoT Technologies. In *Human Agro-Energy Optimization for Business and Industry* (pp. 105–127). IGI Global.

Sampath, B., Sasikumar, C., & Myilsamy, S. (2023). Application of TOPSIS Optimization Technique in the Micro-Machining Process. In Trends, Paradigms, and Advances in Mechatronics Engineering (pp. 162–187). IGI Global.

Saravanan, M., Vasanth, M., Boopathi, S., Sureshkumar, M., & Haribalaji, V. (2022). Optimization of Quench Polish Quench (QPQ) Coating Process Using Taguchi Method. *Key Engineering Materials*, *935*, 83–91. doi:10.4028/p-z569vy

Sathish, T., Sunagar, P., Singh, V., Boopathi, S., Al-Enizi, A. M., Pandit, B., Gupta, M., & Sehgal, S. S. (2023). Characteristics estimation of natural fibre reinforced plastic composites using deep multi-layer perceptron (MLP) technique. *Chemosphere*, *337*, 139346. doi:10.1016/j.chemosphere.2023.139346 PMID:37379988

Selwyn, B., & Leyden, D. (2022). Oligopoly-driven development: The world bank's trading for development in the age of global value chains in perspective. *Competition & Change*, *26*(2), 174–196. doi:10.1177/1024529421995351

Senthil, T., Puviyarasan, M., Babu, S. R., Surakasi, R., Sampath, B., & Associates. (2023). Industrial Robot-Integrated Fused Deposition Modelling for the 3D Printing Process. In Development, Properties, and Industrial Applications of 3D Printed Polymer Composites (pp. 188–210). IGI Global.

Silveira, D., & Vasconcelos, S. (2020). Essays on duopoly competition with asymmetric firms: Is profit maximization always an evolutionary stable strategy? *International Journal of Production Economics*, *225*, 107592. doi:10.1016/j.ijpe.2019.107592

Sun, L., Liu, W., Zhang, H., Jin, Y., & Zhuo, G. (2021). Analysis of the effect of cruise service supply chain network properties on economic profits. *International Journal of Shipping and Transport Logistics*, *13*(6), 569–599. doi:10.1504/IJSTL.2021.118525

Ugandar, R. E., Rahamathunnisa, U., Sajithra, S., Christiana, M. B. V., Palai, B. K., & Boopathi, S. (2023). Hospital Waste Management Using Internet of Things and Deep Learning: Enhanced Efficiency and Sustainability. In M. Arshad (Ed.), (pp. 317–343). Advances in Bioinformatics and Biomedical Engineering. IGI Global. doi:10.4018/978-1-6684-6577-6.ch015

Vanitha, S., Radhika, K., & Boopathi, S. (2023). Artificial Intelligence Techniques in Water Purification and Utilization. In *Human Agro-Energy Optimization for Business and Industry* (pp. 202–218). IGI Global. doi:10.4018/978-1-6684-4118-3.ch010

Venkateswaran, N., Vidhya, K., Ayyannan, M., Chavan, S. M., Sekar, K., & Boopathi, S. (2023). A Study on Smart Energy Management Framework Using Cloud Computing. In 5G, Artificial Intelligence, and Next Generation Internet of Things: Digital Innovation for Green and Sustainable Economies (pp. 189–212). IGI Global. doi:10.4018/978-1-6684-8634-4.ch009

Vennila, T., Karuna, M., Srivastava, B. K., Venugopal, J., Surakasi, R., & Sampath, B. (2022). New Strategies in Treatment and Enzymatic Processes: Ethanol Production From Sugarcane Bagasse. In Human Agro-Energy Optimization for Business and Industry (pp. 219–240). IGI Global.

Wang, J., Zhou, H., & Jin, X. (2021). Risk transmission in complex supply chain network with multi-drivers. *Chaos, Solitons, and Fractals*, *143*, 110259. doi:10.1016/j.chaos.2020.110259

Wardell, D. A., Piketty, M.-G., Lescuyer, G., & Pacheco, P. (2021). *Reviewing initiatives to promote sustainable supply chains: The case of forest-risk commodities*. Academic Press.

Weersink, A., & Fulton, M. (2020). Limits to profit maximization as a guide to behavior change. *Applied Economic Perspectives and Policy*, *42*(1), 67–79. doi:10.1002/aepp.13004

Yang, X.-S. (2020). Nature-inspired optimization algorithms: Challenges and open problems. *Journal of Computational Science*, *46*, 101104. doi:10.1016/j.jocs.2020.101104

Yu, M., Cruz, J. M., Li, D., & Masoumi, A. H. (2022). A multiperiod competitive supply chain framework with environmental policies and investments in sustainable operations. *European Journal of Operational Research*, *300*(1), 112–123. doi:10.1016/j.ejor.2021.07.028

Yuan, H., & Zhou, M. (2020). Profit-maximized collaborative computation offloading and resource allocation in distributed cloud and edge computing systems. *IEEE Transactions on Automation Science and Engineering*, *18*(3), 1277–1287. doi:10.1109/TASE.2020.3000946

Yupapin, P., Trabelsi, Y., Nattappan, A., & Boopathi, S. (2023). Performance improvement of wire-cut electrical discharge machining process using cryogenically treated super-conductive state of Monel-K500 alloy. *Iranian Journal of Science and Technology. Transaction of Mechanical Engineering*, *47*(1), 267–283. doi:10.1007/s40997-022-00513-0

Zhang, Y., Gu, C., Yan, X., & Li, F. (2020). Cournot oligopoly game-based local energy trading considering renewable energy uncertainty costs. *Renewable Energy*, *159*, 1117–1127. doi:10.1016/j.renene.2020.06.066

Chapter 12
Smart Big Data Collection for Intelligent Supply Chain Improvement

G. JayaLakshmi
https://orcid.org/0000-0002-4044-4138
Department of Information Technology, V.R. Siddhartha Engineering College, Kanuru, India

Digvijay Pandey
https://orcid.org/0000-0003-0353-174X
Department of Technical Education, U. P., India

Binay Kumar Pandey
https://orcid.org/0000-0002-4041-1213
Department of Information Technology, College of Technology, Govind Ballabh Pant University of Agriculture and Technology, India

Prabjot Kaur
Birla Institute of Technology, Mesra, India

Darshan A. Mahajan
https://orcid.org/0000-0002-1239-6343
NICMAR University, Pune, India

Sukhvinder Singh Dari
https://orcid.org/0000-0002-6218-6600
Symbiosis Law School, Symbiosis International University, Pune, India

ABSTRACT

Supply chain management is essential to a company's success in today's fiercely competitive business environment, regardless of the industry. Businesses are increasingly turning to big data analytics as a useful tool for supply chain improvement to meet the expanding needs of customers, save operational costs, and boost overall efficiency. In order to improve critical areas including demand forecasting, inventory management, logistics optimization, and risk reduction, research has been conducted on the collecting and use of big data in supply chain management. Big data analytics and supply chain management integration can result in more cost-effective operations, better customer service, and increased resilience to disturbances. Organisations that effectively use big data will gain a competitive advantage in the constantly changing supply chain landscape as technology and data capabilities continue to grow.

DOI: 10.4018/979-8-3693-1347-3.ch012

INTRODUCTION

Supply chain management (SCM), in today's complex and interconnected business environment, has developed into a crucial task for organizations looking to keep a competitive advantage. The gathering and analysis of large data (Kumar, M. S. et al., 2021) is one of the primary facilitators of efficient SCM. Big data, which is the term for enormous and varied collections of information (Pandey, B. K. et al., 2023) created from numerous sources, has the potential to fundamentally alter how businesses plan, carry out, and optimize their supply chain activities (Malhotra, P. et al., 2021). The process of obtaining, storing, and analyzing big data for supply chain management entails gathering information from numerous sources all along the supply chain (Richey, R. G. et al., 2022).

These resources may consist of:

- Internet of Things (IoT) (Kumar Pandey, B. et al., 2021) Sensors: Sensors attached to goods, machines, and other items can deliver real-time information about their whereabouts, state, and performance. For keeping track of the flow of commodities and assets, this information is crucial.
- Enterprise Resource Planning (ERP) Systems: ERP software (Kirubasri, G. et al., 2022) gathers and combines data from a range of corporate operations, such as purchasing, production, and inventory control. A thorough supply chain analysis can be performed using this centralized data. Data from suppliers and partners can offer insights into performance, lead times, and quality. This data comes from suppliers, logistics partners, and other external stakeholders. For managing suppliers and evaluating risks, this information is essential.
- Customer Information: Information on orders, preferences, and feedback from customers is crucial for predicting demand and developing products.
- Social media and market data analysis can assist businesses in better understanding consumer behaviour and adapting to changes in demand.
- Historical Data: For trend analysis, benchmarking, and continuous improvement, records of earlier supply chain operations and performance measures are essential.

Once this data has been gathered, it needs to be processed and examined in order to yield useful insights. To find trends, anomalies, and opportunities in the data, advanced analytics techniques like machine learning (Singh, H. et al., 2022) and predictive modeling (Babu, S. Z. D. et al., 2022, July) are frequently used.

A block diagram in Figure1for a Big Data (Nguyen, Truong et al., 2017) system in supply chain management would encompass the various components and processes involved in leveraging big data analytics to enhance supply chain operations. This block diagram represents the core components and processes in a Big Data system for supply chain management (M. K. Daoud,et al.,2023). Such a system leverages advanced analytics and data-driven insights to optimize supply chain operations, improve efficiency, reduce costs, and enhance overall performance (Wang, C.et al.,2023).

- **Data Sources:**
    - **IoT Devices**: Sensors (Pandey, J. K. et al., 2022) and devices collecting real-time data on products, equipment, and environmental conditions.
    - **Enterprise Systems**: Internal databases and systems containing information on inventory, orders, and logistics.

Figure 1. Components and processes involved in leveraging big data analytics (Varela Rozadosn& Tjahjono, 2014) to enhance supply chain operations

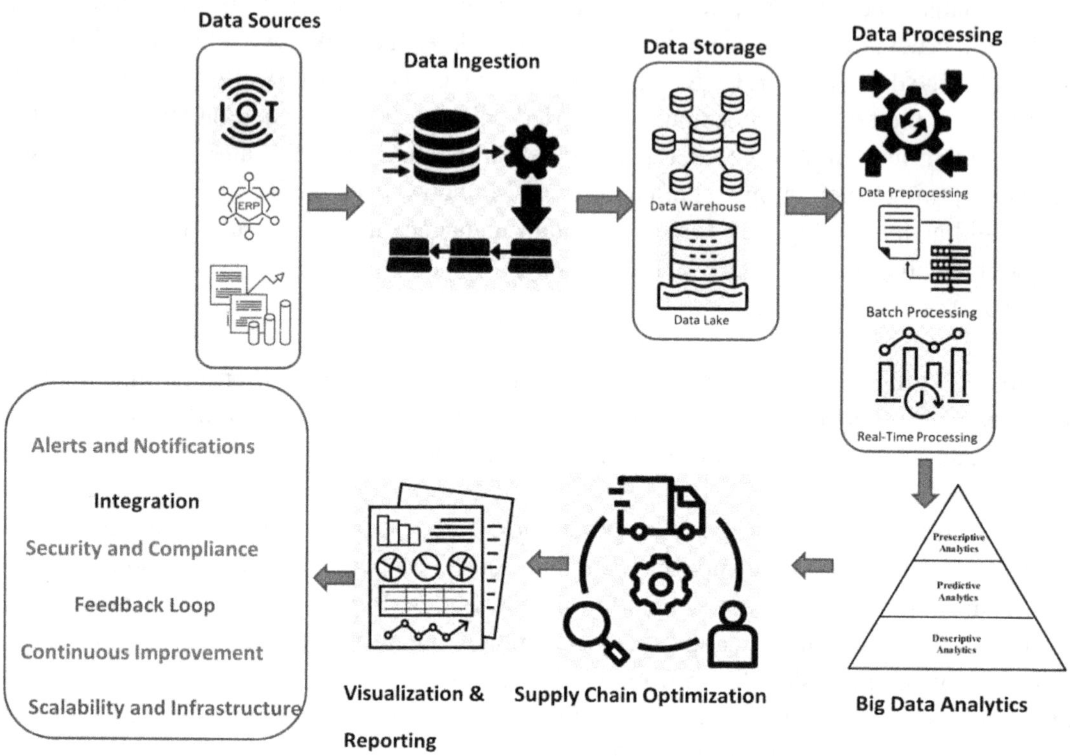

   - **External Data**: Data from external sources, including market trends, weather forecasts, and geopolitical events.
- **Data Ingestion:**

Collect data from various sources and consolidate it into a unified data repository.

- **Data Storage:**
   - **Data Warehouse**: Store structured data for historical analysis.
   - **Data Lake**: Store unstructured or semi-structured data for more in-depth analysis.
- **Data Processing:**
   - **Data Preprocessing**: Clean, normalize, and transform data for analysis.
   - **Batch Processing**: Analyze historical data to identify trends and patterns.
   - **Real-time Processing**: Analyze incoming data for immediate decision-making.
- **Big Data Analytics:**
   - **Descriptive Analytics**: Summarize historical data to gain insights into past performance.
   - **Predictive Analytics**: Use statistical models and machine learning (Khan, B., 2021) to make forecasts.
   - **Prescriptive Analytics**: Recommend optimal actions based on data analysis.

- **Supply Chain Optimization:**
    - **Demand Forecasting**: Predict future demand based on historical and real-time data.
    - **Inventory Optimization**: Determine optimal inventory levels and reorder points.
    - **Route Optimization**: Optimize transportation (Sahani, K. et al., 2023) routes to reduce costs and delivery times.
    - **Supplier Management**: Analyze supplier performance and identify areas for improvement.
- **Visualization and Reporting:**
    - Create interactive dashboards and reports to present key supply chain metrics and insights. Provide data visualization tools for decision-makers.
- **Alerts and Notifications:**
    - Automated alerts based on predefined conditions, such as inventory levels, production delays, or quality issues.
- **Integration:**
    - Integrate with existing ERP (Enterprise Resource Planning) and SCM (Supply Chain Management) systems for seamless data flow.Interface with external systems for data exchange and coordination.
- **Security and Compliance:**
    - Implement robust security measures to protect sensitive supply chain data. Ensure compliance with data privacy regulations, especially if dealing with customer data.
- **Feedback Loop:**
    - Capture feedback from supply chain operators and decision-makers to improve the system's accuracy and effectiveness.
- **Continuous Improvement:**
    - Continuously analyze and refine the system to adapt to changing supply chain dynamics and business goals.
- **Scalability and Infrastructure:**
    - Ensure the system can scale to handle increasing data volumes and user demands. Maintain a robust IT infrastructure capable of supporting big data processing.

RELATED WORK

A literature review on big data collection for supply chain improvement should encompass a variety of research articles and studies that explore different aspects of data collection and its impact on supply chain management. Chae and Olson (2015) discussed the growing importance of big data analytics in supply chain management (Ahmad, A. Y. B.,et al.,2019). It emphasizes the need for collecting data from various sources such as RFID, GPS, and sensors to improve visibility and decision-making in the supply chain. Big data plays important role in enhancing supply chain performance. It emphasizes the importance of data collection from multiple sources, including IoT devices, social media, and supply chain partners, to enable better demand forecasting, inventory management, and logistics optimization. Big data collection and analysis can lead to improved supply chain competitiveness (Ahmad, A. Y. B.,et al.,2023). It emphasizes the integration of various data sources, such as GPS data, social media sentiment analysis, and weather forecasts, for better decision-making (Pandey, B. K., & Pandey, D., 2023). The

Table 1. Selected literature review articles on data analytics

Title and Authors	Journal/Year	Description With Remarks
"Big Data Analytics for Supply Chain Management: A Literature Review and Research Agenda" (Fosso Wamba, Samuel & Akter, Shahriar., 2015) .	Computers & Industrial Engineering, 2020	This comprehensive review discusses the use of big data analytics in supply chain management and suggests a research agenda for the field.
"Big Data and Predictive Analytics for Supply Chain Digitalization: A Literature Review"(Hazen, Benjamin. et al., 2016)	International Journal of Production Research, 2021	This paper provides insights into the use of big data and predictive analytics in supply chain digitalization and offers a review of the literature up to 2020.
"Big Data Analytics in Supply Chain Management: Trends and Related Research" (Rozados, I. V., & Tjahjono, B., 2014)	Expert Systems with Applications, 2020	This study explores trends in big data analytics in supply chain management and reviews related research, highlighting the potential improvements in supply chain operations.
"Big Data and Supply Chain Management: A Review and Bibliometric Analysis.",Gursoy, D., et al.[17]	Annals of Operations Research, 2020	This paper presents a review and bibliometric analysis of research related to big data in supply chain management, offering an overview of key trends and themes.
"Supply Chain Digitalization: An Overview on Performance Enhancing Tools" (Rasool, F. et al., 2022)	International Journal of Production Research, 2021	This article provides an overview of performance-enhancing tools in supply chain digitalization, including the use of big data, and reviews developments up to 2020.

collection and analysis of big data can impact supply chain strategies. It highlights the role of data from RFID, sensors, and GPS in optimizing transportation, inventory management, and demand forecasting (Nguyen, Truong. et al., 2017) .And big data analytics can enhance supply chain agility. It emphasizes the importance of collecting and analyzing data in real-time from various sources, such as IoT devices (Pramanik, S. et al., 2023), to enable rapid response to disruptions (Mandal, Santanu., 2018). The real-time aspect of data collection in transportation and logistics use of GPS data, RFID, and sensor data to improve route optimization, reduce transportation costs, and enhance supply chain visibility (Golinska-Dawson et al., 2023). Big data emphasizes the importance of collecting data from a wide range of sources, including IoT, social media, and weather data, for improving supply chain processes logistics and supply chain management (Wang, G. et al., 2016). The growing importance of data collection from sources such as IoT devices and social media for enhancing supply chain visibility, sustainability, and responsiveness (Chalmeta, R., & Santos-deLeón, N. J., 2020).

The table Table 1 includes some key research papers published. The related work covers the use of big data in supply chains and its impact on improving various aspects of the supply chain management process.

CONTEXT OF DATA IN SUPPLY CHAINS

Data plays a pivotal role within the framework of supply chains. It serves as the critical foundation for informed decision-making, optimization (Pandey, D. et al., 2021), and the overall enhancement of supply chain management efficiency. In the context of supply chains, data can be categorized into various essential types:

1. **Demand Data:**
    - **Sales Data:** This encompasses information concerning the historical and current sales of products, including quantities, locations, and timeframes.
    - **Order Data:** It includes specifics about customer orders, such as order size, frequency, and the specific products ordered.
    - **Market Data:** This pertains to insights into market trends, customer preferences, and competitive dynamics that influence demand.
2. **Inventory Data:**
    - **Stock Levels:** This category deals with data concerning the quantity and location of inventory at different points in the supply chain, including raw materials, work-in-progress, and finished goods.
    - **Replenishment Data:** This pertains to information regarding reorder points, safety stock levels, and inventory turnover rates.
    - **Lead Time Data:** This focuses on data related to the time it takes for inventory to be restocked after depletion.
3. **Logistics and Transportation Data:**
    - **Shipment Data:** This encompasses details about the movement of goods, including carriers, routes, delivery times, and tracking information.
    - **Freight Data:** This deals with information related to shipping costs, modes of transportation, and carrier performance.
    - **Real-time Tracking Data:** This includes data sourced from IoT sensors and GPS devices, delivering real-time insights into the location and condition of shipments.
4. **Supplier and Procurement Data:**
    - **Supplier Performance Data:** This consists of metrics gauging supplier reliability, quality, lead times, and pricing.
    - **Purchase Order Data:** It incorporates details about purchase orders, including quantities, delivery schedules, and agreed-upon terms.
    - **Supplier Risk Data:** This pertains to data concerning geopolitical, economic, and environmental factors that may impact supplier stability.
5. **Quality and Compliance Data:**
    - **Quality Assurance Data:** This includes information about product quality, testing results, and adherence to regulatory standards.
    - **Compliance Data:** This focuses on data associated with regulatory and environmental compliance requirements affecting the supply chain.
6. **Financial Data:**
    - **Cost Data:** This encompasses information regarding the costs linked to various facets of the supply chain, covering manufacturing, transportation, warehousing, and inventory holding costs.
    - **Revenue Data:** It deals with details on sales revenue, pricing strategies, and overall profitability.
7. **Sustainability and Environmental Data:**
    - **Carbon Emissions Data:** This involves insights into the carbon footprint of the supply chain, which can be utilized for measurement and mitigation of environmental impact.

- **Waste Data:** This category includes data related to waste generation and recycling efforts within the supply chain.

8. **Operational Data:**
   - **Performance Metrics:** These are key performance indicators (KPIs) and operational metrics used to assess the efficiency and effectiveness of supply chain processes.
   - **Workforce Data:** This comprises information about the workforce, including labor hours, skills, and training.
9. **Real-time Data:**
   - **IoT and Sensor Data:** This encompasses real-time data derived from IoT devices and sensors that monitor various aspects of the supply chain, such as temperature, humidity, and equipment status.
   - **Big Data:** Large volumes of data from diverse sources, including social media, web scraping, and external market data, which can be harnessed for advanced analytics and real-time decision-making.

In the context of supply chains, data collection, processing, and analysis facilitate instantaneous decision-making, process optimization, demand prediction, cost reduction, enhanced transparency, and the timely and efficient delivery of products. Data-driven supply chain management is of increasing significance as businesses strive to gain a competitive edge and adapt to shifting market conditions. By harnessing data and applying analytics, supply chain professionals can make more informed decisions, reduce costs, minimize risks, and improve overall efficiency. Data-driven supply chain management is vital for staying competitive, meeting customer expectations, and adapting to the dynamic nature of global supply chains.

BIG DATA IN SUPPLY CHAIN MANAGEMENT

Collecting big data for supply chain improvement involves gathering, storing, and processing large volumes of data from various sources within the supply chain (Khan, Yasser, et al.,2022). This data is used for analytics, decision-making, and optimization. Here are key aspects of big data collection for supply chain improvement (B. Muniandi et al., 2019):

1. **Data Sources:** Identify the sources of data within your supply chain. These can include:
   - **IoT Sensors:** Sensors on equipment, vehicles, and storage facilities provide real-time data on temperature, humidity, location, and other conditions.
   - **RFID Tags:** RFID technology helps track the movement and status of products and materials.
   - **ERP Systems:** Enterprise Resource Planning (ERP) systems capture data on orders, inventory, and production.
   - **External Data:** This includes data from market trends, social media, and weather forecasts, which can impact demand and logistics.
2. **Data Integration:** Integrate data from various sources into a central repository or data lake. Ensure compatibility and consistency in data formats and standards.
3. **Data Quality:** Clean and preprocess data to eliminate errors and inconsistencies. Accurate and high-quality data is crucial for reliable analysis and decision-making.

Figure 2. Categorization of supply chains data

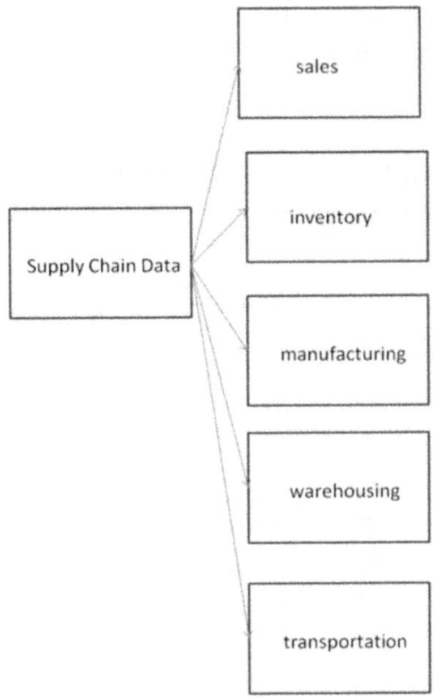

4. **Real-time Data:** Implement systems for collecting and processing data in real-time. This allows for immediate responses to supply chain events and issues.
5. **Cloud Solutions:** Consider cloud-based solutions for data storage and processing. Cloud platforms can provide scalability and accessibility for supply chain data.
6. **Big Data Technologies:** Utilize big data technologies like Hadoop, Apache Spark, and data warehouses to store and analyze large datasets efficiently.
7. **Analytics:** Implement advanced analytics and machine learning algorithms (Gupta, R. et al., 2023) to extract insights from the data. This can help with demand forecasting, predictive maintenance, and process optimization.
8. **Data Security:** Ensure data security and compliance with relevant data protection regulations. Protect sensitive supply chain data from unauthorized access and breaches.
9. **Supplier Collaboration:** Collaborate with key suppliers to share data and implement Vendor-Managed Inventory (VMI) systems. This enables suppliers to restock inventory proactively.
10. **Visualization:** Use data visualization tools and dashboards to provide a clear and intuitive view of supply chain performance. Visual representations make it easier for decision-makers to understand complex data.
11. **Continuous Improvement:** Continuously monitor and evaluate the data collection and analysis process. Seek opportunities for improvement and adapt to changing supply chain dynamics.
12. **Scalability:** Ensure that your data collection and storage infrastructure can scale as the volume of data grows. Scalability is crucial for handling the increasing amounts of data generated by IoT sensors and other sources.

Collecting and analyzing big data in the supply chain can lead to improved decision-making, reduced costs, better customer service, and enhanced efficiency. It provides a competitive advantage by allowing supply chain professionals to make informed choices based on real-time data and advanced analytics.

METHODOLOGY FOR BIG DATA COLLECTION FOR SUPPLY CHAIN IMPROVEMENT

The methodology for collecting big data for supply chain improvement involves a structured approach to gather, process, and leverage data to enhance the efficiency and effectiveness of supply chain operations. Here is a step-by-step methodology:

1. Define Objectives and Goals:
    - Clearly define the objectives of big data collection in your supply chain. What specific areas do you want to improve? Examples include demand forecasting, inventory management, logistics optimization, or supplier collaboration.
2. Identify Data Sources:
    - Identify the sources of data within your supply chain. These can include IoT sensors, RFID technology, ERP systems, external data sources (market trends, social media, weather forecasts), and other relevant data streams.
3. Data Integration:
    - Integrate data from various sources into a centralized repository or data lake. Ensure that data is compatible in terms of formats and standards.
4. Data Quality Assurance:
    - Cleanse and preprocess the data to eliminate errors and inconsistencies. High-quality data is essential for reliable analysis and decision-making.
5. Real-time Data Collection:
    - Implement systems for collecting and processing data in real-time. This allows for immediate responses to supply chain events and issues.
6. Data Storage and Processing:
    - Consider using big data technologies like Hadoop, Apache Spark, or data warehouses for storing and analyzing large datasets efficiently.
7. Data Security and Privacy:
    - Ensure that data is secure (David, S. et al., 2023) and compliant with relevant data protection regulations. Protect sensitive supply chain data from unauthorized access and breaches.
8. Analytics and Machine Learning:
    - Implement advanced analytics and machine learning algorithms to extract insights from the data. These models help with demand forecasting, predictive maintenance, and process optimization.
9. Supplier Collaboration:
    - Collaborate with key suppliers to share data and implement Vendor-Managed Inventory (VMI) systems. This allows suppliers to proactively restock inventory based on real-time demand data.
10. Data Visualization:

- Utilize data visualization tools and dashboards to provide a clear and intuitive view of supply chain performance. Visual representations make it easier for decision-makers to understand complex data.

11. Scalability:
    - Ensure that your data collection and storage infrastructure can scale as the volume of data grows. Scalability is crucial for handling the increasing amounts of data generated by IoT sensors and other sources.
12. Continuous Improvement:
    - Continuously monitor and evaluate the data collection and analysis process. Seek opportunities for improvement and adapt to changing supply chain dynamics.
13. Pilot Projects:
    - Before full-scale implementation, consider conducting pilot projects to test the data collection methods and the impact on specific supply chain processes.
14. Performance Measurement:
    - Establish KPIs and performance metrics to measure the impact of big data on supply chain improvement. Continuously monitor and assess performance against these metrics.
15. Training and Skill Development:
    - Ensure that the supply chain team has the necessary skills and knowledge to work with big data. Training and skill development are essential for leveraging data effectively.

By following this methodology, organizations can effectively collect, process, and leverage big data to enhance their supply chain operations, resulting in better decision-making, cost reduction, improved customer service, and overall supply chain efficiency.

CASE STUDY

Materials and Methods

For the analysis, a dataset of Supply Chains from the business DataCo Global was employed. Important registered activity areas include: commercial distribution, production, sales, and provisioning. Additionally, it enables the connection of organized and unstructured data for the purpose of knowledge creation.

Descriptive Analysis and Visualization

In the commercial world, data is increasingly taking on defining characteristics. DataCo Global business decision depends on it, and as a result, it establishes what businesses do. DataCo Global employed descriptive statistics (Tripathi, R. P. et al., 2023) and data visualization, in particular, can have a significant advantage over those that don't when it comes to statistics as shown in Figure .

To know the number of late deliveries in accordance with the shipping method and region and in order to compare the results of these two versions of the graph, which were created using different Python libraries, the first was an estatic graph created using Matplotlib, while the second was a dynamic graph created using Plotly.

Figure 3. (a) Top 10 products with late deliveries and (b) top 10 products with highest rate of late deliveries

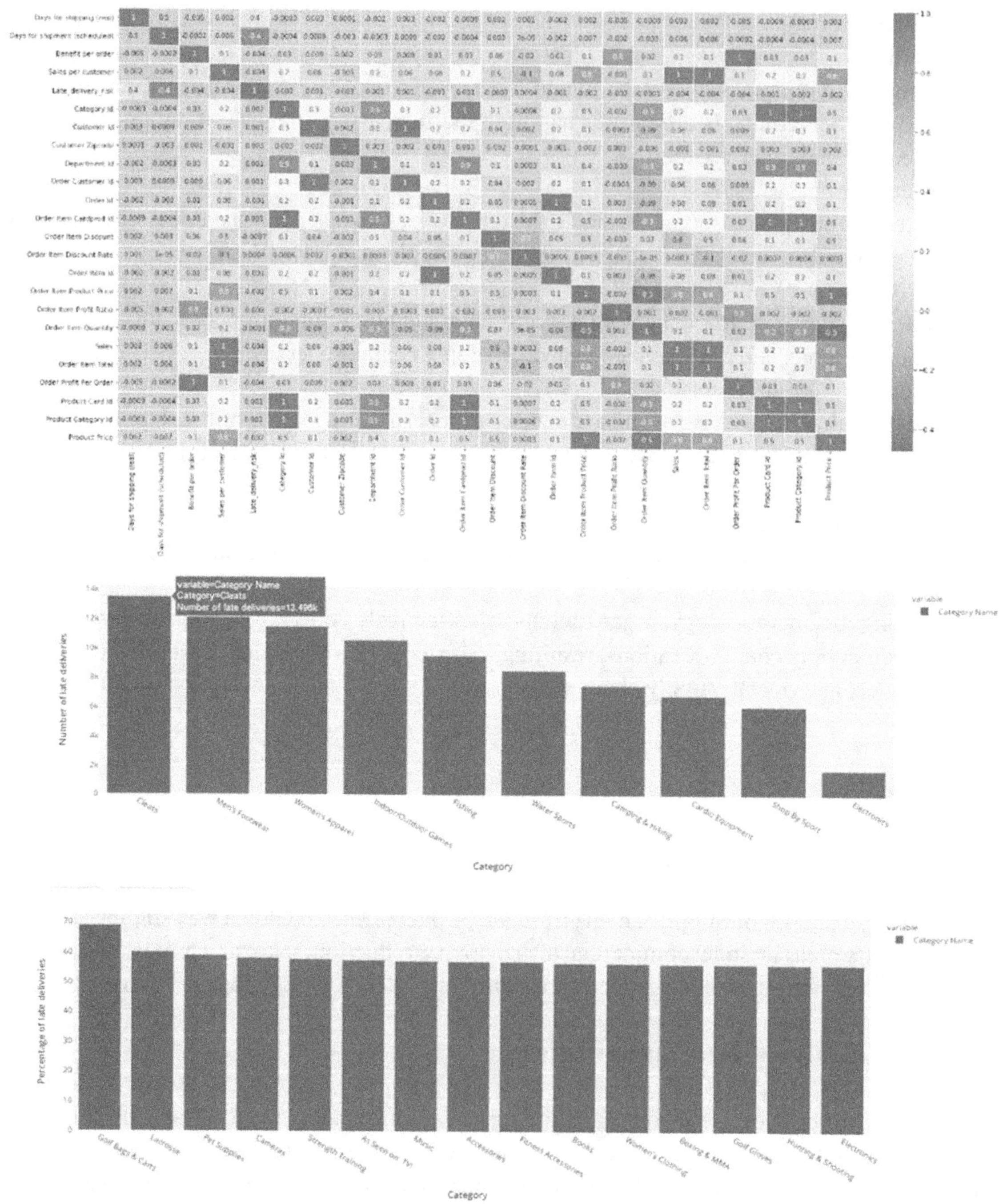

Predictive Statistics

Figure 4. Different types of shipping methods used in all regions

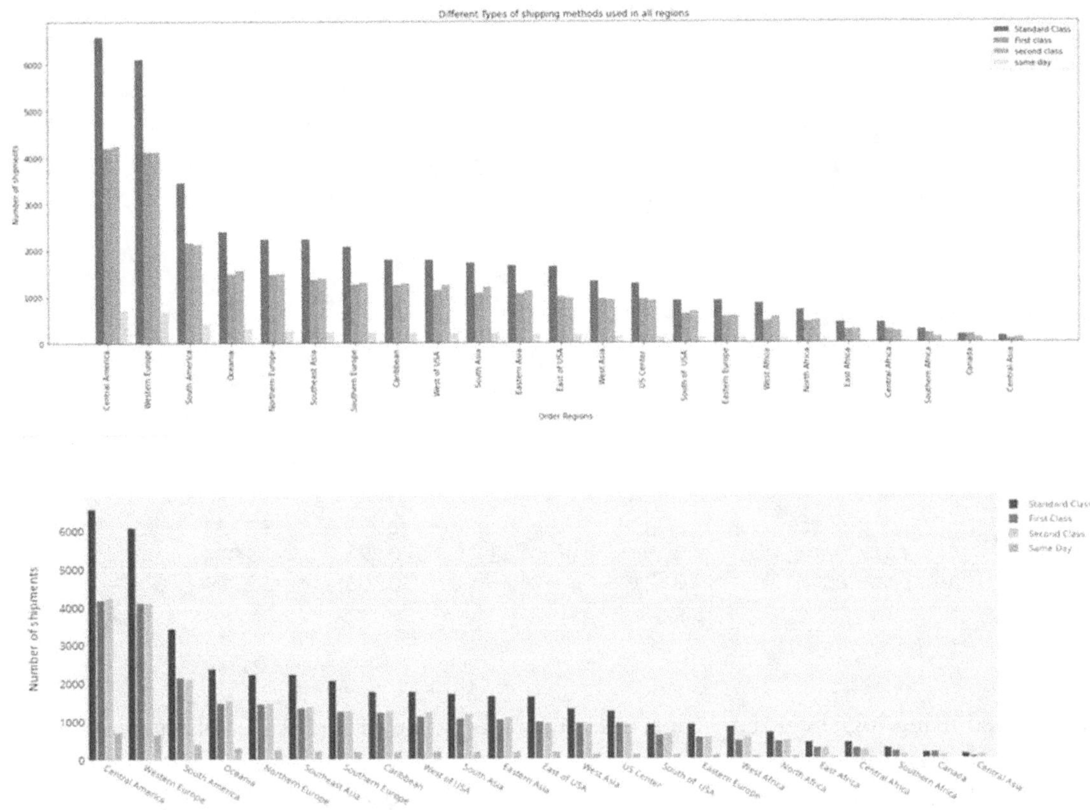

Test of Hypotheses

Hipotesis H0:

- The area to which the delivery is made has no bearing on the delivery being delayed.
- The late delivery is not affected by the kind of shipment.
- Product category and late delivery have no bearing on each other.

Alternative Hipothesis:

- The region where the delivery is made has an impact on the delivery's lateness.
- The type of delivery affects the delayed delivery.
- Influenced by the product category and the delayed delivery

Classification Techniques

Logistic Regression

The columns are selected needed for the model and Feature engineering, one hot encoding using one hot encoding when the category variable is a NOMINAL. Score the model is 0.7531560651338659. The

Figure 5. Logistic regression results

	precision	recall	f1-score	support
0	0.77	0.95	0.85	24680
1	0.50	0.14	0.22	8114
accuracy			0.75	32794
macro avg	0.64	0.55	0.54	32794
weighted avg	0.71	0.75	0.70	32794

Figure 6. Random Forest results

	precision	recall	f1-score	support
0	0.77	0.97	0.86	24680
1	0.53	0.10	0.17	8114
accuracy			0.76	32794
macro avg	0.65	0.53	0.51	32794
weighted avg	0.71	0.76	0.69	32794

model developed using logistical regression has an accuracy rate of 75.59%.Classification_report(Y_test,Y_pred) is shown in Figure 5.

Random Forest is the second algorithm to use. Score of the model is 0.7555345490028664. The model developed using the Random Forest algorithm has an accuracy of 75.76%.

CONCLUSION

This research abstract emphasizes the critical significance that big data analytics and data collection play in advancing the supply chain. Organizations may improve decision-making, efficiency, cut costs, and better meet the needs of today's changing markets by utilizing the potential of big data. For organizations hoping to be resilient and competitive in a world economy that is becoming more complicated, using big data in supply chain management is no longer a choice but a requirement. case study demonstrates how DataCo Global has successfully leveraged big data collection and analysis to optimize its supply chain management. By embracing data-driven decision-making DataCo Global has improved efficiency, reduced costs, and remained agile in the face of market dynamics and disruptions. This study serves as a valuable illustration of how supply chain companies can harness the power of big data to gain a competitive edge and better meet the demands of today's dynamic global markets.

REFERENCES

Ahmad, A. Y. (2019). Empirical Analysis on Accounting Information System Usage in Banking Sector in Jordan. *Academy of Accounting and Financial Studies Journal, 23*(5), 1–9.

Ahmad, A. Y. B., Gongada, T. N., Shrivastava, G., Gabbi, R. S., Islam, S., & Nagaraju, K. (2023). E-Commerce Trend Analysis and Management for Industry 5.0 using User Data Analysis. *International Journal of Intelligent Systems and Applications in Engineering, 11*(11s), 135–150.

Ahmad, A. Y. B., & Kumari, S. S. (2023). Blockchain Implementation in Financial Sector and Cyber Security System. *2023 International Conference on Artificial Intelligence and Smart Communication (AISC),* 586-590. 10.1109/AISC56616.2023.10085045

Babu, S. Z. D., Pandey, D., Naidu, G. T., Sumathi, S., Gupta, A., Bader Alazzam, M., & Pandey, B. K. (2022, July). Analysation of Big Data in Smart Healthcare. In *Artificial Intelligence on Medical Data: Proceedings of International Symposium, ISCMM 2021* (pp. 243-251). Singapore: Springer Nature Singapore.

Chalmeta, R., & Santos-deLeón, N. J. (2020). Sustainable supply chain in the era of industry 4.0 and big data: A systematic analysis of literature and research. *Sustainability (Basel), 12*(10), 4108. doi:10.3390/su12104108

Daoud, M. K., Al-Qeed, M., Ahmad, A. Y. B., & Al-Gasawneh, J. A. (2023). Mobile Marketing: Exploring the Efficacy of User-Centric Strategies for Enhanced Consumer Engagement and Conversion Rates. *International Journal of Membrane Science and Technology, 10*(2), 1252–1262. doi:10.15379/ijmst.vi.1425

Daoud, Alqudah, Al-Qeed, Al Qaied, & Ahmad. (2023). The Relationship Between Mobile Marketing and Customer Perceptions in Jordanian Commercial Banks: The Electronic Quality as A Mediator Variable. *IJMST, 10*(2), 1360-1371.

David, S., Duraipandian, K., Chandrasekaran, D., Pandey, D., Sindhwani, N., & Pandey, B. K. (2023). Impact of blockchain in healthcare system. In *Unleashing the Potentials of Blockchain Technology for Healthcare Industries* (pp. 37–57). Academic Press. doi:10.1016/B978-0-323-99481-1.00004-3

Golinska-Dawson, P., Werner-Lewandowska, K., Kolinska, K., & Kolinski, A. (2023). Impact of market drivers on the digital maturity of logistics processes in a supply chain. *Sustainability (Basel), 15*(4), 3120. doi:10.3390/su15043120

Gupta, R., Mane, M., Bhardwaj, S., Nandekar, U., Afaq, A., Dhabliya, D., & Pandey, B. K. (2023). Use of Artificial Intelligence for Image Processing to Aid Digital Forensics: Legislative Challenges. In *Handbook of Research on Thrust Technologies' Effect on Image Processing* (pp. 433–447). IGI Global. doi:10.4018/978-1-6684-8618-4.ch026

Hazen, B., Skipper, J., Ezell, J., & Boone, C. (2016). Big Data and Predictive Analytics for Supply Chain Sustainability: A Theory-driven Research Agenda. *Computers & Industrial Engineering, 101*, 592–598. Advance online publication. doi:10.1016/j.cie.2016.06.030

Khan, B., Hasan, A., Pandey, D., Ventayen, R. J. M., Pandey, B. K., & Gowwrii, G. (2021). 12 Fusion of Datamining and Artificial Intelligence. *Machine learning and iot for intelligent systems and smart applications*, 201.

Khan, Y. (2022). Application of Internet of Things (IoT) in Sustainable Supply Chain Management. *Sustainability, 15*(1), 694. doi:10.3390/su15010694

Kirubasri, G., Sankar, S., Pandey, D., Pandey, B. K., Nassa, V. K., & Dadheech, P. (2022). Software-defined networking-based Ad hoc networks routing protocols. In *Software defined networking for Ad Hoc networks* (pp. 95–123). Springer International Publishing. doi:10.1007/978-3-030-91149-2_5

Kumar, M. S., Sankar, S., Nassa, V. K., Pandey, D., Pandey, B. K., & Enbeyle, W. (2021). Innovation and creativity for data mining using computational statistics. In *Methodologies and Applications of Computational Statistics for Machine Intelligence* (pp. 223–240). IGI Global. doi:10.4018/978-1-7998-7701-1.ch012

Kumar Pandey, B., Pandey, D., Nassa, V. K., Ahmad, T., Singh, C., George, A. S., & Wakchaure, M. A. (2021). Encryption and steganography-based text extraction in IoT using the EWCTS optimizer. *Imaging Science Journal, 69*(1-4), 38–56. doi:10.1080/13682199.2022.2146885

Malhotra, P., Pandey, D., Pandey, B. K., & Patra, P. M. (2021). Managing agricultural supply chains in COVID-19 lockdown. *International Journal of Quality and Innovation, 5*(2), 109–118. doi:10.1504/IJQI.2021.117181

Mandal, S. (2018). An examination of the importance of big data analytics in supply chain agility development: A dynamic capability perspective. *Management Research Review, 41*(10), 1201–1219. Advance online publication. doi:10.1108/MRR-11-2017-0400

Mishra, D., Gunasekaran, A., Papadopoulos, T., & Childe, S. J. (2018). Big Data and supply chain management: A review and bibliometric analysis. *Annals of Operations Research, 270*(1-2), 313–336. doi:10.1007/s10479-016-2236-y

Muniandi, B., Huang, C.-J., Kuo, C.-C., Yang, T.-F., Chen, K.-H., Lin, Y.-H., Lin, S.-R., & Tsai, T.-Y. (2019, November). A 97% Maximum Efficiency Fully Automated Control Turbo Boost Topology for Battery Chargers. *IEEE Transactions on Circuits and Systems. I, Regular Papers, 66*(11), 4516–4527. doi:10.1109/TCSI.2019.2925374

Nguyen, T., Zhou, L., Spiegler, V., Ieromonachou, P., & Lin, Y. (2017). Big data analytics in supply chain management: A state-of-the-art literature review. *Computers & Operations Research*. Advance online publication. doi:10.1016/j.cor.2017.07.004

Pandey, B. K., & Pandey, D. (2023). Parametric optimization and prediction of enhanced thermoelectric performance in co-doped CaMnO3 using response surface methodology and neural network. *Journal of Materials Science Materials in Electronics, 34*(21), 1589. doi:10.1007/s10854-023-10954-1

Pandey, B. K., Pandey, D., Alkhafaji, M. A., Güneşer, M. T., & Şeker, C. (2023). A Reliable Transmission and Extraction of Textual Information Using Keyless Encryption, Steganography, and Deep Algorithm with Cuckoo Optimization. In *Micro-Electronics and Telecommunication Engineering: Proceedings of 6th ICMETE 2022* (pp. 629–636). Springer Nature Singapore. doi:10.1007/978-981-19-9512-5_57

Pandey, D., Pandey, B. K., & Wairya, S. (2021). Hybrid deep neural network with adaptive galactic swarm optimization for text extraction from scene images. *Soft Computing*, *25*(2), 1563–1580. doi:10.1007/s00500-020-05245-4

Pandey, J. K., Jain, R., Dilip, R., Kumbhkar, M., Jaiswal, S., Pandey, B. K., & Pandey, D. (2022). Investigating Role of IoT in the Development of Smart Application for Security Enhancement. In *IoT Based Smart Applications* (pp. 219–243). Springer International Publishing.

Pramanik, S., Pandey, D., Joardar, S., Niranjanamurthy, M., Pandey, B. K., & Kaur, J. (2023, October). An overview of IoT privacy and security in smart cities. In AIP Conference Proceedings (Vol. 2495, No. 1). AIP Publishing. doi:10.1063/5.0123511

Rasool, F., Greco, M., & Grimaldi, M. (2022). Digital supply chain performance metrics: A literature review. *Measuring Business Excellence*, *26*(1), 23–38. doi:10.1108/MBE-11-2020-0147

Richey, R. G., Roath, A. S., Adams, F. G., & Wieland, A. (2022). A responsiveness view of logistics and supply chain management. *Journal of Business Logistics*, *43*(1), 62–91. doi:10.1111/jbl.12290

Rozados, I. V., & Tjahjono, B. (2014, December). Big data analytics in supply chain management: Trends and related research. In *6th international conference on operations and supply chain management* (Vol. 1, p. 13). Academic Press.

Rozados, V. (2014). *Big Data Analytics in Supply Chain Management: Trends and Related Research*. doi:10.13140/RG.2.1.4935.2563

Sahani, K., Khadka, S. S., Sahani, S. K., Pandey, B. K., & Pandey, D. (2023). A possible underground roadway for transportation facilities in Kathmandu Valley: A racking deformation of underground rectangular structures. *Engineering Reports*, 12821. doi:10.1002/eng2.12821

Sengupta, R., Sengupta, D., Pandey, D., Pandey, B. K., Nassa, V. K., & Dadeech, P. (2021). A Systematic Review of 5G Opportunities, Architecture and Challenges. *Future Trends in 5G and G, 6*, 247.

Singh, H., Pandey, B. K., George, S., Pandey, D., Anand, R., Sindhwani, N., & Dadheech, P. (2022, July). Effective Overview of Different ML Models Used for Prediction of COVID-19 Patients. In *Artificial Intelligence on Medical Data: Proceedings of International Symposium, ISCMM 2021* (pp. 185-192). Singapore: Springer Nature Singapore.

Tripathi, R. P., Sharma, M., Gupta, A. K., Pandey, D., Pandey, B. K., Shahul, A., & George, A. H. (2023). Timely Prediction of Diabetes by Means of Machine Learning Practices. *Augmented Human Research*, *8*(1), 1. doi:10.1007/s41133-023-00062-4

Wamba, S. & Akter, S. (2015). *Big Data Analytics for Supply Chain Management: A Literature Review and Research Agenda*. . doi:10.1007/978-3-319-24626-0_5

Wang, C., Ahmad, S. F., Ayassrah, A. Y. B. A., Awwad, E. M., Irshad, M., Ali, Y. A., ... Han, H. (2023). An empirical evaluation of technology acceptance model for Artificial Intelligence in E-commerce. *Heliyon*, *9*(8), e18349. doi:10.1016/j.heliyon.2023.e18349 PMID:37520947

Wang, G., Gunasekaran, A., Ngai, E. W., & Papadopoulos, T. (2016). Big data analytics in logistics and supply chain management: Certain investigations for research and applications. *International Journal of Production Economics*, *176*, 98–110. doi:10.1016/j.ijpe.2016.03.014

Chapter 13
Post-Pandemic Biometric Challenges and Solutions: A Shocker to Supply Chain

K. Neelima
https://orcid.org/0000-0002-4296-3273
School of Engineering, Mohan Babu University, Tirupati, India

B. Madhavi
School of Engineering and Technology, Sri Padmavathi Mahila Viswavidyala, India

C. Padma
Sri Venkateswara College of Engineering, Tirupati, India

Binay Kumar Pandey
https://orcid.org/0000-0002-4041-1213
Department of Information Technology, College of Technology, Govind Ballabh Pant University of Agriculture and Technology, Pantnagar, India

Gadee Gowwrii
Osmania University, Hyderabad, India

Shyam Sundar Manaktala
Jaipur Engineering College and Research Centre, India

ABSTRACT

The COVID-19 pandemic has imposed several challenges to mankind, among them one being biometric, for attendance of working community and the related demand and supply chain related to biometric companies, developers, investors and customers. Due to many medical constraints, people are now reluctant to use contact-based biometric systems. With the increase in personal and social hygiene to avoid transmission of pathogens via contact, people try to avoid usage of fingerprint, facial-, and voice-based biometrics. Further, if the system is not active then multiple times of access contacts may be necessary. This aspect has to be restricted for avoidance of future pandemic situations.

DOI: 10.4018/979-8-3693-1347-3.ch013

1. INTRODUCTION

The COVID19 (Pandey, D. et al., 2021) pandemic has imposed several challenges to mankind, among them one being biometric for attendance of working community and the related demand and supply chain related to biometric companies, developers, investors and customers. Due to many medical constraints, people are now reluctant to use contact based biometric systems. With the increase in personal and social hygiene so as to avoid transmission of pathogens via contact, people try to avoid usage of finger print, facial and voice based biometrics. Further, if the system is not active then multiple times of access contacts may be necessary (B. Muniandi et al., 2019). This aspect has to be restricted for avoidance of future pandemic situations. Hence with the imposed challenges, arrival of new solutions through renewed opportunities and research are explored. The exploration as a set of new solutions many ways to biometrics were developed such as periocular recognition or non-constrained iris, touchless fingerprint and vein based authentication, face recognition system via a group through video capture, etc. Further the new approach is to utilize the biometrics itself for disease detection with integrated thermal and infrared sensors is used. The location updates are availed from IoT (Pandey, J. K. et al.,2022) approaches where the global positioning system integrated devices are developed. Hybrid biometric devices with multiple ways of biometric in a single device arealso developed. So the higher priority will be for the design and development of biometric devices with the related inventory manufacture and distribution. As the new technologies are invented, further the cost of manufacturing and distribution increases, affecting the supply chain. This chapter details the various challenges imposed due to COVID19 pandemic (Lelisho, M. E. et al.,2023) and the solutions devised as an alternative to them with applicable pros and cons. Also this details the entire framework of design to end-user including the demand and supply aspects.

The COVID19 (Menon, V. et al., 2022) pandemic has imposed several challenges to mankind due to very dangerous life threateningvirus spread across the world. This has changed the dynamics of life in every possible way. Several problems were faced by living people like inequalities based on gender, ethnic races, economy, etc (Neelima K, C Subhas, 2022). There were other areas that are also severely affected like world economy, industriesespecially manufacturing, transport, distribution, medical field, tourism (Saxena, A. et al.,2021), etc. The world as a whole looks upon new ways of touchless biometrics/ scanners everywhere for record of presence and digital payments.

The most affected area is the working environment which had shifted from offices to home. During work hours, the tracking of employee to assigned work has been a major challenge. Even after pandemic, when the working environment has shifted to office, still people are accepting adherence to pandemic time protocols for safety. This has revolutionized the biometric systems in an unexpected manner. The focus is to avoid gathering to as to avoid potential transmission of viruses. This further imposes conditions like hand and device hygiene.

The biometric systems that aim at automatic identity verification of authenticated individuals based on their biological or physical traits. Many systems have to maintain a database (Babu, S. Z. D. et al.,2022) inherently and update as the new authentic individuals add up in the organisation. These details can never be lost so as to enable authentication. The biometric systems do find applications in offices (V.M. Patel, et al, 2016) for identity management (S. Mondal and P. Bours, 2017), forensics for post accident culprit identification (M. Tistarelli and C. Champod. 2017), surveillance for social and welfare management (M. Tistarelli and C. Champod. 2009), etc.

This chapter aims at the discussion on various biometric devices available and their respective pros and cons. The possible solutions to overcome the challenges imposed by pandemic. Further how the related supply chain is affected and ways to overcome it.

2. BIOMETRIC SYSTEMS – A GLIMPSE

In prose, many solutions were proposed for biometric systems starting from traditional to advanced biometric systems. The following are the biometric systems proposed as a solution for authentication. The Broad classification (Pandey, D. et al.,2022) includes touch based and touchless biometric systems. The second category arises due to mandatory use of masks and sanitizers during pandemic and even post pandemic. There are more significant threats due to these imposed conditions for identification (Pandey, B. K. et al.,2021) of personswith masks.

2.1 Touch Based Systems

These biometric systems include a mandatory touch to the sensing system for identification. The usage of such systems was restricted starting from pandemic period. But still as they contributed much to the society prior to pandemic, a note of them doesn't harm (Khan, Yasser, et al.,2023).

2.1.1 Traditional Biometric Systems

The traditional biometric systemsas shown in figure 1 are based on touch based systems include authentic passwords, access cards, etc which serve as an example for token based security systems. These systems were easily deployable and transferable but could be easily hacked or shared which imposed threat to organization (S Carlaw, 2020).

Figure 1. Traditional biometric systems

Figure 2. Fingerprint recognition system

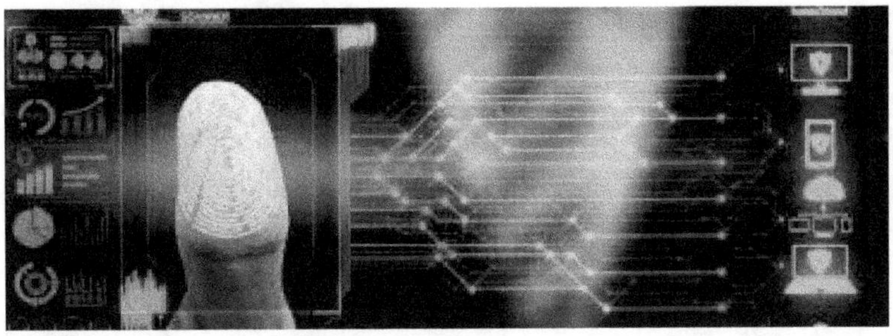

2.1.2 Fingerprint Recognition System

The finger print recognition biometric system as shown in figure 2 works based on the finger print database with various positions of finger or fingers (A. Bera and D. Bhattacharjee, 2017). These use the scanned and stored finger ridges, grooves and valleys for comparison with the current one collected from a smooth surface used to scan with a backlight for clarity.It uses near-infrared or short wave infrared or laser scatter contrast imaging or NIR backlight. It offers advantages like accuracy and ease in database (Kumar, M. S. et al.,2021) collection and validation. But it requires installation and during pandemic it was the system that caused an easy spread of virus (L. Spinoulas, et al, 2020).

2.1.3 Handwritten Signature Biometric System

It is one of the contact based biometric system as shown in figure 3 where the person is asked to write a few words to a sentence or even a simple signature. Based on the writing style, the identification is performed by comparing the present signature with DeepSignDB database and then authentication is performed. This system offers the advantage of easy identification of fake signatures especially at banks but it requires extra handwriting input devices and the collection of handwritten script or signature along with high accuracy trained systems with machine learning (Meslie, Y. et al.,2021) or deep learning algorithms (Pandey, B. K., &Pandey, D. 2023) . Hence this proves to be good for banking sectors and forensics but not for daily usage (R. Tolosana, et al, 2019).

2.2 Touch-Less Biometric Systems

These systems do not require any contact to the biometric system and the authentication is performed based on scan similar to selfie photography.

2.2.1 Sclera Vasculature and Periocular Biometric Recognition System

This identifies the authentic person based on the tendency of veins of the sclera. This accepts the input as the eye and its surrounding region in RGB color image. It uses orthogonal combinatorial local binary coding model or learning label smoothing regularization model combined with cross-entropy and KL divergence loss function to verify the identity from stored database. The advantage offered by this system is the requirement of focussed picture of sclera but it requires high resolution camera and focussed

Figure 3. Handwritten signature biometric system

angles which is usually a time consuming process when the number of persons to be authenticated are large (M. Vitek, et al. 2020).

2.2.2 Gait or Stride Recognition

This system focuses the authentication based on gait and temporal features by using sensors (Vinodhini, V. et al.,2022) like accelerometers and gyroscopes embedded in cell phones. For giat related features, Convolutional neural networks and recurrent neural networks are used whereas for temporal features, a long short-term memory network (LSTM) is used. It offers advantage of minimal additional features requirement but falls short due to relatively low accuracy rate (Q. Zou, et al. 2020).

2.2.3 Palm Recognition Biometric System

This biometric system uses palm images taken as a photo in a contactless mode. It uses a regular generative adversarial network with loss function to aid in learning the features of pal line connectivity for every person two identified palms taken as database. As the number of persons increase, the number of iterations require more for training and acquisition of the model. It offers advantage of contactless biometric but any variations in the palm line may cause forgery of GAN generated patterns (S. Minaee, et al. 2020).

2.2.4 Wrist Vein Biometric Recognition System

This biometric system uses the NIR camera and NIR LED embedded in modern cell phones, to capture the structure of wrist groove lines. It uses algorithms like SIFT, SURF, ORB, etc for feature point acquisition process, tgs-cvbr algorithm for database preparation phase, i.e., for extraction of features and to provide authentication.It offers advantages like real time recognition in contactless manner but has relatively low recognition accuracy (R. Garcia-Martin and R. Sanchez-Reillo, 2020).

2.2.5 Voice Recognition Biometric System

It uses voice as a basis for recognition but if any deviations to voice occur due to changing environmental conditions, then it fails miserably. Its implementation requires Natural Language Processing algorithms, a low to high intensity voice recognition system like mic, deep learning algorithms for training the system, etc (D. Snyder, et al. 2018).

2.2.6 Face Recognition Biometric System

This is the biometric system as shown in figure 4, which is most popular in pre-pandemic era and from pandemic to post pandemic era. It uses facial features as the mode to authenticate the person. The algorithms were drastically improved to identify the person even with various types of masks like clinical mask, cloth mask, plastic mask, transparent mask, etc. It offered advantages like contactless and fast recognition but accuracy decreases with variations in masks wore by the person (M. K. Daoud, et al., 2023). It uses Residual Neural Network with IoT (Pramanik, S. et al., 2023) integrated systems like physi-

Figure 4. Face recognition biometric system

cal layer, edge layer, bounding box, edge computing, etc. The hardware includes the installed cameras, mobile phones, microchips and microcontrollers as per the requirement. Many preprocessing algorithms were developed for face recognition, feature extraction and database storing and mining algorithms, etc (M. Loey, et al. 2020).

3. FUTURE TECHNOLOGIES

To reduce sensor contamination and pathogen transmission, the contactless biometric systems gained more popularity. The research enabled several solutions towards this like new devices for input and output, several machine learning (Singh, H. et al.,2022) and deep learning algorithms that can be integrated, interoperability of touch and touch-less systems, Integrated Augmented Reality and Virtual Reality devices, etc.

Personal hygiene concerns have increased societal resistance to the use of touch-based sensors which enabled design of 2D or 3D touchless fingerprint recognition systems such as those illustrated in Figure 5 (J. Priesnitz, et al, 2021).

Touchless fingerprint sensors capture and process fingerprints by using colour images with improved contrast and sharpness (Ahmad, A. Y. B., (2019)). The research focus was towards the minutiae extractors and comparators. Further the interoperability of touch-based and touchless devices was integrated to overcome some of the challenges like mirroring, colour-to-grayscale conversion or inverted back- and foreground, aspect ratio or deformation estimation, DPI alignment and ridge frequency estimation, etc without degradation in accuracy and reliability.

The fingervein-based recognition sensors prove to be an alternative for robust operation even with variability in skin hydration or presentation attacks especially in ATMs. These utilize the NIR illuminated images of the finger or hand being differently absorbed by hemoglobin and the skin for easy detection of vein patterns (Ahmad, A. Y. B.,ey al.,2023). But the deviations in accuracy might happen due to significant rotation and translation variation due to finger misplacement.

Figure 5. Touchless fingerprints (V. M. Patel, et al, 2016)

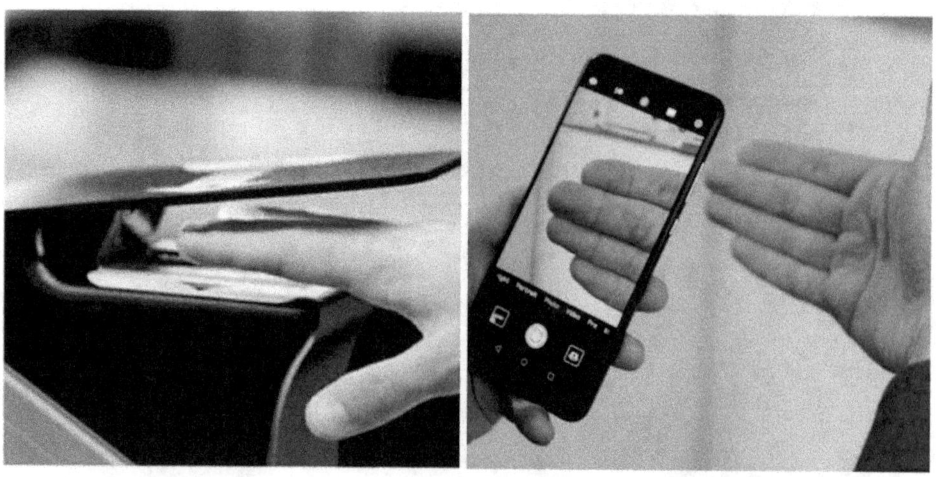

Hence the capture of hand vascular patterns gained popularity where the Bluetooth controlled device captures the images required under challenging environmental conditions, e.g., uncontrolled background or varying illumination, etc. Here the challenges may be replay and presentation attacks.

Due to damage caused to respiratory system by COVID-19 attack, the speech of human was severely impacted due to diminished lung capacity or disease. SO speech based biometric systems had to undergo severe changes like using non-speech sounds recorded from healthy speakers and those infected (Tareke, S. A. et al.,2022) with the COVID19 virus including recordings of coughs, breathing sounds, speech excerpts, etc as an alternative.

The thermal face images could aid in recognising individuals with fever or symptoms of COVID-19 infection (Parthiban, K. et al.,2021). Further the thermal screening equipment was devised.

4. IMPACT ON SOCIETY

Similar to other technologies, biometric recognition systems also do affect the society. The positive aspects of biometric systems include faster border crossing authentication or smartphone or laptop unlocking convenience but due to privacy and security issues, fairness or trustworthiness of biometric systems is varied which have paved way to contact-less approaches for global applications like building access control. The drastic improvements in digitalisation in many sectors like online exams or eHealth systems, has enabled wide acceptance of biometric technologies. But these systems do require security algorithms to avoid personal tracking like issues with personal data access, unauthenticated data erasure, data sharing, etc. If any bias or errors are derived from the biometric technologies for authentication, then negative impacts such as discrimination, and diminish the trust etc can happen. The body temperature checks, contact tracing, COVID testing and handling of results, monitoring presence within the premises, vaccination campaigns, access control, and the use of IT-tools in telework had aided a lot in the development of secured biometric systems (P. Rot, et al, 2020).

5. SHOCKWAVES IN BIOMETRIC SUPPLY CHAIN

The global reaction to pandemic had short-term and long-term implications in biometric related business with a similar magnitude. For all related businesses, a rough sea was foreseen due to limited consumer spending, supply chain disruptions, less amount of manufacturing as less available labour.

Several companies like Alibaba, YITU, Graphen and Google DeepMind, etc have focussed towards development of AI tools integrated biometrics to help detect the virus, diagnose its evolution, track its geographical footprint, project its future, and predict its potential protein structure to find a vaccine for it. So due to outlook retrenchment, reduced investment in modernisation, etc the survival instincts trump the drive to prosperity.

Once any biometric device design is developed, it undergoes the following phases in supply chain. They are

- Planning and Procurement (the phase where the raw materials and critical components are firmly decided, contacted for supply from multiple suppliers with their relevant purchase orders, decision will be made for purchase and delivery of inventories). Here,the blockchain (David, S. et al.,2023) is integrated to track the payment and supply.

- Manufacturing and Production (The organization spans across multiple plants for stock levels, state of equipment, maintenance of records, etc). Here, the priority is to have a seamless invoice generation and fast processing to improve accuracy and speed, reduce overpayments and disintermediation of third party service providers, etc.
- Asset Tracking and Logistics (tracking shipments having partial or full capacity). Here, the integration of Blockchain with IoT (Iyyanar, P. et al.,2023) sensors can be performed to automate decisions to schedule fleets, alternate routes, reduce the freight process errors, etc.
- Compliance and Sustainability (complying with the standards and timelines to follow the norms set by governments and regulators across the world). Here, by integrating IoT (Kumar Pandey, B. et al.,2021) Sensors and biometrics with the underlying networks, organizations can be used to know the proof of source, persons involved, processes and product certifications, etc to ensure quality and reduce redundant paper based audits.
- Distribution and Retail (Deliver of goods ordered to the respective location or organization by using healthy logistics). Here, the biometrics aid in authenticated transfer and distribution of goods without compromising privacy of individuals.

Due to pandemic, all the above were disrupted from small scale to large scale, leading to reinvading of supply chain norms, manufacturing and distribution of inventory for new inventions that require Artificial Intelligence and Machine Learning integrated Biometrics.

6. CONCLUSION

Severe challenges wereimposed by the pandemic to biometric recognition systems and supply chains that had paved way to development of new biometrics technologies. The strict protocols and imposed constraints like use of masks covering the nose and mouth to control the widespread of pathogens enabled the use of facial biometrics. They could degrade the performance of the biometric systems as masks occluded a considerable part of the face. Then other biometric systems like iris recognition gained importance that can use the NIR spectrum with mobile devices. The images can have quality from low to super-resolution for such systems. Further biometric systems included full periocular region. Then hand-based biometric systems were affected due to hygiene practices whose performance was degraded due to dry skin, lower quality fingerprint images for both touch-based and touch-less systems. Vein-based recognition systems were found to be more robust to variations in skin conditions. Many significant changes were seen in input sensing devices, algorithms adopted, etc in the post pandemic era. Still continuous authentication, presentation attack detection, or biometric template protection to ensure security and privacy remain as the challenge to biometric systems. To reinvade the supply chain prior to pandemic, the new technologies like Blockchain, Artificial Intelligence, Machine Learning, etc are mandatory.

REFERENCES

Ahmad, A. Y. B. (2019). Empirical Analysis on Accounting Information System Usage in Banking Sector in Jordan. *Academy of Accounting and Financial Studies Journal, 23*(5), 1–9.

Ahmad, A. Y. B., Gongada, T. N., Shrivastava, G., Gabbi, R. S., Islam, S., & Nagaraju, K. (2023). E-Commerce Trend Analysis and Management for Industry 5.0 using User Data Analysis. *International Journal of Intelligent Systems and Applications in Engineering, 11*(11s), 135–150.

Ahmad, A. Y. B., & Kumari, S. S. (2023). Blockchain Implementation in Financial Sector and Cyber Security System. *2023 International Conference on Artificial Intelligence and Smart Communication (AISC),* 586-590. 10.1109/AISC56616.2023.10085045

Babu, S. Z. D., Pandey, D., Naidu, G. T., Sumathi, S., Gupta, A., Bader Alazzam, M., & Pandey, B. K. (2022, July). Analysation of Big Data in Smart Healthcare. In *Artificial Intelligence on Medical Data: Proceedings of International Symposium, ISCMM 2021* (pp. 243-251). Singapore: Springer Nature Singapore.

Bera, A., & Bhattacharjee, D. (2017). Human identification using selected features from finger geometric profiles. *IEEE Transactions on Systems, Man, and Cybernetics. Systems, 50*, 2017.

Carlaw, S. (2020). Impact on biometrics of COVID-19. *Biometric Technol. Today, 2020*(4), 8–9. doi:10.1016/S0969-4765(20)30050-3

Daoud, Alqudah, Al-Qeed, Al Qaied, & Ahmad. (2023). The Relationship Between Mobile Marketing and Customer Perceptions in Jordanian Commercial Banks: The Electronic Quality as A Mediator Variable. *IJMST, 10*(2), 1360-1371.

Daoud, M. K., Al-Qeed, M., Ahmad, A. Y. B., & Al-Gasawneh, J. A. (2023). Mobile Marketing: Exploring the Efficacy of User-Centric Strategies for Enhanced Consumer Engagement and Conversion Rates. *International Journal of Membrane Science and Technology, 10*(2), 1252–1262. doi:10.15379/ijmst.vi.1425

David, S., Duraipandian, K., Chandrasekaran, D., Pandey, D., Sindhwani, N., & Pandey, B. K. (2023). Impact of blockchain in healthcare system. In *Unleashing the Potentials of Blockchain Technology for Healthcare Industries* (pp. 37–57). Academic Press. doi:10.1016/B978-0-323-99481-1.00004-3

Garcia-Martin, R., & Sanchez-Reillo, R. (2020). Vein biometric recognition on a smartphone. *IEEE Access : Practical Innovations, Open Solutions, 8*, 2020. doi:10.1109/ACCESS.2020.3000044

Iyyanar, P., Anand, R., Shanthi, T., Nassa, V. K., Pandey, B. K., George, A. S., & Pandey, D. (2023). A Real-Time Smart Sewage Cleaning UAV Assistance System Using IoT. In *Handbook of Research on Data-Driven Mathematical Modeling in Smart Cities* (pp. 24–39). IGI Global.

Khan, Y. (2022). Application of Internet of Things (IoT) in Sustainable Supply Chain Management. *Sustainability, 15*(1), 694. doi:10.3390/su15010694

Kumar, M. S., Sankar, S., Nassa, V. K., Pandey, D., Pandey, B. K., & Enbeyle, W. (2021). Innovation and creativity for data mining using computational statistics. In *Methodologies and Applications of Computational Statistics for Machine Intelligence* (pp. 223–240). IGI Global. doi:10.4018/978-1-7998-7701-1.ch012

Kumar Pandey, B., Pandey, D., Nassa, V. K., Ahmad, T., Singh, C., George, A. S., & Wakchaure, M. A. (2021). Encryption and steganography-based text extraction in IoT using the EWCTS optimizer. *Imaging Science Journal*, *69*(1-4), 38–56. doi:10.1080/13682199.2022.2146885

Lelisho, M. E., Pandey, D., Alemu, B. D., Pandey, B. K., & Tareke, S. A. (2023). The negative impact of social media during COVID-19 pandemic. *Trends in Psychology*, *31*(1), 123–142. doi:10.1007/s43076-022-00192-5

Loey, M., Manogaran, G., Taha, M. H. N., & Khalifa, N. E. M. (2020). A hybrid deep transfer learning model with machine learning methods for face mask detection in the era of the COVID-19 pandemic. *Measurement*, *167*, 108288. doi:10.1016/j.measurement.2020.108288 PMID:32834324

Menon, V., Pandey, D., Khosla, D., Kaur, M., Vashishtha, H. K., George, A. S., & Pandey, B. K. (2022). A Study on COVID–19, Its Origin, Phenomenon, Variants, and IoT-Based Framework to Detect the Presence of Coronavirus. In *IoT Based Smart Applications* (pp. 1–13). Springer International Publishing.

Meslie, Y., Enbeyle, W., Pandey, B. K., Pramanik, S., Pandey, D., Dadeech, P., & Saini, A. (2021). Machine intelligence-based trend analysis of COVID-19 for total daily confirmed cases in Asia and Africa. In *Methodologies and Applications of Computational Statistics for Machine Intelligence* (pp. 164–185). IGI Global. doi:10.4018/978-1-7998-7701-1.ch009

MinaeeS.MinaeiM.AbdolrashidiA. (2020) Palm-GAN: generating realistic palmprint images using total-variation regularized GAN. 2020, https://arxiv.org/abs/2003.10834

Mondal, S., & Bours, P. (2017, March). A study on continuous authentication using a combination of keystroke and mouse biometrics. *Neurocomputing*, *230*, 1–22. doi:10.1016/j.neucom.2016.11.031

Muniandi, B., Huang, C.-J., Kuo, C.-C., Yang, T.-F., Chen, K.-H., Lin, Y.-H., Lin, S.-R., & Tsai, T.-Y. (2019, November). A 97% Maximum Efficiency Fully Automated Control Turbo Boost Topology for Battery Chargers. *IEEE Transactions on Circuits and Systems. I, Regular Papers*, *66*(11), 4516–4527. doi:10.1109/TCSI.2019.2925374

Neelima, K., & Chennapalli, S. (2022). Post-Pandemic Global Inequalities: Causes and Measures. In S. Deo & A. Kumar (Eds.), *Emerging Trends and Insights on Economic Inequality in the Wake of Global Crises* (pp. 40–55). IGI Global. doi:10.4018/978-1-6684-5289-9.ch003

Pandey, B. K., & Pandey, D. (2023). Parametric optimization and prediction of enhanced thermoelectric performance in co-doped CaMnO3 using response surface methodology and neural network. *Journal of Materials Science Materials in Electronics*, *34*(21), 1589. doi:10.1007/s10854-023-10954-1

Pandey, B. K., Pandey, D., Wariya, S., Aggarwal, G., & Rastogi, R. (2021). Deep learning and particle swarm optimisation-based techniques for visually impaired humans' text recognition and identification. *Augmented Human Research*, *6*(1), 1–14. doi:10.1007/s41133-021-00051-5

Pandey, D., Ogunmola, G. A., Enbeyle, W., Abdullahi, M., Pandey, B. K., & Pramanik, S. (2021). COVID-19: A framework for effective delivering of online classes during lockdown. *Human Arenas*, 1-15.

Pandey, D., Wairya, S., Sharma, M., Gupta, A. K., Kakkar, R., & Pandey, B. K. (2022). An approach for object tracking, categorization, and autopilot guidance for passive homing missiles. *Aerospace Systems*, *5*(4), 553–566. doi:10.1007/s42401-022-00150-0

Pandey, J. K., Jain, R., Dilip, R., Kumbhkar, M., Jaiswal, S., Pandey, B. K., & Pandey, D. (2022). Investigating Role of IoT in the Development of Smart Application for Security Enhancement. In *IoT Based Smart Applications* (pp. 219–243). Springer International Publishing.

Parthiban, K., Pandey, D., & Pandey, B. K. (2021). Impact of SARS-CoV-2 in online education, predicting and contrasting mental stress of young students: A machine learning approach. *Augmented Human Research*, *6*(1), 10. doi:10.1007/s41133-021-00048-0

Patel, V. M., Chellappa, R., Chandra, D., & Barbello, B. (2016, July). Continuous user authentication on mobile devices: Recent progress and remaining challenges. *IEEE Signal Processing Magazine*, *33*(4), 49–61. doi:10.1109/MSP.2016.2555335

Pramanik, S., Pandey, D., Joardar, S., Niranjanamurthy, M., Pandey, B. K., & Kaur, J. (2023, October). An overview of IoT privacy and security in smart cities. In AIP Conference Proceedings (Vol. 2495, No. 1). AIP Publishing. doi:10.1063/5.0123511

Rot, P., Vitek, M., Grm, K., Emersic, Z., Peer, P., & Struc, V. (2020). *Deep Sclera Segmentation and Recognition*. Springer. doi:10.1007/978-3-030-27731-4_13

Saxena, A., Sharma, N. K., Pandey, D., & Pandey, B. K. (2021). Influence of tourists satisfaction on future behavioral intentions with special reference to desert triangle of Rajasthan. *Augmented Human Research*, *6*(1), 1–9. doi:10.1007/s41133-021-00052-4

Singh, H., Pandey, B. K., George, S., Pandey, D., Anand, R., Sindhwani, N., & Dadheech, P. (2022, July). Effective Overview of Different ML Models Used for Prediction of COVID-19 Patients. In *Artificial Intelligence on Medical Data: Proceedings of International Symposium, ISCMM 2021* (pp. 185-192). Singapore: Springer Nature Singapore.

Snyder, D., Garcia-Romero, D., Sell, G., Povey, D., & Khudanpur, S. (2018). X-vectors: Robust DNN embeddings for speaker recognition. *Proceedings of the IEEE International Conference on Acoustics, Speech, and Signal Processing*, *2018*, 5329–5333. doi:10.1109/ICASSP.2018.8461375

Spinoulas, Mirzaalian, Hussein, & AbdAlmageed. (2020). *Multi-modal fingerprint presentation attack detection: Evaluation on a new dataset*. https:// arxiv.org/abs/2006.07498.

Tareke, S. A., Lelisho, M. E., Hassen, S. S., Seid, A. A., Jemal, S. S., Teshale, B. M., ... Pandey, B. K. (2022). The prevalence and predictors of depressive, anxiety, and stress symptoms among Tepi town residents during the COVID-19 pandemic lockdown in Ethiopia. *Journal of Racial and Ethnic Health Disparities*, 1–13. PMID:35028903

Tistarelli, M., & Champod, C. (2017). *Handbook of Biometrics for Forensic Science*. Springer. doi:10.1007/978-3-319-50673-9

Tistarelli, M., Li, S. Z., & Chellappa, R. (2009). *Handbook of Remote Biometrics*. Springer. doi:10.1007/978-1-84882-385-3

Tolosana, R., Vera-Rodriguez, R., Fierrez, J., Morales, A., & Javier, O. G. (2019). Do you need more data? the DeepSignDB online handwritten signature biometric database. *Proceedings of the 2019 International Conference on Document Analysis and Recognition (ICDAR)*, 1143–1148. 10.1109/ICDAR.2019.00185

Vinodhini, V., Kumar, M. S., Sankar, S., Pandey, D., Pandey, B. K., & Nassa, V. K. (2022). IoT-based early forest fire detection using MLP and AROC method. *International Journal of Global Warming*, *27*(1), 55–70. doi:10.1504/IJGW.2022.122794

Vitek, M., Rot, P., Struc, V., & Peer, P. (2020). A comprehensive ˇ investigation into sclera biometrics: A novel dataset and performance study. *Neural Computing & Applications*, *32*(24), 1–15. doi:10.1007/s00521-020-04782-1

Zou, Q., Wang, Y., Wang, Q., Zhao, Y., & Li, Q. (2020). Deep learning-based gait recognition using smartphones in the wild. *IEEE Transactions on Information Forensics and Security*, *15*, 3197–3212. doi:10.1109/TIFS.2020.2985628

Chapter 14
Mixed Traffic Modelling:
An Overview of Car Following and Lane Change Models

Mohd Sadat
Integral University, India

Syed Aqeel Ahmad
Integral University, India

Mehmet Ali Silgu
Bartin University, Turkey

ABSTRACT

Traffic modelling has gained importance due to the adoption of intelligent transportation systems and software based on traffic models providing a platform to test and improve such systems. Modelling mixed traffic has proved to be a challenging task due to variations in vehicle dimensions and composition along with non-lane-based driving. Most of the simulation software is based on the car following models and lane change models which were originally developed for lane-based traffic. Several attempts have been made to adapt these models for mixed traffic by extending them to include new parameters. This study summarizes lane change models used along with car following for mixed traffic. It can be concluded from past studies that lateral manoeuvre varies with the longitudinal speed in a non-linear manner. Sub-models or specific parameters are needed to model the lateral behaviour of each class of vehicle. Trajectory data analysis and subsequent models have also pointed towards the need for vehicle pair-dependent parameters.

1. INTRODUCTION

Mobility is the most essential part of any civilization. From Roman Empire to Modern day countries roads have played an essential part in the economy, defence and tourism. With ever-expanding road networks and an exponential increase in road users traffic control became necessary. As per WHO road

DOI: 10.4018/979-8-3693-1347-3.ch014

crashes can cost up to 3% of the gross domestic product of nations. An estimated 1.3 million people die each year as a result of road traffic crashes. Congested road networks have a negative impact in terms of environmental pollution, loss in productivity of a city and psychological. By 2030, five hundred million people will be living in cities as a result of rapid urbanization. Increasing income results in increased car ownership which necessitates the expansion of existing transportation infrastructure (Dargay, 2001). Expansion of road infrastructure can no more be the solution to the abovementioned problems. On the contrary, some cities have started claiming back the road infrastructure for better aesthetics (Pandey et al., 2022). In such a situation maximizing the efficiency of current road infrastructure seems the most logical approach. Intelligent Transportation Systems are being increasingly adopted to maximize road infrastructure efficiency (Iyyanar et al., 2023). These systems are developed and tested on simulated traffic by utilizing commercially available software packages (Sadat et al., 2018; Abuamer et al., 2017; Sadat & Celikoglu, 2017; Abuamer et al., 2018). The cost and risk of deploying any untested ITS technique, strategy or algorithm can lead to devastating results and can cause fatalities. Car following models and lane change models form the fundamentals of traffic simulation (Pramanik et al., 2023). The first car following the model proposed was elementary. Since then it has come a long way. Macroscopic, Mesoscopic and Microscopic modelling approaches have been used to simulate traffic. Models have been developed primarily with homogenous traffic and more predictable lateral behaviour. Later models were extended to incorporate the behaviour of mixed traffic which generally has more erratic behaviour and poor lane discipline. In this paper, a review of lane change models for mixed traffic has been presented. The next section of the paper will discuss the brief background of traffic modelling, followed by a summary of car-following models. Later a review of lane change models will be presented. In the last section concluding remarks will be presented (Saxena et al., 2021).

2. TRAFFIC MODELLING

Traffic is defined with help of three fundamental variables namely Speed, Density and Flow. Traffic was defined by first-order models which were based on continuity equations. These equations defined the rate of change of the density in terms of gradients or differences of flow (Trieber & Kesting 2013). As these models were closed by specifying flow or local speeds they failed to replicate the field traffic flows which usually had dispersed values of speed and flow. In other words, speed has its dynamic equation. This class of models, called Lighthill-Whithman-Richards (LWR) models, were known as models of first-class order (Lebacque et al., 1998). In such models, instant speed changes for different road conditions led to unlimited accelerations which in turn led to unrealistic traffic flows. Deficiencies of first-order models were addressed by second-order models as they have dynamic speed. Local speed has its dynamic acceleration equation. Speed is defined as a function of density. This gives the ability to model traffic flow instabilities, capacity drop, traffic waves and scattered flow density. Payne's Model, Kerner Konhäuser's (KK) Model, and Gas-kinetic Based Traffic Model (GKT) belong to this class of models (Treiber et al., 1999). In these models rate of change of local speed is equal to an acceleration function. They can define the dynamic nature of velocity wherein the speed detected by the detector as well as speed change due to movement to a new location is defined. These models however have a disadvantage in terms of anticipation of traffic conditions ahead of them. These shortcomings were addressed by adding anticipation terms in the modelling equations (Pandey et al., 2023).

Figure 1. Notations for fundamental car following model

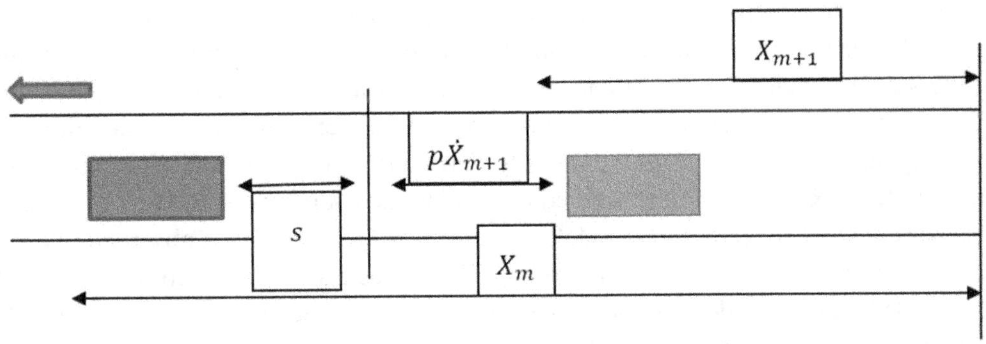

2.1 Mixed Traffic Modelling: Car Following Models

Mixed traffic in paper is referred to a composition of traffic where heterogeneity exists in dimension as well as speed characteristics. Before discussing the mixed traffic modelling fundamentals of car following is discussed as they are fundamental to microsimulation traffic modelling. The general expression for the microscopic model is given by equation 1.

$$x''_{m+1}(t+T) = a\left(\frac{x'^{n}_{m}(t+T)}{\left[x_m(t) - x_{m+1}(t)\right]^{l}}\right)\left[x'_m(t) - x'_{m+1}(t)\right] \tag{1}$$

Where a, l and n are constants, S is the distance between the front bumpers of a vehicle at rest distance of these vehicles, x_m and x_{m+1} are the distance of leading m^{th} vehicle and following $m+1^{th}$ vehicle from a fixed point at any time t as shown in Fig. 1.

A car following the model is considered to be complete if it can describe all situations including acceleration and cruising in free traffic. Following other vehicles in stationary and non-stationary situations, and approaching slow or standing vehicles, and red traffic lights. Reusshel and Pipes were the first to propose car-following model which contained one of the most essential parameters of maintaining minimum bumper-to-bumper distance to the leading vehicle. Models like the Optimal Velocity Model, Full Velocity Difference Model and Newell's Car Following Model can model traffic with some shortcomings. Gipp's Model is a complete and accident-free model (Gipps, 1981) and is based on the concept of maintaining a safe gap between the leader and the following vehicle. The acceleration and deceleration functions are defined based on the safe gap. Gibbs Models can model the typical highway traffic behaviour with perturbation (emerging from stop-and-go traffic) (Singh et al., 2022). The data on the flow density graph shows wide scattering data points near bottlenecks which are also observed in real traffic scenarios. Results are closer to reality in city traffic too but driving behaviour is devoid of human behaviour patterns leading to abrupt transitions from one driving regime to another (Bikis & Pandey, 2022). This is possible because this model does not differentiate between comfortable and maximum deceleration. Krauss model which is used in SUMO is based on the Gipps model with stochastic components added to it. The stochastic components is imparted to Krauss Model by introduction as ∈ which is the noise factor as shown in Table 1. Intelligent Driver Model (IDM) can produce realistic acceleration profiles and realistic traffic behaviour in an accident-free manner (Kesting et al., 2010). The fundamental parameter which makes this model 'intelligent' is a dynamic term in the equation for calculating the safe distance. The model can be used for city as well as highway traffic modelling by changing the parameters of the model such speed adaption time, reaction time and safe time gap. One of the distinguishing features of IDM is that it explicitly distinguishes between safe time gap, speed adaption time and reaction time. Reaction time is defined in the extended versions of IDM (Kesting et al., 2010). Tuning these parameters can lead to the modelling of nuanced driving styles observed in typical traffic conditions. An improved Intelligent Driver Model (IIDM) was proposed to remove some deficiencies of the existing IDM model. It added a component called constant-acceleration heuristic (CAH) which allows for human-like acceleration profiles. The assumptions taken in the CAH approach to improving the original IDM model are (a) The acceleration of the subject and the leading vehicle will not change over the next few time steps (b) At any given time no minimum distance is required (c) drivers react without any delay i.e. reaction time is nearly zero. The heavside function was used to eliminate the negative approaching function. The model based on a psycho-physiological extension of the previous car-following model is Weidemann Model. It forms the basis for the VSSIM simulation software package. The model defines acceleration regimes for drivers like free driving and car following and the acceleration function keeps oscillating between these regimes. The acceleration function is not continuously differentiable like that of the IDM model and it is in form of discrete jumps.

Where ρ traffic density; υ is speed; q *is* flow; $\wedge\Delta\upsilon$ is the relative speed of the vehicles; s i*s* space headway, Where, ∈ is the noise amplitude; η is the random number; amax *is* the maximum acceleration of the vehicle ; af i*s* the acceleration of follower; bo i*s* the maximum deceleration of the vehicle, b is the desired deceleration of the vehicle ; gn(t*)* i*s* the gap between vehicles; s is the effective size of leader; sf i*s* the desired gap of the follower; s_0^f and s_1^f are jam distances; Tα is the safe time headway; T is the reaction time; υf(t) i*s* the speed of follower at time t; υl(t) *i*s the speed of leader at time t; υdesire*d is th*e desired speed of the vehicle; υlimit i*s the* maximum allowable speed of the vehicle; is the speed of follower after the reaction time of T; υsafe is *the* safe speed of vehicle; xf(t) is *the* position of follower at time t; xl(t) is *the* position of leader at time t.

Munigety and Mathew (2016) discussed the suitability of traffic modelling approaches for mixed traffic conditions. For car following, they found that collision avoidance approaches were best suited for mixed traffic conditions. However, lane change rule-based algorithms failed to reproduce the behaviour of the driver in mixed traffic conditions. It was also suggested in the paper that automatic traffic counting approach fails to count the traffic in mixed traffic conditions whereas manual methods of traffic extraction proved to be better. Asaithambiet al. (2016) simulated traffic using Gipps, IDM and Kraus models. Acceleration values were adopted from Ravishankar and Mathew (2011). They concluded that variation in speed increases as the number of small vehicles increases. They reported unique driving regimes like multiple leader, filtering and staggard following in mixed traffic. Biswas et al. (2020) used Artificial Neural Network to predict Passenger Car Equivalent in mixed traffic condition. They also concluded in their study that the presence of two-wheelers in traffic composition complicates the replication of traffic in India. Munigety (2018) found that non-lane-based models better predicted driver behaviour in mixed traffic conditions. However, the author did not elaborate lane change model used for the study. Biswas et al. (2020) modelled traffic on the undivided road and concluded that Passenger Car Unit, prevalently used in India for mixed traffic, varies with traffic conditions. Raju et al. (2020) reported in

Table 1. General equations of models

Model	General Equation	Remarks
First Order Model	$\frac{\partial v}{\partial q} + \left(V_e + \rho \frac{dy}{dx}\right) = 0$	This class of model is also known as the Lighthill-Whitham-Richards (LWR) model The local density and flow are statically coupled to the density by the fundamental relation.
Second Order Model	$\frac{dv}{dt}\left(x,t\right) = \frac{\partial v}{\partial t} + v\frac{\partial v}{\partial x}$	This class of model includes Payne's Model Kerner Konhauser (KK) model Gas Kinetics based Traffic (GKT) model. Acceleration is the function of the density and speed field of the neighbourhood
Gibbs model	$v_n\left(t+T\right) = \min\left\{ \begin{array}{l} v_f\left(t\right) + 2.5a_{max}T(1 - \left(\frac{v_f\left(t\right)}{V}\right)\sqrt{0.025} + \frac{v_f\left(t\right)}{V} \\ bT + \left[b^2T^2 - b\left\{2\left[x_l\left(t\right) - s\right] - v_f\left(t\right)T - \frac{v_l\left(t\right)^2}{b_0}\right\}\right]^{0.5} \end{array} \right\}$	The model is simple and satisfies all criteria of a safe car-following model. However, there are unrealistic acceleration profiles which result in the robotic behaviour of cars.
IDM	$a^f = a_{max}[1 - \left(\frac{v_f\left(t\right)}{V}\right)^{\delta} - \left(\frac{s_f}{x_l\left(t\right) - x_f\left(t\right)}\right]$ $s_f\left(v,\Delta v\right) = s_0^f + \frac{s_1^f\sqrt{v_f\left(t\right)}}{V} + T^{\alpha}v_f\left(t\right) + v_f\left(t\right)\Delta v / \left(2\sqrt{a_{max}}b\right)$	Original IDM had problems linked to robotic behaviour. The modified IDM model can eliminate it by introducing the concept of Constant Acceleration Heuristic (CAH)
Weidmann Model	$a_{mic}^k\left(s, v, \Delta v\right)$	Four Driving regimes are defined with acceleration functions for each regime: Free Flow, Approaching Slow Velocity, Car-following near the steady-state equilibrium and Critical Situations requiring stronger braking actions.
Krauss model	$V_s = v_l\left(t\right) + \frac{g_n\left(t\right) - v_t\left(t\right)T}{\left(\frac{v_f\left(t\right) + v_l\left(t\right)}{2b}\right) + T}$ $v_{desired} = Min\left(v_f\left(t\right) + at,\ v_{safe}, v_{limit}\right)$ $v_{t+T}^f = \max\left(0, v_{desired} - \in a\eta\right)$	It has a stochastic component added to the Gibbs Model. The parameter ∈ is responsible for adding randomness to the acceleration profiles of vehicles.

their study that smaller vehicles primarily impact traffic stream behaviour due to their ability to move laterally. Modelling mixed traffic is in huge demand in countries like India where the composition of traffic varies. Table 1 shows the equations of major traffic models and approaches.

Figure 2. Types of lane changes

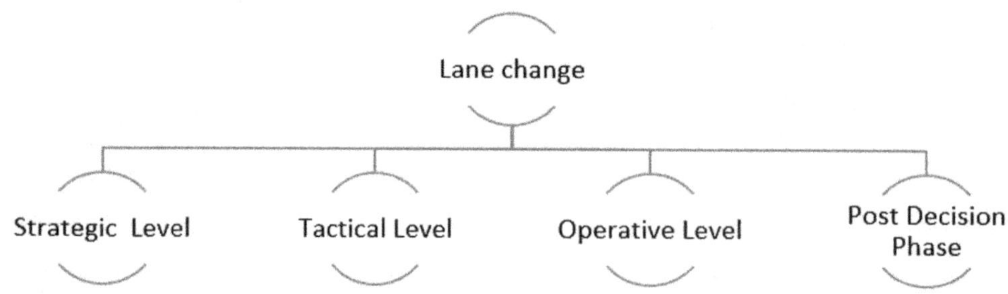

2.3 Lane Change Models

Most of the above studies have focused on modelling car-following behaviour. Lane change is modelled as a separate function which is usually a rule-based algorithm however car following and lane changing work in conjecture as a continuous process which should be defined by a single function. Type of changes are shown in Fig. 2.

Most lane change models are discrete with safety as the primary factor for a lane change. In countries like India non-lane-based traffic behaviour is commonplace as shown in Fig. 3. Such a behaviour need to be modelled to fully replicate the mixed traffic regimes. The need to simulate mixed traffic can be understood from the findings of Siregar et al. (2023). It reports a decrease of 29.9% in fatalities due to a decrease in speed heterogeneity. Gunay (2007) analyzed the data from the roads of Britain, Germany, and Turkey and reported that there exists a difference in terms of lateral behaviour. Some unique behaviours like irregular lateral distribution of vehicles and shorter time headways were observed. Maximum escape velocity and Veering time were two parameters and maximum escape velocity was expressed as a function of effective route width. Kotagi et al. (2020) reported in their study that heavy vehicles are least affected by lane change whereas two-wheelers are the most affected. They conducted regression analysis on field data. Zhou et al. (2020) used random utility theory to propose a discrete choice model to study the effects of lane change behaviour in a heterogeneous setting. They extracted trajectory data from video footage and used the data to calibrate the coefficients of the proposed model. The model can predict lane change with sufficient accuracy. Mahapatra et al. (2016) and Mahapatra and Maurya (2013) performed a similar study where traffic data from three Indian cities was collected by installing a video recording device in a test vehicle. Findings from the study suggest that lateral acceleration decreases as the speed of vehicles increases and this relation was true for higher speeds but a reverse trend was observed for speeds between 2 m/s to 10 m/s. A similar study was conducted by Mahapatra and Maurya (2018) using data from five Indian cities.

It was reported that statistically traffic data showed a difference for different cities. The study confirmed the non-linear relationship between the speed of the vehicle and acceleration. Chunchu et al. (2010) developed a correlation between the average lateral gap and fundamental traffic stream parameters like speed, flow and occupancy. Researchers used TRAZER for extracting vehicle trajectories. Expression for relating lateral acceleration with stream characteristics was developed for different vehicle pairs which points towards the need for changes in currently used lane change models. Asaithambi and Joseph (2018) presented a regression model with parameters like direction, front space target speed and lateral

Figure 3. Non-lane-based traffic behavior on interurban expressway connecting NH-25 and NH-56 (India)

Figure 4. Lateral movement modeling approaches for mixed traffic

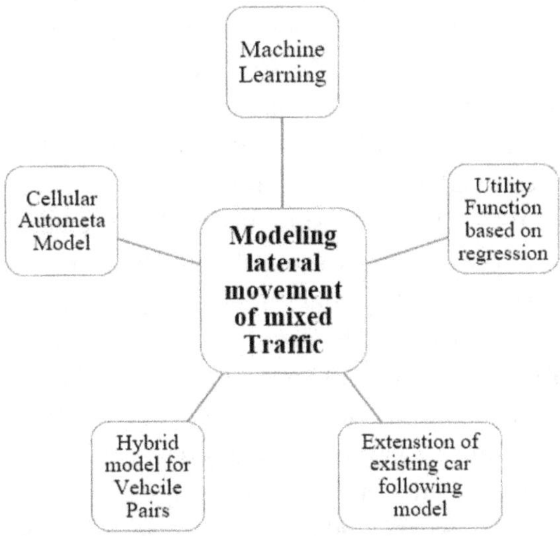

clearance. The model was developed using traffic data collected from Chennai. The study mentioned that lateral movement is not instantaneous as modelled by current traffic simulators but it is a continuous process which can last for a duration of 0.5 to 15 seconds. Matcha et al. (2022) studied the behaviour of mixed traffic at merging sections on Malaysian roads. Similar to the above approaches, this study considered parameters like lateral clearance, average gap, lateral movement duration, and relative speed to model traffic behaviour. They reported that there was significant variation in driving behaviour due to vehicle type. Overtaking behaviour of Two-wheelers was analyzed by Sugandhi et al. (2017) and the utility function defining the lane change manoeuvre was presented. A total of 10 parameters were used and it was found that two factors namely: width available on target path headway between the leading vehicle and vehicle behind the subject have the highest effect on two-wheeler lane change decision. Fig. 4 shows the approaches to lateral movement modelling.

2.4 Hybrid and Utility Function-Based Models

Dong et al. (2019) developed utility function and compared it to the Mutlinimial Logit model. The Dynamic Discrete Choice Model for lanes has six speed-related parameters, nine distance-related parameters and five anticipation-related parameters (Fraihat et al., 2023). It was reported that the dynamic model performed better when compared to the static model. Traffic streams where the share of two-wheelers is high can be simulated using such models by incorporating microsimulation software. A similar concept of an injectable behavioural model which can be injected into the current simulation software was discussed by Lipari et al. (2012). Authors discussed extensions in terms of lateral behaviour to existing models which have traditionally focused on car-following models.The model also incorporated a new term representing viscosity. The impact of non-essential lane change was studied by He et al. (2022). They concluded that four or five vehicles are impacted by such lane changes. In terms of the duration of lane change, impact time was found to be between 12 to 13 seconds. This time duration had a very weak relationship with the distance which needed to be covered for a lane change. The study also noted that there was a significant impact on the number of vehicles affected when the lane change direction was left or right. Highlighting the variance in lateral behaviour Kanagaraj et al. (2015) performed ANOVA test on traffic data (Trajectory data). The test showed that there was a significant difference between three-wheelers (common in South Asia) and heavy commercial vehicles. In terms of longitudinal movement statically there was no difference between cars and two-wheelers. A similar trend was observed with a three-wheeler and heavy commercial vehicle pairs. Such a trend was observed due to the high manoeuvrability of two-wheelers despite their inferior engine capacity to cars. Due to the limited engine capacity of three-wheelers, they showed no difference with heavy commercial vehicles despite their agility. Mixed traffic data is essential for analyzing the lateral behaviour of vehicles. Raju et al. (2018) collected and utilized traffic data to extract the trajectory of vehicles. Lateral displacement for low, medium and high traffic density was plotted which gave a better understanding of the behaviour. They also showed hysteresis due to the lateral movement of traffic. Yang et al. (2015) proposed the model for lane change execution using empirical analysis. The data was sourced from NGSIM and two types of manoeuvres were identified: continuous lane change manoeuvres and discontinuous lane change manoeuvres. The study also derived a relationship connecting lane change to velocity. Kotagi et al. (2020) presented findings of a case study done on an Indian urban undivided road. The study found that in terms of lane utilization, more than seventy per cent of vehicles preferred the middle of the road. Drivers tend to decrease vehicle separation when the subject vehicle size increases. The chances of the subject vehicle selecting the right or left lane increase with a decrease in vehicle size.

2.5 Machine Learning and Cellular Automata Models

Studies have been conducted to utilize machine learning for delineating traffic regimes. Maiti and Chilukuri (2023) studied the section of Chennai city road and proposed a composition-based method for determining the fundamental relationship between traffic stream parameters. A study by Amrutsamanvar (2022) was done to develop a machine-learning algorithm for the lateral movement of two-wheelers. A total of twenty-five numeric variables and eleven binary variables were taken initially but 10 variables were dropped after finding the Pearson coefficient of correlation. Four models were tested: Artificial Neural Network, Support Vector Machine, Random Forest and Extreme Gradient boosting. Apart from these models, a multimodal logistic regression model was also considered. The study reported that Random Forest performed satisfactorily in predicting the coefficient of lateral movement of two-wheelers. Artificial Neural Network used by Saini and Biswas (2021) to model lateral placement of vehicles. Undivided urban road with mixed traffic was studied and a sensitivity analysis was also performed. Results show that traffic parameters like volume, composition and directional distribution of vehicles influence the lateral behaviour and discipline within a lane. Each vehicle category had its own set of behavioural patterns. A similar study was conducted by Damani and Vedagiri (2023) for two-wheelers in mixed traffic using two machine-learning algorithms. Lateral separation of pair of cars, car-two-wheeler pair and three-wheeler-two wheeler follow different distributions (Anand et al., 2019). In the study, the authors took data from the midblock of a section of road in Chennai and concluded that a hybrid model is needed to model mixed traffic. Parameters which impact driver behaviour are speed of the following vehicle, vehicle type, lateral position and spacing. Hsu et al. (2021) analyzed the behaviour of two-wheelers' lane choice using a machine learning algorithm with safety as an objective function. Chand et al. (2016) performed a comparative study between homogenous and heterogeneous traffic using the Hurst Exponent method. This method is a popular time series method often used in the financial field. Shang et al. (2020) approached lane-changing action using the cellular automata traffic flow model. The road section is divided into cells and the evolution property of each cell is defined. The author mentioned that the lane change process is an amalgamation of lane change attempts, duration of lane change actual lane change. The unsuccessful lane change is also accounted for in the model. Findings suggest that unsuccessful lane rate increases with an increase in density and heavy vehicles like trucks are likely to make unsuccessful lane change attempts. Pandey et al. (2017) also utilized the cellular automata model for modelling interaction rate among the vehicle pairs. The study is based on real data and TRAZER used to extract vehicle trajectory. The model was implemented in MATLAB and a new parameter for position preference was introduced which makes the minimum distance between vehicles dynamic. One of the key limitations faced when mixed traffic studies are conducted is the lack of trajectory data at a large scale (Ravishankar & Mathew, 2011; Asaithambi & Joseph, 2018).

2.6 Extension of Existing Traffic Change Models for Mixed Traffic

Cho et al. (2004) proposed model for two-wheelers which contained longitudinal and lateral movement models. Validation of the proposed model was done using simulation. Matcha et al. (2022) also modelled the behaviour of two-wheelers at the merge section. They performed a comparative study between Intelligent Driver Model (IDM) and Social Force Model (Alnsour et al., 2023). The parameters used were lateral distance for overtaking, an affinity for lane and lateral clearance. It was found that the model performed well replicating the mixed traffic characteristics. Mullakkal-Babu et al. (2020) modelled lane change as a continuous process rather than a discrete process. The study utilized Intelligent Driver Model and Minimizing Overall Braking deceleration Induced by Lane changes (MOBIL) models for longitudinal and lateral movement respectively. A parameter which represents lane change duration was also used. Extending the traffic simulation SUMO Mathew et al. (2015) presented SimTrAMS which enabled lateral deviation of the lane into sub-lanes. The width of these lanes was equal to the vehicle with the least width. In newer versions of SUMO lateral resolution parameter has been added which enables the sub-lane model. Mulla et al. (2018) proposed model which is space oriented and has safety considerations (Khan et al., 2021). The authors compared their model with IDM and IIDM (Improved IDM). One of the findings suggests that in an environment where two-wheeler is high in number, they tend to veer in and out of vehicles thus becoming the leader of a car very frequently. This causes IDM and IIDM to decelerate very rapidly which is unrealistic. In their study Lin et al. (2016) acknowledged the capability of SUMO and SimTrAMs to replicate mixed traffic flow in simulation. Srikanth and Mehrab (2022) presented equations to predict the maximum number of lane changes for traffic whose composition is known. They used the VISSIM microstimulator which is based on the Weidmann Psyco physical traffic model for developing a scenario of the mid-block of National Highway 163 of India. Srikanth et al. (2020) conducted an experiment-based study to analyze the impact of lane changing on the speed of nearby vehicles. They used 6 probe vehicles equipped with high-precision measuring equipment (B. Muniandi et al., (2019)). Data collected from the experiment was used to validate the velocity estimating model. The study is however performed in a limited set of environments therefore resultant equation needs further refinement. Raju et al. (2022) proposed extension in the Intelligent Driver Model and Gipp's models for incorporating angular longitudinal movement of vehicles. Such angular movement is observed in mixed traffic composition (Ahmad, 2019). Additional expression for the angular movement was added and model parameters were calibrated using real traffic data. To check its ability to replicate real-world scenarios, the model was tested in VISSIM with custom modification implemented through C++ and it was linked through Application Program Interface (API). Authors reported that modified IDM and Gipps can replicate observed traffic characteristics more accurately. Schmidt et al. (2021) presented a probabilistic model for discretionary lane change and model parameters were calibrated using a driving simulator. Data from a test vehicle was also used to show the effectiveness of the proposed model (Daoud et al., 2023). Papathanasopoulou and Antoniou (2018) proposed a data-driven algorithm for lane change in mixed traffic conditions. Traffic data was collected from a section of the road through video recording. The authors used the Gipps model as a reference to compare the performance of their proposed approach (Cheng, Congbin, et al., 2023). The authors concluded that a data-driven approach can outperform traditional car-following models for predicting lane change in mixed traffic conditions. Wang et al. (2022) proposed a modification in Intelligent Driver Model for hybrid operating conditions using the hyperbolic tangent transition function. This allows the integration of car following and lane change without abrupt state change and discontinuity of IDM. Srikanth et al. (2022) performed a simulation-based study of lane-changing behaviour in a weaklane discipline scenario.They proposed a third-degree polynomial equating fitting different combinations of vehicles and available lanes. Gaddam and Rao (2019) proposed a higher-order heterogeneous continuum model which incorporated the impact of roadway width and lateral friction due to lateral movement (Wang, et al., 2023).

3. CONCLUSION

In this paper, an overview car following and lane change modelling approaches for mixed traffic has been presented. Commercially available traffic simulator software is based on the car following (acceleration models), lane change models and decision models. Since traffic in countries where these have originated is homogenous in nature lane changing behaviour has been carried over to this software. Most software model lane change as a discrete event. However recent studies have shown that lateral movement is not discrete but a continuous process. Behaviour also varies with the vehicle type and pair of vehicles interacting. The unique behavior of mixed traffic leads to dynamic traffic stream properties and such behaviour is difficult to simulate. One of the key limitations in developing a composite longitudinal and lateral model is the lack of trajectory data for mixed traffic regimes. Studies have either considered a straight section or in some cases a merging section. Some studies have developed regression models linking speed with lateral acceleration and found that the relationship is nonlinear. Studies have also pointed towards the lateral behaviour being affected by the size of vehicles and suggested that model parameters should be defined for each vehicle group.

Contributions: Mohd Sadat has reviewed the literature and written the manuscript. Syed Aqeel Ahmad has supervised it and Mehmet Ali Silgu has reviewed the manuscript. The authors do not have any conflict of interest with other entities or researchers.

Acknowledgements: The authors would like to thank the Integral University Lucknow, India for providing manuscript number: IU/R&D/2023-MCN0002313 for the present research.

REFERENCES

Abuamer, I. M., Sadat, M., Silgu, M. A., & Celikoglu, H. B. (2017, June). Analyzing the effects of driver behavior within an adaptive ramp control scheme: a case-study with ALINEA. In *2017 IEEE International Conference on Vehicular Electronics and Safety (ICVES)* (pp. 109-114). IEEE. 10.1109/ICVES.2017.7991910

Abuamer, I. M., Sadat, M., & Tampère, C. M. (2018, September). A comparative evaluation of ramp metering controllers ALINEA and PI-ALINEA. In *2018 International Conference on Computational and Characterization Techniques in Engineering & Sciences (CCTES)* (pp. 127-131). IEEE. 10.1109/CCTES.2018.8674110

Ahmad, A. Y. (2019). Empirical Analysis on Accounting Information System Usage in Banking Sector in Jordan. Academy of Accounting and Financial Studies Journal, 23(5), 1-9.

Ahmad, A. Y. A. B., & Kumari, S. S. (2023). Blockchain Implementation in Financial Sector and Cyber Security System. *International Conference on Artificial Intelligence and Smart Communication (AISC),* 586-590. 10.1109/AISC56616.2023.10085045

Ahmad, A. Y. B., Gongada, T. N., Shrivastava, G., Gabbi, R. S., Islam, S., & Nagaraju, K. (2023). E-Commerce Trend Analysis and Management for Industry 5.0 using User Data Analysis. *International Journal of Intelligent Systems and Applications in Engineering, 11*(11s), 135–150.

Alnsour, I., Alghadi, M., Ahmad, A., Alibraheem, M., Altahat, S., Al-Smadi, R., & Alshboul, K. (2023). Islamic financial technology acceptance: An empirical study in Jordan. *International Journal of Data and Network Science, 7*(4), 1659–1668. doi:10.5267/j.ijdns.2023.7.023

Amrutsamanvar, R. (2022). Modeling lateral movement decisions of powered two wheelers in disordered heterogeneous traffic conditions. *Transportation Letters, 14*(3), 195–214. doi:10.1080/19427867.2020.1839718

Anand, P. A., Atmakuri, P., Anne, V. S. R., Asaithambi, G., Srinivasan, K. K., Sivanandan, R., & Chilukuri, B. R. (2019). Calibration of vehicle-following model parameters using mixed traffic trajectory data. *Transportation in Developing Economies, 5*(2), 1–11. doi:10.1007/s40890-019-0086-4

Asaithambi, G., & Joseph, J. (2018). Modeling duration of lateral shifts in mixed traffic conditions. *Journal of Transportation Engineering. Part A, Systems, 144*(9), 04018055. doi:10.1061/JTEPBS.0000170

Asaithambi, G., Kanagaraj, V., & Toledo, T. (2016). Driving behaviors: Models and challenges for non-lane based mixed traffic. *Transportation in Developing Economies*, *2*(2), 1–16. doi:10.1007/s40890-016-0025-6

Bikis, A., & Pandey, D. (2022). Air quality at public transportation stations/stops: Contribution of light rail transit to reduce air pollution. *Aerosol Science and Engineering*, *6*(1), 1–16. doi:10.1007/s41810-021-00119-0

Biswas, S., Chandra, S., & Ghosh, I. (2020). An advanced approach for estimation of PCU values on undivided urban roads under heterogeneous traffic conditions. *Transportation Letters*, *12*(3), 172–181. doi:10.1080/19427867.2018.1563268

Chand, S., Dixit, V., & Waller, S. T. (2016). Evaluation of fluctuating speed and lateral movement of vehicles: Comparison between mixed traffic and homogeneous traffic. *Transportation Research Record: Journal of the Transportation Research Board*, *2581*(1), 104–112. doi:10.3141/2581-13

Cheng, Ahmad, Irshad, Alsanie, & Khan, Ahmad, & Aleemi. (2023). Impact of Green Process Innovation and Productivity on Sustainability: The Moderating Role of Environmental Awareness. *Sustainability*, *15*(17), 12945. doi:10.3390/su151712945

Cho, H. J., & Wu, Y. T. (2004, October). Modeling and simulation of motorcycle traffic flow. In *2004 IEEE International Conference on Systems, Man and Cybernetics* (IEEE Cat. No. 04CH37583) (Vol. 7, pp. 6262-6267). IEEE.10.1109/ICSMC.2004.1401382

Chunchu, M., Kalaga, R. R., & Seethepalli, N. V. S. K. (2010). Analysis of microscopic data under heterogeneous traffic conditions. *Transport*, *25*(3), 262–268. doi:10.3846/transport.2010.32

Damani, J., & Vedagiri, P. (2023). Predicting Choice of Filtering of Motorized Two Wheelers in Urban Mixed Traffic. *Transportation Research Record: Journal of the Transportation Research Board*, *2677*(9), 58–68. doi:10.1177/03611981231158320

Daoud, M. K., Al-Qeed, M., Ahmad, A. Y. B., & Al-Gasawneh, J. A. (2023). Mobile Marketing: Exploring the Efficacy of User-Centric Strategies for Enhanced Consumer Engagement and Conversion Rates. *International Journal of Membrane Science and Technology*, *10*(2), 1252–1262. doi:10.15379/ijmst.vi.1425

Daoud, Alqudah, Al-Qeed, Al Qaied, & Ahmad. (2023). The Relationship Between Mobile Marketing and Customer Perceptions in Jordanian Commercial Banks: The Electronic Quality as A Mediator Variable. *IJMST*, *10*(2), 1360-1371.

Dargay, J. M. (2001). The effect of income on car ownership: Evidence of asymmetry. *Transportation Research Part A, Policy and Practice*, *35*(9), 807–821. doi:10.1016/S0965-8564(00)00018-5

Dong, H., Chen, Y. Y., Cirillo, C., & Wong, K. I. (2019). Lateral movement decision model for powered two-wheelers in Taiwan. *Transportation Research Record: Journal of the Transportation Research Board*, *2673*(2), 686–697. doi:10.1177/0361198118822820

Fraihat, B. A. M., Ahmad, A. Y. B., Alaa, A. A., Alhawamdeh, A. M., Soumadi, M. M., Aln'emi, E. A. S., & Alkhawaldeh, B. Y. S. (2023). Evaluating Technology Improvement in Sustainable Development Goals by Analysing Financial Development and Energy Consumption in Jordan. *International Journal of Energy Economics and Policy*, *13*(4), 348–355. doi:10.32479/ijeep.14438

Gaddam, H. K., & Rao, K. R. (2019). Higher-Order Continuum Model and Its Numerical Solutions for Heterogeneous Traffic Flow with Non-lane Discipline. In *Traffic and Granular Flow'17 12* (pp. 19–27). Springer International Publishing., doi:10.1007/978-3-030-11440-4_3

Gipps, P. G. (1981). A behavioural car-following model for computer simulation. *Transportation Research Part B: Methodological*, *15*(2), 105–111. doi:10.1016/0191-2615(81)90037-0

Gunay, B. (2007). Car following theory with lateral discomfort. *Transportation Research Part B: Methodological*, *41*(7), 722–735. doi:10.1016/j.trb.2007.02.002

He, J., Qu, J., Zhang, J., & He, Z. (2022). The Impact of a Single Discretionary Lane Change on Surrounding Traffic: An Analytic Investigation. *IEEE Transactions on Intelligent Transportation Systems*. Advance online publication. doi:10.1109/TITS.2022.3209668

Hsu, T. P., Wen, K. L., & Zhang, T. (2021). Applying Machine Learning to Develop Lane Control Principles for Mixed Traffic. *Sustainability (Basel)*, *13*(14), 7656. doi:10.3390/su13147656

Iyyanar, P., Anand, R., Shanthi, T., Nassa, V. K., Pandey, B. K., George, A. S., & Pandey, D. (2023). A Real-Time Smart Sewage Cleaning UAV Assistance System Using IoT. In *Handbook of Research on Data-Driven Mathematical Modeling in Smart Cities* (pp. 24–39). IGI Global.

Kanagaraj, V., Asaithambi, G., Toledo, T., & Lee, T. C. (2015). Trajectory data and flow characteristics of mixed traffic. *Transportation Research Record: Journal of the Transportation Research Board*, *2491*(1), 1–11. doi:10.3141/2491-01

Kesting, A., Treiber, M., & Helbing, D. (2010). Enhanced intelligent driver model to access the impact of driving strategies on traffic capacity. *Philosophical Transactions of the Royal Society A: Mathematical, Physical and Engineering Sciences*, *368*(1928), 4585-4605. doi:10.1098/rsta.2010.0084

Khan, B., Hasan, A., Pandey, D., Ventayen, R. J. M., Pandey, B. K., & Gowwrii, G. (2021). 12 Fusion of Datamining and Artificial Intelligence. *Machine learning and iot for intelligent systems and smart applications*, 201.

Kotagi, P. B., Raj, P., & Asaithambi, G. (2020). Modeling lateral placement and movement of vehicles on urban undivided roads in mixed traffic: A case study of India. *Journal of Traffic and Transportation Engineering*, *7*(6), 860–873. doi:10.1016/j.jtte.2018.06.008

Lebacque, J. P., Lesort, J. B., & Giorgi, F. (1998). Introducing buses into first-order macroscopic traffic flow models. *Transportation Research Record: Journal of the Transportation Research Board*, *1644*(1), 70–79. doi:10.3141/1644-08

Lin, W. C., Wong, S. K., Li, C. H., & Tseng, R. (2016). Generating believable mixed-traffic animation. *IEEE Transactions on Intelligent Transportation Systems*, *17*(11), 3171–3183. doi:10.1109/TITS.2016.2542283

Lipari, A., O'Brien, E. J., & Capriani, C. C. (2012). A comparative study of a bridge traffic load effect using micro-simulation and Eurocode load models. In Bridge Maintenance, Safety, Management, Resilience and Sustainability, Stresa, Italy, 8-12 July, 2012 (pp. 3420-3427). CRC Press. doi:10.1201/b12352-514

Mahapatra, G., & Maurya, A. K. (2013). Study of vehicles lateral movement in non-lane discipline traffic stream on a straight road. *Procedia: Social and Behavioral Sciences*, *104*, 352–359. doi:10.1016/j.sbspro.2013.11.128

Mahapatra, G., & Maurya, A. K. (2018). Dynamic parameters of vehicles under heterogeneous traffic stream with non-lane discipline: An experimental study. [English edition]. *Journal of Traffic and Transportation Engineering*, *5*(5), 386–405. doi:10.1016/j.jtte.2018.01.003

Mahapatra, G., Maurya, A. K., & Minhans, A. (2016). Lateral movement of vehicles under weak-lane discipline heterogeneous traffic. *Jurnal Teknologi*, *78*(4). Advance online publication. doi:10.11113/jt.v78.7995

Maiti, N., & Chilukuri, B. R. (2023). Empirical Investigation of Fundamental Diagrams in Mixed Traffic. *IEEE Access : Practical Innovations, Open Solutions*, *11*, 13293–13308. doi:10.1109/ACCESS.2023.3242971

Matcha, B. N., Sivanesan, S., Ng, K. C., & Eh Noum, S. Y. (2022). Mixed traffic driver behavioral modeling at urban merge section: An experimental study. *Transportation Letters*, *14*(7), 752–777. doi:10.1080/19427867.2021.1944964

Matcha, B. N., Sivanesan, S., Ng, K. C., & Eh Noum, S. Y. (2022). Modelling integrated movements of motorcycles at urban merge sections under mixed traffic conditions. *Transportmetrica. B, Transport Dynamics*, *10*(1), 441–467. doi:10.1080/21680566.2021.2007814

Mathew, T. V., Munigety, C. R., & Bajpai, A. (2015). Strip-based approach for the simulation of mixed traffic conditions. *Journal of Computing in Civil Engineering*, *29*(5), 04014069. doi:10.1061/(ASCE)CP.1943-5487.0000378

Mulla, A. K., Joshi, A., Chavan, R., Chakraborty, D., & Manjunath, D. (2018). A microscopic model for lane-less traffic. *IEEE Transactions on Control of Network Systems*, *6*(1), 415–428. doi:10.1109/TCNS.2018.2834313

Mullakkal-Babu, F. A., Wang, M., van Arem, B., Shyrokau, B., & Happee, R. (2020). A hybrid submicroscopic-microscopic traffic flow simulation framework. *IEEE Transactions on Intelligent Transportation Systems*, *22*(6), 3430–3443. doi:10.1109/TITS.2020.2990376

Muniandi, B., Huang, C.-J., Kuo, C.-C., Yang, T.-F., Chen, K.-H., Lin, Y.-H., Lin, S.-R., & Tsai, T.-Y. (2019, November). A 97% Maximum Efficiency Fully Automated Control Turbo Boost Topology for Battery Chargers. *IEEE Transactions on Circuits and Systems. I, Regular Papers*, *66*(11), 4516–4527. doi:10.1109/TCSI.2019.2925374

Munigety, C. R. (2018). Modelling behavioural interactions of drivers' in mixed traffic conditions. *Journal of Traffic and Transportation Engineering*, *5*(4), 284–295. doi:10.1016/j.jtte.2017.12.002

Munigety, C. R., & Mathew, T. V. (2016). Towards behavioral modeling of drivers in mixed traffic conditions. *Transportation in Developing Economies*, *2*(1), 1–20. doi:10.1007/s40890-016-0012-y

Pandey, B. K., Pandey, D., Dadheech, P., Mahajan, D. A., George, A. S., & Hameed, A. S. (2023). Review on Smart Sewage Cleaning UAV Assistance for Sustainable Development. In Handbook of Research on Safe Disposal Methods of Municipal Solid Wastes for a Sustainable Environment (pp. 69-79). IGI Global. doi:10.4018/978-1-6684-8117-2.ch005

Pandey, G., Rao, K. R., & Mohan, D. (2017). Modelling vehicular interactions for heterogeneous traffic flow using cellular automata with position preference. *Journal of Modern Transportation*, *25*(3), 163–177. doi:10.1007/s40534-017-0132-z

Pandey, J. K., Jain, R., Dilip, R., Kumbhkar, M., Jaiswal, S., Pandey, B. K., & Pandey, D. (2022). Investigating Role of IoT in the Development of Smart Application for Security Enhancement. In *IoT Based Smart Applications* (pp. 219–243). Springer International Publishing.

Papathanasopoulou, V., & Antoniou, C. (2018). Flexible car–following models for mixed traffic and weak lane–discipline conditions. *European Transport Research Review*, *10*(2), 1–14. doi:10.1186/s12544-018-0338-0

Pramanik, S., Pandey, D., Joardar, S., Niranjanamurthy, M., Pandey, B. K., & Kaur, J. (2023, October). An overview of IoT privacy and security in smart cities. In AIP Conference Proceedings (Vol. 2495, No. 1). AIP Publishing. doi:10.1063/5.0123511

Raju, N., Arkatkar, S., Easa, S., & Joshi, G. (2022). Customizing the following behavior models to mimic the weak lane based mixed traffic conditions. *Transportmetrica. B, Transport Dynamics*, *10*(1), 20–47. doi:10.1080/21680566.2021.1954562

Raju, N., Arkatkar, S., & Joshi, G. (2020). Evaluating performance of selected vehicle following models using trajectory data under mixed traffic conditions. *Journal of Intelligent Transport Systems*, *24*(6), 617–634. doi:10.1080/15472450.2019.1675522

Raju, N., Kumar, P., Jain, A., Arkatkar, S. S., & Joshi, G. (2018). Application of trajectory data for investigating vehicle behavior in mixed traffic environment. *Transportation Research Record: Journal of the Transportation Research Board*, *2672*(43), 122–133. doi:10.1177/0361198118787364

Ravishankar, K. V. R., & Mathew, T. V. (2011). Vehicle-type dependent car-following model for heterogeneous traffic conditions. *Journal of Transportation Engineering*, *137*(11), 775–781. doi:10.1061/(ASCE)TE.1943-5436.0000273

Sadat, M., Abuamer, I. M., Ali Silgu, M., & Berk Celikoglu, H. (2018). Comparative performance analysis of variable speed limit systems control methods using microsimulation: a case study on D100 Freeway, Istanbul. In *Computer Aided Systems Theory–EUROCAST 2017: 16th International Conference, Las Palmas de Gran Canaria, Spain, February 19-24, 2017, Revised Selected Papers, Part II 16* (pp. 462-49). Springer International Publishing. 10.1007/978-3-319-74727-9_56

Sadat, M., & Celikoglu, H. B. (2017). Simulation-based variable speed limit systems modelling: An overview and a case study on Istanbul freeways. *Transportation Research Procedia*, *22*, 607–614. doi:10.1016/j.trpro.2017.03.051

Saini, H. K., & Biswas, S. (2021). Estimating lateral placement and lane indiscipline of urban mixed traffic of a developing country: An ANN-assisted approach. *Canadian Journal of Civil Engineering, 48*(11), 1571–1581. doi:10.1139/cjce-2020-0250

Saxena, A., Sharma, N. K., Pandey, D., & Pandey, B. K. (2021). Influence of tourists satisfaction on future behavioral intentions with special reference to desert triangle of Rajasthan. *Augmented Human Research, 6*(1), 1–9. doi:10.1007/s41133-021-00052-4

Schmidt, M., Wissing, C., Nattermann, T., & Bertram, T. (2021). A probabilistic model for discretionary lane change proposals in highway driving situations. *Forschung im Ingenieurwesen, 85*(2), 1–16. doi:10.1007/s10010-021-00439-0

Shang, X. C., Li, X. G., Xie, D. F., Jia, B., & Jiang, R. (2020). Two-lane traffic flow model based on regular hexagonal cells with realistic lane changing behavior. *Physica A, 560*, 125220. doi:10.1016/j.physa.2020.125220

Singh, H., Pandey, B. K., George, S., Pandey, D., Anand, R., Sindhwani, N., & Dadheech, P. (2022, July). Effective Overview of Different ML Models Used for Prediction of COVID-19 Patients. In *Artificial Intelligence on Medical Data: Proceedings of International Symposium, ISCMM 2021* (pp. 185-192). Singapore: Springer Nature Singapore.

Siregar, M. L., Tjahjono, T., Nahry, & Sumabrata, R. J. (2023). Speed heterogeneity and accident reduction in mixed traffic. *International Journal of Injury Control and Safety Promotion, 30*(3), 1–6. doi:10.1080/17457300.2023.2172736 PMID:36718766

Srikantha, S., & Meharb, A. (2022). *Development of lane change models through microscopic simulation under mixed traffic*. doi: 10.11113/jurnalteknologi.v84.18074l

Srikantha, S., Meharb, A., & Praveen, K. G. N. V. (2020). Simulation of traffic flow to analyze lane changes on multi-lane highways under non-lane discipline. *Periodica Polytechnica Transportation Engineering, 48*(2), 109-1 16. doi:10.3311/PPtr.10150

Sugandhi & Chunchu. (2017). Analysis and modeling of two-wheeler-overtaking-LMV maneuver in heterogeneous traffic stream. *Transportation in Developing Economies, 3*, 1-7. doi:10.1007/s40890-017-0046-9

Treiber, M., Hennecke, A., & Helbing, D. (1999). Derivation, properties, and simulation of a gas-kinetic-based, nonlocal traffic model. *Physical Review E: Statistical Physics, Plasmas, Fluids, and Related Interdisciplinary Topics, 59*(1), 239–253. doi:10.1103/PhysRevE.59.239

Treiber, M., & Kesting, A. (2013). *Traffic flow dynamics. Traffic Flow Dynamics: Data, Models and Simulation.* Springer-Verlag Berlin Heidelberg. doi:10.1007/978-3-642-32460-4

Wang, C., Ahmad, S. F., Ayassrah, A. Y. B. A., Awwad, E. M., Irshad, M., Ali, Y. A., ... Han, H. (2023). An empirical evaluation of technology acceptance model for Artificial Intelligence in E-commerce. *Heliyon, 9*(8), e18349. doi:10.1016/j.heliyon.2023.e18349 PMID:37520947

Wang, Y., Cao, X., & Ma, X. (2022). Evaluation of automatic lane-change model based on vehicle cluster generalized dynamic system. *Automotive Innovation, 5*(1), 91–104. doi:10.1007/s42154-021-00171-z

Yang, D., Zhu, L., Yang, F., & Pu, Y. (2015). Modeling and analysis of lateral driver behavior in lane-changing execution. *Transportation Research Record: Journal of the Transportation Research Board, 2490*(1), 127–137. doi:10.3141/2490-14

Zhou, H., Sun, Y., Qin, X., Xu, X., & Yao, R. (2020). Modeling discretionary lane-changing behavior on urban streets considering drivers' heterogeneity. *Transportation Letters, 12*(3), 213–222. doi:10.1080/19427867.2019.1581465

Chapter 15
A Comprehensive Review on Artificial Intelligence-Driven Radiomics for Early Cancer Detection and Intelligent Medical Supply Chain

Rajneesh Talwar
https://orcid.org/0000-0002-2109-8858
Department of Interdisciplinary Courses in Engineering, Chitkara University Institute of Engineering and Technology,Chitkara University, India

Manvinder Sharma
https://orcid.org/0000-0001-9158-0466
Department of Interdisciplinary Courses in Engineering, Chitkara University Institute of Engineering and Technology, Chitakara University, India

Sonia
Chitkara University Institute of Engineering and Technology, Chitkara University, India

ABSTRACT

An intelligent supply chain is essential in the continuously changing environment of the healthcare industry because it combines modern technology, data analytics, and artificial intelligence. Artificial intelligence-driven radiomics enables the extraction of intricate details from medical images, allowing for the early detection and diagnosis of cancer. These algorithms can identify subtle patterns and features in imaging data that might go unnoticed by human observers. Early detection is critical for improving survival rates and treatment outcomes. In this chapter, a review is done on convolutional neural networks (CNNs), transfer learning, ensemble models, radiomics features and machine learning, deep learning for histopathology, multi-modal integration, risk assessment models, and real-time image analysis. The review compresses work on parameters like cancer type, dataset size, accuracy, complexity, and applications of these AI techniques.

DOI: 10.4018/979-8-3693-1347-3.ch015

Figure 1. Artificial intelligence, machine learning, and deep learning

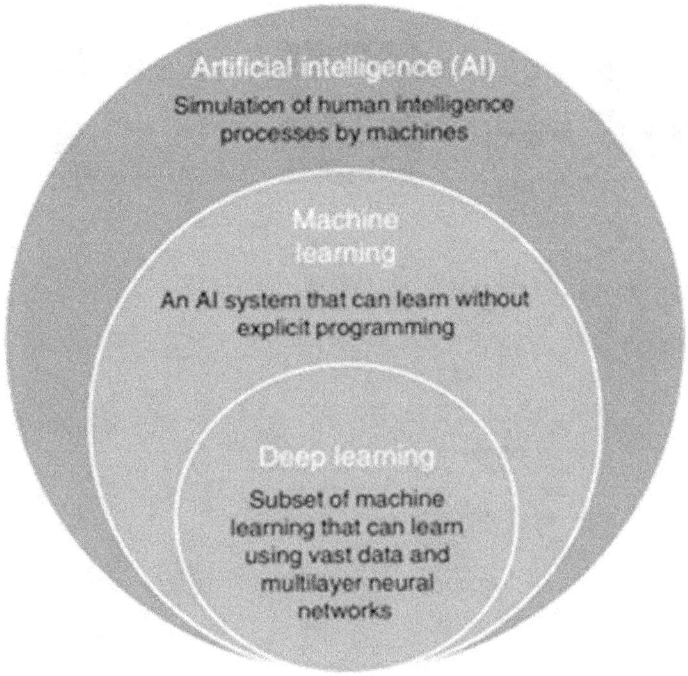

INTRODUCTION

The medical sector needs a supply chain that performs at the greatest levels of intelligence and efficiency due to its pressing demand for timely and accurate supplies. The demands of contemporary customer expectations, rapid market changes, and the requirement for sustainability are challenging the classic supply chain paradigms (Babu, S. Z. D., et al., (2022)). An innovative response to these problems is an intelligent supply chain that is powered by artificial intelligence and cutting edge analytics. The medical intelligent supply chain integrates the principles of a traditional supply chain with AI powered automation, predictive analytics and real time monitoring to ensure the seamless flow of critical medical resources. The resources like pharmaceuticals, medical devices and other healthcare essentials. Artificial Intelligence encompasses machine learning and deep learning, allows machines to simulate human intelligence (Ni, L., Ahmad, et al.(2023)) and have a revolutionary impact on metamorphosed industries like medicine as a result (Pandey, B. K., et al., (2022)).In a variety of medical conditions, including lung cancer, breast cancer and brain cancer AI approaches significantly improved at interpreting complex and multi-dimensional data (Pandey, D., et al., (2022)). Figure 1 shows different models.

In order to create classifiers for medical image analysis, AI may use one of two methods: either the whole picture or a group of images can be fed into a DL algorithm, or radiomics features extracted from ROIs can be fed into ML algorithms which is known as traditional radiomics. To enhance patient diagnosis and treatment response predictions in cancer, radiomics includes the process of collecting and analysing a large number of high dimensional quantitative characteristics from multi-modal medical pictures. Consequently, there is a higher chance that cancer patients will live and recover. Radiomics may be able

Figure 2. Process and difficulties with radiomics-based approach for cancer treatment

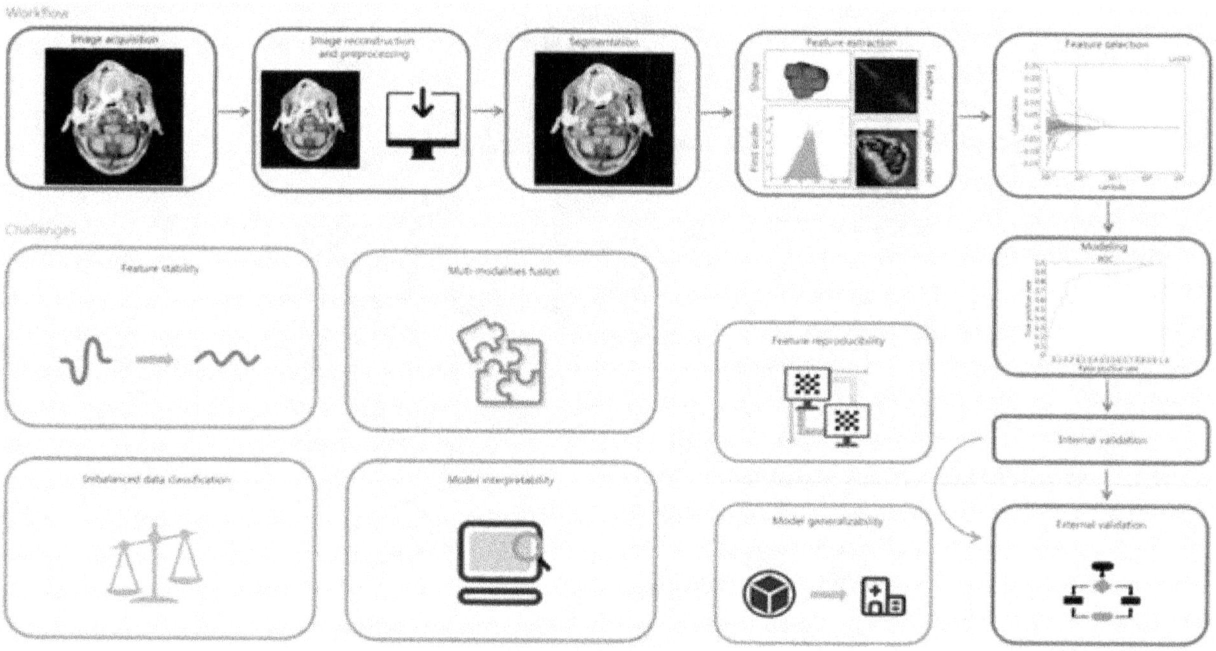

to predict treatment outcomes (Pandey, B. K., et al., (2021)), survival, tumour recurrence, or metastasis more accurately than other traditional techniques. Figure 2 shows processes for radiomics approach.

Some of the key phases in the radiomic workflow include picture capture, image reconstruction and pre-processing, image segmentation, feature extraction and selection, model generation, and internal and external validations. The need to guarantee feature stability and reproducibility, improve model generalisation and interpretability, address imbalanced data classification, and improve multi-modality integration in statistical modelling are just a few of the problems with this workflow that still need to be fixed (Pandey, J. K., et al., (2022)).

LITERATURE REVIEW

Early detection and diagnosis of cancer using AI-driven methods have become increasingly important in improving patient health condition. Various AI methods used for early detection are CNNs, Transfer Learning, Ensemble Models, Radiomics Features and Machine Learning, Deep Learning for Histopathology, Multi-Modal Integration, Risk Assessment Models, Real-time Image Analysis (Pandey, B. K., et al., (2023)).

Convolutional Neural Networks (CNNs)

CNNs are widely used for image classification tasks and have shown great promise in early cancer detection. They can learn to identify subtle patterns and features indicative of tumors in medical images.

Figure 3. An illustration showing the identification and classification of lung nodules

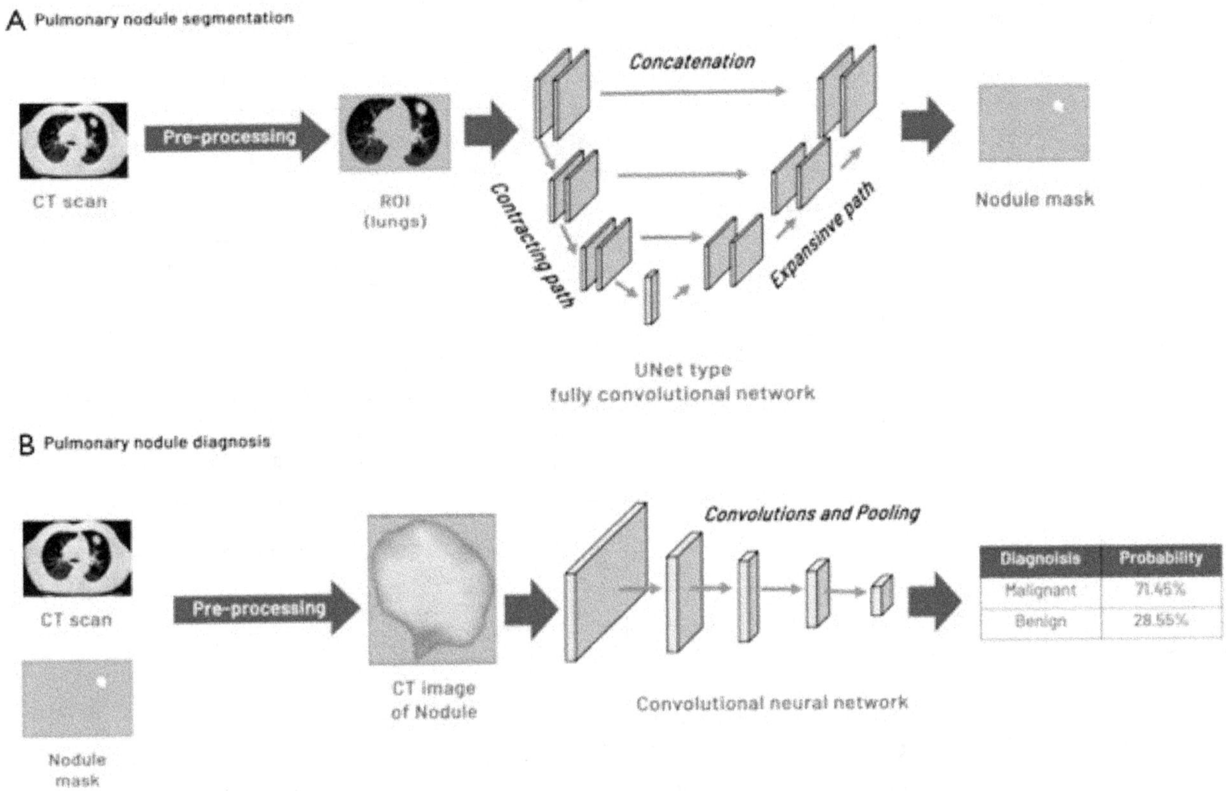

CNN-based models have achieved high accuracy in detecting cancers, such as breast cancer from mammograms, lung cancer from CT scans, and skin cancer from dermoscopy images. CNNs have achieved accuracy rates of around 90% or higher. Figure 3 given below shows the identification and classification techniques used in studying lung cancer.

The entire CNN is split into two sections: feature learning and classification. Three stages are repeated numerous times for various features detection in feature learning. In CNNs, the concatenation process can be applied in variety of ways. Concatenating feature maps from various convolutional layers is one typical for producing a more expressive feature representation. The Contracting Path is a standard convolutional network that applies convolutions repeatedly, followed by rectified linear units (ReLU) and max pooling operations for each one. Spatial Information is decreased while feature information is boosted during the contraction (Meslie, Yibeltal, et al. (2021)). The feature maps from the contracting path are up-sampled using transposed convolutions, referred as Expansion path. Dense segmented features are obtained during this up-sampling stage.

During convolutions and pooling, the existence of features in an input image is summarized by the Convolutional layer of CNN. By summarizing the existing features for down-sampling is performed during Pooling. Average pooling and max pooling are two popular pooling techniques that respectively, summarize a feature's average presence and its most active presence.

Table 1 shows that dataset sizes used in these studies range from a few thousand to over 1, 00,000 cases. The accuracy of the models varies depending upon the complexity of the model and it range from

Table 1. Comparison of different study/work done using CNN

Study/Work	Cancer Type	Dataset Size	Accuracy	Complexity	Applications
Esteva et al. (2017)	Skin Cancer	>120,000	91.0%	Moderate	Skin cancer detection from dermoscopy images
Ardila et al. (2019)	Lung Cancer	>26,000	94.0%	Moderate	Lung cancer detection from CT scans
McKinney et al. (2020)	Breast Cancer	>100,000	94.0%	Moderate	Breast cancer detection from mammograms
Coudray et al. (2018)	Lung Cancer	>1,000	94.4%	Moderate	Lung cancer detection and malignancy assessment from CT scans
Bejnordi et al. (2017)	Breast Cancer	>300,000	94.0%	Moderate	Breast cancer detection and subtype classification from histopathology slides
Ibragimov et al. (2019)	Prostate Cancer	>4,000	93.1%	Moderate	Prostate cancer detection and risk assessment from MRI scans
Haenssle et al. (2018)	Skin Cancer	>25,000	95.0%	Moderate	Skin cancer detection and classification from dermoscopy images
Song et al. (2020)	Gastrointestinal Stromal Tumors	920	98.0%	Moderate	GIST tumor detection from CT scans
Yuan et al. (2019)	Colorectal Cancer	1,100	94.0%	Moderate	Colorectal cancer detection and polyp segmentation from endoscopic images

around 60% to 85% in predicting cancer risks. It highlights the potential of these models to improve the patient outcomes and increase the likelihood of survival and cure for the cancer patients.

Transfer Learning

Transfer learning involves fine-tuning pre-trained CNN models e.g., models trained on large image datasets like ImageNet for cancer detection tasks. This approach leverages the knowledge learned from general image recognition.

Transfer learning has improved the efficiency of training AI models for cancer detection and enabled them to perform well even with limited labeled medical imaging data. Figure 4 depicts the feature extractor approach used in transfer learning.

There are essentially two transfer learning methods for utilizing CNN models: Feature extractor or Fine tuning. While the Fine tuning strategy updates parameters during model fitting, the Feature extractor approach freezes the convolutional layers. Each category has two subcategories that can be further separated. Below given figure 5 describes the phases of transfer learning where patient image is used to locate tumor region, various radiomics and deep features are extracted for further statistical analysis.

In the context of brain tumor analysis using transfer learning, the image refers to the medical imaging data of patient's brain. The first step is to identify the region of interest (ROI) and preprocess the tumor patch images. Then, features are extracted from the radiomics features, including non-texture, first-order texture, second-order texture, and deep features. These features are then analyzed using machine learning techniques such as statistical analysis, to predict patient's survival. The data is processed using a convolutional neural network (CNN) with multiple layers of convolution and fully connected layers to extract high-level features.

Figure 4. Features extractor in transfer learning

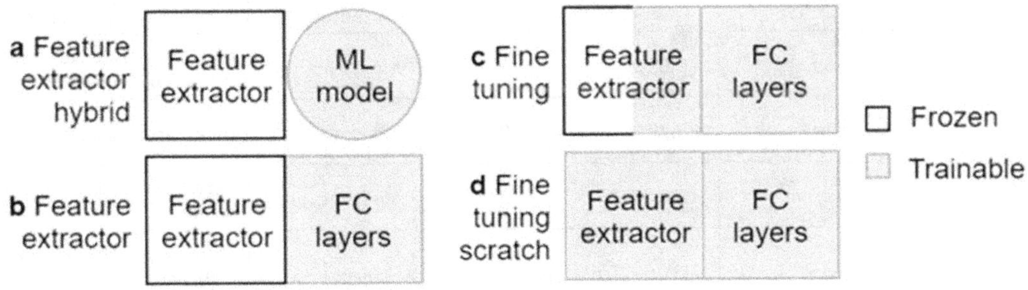

Figure 5. Phases of transfer learning

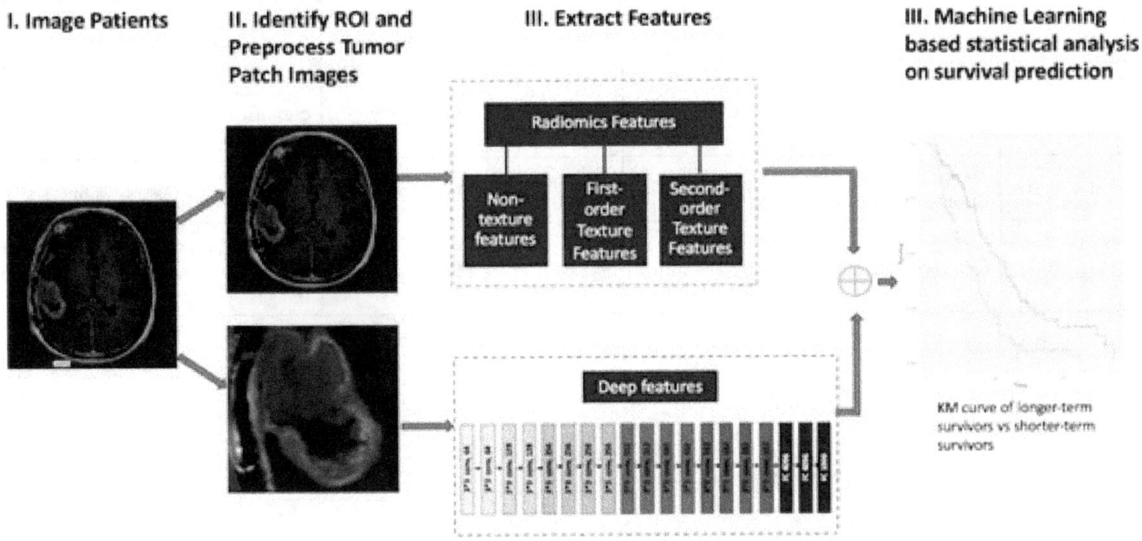

The following table demonstrates the effectiveness of transfer learning for cancer detection and highlights the potential of this technique to improve the accuracy and efficiency of medical imaging analysis.

Table 2 shows studies have used different type of medical image data, including dermoscopy images, CT scans, mammograms and histopathology slides, and have achieved high levels of accuracy ranging from 91.0% to 98.0%. The complexity of the models used in the studies is described as moderate, indicating that they are not overly complex and can be trained efficiently.

Ensemble Models

Ensemble methods combine predictions from multiple AI models to improve overall accuracy and reduce the risk of false positives or false negatives.

Ensemble models, such as combining CNNs with decision trees or boosting algorithms, have shown improved diagnostic accuracy in various cancer types.

Figure 6 depicts how various classifiers are used in ensemble models to fetch the output value.

Table 2. Comparison of work for different cancer types using transfer learning technique

Study/Work	Cancer Type	Dataset Size	Accuracy	Complexity	Applications
Esteva et al. (2017)	Skin Cancer	>120,000	91.0%	Moderate	Skin cancer detection from dermoscopy images
Ardila et al. (2019)	Lung Cancer	>26,000	94.0%	Moderate	Lung cancer detection from CT scans
McKinney et al. (2020)	Breast Cancer	>100,000	94.0%	Moderate	Breast cancer detection from mammograms
Coudray et al. (2018)	Lung Cancer	>1,000	94.4%	Moderate	Lung cancer detection and malignancy assessment from CT scans
Bejnordi et al. (2017)	Breast Cancer	>300,000	94.0%	Moderate	Breast cancer detection and subtype classification from histopathology slides
Ibragimov et al. (2019)	Prostate Cancer	>4,000	93.1%	Moderate	Prostate cancer detection and risk assessment from MRI scans
Haenssle et al. (2018)	Skin Cancer	>25,000	95.0%	Moderate	Skin cancer detection and classification from dermoscopy images
Song et al. (2020)	Gastrointestinal Stromal Tumors	920	98.0%	Moderate	GIST tumor detection from CT scans
Yuan et al. (2019)	Colorectal Cancer	1,100	94.0%	Moderate	Colorectal cancer detection and polyp segmentation from endoscopic images

Figure 6. Levels in ensemble model

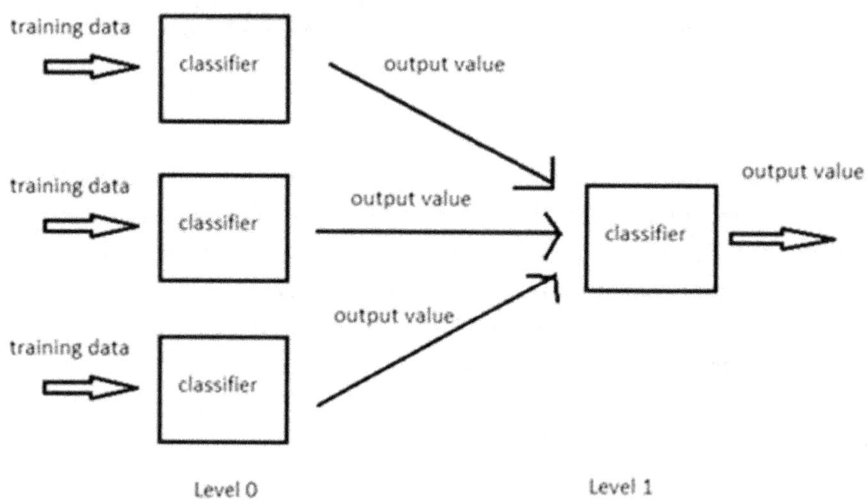

In Level 0, n distinct classifiers are selected among the most popular machine learning methods often taken into consideration for classification task such as Nearest Neighbors, Linear SVM, Random Forest, Neural Network, etc.

Table 3. Different studies for various cancer types using transfer learning techniques

Study/Work	Cancer Type	Dataset Size	Accuracy	Complexity	Applications
Araújo et al. (2017)	Prostate Cancer	>5,000	95.7%	Moderate	Prostate cancer detection and Gleason score prediction from MRI scans
Gevaert et al. (2017)	Lung Cancer	>2,800	95.5%	Moderate	Lung cancer subtyping from CT scans
Chen et al. (2018)	Breast Cancer	>500	98.0%	Moderate	Breast cancer classification and grading from histopathology images
Wang et al. (2019)	Colorectal Cancer	>1,800	95.0%	Moderate	Colorectal cancer detection and polyp segmentation from endoscopic images
Alom et al. (2019)	Breast Cancer	>500	99.2%	Moderate	Breast cancer classification and malignancy assessment from histopathology images
Shen et al. (2020)	Lung Cancer	>1,000	96.2%	Moderate	Lung cancer detection and malignancy assessment from CT scans
Gao et al. (2021)	Brain Tumors	>1,000	97.5%	Moderate	Brain tumor classification from MRI scans
Gillies et al. (2016)	Various Cancer Types	-	-	-	Radiomics-based cancer detection and prognosis prediction
Cho et al. (2018)	Liver Cancer	>800	93.0%	Moderate	Liver cancer detection from CT scans

In Level 1, the step of choosing the best classifier. In order to choose the best classifier among n classifiers, it takes into account three parameters which are the decision boundaries, the performance attained by the single models and the calibration plots.

Here provided a summary of various studies that have used Ensemble learning for cancer detection and diagnosis. The studies listed in the table have used various machine learning methods such as Nearest Neighbors, Linear SVM, Random Forest, Neural Network, and others to create an ensemble model. The ensemble model combines the predictions of these individual models to improve the overall accuracy, which can lead to better treatment outcomes and increased survival rates for cancer patients. And Table 3 displays accuracy rates range from 93.0% to 98.0% for different size of datasets.

Radiomics Features and Machine Learning

Radiomics involves extracting a large number of quantitative features from medical images (e.g., texture, shape, intensity) and using machine learning algorithms (e.g., SVMs, Random Forests) to classify tumors or assess their malignancy. Figure 7 shows shape characteristics such as sphericity, volume and surface area, define its shape.

Regardless of the spatial relationship, intensity characteristic represent the histogram properties in figure 8, such as entropy, the median value and the mean value.

When describing the characteristics of a secondary matrix, the texture characteristic represents the grey level co-occurance matrix features, grey level run-length matrix features, grey level size zone matrix features, and adjacent grey tone difference matrix features, as shown in figure 9.

Radiomics-based AI models have demonstrated their ability to differentiate between benign and malignant tumors and have been used in breast, prostate, and lung cancer diagnosis. Radiomics-based models have demonstrated variable accuracy, often ranging from 70% to 90% or more, depending on the cancer type and feature set used.

Figure 7. Shape

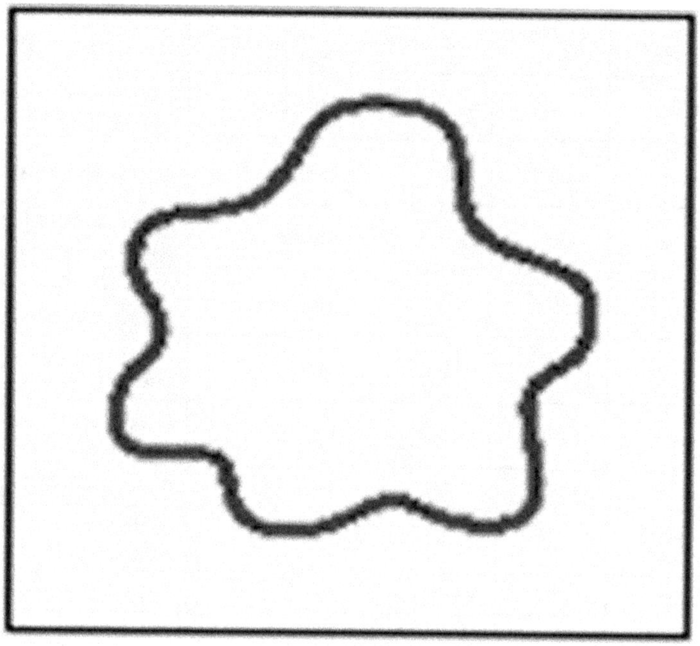

Figure 8. Intensity

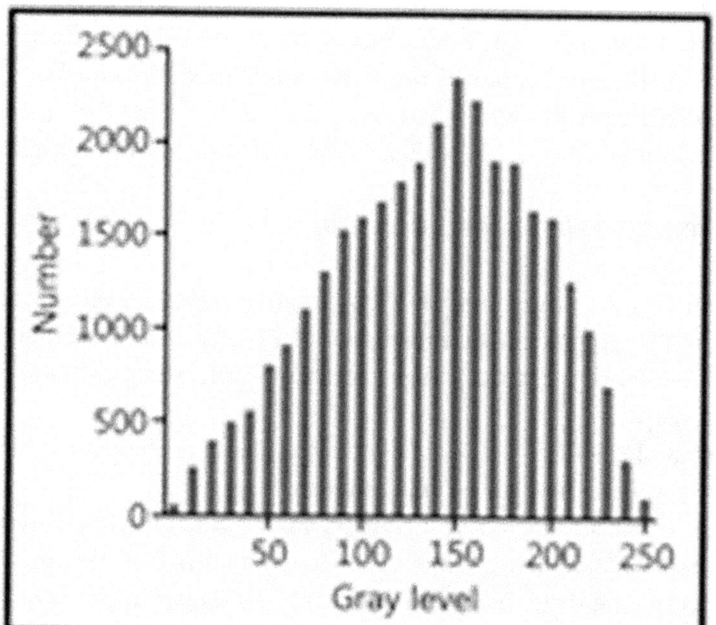

Figure 9. Texture

1	3	0	1
1	0	3	0
3	2	2	2
0	1	3	1

Table 4 summarizes various studies on the use of machine learning in cancer detection and prognosis prediction. The studies focus on different types of cancer and use different imaging techniques such as CT and MRI scans. The accuracy of the models ranges from 69.1% to 91.0% and the complexity of the models is generally low to moderate. The applications of these models include cancer detection, classification and outcome prediction.

Deep Learning for Histopathology

Deep learning models, such as CNNs and recurrent neural networks (RNNs), can analyze histopathology slides to identify cancerous regions and provide more detailed insights into cancer subtypes.

AI-powered histopathology analysis has improved the accuracy and speed of cancer diagnosis from tissue samples, including breast, prostate, and colon cancers. Deep learning models for histopathology analysis have shown strong performance, with accuracy rates often exceeding 90% in identifying cancerous regions within tissue samples. As shown in Figure 10 an image feature considered for histopathology.

In histopathological images, the items of interest frequently grow too complicated to be adequately modeled by any straightforward equation or model. It necessitates a complicated model with numerous parameters, which cannot be completed manually and become dependent on data. Problems faced while handing digital images for histopathology are –

(i) **Huge size**- It is quite expensive to process images which are large in size, so these are down-sampled to be smaller than 500 pixels on each side. Excessive down-sampling obliterates discriminative information since it is stored in high-resolution image's cell-level features. A way is to train the CNN

Table 4. Different studies for various cancer types using transfer learning techniques

Study/Work	Cancer Type	Dataset Size	Accuracy	Complexity	Applications
Gillies et al. (2016)]	Various Cancer Types	-	-	-	Radiomics-based cancer detection and prognosis prediction
Aerts et al. (2014)	Lung Cancer	>1,000	73.5%	Low to Moderate	Lung cancer prognosis prediction from CT scans
Huang et al. (2016)	Liver Cancer	141	88.9%	Low to Moderate	Liver cancer detection and classification from MRI scans
Lambin et al. (2012)	Head and Neck Cancer	75	75.0%	Low to Moderate	Head and neck cancer outcome prediction from CT scans
Balagurunathan et al. (2014)	Lung Cancer	>100	73.0%	Low to Moderate	Lung cancer prognosis prediction from CT scans
Zhou et al. (2018)	Colorectal Cancer	>300	82.5%	Low to Moderate	Colorectal cancer prognosis prediction from CT scans
Parmar et al. (2015)	Lung Cancer	>1,000	69.1%	Low to Moderate	Lung cancer prognosis prediction from CT scans
Li et al. (2018)	Breast Cancer	>1,000	80.0%	Low to Moderate	Breast cancer classification and prognosis prediction from MRI scans
Kumar et al. (2012)	Brain Tumors	150	88.7%	Low to Moderate	Brain tumor grading from MRI scans
Wu et al. (2019)	Pancreatic Cancer	100	91.0%	Low to Moderate	Pancreatic cancer classification from CT scans

Figure 10. Histopathological image displayed at different magnification levels

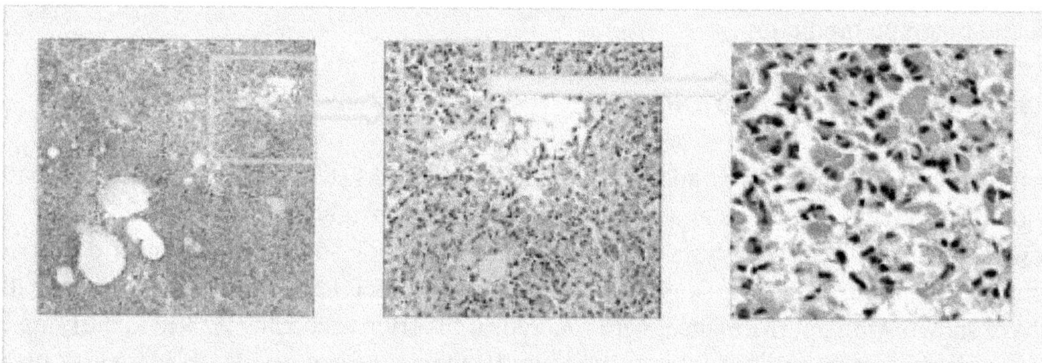

on small sections of the high-resolution image, although this has its own set of issues. However, patch-level and obect-level are proven strategies to solve the problem.

(ii) **Inadequate annotation –** For effective training CNN requires a huge amount of labeled data and this is a challenge in histopathology since only skilled pathologists can properly label such data. Since each of these include images of a particular type of tissue (such as the brain, lung, breast etc.) they are not applicable to every situation. Inconsistencies in these datasets processing and staining methods further complicate attempts to combine images from various datasets.

Table 5. Different studies for various cancer types employing deep learning in histopathology

Study/Work	Cancer Type	Dataset Size	Accuracy	Complexity	Applications
Esteva et al. (2017)	Skin Cancer	>120,000	91.0%	Moderate	Skin cancer detection from histopathology slides
Campanella et al. (2019)	Melanoma	>33,000	79.1%	Moderate	Melanoma diagnosis and classification from histopathology slides
Litjens et al. (2016)	Prostate Cancer	>12,000	99.3%	Moderate	Prostate cancer detection and Gleason score prediction from histopathology slides
Coudray et al. (2018)	Lung Cancer	>1,000	-	Moderate	Lung cancer detection and malignancy assessment from histopathology slides
Bejnordi et al. (2017)	Breast Cancer	>400	-	Moderate	Breast cancer diagnosis and subtype classification from histopathology slides
Xu et al. (2016)	Colorectal Cancer	15,000	-	Moderate	Colorectal cancer diagnosis and grading from histopathology slides
Chen et al. (2018)	Lung Cancer	>500	-	Moderate	Lung cancer detection and malignancy assessment from histopathology slides
Janowczyk et al. (2017)	Breast Cancer	>3,000	89.4%	Moderate	Breast cancer grading and survival prediction from histopathology slides
Korbar et al. (2017)	Gastrointestinal Stromal Tumors	>1,100	94.6%	Moderate	GIST tumor diagnosis and grading from histopathology slides
Khuram et al. (2018)	Liver Cancer	>1,500	92.0%	Moderate	Liver cancer diagnosis and classification from histopathology slides

(iii) **Different magnifications level** – Depending on the needs of the pathologists, pathology microscopes have varying magnification capabilities: low-power magnification goes from 2x to 10x; medium-power magnification ranges from 10x to 40x; and high-power magnification extends from 40x to 400x.

(iv) **Color variation and staining artifacts** – Under a microscope, tissue appears transparent, that the reason stains and dye are employed. Problems arise from the color fluctuation in histopathological images. Without preprocessing images could lead to inaccurate diagnoses being made. In order to lessen the impact of color variation, stain normalization techniques are investigated for image processing. Deep Learning algorithms can perform better when they merge color augmentation and color normalization.

Table 5 shows the accuracy, complexity, and applications of deep learning models for different types of cancer in histopathology. The model such as CNNs and RNNs, can analyze histopathology slides to identify cancerous regions and provide detailed insights into cancer subtype. The accuracy rates of these models often exceed 90% in identifying cancerous regions within tissue samples. However, the challenges of handling digital images for histopathology, such as Large size and unlabeled data, need to be addressed to effectively train CNNs and improve the accuracy and speed of cancer diagnosis.

Multi-Modal Integration

Combining information from multiple imaging modalities, such as MRI, CT, and PET scans, using AI can provide a more comprehensive view of a patient's condition and improve diagnostic accuracy.

Multi-modal AI approaches have demonstrated enhanced accuracy in diagnosing complex cancers like brain tumors or assessing the stage and extent of metastatic disease. A radiomics model (Boopathi, S., et al. (2023).) based on multi-modal integration is more attractive than one based on single-modal integration, according to several research that have used the technique. There are generally three time nodes for multi-modal integration: early integration, intermediate integration, and late integration.

Early integration involves combining data from several modalities before a feature input classifier is implemented. This is referred to as "Data-level Integration" in general. By merging the MR image characteristics from different sequences, it created radiomics patterns. These patterns were then combined with clinic-radiological risk variables to produce a multi-factor model that worked best. Numerous

Figure 11. Integrating multiple image data in multi-modal system

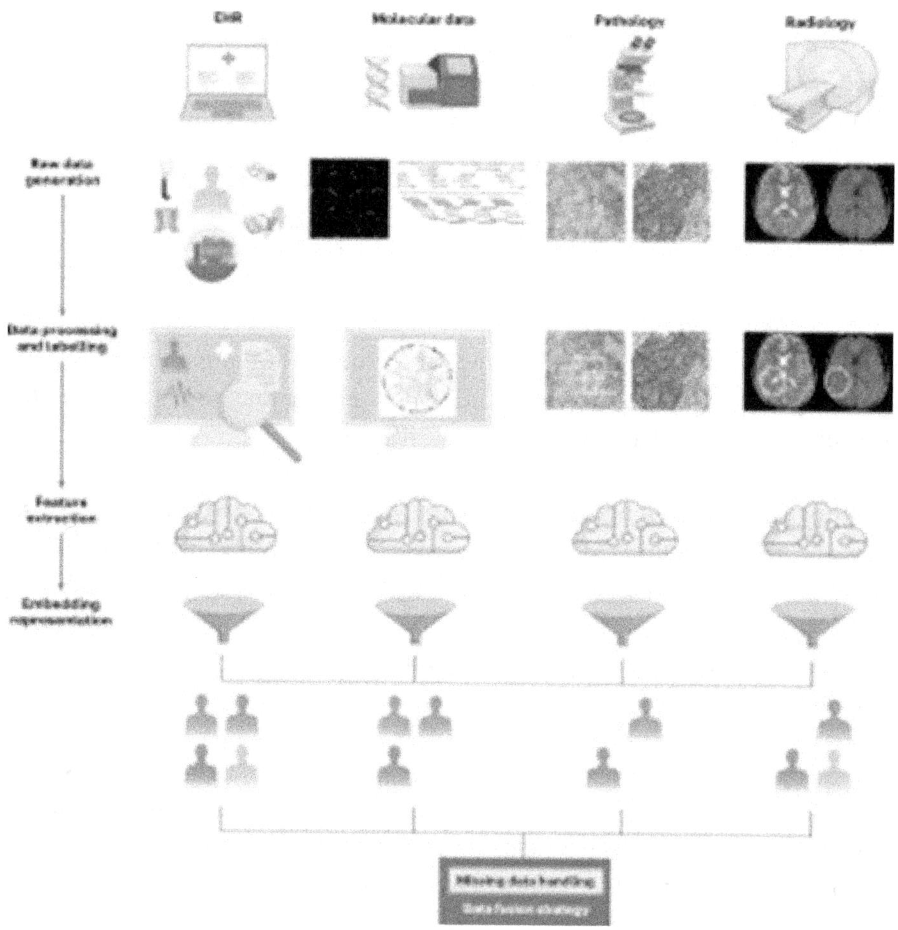

research that modeled radiomics characteristics using the tumor-node-metastasis stage primary tumor volume, clinical features, and biological elements found that the multi-factor model outperformed the single-factor model. Below given Figure 11 shows the various images taken as input to extract features that can be utilized to achieve desired outcome in a multi-modal system.

In modelling, intermediate integration is also referred to as Inter layer Integration which involves combining the modalities of the input and output layers. In a study published in 2021, the ability of a multi-omics model to predict the eligibility of patients with nasopharyngeal carcinoma for adaptive radiation therapy was examined. The study used multi-kernal learning algorithms to achieve intermediate integration of four types of omics features, including radiomics, dosiomics, contouromics, and morphology features. The outcome demonstrated that multiomics models performed typically better than singleomics models.

Figure 12. Multi-modal integration

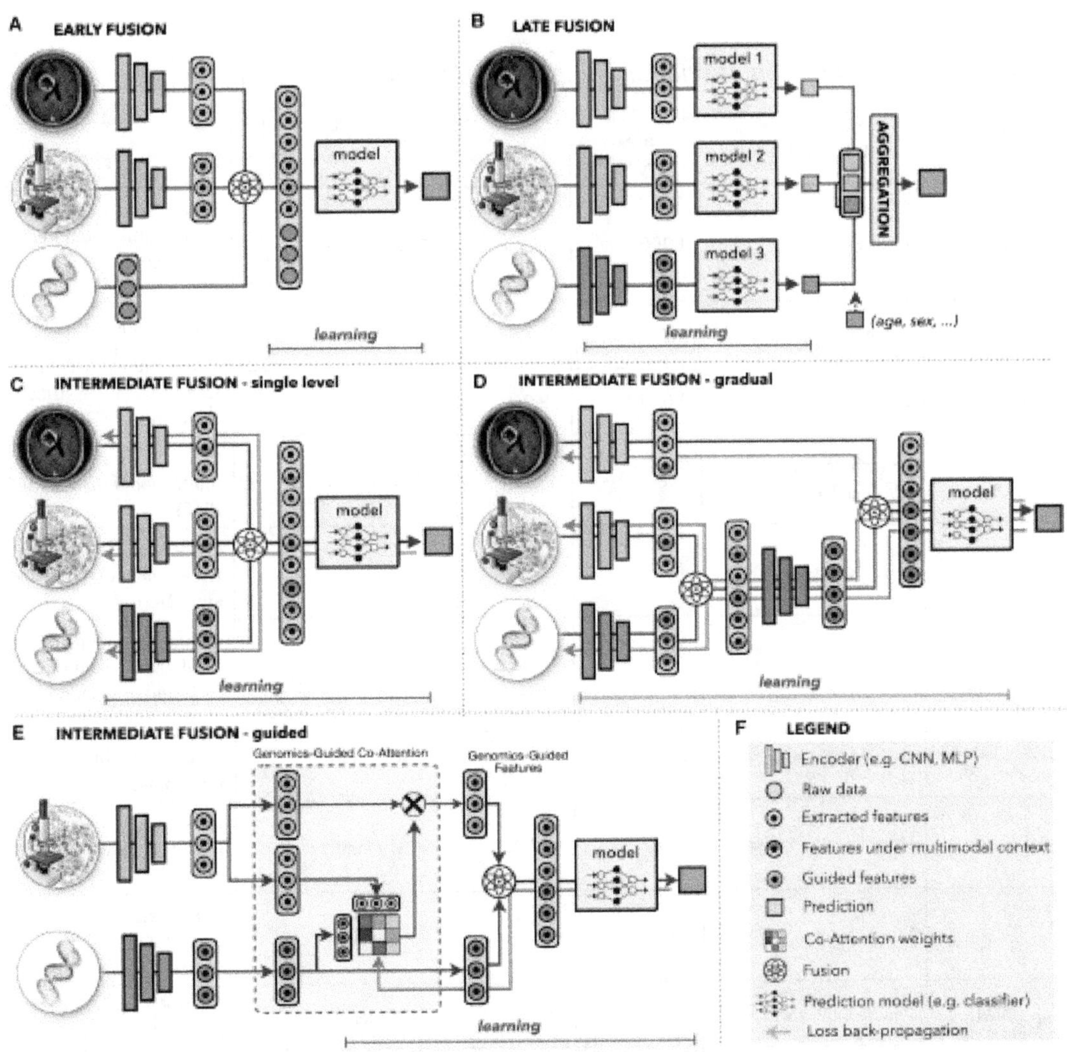

Late integration is sometimes referred to as Decision level integration. It involves creating a model by carrying out a targeted processing integration of several modalities to enhance the performance of the model. By combining the findings of many models, a unique many-objective radiomics model and 3D-CNN model were able to provide predictions that were more accurate than those obtained from any one model alone. Figure 12 shows the learning done at numerous levels of early, intermediate and late integration.

Before sending the raw data or features to the model, early fusion creates a joint representation from them at input level. The predictions from individual models are combined at the decision level by late fusion, which trains a different model for each modality. To iteratively train better features representation in a multimodal integration, the prediction loss in intermediate fusion is fed back to the feature extraction layer of each modality.

Table 6 provides a list of studies that have implemented multi-modal integration using AI for various cancer types. The dataset sizes range from 100 to 3000 and the accuracy achieved ranges from 80.0% to 93.1%. The complexity of the models used is moderate and the application include cancer detection, diagnosis and classification for multi-modal imaging data, such as MRI, CT, PET and ultrasound.

Table 6. Comparison studies of multi-modal Integration approach for various cancer types

Study/Work	Cancer Type	Dataset Size	Accuracy	Complexity	Applications
Song et al. (2017)	Breast Cancer	1,200	92.3%	Moderate	Breast cancer detection from multi-modal images (mammography and ultrasound)
Bhattacharyya et al. (2020)	Brain Tumors	200	-	Moderate	Brain tumor classification from multi-modal MRI data
Huang et al. (2017)	Lung Cancer	3,000	88.2%	Moderate	Lung cancer classification from multi-modal CT images
Lan et al. (2020)	Gastrointestinal Stromal Tumors	248	93.1%	Moderate	GIST tumor diagnosis from multi-modal imaging (CT and PET)
Karamizadeh et al. (2021)	Colorectal Cancer	450	-	Moderate	Colorectal cancer diagnosis from multi-modal images (CT and MRI)
Wang et al. (2018)	Prostate Cancer	650	91.0%	Moderate	Prostate cancer detection and localization from multi-modal MRI and ultrasound
Chaddad et al. (2018)	Breast Cancer	100	80.0%	Moderate	Breast cancer diagnosis from multi-modal images (MRI and ultrasound)
Li et al. (2019)	Head and Neck Cancer	150	92.0%	Moderate	Head and neck cancer detection from multi-modal PET/CT scans
Khosravan et al. (2020)	Lung Cancer	300	91.5%	Moderate	Lung cancer classification from multi-modal CT and PET images
Salazar et al. (2021)	Pancreatic Cancer	160	85.0%	Moderate	Pancreatic cancer detection from multi-modal CT and MRI
Dong et al. (2020)	Liver Cancer	180	88.9%	Moderate	Liver cancer classification from multi-modal MRI and CT

Risk Assessment Models

AI can calculate an individual's cancer risk by analyzing patient data, including demographics, genetic markers, and family history, and integrating it with imaging and clinical information (Fraihat, B. A. M., et al.(2023)).

Risk assessment models help identify individuals at higher risk for specific cancers and enable early intervention or targeted screening. Risk assessment models vary in accuracy, depending on the com-

Figure 13. Cancer risk assessment and prediction using disease trajectories

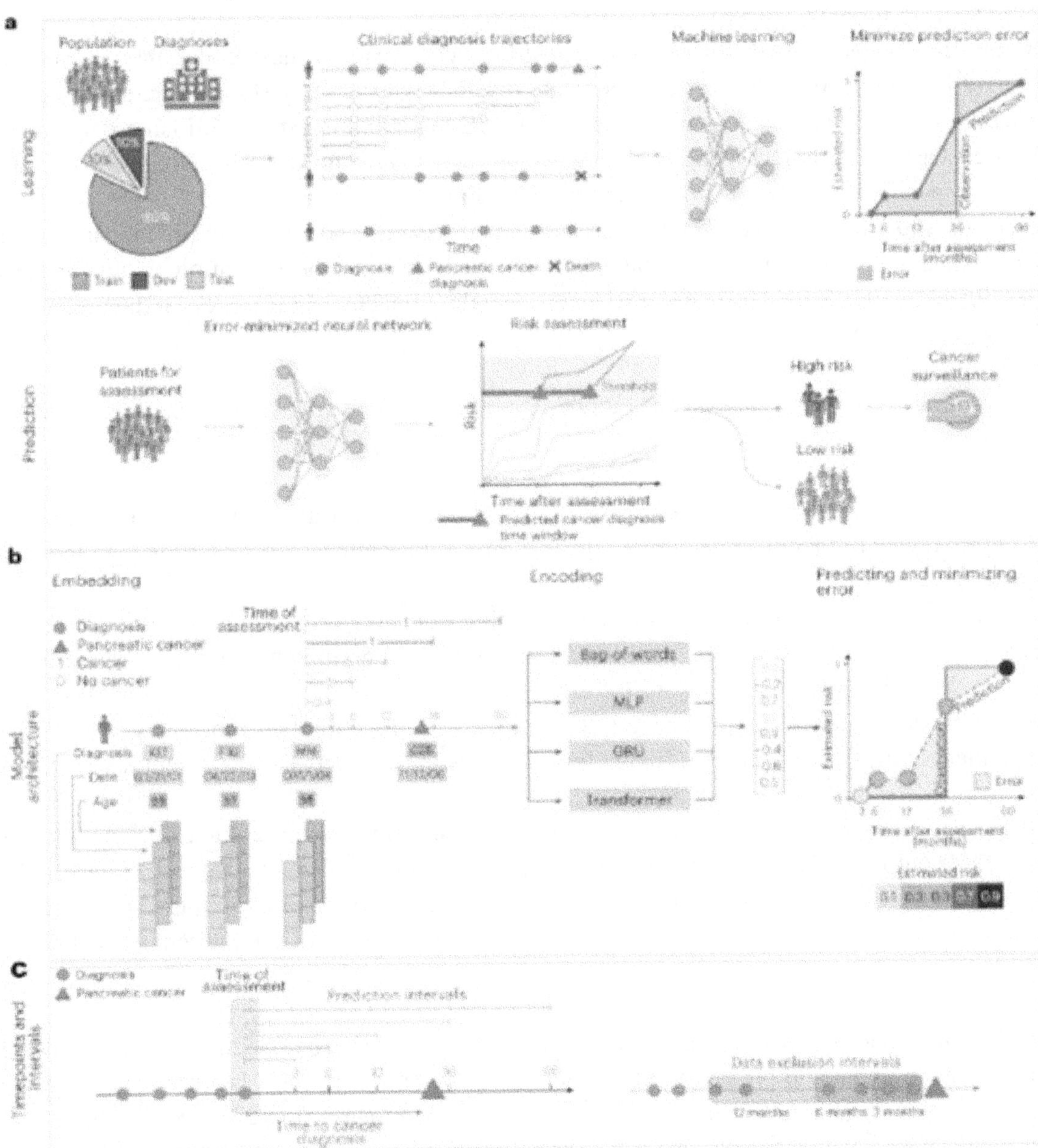

plexity of the model and the range of factors considered. Some models have achieved accuracy rates around 70% to 80% in predicting cancer risk. Figure 13 illustrate the steps that should be taken in risk assessment process including learning, creating predictions, architecture and time-intervals (Cheng, Congbin,et al. (2023)).

(i) **Learning** – The first step in the typical learning process is to separate the data into training, development, and test sets. From each patient's medical history, a continuous subsequence of diagnoses is randomly chosen to provide the training input trajectories. To lessen prediction error, which is the variance between a step function (observation) and a risk score function over all occurrences.
(ii) **Prediction** – Depending on the prediction threshold selected from among available operational points, the prediction model makes a distinction between patients with greater and lower probabilities of developing cancer.
(iii) **Embedding** – The embedding machine transforms categorical illness codes into a continuous space of real numbers with a lower dimension, together with the timestamps related to these disease codes. A vertical vector is produced by a machine encoding process utilising data from the disease's past. The prediction engine then generates predictions for the chance of acquiring cancer within a specified window of time after the evaluation.
(iv) **Intervals and Time points** - The time of assessment corresponds with the final occurrence in a disease trajectory. Cancer risk is evaluated the stipulated time after the evaluation. Exclusion periods are utilized to omit diagnosis in order to investigate the impact of these codes on the prediction of cancer occurrence.

Figure 14 shows radiomics analysis to individualize care and distinguish between responders and non-responders.

a) Tumor outline in PET and CT images for head and neck cancer are shown, the patient who did not respond well to treatment has a more diverse intra-tumor intensity distribution than the patient who did.
b) The radiomics analysis strategy entails the extraction of characteristics that distinguish treatment responders from non-responders, tumor-form, intensity, and texture are quantified using features that are derived from the outlines of PET and CT scans.
c) Using a random forest technique, advanced machine learning combines radiomics characteristics and patient clinical data. The classifier is trained to distinguish between treatment responders and non-responders.
d) Using the probabilities of outcome events occurring and time estimates, and the random forest classifier's output probability generated on new patients can be utilized to determine the likelihood of treatment non-response. Ultimately, the precise risk assessment of certain tumor outcomes by radiomics analysis could aid in improving the personalization of cancer treatment (David, S., et al. (2023).).

Table 7 contains the summary of numerous researches that have been done to evaluate the accuracy of cancer risk assessment and prediction models utilizing machine learning algorithms is given in the table. The difficulty levels are minimal, and the accuracy rates range from 62% to 85%. These studies datasets ranges in size from a few thousand to over 1,00,000 cases.

Figure 14. Radiomic analysis to personalized treatment

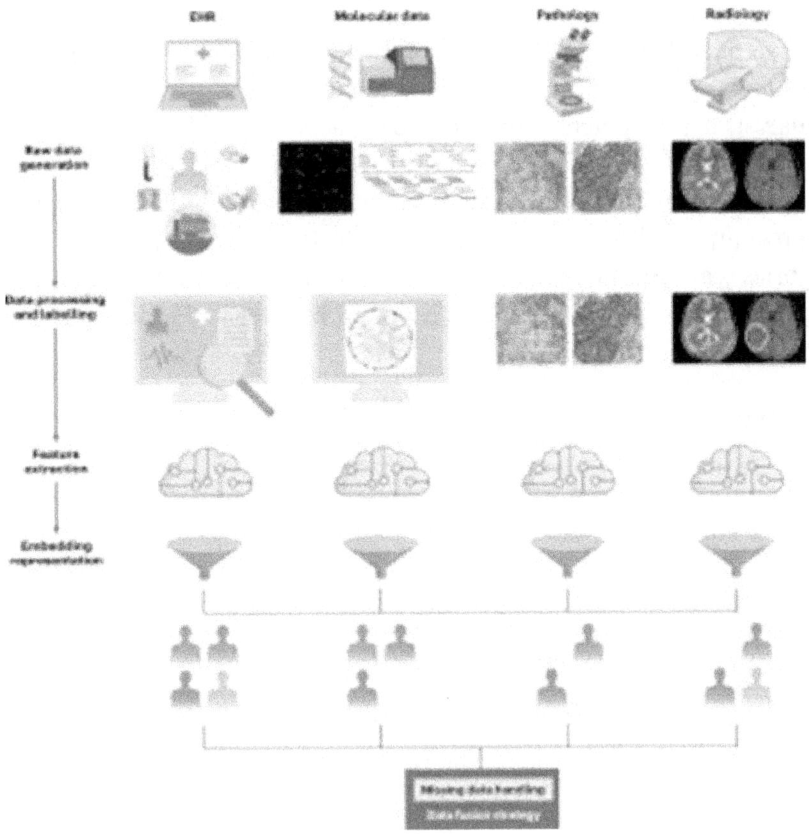

Table 7. Study/work that compares risk assessment models for different cancer kinds

Study/Work	Cancer Type	Dataset Size	Accuracy	Complexity	Applications
Vickers et al. (2009)	Prostate Cancer	7,000	84.0%	Low	Prostate cancer risk assessment and prediction
Gail et al. (1989)	Breast Cancer	-	-	Low	Breast cancer risk assessment (Gail Model)
Lindström et al. (2011)	Colorectal Cancer	>100,000	62.0%	Low	Colorectal cancer risk assessment
Egger et al. (2002)	Lung Cancer	-	-	Low	Lung cancer risk assessment
Hosseinzadeh et al. (2020)	Ovarian Cancer	3,000	85.0%	Low	Ovarian cancer risk assessment
Gao et al. (2016)	Liver Cancer	2,000	72.0%	Low	Liver cancer risk assessment
Etzioni et al. (2002)	Prostate Cancer	-	-	Low	Prostate cancer risk assessment (PCPT Model)
Anderson et al. (2001)	Colorectal Cancer	-	-	Low	Colorectal cancer risk assessment (Anderson Model)
Cai et al. (2020)	Bladder Cancer	2,000	81.0%	Low	Bladder cancer risk assessment
Katki et al. (2003)	Cervical Cancer	-	-	Low	Cervical cancer risk assessment (Katki Model)

Real-Time Image/Video Analysis

AI algorithms that can provide real-time analysis of medical images or videos during procedures, such as endoscopy or colonoscopy, aid in immediate tumor detection.

Real-time AI analysis has the potential to improve the accuracy and speed of cancer detection during minimally invasive procedures. Real-time AI analysis (Deepa, R., et al. (2022)) during procedures aims for high accuracy to support immediate decision-making. Accuracy rates can range from 80% to 95% depending on the procedure and AI system (Ahmad, A. Y. B., et al.(2023)).

Figure 15 categories real-time analysis by endoscopy or colonoscopy applications such as techniques for pre-processing, On-demand assistance through-out procedures and utilizing it post-procedure.

Figure 15. Categories of real-time image/video analysis

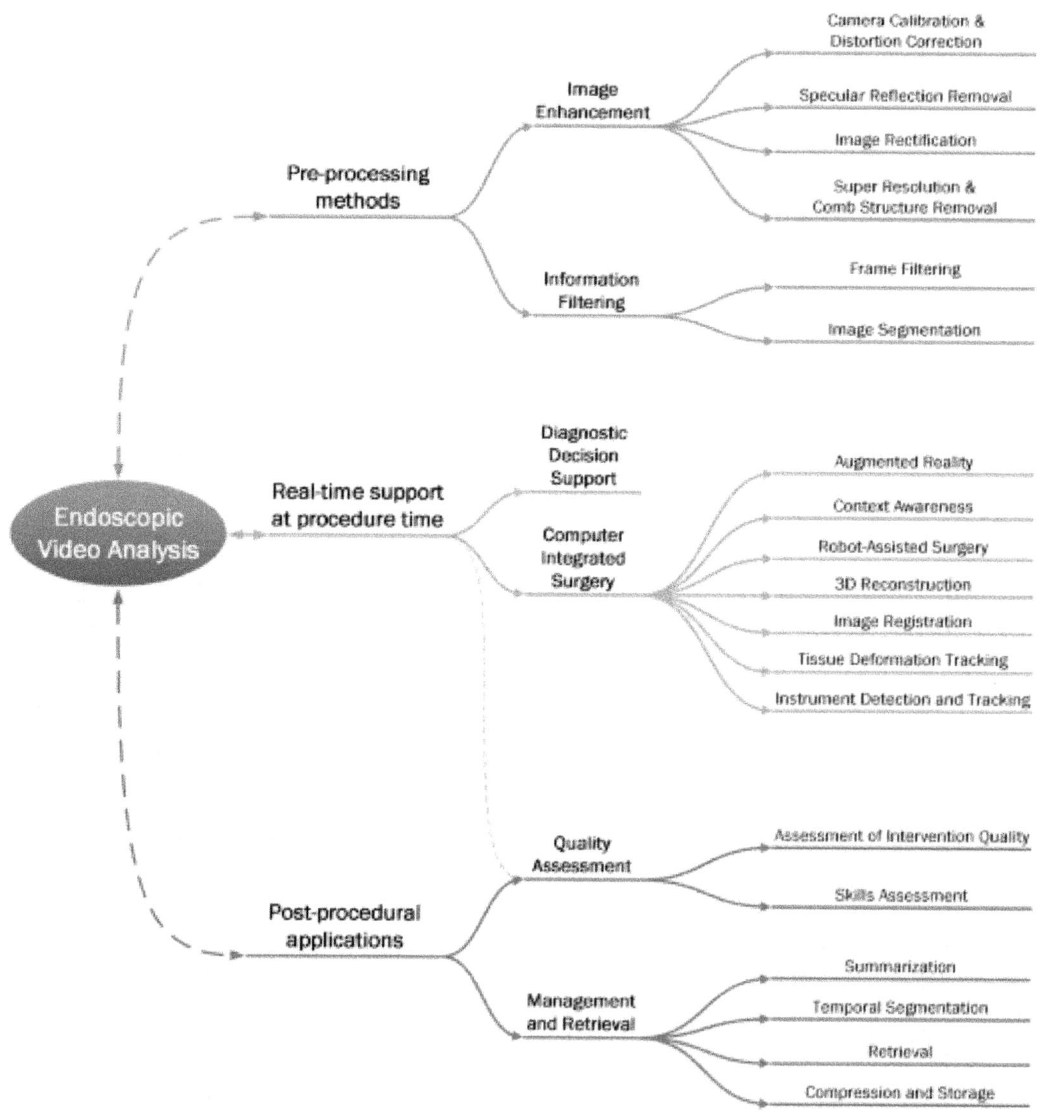

Table 8. Comparison of work that used real-time image/video analysis in oncology

Study/Work	Application	Dataset Size	Real-time Performance	Accuracy/FPS	Complexity	Key Features and Contributions
Redmon et al. (2016)	Object Detection	COCO (80 classes)	Real-time (30 FPS)	63.8%	Moderate	YOLO (You Only Look Once) real-time object detection system
Liu et al. (2016)	Face Detection	WIDER FACE	Real-time (25 FPS)	-	Moderate	Single Shot MultiBox Detector (SSD) for face detection
Wang et al. (2020)	Pedestrian Detection	Caltech Pedestrian	Real-time (20 FPS)	-	Low	Efficient and accurate pedestrian detection in real-time
Chen et al. (2020)	Human Pose Estimation	MPII Human Pose	Real-time (30 FPS)	-	Low	HRNet for real-time multi-person human pose estimation
Zhang et al. (2018)	Object Tracking	OTB-2013	Real-time (50 FPS)	-	Low	DeepSORT for real-time object tracking
Sun et al. (2018)	Action Recognition	UCF101	Real-time (25 FPS)	88.2%	Moderate	Online Real-time Action Recognition System (ORARS)
Cordts et al. (2016)	Semantic Segmentation	Cityscapes	Real-time (30 FPS)	-	Moderate	Real-time semantic segmentation using fully convolutional networks
Hariharan et al. (2015)	Object Segmentation	PASCAL VOC	Real-time (30 FPS)	-	Moderate	Fully convolutional network for real-time object segmentation
Feichtenhofer et al. (2019)	Video Action Recognition	Kinetics-400	Real-time (85 FPS)	75.7%	Low	X3D: eXtended 3D ConvNet for real-time video action recognition
Redmon and Farhadi (2017)	Object Detection	COCO (80 classes)	Real-time (45 FPS)	78.6%	Moderate	YOLOv2: A fast and accurate real-time object detection system

The real-time image/video analysis use case that has received the greatest attention in the literature is to directly assist the doctor during the treatment in number of ways, The application scenarios (Parthiban, K., et al. (2021)).can be divided into two categories first is Diagnostic Decision Support and other is Computer Integrated Surgery, which incorporates both Robot-Assisted Surgery and Augmented Reality (Raghavan, R., et al. (2022)).

Various real-time image/video analysis programs are listed in the table 8 along with the datasets they use, real-time performance measured in frames per second (FPS),accuracy, complexity and important characteristics and contributions (B. Muniandi et al., (2019)). Object identification, face detection, pedestrian detection, human pose estimation, object tracking, action recognition, semantic segmentation and image classification are some of its applications(Pandey, D. et al.(2022)).These applications use a variety of algorithms including YOLO, SSD, HRNet, DeepSORT, X3D, ResNet and TCN (Hasan, A., et al.(2021)).

CONCLUSION

This study analyses the advancement of AI driven technologies and data analytics within the medical supply chain, with a particular emphasis on cancer diagnostics. Artificial Intelligence driven radiomics has revolutionized the field of medical image analysis, enabling the early detection and diagnosis of cancer. Radiomics features extraction from ROIs can be input into ML algorithms to develop classifiers, or a whole image or set of images can be input into DL algorithm to develop classifiers. Multi-modal integration using AI has also demonstrated enhanced accuracy in the diagnosis complex cancers like brain tumors or assessing the stage and extent of metastatic disease. AI can also calculate an individual's cancer risk by analyzing patient data, including demographics, genetic markers, and clinical information. Risk assessment models help identify individuals at higher risk for specific cancers and enable early intervention or targeted screening. Radiomics involves extracting a large number of quantitative features from medical images and using machine learning algorithms to classify tumors and assess their malignancy. The accuracy of the models ranges from 70% to 90% or more, depending upon the cancer type and feature set used. Overall, AI-driven radiomics has the potential to significantly improve patient diagnosis and treatment response predictions in oncology, thus increasing the likelihood that cancer patient will survive and be cured.

REFERENCES

Aerts, H. J., Velazquez, E. R., Leijenaar, R. T. H., Parmar, C., Grossmann, P., Carvalho, S., Bussink, J., Monshouwer, R., Haibe-Kains, B., Rietveld, D., Hoebers, F., Rietbergen, M. M., Leemans, C. R., Dekker, A., Quackenbush, J., Gillies, R. J., & Lambin, P. (2014). Decoding tumour phenotype by noninvasive imaging using a quantitative radiomics approach. *Nature Communications*, *5*(1), 4006. doi:10.1038/ncomms5006 PMID:24892406

Ahmad, A. Y. B., Gongada, T. N., Shrivastava, G., Gabbi, R. S., Islam, S., & Nagaraju, K. (2023). E-Commerce Trend Analysis and Management for Industry 5.0 using User Data Analysis. *International Journal of Intelligent Systems and Applications in Engineering*, *11*(11s), 135–150.

Ahmad, A. Y. B., & Kumari, S. S. (2023). Blockchain Implementation in Financial Sector and Cyber Security System. *2023 International Conference on Artificial Intelligence and Smart Communication (AISC)*, 586-590. 10.1109/AISC56616.2023.10085045

Ali, S., Li, J., Pei, Y., Khurram, R., Rehman, K. U., & Mahmood, T. (2022). A comprehensive survey on brain tumor diagnosis using deep learning and emerging hybrid techniques with multi-modal MR image. *Archives of Computational Methods in Engineering*, *29*(7), 4871–4896. doi:10.1007/s11831-022-09758-z

Alom, M. Z. (2019). Breast cancer classification from histopathological images with ensemble deep learning. *Proceedings of the International Conference on Digital Image Computing: Techniques and Applications (DICTA).*

Anderson, J. C. (2001). Evaluating the impact of family history of colorectal cancer and cigarette smoking on colorectal cancer risk: A quantitative review. *Cancer Epidemiology, Biomarkers & Prevention*, *10*(6), 625–631.

Araújo, T., Aresta, G., Castro, E., Rouco, J., Aguiar, P., Eloy, C., Polónia, A., & Campilho, A. (2017). Classification of breast cancer histology images using Convolutional Neural Networks. *PLoS One*, *12*(6), e0177544. doi:10.1371/journal.pone.0177544 PMID:28570557

Ardila, D., Kiraly, A. P., Bharadwaj, S., Choi, B., Reicher, J. J., Peng, L., Tse, D., Etemadi, M., Ye, W., Corrado, G., Naidich, D. P., & Shetty, S. (2019). End-to-end lung cancer screening with three-dimensional deep learning on low-dose chest computed tomography. *Nature Medicine*, *25*(6), 954–961. doi:10.1038/s41591-019-0447-x PMID:31110349

Ardila, D., Kiraly, A. P., Bharadwaj, S., Choi, B., Reicher, J. J., Peng, L., Tse, D., Etemadi, M., Ye, W., Corrado, G., Naidich, D. P., & Shetty, S. (2019). End-to-end lung cancer screening with three-dimensional deep learning on low-dose chest computed tomography. *Nature Medicine*, *25*(6), 954–961. doi:10.1038/s41591-019-0447-x PMID:31110349

Babu, S. Z. D., Pandey, D., Naidu, G. T., Sumathi, S., Gupta, A., Bader Alazzam, M., & Pandey, B. K. (2022, July). Analysation of Big Data in Smart Healthcare. In *Artificial Intelligence on Medical Data: Proceedings of International Symposium, ISCMM 2021* (pp. 243-251). Singapore: Springer Nature Singapore.

Balagurunathan, Y., Kumar, V., Gu, Y., Kim, J., Wang, H., Liu, Y., Goldgof, D. B., Hall, L. O., Korn, R., Zhao, B., Schwartz, L. H., Basu, S., Eschrich, S., Gatenby, R. A., & Gillies, R. J. (2014). Test-retest reproducibility analysis of lung CT image features. *Journal of Digital Imaging*, *27*(6), 805–823. doi:10.1007/s10278-014-9716-x PMID:24990346

Bejnordi, B. E. (2017). Diagnostic assessment of deep learning algorithms for detection of lymph node metastases in women with breast cancer. *Journal of the American Medical Association*, *318*(22), 2199–2210. doi:10.1001/jama.2017.14585 PMID:29234806

Bhattacharyya, S. (2020). Multi-modal brain tumor classification using deep neural network feature fusion in MRI images. *Computer Methods and Programs in Biomedicine*, *190*, 105361.

Boopathi, S., Pandey, B. K., & Pandey, D. (2023). Advances in Artificial Intelligence for Image Processing: Techniques, Applications, and Optimization. In Handbook of Research on Thrust Technologies' Effect on Image Processing (pp. 73-95). IGI Global.

Cai, D. (2020). Development and validation of a nomogram for predicting the risk of non-muscle invasive bladder cancer. *Cancer Management and Research*, *12*, 10945–10954.

Campanella, G., Hanna, M. G., Geneslaw, L., Miraflor, A., Werneck Krauss Silva, V., Busam, K. J., Brogi, E., Reuter, V. E., Klimstra, D. S., & Fuchs, T. J. (2019). Clinical-grade computational pathology using weakly supervised deep learning on whole slide images. *Nature Medicine*, *25*(8), 1301–1309. doi:10.1038/s41591-019-0508-1 PMID:31308507

Chaddad, A. (2018). Fusion of multi-modal imaging and clinicopathological data in computer-assisted breast histopathology. *Proceedings of the IEEE International Conference on Acoustics, Speech, and Signal Processing*, *2018*, 2587–2591.

Chen, C. (2018). Differential diagnosis of breast cancer using quantitative, label-free and molecular vibrational imaging. *Biomedical Optics Express*, *9*(12), 5952–5969. PMID:31065447

Chen, Y. (2020). HRNet: Deep High-Resolution Representation Learning for Human Pose Estimation. *Proceedings of the IEEE/CVF Conference on Computer Vision and Pattern Recognition (CVPR)*.

Cheng, Ahmad, Irshad, Alsanie, & Khan, Ahmad, & Aleemi. (2023). Impact of Green Process Innovation and Productivity on Sustainability: The Moderating Role of Environmental Awareness. *Sustainability*, *15*(17), 12945. doi:10.3390/su151712945

Cordts, M. (2016). The Cityscapes Dataset for Semantic Urban Scene Understanding. *Proceedings of the IEEE Conference on Computer Vision and Pattern Recognition (CVPR)*. 10.1109/CVPR.2016.350

Coudray, N., Ocampo, P. S., Sakellaropoulos, T., Narula, N., Snuderl, M., Fenyö, D., Moreira, A. L., Razavian, N., & Tsirigos, A. (2018). Classification and mutation prediction from non-small cell lung cancer histopathology images using deep learning. *Nature Medicine*, *24*(10), 1559–1567. doi:10.1038/s41591-018-0177-5 PMID:30224757

David, S., Duraipandian, K., Chandrasekaran, D., Pandey, D., Sindhwani, N., & Pandey, B. K. (2023). Impact of blockchain in healthcare system. In *Unleashing the Potentials of Blockchain Technology for Healthcare Industries* (pp. 37–57). Academic Press. doi:10.1016/B978-0-323-99481-1.00004-3

Deepa, R., Anand, R., Pandey, D., Pandey, B. K., & Karki, B. (2022). Comprehensive performance analysis of classifiers in diagnosis of epilepsy. *Mathematical Problems in Engineering*, *2022*, 2022. doi:10.1155/2022/1559312

Dong, F. (2020). Joint fine-tuning deep learning for pancreatic ductal adenocarcinoma segmentation in CT and MRI images. *IEEE Journal of Biomedical and Health Informatics*, *24*(7), 2071–2080.

Esteva, A., Kuprel, B., Novoa, R. A., Ko, J., Swetter, S. M., Blau, H. M., & Thrun, S. (2017). Dermatologist-level classification of skin cancer with deep neural networks. *Nature*, *542*(7639), 115–118. doi:10.1038/nature21056 PMID:28117445

Etzioni, R. (2002). The prostate cancer prevention trial: Predictive power of prostate cancer risk calculators. *Urology*, *59*(6), 889–895. PMID:12031375

Feichtenhofer, C. (2019). X3D: eXtended 3D ConvNet for Video Action Recognition. *Proceedings of the IEEE International Conference on Computer Vision (ICCV)*.

Fraihat, B. A. M., Ahmad, A. Y. B., Alaa, A. A., Alhawamdeh, A. M., Soumadi, M. M., Aln'emi, E. A. S., & Alkhawaldeh, B. Y. S. (2023). Evaluating Technology Improvement in Sustainable Development Goals by Analysing Financial Development and Energy Consumption in Jordan. *International Journal of Energy Economics and Policy, 13*(4), 348–355. doi:10.32479/ijeep.14438

Gail, M. H., Brinton, L. A., Byar, D. P., Corle, D. K., Green, S. B., Schairer, C., & Mulvihill, J. J. (1989). Projecting individualized probabilities of developing breast cancer for white females who are being examined annually. *Journal of the National Cancer Institute, 81*(24), 1879–1886. doi:10.1093/jnci/81.24.1879 PMID:2593165

Gao, X. (2021). Brain tumor classification using capsule networks and ensemble methods. *Computers in Biology and Medicine, 136*, 104722.

Gevaert, O., Mitchell, L. A., Achrol, A. S., Xu, J., Echegaray, S., Steinberg, G. K., Cheshier, S. H., Napel, S., Zaharchuk, G., & Plevritis, S. K. (2017). Glioblastoma multiforme: Exploratory radiogenomic analysis by using quantitative image features. *Radiology, 273*(1), 168–174. doi:10.1148/radiol.14131731 PMID:24827998

Gillies, R. J., Kinahan, P. E., & Hricak, H. (2016). Radiomics: Images are more than pictures, they are data. *Radiology, 278*(2), 563–577. doi:10.1148/radiol.2015151169 PMID:26579733

Gupta, A., Anand, R., Pandey, D., Sindhwani, N., Wairya, S., Pandey, B. K., & Sharma, M. (2021). Prediction of breast cancer using extremely randomized clustering forests (ERCF) technique: Prediction of breast cancer. *International Journal of Distributed Systems and Technologies, 12*(4), 1–15. doi:10.4018/IJDST.287859

Gupta, A. K., Sharma, M., Sharma, A., & Menon, V. (2022). A study on SARS-CoV-2 (COVID-19) and machine learning based approach to detect COVID-19 through X-ray images. *International Journal of Image and Graphics, 22*(03), 2140010. doi:10.1142/S0219467821400106

Haenssle, H. A., Fink, C., Schneiderbauer, R., Toberer, F., Buhl, T., Blum, A., Kalloo, A., Hassen, A. B. H., Thomas, L., Enk, A., Uhlmann, L., Alt, C., Arenbergerova, M., Bakos, R., Baltzer, A., Bertlich, I., Blum, A., Bokor-Billmann, T., Bowling, J., ... Zalaudek, I. (2018). Man against machine: Diagnostic performance of a deep learning convolutional neural network for dermoscopic melanoma recognition in comparison to 58 dermatologists. *Annals of Oncology : Official Journal of the European Society for Medical Oncology, 29*(8), 1836–1842. doi:10.1093/annonc/mdy166 PMID:29846502

Hariharan, B. (2015). Hypercolumns for Object Segmentation and Fine-grained Localization. *Proceedings of the IEEE Conference on Computer Vision and Pattern Recognition (CVPR).* 10.1109/CVPR.2015.7298642

Hasan, A., Pandey, D., & Khan, A. (2021). Application of EEG time-varying networks in the evaluation of dynamic functional brain networks. *Augmented Human Research, 6*(1), 1–8. doi:10.1007/s41133-021-00046-2

Hosseinzadeh, F. (2020). A machine learning approach for early detection and prediction of ovarian cancer. *BMC Medical Informatics and Decision Making, 20*(1), 1–10. PMID:31906929

Huang, X. (2017). Lung cancer malignancy identification using a multi-scale vessel-based radiomic algorithm. *Computerized Medical Imaging and Graphics*, *59*, 29–35.

Huang, Y. Q., Liang, C., He, L., Tian, J., Liang, C., Chen, X., Ma, Z., & Liu, Z. (2016). Development and validation of a radiomics nomogram for preoperative prediction of lymph node metastasis in colorectal cancer. *Journal of Clinical Oncology*, *34*(18), 2157–2164. doi:10.1200/JCO.2015.65.9128 PMID:27138577

Ibragimov, B. (2019). Supervised learning-based multimodal MRI brain tumor classification using texture features from supervoxels. *Computerized Medical Imaging and Graphics*, *72*, 32–43.

Janowczyk, A. (2017). Deep learning for digital pathology image analysis: A comprehensive tutorial with selected use cases. *Journal of Pathology Informatics*, *8*, 7. PMID:27563488

Karamizadeh, S. (2021). A novel multimodal approach for colorectal cancer classification using CT and MRI images. *Computerized Medical Imaging and Graphics*, *90*, 101869.

Kaur, N., & Sharma, M. (2017, August). Brain tumor detection using self-adaptive K-means clustering. In *2017 international conference on energy, communication, data analytics and soft computing (ICECDS)* (pp. 1861-1865). IEEE.

Kaur, S. P., & Sharma, M. (2015). Radially optimized zone-divided energy-aware wireless sensor networks (WSN) protocol using BA (bat algorithm). *Journal of the Institution of Electronics and Telecommunication Engineers*, *61*(2), 170–179. doi:10.1080/03772063.2014.999833

Khosla, D., Sharma, M., Sharma, A., Budhiraja, A., & Singh, S. (2019). Blockchain based supply chain management: An overview. *Int. J. Control Automat*, *12*(5), 424–430.

Khosla, D., Singh, S., Sharma, M., Sharma, A., Bharti, G., & Rajput, G. (2022). A Review on Virtual Reality and Applications for Next Generation Systems and Society 5.0. *Machine Intelligence and Data Science Applications: Proceedings of MIDAS 2021*, 303-312.

Khosravan, N. (2020). Multi-modal classification of lung nodules in CT scans: Effects of class distribution and data augmentation. *Journal of Medical Imaging (Bellingham, Wash.)*, *7*(3), 034001. PMID:32509915

Khuram, A. (2018). Machine learning-based differentiation between benign and malignant GIST using heterogeneous textural features and robust binary classifiers. *Computer Methods and Programs in Biomedicine*, *154*, 89–98.

Kim, W., Cho, S. K., Shin, S. W., Hyun, D., Lee, M. W., & Rhim, H. (2019). Combination therapy of transarterial chemoembolization (TACE) and radiofrequency ablation (RFA) for small hepatocellular carcinoma: Comparison with TACE or RFA monotherapy. *Abdominal Radiology*, *44*(6), 2283–2292. doi:10.1007/s00261-019-01952-1 PMID:30806742

Korbar, B., Olofson, A. M., Miraflor, A. P., Nicka, C. M., Suriawinata, M. A., Torresani, L., Suriawinata, A. A., & Hassanpour, S. (2017). Deep learning for classification of colorectal polyps on whole-slide images. *Journal of Pathology Informatics*, *8*(1), 30. doi:10.4103/jpi.jpi_34_17 PMID:28828201

Kukreja, V., & Dhiman, P. (2020, September). A Deep Neural Network based disease detection scheme for Citrus fruits. In *2020 International conference on smart electronics and communication (ICOSEC)* (pp. 97-101). IEEE. 10.1109/ICOSEC49089.2020.9215359

Kumar Pandey, B., Pandey, D., Nassa, V. K., Ahmad, T., Singh, C., George, A. S., & Wakchaure, M. A. (2021). Encryption and steganography-based text extraction in IoT using the EWCTS optimizer. *Imaging Science Journal*, *69*(1-4), 38–56. doi:10.1080/13682199.2022.2146885

Li, H. (2018). Machine learning for classifying malignant and benign breast lesions in MRI images. *Proceedings of the SPIE Medical Imaging*, *10575*, 1057519.

Li, H. (2019). A deep joint model for segmentation and diagnosis in individual head and neck CT scans with human papillomavirus status. *International Journal of Computer Assisted Radiology and Surgery*, *14*(3), 515–525.

Lindström, S. (2011). A comprehensive survey of genetic variation in 20,691 subjects from four large cohorts. *PLoS One*, *6*(8), e23133. PMID:21850257

Liu, W. (2016). SSD: Single Shot MultiBox Detector. *European Conference on Computer Vision (ECCV)*.

Ma, Y., Xu, T., Huang, X., Wang, X., Li, C., Jerwick, J., Ning, Y., Zeng, X., Wang, B., Wang, Y., Zhang, Z., Zhang, X., & Zhou, C. (2019). Computer-aided diagnosis of label-free 3-D optical coherence microscopy images of human cervical tissue. *IEEE Transactions on Biomedical Engineering*, *66*(9), 2447–2456. doi:10.1109/TBME.2018.2890167 PMID:30605087

McKinney, S. M., Sieniek, M., Godbole, V., Godwin, J., Antropova, N., Ashrafian, H., Back, T., Chesus, M., Corrado, G. S., Darzi, A., Etemadi, M., Garcia-Vicente, F., Gilbert, F. J., Halling-Brown, M., Hassabis, D., Jansen, S., Karthikesalingam, A., Kelly, C. J., King, D., ... Shetty, S. (2020). International evaluation of an AI system for breast cancer screening. *Nature*, *577*(7788), 89–94. doi:10.1038/s41586-019-1799-6 PMID:31894144

Meslie, Y., Enbeyle, W., Pandey, B. K., Pramanik, S., Pandey, D., Dadeech, P., Belay, A., & Saini, A. (2021). Machine intelligence-based trend analysis of COVID-19 for total daily confirmed cases in Asia and Africa. In *Methodologies and Applications of Computational Statistics for Machine Intelligence* (pp. 164–185). IGI Global. doi:10.4018/978-1-7998-7701-1.ch009

Muniandi, B., Huang, C.-J., Kuo, C.-C., Yang, T.-F., Chen, K.-H., Lin, Y.-H., Lin, S.-R., & Tsai, T.-Y. (2019, November). A 97% Maximum Efficiency Fully Automated Control Turbo Boost Topology for Battery Chargers. *IEEE Transactions on Circuits and Systems. I, Regular Papers*, *66*(11), 4516–4527. doi:10.1109/TCSI.2019.2925374

Ni, L., Ahmad, S. F., Alshammari, T. O., Liang, H., Alsanie, G., Irshad, M., Alyafi-AlZahri, R., Bin-Saeed, R. H., Al-Abyadh, M. H. A., Abu Bakir, S. M. M., & Ayassrah, A. Y. B. A. (2023). The role of environmental regulation and green human capital towards sustainable development: The mediating role of green innovation and industry upgradation. *Journal of Cleaner Production*, *421*, 138497. doi:10.1016/j.jclepro.2023.138497

Pandey, B. K., Mane, D., Nassa, V. K. K., Pandey, D., Dutta, S., Ventayen, R. J. M., & Rastogi, R. (2021). Secure text extraction from complex degraded images by applying steganography and deep learning. In *Multidisciplinary approach to modern digital steganography* (pp. 146–163). IGI Global. doi:10.4018/978-1-7998-7160-6.ch007

Pandey, B. K., Pandey, D., & Agarwal, A. (2022). Encrypted information transmission by enhanced steganography and image transformation. *International Journal of Distributed Artificial Intelligence, 14*(1), 1–14. doi:10.4018/IJDAI.297110

Pandey, B. K., Pandey, D., Gupta, A., Nassa, V. K., Dadheech, P., & George, A. S. (2023). Secret data transmission using advanced morphological component analysis and steganography. In *Role of Data-Intensive Distributed Computing Systems in Designing Data Solutions* (pp. 21–44). Springer International Publishing. doi:10.1007/978-3-031-15542-0_2

Pandey, B. K., Pandey, D., Nassa, V. K., George, S., Aremu, B., Dadeech, P., & Gupta, A. (2022, July). Effective and secure transmission of health information using advanced morphological component analysis and image hiding. In *Artificial Intelligence on Medical Data: Proceedings of International Symposium, ISCMM 2021* (pp. 223-230). Singapore: Springer Nature Singapore.

Pandey, B. K., Pandey, D., Wairya, S., & Agarwal, G. (2021). An advanced morphological component analysis, steganography, and deep learning-based system to transmit secure textual data. *International Journal of Distributed Artificial Intelligence, 13*(2), 40–62. doi:10.4018/IJDAI.2021070104

Pandey, B. K., Pandey, D., Wairya, S., Agarwal, G., Dadeech, P., Dogiwal, S. R., & Pramanik, S. (2022). Application of integrated steganography and image compressing techniques for confidential information transmission. *Cyber Security and Network Security*, 169-191.

Pandey, B. K., Pandey, D., Wariya, S., & Agarwal, G. (2021). A deep neural network-based approach for extracting textual images from deteriorate images. *EAI Endorsed Transactions on Industrial Networks and Intelligent Systems, 8*(28), e3–e3. doi:10.4108/eai.17-9-2021.170961

Pandey, D., Nassa, V. K., Jhamb, A., Mahto, D., Pandey, B. K., George, A. H., & Bandyopadhyay, S. K. (2021). An integration of keyless encryption, steganography, and artificial intelligence for the secure transmission of stego images. In *Multidisciplinary approach to modern digital steganography* (pp. 211–234). IGI Global. doi:10.4018/978-1-7998-7160-6.ch010

Pandey, D., & Pandey, B. K. (2022). An efficient deep neural network with adaptive galactic swarm optimization for complex image text extraction. In *Process Mining Techniques for Pattern Recognition* (pp. 121–137). CRC Press. doi:10.1201/9781003169550-10

Pandey, D., Pandey, B. K., & Wairya, S. (2021). Hybrid deep neural network with adaptive galactic swarm optimization for text extraction from scene images. *Soft Computing, 25*(2), 1563–1580. doi:10.1007/s00500-020-05245-4

Pandey, J. K., Jain, R., Dilip, R., Kumbhkar, M., Jaiswal, S., Pandey, B. K., & Pandey, D. (2022). Investigating Role of IoT in the Development of Smart Application for Security Enhancement. In *IoT Based Smart Applications* (pp. 219–243). Springer International Publishing.

Parthiban, K., Pandey, D., & Pandey, B. K. (2021). Impact of SARS-CoV-2 in online education, predicting and contrasting mental stress of young students: A machine learning approach. *Augmented Human Research, 6*(1), 10. doi:10.1007/s41133-021-00048-0

Raghavan, R., Verma, D. C., Pandey, D., Anand, R., Pandey, B. K., & Singh, H. (2022). Optimized building extraction from high-resolution satellite imagery using deep learning. *Multimedia Tools and Applications*, *81*(29), 42309–42323. doi:10.1007/s11042-022-13493-9

Rani, S., Koundal, D., Kavita, F., Ijaz, M. F., Elhoseny, M., & Alghamdi, M. I. (2021). An optimized framework for WSN routing in the context of industry 4.0. *Sensors (Basel)*, *21*(19), 6474. doi:10.3390/s21196474 PMID:34640792

Redmon, J., & Farhadi, A. (2017). YOLOv2: A Fast and Accurate Object Detector. arXiv preprint arXiv:1612.08242.

Sharma, M., Gupta, A. K., Singh, J., Mittal, R., Singh, H., & Pandey, D. (2022, December). Effects of slot shape in performance of SIW based Leaky Wave Antenna. In *2022 International Conference on Computational Modelling, Simulation and Optimization (ICCMSO)* (pp. 268-273). IEEE. 10.1109/ICCMSO58359.2022.00060

Sharma, M., Pandey, D., Palta, P., & Pandey, B. K. (2022). Design and power dissipation consideration of PFAL CMOS V/S conventional CMOS based 2: 1 multiplexer and full adder. *Silicon*, *14*(8), 4401–4410. doi:10.1007/s12633-021-01221-1

Sharma, M., Saripalli, S. R., Gupta, A. K., Talwar, R., Dadheech, P., & Kanike, U. K. (2023). Real-Time Pothole Detection During Rainy Weather Using Dashboard Cameras for Driverless Cars. In *Handbook of Research on Thrust Technologies' Effect on Image Processing* (pp. 384–394). IGI Global. doi:10.4018/978-1-6684-8618-4.ch023

Sharma, M., Sharma, B., Gupta, A. K., Khosla, D., Goyal, S., & Pandey, D. (2021). A study and novel AI/ML-based framework to detect COVID-19 virus using smartphone embedded sensors. In *Sustainability Measures for COVID-19 Pandemic* (pp. 59–74). Springer Nature Singapore. doi:10.1007/978-981-16-3227-3_4

Sharma, M., Sharma, B., Gupta, A. K., & Pandey, D. (2023). Recent developments of image processing to improve explosive detection methodologies and spectroscopic imaging techniques for explosive and drug detection. *Multimedia Tools and Applications*, *82*(5), 6849–6865. doi:10.1007/s11042-022-13578-5

Sharma, M., & Singh, H. (2022). Contactless methods for respiration monitoring and design of SIW-LWA for real-time respiratory rate monitoring. *Journal of the Institution of Electronics and Telecommunication Engineers*, 1–11. doi:10.1080/03772063.2022.2069167

Sharma, M., Singh, H., & Pandey, D. (2022). Parametric considerations and dielectric materials impacts on the performance of 10 GHzSIW-LWA for respiration monitoring. *Journal of Electronic Materials*, *51*(5), 2131–2141. doi:10.1007/s11664-022-09482-1

Song, W. (2020). Automated detection and classification of gastrointestinal stromal tumors using deep learning. *BioMed Research International.*

Sun, L. (2018). Online Real-Time Action Recognition System for Untrimmed Videos. *Proceedings of the European Conference on Computer Vision (ECCV).*

Talwar, R., Sharma, M., Singh, H., & Sagar, P. (2023). A Comparative Analysis on Image Processing-Based Algorithms and Approaches in Healthcare. In *Handbook of Research on Thrust Technologies' Effect on Image Processing* (pp. 1–14). IGI Global. doi:10.4018/978-1-6684-8618-4.ch001

Vickers, A. J. (2009). An empirical evaluation of the Gail model for breast cancer risk prediction in the Nurses' Health Study. *Journal of the National Cancer Institute*, *101*(14), 1014–1023.

Wang, H. (2018). Multi-modal 3D U-net for bladder and prostate segmentation on MRI and CT images. *Proceedings of the IEEE Conference on Computer Vision and Pattern Recognition Workshops*, 1176-1179.

Wang, Y. (2020). Efficient and Accurate Pedestrian Detection in Real-Time: A Survey. *arXiv preprint arXiv:2009.00936*.

Wu, W. (2019). Development of a multipara-metric radiomics model for preoperative evaluation of early recurrence in advanced-stage colorectal cancer. *Journal of Clinical Oncology*, *37*(18), 1522–1531.

Xu, J. (2016). Deep learning for histopathological image analysis: Towards computerized diagnosis aided by deep learning—review. *Medical Image Analysis*, *32*, 177–196.

Xu, Y., Jia, Z., Ai, Y., Zhang, F., Lai, M., Eric, I., & Chang, C. (2015, April). Deep convolutional activation features for large scale brain tumor histopathology image classification and segmentation. In *2015 IEEE international conference on acoustics, speech and signal processing (ICASSP)* (pp. 947-951). IEEE.

Yuan, Y. (2019). A benchmark for endoluminal scene segmentation of gastroscopic images. *Computerized Medical Imaging and Graphics*, *77*, 101642.

Zhang, L. (2018). DeepSORT: A Simple Online and Realtime Tracking Approach with Minimalistic Model Design. *arXiv preprint arXiv:1812.00442*.

Zhou, M., Scott, J., Chaudhury, B., Hall, L., Goldgof, D., Yeom, K. W., Iv, M., Ou, Y., Kalpathy-Cramer, J., Napel, S., Gillies, R., Gevaert, O., & Gatenby, R. (2018). Radiomics in brain tumor: Image assessment, quantitative feature descriptors, and machine-learning approaches. *AJNR. American Journal of Neuroradiology*, *39*(2), 208–216. doi:10.3174/ajnr.A5391 PMID:28982791

Chapter 16
Assessment of the Manufacturing Quality of Metallic Surface Finishes in Artificial Intelligence

Suresh Kumar Sahani
MIT Campus, Janakpurdham, Nepal

Kameshwar Sahani
Kathmandu University, Nepal

Darshan A. Mahajan
https://orcid.org/0000-0002-1239-6343
NICMAR University, Pune, India

Tamanna M. Prajapati
Shri D.N. Institute of Computer Applications, India

Sukhvinder Singh Dari
https://orcid.org/0000-0002-6218-6600
Symbiosis Law School, Symbiosis International University, India

Dharmesh Dhabliya
https://orcid.org/0000-0002-6340-2993
Department of Information Technology, Vishwakarma Institute of Information Technology, India

Pankaj Dadheech
https://orcid.org/0000-0001-5783-1989
Swami Keshvanand Institute of Technology, Management, and Gramothan, India

ABSTRACT

This chapter describes a prototype of a system that automatically checks the surface of precision ground metallic surfaces. It specifically focuses on bearing rolls. The authors study and test how light bounces off the surface using optical experiments. The aim is to figure out how to make things look sharp and bright, so it's easy to see the contrast between surfaces that are damaged and those that aren't. A new method for choosing a value to separate different parts of an image is presented. In addition, the text explores various search methods that go through a list one by one and have been made available to the public. These algorithms are used to find the most suitable group of traits for organizing or categorizing something. The text also looks at how much computer power these algorithms need. Finally, the authors display the results of sorting 540 blemished pictures.

DOI: 10.4018/979-8-3693-1347-3.ch016

1. INTRODUCTION

In businesses, more and more people want machines that check products to make sure they are good enough. Therefore, the use of techniques to modify images is crucial in this expanding area. The things that customers want are fair because when something is low quality, it can end up being expensive. This is because you have to pay for it initially, and then also pay to fix it later. When humans evaluate how good a product is in tasks that are done over and over again, like checking textiles, they can only be completely accurate about 80% of the time. So, if we use a machine (B. Smith, et al. (1993)) instead of people to look for problems, it will usually do a better job and be cheaper. You can find information on automated visual inspection in a survey called (T. S. Newman, et al. (1995)). In easy words, some recent papers have been published about checking the surface of steel products. Most of these papers focus on flat objects.

This paper describes a machine that can automatically inspect the look of bearing rolls. These rolls are very smooth and have precise surfaces. A simple explanation of how an automated solution for checking bearing rolls in real-time works can be seen in Figure 1.

It has five main parts.

A setup is described in Section 3 that can capture images of surfaces. It includes the necessary equipment such as a camera, lighting, and frame-grabber. Identifying mistakes or errors (refer to Section 4). breaking down an image into separate parts or regions based on its content extracting characteristics or properties from data feature selection is a process described in Section 5. 3

Categorizing means sorting things into different groups (check Section 5 for more information). I'm sorry, but I need a text to rewrite it in simple words. Please provide the text you would like me to simplify.

The problem we are currently facing is described in Section 2. This text explains what the inspection system needs to do and what kinds of defects it should look for. The way the optical arrangement is built is determined by studying how light reflects off of surfaces. You can find more information about this in Section 3 of the document. This modeling is influenced by the works of references 5, 6, and 7. Scientists conducted tests in a lab to check if the model was correct and to find the best place for the lights. To check one roll, about 7 million bytes of data need to be analyzed. As a result, in the first step, an old statistical method (found in Section 4) is used to find problems in the collected data. These parts

Figure 1. System concept

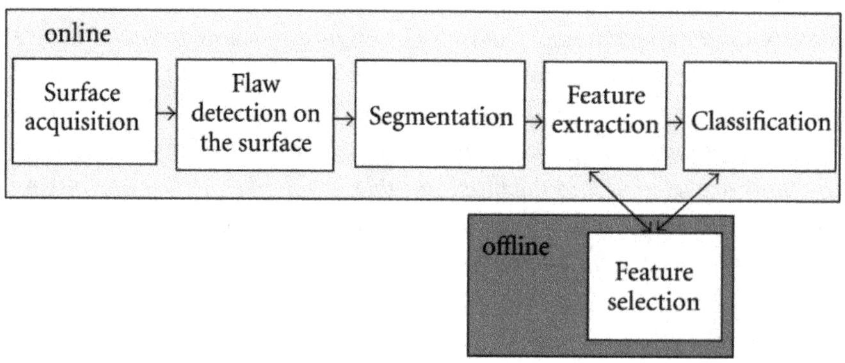

Figure 2. Different bearing rolls

of the information are taken out and sent as smaller pictures for additional work. This way, we reduce the data by about 100 times.

The different types of problems in the sub images are explained in Section 5. These pictures are divided into parts to detect the problem from everything around it, so that we can figure out its specific features. During online processing, we use these characteristics to group things together. Finding the best set of characteristics for classification is a difficult job and is done in advance. To achieve this goal, we conducted a study comparing different methods for choosing the most important features in a sequence. We also tested these methods using real data from this particular application. The paper concludes with a short summary and suggests topics for further study.

2. PROBLEM STATEMENT

To make good bearings, the surfaces of the rolls have to be smooth and without any problems that may happen while making them. To make sure that bearings can last a long time and don't cause much rubbing, any rolls with faults bigger than 0. 1 mm should be taken out of the production batch. This means that small defects are easier to see than big defects. The bearing rolls come in different sizes. The size can be from 45 to 100 mm long, and from 30 to 45 mm wide. Picture 2 shows the different positions. The time it takes to find and categorize all issues on a small bearing roll is 1. 2 seconds as a result, the amount of data checked in 100% inspection is equal to around 6 megabytes per second.

After the process of grinding, a quick look is taken at the object to check for any visible issues or problems. Right now, the rough surface looks very shiny and is not affected by any bumps or imperfections caused by the liquid used for corrosion protection.

2.1. Characteristic of Flaws

The imperfections on the metal surface are determined by how it is treated in the end.

There are three main reasons for uneven surfaces in this situation:

(i) Material defects (Pandey, B. K., & Pandey, D., 2023) are flaws that are already in the material before grinding.

(ii) Problems that occur during the process of grinding.

Rubbing marks caused by touching or moving objects.

According to the people who check the products, they have found five different types of problems that occurred during production. So, the first three classes make the surface less rough.

(1) Class 1 material flaws are barely noticeable and appear as a pale shade of gray. The brightness of the flaw increases towards the edge. They don't have a particular shape or size. These mistakes are already there in the empty area and they appear like a gap in the surface of the rolling bearing.

Grinding flaws (class 2) happen when the bearing roll comes out of the grinding machine after being ground. They usually look like a triangle with a main direction. The error's gray value in class 1 is more consistent and lower than in this case. How these flaws look really depends on how the light shines on them (see Section 3). The surface is not smooth.

Scratches (class 3): Scratches happen when the rough particles on a grinding wheel rub against a surface. They look very thin and long with a low, mostly gray color. Most of them are oriented between 60 and 120 degrees. They also make the surface less rough.

Chafe marks (class 4): Chafe marks occur when the manipulators touch something excessively. They don't have a specific shape, but the object is usually not consistent or uniform. These flaws actually make the surface smoother.

Spots in class 5 are puzzling. We don't understand how they are created. The cleaning process cannot remove them until they are visually checked. Small spots that are gray in color become visible. They don't make the surface smoother or rougher.

Another problem with this task is that defect types 4 and 5 should not result in a part being taken out of the production group. This puts more expectations on the algorithms used for classification.

2. OPTICAL ARRANGEMENT AND EXPERIMENTAL SETUP

Good lighting can make surface defects easier to see. The position of the light source has a big effect on how clear the image is, especially for mistakes in class 2 and class 3. These flaws are identified by an ongoing change in the surface's structure, which lowers the measurement of how rough it is. So, the best way for the light to hit the surface is determined by its shape. Because of this, we have analyzed and tested how the surface reflects light using models and optical tests.

3.1. Reflection Model

The surface is made up of many small parts called microfacets. These microfacets form a larger section of the surface, which has a general direction called the mean normal vector n. When studying how surfaces reflect light, we look at how bumpy the surface is by examining the angles of the tiny parts that make up the surface. Each small part of a surface is described by a slope, which is the angle at which it is tilted in relation to the overall angle of the surface. The surface is explained by the measure of how spread out or concentrated the data is around the average value.

Neymar and his friends. This text compares the Beckmann-Spizz chino.

Figure 3. Three reflection components

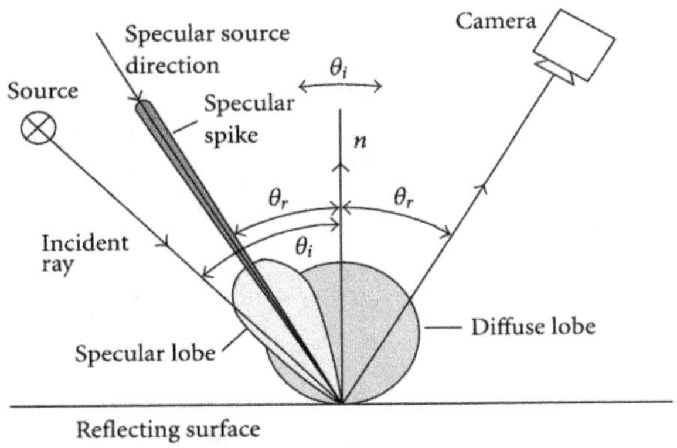

We switched from using one model to another for how light behaves on surfaces. We also created a new way to measure how surfaces reflect light, both for smooth and bumpy surfaces. This framework is made up of three parts that involve light: the light that is scattered, the light that is focused, and the light that is concentrated. These three sections are shown in Figure 3. The brightness is found where the curves on the sensor intersect. This is where the light comes from and starts.

When the surface reflects light towards the camera, it creates a picture that is bright.

$I_{im} = I_{dl} + I_{sl} + I_{ss}.$

The diffuse projection may be a portion of the Lambertson show that speaks to the scattered light. A Torrance-Sparrow model is a tool used to make predictions about the specular lobe.

$$I_{sl} = K_{sl} \exp\left(-\frac{\alpha^2}{2\sigma_\alpha^2}\right) F\left(\theta_i', \eta'\right) G\left(\theta_i, \theta_r, \phi_r\right), \tag{1}$$

$K_s l$ represents how big the shiny spot is, and the exponential part talks about how the small surfaces are arranged in a curved shape, assuming a regular pattern (P. Beckmann and A. Spizzochino (1963)).

The Fresnel coefficient is a symbol for $F(\theta_i, \eta)$, which shows the relationship between the angle at which light hits a surface (θ_i) and the speed at which it moves through a material (η). In books and articles, it is noticed that, for metals, the Fresnel coefficient measures the amount of light reflection at the boundary between the metal and another material. stays mostly the same until the angle of incidence θ_i is close to 75 degrees. So, in this application, we assume that this coefficient stays the same.

The geometric attenuation factor $G(\theta_i, \theta_r, \varphi_r)$ (K. E. Torrance. et al.(1967)) represents how neighboring facets block or hide other facets. θ_r and φ_r indicate the camera's direction.

The value of G is equal to one when the way we are looking and the average direction are alike.

Specular spike is a really sharp part that can be simplified as a delta function.

Figure 4. Coordinate system for the reflection model (adopted from Torrence and Sparrow (1967)

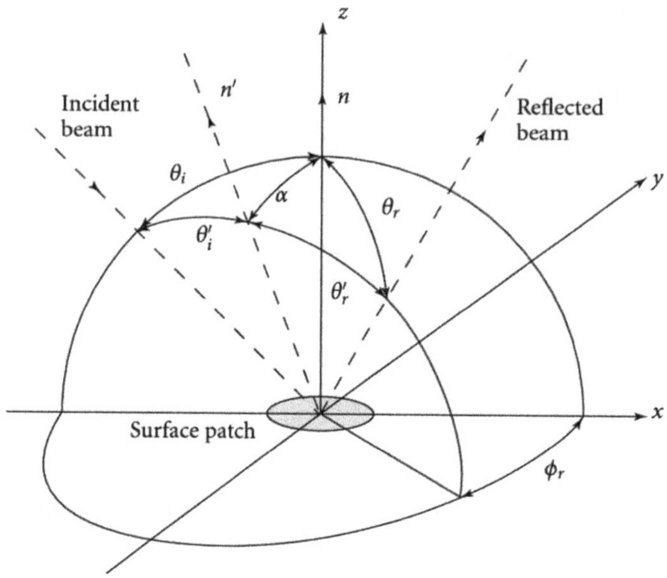

$I_{ss} = K_{ss}\delta(\theta i \_ \theta r)\delta_{(}\phi r)$ (2)

KSS r_{ep}resents the power of the shiny point part.

The model uses a coordinate system, as seen in Figure 4.

The ratio Ks*l/Kss d*epends on how rough the surface. For surfaces that are not smooth, the shiny part is much more noticeable than the tiny shiny spot. This only happens when the roughness of the surface is more than 1. 5 times the wavelength of the light. smoothness is high.

$Id_l = Kd_l \cos\theta i,$ (3)

The angle at which the incident wave hits the object, the equation for the diffuse lobe radiation pattern can be written as Kdl = θi the angle at which the light rays hit something.

The specular lobe is there because it has a simpler math equation. The flaws on the surface only affect how smooth or rough it looks when light reflects off it. So, when light hits an object, it can bounce off in different ways. One of these ways is called specular lobe component, which helps us understand how light reflects off a smooth surface differently from other surfaces. The brightness or shininess of a surface that is undamaged and has faults.

3.2. Measurements of Surface Roughness

We checked if the reflection model worked by measuring how smooth the surface was. We used a special machine called a topography measuring apparatus to measure the height of the flaws on the surface, as well as the nearby surface that didn't have any errors. We used a machine called the Wyo NT-1000,

Figure 5. 3D profile of a scratch

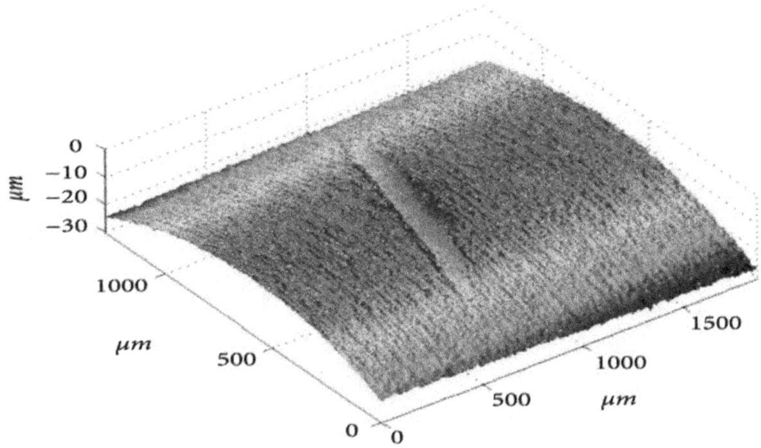

Figure 6. Roughness profiles of a grinding flaw and a scratch

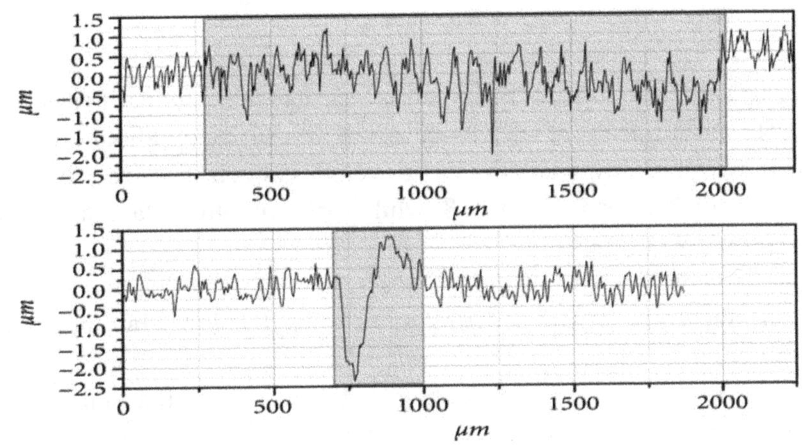

which was made by a company called Veto Instruments, Inc. In New York, which is in the United States. Figure 5 displays the bumpy surface of a scratch in a 3D format.

In simpler terms, the way light reflects off machined surfaces can be divided into two functions: one that reflects parallel to the direction the surface was machined, and another that reflects perpendicular to it. In the suggested plan (as shown in Figure 10), the camera, the light source, and the roll's axis are all on the same flat surface. So, we don't need to worry about the reflection function that goes in the same direction as the machine. Instead, we focus on figuring out how the reflection function works in the area where the optical setup is. text is about simplifying another text by using simpler words.

Figure 6 shows the roughness profiles for a scratch and grinding mistake measured in the same direction as the roll axis. Both problems make the surface rougher.

Figure 7.

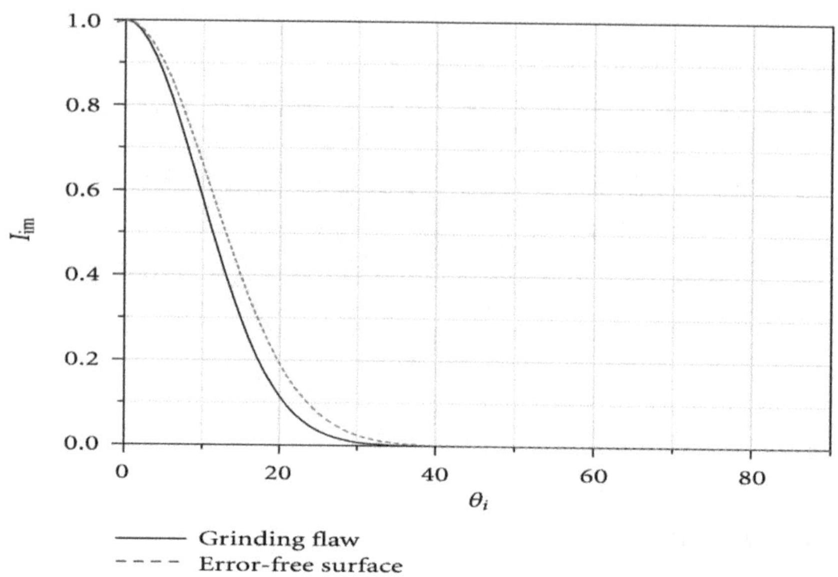

The amount of variation in the slopes of the errors is less than the amount of variation in the slopes of the intact surface. A flawed surface is at least twice as tall as a surface without errors. The main waves on the rough surface move more slowly and the inclines are less steep. These effects cause a lower value of σα. The measured grinding error value is 4. 8, while for a smooth surface it is 5. 5 This difference makes the reflection property change.

We calculate and show the strength of the reflection in a specific direction using a mathematical model in Figure 7. The angle you look at something is always 0 degrees, but the angle that something comes from can be different.

The difference in the brightness of the reflections between a smooth surface and a surface with a grinding flaw shows how rough the surfaces are. The biggest difference occurs when the angle of light is between 10 and 30 degrees. So, having a light angle in this range should give the best contrast.

3.3. Optical Measurements

We calculate and show the strength of the reflection in a specific direction using a mathematical model in Figure 7. The angle you look at something is always 0 degrees, but the angle that something comes from can be different. The difference in the brightness of the reflections between a smooth surface and a surface with a grinding flaw shows how rough the surfaces are. The biggest difference occurs when the angle of light is between 10 and 30 degrees. So, having a light angle in this range should give the best contrast. A surface that is not smooth causes less light to bounce into the camera. The biggest difference between a damaged area and a normal area can be seen when the light is shining from an angle between 10 degrees and 40 degrees. This experiment's outcome matches the prediction from the model (refer to Figure 7), even though there were some simplifications and assumptions made in (Pandey, Pandey, &

Figure 8. Shows the intensity measurement for both a smooth surface with no errors and a surface with grinding errors. In this case, we are fixing the viewing direction at 0 degrees and changing the direction of the light source.

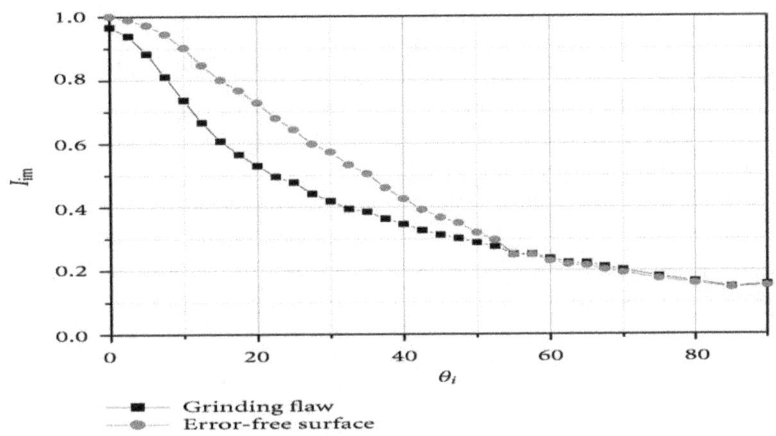

Wairya, 2021; Torrance & Sparrow, 1967). The reflection model calculates how bright something looks when light hits it and bounces back. It compares the brightness of a smooth surface with no mistakes to the brightness of a surface with grinding mistakes. It only considers the straight, shiny part of the light.

3.4. Applying Ideas and Concepts in a Real-World Setting for the Production Environment

The bearing roll is made bright on both sides with a strong light to ensure that the entire surface is evenly lit. The light hits the surface from different angles because of the shape of the light source. Figure 9 shows this.

Furthermore, the way the light is spread out on the roll is different for every source of light. The left side of the stage is mostly lit up by the light on the left, and the same goes for the other side. Through experimentation, it has been found that the ideal illumination angle is 45 degrees, as determined by scientific testing. This means that when considering the way things are put together and how big they are, β equals 14 degrees.

The value of γ is 65 degrees, and the value of δ is 18 degrees. Therefore, for most of the light rays, the angle at which they hit an object is between 18 degrees and 32 degrees.

Alpha plus beta equals 59 degrees.

Additionally, the brightness on the roll is different for each light source. The left side of the stage is mostly brightened by the light on the left, and the right side is also brightened by a light on the right. We found through experiments that the best angle of illumination is 45 degrees. This means that when considering the shape and size, β is equal to 14 degrees. The value of γ is 65 degrees and the value of δ is 18 degrees. Therefore, the angle that most of the light rays hit is between 18 degrees and the sum of alpha and beta, which is 59 degrees.

Figure 9. Arrangement of the light sources

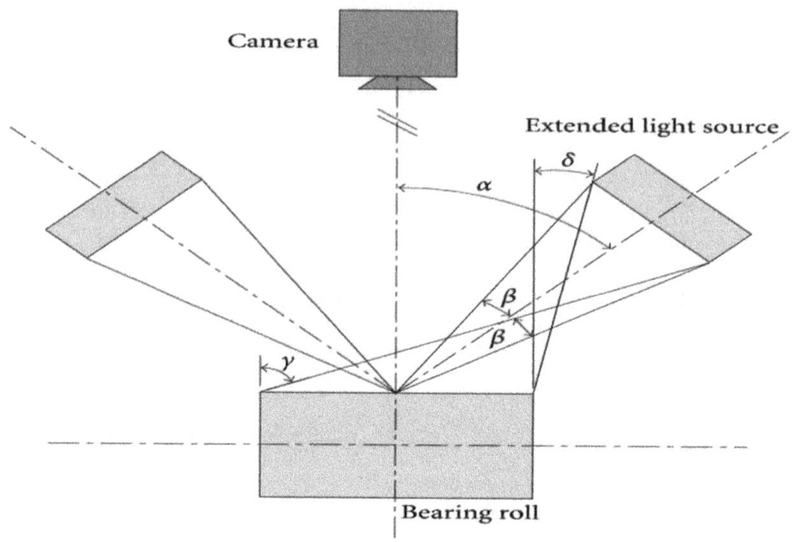

3.5. Experimental Setup

A camera with a black and white sensor and 2048 small dots is used. Around 3500 lines are scanned to measure the perimeter of the small rolls. We pick a time interval that is shorter than half the size of the smallest defect we want to find. The size of each pixel is 0. 049 mm horizontally and 0. 027 mm vertically. The way the parts are set up is displayed in Figure 10.

3. FLAW DETECTION

The problems need to be found on the surface image that was obtained, where they are hidden in a mostly even pattern. The unevenness of the ground makes a picture with different patterns and colors. In simpler terms, structural textures are made up of repeating patterns that happen in a certain predictable way.

In the first part, we look for areas with possible mistakes by moving a window across the entire surface. In this window, we use less information to find out if there is a problem or not. When areas have values that go beyond limits, they are separated into smaller pictures for additional work. This step reduces the data size by around 1/100. In simple terms, there are two main ways to analyze textural features in research: either by looking at the arrangement of elements in a space or by studying the frequency of patterns in that space. The hardest part is finding the right characteristics that describe the flaws well. Because this application requires quick processing, only basic statistical features of the space are calculated. These features include the average, variability, asymmetry, and shape of the data. They can find flaws on surfaces even if the contrast is not very strong.

Figure 10. Experimental arrangement

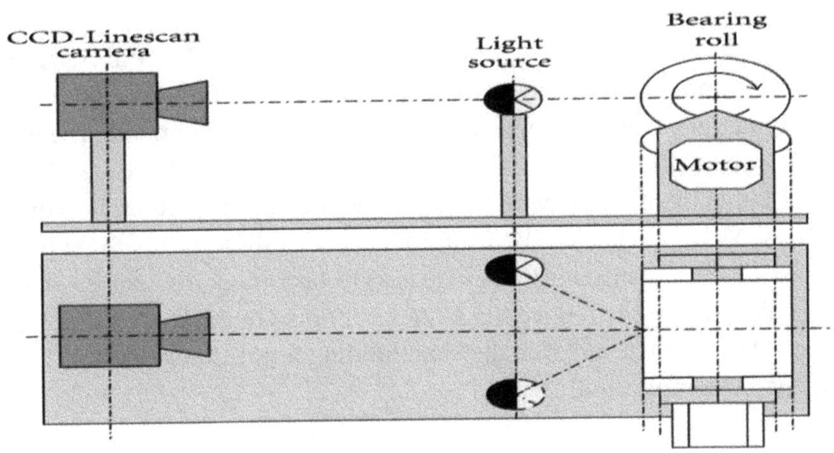

5. CLASSIFICATION

The irregularities that are found are sorted into groups based on their specific features. So, each small image is explained by a list of characteristics, where *xi* is the description number *i* and *N* is the total number of all the features. To achieve this, we divide the differences in the small images and extract their characteristics. We do not know which features are the best for classification beforehand. Therefore, the characteristics need to be chosen beforehand from a big group to achieve the best classification results.

Figure 11. (a) Showcasing a mistake in grinding, (b) a graph that shows the distribution of something, (c) a black and white image after using a filter and setting a certain level, and (d) a graph that has been made smoother with a gray line indicating the level we set. The value of T is 149

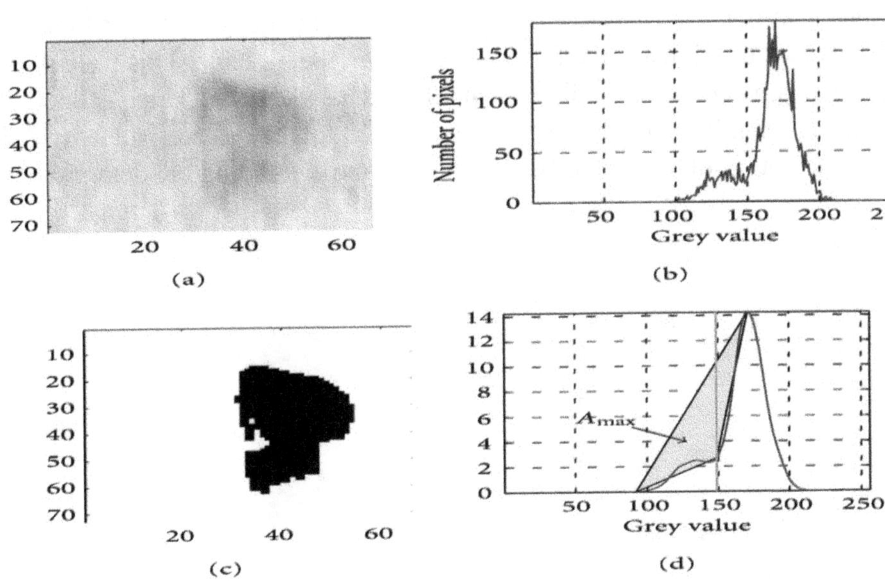

5.1 Segmentation

The most popular technique for dividing an image (Kumar Pandey, B. et al., 2021) into segments is called thresholding. The limit is calculated from the histogram. The flaw and the surrounding statistical texture might have similar gray values, so when we make the histogram smoother, there is only one peak. Some problems in this application have very little difference between the colors, which makes the graph look uneven. We think that the mistake, which is a similar area in the picture, is shown at the end of the histogram (Ahmad, A. Y. B., et al. (2023)). Therefore, the threshold needs to be positioned where the shape of the data distribution changes from being steep to becoming a gradually declining tail. Before deciding on a threshold, we need to reduce the amount of noise in the histogram by using a smoothing technique. This is needed to make sure that the shareholding algorithm works well.

The histogram $H(i)$ is complicated.

$$H(i) = H(i) * g(i, \sigma) \tag{4}$$

with a one-dimensional Gaussian kernel

$$g\left(i,\sigma\right) = \frac{1}{\sqrt{2\pi\sigma^2}} \exp\left(-\frac{i^2}{2\sigma^2}\right), \tag{5}$$

Where is the gray value, is the width of the kernel, and ~ ()$i\sigma$Hi means the histogram that has been smoothed. To make sure the algorithm works well, we need to pick the right value for σ. A very big σ value will make things too smooth in a bad way.

This means that if the value is too low, the smoothing won't be enough.

After the histogram has been made smoother, the threshold algorithm is used to find the value that maximizes the area of a triangle. side of the histogram $p_2 = [x_2, y_2]$ can be used to calculate the width of the histogram peak.

The points x_2 and y_2 are selected to create the bottom line of the triangle. We are looking for the point on the histogram at p3 = [*xi*, *yi*] that is the farthest away from the baseline. This means finding the biggest area that the three points make. But, discovering the enclosed area Ai happened before discovering the regular distance. To calculate the area Ai, you need to multiply the x and y values of three points, p_1, p_2, and p_3. Take half of the result to get the final area. This means finding the determinant.

$$A_i = \frac{1}{2}\begin{vmatrix} x_i & y_i & 1 \\ x_1 & y_1 & 1 \\ x_2 & y_2 & 1 \end{vmatrix}, \tag{6}$$

or

$$A_i = \frac{1}{2}\left[x_i\left(y_1 - y_2\right) - y_i\left(x_1 - x_2\right) + \left(x_1 y_2 - x_2 y_1\right)\right]. \tag{7}$$

This math equation can be made simpler because **p**1 and **p**2 are constant means staying the same, and during the search means while looking for something

$$A_i = x_i c_0 + y_i c_1 + c_2 \tag{8}$$

The threshold value T is

$$T = x_i | x_2 < x_i < x_2 \wedge A_i = \max(A_i) \tag{9}$$

The picture in Figure 11 shows the outcome of the segmentation.

The way we generated the threshold helps to separate the flaw into smaller parts. But the algorithm has a big advantage: it doesn't matter how many peaks are in the histogram. In a bimodal histogram, the threshold level is chosen at the lowest point between the two peaks. When the difference in brightness between parts of the image is small, the threshold level that is chosen is where the different categories (defects/background) of the histogram meet. If the flaw creates a bigger peak than the surrounding peaks, this method does not work. However, in this app, the area around it always has the most influence.

5.2 Feature Extraction

The segmentation creates a clear and distinct object in the smaller image. This is important for the next action where we calculate features for describing shape and descriptors that are dependent on gray values. The methods used to calculate different features can be found in (Gonzalez & Woods, 1992; Pernkopf, 2002; Sonka et al., 1999) and are listed in Table 1. In total, we collected 54 details of each problem in an initial stage.

Basically, there were four different ways to take out features. These were different ways of measuring and describing things using statistics, shapes, and lines. (1) Features based on regions: basic descriptors based on the binary image. These features refer to either all parts that are obtained after dividing something into smaller parts or to the biggest part that was extracted using a specific method called region labeling algorithm explained in a paper by Sanka et al. Rephrase this text using easier words: (M. Sonka, et al.(1999)). The given passage in simpler words: The passage says that it is important to communicate effectively with others. Communication is about clearly sharing our thoughts, ideas, and feelings, and also actively listening to what others have to say. Being able to communicate well with others can assist in forming strong connections and solving disagreements (Raghavan, R., et al.(2022)). Most of the features are created from the shapes seen in different areas and from moments that stay the same no matter how the objects are moved. Statistical features are numbers that describe an image or a flaw and its background. Furthermore, the relationship between the average and the variability of the flaw in comparison to the surrounding background are used as characteristics.

The shape of the largest part in the black and white image is explained using Fourier descriptors. So, the shape is shown as a closed line $c(i)$ $\vec{c}(i) = (c_x(i), c_y(i))$, where i=L is the length of a curve, and cx(i) and cy(i) are the x and y co-ordinates. The Fourier descriptors are calculated for the x and y coordinates. From these descriptors, the first few descriptors that are invariant to translation, rotation, and magnification are used.

This is a way to see how the flaw looks.

Gradient features refer to the way that the brightness of an image changes quickly between nearby pixels.

The equation can be made simpler because p1 and p2 are used to find the highest change in both directions. This helps to determine whether there are flaws that are hard to see or flaws that are easy to see.

5.3 Feature Selection

In everyday classification problems, we often don't know what features are important for classification beforehand. So, the job of feature selection is to pick out only the most important features from a bunch (Pandey, D., et al. (2021)), so that it helps improve the way things are classified. Many different ways of doing things exist, and they usually have four basic steps.

One way to create the next group of features *X*. A way to judge how good *X* is. A stopping criterion is a condition that determines when to stop a search. It can be based on how it's made or how it's tested; text). Selected subset means a smaller group of things that have been chosen or picked out from a larger group. Feature selection is done in opine, which means only the chosen features are used for classifying things online. The most ideal group or selection is selected from the set

$$X = \{x_i | \, i=1,\dots,d; \, x_i \in Y\} \tag{10}$$

$$Y = \{y_i | \, i=1,\dots,D\} \tag{11}$$

One way to create the next group of features *X*. A way to judge how good *X* is. A stopping criterion is a condition that determines when to stop a search. It can be based on how it's made or how it's tested; text). Selected subset means a smaller group of things that have been chosen or picked out from a larger group. Feature selection is done in opine, which means only the chosen features are used for classifying things online (Pandey, B. K, et al. (2022)). The most ideal group or selection

The total amount of space within all segments. The total length of all the lines that make up the edges of a shape. Compactness means that all segments are short and do not take up much space. Center of gravity in x refers to the point at which the weight of an object is evenly distributed. Center of gravity in y refers to the position in which the total weight of an object is considered to be concentrated vertically, along the y-axis. The smallest amount in polar measurement. Polar measure maximum can be rewritten as finding the highest value in a polar measurement. Polar measure is a way to describe the position or direction of something using angles and distances. The ratio of how wide something is compared to how tall it is in all parts.

The measurement of how tall each part is. The measurement of how wide all parts are. All parts are round (Pandey, B.K., et al. (2021)),. The amount of stops in the side-to-side view. The amount of things that stop or get interrupted when we show them on a straight up and down view. The number of empty spaces within the object. Number of empty spaces inside the object. Amount of things The size of the biggest part The total length of the longest segment's outer edge. The way in which the biggest part is pointed. The size of the rectangle that can contain the longest segment. The size of the rectangular shape that can fit around the longest segment. The biggest rectangle-like shape

The larges segment is compact.

Axis ratio is when you compare the longest side to the shortest side of a rectangle that is around an object. The straight line that best represents the length of the longest segment when projected onto a flat surface. The a1 is a number that helps find the line that fits best with the longest flat line. The angle of the regression line is the slope of the line that shows the direction of the longest segment when it is projected horizontally. The absolute error is the difference between the position of the regression line and where it intersects the horizontal axis. The b0 value is the number that calculates the horizontal projection of the longest part in a second-order fit analysis. The b1 of the second-order fit is the steepness of the line that shows the longest segment when it is laid horizontally. The "b2" term in the second-order fit refers to the longest horizontal part of a line. The difference between the actual horizontal projection and the predicted horizontal projection using a second-order fit can be explained like this: It means comparing the actual measurement of something going sideways (horizontal) to the estimate made using a specific mathematical method called second-order fit. The proportion of the areas

Eccentricity means being different or strange in an unusual way. It refers to having unconventional habits, behaviors, or thoughts that deviate from what is considered normal or typical. The ratio of the area of a shape to its width. The overall color of all sections is gray, but not too dark or too light. The standard deviation tells us how different or spread out all the segments are. The usual level of lightness of the color that forms the background.

The background's standard deviation tells us how much the numbers in the background deviate from their average value. The relationship between the average length of the segments and the background. The ratio is used to compare how much the segments differ from each other compared to how much they differ from the background. The darkest shade of gray in the picture. The lightest gray color in the picture. The fourth order moment of the image measures the distribution of pixel intensities in the image. Skewness of the image refers to how the image looks different and uneven compared to a balanced and symmetrical image. The standard deviation of the image shows how much the pixel values differ from the average value. The typical or usual worth of the picture. The second harmonic coefficient of the Fourier descriptor

The third harmonic coefficient of the Fourier descriptor is a number that shows how much the third harmonic is important in representing a signal or shape using Fourier series.

The fourth harmonic coefficient of the Fourier descriptor is a number that tells us about the shape or pattern of something. The fifth harmonic coefficient of the Fourier descriptor is a number that tells us about a specific part of a math formula called the Fourier descriptor. The steepest incline in the sideways direction. The highest amount of change going upwards or downwards.

The process of looking carefully at smooth and detailed metal surfaces made by machines to make sure they are accurate and precise.

When J is higher, it means the subset is better. The problem of feature selection is about finding a smaller set of features from a larger set. We want to choose only a certain number of features and find the best combination of those features.

When J is higher, it means the subset is better. The problem of feature selection is to pick a set of features from the available options so that the number of chosen features is a specific value and a certain measure called J is the highest possible.

$$J\left(X^{opt}\right) = \max_{X \subseteq Y, |X| = d} J\left(X\right). \tag{12}$$

The evaluation criterion J is suggested to be the measure of how well someone or something performs. Unfortunately, this is a difficult task for the computer. A rule is a guideline or a regulation that needs to be followed. There are other ways to evaluate, but Dash and Liu (1997) discovered that the most accurate way to choose the subset is to use the same classifier as the online application.

We did a lot of research using not-so-great methods for picking out the most important features in order. Additionally, genetic algorithms were used on the same set of data to choose which features to include. Sequential feature selection algorithms are a type of method that looks for the best set of features in a step-by-step way. It does this by searching for the subset of features that is not perfect but still pretty good. The forward methods begin with nothing and add features until they find a reason to stop looking. The backward algorithms are the opposite or contrasting versions. They start with all the features chosen and then remove features one by one. The famous not-too-good step-by-step algorithms are listed, and then we talk about how they compare to each other.

Sequential forward selection (SFS) is a method where, in each step, we add one feature from the remaining features to a smaller group called the subset. We do this in a way that the subset is chosen to have the best possible score according to a certain evaluation measure J.

Sequential backward selection (SBS) is a method where, in each step, one feature is removed from the set of features.

This means that we are not including a certain characteristic because it does not work well, only keeping the ones that give the best outcome.

The SFS algorithm is utilized to gradually increase the number of selected features by adding l features in the Plus l-take away r selection process. Next, the SBS algorithm removes some characteristics. GSFS(r) differentiates itself from the SFS method by incorporating the simultaneous inclusion of multiple features, rather than a sequential addition of one feature at a time.

GSBS (r) is the opposite of GSFS.

The PTA and GTA methods are different because PTA uses SFS and SBS procedures, while GTA uses GSFS and GSBS algorithms. Sequential forward floating selection (SFFS) is a method that adds new features to a process using the SFS procedure. Afterwards, we exclude certain bad things from the updated group of things. So, the l and r values are not necessary.

SBFS is a process where we start with a big pool of options and systematically remove one option at a time until we are left with the best option. This method is the exact opposite of the SFFS method.

The AS FFS algorithm is similar to the SFFS method, but instead of using the SFS and SBS methods, it uses their generalized versions called GSFS and GSBS. The quantity or size.

We compared the methods by looking at how well they performed using the 3NN classification result as a measure. The group could only have a maximum of 22 members. We measure the performance by combining four classification results from four different parts of the dataset. The AS BFS algorithm works in the opposite way compared to the AS FFS algorithm. The SFFS and SBFS algorithms are described in a research paper by Pupil et al. Please rewrite the following text in simpler words: (P. Pudil, J. (1997)). Change this passage into simpler language. The new adaptive floating algorithms (AS FFS, AS BFS) are explained in a recent publication. The explanations for all other sequential methods can be found in references 14 and 18. There are some interesting studies comparing different feature selection algorithms that are mentioned in references (A. K. Jain and D. Zongker (1997)). The researchers used special programs to select the best features from a collection of 540 images that showed different

Figure 12. The outcomes of various techniques employed for choosing characteristics

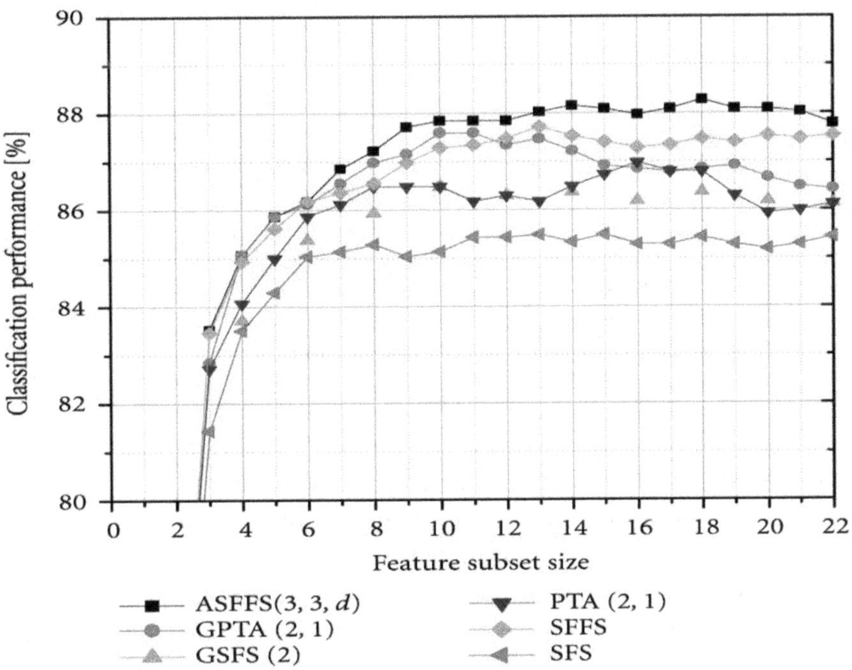

types of flaws on a surface (Sharma, M., et al.(2023)). They made sure that each type of flaw had the same number of images. They also looked at a total of 54 different characteristics in each image. The researchers evaluated different methods to choose important features based on how well they helped classify things accurately. The way the 3-nearest-neighbor decision rule works is used to find the best solution (Khan, Yasser, et al. (2022)). The performance of the sequential forward algorithms is shown in Figure 13. Usually, the floating algorithms work better than the algorithms that are not floating. The AS FFS (3,3'd) method is only slightly different from the classical floating algorithm (SFFS). For a small number of elements,

For the AS FFS (3,3,d) method, we performed several optimization runs for each sub-set size d. We have made a list of the top outcomes we achieved. With the current parameter setting, we can figure out in real time how well a smaller amount of information can predict results. If you want to know more, check out (P. Somol, et al.(1999)).

In order to assess the accuracy of the AS FFS (3,3,d) algorithm, we utilized the three nearest neighbors decision rule as depicted in Figure 14 to evaluate its performance.

The level of performance demonstrated by both the generalized PTA method and the AS FFS algorithm is roughly similar. The graph in Figure 12 displays the number of evaluations conducted by various algorithms during the optimization process. The total number of algorithms that do not change remains the same for a specific parameter setting. The number depends on the training set because the algorithms can change their values. - Three times more expenses are incurred when using the adaptive floating algorithm with the preferred settings compared to the regular floating algorithm. Because the training set was too specific, the chosen features for the best classification of the training data do not

Figure 13. Appropriate number of evaluations for different sequential selection algorithms

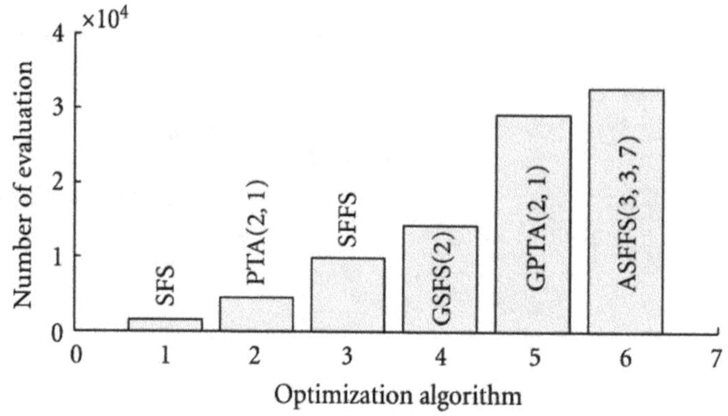

work as well on the separate test data. In real life, we need to check if the feature selection optimization worked by testing it on a set of objects. As a result, there are various ways proposed in the writing (R. Kohavi, et al. (1995)). The average of the four highest scores from four different sets of information is calculated. Then, the estimated rankings of the best feature combinations for the remaining test data are added together. This information is displayed in Figure 13. Result than a larger subset of features is known as the "curse of dimensionality." This phenomenon occurs when the dimensionality of a dataset increases, meaning there are more features to consider. In some cases, having a smaller set of features can actually lead to better outcomes or results compared to using a larger set of features. This can be due

Figure 14.

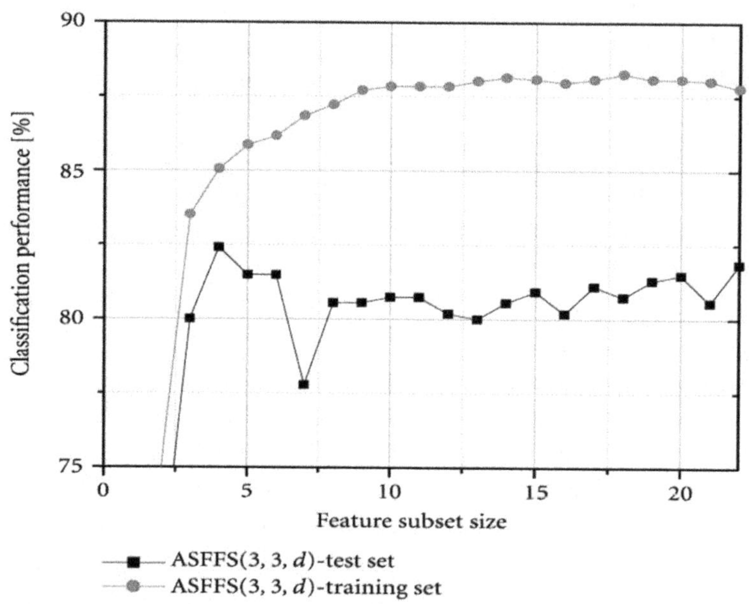

to a variety of reasons, such as reduced noise, improved simplicity, or better generalization abilities. In summary, the curse of dimensionality refers to the situation where a smaller subset of features outperforms a larger subset in achieving desirable outcomes. The performance of the classification on the test data is clear. The top to choose the best size of the feature subset We measure how well the training data is classified. subset containing 18 features (Madhumathy, P., & Pandey, D. (2022)). This means that the test data performs the best when using a set of 18 specific features.

The subset has about 4 items. Because of that, the features that are selected are the ones using numbers 19, 22, 24, and 41 from Table 1.

We need to consider different problems that do not agree with each other. If you don't include enough information, you might not be able to tell if there is discrimination happening. Otherwise, having fewer things to work with means it's easier and the classifier works better overall.

5.4. Statistical Classification

Before categorizing, the qualities were adjusted (Pandey, Nassa, Jhamb, Mahto, Pandey, George, & Bandyopadhyay, 2021) based on their average values and variations. We use the equation below to make each feature xmn have a standard range.

$$x_{mn} = \frac{x'_{mn} - \mu_n}{\sigma_n}, m = 1,2,\ldots,M, n = 1,2,\ldots,N, \tag{13}$$

Where

$$\mu_n = \frac{1}{M}\sum_{m=1}^{M} x'_{mn}, \sigma_n = \sqrt{\frac{1}{M}\sum_{m=1}^{M}\left(x'_{mn} - \mu_n\right)^2}, \tag{14}$$

Are the average value and the level of spread for a set of data, where N is the number of different characteristics that are being measured and M is the total number of measurements. This scaling approach makes sure that all the different features have the same statistical properties, with an average of 0 and a standard deviation of 1.

In classification, we put objects into different groups based on their characteristics. The Bayes decision rule is a basic way to analyze patterns in statistics.

Patterns x belong to class ωj as

$$X \rightarrow \omega j \text{ if } P(\omega j|_X) = \max_{=1} P\left(\omega_i \middle| X\right), \tag{15}$$

In simpler terms, the text means that "t" represents the number of different classes. "$P(\omega i \mid x)$" refers to the probability of a certain class "ωi" given some data "x". This probability is calculated by using a function called the probability density function "$p(x \mid \omega i)$".

Table 1. A table that categorizes a group of 108 observations into different classes using a decision rule known as three nearest neighbors

Correct Class			Predicted Class		
	1	2	3	4	5
1	94	1	2	0	11
	17.41%	0.19%	0.37%	0.00%	2.04%
2	0	95	3	10	0
	0.00%	17.59%	0.56%	1.85%	0.00%
3	3	1	94	3	7
	0.56%	0.19%	17.41%	0.56%	1.30%
4	0	10	5	88	5
	0.00%	1.85%	0.93%	16.30%	0.93%
5	8	1	7	2	90
	1.48%	0.19%	1.30%	0.37%	16.67%

$$P\left(\omega_i \middle| X\right) = \frac{p\left(X \middle| \omega_i\right) P\left(\omega_i\right)}{\sum_{j=1}^{t} p\left(X \middle| \omega_j\right) P\left(\omega_j\right)}. \tag{16}$$

Different ways of organizing or categorizing things were created by making educated guesses about the likelihood of belonging to a certain category and the overall probability of each category. Simple decision rules take this probability density function and represent it in a mathematical form. The multivariate normal density distribution is often used. It is described by the average value (mean) and how spread out the data is (covariance) for each class. This results in the famous decision rules for minimum distance and Mahala Nobis distance mentioned in reference (Khan, 2022). Changed to non-parametric decision rules. This is done to better separate the classes and improve the accuracy of the classification.

Not as effective as the k-nearest-neighbor (kNN) method. The kNN decision rule tries to estimate the probability of a particular outcome (*ωi*) based on the input data (*x*). A group of known examples with labels is provided. We find the k-nearest examples to the unknown object. The new item is given the classification of the class that appears most often among its nearby items.

$$X \rightarrow \omega j \text{ if } k_j = \max_{i=1,\ldots,t} k_i. \tag{17}$$

If the training set is small, the kNN decision rule will be a pretty good estimate of the Bayes rule. Randy and Jain suggest trying out various values of k to determine the most effective one for the classification. For the classification experiments, we took 108 samples of each of the 5 types of problems and used four established features to classify them. To classify, we take out the object we want to identify from the group of similar objects used to make decisions in the kNN rule. In this way, 85. 37% of the information is sorted correctly (refer to Table 2).

The important parts of the classification table:

(i) When objects in class 1 are incorrectly labeled, they are often mistakenly assigned to class 5, and the same happens for objects in class 5 being assigned to class 1. If an observation from class 3 is misclassified, it is usually labeled as belonging to class 5. Objects in both second and fourth grade also cause a lot of problems. The classification result is not good because if the bearing rolls have flaws of type 4 or 5, they should not be taken out of the production lot. So, we should add a rejection category to the classification.

6. CONCLUSION AND RECOMMENDATIONS

When there is a mistake, the way the surface looks can affect how it reflects light. This was proven using a method that measures how light reflects off an object. The accuracy of the findings was confirmed through optical tests. In addition, we looked into finding the best angle to position the light source so that the bearing roll would be evenly lit.

The second part of the text is about finding mistakes, dividing things into smaller parts, picking out important details, choosing what's relevant, and grouping things into categories. A strong and flexible method of dividing data into segments, which can be used on datasets with only one or two peaks, was demonstrated. This method involves finding the largest triangle shape within the data and using it to determine where to split the dataset. To identify the flaws, we looked at certain characteristics. We then used algorithms to find the most important characteristics for classifying the flaws effectively. So, we did a study comparing different ways of choosing features that are not the best. It was demonstrated that using only a few specific characteristics gives better results when predicting categories in a different set of data.

The future research will concentrate on creating algorithms that can classify defects. There are many different classification methods that might work better than the current kNN decision rule. We will focus on Bayesian network classifiers, which are currently considered the best decision rules. Furthermore, using a mix of different classifiers could improve the accuracy of classification.

REFERENCES

Ahmad, A. Y. B., Gongada, T. N., Shrivastava, G., Gabbi, R. S., Islam, S., & Nagaraju, K. (2023). E-Commerce Trend Analysis and Management for Industry 5.0 using User Data Analysis. *International Journal of Intelligent Systems and Applications in Engineering*, *11*(11s), 135–150.

Beckmann, P., & Spizzochino, A. (1963). *The Scattering of Electro-magnetic Waves from Rough Surfaces*. Pergamon.

Dash, M., & Liu, H. (1997). Feature selection for classification. *Intelligent Data Analysis*, *1*(3), 131–156. doi:10.3233/IDA-1997-1302

Devijver, P. A., & Kittler, J. (1982). *Pattern Recognition: A Statistical Approach*. Prentice-Hall.

Gonzalez, R. C., & Woods, R. E. (1992). *Digital Image Processing*. Addison-Wesley.

Jain, A. K., & Zongker, D. (1997). Feature selection: Evaluation, ap-plication, and small sample performance. *IEEE Transactions on Pattern Analysis and Machine Intelligence, 19*(2), 153–158. doi:10.1109/34.574797

Khan, Y. (2022). Application of Internet of Things (IoT) in Sustainable Supply Chain Management. *Sustainability, 15*(1), 694. doi:10.3390/su15010694

Kohavi, R. (1995). A study of cross-validation and bootstrap for ac-curacy estimation and model selection. *Proc. of the 14th International Joint Conference on Artificial Intelligence*, 1137–1143.

Kumar Pandey, B., Pandey, D., Nassa, V. K., Ahmad, T., Singh, C., George, A. S., & Wakchaure, M. A. (2021). Encryption and steganography-based text extraction in IoT using the EWCTS optimizer. *Imaging Science Journal, 69*(1-4), 38–56. doi:10.1080/13682199.2022.2146885

Madhumathy, P., & Pandey, D. (2022). Deep learning based photo acoustic imaging for non-invasive imaging. *Multimedia Tools and Applications, 81*(5), 7501–7518. doi:10.1007/s11042-022-11903-6

Newman, T. S., & Jain, A. K. (1995). A survey of automated visual inspection. *Computer Vision and Image Understanding, 61*(2), 231–262. doi:10.1006/cviu.1995.1017

Ni, L., Ahmad, S. F., Alshammari, T. O., Liang, H., Alsanie, G., Irshad, M., Alyafi-AlZahri, R., Bin-Saeed, R. H., Al-Abyadh, M. H. A., Abu Bakir, S. M. M., & Ayassrah, A. Y. B. A. (2023). The role of environmental regulation and green human capital towards sustainable development: The mediating role of green innovation and industry upgradation. *Journal of Cleaner Production, 421*, 138497. doi:10.1016/j.jclepro.2023.138497

Pandey, B. K., Mane, D., Nassa, V. K. K., Pandey, D., Dutta, S., Ventayen, R. J. M., & Rastogi, R. (2021). Secure text extraction from complex degraded images by applying steganography and deep learning. In *Multidisciplinary approach to modern digital steganography* (pp. 146–163). IGI Global. doi:10.4018/978-1-7998-7160-6.ch007

Pandey, B. K., & Pandey, D. (2023). Parametric optimization and prediction of enhanced thermoelectric performance in co-doped CaMnO3 using response surface methodology and neural network. *Journal of Materials Science Materials in Electronics, 34*(21), 1589. doi:10.1007/s10854-023-10954-1

Pandey, B. K., Pandey, D., Nassa, V. K., George, S., Aremu, B., Dadeech, P., & Gupta, A. (2022, July). Effective and secure transmission of health information using advanced morphological component analysis and image hiding. In *Artificial Intelligence on Medical Data: Proceedings of International Symposium, ISCMM 2021* (pp. 223-230). Singapore: Springer Nature Singapore.

Pandey, B. K., Pandey, D., Wairya, S., & Agarwal, G. (2021). An advanced morphological component analysis, steganography, and deep learning-based system to transmit secure textual data. *International Journal of Distributed Artificial Intelligence, 13*(2), 40–62. doi:10.4018/IJDAI.2021070104

Pandey, B. K., Pandey, D., Wairya, S., Agarwal, G., Dadeech, P., Dogiwal, S. R., & Pramanik, S. (2022). Application of integrated steganography and image compressing techniques for confidential information transmission. *Cyber Security and Network Security*, 169-191.

Pandey, B. K., Pandey, D., Wariya, S., & Agarwal, G. (2021). A deep neural network-based approach for extracting textual images from deteriorate images. *EAI Endorsed Transactions on Industrial Networks and Intelligent Systems*, *8*(28), e3–e3. doi:10.4108/eai.17-9-2021.170961

Pandey, B. K., Pandey, D., Wariya, S., Aggarwal, G., & Rastogi, R. (2021). Deep learning and particle swarm optimisation-based techniques for visually impaired humans' text recognition and identification. *Augmented Human Research*, *6*(1), 1–14. doi:10.1007/s41133-021-00051-5

Pandey, D., Nassa, V. K., Jhamb, A., Mahto, D., Pandey, B. K., George, A. H., & Bandyopadhyay, S. K. (2021). An integration of keyless encryption, steganography, and artificial intelligence for the secure transmission of stego images. In *Multidisciplinary approach to modern digital steganography* (pp. 211–234). IGI Global. doi:10.4018/978-1-7998-7160-6.ch010

Pandey, D., Nassa, V. K., Jhamb, A., Mahto, D., Pandey, B. K., George, A. H., & Bandyopadhyay, S. K. (2021). An integration of keyless encryption, steganography, and artificial intelligence for the secure transmission of stego images. In *Multidisciplinary approach to modern digital steganography* (pp. 211–234). IGI Global. doi:10.4018/978-1-7998-7160-6.ch010

Pandey, D., Pandey, B. K., & Wairya, S. (2021). Hybrid deep neural network with adaptive galactic swarm optimization for text extraction from scene images. *Soft Computing*, *25*(2), 1563–1580. doi:10.1007/s00500-020-05245-4

Pandey, D., Wairya, S., Pradhan, B., & Wangmo. (2022). Understanding COVID-19 response by twitter users: A text analysis approach. *Heliyon*, *8*(8), e09994. doi:10.1016/j.heliyon.2022.e09994 PMID:35873536

Pernkopf, F. (2002). *Automatic visual inspection of metallic surfaces* [Ph.D. thesis]. University of Leoben, Leoben, Austria.

Pudil, P., Novovicovˇa, J., & Kittler, J. (1994). Floating search methods in feature selection. *Pattern Recognition Letters*, *15*(11), 1119–1125. doi:10.1016/0167-8655(94)90127-9

Raghavan, R., Verma, D. C., Pandey, D., Anand, R., Pandey, B. K., & Singh, H. (2022). Optimized building extraction from high-resolution satellite imagery using deep learning. *Multimedia Tools and Applications*, *81*(29), 42309–42323. doi:10.1007/s11042-022-13493-9

Sharma, M., Sharma, B., Gupta, A. K., & Pandey, D. (2023). Recent developments of image processing to improve explosive detection methodologies and spectroscopic imaging techniques for explosive and drug detection. *Multimedia Tools and Applications*, *82*(5), 6849–6865. doi:10.1007/s11042-022-13578-5

Smith, B. (1993). Making war on defects: Six-sigma design. *IEEE Spectrum*, *30*(9), 43–47. doi:10.1109/6.275174

Somol, P., Pudil, P., Novovicovˇa, J., & Paclík, P. (1999). ´ and P. Pacl'ık, "Adaptive floating search methods in feature selection,". *Pattern Recognition Letters*, *20*(11–13), 1157–1163. doi:10.1016/S0167-8655(99)00083-5

Sonka, M., Hlavac, V., & Boyle, R. (1999). *Image Processing, Analy-sis, and Machine Vision* (2nd ed.). International Thomson Publishing.

Torrance, K. E., & Sparrow, E. M. (1967). Theory for o-specular reflection from roughened surfaces. *Journal of the Optical Society of America*, *57*(9), 1105–1114. doi:10.1364/JOSA.57.001105

Compilation of References

Abedinnia, H., Glock, C. H., Grosse, E. H., & Schneider, M. (2017). Machine Scheduling Problems in Production: A Tertiary Study. *Computers & Industrial Engineering*, *111*, 403–416. doi:10.1016/j.cie.2017.06.026

Abidi, M. H., Mohammed, M. K., & Alkhalefah, H. (2022, March 14). Predictive Maintenance Planning for Industry 4.0 Using Machine Learning for Sustainable Manufacturing. *Sustainability (Basel)*, *14*(6), 3387. doi:10.3390/su14063387

Abuamer, I. M., Sadat, M., Silgu, M. A., & Celikoglu, H. B. (2017, June). Analyzing the effects of driver behavior within an adaptive ramp control scheme: a case-study with ALINEA. In *2017 IEEE International Conference on Vehicular Electronics and Safety (ICVES)* (pp. 109-114). IEEE. 10.1109/ICVES.2017.7991910

Abuamer, I. M., Sadat, M., & Tampère, C. M. (2018, September). A comparative evaluation of ramp metering controllers ALINEA and PI-ALINEA. In *2018 International Conference on Computational and Characterization Techniques in Engineering & Sciences (CCTES)* (pp. 127-131). IEEE. 10.1109/CCTES.2018.8674110

Aerts, H. J., Velazquez, E. R., Leijenaar, R. T. H., Parmar, C., Grossmann, P., Carvalho, S., Bussink, J., Monshouwer, R., Haibe-Kains, B., Rietveld, D., Hoebers, F., Rietbergen, M. M., Leemans, C. R., Dekker, A., Quackenbush, J., Gillies, R. J., & Lambin, P. (2014). Decoding tumour phenotype by noninvasive imaging using a quantitative radiomics approach. *Nature Communications*, *5*(1), 4006. doi:10.1038/ncomms5006 PMID:24892406

Ahmad, A. Y. (2019). Empirical Analysis on Accounting Information System Usage in Banking Sector in Jordan. Academy of Accounting and Financial Studies Journal, 23(5), 1-9.

Ahmad, A. Y. A. B. (2019). Empirical Analysis on Accounting Information System Usage in Banking Sector in Jordan. *Academy of Accounting and Financial Studies Journal*, *23*(5), 1–9.

Ahmad, A. Y. A. B., Gongada, T. N., Shrivastava, G., Gabbi, R. S., Islam, S., & Nagaraju, K. (2023). E-Commerce Trend Analysis and Management for Industry 5.0 using User Data Analysis. *International Journal of Intelligent Systems and Applications in Engineering*, *11*(11s), 135–150.

Ahmad, A. Y. A. B., & Kumari, S. S. (2023). Blockchain Implementation in Financial Sector and Cyber Security System. *2023 International Conference on Artificial Intelligence and Smart Communication (AISC),* 586-590. 10.1109/AISC56616.2023.10085045

Ali, M., Haider, M. N., Lashari, S. A., Sharif, W., Khan, A., & Ramli, D. A. (2022). Stacking Classifier with Random Forest functioning as a Meta Classifier for Diabetes Diseases Classification. *Procedia Computer Science*, *207*, 3459–3468. doi:10.1016/j.procs.2022.09.404

Ali, S., Li, J., Pei, Y., Khurram, R., Rehman, K. U., & Mahmood, T. (2022). A comprehensive survey on brain tumor diagnosis using deep learning and emerging hybrid techniques with multi-modal MR image. *Archives of Computational Methods in Engineering*, *29*(7), 4871–4896. doi:10.1007/s11831-022-09758-z

Alnsour, I., Alghadi, M., Ahmad, A., Alibraheem, M., Altahat, S., Al-Smadi, R., & Alshboul, K. (2023). Islamic financial technology acceptance: An empirical study in Jordan. *International Journal of Data and Network Science*, *7*(4), 1659–1668. doi:10.5267/j.ijdns.2023.7.023

Alom, M. Z. (2019). Breast cancer classification from histopathological images with ensemble deep learning. *Proceedings of the International Conference on Digital Image Computing: Techniques and Applications (DICTA).*

Amrutsamanvar, R. (2022). Modeling lateral movement decisions of powered two wheelers in disordered heterogeneous traffic conditions. *Transportation Letters*, *14*(3), 195–214. doi:10.1080/19427867.2020.1839718

Anand, P. A., Atmakuri, P., Anne, V. S. R., Asaithambi, G., Srinivasan, K. K., Sivanandan, R., & Chilukuri, B. R. (2019). Calibration of vehicle-following model parameters using mixed traffic trajectory data. *Transportation in Developing Economies*, *5*(2), 1–11. doi:10.1007/s40890-019-0086-4

Anand, R., Khan, B., Nassa, V. K., Pandey, D., Dhabliya, D., Pandey, B. K., & Dadheech, P. (2023). Hybrid convolutional neural network (CNN) for Kennedy Space Center hyperspectral image. *Aerospace Systems*, *6*(1), 71–78. doi:10.1007/s42401-022-00168-4

Anand, R., Lakshmi, S. V., Pandey, D., & Pandey, B. K. (2023). An enhanced ResNet-50 deep learning model for arrhythmia detection using electrocardiogram biomedical indicators. *Evolving Systems*, 1–15. doi:10.1007/s12530-023-09559-0

Anand, R., Singh, J., Pandey, D., Pandey, B. K., Nassa, V. K., & Pramanik, S. (2022). Modern technique for interactive communication in LEACH-based ad hoc wireless sensor network. In *Software Defined Networking for Ad Hoc Networks* (pp. 55–73). Springer International Publishing. doi:10.1007/978-3-030-91149-2_3

Anderson, J. C. (2001). Evaluating the impact of family history of colorectal cancer and cigarette smoking on colorectal cancer risk: A quantitative review. *Cancer Epidemiology, Biomarkers & Prevention*, *10*(6), 625–631.

Araújo, T., Aresta, G., Castro, E., Rouco, J., Aguiar, P., Eloy, C., Polónia, A., & Campilho, A. (2017). Classification of breast cancer histology images using Convolutional Neural Networks. *PLoS One*, *12*(6), e0177544. doi:10.1371/journal.pone.0177544 PMID:28570557

Ardila, D., Kiraly, A. P., Bharadwaj, S., Choi, B., Reicher, J. J., Peng, L., Tse, D., Etemadi, M., Ye, W., Corrado, G., Naidich, D. P., & Shetty, S. (2019). End-to-end lung cancer screening with three-dimensional deep learning on low-dose chest computed tomography. *Nature Medicine*, *25*(6), 954–961. doi:10.1038/s41591-019-0447-x PMID:31110349

Arief Daulay. (2023, June 3). Review of Literature on Improving the KNN Algorithm. *Transactions on Machine Learning and Artificial Intelligence*, *11*(3). Advance online publication. doi:10.14738/tecs.113.14768

Arockia Panimalar, S., & Krishnakumar, A. (2023, November). Customer churn prediction model in cloud environment using DFE-WUNB: ANN deep feature extraction with Weight Updated Tuned Naïve Bayes classification with Block-Jacobi SVD dimensionality reduction. *Engineering Applications of Artificial Intelligence*, *126*, 107015. doi:10.1016/j.engappai.2023.107015

Asaithambi, G., & Joseph, J. (2018). Modeling duration of lateral shifts in mixed traffic conditions. *Journal of Transportation Engineering. Part A, Systems*, *144*(9), 04018055. doi:10.1061/JTEPBS.0000170

Asaithambi, G., Kanagaraj, V., & Toledo, T. (2016). Driving behaviors: Models and challenges for non-lane based mixed traffic. *Transportation in Developing Economies*, *2*(2), 1–16. doi:10.1007/s40890-016-0025-6

Awad, A., Pang, W., Lusseau, D., & Coghill, G. M. (2023). A survey on physarum polycephalum intelligent foraging behaviour and bio-inspired applications. *Artificial Intelligence Review*, *56*(1), 1–26. doi:10.1007/s10462-021-10112-1

Awuzie, B., & McDermott, P. (2017). An Abductive Approach to Qualitative Built Environment Research. *Qualitative Research Journal*, *17*(4), 356–372. doi:10.1108/QRJ-08-2016-0048

Ayenew, B., Pandey, D., Yitayew, M., Etana, D., Binay Kumar, P., & Verma, N. (2020). Risk for surge maternal mortality and morbidity during the ongoing corona virus pandemic. *Medlife Clinics*, *2*(1), 1012.

Ayvaz, S., & Alpay, K. (2021, July). Predictive maintenance system for production lines in manufacturing: A machine learning approach using IoT data in real-time. *Expert Systems with Applications*, *173*, 114598. doi:10.1016/j.eswa.2021.114598

Babu, B. S., Kamalakannan, J., Meenatchi, N., Karthik, S., & Boopathi, S. (2022). Economic impacts and reliability evaluation of battery by adopting Electric Vehicle. *IEEE Explore*, 1–6.

Babu, S. Z. D., Pandey, D., Naidu, G. T., Sumathi, S., Gupta, A., Bader Alazzam, M., & Pandey, B. K. (2022, July). Analysation of Big Data in Smart Healthcare. In *Artificial Intelligence on Medical Data: Proceedings of International Symposium, ISCMM 2021* (pp. 243-251). Singapore: Springer Nature Singapore.

Bai, C., & Sarkis, J. (2020). A supply chain transparency and sustainability technology appraisal model for blockchain technology. *International Journal of Production Research*, *58*(7), 2142–2162. doi:10.1080/00207543.2019.1708989

Balagurunathan, Y., Kumar, V., Gu, Y., Kim, J., Wang, H., Liu, Y., Goldgof, D. B., Hall, L. O., Korn, R., Zhao, B., Schwartz, L. H., Basu, S., Eschrich, S., Gatenby, R. A., & Gillies, R. J. (2014). Test-retest reproducibility analysis of lung CT image features. *Journal of Digital Imaging*, *27*(6), 805–823. doi:10.1007/s10278-014-9716-x PMID:24990346

Barták, R., Salido, M. A., & Rossi, F. (2010). Constraint Satisfaction Techniques in Planning and Scheduling. *Journal of Intelligent Manufacturing*, *21*(1), 5–15. doi:10.1007/s10845-008-0203-4

Bassiouni, M. M., Chakrabortty, R. K., Hussain, O. K., & Rahman, H. F. (2023, January). Advanced deep learning approaches to predict supply chain risks under COVID-19 restrictions. *Expert Systems with Applications*, *211*, 118604. doi:10.1016/j.eswa.2022.118604 PMID:35999828

BeaufilsT.WenzL. (2021). The SPIN covid19 RMRIO dataset: Global trade network data for the years 2016-2026 reflecting macroeconomic effects of the covid19 pandemic - B. Data for 2020 - 2026 - Covid scenario (2.0) [Data set]. Zenodo. doi:10.5281/zenodo.5713825

Beckmann, P., & Spizzochino, A. (1963). *The Scattering of Electro-magnetic Waves from Rough Surfaces*. Pergamon.

Bejnordi, B. E. (2017). Diagnostic assessment of deep learning algorithms for detection of lymph node metastases in women with breast cancer. *Journal of the American Medical Association*, *318*(22), 2199–2210. doi:10.1001/jama.2017.14585 PMID:29234806

Ben-Daya, M., Hassini, E., & Bahroun, Z. (2019). Internet of Things and Supply ChainManagement: A Literature Review. *International Journal of Production Research*, *57*(15-16), 4719–4742. doi:10.1080/00207543.2017.1402140

Bennett, C. C., & Hauser, K. (2013). Artificial Intelligence Framework for SimulatingClinical Decision-Making: A Markov Decision Process Approach. *Artificial Intelligence in Medicine*, *57*(1), 9–19. doi:10.1016/j.artmed.2012.12.003 PMID:23287490

Bera, A., & Bhattacharjee, D. (2017). Human identification using selected features from finger geometric profiles. *IEEE Transactions on Systems, Man, and Cybernetics. Systems*, *50*, 2017.

Berente, N., Gu, B., Recker, J., & Santhanam, R. (2021). Managing Artificial Intelligence. *Management Information Systems Quarterly*, *45*, 1433–1450.

Bessant, Y. A., Jency, J. G., Sagayam, K. M., Jone, A. A. A., Pandey, D., & Pandey, B. K. (2023). Improved parallel matrix multiplication using Strassen and Urdhvatiryagbhyam method. *CCF Transactions on High Performance Computing*, *5*(2), 1–14. doi:10.1007/s42514-023-00149-9

Bhandari, R. (2014). Impact of technology on logistics and supply chain management. *IOSR Journal of Business and Management*, *2*, 19–24.

Bhattacharyya, S. (2020). Multi-modal brain tumor classification using deep neural network feature fusion in MRI images. *Computer Methods and Programs in Biomedicine*, *190*, 105361.

Bikis, A., & Pandey, D. (2022). Air quality at public transportation stations/stops: Contribution of light rail transit to reduce air pollution. *Aerosol Science and Engineering*, *6*(1), 1–16. doi:10.1007/s41810-021-00119-0

Bi, L., Fili, M., & Hu, G. (2022, May 31). COVID-19 forecasting and intervention planning using gated recurrent unit and evolutionary algorithm. *Neural Computing & Applications*, *34*(20), 17561–17579. doi:10.1007/s00521-022-07394-z PMID:35669538

Biswas, S., Chandra, S., & Ghosh, I. (2020). An advanced approach for estimation of PCU values on undivided urban roads under heterogeneous traffic conditions. *Transportation Letters*, *12*(3), 172–181. doi:10.1080/19427867.2018.1563268

Boopathi, S., Kumar, P. K. S., Meena, R. S., & Sudhakar, M. (2023). Sustainable Developments of Modern Soil-Less Agro-Cultivation Systems: Aquaponic Culture. In Human Agro-Energy Optimization for Business and Industry (pp. 69–87). IGI Global.

Boopathi, S., Pandey, B. K., & Pandey, D. (2023). Advances in Artificial Intelligence for Image Processing: Techniques, Applications, and Optimization. In Handbook of Research on Thrust Technologies' Effect on Image Processing (pp. 73-95). IGI Global.

Boopathi, S., Pandey, B. K., & Pandey, D. (2023). Advances in Artificial Intelligence for Image Processing: Techniques, Applications, and Optimization. In Handbook of Research on Thrust Technologies' Effect on Image Processing (pp. 73–95). IGI Global.

Boopathi, S. (2019). Experimental investigation and parameter analysis of LPG refrigeration system using Taguchi method. *SN Applied Sciences*, *1*(8), 892. doi:10.1007/s42452-019-0925-2

Boopathi, S. (2022). Experimental investigation and multi-objective optimization of cryogenic Friction-stir-welding of AA2014 and AZ31B alloys using MOORA technique. *Materials Today. Communications*, *33*, 104937. doi:10.1016/j.mtcomm.2022.104937

Boopathi, S., Hari balaji, V., Mageswari, M., & Asif, M. M. (2022). Influences of Boron Carbide Particles on the Wear Rate and Tensile Strength of AA2014 Surface Composite Fabricated by Friction-Stir Processing. *Mater-Tehnol.Si. Materials Technology*, *56*(3), 263–270.

Boopathi, S., Kumaresan, A., & Manohar, N., & KrishnaMoorthi, R. (2017). Review on Effect of Process Parameters—Friction Stir Welding Process. *International Research Journal of Engineering and Technology*, *4*(7), 272–278.

Boopathi, S., Myilsamy, S., & Sukkasamy, S. (2021). *Experimental Investigation and Multi-Objective Optimization of Cryogenically Cooled Near-Dry Wire-Cut EDM Using TOPSIS Technique*. IJAMT.

Boopathi, S., Pandey, B. K., & Pandey, D. (2023). Advances in artificial intelligence for image processing: techniques, applications, and optimization. In *Handbook of research on thrust technologies' effect on image processing* (pp. 73–95). IGI Global. doi:10.4018/978-1-6684-8618-4.ch006

Boopathi, S., & Sivakumar, K. (2013). Experimental investigation and parameter optimization of near-dry wire-cut electrical discharge machining using multi-objective evolutionary algorithm. *International Journal of Advanced Manufacturing Technology*, *67*(9–12), 2639–2655. doi:10.1007/s00170-012-4680-4

Boopathi, S., & Sivakumar, K. (2016). Optimal parameter prediction of oxygen-mist near-dry wire-cut EDM. *Inderscience: International Journal of Manufacturing Technology and Management*, *30*(3–4), 164–178. doi:10.1504/IJMTM.2016.077812

Boopathi, S., Sureshkumar, M., & Sathiskumar, S. (2022). Parametric Optimization of LPG Refrigeration System Using Artificial Bee Colony Algorithm. *International Conference on Recent Advances in Mechanical Engineering Research and Development*, 97–105.

Bringsjord, S., Govindarajulu, N. S., & Sundar, N. (2020). *Stanford Encyclopedia of Philosophy*. Retrieved from The Stanford Encyclopedia of Philosophy: https://plato.stanford.edu/entries/artificial-intelligence/# HistAI

Bughin, J., Hazan, E., Ramaswamy, S., Chui, M., Allas, T., Dahlstrom, P., & Trench, M. (2017). *Artificial Intelligence: The Next Digital Frontier?* McKinsey Global Institute. Retrieved on August 19, 2023 from https://www.mckinsey.com/~/media/mckinsey/industries/advanced%20electronics/our %20insights/how%20artificial%20intelligence%20can%20deliver%20real%20value%20to%20companies/mgi-artificial-intelligence-discussion-paper.ashx

Burstein, G., & Zuckerman, I. (2023, February 6). Deconstructing Risk Factors for Predicting Risk Assessment in Supply Chains Using Machine Learning. *Journal of Risk and Financial Management*, *16*(2), 97. doi:10.3390/jrfm16020097

Caballero, S., & Rice, J.B. (2018). *Artificial Intelligence/Machine Learning + Supply Chain Planning*. MIT's Center for Transportation and Logistics.

Cai, D. (2020). Development and validation of a nomogram for predicting the risk of non-muscle invasive bladder cancer. *Cancer Management and Research*, *12*, 10945–10954.

Camargo, L. R., Pereira, S. C. F., & Scarpin, M. R. S. (2020). Fast and Ultra-Fast Fashion Supply Chain Management: An Exploratory Research. *International Journal of Retail & Distribution Management*, *48*(6), 537–553. doi:10.1108/IJRDM-04-2019-0133

Campanella, G., Hanna, M. G., Geneslaw, L., Miraflor, A., Werneck Krauss Silva, V., Busam, K. J., Brogi, E., Reuter, V. E., Klimstra, D. S., & Fuchs, T. J. (2019). Clinical-grade computational pathology using weakly supervised deep learning on whole slide images. *Nature Medicine*, *25*(8), 1301–1309. doi:10.1038/s41591-019-0508-1 PMID:31308507

Cano-Marin, E., Ribeiro-Soriano, D., Mardani, A., & Blanco Gonzalez-Tejero, C. (2023, September). Exploring the challenges of the COVID-19 vaccine supply chain using social media analytics: A global perspective. *Sustainable Technology and Entrepreneurship*, *2*(3), 100047. doi:10.1016/j.stae.2023.100047

Carlaw, S. (2020). Impact on biometrics of COVID-19. *Biometric Technol. Today*, *2020*(4), 8–9. doi:10.1016/S0969-4765(20)30050-3

Cavalcante, I. M., Frazzon, E. M., Forcellini, F. A., & Ivanov, D. (2019, December). A supervised machine learning approach to data-driven simulation of resilient supplier selection in digital manufacturing. *International Journal of Information Management*, *49*, 86–97. doi:10.1016/j.ijinfomgt.2019.03.004

Chaddad, A. (2018). Fusion of multi-modal imaging and clinicopathological data in computer-assisted breast histopathology. *Proceedings of the IEEE International Conference on Acoustics, Speech, and Signal Processing*, *2018*, 2587–2591.

Chalmeta, R., & Santos-deLeón, N. J. (2020). Sustainable supply chain in the era of industry 4.0 and big data: A systematic analysis of literature and research. *Sustainability (Basel)*, *12*(10), 4108. doi:10.3390/su12104108

Chand, S., Dixit, V., & Waller, S. T. (2016). Evaluation of fluctuating speed and lateral movement of vehicles: Comparison between mixed traffic and homogeneous traffic. *Transportation Research Record: Journal of the Transportation Research Board*, *2581*(1), 104–112. doi:10.3141/2581-13

Charran, E., & Sweetman, S. (2019). *AI Maturity and Organizations: Understanding AI Maturity and Organizations.* Microsoft Inc.

Chen, C. (2018). Differential diagnosis of breast cancer using quantitative, label-free and molecular vibrational imaging. *Biomedical Optics Express*, *9*(12), 5952–5969. PMID:31065447

Cheng, Ahmad, Irshad, Alsanie, & Khan, Ahmad, & Aleemi. (2023). Impact of Green Process Innovation and Productivity on Sustainability: The Moderating Role of Environmental Awareness. *Sustainability*, *15*(17), 12945. doi:10.3390/su151712945

Cheng, J. C., Chen, W., Chen, K., & Wang, Q. (2020, April). Data-driven predictive maintenance planning framework for MEP components based on BIM and IoT using machine learning algorithms. *Automation in Construction*, *112*, 103087. doi:10.1016/j.autcon.2020.103087

Chen, P. Y., & Wang, F. K. (2020). Artificial intelligence for supply chain management: A comprehensive literature review and research agenda. *Expert Systems with Applications*, *162*, 113955.

Chen, T., & Guestrin, C. (2016, August 13). XGBoost. *Proceedings of the 22nd ACM SIGKDD International Conference on Knowledge Discovery and Data Mining*. 10.1145/2939672.2939785

Chen, Y. (2020). HRNet: Deep High-Resolution Representation Learning for Human Pose Estimation. *Proceedings of the IEEE/CVF Conference on Computer Vision and Pattern Recognition (CVPR).*

Chen, Y., Wang, Y., & Xu, D. (2019). Demand forecasting for perishable food supply chains with long short-term memory networks. *Computers & Industrial Engineering*, *132*, 1–9.

Cho, H. J., & Wu, Y. T. (2004, October). Modeling and simulation of motorcycle traffic flow. In *2004 IEEE International Conference on Systems, Man and Cybernetics* (IEEE Cat. No. 04CH37583) (Vol. 7, pp. 6262-6267). IEEE.10.1109/ICSMC.2004.1401382

Choi, T.-M. (2019). Blockchain-technology-supported platforms for diamond authentication and certification in luxury supply chains. *Transportation Research Part E, Logistics and Transportation Review*, *128*, 17–29. doi:10.1016/j.tre.2019.05.011

Chopra, S., & Meindl, P. (2016). *Supply chain management: Strategy, planning, and operation.* Pearson.

Chopra, N., & Ansari, M. M. (2022). Golden jackal optimization: A novel nature-inspired optimizer for engineering applications. *Expert Systems with Applications*, *198*, 116924. doi:10.1016/j.eswa.2022.116924

Christopher, M. (2016). *Logistics & Supply Chain Management.* Pearson Education Limited.

Chu, D., Ma, W., Yang, Z., Li, J., Deng, Y., & Cheong, K. H. (2021). A Physarum-inspired algorithm for logistics optimization: From the perspective of effective distance. *Swarm and Evolutionary Computation*, *64*, 100890. doi:10.1016/j.swevo.2021.100890

Chunchu, M., Kalaga, R. R., & Seethepalli, N. V. S. K. (2010). Analysis of microscopic data under heterogeneous traffic conditions. *Transport*, *25*(3), 262–268. doi:10.3846/transport.2010.32

Coandă, P., Avram, M., & Constantin, V. (2020, December 1). A state of the art of predictive maintenance techniques. *IOP Conference Series. Materials Science and Engineering*, *997*(1), 012039. doi:10.1088/1757-899X/997/1/012039

Coe, N. M., & Yang, C. (2022). Mobile gaming production networks, platform business groups, and the market power of China's Tencent. *Annals of the American Association of Geographers*, *112*(2), 307–330. doi:10.1080/24694452.2021.1933887

Concern levels on possible drug supply chain disruption due to COVID-19 2020. (2020, April 8). Statista. https://www.statista.com/statistics/1110180/concern-on-drug-supply-chain-disruption-due-to-covid-19/

Conde, M. L., & Twinn, I. (2019). *How Artificial Intelligence is Making Transport Safer, Cleaner, More Reliable and Efficient in Emerging Markets (No. 33387)*. The World Bank.

Cordts, M. (2016). The Cityscapes Dataset for Semantic Urban Scene Understanding. *Proceedings of the IEEE Conference on Computer Vision and Pattern Recognition (CVPR)*. 10.1109/CVPR.2016.350

Cottrill, K. (2018). The Benefits of Blockchain: Fact or wishful thinking. *Supply Chain Manag. Rev.*, *22*, 20–25.

Coudray, N., Ocampo, P. S., Sakellaropoulos, T., Narula, N., Snuderl, M., Fenyö, D., Moreira, A. L., Razavian, N., & Tsirigos, A. (2018). Classification and mutation prediction from non-small cell lung cancer histopathology images using deep learning. *Nature Medicine*, *24*(10), 1559–1567. doi:10.1038/s41591-018-0177-5 PMID:30224757

Craighead, C. W., Ketchen, D. J. Jr, & Darby, J. L. (2020). Pandemics and supply chain management research: Toward a theoretical toolbox. *Decision Sciences*, *51*(4), 838–866. doi:10.1111/deci.12468 PMID:34234384

Cundell, T., Guilfoyle, D., Kreil, T. R., & Sawant, A. (2020). Controls to Minimize Disruption of the Pharmaceutical Supply Chain During the COVID-19 Pandemic. *PDA Journal of Pharmaceutical Science and Technology*, *74*(4), 468–494. doi:10.5731/pdajpst.2020.012021 PMID:32467176

Damani, J., & Vedagiri, P. (2023). Predicting Choice of Filtering of Motorized Two Wheelers in Urban Mixed Traffic. *Transportation Research Record: Journal of the Transportation Research Board*, *2677*(9), 58–68. doi:10.1177/03611981231158320

Daoud, Alqudah, Al-Qeed, Al Qaied, & Ahmad. (2023). The Relationship Between Mobile Marketing and Customer Perceptions in Jordanian Commercial Banks: The Electronic Quality as A Mediator Variable. *IJMST, 10*(2), 1360-1371.

Daoud, M. K., Al-Qeed, M., Ahmad, A. Y. B., & Al-Gasawneh, J. A. (2023). Mobile Marketing: Exploring the Efficacy of User-Centric Strategies for Enhanced Consumer Engagement and Conversion Rates. *International Journal of Membrane Science and Technology*, *10*(2), 1252–1262. doi:10.15379/ijmst.vi.1425

Dargay, J. M. (2001). The effect of income on car ownership: Evidence of asymmetry. *Transportation Research Part A, Policy and Practice*, *35*(9), 807–821. doi:10.1016/S0965-8564(00)00018-5

Dash, M., & Liu, H. (1997). Feature selection for classification. *Intelligent Data Analysis*, *1*(3), 131–156. doi:10.3233/IDA-1997-1302

Data_Sheet_1_From Farm to Fork: Early Impacts of COVID-19 on Food Supply Chain. pdf. (2023, May 30). Figshare. https://figshare.com/articles/dataset/Data_Sheet_1_From_Farm_to_Fork_Early_Impacts_of_COVID-19_on_Food_Supply_Chain_pdf/16928122

David, S., Duraipandian, K., Chandrasekaran, D., Pandey, D., Sindhwani, N., & Pandey, B. K. (2023). Impact of blockchain in healthcare system. In *Unleashing the Potentials of Blockchain Technology for Healthcare Industries* (pp. 37–57). Academic Press. doi:10.1016/B978-0-323-99481-1.00004-3

De Sousa Jabbour, A. B. L., Gunasekaran, A., Mendoza-Tello, J. C., & Lopes de Sousa Jabbour, C. J. (2018). The impact of green supply chain management and green innovation on environmental performance: The role of process control and environmental culture. *International Journal of Production Economics, 204*, 383–392.

Deepa, R., Anand, R., Pandey, D., Pandey, B. K., & Karki, B. (2022). Comprehensive performance analysis of classifiers in diagnosis of epilepsy. *Mathematical Problems in Engineering, 2022*, 2022. doi:10.1155/2022/1559312

Devijver, P. A., & Kittler, J. (1982). *Pattern Recognition: A Statistical Approach*. Prentice-Hall.

Dey, A., & Nair, A. (2019). Applications of artificial intelligence in supply chain management: A review. *International Journal of Information Management, 46*, 216–225.

Dhanya, D., Kumar, S. S., Thilagavathy, A., Prasad, D., & Boopathi, S. (2023). Data Analytics and Artificial Intelligence in the Circular Economy: Case Studies. In Intelligent Engineering Applications and Applied Sciences for Sustainability (pp. 40–58). IGI Global.

Dong, F. (2020). Joint fine-tuning deep learning for pancreatic ductal adenocarcinoma segmentation in CT and MRI images. *IEEE Journal of Biomedical and Health Informatics, 24*(7), 2071–2080.

Dong, H., Chen, Y. Y., Cirillo, C., & Wong, K. I. (2019). Lateral movement decision model for powered two-wheelers in Taiwan. *Transportation Research Record: Journal of the Transportation Research Board, 2673*(2), 686–697. doi:10.1177/0361198118822820

Dwivedi, Y. K., Hughes, L., Ismagilova, E., Aarts, G., Coombs, C., Crick, T., & Williams, M. D. (2021). Artificial Intelligence (AI): Multidisciplinary Perspectives on Emerging Challenges, Opportunities, and Agenda for Research, Practice and Policy. *International Journal of Information Management, 57*, 101994. Advance online publication. doi:10.1016/j.ijinfomgt.2019.08.002

El Jaouhari, A., Arif, J., Fellaki, S., Amejwal, M., & Azzouz, K. (2022). Lean Supply ChainManagement and Industry 4.0 Interrelationships: The Status Quo and Future Perspectives. *International Journal of Lean Six Sigma*. Advance online publication. doi:10.1108/IJLSS-11-2021-0192

Esteva, A., Kuprel, B., Novoa, R. A., Ko, J., Swetter, S. M., Blau, H. M., & Thrun, S. (2017). Dermatologist-level classification of skin cancer with deep neural networks. *Nature, 542*(7639), 115–118. doi:10.1038/nature21056 PMID:28117445

Etzioni, R. (2002). The prostate cancer prevention trial: Predictive power of prostate cancer risk calculators. *Urology, 59*(6), 889–895. PMID:12031375

Fatorachian, H., & Kazemi, H. (2021). Impact of Industry 4.0 on supply chain performance. *Production Planning and Control, 32*(1), 63–81. doi:10.1080/09537287.2020.1712487

Fawcett, S. E., Ellram, L. M., & Ogden, J. A. (2014). *Supply chain management: From vision to implementation*. Pearson.

Feichtenhofer, C. (2019). X3D: eXtended 3D ConvNet for Video Action Recognition. *Proceedings of the IEEE International Conference on Computer Vision (ICCV).*

Fosso Wamba, S., & Akter, S. (2019). Understanding Supply Chain Analytics Capabilities and Agility for Data-Rich Environments. *International Journal of Operations & Production Management, 39*(6/7/8), 887–912. doi:10.1108/IJOPM-01-2019-0025

Fourtane, S. (2021). *Artificial Intelligence to Play Instrumental Role in Future of Higher Education*. Fierce Education. Retrieved on August 19, 2023 from https://www.fierceeducation.com/administration/artificial-intelligence-to-play-instrumental-role-future-higher-education

Fraihat, B. A. M., Ahmad, A. Y. B., Alaa, A. A., Alhawamdeh, A. M., Soumadi, M. M., Aln'emi, E. A. S., & Alkhawaldeh, B. Y. S. (2023). Evaluating Technology Improvement in Sustainable Development Goals by Analysing Financial Development and Energy Consumption in Jordan. *International Journal of Energy Economics and Policy*, *13*(4), 348–355. doi:10.32479/ijeep.14438

Gaddam, H. K., & Rao, K. R. (2019). Higher-Order Continuum Model and Its Numerical Solutions for Heterogeneous Traffic Flow with Non-lane Discipline. In *Traffic and Granular Flow'17 12* (pp. 19–27). Springer International Publishing., doi:10.1007/978-3-030-11440-4_3

Gail, M. H., Brinton, L. A., Byar, D. P., Corle, D. K., Green, S. B., Schairer, C., & Mulvihill, J. J. (1989). Projecting individualized probabilities of developing breast cancer for white females who are being examined annually. *Journal of the National Cancer Institute*, *81*(24), 1879–1886. doi:10.1093/jnci/81.24.1879 PMID:2593165

Gao, C., Liu, C., Schenz, D., Li, X., Zhang, Z., Jusup, M., Wang, Z., Beekman, M., & Nakagaki, T. (2019). Does being multi-headed make you better at solving problems? A survey of Physarum-based models and computations. *Physics of Life Reviews*, *29*, 1–26. doi:10.1016/j.plrev.2018.05.002 PMID:29857934

Gao, X. (2021). Brain tumor classification using capsule networks and ensemble methods. *Computers in Biology and Medicine*, *136*, 104722.

Garcia-Martin, R., & Sanchez-Reillo, R. (2020). Vein biometric recognition on a smartphone. *IEEE Access : Practical Innovations, Open Solutions*, *8*, 2020. doi:10.1109/ACCESS.2020.3000044

Gartner. (2019). *Gartner's top 10 strategic technology trends for 2019*. Author.

Gesing, B., Peterson, S.J., & Michelsen, D. (2018). *Artificial intelligence in logistics: A collaborative report by DHL and IBM on implications and use cases for the logistics industry*. Troisdorf: DHL Customer Solutions & Innovation.

Gevaert, O., Mitchell, L. A., Achrol, A. S., Xu, J., Echegaray, S., Steinberg, G. K., Cheshier, S. H., Napel, S., Zaharchuk, G., & Plevritis, S. K. (2017). Glioblastoma multiforme: Exploratory radiogenomic analysis by using quantitative image features. *Radiology*, *273*(1), 168–174. doi:10.1148/radiol.14131731 PMID:24827998

Ghadge, A., Er Kara, M., Moradlou, H., & Goswami, M. (2020). The impact of Industry 4.0 implementation on supply chains. *Journal of Manufacturing Technology Management*, *31*(4), 669–686. doi:10.1108/JMTM-10-2019-0368

Ghadge, A., Mogale, D. G., Bourlakis, M., Maiyar, L. M., & Moradlou, H. (2022). Link between Industry 4.0 and green supplychain management: Evidence from the automotive industry. *Computers & Industrial Engineering*, *169*, 108303. doi:10.1016/j.cie.2022.108303

Ghaffari, A., & Rabbani, M. (2019). A comprehensive review of applications of artificial intelligence and machine learning in supply chain management. *Computers & Industrial Engineering*, *137*, 106027.

Gillies, R. J., Kinahan, P. E., & Hricak, H. (2016). Radiomics: Images are more than pictures, they are data. *Radiology*, *278*(2), 563–577. doi:10.1148/radiol.2015151169 PMID:26579733

Gipps, P. G. (1981). A behavioural car-following model for computer simulation. *Transportation Research Part B: Methodological*, *15*(2), 105–111. doi:10.1016/0191-2615(81)90037-0

Glasheen, J. (2020). *What is Order Management?* Retrieved from IBM: https://www.ibm.com/in-en/supply-chain/order-management

Golinska-Dawson, P., Werner-Lewandowska, K., Kolinska, K., & Kolinski, A. (2023). Impact of market drivers on the digital maturity of logistics processes in a supply chain. *Sustainability (Basel)*, *15*(4), 3120. doi:10.3390/su15043120

Gong, Y., Yang, Z., & Pan, J. (2020). An optimization model for warehouse layout design based on genetic algorithm. *International Journal of Industrial Engineering Computations*, *11*(4), 573–586.

Gonzalez, R. C., & Woods, R. E. (1992). *Digital Image Processing*. Addison-Wesley.

Gowri, N. V., Dwivedi, J. N., Krishnaveni, K., Boopathi, S., Palaniappan, M., & Medikondu, N. R. (2023). Experimental investigation and multi-objective optimization of eco-friendly near-dry electrical discharge machining of shape memory alloy using Cu/SiC/Gr composite electrode. *Environmental Science and Pollution Research International*, *30*(49), 1–19. doi:10.1007/s11356-023-26983-6 PMID:37126160

Gülen, K. (2023). Unleashing the Power of AI with the Rise of Intelligent Supply Chain Management. In *Artificial Intelligence, Industry, Transportation & Logistics*. https://dataconomy.com/2023/01/artificial-intelligence-supply-chain

Gunasekaran, A., & Ngai, E. W. T. (2017). The future of operations management: An outlook and analysis. *International Journal of Production Economics*, *193*, 612–624.

Gunasekaran, K., Boopathi, S., & Sureshkumar, M. (2022). Analysis of a Cryogenically Cooled Near-Dry WEDM Process using Different Dielectrics. *Mater-Tehnol.Si. Materials Technology*, *56*(2), 179–186.

Gunay, B. (2007). Car following theory with lateral discomfort. *Transportation Research Part B: Methodological*, *41*(7), 722–735. doi:10.1016/j.trb.2007.02.002

Gunning, D., & Aha, D. W. (2019, June). DARPA's Explainable Artificial Intelligence Program. *AI Magazine*, *40*(2), 44–58. doi:10.1609/aimag.v40i2.2850

Gupta, A. K., Sharma, M., Sharma, A., & Menon, V. (2022). A study on SARS-CoV-2 (COVID-19) and machine learning based approach to detect COVID-19 through X-ray images. *International Journal of Image and Graphics*, *22*(03), 2140010. doi:10.1142/S0219467821400106

Gupta, A., Anand, R., Pandey, D., Sindhwani, N., Wairya, S., Pandey, B. K., & Sharma, M. (2021). Prediction of breast cancer using extremely randomized clustering forests (ERCF) technique: Prediction of breast cancer. *International Journal of Distributed Systems and Technologies*, *12*(4), 1–15. doi:10.4018/IJDST.287859

Gupta, R., Mane, M., Bhardwaj, S., Nandekar, U., Afaq, A., Dhabliya, D., & Pandey, B. K. (2023). Use of Artificial Intelligence for Image Processing to Aid Digital Forensics: Legislative Challenges. In *Handbook of Research on Thrust Technologies' Effect on Image Processing* (pp. 433–447). IGI Global. doi:10.4018/978-1-6684-8618-4.ch026

Haenlein, M., & Kaplan, A. (2019). A Brief History of Artificial Intelligence: On the Past, Present, and Future of Artificial Intelligence. *California Management Review*, *61*(4), 5–14. doi:10.1177/0008125619864925

Haenssle, H. A., Fink, C., Schneiderbauer, R., Toberer, F., Buhl, T., Blum, A., Kalloo, A., Hassen, A. B. H., Thomas, L., Enk, A., Uhlmann, L., Alt, C., Arenbergerova, M., Bakos, R., Baltzer, A., Bertlich, I., Blum, A., Bokor-Billmann, T., Bowling, J., ... Zalaudek, I. (2018). Man against machine: Diagnostic performance of a deep learning convolutional neural network for dermoscopic melanoma recognition in comparison to 58 dermatologists. *Annals of Oncology : Official Journal of the European Society for Medical Oncology*, *29*(8), 1836–1842. doi:10.1093/annonc/mdy166 PMID:29846502

Hall, D., Lister, J., & Mercer, H. (2020). *Privatised and unprepared: The NHS supply chain*. Academic Press.

Hariharan, B. (2015). Hypercolumns for Object Segmentation and Fine-grained Localization. *Proceedings of the IEEE Conference on Computer Vision and Pattern Recognition (CVPR)*. 10.1109/CVPR.2015.7298642

Hartmann, J., & Moeller, S. (2014). Chain Liability in Multitier Supply Chains? Responsibility Attributions for Unsustainable Supplier Behavior. *Journal of Operations Management*, *32*(5), 281–294. doi:10.1016/j.jom.2014.01.005

Hasan, A., Pandey, D., & Khan, A. (2021). Application of EEG time-varying networks in the evaluation of dynamic functional brain networks. *Augmented Human Research, 6*(1), 1–8. doi:10.1007/s41133-021-00046-2

Hashemian, H. M., & Bean, W. C. (2011, October). State-of-the-Art Predictive Maintenance Techniques*. *IEEE Transactions on Instrumentation and Measurement, 60*(10), 3480–3492. doi:10.1109/TIM.2009.2036347

Hazen, B., Skipper, J., Ezell, J., & Boone, C. (2016). Big Data and Predictive Analytics for Supply Chain Sustainability: A Theory-driven Research Agenda. *Computers & Industrial Engineering, 101*, 592–598. Advance online publication. doi:10.1016/j.cie.2016.06.030

Heikkilä, J., & Lintukangas, K. (2020). Machine learning in supply chain management: A literature review. *International Journal of Production Economics, 230*, 107786.

He, J., Qu, J., Zhang, J., & He, Z. (2022). The Impact of a Single Discretionary Lane Change on Surrounding Traffic: An Analytic Investigation. *IEEE Transactions on Intelligent Transportation Systems*. Advance online publication. doi:10.1109/TITS.2022.3209668

Hellingrath, B., & Lechtenberg S. (2019). Applications of Artificial Intelligence in Supply Chain Management and Logistics: Focusing onto Recognition for Supply Chain Execution. *The Art of Structuring,* 283-296. doi:10.1007/978-3-030-06234-7_27

Helo, P., & Hao, Y. (2019). Blockchains in operations and supply chains: A model and reference implementation. *Computers & Industrial Engineering, 136*, 242–251. doi:10.1016/j.cie.2019.07.023

Heydarbakian, S., & Spehri, M. (2022). Interpretable Machine Learning to Improve Supply Chain Resilience, An Industry 4.0 Recipe. *IFAC-PapersOnLine, 55*(10), 2834–2839. doi:10.1016/j.ifacol.2022.10.160

Hoffmann, R. (2019). *9 Benefits of Artificial Intelligence on Customer Service*. Business.com. Retrieved on August 19, 2023 from https://www.business.com/articles/artificial-intelligence-customer-service/

Hosseinzadeh, F. (2020). A machine learning approach for early detection and prediction of ovarian cancer. *BMC Medical Informatics and Decision Making, 20*(1), 1–10. PMID:31906929

Hsu, T. P., Wen, K. L., & Zhang, T. (2021). Applying Machine Learning to Develop Lane Control Principles for Mixed Traffic. *Sustainability (Basel), 13*(14), 7656. doi:10.3390/su13147656

Huang, M., & Rust, R. (2018). Artificial Intelligence in Service. *Journal of Service Research, 21*(2), 155–172. doi:10.1177/1094670517752459

Huang, X. (2017). Lung cancer malignancy identification using a multi-scale vessel-based radiomic algorithm. *Computerized Medical Imaging and Graphics, 59*, 29–35.

Huang, X., Zhang, B., & Li, C. (2021). Platform profit maximization on service provisioning in mobile edge computing. *IEEE Transactions on Vehicular Technology, 70*(12), 13364–13376. doi:10.1109/TVT.2021.3124483

Huang, Y. Q., Liang, C., He, L., Tian, J., Liang, C., Chen, X., Ma, Z., & Liu, Z. (2016). Development and validation of a radiomics nomogram for preoperative prediction of lymph node metastasis in colorectal cancer. *Journal of Clinical Oncology, 34*(18), 2157–2164. doi:10.1200/JCO.2015.65.9128 PMID:27138577

Hua, X., Yao, H., Wang, Z., Li, B., & Wang, H. (2021). A wireless weak-connected network routing algorithm inspired by Physarum polycephalum. *Computers & Electrical Engineering, 91*, 107083. doi:10.1016/j.compeleceng.2021.107083

Hugos, M. H. (2017). *Essentials of supply chain management*. John Wiley & Sons.

Ibragimov, B. (2019). Supervised learning-based multimodal MRI brain tumor classification using texture features from supervoxels. *Computerized Medical Imaging and Graphics*, *72*, 32–43.

Iyyanar, P., Anand, R., Shanthi, T., Nassa, V. K., Pandey, B. K., George, A. S., & Pandey, D. (2023). A Real-Time Smart Sewage Cleaning UAV Assistance System Using IoT. In *Handbook of Research on Data-Driven Mathematical Modeling in Smart Cities* (pp. 24–39). IGI Global.

Jabbour, C. J. C., Fiorini, P. D., Ndubisi, N. O., Queiroz, M. M., & Piato, E. L. (2020). Digitally Enabled Sustainable Supply Chains in the 21st Century: A Review and a ResearchAgenda. *The Science of the Total Environment*, *725*, 138177. Advance online publication. doi:10.1016/j.scitotenv.2020.138177 PMID:32302825

Jain, A. K., & Zongker, D. (1997). Feature selection: Evaluation, ap-plication, and small sample performance. *IEEE Transactions on Pattern Analysis and Machine Intelligence*, *19*(2), 153–158. doi:10.1109/34.574797

Jain, V., Kumar, S., Soni, U., & Chandra, C. (2017). Supply chain resilience: Model development and empirical analysis. *International Journal of Production Research*, *55*(22), 6779–6800. doi:10.1080/00207543.2017.1349947

Jakupović, A., Pavlić, M., & Han, Z. D. (2014). Formalization Method for the Text Expressed Knowledge. *Expert Systems with Applications*, *41*(11), 5308–5322. doi:10.1016/j.eswa.2014.03.006

Janowczyk, A. (2017). Deep learning for digital pathology image analysis: A comprehensive tutorial with selected use cases. *Journal of Pathology Informatics*, *8*, 7. PMID:27563488

Janvier-James, A. M. (2012). A new introduction to supply chains and supply chain management: Definitions and theories perspective. *International Business Research*, *5*(1), 194–207. Retrieved August 19, 2023, from. doi:10.5539/ibr.v5n1p194

Jassim, M. S., Coskuner, G., Sultana, N., & Hossain, S. Z. (2023, January). Forecasting domestic waste generation during successive COVID-19 lockdowns by Bidirectional LSTM super learner neural network. *Applied Soft Computing*, *133*, 109908. doi:10.1016/j.asoc.2022.109908

Ji, Y., Lin, Z., & Rong, T. (2019). AdaptiveSLA: A two-stage scheduling framework for SLA profit maximization in multi-tenant database. *Journal of Physics: Conference Series*, *1187*(5), 052002. doi:10.1088/1742-6596/1187/5/052002

Kalavathy, K. S., Swapna, H. R., Nallasivam, A., Pandey, D., Mahajan, D. A., & Dadheech, P. (2023). An Empirical Investigation on the Influence of Social Networks on Purchase Decision Making: An Indian Perspective. In *Social Media and Online Consumer Decision Making in the Fashion Industry* (pp. 26–43). IGI Global. doi:10.4018/978-1-6684-8753-2.ch002

Kalidas, R., Boopathi, S., Sivakumar, K., & Mohankumar, P. (2012). Optimization of Machining Parameters of WEDM Process Based On the Taguchi Method. *IJEST*, *6*(1).

Kaminsky, P., Simchi-Levi, E., & Simchi-Levi, D. (2003). *Designing and Managing the Supply Chain* (Vol. 2). New York: McGraw Hill Professional.

Kaminsky, P., Simchi-Levi, E., &Simchi-Levi, D. (2003). *Designing and Managing the Supply Chain* (Vol. 2). New York: McGraw Hill Professional.

Kanagaraj, V., Asaithambi, G., Toledo, T., & Lee, T. C. (2015). Trajectory data and flow characteristics of mixed traffic. *Transportation Research Record: Journal of the Transportation Research Board*, *2491*(1), 1–11. doi:10.3141/2491-01

Kannan, V. R., & Tan, K. C. (2015). Big data for supply chain management in the service and manufacturing sectors: Challenges, opportunities, and future perspectives. *Computers & Industrial Engineering*, *101*, 572–591.

Karamizadeh, S. (2021). A novel multimodal approach for colorectal cancer classification using CT and MRI images. *Computerized Medical Imaging and Graphics*, *90*, 101869.

Kaur, N., & Sharma, M. (2017, August). Brain tumor detection using self-adaptive K-means clustering. In *2017 international conference on energy, communication, data analytics and soft computing (ICECDS)* (pp. 1861-1865). IEEE.

Kaur, S. P., & Sharma, M. (2015). Radially optimized zone-divided energy-aware wireless sensor networks (WSN) protocol using BA (bat algorithm). *Journal of the Institution of Electronics and Telecommunication Engineers*, *61*(2), 170–179. doi:10.1080/03772063.2014.999833

Kesting, A., Treiber, M., & Helbing, D. (2010). Enhanced intelligent driver model to access the impact of driving strategies on traffic capacity. *Philosophical Transactions of the Royal Society A: Mathematical, Physical and Engineering Sciences, 368*(1928), 4585-4605. doi:10.1098/rsta.2010.0084

Ketchen, D. J. Jr, Crook, R. T., & Craighead, C. W. (2014). From supply chains to supply ecosystems: Implications for strategic sourcing research and practice. *Journal of Business Logistics*, *35*(3), 165–171. doi:10.1111/jbl.12057

Khan, B., Hasan, A., Pandey, D., Ventayen, R. J. M., Pandey, B. K., & Gowwrii, G. (2021). 12 Fusion of Datamining and Artificial Intelligence. *Machine learning and iot for intelligent systems and smart applications*, 201.

Khan, Y. (2022). Application of Internet of Things (IoT) in Sustainable Supply Chain Management. *Sustainability, 15*(1), 694. doi:10.3390/su15010694

Khasis, D. (2019). *Four Ways AI Is Impacting Logistics and Supply Chain Management.* Retrieved from Supply Chain Brain. Retrieved on August 19, 2023 from https://www.supplychainbrain.com/blogs/1-think-tank/post/30045-four-ways-ai-is-impacting-logistics-and-supply-chain-management

Khosla, D., Sharma, M., Sharma, A., Budhiraja, A., & Singh, S. (2019). Blockchain based supply chain management: An overview. *Int. J. Control Automat*, *12*(5), 424–430.

Khosla, D., Singh, S., Sharma, M., Sharma, A., Bharti, G., & Rajput, G. (2022). A Review on Virtual Reality and Applications for Next Generation Systems and Society 5.0. *Machine Intelligence and Data Science Applications: Proceedings of MIDAS 2021*, 303-312.

Khosravan, N. (2020). Multi-modal classification of lung nodules in CT scans: Effects of class distribution and data augmentation. *Journal of Medical Imaging (Bellingham, Wash.)*, *7*(3), 034001. PMID:32509915

Khuram, A. (2018). Machine learning-based differentiation between benign and malignant GIST using heterogeneous textural features and robust binary classifiers. *Computer Methods and Programs in Biomedicine*, *154*, 89–98.

Kim, W., Cho, S. K., Shin, S. W., Hyun, D., Lee, M. W., & Rhim, H. (2019). Combination therapy of transarterial chemoembolization (TACE) and radiofrequency ablation (RFA) for small hepatocellular carcinoma: Comparison with TACE or RFA monotherapy. *Abdominal Radiology*, *44*(6), 2283–2292. doi:10.1007/s00261-019-01952-1 PMID:30806742

Kirubasri, G., Sankar, S., Pandey, D., Pandey, B. K., Nassa, V. K., & Dadheech, P. (2022). Software-defined networking-based Ad hoc networks routing protocols. In *Software defined networking for Ad Hoc networks* (pp. 95–123). Springer International Publishing. doi:10.1007/978-3-030-91149-2_5

Kohavi, R. (1995). A study of cross-validation and bootstrap for ac-curacy estimation and model selection. *Proc. of the 14th International Joint Conference on Artificial Intelligence*, 1137–1143.

Koot, M., Mes, M. R. K., & Iacob, M. E. (2020). A systematic literature review of supply chain decision making supported by the Internet of things and big data analytics. *Computers & Industrial Engineering*, *154*, 107076. doi:10.1016/j.cie.2020.107076

Korbar, B., Olofson, A. M., Miraflor, A. P., Nicka, C. M., Suriawinata, M. A., Torresani, L., Suriawinata, A. A., & Hassanpour, S. (2017). Deep learning for classification of colorectal polyps on whole-slide images. *Journal of Pathology Informatics*, *8*(1), 30. doi:10.4103/jpi.jpi_34_17 PMID:28828201

Kotagi, P. B., Raj, P., & Asaithambi, G. (2020). Modeling lateral placement and movement of vehicles on urban undivided roads in mixed traffic: A case study of India. *Journal of Traffic and Transportation Engineering*, *7*(6), 860–873. doi:10.1016/j.jtte.2018.06.008

Kourou, K., & Themis, E. (2015). Machine learning applications in cancer prognosis and prediction. *Computational and Structural Biotechnology Journal*, *1*(3), 8–17. doi:10.1016/j.csbj.2014.11.005 PMID:25750696

Kreipl, S., & Pinedo, M. (2004). Planning and Scheduling in Supply Chains: An Overview of Issues in Practice. *Production and Operations Management*, *13*(1), 77–92. doi:10.1111/j.1937-5956.2004.tb00146.x

Kukreja, V., & Dhiman, P. (2020, September). A Deep Neural Network based disease detection scheme for Citrus fruits. In *2020 International conference on smart electronics and communication (ICOSEC)* (pp. 97-101). IEEE. 10.1109/ICOSEC49089.2020.9215359

Kumar Pandey, B., Pandey, D., Nassa, V. K., Ahmad, T., Singh, C., George, A. S., & Wakchaure, M. A. (2021). Encryption and steganography-based text extraction in IoT using the EWCTS optimizer. *Imaging Science Journal*, *69*(1-4), 38–56. doi:10.1080/13682199.2022.2146885

Kumar, A., Khan, M. A., & Singh, S. (2022). A fuzzy logic-based approach to supplier selection for green supply chain management. *International Journal of Advanced Manufacturing Technology*, *120*(9-12), 2021–2035.

Kumara, V., Mohanaprakash, T., Fairooz, S., Jamal, K., Babu, T., & Sampath, B. (2023). Experimental Study on a Reliable Smart Hydroponics System. In *Human Agro-Energy Optimization for Business and Industry* (pp. 27–45). IGI Global. doi:10.4018/978-1-6684-4118-3.ch002

Kumar, M. S., Sankar, S., Nassa, V. K., Pandey, D., Pandey, B. K., & Enbeyle, W. (2021). Innovation and creativity for data mining using computational statistics. In *Methodologies and Applications of Computational Statistics for Machine Intelligence* (pp. 223–240). IGI Global. doi:10.4018/978-1-7998-7701-1.ch012

Kumar, P. R., Meenakshi, S., Shalini, S., Devi, S. R., & Boopathi, S. (2023). Soil Quality Prediction in Context Learning Approaches Using Deep Learning and Blockchain for Smart Agriculture. In R. Kumar, A. B. Abdul Hamid, & N. I. Binti Ya'akub (Eds.), (pp. 1–26). Advances in Computational Intelligence and Robotics. IGI Global. doi:10.4018/978-1-6684-9151-5.ch001

Kumar, S., & Kumar, H. (2023, December). Classification of COVID-19 X-ray images using transfer learning with visual geometrical groups and novel sequential convolutional neural networks. *MethodsX*, *11*, 102295. doi:10.1016/j.mex.2023.102295 PMID:37539339

Kusiak, A. (2019). Fundamentals of Smart Manufacturing: A Multi-Thread Perspective. *Annual Reviews in Control*, *47*, 214–220. doi:10.1016/j.arcontrol.2019.02.001

Kusi-Sarpong, S., Sarkis, J., & Wang, X. (2019). Exploring the role of artificial intelligence in supply chain management. *Journal of Cleaner Production*, *208*, 1452–1468.

Lebacque, J. P., Lesort, J. B., & Giorgi, F. (1998). Introducing buses into first-order macroscopic traffic flow models. *Transportation Research Record: Journal of the Transportation Research Board*, *1644*(1), 70–79. doi:10.3141/1644-08

Lee, H. L. (2004). The triple-a supply chain. *Harvard Business Review*, *82*(10), 102–112. PMID:15559579

Lee, J., & Mitici, M. (2023, February). Deep reinforcement learning for predictive aircraft maintenance using probabilistic Remaining-Useful-Life prognostics. *Reliability Engineering & System Safety*, *230*, 108908. doi:10.1016/j.ress.2022.108908

Lee, J., Wu, F., Zhao, W., Ghaffari, M., Liao, L., & Siegel, D. (2014, January). Prognostics and health management design for rotary machinery systems—Reviews, methodology and applications. *Mechanical Systems and Signal Processing*, *42*(1–2), 314–334. doi:10.1016/j.ymssp.2013.06.004

Lelisho, M. E., Pandey, D., Alemu, B. D., Pandey, B. K., & Tareke, S. A. (2023). The negative impact of social media during COVID-19 pandemic. *Trends in Psychology*, *31*(1), 123–142. doi:10.1007/s43076-022-00192-5

Liao, S. P. S. H. T., & Wu, X. (2020). The Role of Big Data and Artificial Intelligence in Education and Education Research: A Literature Mapping. In *6th International Conference on and Social Science Research* (pp. 241-245). Academic Press.

Li, D., Zhi, B., Schoenherr, T., & Wang, X. (2023, March 28). Developing capabilities for supply chain resilience in a post-COVID world: A machine learning-based thematic analysis. *IISE Transactions*, *55*(12), 1256–1276. doi:10.1080/24725854.2023.2176951

Li, H. (2018). Machine learning for classifying malignant and benign breast lesions in MRI images. *Proceedings of the SPIE Medical Imaging*, *10575*, 1057519.

Li, H. (2019). A deep joint model for segmentation and diagnosis in individual head and neck CT scans with human papillomavirus status. *International Journal of Computer Assisted Radiology and Surgery*, *14*(3), 515–525.

Lindström, S. (2011). A comprehensive survey of genetic variation in 20,691 subjects from four large cohorts. *PLoS One*, *6*(8), e23133. PMID:21850257

Lin, W. C., Wong, S. K., Li, C. H., & Tseng, R. (2016). Generating believable mixed-traffic animation. *IEEE Transactions on Intelligent Transportation Systems*, *17*(11), 3171–3183. doi:10.1109/TITS.2016.2542283

Lipari, A., O'Brien, E. J., & Capriani, C. C. (2012). A comparative study of a bridge traffic load effect using micro-simulation and Eurocode load models. In Bridge Maintenance, Safety, Management, Resilience and Sustainability, Stresa, Italy, 8-12 July, 2012 (pp. 3420-3427). CRC Press. doi:10.1201/b12352-514

Littman, M., Ajunwa, I., Berger, G., Boutilier, C., Currie, M., Doshi-Velez, F., Hadfield, G., Horowitz, M., Isbell, C., Kitano, H., Levy, K., Lyons, T., Mitchell, M., Shah, J., Sloman, S., Vallor, S., & Walsh, T. (2021). *Gathering Strength, Gathering Storms: The One Hundred Year Study on Artificial Intelligence (AI100) 2021 Study Panel Report*. The Stanford University. Retrieved on August 19, 2023 from https://ai100.stanford.edu/2021-report

Liu, C., Shu, T., Chen, S., Wang, S., Lai, K. K., & Gan, L. (2016). An improved grey neural network model for predicting transportation disruptions. *Expert Systems with Applications*, *45*, 331–340. doi:10.1016/j.eswa.2015.09.052

Liu, C., Zhu, H., Tang, D., Nie, Q., Zhou, T., Wang, L., & Song, Y. (2022, October). Probing an intelligent predictive maintenance approach with deep learning and augmented reality for machine tools in IoT-enabled manufacturing. *Robotics and Computer-integrated Manufacturing*, *77*, 102357. doi:10.1016/j.rcim.2022.102357

Liu, W. (2016). SSD: Single Shot MultiBox Detector. *European Conference on Computer Vision (ECCV)*.

Liu, Z. Y., & Li, Z. P. (2020). A blockchain-based framework of cross-border e-commerce supply chain. *International Journal of Information Management*, *52*, 102059. doi:10.1016/j.ijinfomgt.2019.102059

Li, Y., Diabat, A., & Lu, C. C. (2020). Leagile Supplier Selection in Chinese Textile Industries: A DEMATEL Approach. *Annals of Operations Research, 287*(1), 303–322. doi:10.1007/s10479-019-03453-2

Loey, M., Manogaran, G., Taha, M. H. N., & Khalifa, N. E. M. (2020). A hybrid deep transfer learning model with machine learning methods for face mask detection in the era of the COVID-19 pandemic. *Measurement, 167*, 108288. doi:10.1016/j.measurement.2020.108288 PMID:32834324

Long, D., & Magerko, B. (2020). What Is AI Literacy? Competencies and Design Considerations. In *Proceedings of the 2020 CHI Conference on Human Factors in Computing Systems* (pp. 1-16). Association for Computing Machinery. Retrieved on August 19, 2023 from https://doi.org/10.1145/3313831.3376727

Lopes de Sousa Jabbour, A. B., Jabbour, C. J. C., Godinho Filho, M., & Roubaud, D. (2018). Industry 4.0 and the circular economy: A proposed research agenda and original roadmap for sustainable operations. *Annals of Operations Research, 270*(1-2), 273–286. doi:10.1007/s10479-018-2772-8

Lundberg, S., & Lee, S. I. (2017, May 22). *A Unified Approach to Interpreting Model Predictions*. arXiv.org. https://arxiv.org/abs/1705.07874v2

Ma, C., Li, W., Cao, J., Du, J., Li, Q., & Gravina, R. (2020, January). Adaptive sliding window based activity recognition for assisted livings. *Information Fusion, 53*, 55–65. doi:10.1016/j.inffus.2019.06.013

Machado, C. G., Winroth, M. P., & Ribeiro da Silva, E. H. D. (2020). Sustainable manufacturing in Industry 4.0: An emerging research agenda. *International Journal of Production Research, 58*(5), 1462–1484. doi:10.1080/00207543.2019.1652777

Madhumathy, P., & Pandey, D. (2022). Deep learning based photo acoustic imaging for non-invasive imaging. *Multimedia Tools and Applications, 81*(5), 7501–7518. doi:10.1007/s11042-022-11903-6

Mahapatra, G., & Maurya, A. K. (2013). Study of vehicles lateral movement in non-lane discipline traffic stream on a straight road. *Procedia: Social and Behavioral Sciences, 104*, 352–359. doi:10.1016/j.sbspro.2013.11.128

Mahapatra, G., & Maurya, A. K. (2018). Dynamic parameters of vehicles under heterogeneous traffic stream with non-lane discipline: An experimental study. [English edition]. *Journal of Traffic and Transportation Engineering, 5*(5), 386–405. doi:10.1016/j.jtte.2018.01.003

Mahapatra, G., Maurya, A. K., & Minhans, A. (2016). Lateral movement of vehicles under weak-lane discipline heterogeneous traffic. *Jurnal Teknologi, 78*(4). Advance online publication. doi:10.11113/jt.v78.7995

Maiti, N., & Chilukuri, B. R. (2023). Empirical Investigation of Fundamental Diagrams in Mixed Traffic. *IEEE Access : Practical Innovations, Open Solutions, 11*, 13293–13308. doi:10.1109/ACCESS.2023.3242971

Ma, J., Ning, N., & Xu, T. (2021). Analyzing the chinese telecommunication industry based on oligopoly game and dynamic evolution. *International Journal of Bifurcation and Chaos in Applied Sciences and Engineering, 31*(14), 2150238. doi:10.1142/S0218127421502382

Makkar, S., Devi, G. N.R., & Solanki, V.K. (2019). Applications of Machine Learning Techniques in Supply Chain Optimization. *ICICCT 2019 – System Reliability, Quality Control, Safety, Maintenance and Management*, 861–869.

Malhotra, P., Pandey, D., Pandey, B. K., & Patra, P. M. (2021). Managing agricultural supply chains in COVID-19 lockdown. *International Journal of Quality and Innovation, 5*(2), 109–118. doi:10.1504/IJQI.2021.117181

Manavalan, E., & Jayakrishna, K. (2019). A review of Internet of Things (IoT) embedded sustainable supply chain for industry 4.0 requirements. *Computers & Industrial Engineering, 127*, 925–953. doi:10.1016/j.cie.2018.11.030

Mandal, S. (2018). An examination of the importance of big data analytics in supply chain agility development: A dynamic capability perspective. *Management Research Review*, *41*(10), 1201–1219. Advance online publication. doi:10.1108/MRR-11-2017-0400

Manyika, J., & Michael, C. (2017). *A Future That Works: Automation, Employment, and Productivity*. McKinsey & Co.

Manzella, F., Pagliarini, G., Sciavicco, G., & Stan, I. (2023, March). The voice of COVID-19: Breath and cough recording classification with temporal decision trees and random forests. *Artificial Intelligence in Medicine*, *137*, 102486. doi:10.1016/j.artmed.2022.102486 PMID:36868683

Matcha, B. N., Sivanesan, S., Ng, K. C., & Eh Noum, S. Y. (2022). Mixed traffic driver behavioral modeling at urban merge section: An experimental study. *Transportation Letters*, *14*(7), 752–777. doi:10.1080/19427867.2021.1944964

Matcha, B. N., Sivanesan, S., Ng, K. C., & Eh Noum, S. Y. (2022). Modelling integrated movements of motorcycles at urban merge sections under mixed traffic conditions. *Transportmetrica. B, Transport Dynamics*, *10*(1), 441–467. doi:10.1080/21680566.2021.2007814

Mathew, T. V., Munigety, C. R., & Bajpai, A. (2015). Strip-based approach for the simulation of mixed traffic conditions. *Journal of Computing in Civil Engineering*, *29*(5), 04014069. doi:10.1061/(ASCE)CP.1943-5487.0000378

Ma, Y., Xu, T., Huang, X., Wang, X., Li, C., Jerwick, J., Ning, Y., Zeng, X., Wang, B., Wang, Y., Zhang, Z., Zhang, X., & Zhou, C. (2019). Computer-aided diagnosis of label-free 3-D optical coherence microscopy images of human cervical tissue. *IEEE Transactions on Biomedical Engineering*, *66*(9), 2447–2456. doi:10.1109/TBME.2018.2890167 PMID:30605087

McKinney, S. M., Sieniek, M., Godbole, V., Godwin, J., Antropova, N., Ashrafian, H., Back, T., Chesus, M., Corrado, G. S., Darzi, A., Etemadi, M., Garcia-Vicente, F., Gilbert, F. J., Halling-Brown, M., Hassabis, D., Jansen, S., Karthikesalingam, A., Kelly, C. J., King, D., ... Shetty, S. (2020). International evaluation of an AI system for breast cancer screening. *Nature*, *577*(7788), 89–94. doi:10.1038/s41586-019-1799-6 PMID:31894144

McKinsey & Company. (2021). *Succeeding in the AI Supply-Chain Revolution*. https://www.mckinsey.com/industries/metals-and-mining/our-insights/succeeding-inthe-ai-supply-chain-revolution

Mena, C., Melnyk, S. A., Baghersad, M., & Zobel, C. W. (2020). Sourcing decisions under conditions of risk and resilience: A behavioral study. *Decision Sciences*, *51*(4), 985–1014. doi:10.1111/deci.12403

Menon, V., Pandey, D., Khosla, D., Kaur, M., Vashishtha, H. K., George, A. S., & Pandey, B. K. (2022). A Study on COVID–19, Its Origin, Phenomenon, Variants, and IoT-Based Framework to Detect the Presence of Coronavirus. In *IoT Based Smart Applications* (pp. 1–13). Springer International Publishing.

Mercuri, F., della Corte, G., & Ricci, F. (2021). Blockchain technology and sustainable business models: A case study of Devoleum. *Sustainability (Basel)*, *13*(10), 5619. doi:10.3390/su13105619

Meslie, Y., Enbeyle, W., Pandey, B. K., Pramanik, S., Pandey, D., Dadeech, P., & Saini, A. (2021). Machine intelligence-based trend analysis of COVID-19 for total daily confirmed cases in Asia and Africa. In *Methodologies and Applications of Computational Statistics for Machine Intelligence* (pp. 164–185). IGI Global. doi:10.4018/978-1-7998-7701-1.ch009

Microsoft Azure Predictive Maintenance. (n.d.). Microsoft Azure Predictive Maintenance | Kaggle. https:///datasets/arnabbiswas1/microsoft-azure-predictive-maintenance

Min, H. (2015). *The Essentials of Supply Chain Management*. Pearson Education Ltd.

Min, H. (2015). *The Essentials of Supply Chain Management*. Pearson Education LTD.

MinaeeS.MinaeiM.AbdolrashidiA. (2020) Palm-GAN: generating realistic palmprint images using total-variation regularized GAN. 2020, https://arxiv.org/abs/2003.10834

Min, H. (2019). Artificial intelligence in supply chain management: Theory and applications. *International Journal of Logistics*, *13*(1), 13–39. doi:10.1080/13675560902736537

Mishra, D., Gunasekaran, A., Papadopoulos, T., & Childe, S. J. (2018). Big Data and supply chain management: A review and bibliometric analysis. *Annals of Operations Research*, *270*(1-2), 313–336. doi:10.1007/s10479-016-2236-y

Mohanty, A., Venkateswaran, N., Ranjit, P., Tripathi, M. A., & Boopathi, S. (2023). Innovative Strategy for Profitable Automobile Industries: Working Capital Management. In Handbook of Research on Designing Sustainable Supply Chains to Achieve a Circular Economy (pp. 412–428). IGI Global.

Mohsen, B. (2022). Role of Big Data in Supply Chain Management. *International Journal of Management*, *13*, 24–40.

Mohsen, B. (2023). Developments of Digital Technologies Related to Supply Chain Management. *The 13th International Symposium on Frontiers in Ambient and Mobile Systems (FAMS 2023)*. 10.1016/j.procs.2023.03.105

Mondal, S., & Bours, P. (2017, March). A study on continuous authentication using a combination of keystroke and mouse biometrics. *Neurocomputing*, *230*, 1–22. doi:10.1016/j.neucom.2016.11.031

Moosavi, J., Fathollahi-Fard, A. M., & Dulebenets, M. A. (2022, June). Supply chain disruption during the COVID-19 pandemic: Recognizing potential disruption management strategies. *International Journal of Disaster Risk Reduction*, *75*, 102983. doi:10.1016/j.ijdrr.2022.102983 PMID:35475018

Mostofi, A. (2022). *Select issues in designing license contracts of strategic alliances in the pharmaceutical supply chain* [PhD Thesis]. Open Access Te Herenga Waka-Victoria University of Wellington.

Mulla, A. K., Joshi, A., Chavan, R., Chakraborty, D., & Manjunath, D. (2018). A microscopic model for lane-less traffic. *IEEE Transactions on Control of Network Systems*, *6*(1), 415–428. doi:10.1109/TCNS.2018.2834313

Mullakkal-Babu, F. A., Wang, M., van Arem, B., Shyrokau, B., & Happee, R. (2020). A hybrid submicroscopic-microscopic traffic flow simulation framework. *IEEE Transactions on Intelligent Transportation Systems*, *22*(6), 3430–3443. doi:10.1109/TITS.2020.2990376

Müller, J. M., & Voigt, K. I. (2018). The impact of industry 4.0 on supply chains in engineer-to-order industries-an exploratory case study. *IFAC-PapersOnLine*, *51*(11), 122–127. doi:10.1016/j.ifacol.2018.08.245

Muniandi, B., Huang, C.-J., Kuo, C.-C., Yang, T.-F., Chen, K.-H., Lin, Y.-H., Lin, S.-R., & Tsai, T.-Y. (2019, November). A 97% Maximum Efficiency Fully Automated Control Turbo Boost Topology for Battery Chargers. *IEEE Transactions on Circuits and Systems. I, Regular Papers*, *66*(11), 4516–4527. doi:10.1109/TCSI.2019.2925374

Munigety, C. R. (2018). Modelling behavioural interactions of drivers' in mixed traffic conditions. *Journal of Traffic and Transportation Engineering*, *5*(4), 284–295. doi:10.1016/j.jtte.2017.12.002

Munigety, C. R., & Mathew, T. V. (2016). Towards behavioral modeling of drivers in mixed traffic conditions. *Transportation in Developing Economies*, *2*(1), 1–20. doi:10.1007/s40890-016-0012-y

Myilsamy Sureshkumar, Boopathi, & Sabareesh. (2018). The improving Wear Resistance Properties of Molybdenum Alloy Under Cryogenic Treatment. *International Journal of Mechanical and Production Engineering Research and Development*, *8*(7), 724–728.

Nagurney, A., Besik, D., & Nagurney, L. S. (2019). Global supply chain networks and tariff rate quotas: Equilibrium analysis with application to agricultural products. *Journal of Global Optimization*, *75*(2), 439–460. doi:10.1007/s10898-019-00794-x

Naim, A., & ... (2021). New Trends in Business Process Management: Applications of Green Information Technologies. *British Journal of Environmental Studies*, *1*(1), 12–23.

National Academies of Sciences, Engineering, and Medicine. (2018). *The Integration of the Humanities and Arts with Sciences, Engineering, and Medicine in Higher Education: Branches from the Same Tree.* Retrieved on August 8, 2023 from https://www.nationalacademies.org/our-work/the-integration-of-the-humanities-and-arts-with-sciences-engineering-and-medicine-in-higher-education#:~:text=In%20its%202018%20report%20The%20Integration%20of% 20the,active%20and%20informed%20members%20of%20a%20modern%20democracy

National Academies of Sciences, Engineering, and Medicine. (2018). *The Integration of the Humanities and Arts with Sciences, Engineering, and Medicine in Higher Education: Branches from the Same Tree.* Retrieved on August 8, 2023 from https://www.nationalacademies.org/our-work/the-integration-of-the-humanities-and-arts-with-sciences-engineering-and-medicine-in-higher-education#:~:text=In%20its%202018%20report%20The%20Integration%20of%20the,active%20and%20informed%20members%20of%20a%20modern%20democracy

Nayak, R., & Choudhary, S. (2022). Operational Excellence in Humanitarian Logistics and Supply Chain Management through Leagile Framework: A Case Study from a Non-Mature Economy. *Production Planning and Control*, *33*(6-7), 606–621. doi:10.1080/09537287.2020.1834135

Neelima, K., & Chennapalli, S. (2022). Post-Pandemic Global Inequalities: Causes and Measures. In S. Deo & A. Kumar (Eds.), *Emerging Trends and Insights on Economic Inequality in the Wake of Global Crises* (pp. 40–55). IGI Global. doi:10.4018/978-1-6684-5289-9.ch003

Newman, T. S., & Jain, A. K. (1995). A survey of automated visual inspection. *Computer Vision and Image Understanding*, *61*(2), 231–262. doi:10.1006/cviu.1995.1017

Nguyen, T., Zhou, L., Spiegler, V., Ieromonachou, P., & Lin, Y. (2017). Big data analytics in supply chain management: A state-of-the-art literature review. *Computers & Operations Research*. Advance online publication. doi:10.1016/j.cor.2017.07.004

Ni, L., Ahmad, S. F., Alshammari, T. O., Liang, H., Alsanie, G., Irshad, M., Alyafi-AlZahri, R., BinSaeed, R. H., Al-Abyadh, M. H. A., Abu Bakir, S. M. M., & Ayassrah, A. Y. B. A. (2023). The role of environmental regulation and green human capital towards sustainable development: The mediating role of green innovation and industry upgradation. *Journal of Cleaner Production*, *421*, 138497. doi:10.1016/j.jclepro.2023.138497

Nishanth, J., Deshmukh, M. A., Kushwah, R., Kushwaha, K. K., Balaji, S., & Sampath, B. (2023). Particle Swarm Optimization of Hybrid Renewable Energy Systems. In *Intelligent Engineering Applications and Applied Sciences for Sustainability* (pp. 291–308). IGI Global. doi:10.4018/979-8-3693-0044-2.ch016

Nishitha, P., & Pandey, D. (2021). A study on student perception towards online education during covid-19 crisis. *Augmented Human Research*, *6*(1), 16. doi:10.1007/s41133-021-00055-1

Nunes, P., Santos, J., & Rocha, E. (2023, February). Challenges in predictive maintenance –A review. *CIRP Journal of Manufacturing Science and Technology*, *40*, 53–67. doi:10.1016/j.cirpj.2022.11.004

Pagano, D. (2023, March). A predictive maintenance model using Long Short-Term Memory Neural Networks and Bayesian inference. *Decision Analytics Journal*, *6*, 100174. doi:10.1016/j.dajour.2023.100174

Palaniappan, M., Tirlangi, S., Mohamed, M. J. S., Moorthy, R. S., Valeti, S. V., & Boopathi, S. (2023). Fused Deposition Modelling of Polylactic Acid (PLA)-Based Polymer Composites: A Case Study. In Development, Properties, and Industrial Applications of 3D Printed Polymer Composites (pp. 66–85). IGI Global.

Panagou, S., Fruggiero, F., Lerra, M., Vecchio, C. D., Menchetti, F., Piedimonte, L., Natale, O. R., & Passariello, S. (2022). Feature investigation with Digital Twin for predictive maintenance following a machine learning approach. *IFAC-PapersOnLine*, *55*(2), 132–137. doi:10.1016/j.ifacol.2022.04.182

Pandey, B. K., Pandey, D., Dadheech, P., Mahajan, D. A., George, A. S., & Hameed, A. S. (2023). Review on Smart Sewage Cleaning UAV Assistance for Sustainable Development. In Handbook of Research on Safe Disposal Methods of Municipal Solid Wastes for a Sustainable Environment (pp. 69-79). IGI Global. doi:10.4018/978-1-6684-8117-2.ch005

Pandey, B. K., Pandey, D., Nassa, V. K., George, S., Aremu, B., Dadeech, P., & Gupta, A. (2022, July). Effective and secure transmission of health information using advanced morphological component analysis and image hiding. In *Artificial Intelligence on Medical Data: Proceedings of International Symposium, ISCMM 2021* (pp. 223-230). Singapore: Springer Nature Singapore.

Pandey, B. K., Pandey, D., Wairya, S., Agarwal, G., Dadeech, P., Dogiwal, S. R., & Pramanik, S. (2022). Application of integrated steganography and image compressing techniques for confidential information transmission. *Cyber Security and Network Security*, 169-191.

Pandey, B. K., Pandey, D., Wairya, S., Agarwal, G., Dadeech, P., Dogiwal, S. R., & Pramanik, S. (2022a). Application of integrated steganography and image compressing techniques for confidential information transmission. *Cyber Security and Network Security*, 169-191.

Pandey, D., Hasan, A., Pandey, B. K., Lelisho, M. E., George, A. H., & Shahul, A. (2023). COVID-19 epidemic anxiety, mental stress, and sleep disorders in developing country university students. *CSI Transactions on ICT*, 1-9.

Pandey, D., Ogunmola, G. A., Enbeyle, W., Abdullahi, M., Pandey, B. K., & Pramanik, S. (2021). COVID-19: A framework for effective delivering of online classes during lockdown. *Human Arenas*, 1-15.

Pandey, D., Pandey, B. K., Sindhwani, N., Anand, R., Nassa, V. K., & Dadheech, P. (2022). An Interdisciplinary Approach in the Post-COVID-19 Pandemic Era. *An Interdisciplinary Approach in the Post-COVID-19 Pandemic Era*, 1-290.

Pandey, D., Verma, N., Islam, T., Enbeyle, W., Pandey, B. K., & Patra, P. (2021). The Response of Consumer Food Price Index (CFPI) Due To The Impact of Pandemic Covid-19 On Indian Agriculture Sector. *Hyperion International Journal of Econophysics & New Economy, 14*(1).

Pandey, B. K., Mane, D., Nassa, V. K. K., Pandey, D., Dutta, S., Ventayen, R. J. M., & Rastogi, R. (2021). Secure text extraction from complex degraded images by applying steganography and deep learning. In *Multidisciplinary approach to modern digital steganography* (pp. 146–163). IGI Global. doi:10.4018/978-1-7998-7160-6.ch007

Pandey, B. K., & Pandey, D. (2023). Parametric optimization and prediction of enhanced thermoelectric performance in co-doped CaMnO3 using response surface methodology and neural network. *Journal of Materials Science Materials in Electronics*, *34*(21), 1589. doi:10.1007/s10854-023-10954-1

Pandey, B. K., Pandey, D., & Agarwal, A. (2022). Encrypted information transmission by enhanced steganography and image transformation. *International Journal of Distributed Artificial Intelligence*, *14*(1), 1–14. doi:10.4018/IJDAI.297110

Pandey, B. K., Pandey, D., Alkhafaji, M. A., Güneşer, M. T., & Şeker, C. (2023). A Reliable Transmission and Extraction of Textual Information Using Keyless Encryption, Steganography, and Deep Algorithm with Cuckoo Optimization. In *Micro-Electronics and Telecommunication Engineering: Proceedings of 6th ICMETE 2022* (pp. 629–636). Springer Nature Singapore. doi:10.1007/978-981-19-9512-5_57

Pandey, B. K., Pandey, D., Gupta, A., Nassa, V. K., Dadheech, P., & George, A. S. (2023). Secret data transmission using advanced morphological component analysis and steganography. In *Role of Data-Intensive Distributed Computing Systems in Designing Data Solutions* (pp. 21–44). Springer International Publishing. doi:10.1007/978-3-031-15542-0_2

Pandey, B. K., Pandey, D., Wairya, S., & Agarwal, G. (2021a). An advanced morphological component analysis, steganography, and deep learning-based system to transmit secure textual data. *International Journal of Distributed Artificial Intelligence, 13*(2), 40–62. doi:10.4018/IJDAI.2021070104

Pandey, B. K., Pandey, D., Wariya, S., & Agarwal, G. (2021). A deep neural network-based approach for extracting textual images from deteriorate images. *EAI Endorsed Transactions on Industrial Networks and Intelligent Systems, 8*(28), e3–e3. doi:10.4108/eai.17-9-2021.170961

Pandey, B. K., Pandey, D., Wariya, S., Aggarwal, G., & Rastogi, R. (2021). Deep learning and particle swarm optimisation-based techniques for visually impaired humans' text recognition and identification. *Augmented Human Research, 6*(1), 1–14. doi:10.1007/s41133-021-00051-5

Pandey, D., Nassa, V. K., Jhamb, A., Mahto, D., Pandey, B. K., George, A. H., & Bandyopadhyay, S. K. (2021). An integration of keyless encryption, steganography, and artificial intelligence for the secure transmission of stego images. In *Multidisciplinary approach to modern digital steganography* (pp. 211–234). IGI Global. doi:10.4018/978-1-7998-7160-6.ch010

Pandey, D., & Pandey, B. K. (2022). An efficient deep neural network with adaptive galactic swarm optimization for complex image text extraction. In *Process Mining Techniques for Pattern Recognition* (pp. 121–137). CRC Press. doi:10.1201/9781003169550-10

Pandey, D., Pandey, B. K., & Wairya, S. (2021a). Hybrid deep neural network with adaptive galactic swarm optimization for text extraction from scene images. *Soft Computing, 25*(2), 1563–1580. doi:10.1007/s00500-020-05245-4

Pandey, D., Wairya, S., Pradhan, B., & Wangmo. (2022). Understanding COVID-19 response by twitter users: A text analysis approach. *Heliyon, 8*(8), e09994. doi:10.1016/j.heliyon.2022.e09994 PMID:35873536

Pandey, D., Wairya, S., Sharma, M., Gupta, A. K., Kakkar, R., & Pandey, B. K. (2022). An approach for object tracking, categorization, and autopilot guidance for passive homing missiles. *Aerospace Systems, 5*(4), 553–566. doi:10.1007/s42401-022-00150-0

Pandey, G., Rao, K. R., & Mohan, D. (2017). Modelling vehicular interactions for heterogeneous traffic flow using cellular automata with position preference. *Journal of Modern Transportation, 25*(3), 163–177. doi:10.1007/s40534-017-0132-z

Pandey, J. K., Jain, R., Dilip, R., Kumbhkar, M., Jaiswal, S., Pandey, B. K., & Pandey, D. (2022). Investigating Role of IoT in the Development of Smart Application for Security Enhancement. In *IoT Based Smart Applications* (pp. 219–243). Springer International Publishing.

Papathanasopoulou, V., & Antoniou, C. (2018). Flexible car–following models for mixed traffic and weak lane–discipline conditions. *European Transport Research Review, 10*(2), 1–14. doi:10.1186/s12544-018-0338-0

Parthiban, K., Pandey, D., & Pandey, B. K. (2021). Impact of SARS-CoV-2 in online education, predicting and contrasting mental stress of young students: A machine learning approach. *Augmented Human Research, 6*(1), 10. doi:10.1007/s41133-021-00048-0

Patel, V. M., Chellappa, R., Chandra, D., & Barbello, B. (2016, July). Continuous user authentication on mobile devices: Recent progress and remaining challenges. *IEEE Signal Processing Magazine*, *33*(4), 49–61. doi:10.1109/MSP.2016.2555335

Pernkopf, F. (2002). *Automatic visual inspection of metallic surfaces* [Ph.D. thesis]. University of Leoben, Leoben, Austria.

Perussi, J. B., Gressler, F., & Seleme, R. (2019). Supply chain 4.0: Autonomous vehicles and equipment to meet demand. *Int. J. Supply Chain.*, *8*, 33–41.

Pournader, M., Ghaderi, H., Hassanzadegan, A., & Fahimnia, B. (2021). Artificial Intelligence Applications in Supply Chain Management. *International Journal of Production Economics*, *241*, 108250. Advance online publication. doi:10.1016/j.ijpe.2021.108250

Pramanik, S., Pandey, D., Joardar, S., Niranjanamurthy, M., Pandey, B. K., & Kaur, J. (2023, October). An overview of IoT privacy and security in smart cities. In AIP Conference Proceedings (Vol. 2495, No. 1). AIP Publishing. doi:10.1063/5.0123511

Preindl, R., Nikolopoulos, K., & Litsiou, K. (2020). Transformation strategies for the supply chain: The impact of industry 4.0 and digital transformation. *Supply Chain. Forum Int. J.*, *21*(1), 26–34. doi:10.1080/16258312.2020.1716633

Prihatno, A. T., Nurcahyanto, H., & Jang, Y. M. (2021, April 13). Predictive Maintenance of Relative Humidity Using Random Forest Method. *2021 International Conference on Artificial Intelligence in Information and Communication (ICAIIC)*. 10.1109/ICAIIC51459.2021.9415213

Pudil, P., Novovicovˇa, J., & Kittler, J. (1994). Floating search methods in feature selection. *Pattern Recognition Letters*, *15*(11), 1119–1125. doi:10.1016/0167-8655(94)90127-9

Queiroz, M. M., & Wamba, S. F. (2019). Blockchain adoption challenges in supply chain: An empirical investigation of the main drivers in India and the USA. *International Journal of Information Management*, *46*, 70–82. doi:10.1016/j.ijinfomgt.2018.11.021

Radwan, E., Alattar, E., Radwan, A., Radwan, W., Alajez, M., Pandey, D., & Jebreen, K. (2023). Knowledge, attitudes, and practices of palestinian students toward COVID-19: a cross-sectional study during the first wave of the COVID-19 pandemic. *Human Arenas*, 1-22.

Raghavan, R., Verma, D. C., Pandey, D., Anand, R., Pandey, B. K., & Singh, H. (2022). Optimized building extraction from high-resolution satellite imagery using deep learning. *Multimedia Tools and Applications*, *81*(29), 42309–42323. doi:10.1007/s11042-022-13493-9

Rahimi, A., & Alemtabriz, A. (2022). Providing a Model of Leagile Hybrid Paradigm Practices and Its Impact on Supply Chain Performance. *International Journal of Lean Six Sigma*, *13*(6), 1308–1345. doi:10.1108/IJLSS-04-2021-0073

Raju, N., Arkatkar, S., Easa, S., & Joshi, G. (2022). Customizing the following behavior models to mimic the weak lane based mixed traffic conditions. *Transportmetrica. B, Transport Dynamics*, *10*(1), 20–47. doi:10.1080/21680566.2021.1954562

Raju, N., Arkatkar, S., & Joshi, G. (2020). Evaluating performance of selected vehicle following models using trajectory data under mixed traffic conditions. *Journal of Intelligent Transport Systems*, *24*(6), 617–634. doi:10.1080/15472450.2019.1675522

Raju, N., Kumar, P., Jain, A., Arkatkar, S. S., & Joshi, G. (2018). Application of trajectory data for investigating vehicle behavior in mixed traffic environment. *Transportation Research Record: Journal of the Transportation Research Board*, *2672*(43), 122–133. doi:10.1177/0361198118787364

Rani, S., Koundal, D., Kavita, F., Ijaz, M. F., Elhoseny, M., & Alghamdi, M. I. (2021). An optimized framework for WSN routing in the context of industry 4.0. *Sensors (Basel), 21*(19), 6474. doi:10.3390/s21196474 PMID:34640792

Rashed, Y. (2017). *Internet of Things and Modern Supply Chain Management* [Unpublished Master Thesis]. Tampere University of Technology.

Rasool, F., Greco, M., & Grimaldi, M. (2022). Digital supply chain performance metrics: A literature review. *Measuring Business Excellence, 26*(1), 23–38. doi:10.1108/MBE-11-2020-0147

Ravisankar, A., Sampath, B., & Asif, M. M. (2023). Economic Studies on Automobile Management: Working Capital and Investment Analysis. In Multidisciplinary Approaches to Organizational Governance During Health Crises (pp. 169–198). IGI Global.

Ravishankar, K. V. R., & Mathew, T. V. (2011). Vehicle-type dependent car-following model for heterogeneous traffic conditions. *Journal of Transportation Engineering, 137*(11), 775–781. doi:10.1061/(ASCE)TE.1943-5436.0000273

Redmon, J., & Farhadi, A. (2017). YOLOv2: A Fast and Accurate Object Detector. arXiv preprint arXiv:1612.08242.

Richey, R. G., Roath, A. S., Adams, F. G., & Wieland, A. (2022). A responsiveness view of logistics and supply chain management. *Journal of Business Logistics, 43*(1), 62–91. doi:10.1111/jbl.12290

Rosen, M. A. (2012). Engineering sustainability: A technical approach to sustainability. *Sustainability (Basel), 4*(9), 2270–2292. doi:10.3390/su4092270

Rostami, O., Tavakoli, M., & Tajally, A., & GhanavatiNejad, M. (2022). A Goal Programming-Based Fuzzy Best-Worst Method for the Viable Supplier Selection Problem: A Case Study. *Soft Computing*, 1–26. doi:10.1007/s00500-022-07572-0 PMID:36373094

Rot, P., Vitek, M., Grm, K., Emersic, Z., Peer, P., & Struc, V. (2020). *Deep Sclera Segmentation and Recognition.* Springer. doi:10.1007/978-3-030-27731-4_13

Rozados, I. V., & Tjahjono, B. (2014, December). Big data analytics in supply chain management: Trends and related research. In *6th international conference on operations and supply chain management* (Vol. 1, p. 13). Academic Press.

Rozados, V. (2014). *Big Data Analytics in Supply Chain Management: Trends and Related Research.* doi:10.13140/RG.2.1.4935.2563

Russell, S. J., & Norvig, P. (2016). *Artificial Intelligence: A Modern Approach.* Pearson Education Limited.

Ryan, M. (2017). *Service Management: An Integrated Approach.* Larsen and Keller Education.

Saberi, S., Kouhizadeh, M., Sarkis, J., & Shen, L. (2019). Blockchain technology and its relationships to sustainable supply chain management. *International Journal of Production Research, 57*(7), 2117–2135. doi:10.1080/00207543.2018.1533261

Sadat, M., Abuamer, I. M., Ali Silgu, M., & Berk Celikoglu, H. (2018). Comparative performance analysis of variable speed limit systems control methods using microsimulation: a case study on D100 Freeway, Istanbul. In *Computer Aided Systems Theory–EUROCAST 2017: 16th International Conference, Las Palmas de Gran Canaria, Spain, February 19-24, 2017, Revised Selected Papers, Part II 16* (pp. 462-49). Springer International Publishing. 10.1007/978-3-319-74727-9_56

Sadat, M., & Celikoglu, H. B. (2017). Simulation-based variable speed limit systems modelling: An overview and a case study on Istanbul freeways. *Transportation Research Procedia, 22*, 607–614. doi:10.1016/j.trpro.2017.03.051

Sahani, K., Khadka, S. S., Sahani, S. K., Pandey, B. K., & Pandey, D. (2023). A possible underground roadway for transportation facilities in Kathmandu Valley: A racking deformation of underground rectangular structures. *Engineering Reports*, 12821. doi:10.1002/eng2.12821

Saini, H. K., & Biswas, S. (2021). Estimating lateral placement and lane indiscipline of urban mixed traffic of a developing country: An ANN-assisted approach. *Canadian Journal of Civil Engineering*, *48*(11), 1571–1581. doi:10.1139/cjce-2020-0250

Salim, K., Hebri, R. S. A., & Besma, S. (2022, December 31). Classification Predictive Maintenance Using XGboost with Genetic Algorithm. *Revue D'Intelligence Artificielle*, *36*(6), 833–845. doi:10.18280/ria.360603

Samikannu, R., Koshariya, A. K., Poornima, E., Ramesh, S., Kumar, A., & Boopathi, S. (2022). Sustainable Development in Modern Aquaponics Cultivation Systems Using IoT Technologies. In *Human Agro-Energy Optimization for Business and Industry* (pp. 105–127). IGI Global.

Sampath, B., Sasikumar, C., & Myilsamy, S. (2023). Application of TOPSIS Optimization Technique in the Micro-Machining Process. In Trends, Paradigms, and Advances in Mechatronics Engineering (pp. 162–187). IGI Global.

Sangeetha, G. M., & Prashanth. (2015, July 1). Training the SVM to Larger Dataset Applications using the SVM Sampling Technique. *Indian Journal of Science and Technology*, *8*(15). Advance online publication. doi:10.17485/ijst/2015/v8i15/88281

Saravanan, M., Vasanth, M., Boopathi, S., Sureshkumar, M., & Haribalaji, V. (2022). Optimization of Quench Polish Quench (QPQ) Coating Process Using Taguchi Method. *Key Engineering Materials*, *935*, 83–91. doi:10.4028/p-z569vy

Sathish, T., Sunagar, P., Singh, V., Boopathi, S., Al-Enizi, A. M., Pandit, B., Gupta, M., & Sehgal, S. S. (2023). Characteristics estimation of natural fibre reinforced plastic composites using deep multi-layer perceptron (MLP) technique. *Chemosphere*, *337*, 139346. doi:10.1016/j.chemosphere.2023.139346 PMID:37379988

Saxena, A., Sharma, N. K., Pandey, D., & Pandey, B. K. (2021). Influence of tourists satisfaction on future behavioral intentions with special reference to desert triangle of Rajasthan. *Augmented Human Research*, *6*(1), 1–9. doi:10.1007/s41133-021-00052-4

Schmidt, M., Wissing, C., Nattermann, T., & Bertram, T. (2021). A probabilistic model for discretionary lane change proposals in highway driving situations. *Forschung im Ingenieurwesen*, *85*(2), 1–16. doi:10.1007/s10010-021-00439-0

Scholten, K., Sharkey Scott, P., & Fynes, B. (2014). Mitigation Processes—Antecedents for Building Supply Chain Resilience. *Supply Chain Management*, *19*(2), 211–228. doi:10.1108/SCM-06-2013-0191

Scuotto, V., Caputo, F., Villasalero, M., & del Giudice, M. (2017). A multiple buyer–supplier relationship in the context of SMEs' digital supply chain management. *Production Planning and Control*, *28*(16), 1378–1388. doi:10.1080/09537287.2017.1375149

Selwyn, B., & Leyden, D. (2022). Oligopoly-driven development: The world bank's trading for development in the age of global value chains in perspective. *Competition & Change*, *26*(2), 174–196. doi:10.1177/1024529421995351

Sengupta, R., Sengupta, D., Pandey, D., Pandey, B. K., Nassa, V. K., & Dadeech, P. (2021). A Systematic Review of 5G Opportunities, Architecture and Challenges. *Future Trends in 5G and G, 6*, 247.

Senthil, T., Puviyarasan, M., Babu, S. R., Surakasi, R., Sampath, B., & Associates. (2023). Industrial Robot-Integrated Fused Deposition Modelling for the 3D Printing Process. In Development, Properties, and Industrial Applications of 3D Printed Polymer Composites (pp. 188–210). IGI Global.

Shang, X. C., Li, X. G., Xie, D. F., Jia, B., & Jiang, R. (2020). Two-lane traffic flow model based on regular hexagonal cells with realistic lane changing behavior. *Physica A*, *560*, 125220. doi:10.1016/j.physa.2020.125220

Shao, X. F., Liu, W., Li, Y., Chaudhry, H. R., & Yue, X. G. (2021). Multistage implementation framework for smart supply chain management under industry 4.0. *Technological Forecasting and Social Change*, *162*, 120354. doi:10.1016/j.techfore.2020.120354 PMID:33041379

Sharma, M., Gupta, A. K., Singh, J., Mittal, R., Singh, H., & Pandey, D. (2022, December). Effects of slot shape in performance of SIW based Leaky Wave Antenna. In *2022 International Conference on Computational Modelling, Simulation and Optimization (ICCMSO)* (pp. 268-273). IEEE. 10.1109/ICCMSO58359.2022.00060

Sharma, M., Pandey, D., Palta, P., & Pandey, B. K. (2022). Design and power dissipation consideration of PFAL CMOS V/S conventional CMOS based 2: 1 multiplexer and full adder. *Silicon*, *14*(8), 4401–4410. doi:10.1007/s12633-021-01221-1

Sharma, M., Saripalli, S. R., Gupta, A. K., Talwar, R., Dadheech, P., & Kanike, U. K. (2023). Real-Time Pothole Detection During Rainy Weather Using Dashboard Cameras for Driverless Cars. In *Handbook of Research on Thrust Technologies' Effect on Image Processing* (pp. 384–394). IGI Global. doi:10.4018/978-1-6684-8618-4.ch023

Sharma, M., Sharma, B., Gupta, A. K., Khosla, D., Goyal, S., & Pandey, D. (2021). A study and novel AI/ML-based framework to detect COVID-19 virus using smartphone embedded sensors. In *Sustainability Measures for COVID-19 Pandemic* (pp. 59–74). Springer Nature Singapore. doi:10.1007/978-981-16-3227-3_4

Sharma, M., Sharma, B., Gupta, A. K., & Pandey, D. (2023). Recent developments of image processing to improve explosive detection methodologies and spectroscopic imaging techniques for explosive and drug detection. *Multimedia Tools and Applications*, *82*(5), 6849–6865. doi:10.1007/s11042-022-13578-5

Sharma, M., & Singh, H. (2022). Contactless methods for respiration monitoring and design of SIW-LWA for real-time respiratory rate monitoring. *Journal of the Institution of Electronics and Telecommunication Engineers*, 1–11. doi:10.1080/03772063.2022.2069167

Sharma, M., Singh, H., & Pandey, D. (2022). Parametric considerations and dielectric materials impacts on the performance of 10 GHzSIW-LWA for respiration monitoring. *Journal of Electronic Materials*, *51*(5), 2131–2141. doi:10.1007/s11664-022-09482-1

Sheng, J., Amankwah-Amoah, J., Khan, Z., & Wang, X. (2020). COVID-19 pandemic in the new era of big data analytics: Methodological innovations and future research directions. *British Journal of Management*, *32*(4), 1164–1183. doi:10.1111/1467-8551.12441

Siau, K., & Weiyu, W. (2018). Building Trust in Artificial Intelligence, Machine Learning, and Robotics. *Cutter Business Technology Journal*, *31*(2), 47–53.

Silva, D. F., Batista, G. E. A. P. A., & Keogh, E. (2016, December). Prefix and Suffix Invariant Dynamic Time Warping. *2016 IEEE 16th International Conference on Data Mining (ICDM)*. 10.1109/ICDM.2016.0161

Silveira, D., & Vasconcelos, S. (2020). Essays on duopoly competition with asymmetric firms: Is profit maximization always an evolutionary stable strategy? *International Journal of Production Economics*, *225*, 107592. doi:10.1016/j.ijpe.2019.107592

Singh, H., Pandey, B. K., George, S., Pandey, D., Anand, R., Sindhwani, N., & Dadheech, P. (2022, July). Effective Overview of Different ML Models Used for Prediction of COVID-19 Patients. In *Artificial Intelligence on Medical Data: Proceedings of International Symposium, ISCMM 2021* (pp. 185-192). Singapore: Springer Nature Singapore.

Singh, H., Pandey, D., Kakkar, R., & Sharma, M. (n.d.). Investigations on Genetically Engineered Bioweapons & Computer Based Techniques for Counter Measure and Mathematical Modeling for Prediction of Novel Sars-Cov-2. *Vice Chancellor's Message*, 1.

Singh, J., Pandey, D., & Singh, A. K. (2023). Event detection from real-time twitter streaming data using community detection algorithm. *Multimedia Tools and Applications*, 1–28. doi:10.1007/s11042-023-16263-3

Siregar, M. L., Tjahjono, T., Nahry, & Sumabrata, R. J. (2023). Speed heterogeneity and accident reduction in mixed traffic. *International Journal of Injury Control and Safety Promotion*, *30*(3), 1–6. doi:10.1080/17457300.2023.2172736 PMID:36718766

Smith, B. (1993). Making war on defects: Six-sigma design. *IEEE Spectrum*, *30*(9), 43–47. doi:10.1109/6.275174

Smithies, J. (2017). Artificial Intelligence, Digital Humanities, and the Automation of Labour. In The Digital Humanities and the Digital Modern (pp. 79-111). Palgrave Macmillan. doi:10.1057/978-1-137-49944-8_4

Snyder, D., Garcia-Romero, D., Sell, G., Povey, D., & Khudanpur, S. (2018). X-vectors: Robust DNN embeddings for speaker recognition. *Proceedings of the IEEE International Conference on Acoustics, Speech, and Signal Processing*, *2018*, 5329–5333. doi:10.1109/ICASSP.2018.8461375

Somol, P., Pudil, P., Novovicovˇa, J., & Paclík, P. (1999). ´ and P. Pacl'ık, "Adaptive floating search methods in feature selection,". *Pattern Recognition Letters*, *20*(11–13), 1157–1163. doi:10.1016/S0167-8655(99)00083-5

Song, W. (2020). Automated detection and classification of gastrointestinal stromal tumors using deep learning. *BioMed Research International*.

Sonka, M., Hlavac, V., & Boyle, R. (1999). *Image Processing, Analy-sis, and Machine Vision* (2nd ed.). International Thomson Publishing.

Spinoulas, Mirzaalian, Hussein, & AbdAlmageed. (2020). *Multi-modal fingerprint presentation attack detection: Evaluation on a new dataset*. https:// arxiv.org/abs/2006.07498.

Srikantha, S., & Meharb, A. (2022). *Development of lane change models through microscopic simulation under mixed traffic*. doi: 10.11113/jurnalteknologi.v84.18074l

Srikantha, S., Meharb, A., & Praveen, K. G. N. V. (2020). Simulation of traffic flow to analyze lane changes on multi-lane highways under non-lane discipline. *Periodica Polytechnica Transportation Engineering, 48*(2), 109-1 16. doi:10.3311/PPtr.10150

SrivastavaJ.SharanA. (2022, July 5). *SMOTEEN Hybrid Sampling Based Improved Phishing Website Detection*. doi:10.36227/techrxiv.20207765.v1

Steurtewagen, B., & Van den Poel, D. (2021, September). Adding interpretability to predictive maintenance by machine learning on sensor data. *Computers & Chemical Engineering*, *152*, 107381. doi:10.1016/j.compchemeng.2021.107381

Stoyanov, S. (2021). Integration of Artificial Intelligence in the Supply Chain Management. *Journal Scientific and Applied Research*, *20*(1), 53–59. doi:10.46687/jsar.v20i1.305

Strusani, D., & Houngbonon, G. V. (2019). The role of Artificial Intelligence in supporting development in emerging markets. *International Finance Corporation World Bank Group*. Retrieved from www.ifc.org/thought.leadership

Sugandhi & Chunchu. (2017). Analysis and modeling of two-wheeler-overtaking-LMV maneuver in heterogeneous traffic stream. *Transportation in Developing Economies, 3*, 1-7. doi:10.1007/s40890-017-0046-9

Sun, L. (2018). Online Real-Time Action Recognition System for Untrimmed Videos. *Proceedings of the European Conference on Computer Vision (ECCV).*

Sun, L., Liu, W., Zhang, H., Jin, Y., & Zhuo, G. (2021). Analysis of the effect of cruise service supply chain network properties on economic profits. *International Journal of Shipping and Transport Logistics*, *13*(6), 569–599. doi:10.1504/IJSTL.2021.118525

Swapna, H. R., Singh, S., Madaan, G., Mishra, S., Pandey, D., & Kanike, U. K. (2023). Globalization and Emerging Opportunities and Challenges in Sustainable Environment in Industry 4.0. Handbook of Research on Safe Disposal Methods of Municipal Solid Wastes for a Sustainable Environment, 48-68.

Talwar, R., Sharma, M., Singh, H., & Sagar, P. (2023). A Comparative Analysis on Image Processing-Based Algorithms and Approaches in Healthcare. In *Handbook of Research on Thrust Technologies' Effect on Image Processing* (pp. 1–14). IGI Global. doi:10.4018/978-1-6684-8618-4.ch001

Tama, B. A., Kweka, B. J., Park, Y., & Rhee, K. H. (2017). A critical review of blockchain and its current applications. *Proceedings of the 2017 International Conference on Electrical Engineering and Computer Science*, 109–113. 10.1109/ICECOS.2017.8167115

Tang, J., & Salonitis, K. (2021). A Deep Reinforcement Learning Based Scheduling Policy for Reconfigurable Manufacturing Systems. *Procedia CIRP*, *103*, 1–7. doi:10.1016/j.procir.2021.09.089

Tapscott, D., & Euchner, J. (2019). Blockchain and the Internet of Value. *Research Technology Management*, *62*(1), 12–19. doi:10.1080/08956308.2019.1541711

Tapscott, D., & Tapscott, A. (2016). *Blockchain Revolution: How the Technology behind Bitcoin Is Changing Money, Business and the World.* Penguin Random House.

Tareke, S. A., Lelisho, M. E., Hassen, S. S., Seid, A. A., Jemal, S. S., Teshale, B. M., ... Pandey, B. K. (2022). The prevalence and predictors of depressive, anxiety, and stress symptoms among Tepi town residents during the COVID-19 pandemic lockdown in Ethiopia. *Journal of Racial and Ethnic Health Disparities*, 1–13. PMID:35028903

TASNIM. (2020, June). Disruption in Global Food Supply Chain (FSCs) Due to Covid-19 Pandemic and Impact of Digitalization Through Block Chain Technology in FSCs Management. *European Journal of Business and Management.* Advance online publication. doi:10.7176/EJBM/12-17-08

Thomas, R. (2019). *AI Is Not Magic: It's Time to Demystify and Apply.* IBM Think Blog. Retrieved on August 19, 2023 from https://www.ibm.com/blogs/think/2019/03/ai-is-not-magic

Tirkolaee, E. B., Aydin, N. S., & Mahdavi, I. (2022). A Hybrid Biobjective MarkovChain-Based Optimization Model for Sustainable Aggregate Production Planning. *IEEE Transactions on Engineering Management*, 1–11. doi:10.1109/TEM.2022.3210879

Tistarelli, M., & Champod, C. (2017). *Handbook of Biometrics for Forensic Science.* Springer. doi:10.1007/978-3-319-50673-9

Tistarelli, M., Li, S. Z., & Chellappa, R. (2009). *Handbook of Remote Biometrics.* Springer. doi:10.1007/978-1-84882-385-3

Tolosana, R., Vera-Rodriguez, R., Fierrez, J., Morales, A., & Javier, O. G. (2019). Do you need more data? the DeepSignDB online handwritten signature biometric database. *Proceedings of the 2019 International Conference on Document Analysis and Recognition (ICDAR)*, 1143–1148. 10.1109/ICDAR.2019.00185

Torrance, K. E., & Sparrow, E. M. (1967). Theory for o-specular reflection from roughened surfaces. *Journal of the Optical Society of America*, *57*(9), 1105–1114. doi:10.1364/JOSA.57.001105

Treiber, M., & Kesting, A. (2013). *Traffic flow dynamics. Traffic Flow Dynamics: Data, Models and Simulation.* Springer-Verlag Berlin Heidelberg. doi:10.1007/978-3-642-32460-4

Treiber, M., Hennecke, A., & Helbing, D. (1999). Derivation, properties, and simulation of a gas-kinetic-based, nonlocal traffic model. *Physical Review E: Statistical Physics, Plasmas, Fluids, and Related Interdisciplinary Topics, 59*(1), 239–253. doi:10.1103/PhysRevE.59.239

Treiblmaier, H. (2018). The impact of the blockchain on the supply chain: A theory-based research framework and a call for action. *Supply Chain Management, 23*(6), 545–559. doi:10.1108/SCM-01-2018-0029

Tripathi, R. P., Sharma, M., Gupta, A. K., Pandey, D., Pandey, B. K., Shahul, A., & George, A. H. (2023). Timely Prediction of Diabetes by Means of Machine Learning Practices. *Augmented Human Research, 8*(1), 1. doi:10.1007/s41133-023-00062-4

Tseng, C.-T., & Shang, S. S. C. (2021). Exploring the sustainability of the intermediary role in blockchain. *Sustainability (Basel), 13*(4), 1936. doi:10.3390/su13041936

Ugandar, R. E., Rahamathunnisa, U., Sajithra, S., Christiana, M. B. V., Palai, B. K., & Boopathi, S. (2023). Hospital Waste Management Using Internet of Things and Deep Learning: Enhanced Efficiency and Sustainability. In M. Arshad (Ed.), (pp. 317–343). Advances in Bioinformatics and Biomedical Engineering. IGI Global. doi:10.4018/978-1-6684-6577-6.ch015

Vanitha, S., Radhika, K., & Boopathi, S. (2023). Artificial Intelligence Techniques in Water Purification and Utilization. In *Human Agro-Energy Optimization for Business and Industry* (pp. 202–218). IGI Global. doi:10.4018/978-1-6684-4118-3.ch010

Venkateswaran, N., Vidhya, K., Ayyannan, M., Chavan, S. M., Sekar, K., & Boopathi, S. (2023). A Study on Smart Energy Management Framework Using Cloud Computing. In 5G, Artificial Intelligence, and Next Generation Internet of Things: Digital Innovation for Green and Sustainable Economies (pp. 189–212). IGI Global. doi:10.4018/978-1-6684-8634-4.ch009

Vennila, T., Karuna, M., Srivastava, B. K., Venugopal, J., Surakasi, R., & Sampath, B. (2022). New Strategies in Treatment and Enzymatic Processes: Ethanol Production From Sugarcane Bagasse. In Human Agro-Energy Optimization for Business and Industry (pp. 219–240). IGI Global.

Vickers, A. J. (2009). An empirical evaluation of the Gail model for breast cancer risk prediction in the Nurses' Health Study. *Journal of the National Cancer Institute, 101*(14), 1014–1023.

Vinodhini, V., Kumar, M. S., Sankar, S., Pandey, D., Pandey, B. K., & Nassa, V. K. (2022). IoT-based early forest fire detection using MLP and AROC method. *International Journal of Global Warming, 27*(1), 55–70. doi:10.1504/IJGW.2022.122794

Vitek, M., Rot, P., Struc, V., & Peer, P. (2020). A comprehensive ˇ investigation into sclera biometrics: A novel dataset and performance study. *Neural Computing & Applications, 32*(24), 1–15. doi:10.1007/s00521-020-04782-1

Wamba, S. & Akter, S. (2015). *Big Data Analytics for Supply Chain Management: A Literature Review and Research Agenda.* . doi:10.1007/978-3-319-24626-0_5

Wamba, S. F., & Queiroz, M. M. (2022). A Framework Based on Blockchain, Artificial Intelligence, and Big Data Analytics to Leverage Supply Chain Resilience considering the COVID-19. *IFAC-PapersOnLine, 55*(10), 2396–2401. doi:10.1016/j.ifacol.2022.10.067

Wang, Y. (2020). Efficient and Accurate Pedestrian Detection in Real-Time: A Survey. *arXiv preprint arXiv:2009.00936.*

Wang, C., Ahmad, S. F., Ayassrah, A. Y. B. A., Awwad, E. M., Irshad, M., Ali, Y. A., ... Han, H. (2023). An empirical evaluation of technology acceptance model for Artificial Intelligence in E-commerce. *Heliyon*, *9*(8), e18349. doi:10.1016/j.heliyon.2023.e18349 PMID:37520947

Wang, F., Chen, J., & Guan, X. (2021). A deep reinforcement learning-based approach for dynamic vehicle routing in city logistics. *Transportation Research Part E, Logistics and Transportation Review*, *149*, 1–18.

Wang, G., Gunasekaran, A., Ngai, E. W., & Papadopoulos, T. (2016). Big data analytics in logistics and supply chain management: Certain investigations for research and applications. *International Journal of Production Economics*, *176*, 98–110. doi:10.1016/j.ijpe.2016.03.014

Wang, H. (2018). Multi-modal 3D U-net for bladder and prostate segmentation on MRI and CT images. *Proceedings of the IEEE Conference on Computer Vision and Pattern Recognition Workshops*, 1176-1179.

Wang, J., Zhou, H., & Jin, X. (2021). Risk transmission in complex supply chain network with multi-drivers. *Chaos, Solitons, and Fractals*, *143*, 110259. doi:10.1016/j.chaos.2020.110259

Wang, L., & Zhou, L. (2019). The effects of artificial intelligence on supply chain agility: A conceptual framework. *Journal of Cleaner Production*, *236*, 117619.

Wang, X., Jin, Y., Schmitt, S., & Olhofer, M. (2023, July 13). Recent Advances in Bayesian Optimization. *ACM Computing Surveys*, *55*(13s), 1–36. doi:10.1145/3582078

Wang, X., Kumar, V., Kumari, A., & Kuzmin, E. (2022). Impact of Digital Technology on Supply Chain Efficiency in Manufacturing Industry. In V. Kumar, J. Leng, V. Akberdina, & E. Kuzmin (Eds.), *Digital Transformation in Industry. Lecture Notes in Information Systems and Organisation* (Vol. 54, pp. 347–371). Springer. doi:10.1007/978-3-030-94617-3_25

Wang, Y., Cao, X., & Ma, X. (2022). Evaluation of automatic lane-change model based on vehicle cluster generalized dynamic system. *Automotive Innovation*, *5*(1), 91–104. doi:10.1007/s42154-021-00171-z

Wardell, D. A., Piketty, M.-G., Lescuyer, G., & Pacheco, P. (2021). *Reviewing initiatives to promote sustainable supply chains: The case of forest-risk commodities*. Academic Press.

Weersink, A., & Fulton, M. (2020). Limits to profit maximization as a guide to behavior change. *Applied Economic Perspectives and Policy*, *42*(1), 67–79. doi:10.1002/aepp.13004

Wenzel, H., Smit, D., & Sardesa, S. (2019). A Literature Review on Machine Learning in Supply Chain Management. In W. Kersten, T. Blecker, & C. Ringle (Eds.), *Artificial Intelligence and Digital Transformation in Supply Chain Management* (Vol. 27, pp. 413–441). Innovative Approaches for Supply Chains., doi:10.15480/882.2478

Wu, W. (2019). Development of a multipara-metric radiomics model for preoperative evaluation of early recurrence in advanced-stage colorectal cancer. *Journal of Clinical Oncology*, *37*(18), 1522–1531.

Xie, Y., Yin, Y., Xue, W., Shi, H., & Chong, D. (2020). Intelligent Supply Chain PerformanceMeasurement in Industry 4.0. *Systems Research and Behavioral Science*, *37*(4), 711–718. doi:10.1002/sres.2712

Xu, Y., Jia, Z., Ai, Y., Zhang, F., Lai, M., Eric, I., & Chang, C. (2015, April). Deep convolutional activation features for large scale brain tumor histopathology image classification and segmentation. In *2015 IEEE international conference on acoustics, speech and signal processing (ICASSP)* (pp. 947-951). IEEE.

Xu, J. (2016). Deep learning for histopathological image analysis: Towards computerized diagnosis aided by deep learning—review. *Medical Image Analysis*, *32*, 177–196.

Xu, W., Xiong, S., & Proverbs, D. (2022, February 17). Evaluating Agricultural Food Supply Chain Resilience in the Context of the COVID-19 Pandemic. *International Journal of Information Systems and Supply Chain Management, 15*(1), 1–18. doi:10.4018/IJISSCM.287132

Yang, D., Zhu, L., Yang, F., & Pu, Y. (2015). Modeling and analysis of lateral driver behavior in lane-changing execution. *Transportation Research Record: Journal of the Transportation Research Board, 2490*(1), 127–137. doi:10.3141/2490-14

Yang, X.-S. (2020). Nature-inspired optimization algorithms: Challenges and open problems. *Journal of Computational Science, 46*, 101104. doi:10.1016/j.jocs.2020.101104

Yuan, H., & Zhou, M. (2020). Profit-maximized collaborative computation offloading and resource allocation in distributed cloud and edge computing systems. *IEEE Transactions on Automation Science and Engineering, 18*(3), 1277–1287. doi:10.1109/TASE.2020.3000946

Yuan, Y. (2019). A benchmark for endoluminal scene segmentation of gastroscopic images. *Computerized Medical Imaging and Graphics, 77*, 101642.

Yu, M., Cruz, J. M., Li, D., & Masoumi, A. H. (2022). A multiperiod competitive supply chain framework with environmental policies and investments in sustainable operations. *European Journal of Operational Research, 300*(1), 112–123. doi:10.1016/j.ejor.2021.07.028

Yupapin, P., Trabelsi, Y., Nattappan, A., & Boopathi, S. (2023). Performance improvement of wire-cut electrical discharge machining process using cryogenically treated super-conductive state of Monel-K500 alloy. *Iranian Journal of Science and Technology. Transaction of Mechanical Engineering, 47*(1), 267–283. doi:10.1007/s40997-022-00513-0

Yu, Y., Wang, X., Zhong, R. Y., & Huang, G. Q. (2017). E-Commerce Logistics in SupplyChain Management: Implementations and Future Perspective in Furniture Industry. *Industrial Management & Data Systems, 117*, 2263–2286. doi:10.1108/IMDS-09-2016-0398

Zakur, Y. A., Mallik, B. B., Zakoor, Y. A., & Pandey, D. (2023). Survey on the Artificial Intelligence and Machine Learning Techniques on the Applications of Wastewater Treatment for Sustainable Environment. In *Handbook of Research on Safe Disposal Methods of Municipal Solid Wastes for a Sustainable Environment* (pp. 241–248). IGI Global. doi:10.4018/978-1-6684-8117-2.ch017

Zamani, E. D., Smyth, C., Gupta, S., & Dennehy, D. (2022). Artificial Intelligence and BigData Analytics for Supply Chain Resilience: A Systematic Literature Review. *Annals of Operations Research*, 1–28. doi:10.1007/s10479-022-04983-y PMID:36212520

Zarbakhshnia, N., Soleimani, H., & Ghaderi, H. (2018). Sustainable Third-Party Reverse Logistics Provider Evaluation and Selection Using Fuzzy SWARA and Developed Fuzzy COPRAS in the Presence of Risk Criteria. *Applied Soft Computing, 65*, 307–319. doi:10.1016/j.asoc.2018.01.023

Zhang, L. (2018). DeepSORT: A Simple Online and Realtime Tracking Approach with Minimalistic Model Design. *arXiv preprint arXiv:1812.00442.*

Zhang, F., Wu, X., Tang, C. S., Feng, T., & Dai, Y. (2020). Evolution of operations management research: From managing flows to building capabilities. *Production and Operations Management, 29*(10), 2219–2229. doi:10.1111/poms.13231

Zhang, M., Yu, X., & Li, H. (2021). Optimization model and algorithm for green supply chain transportation routing problem based on artificial intelligence. *International Journal of Advanced Manufacturing Technology, 115*(1-4), 57–76.

Zhang, Y., Gu, C., Yan, X., & Li, F. (2020). Cournot oligopoly game-based local energy trading considering renewable energy uncertainty costs. *Renewable Energy, 159*, 1117–1127. doi:10.1016/j.renene.2020.06.066

Zhao, G., Liu, S., Lopez, C., Lu, H., Elgueta, S., Chen, H., & Boshkoska, B. M. (2019). Blockchain technology in agri-food value chain management: A synthesis of applications, challenges and future research directions. *Computers in Industry*, *109*, 83–99. doi:10.1016/j.compind.2019.04.002

Zhou, H., Sun, Y., Qin, X., Xu, X., & Yao, R. (2020). Modeling discretionary lane-changing behavior on urban streets considering drivers' heterogeneity. *Transportation Letters*, *12*(3), 213–222. doi:10.1080/19427867.2019.1581465

Zhou, L., Pan, S., Wang, J., & Vasilakos, A. V. (2017). Machine learning on big data: Opportunities and challenges. *Neurocomputing*, *237*, 350–361. doi:10.1016/j.neucom.2017.01.026

Zhou, M., Scott, J., Chaudhury, B., Hall, L., Goldgof, D., Yeom, K. W., Iv, M., Ou, Y., Kalpathy-Cramer, J., Napel, S., Gillies, R., Gevaert, O., & Gatenby, R. (2018). Radiomics in brain tumor: Image assessment, quantitative feature descriptors, and machine-learning approaches. *AJNR. American Journal of Neuroradiology*, *39*(2), 208–216. doi:10.3174/ajnr.A5391 PMID:28982791

Zouari, D., Ruel, S., & Viale, L. (2021). Does Digitalizing the Supply Chain Contribute toIts Resilience? *International Journal of Physical Distribution & Logistics Management*, *51*(2), 149–180. doi:10.1108/IJPDLM-01-2020-0038

Zou, Q., Wang, Y., Wang, Q., Zhao, Y., & Li, Q. (2020). Deep learning-based gait recognition using smartphones in the wild. *IEEE Transactions on Information Forensics and Security*, *15*, 3197–3212. doi:10.1109/TIFS.2020.2985628

About the Contributors

Uday Kumar Kanike finished a Doctorate from Georgia State University in 2023.

Digvijay Pandey is a Lecturer, Department of Technical Education, Research Scholar, IET Lucknow, India.

* * *

Rashi Agarwal previously worked in ST Microelectronics, Noida before following the passion towards teaching and research. She is currently an Associate Professor in the Department of CSE at HBTU, Kanpur. She has a Youtube channel for Image processing lab work which has more that 3 million views.

Syed Aqeel Ahmad is currently working as a Professor and head of the Department of Civil Engineering, at Integral University, Lucknow, India. He has more than 20 research papers and is currently working in the field of Traffic Engineering. He also works as a consultant to various national as well as state transportation authorities.

M. Beulah Viji Christiana, Professor, Department of Management Studies, Panimalar Engineering College affiliated to Anna University, has a got a rich teaching experience which spans over 23 years. She is an experienced and innovative student focused professional and mentor with a proven track record of excellent teaching skills. Her academic qualification encompasses Post Graduate degrees in English Literature and Business Administration from Madurai Kamaraj University and she received her M.Phil in Management Studies from Bharathidasan University. She was awarded Ph.D in Management Studies from Mother Teresa Women's University, Kodaikanal . She has published more than 40 research articles in various national and international journals of repute as well as in conferences. Known for her extensive exposure in mentoring students through igniting their creative and innovative ability as well in stimulating them to think logically and analytically, she has guided many students in their research projects pertaining to the various functional areas of management. Besides she is also known for her role as a reviewer in various journals and books and she has authored five books.

Sampath Boopathi an accomplished individual with a strong academic background and extensive research experience. He completed his undergraduate studies in Mechanical Engineering and pursued his postgraduate studies in the field of Computer-Aided Design. Dr. Boopathi obtained his Ph.D. from Anna University, focusing his research on Manufacturing and optimization. Throughout his career, Dr. Boopathi has made significant contributions to the field of engineering. He has authored and published over 160 research articles in internationally peer-reviewed journals, highlighting his expertise and dedication to advancing knowledge in his area of specialization. His research output demonstrates his commitment to conducting rigorous and impactful research. In addition to his research publications, Dr. Boopathi has also been granted one patent and has three published patents to his name. This indicates his innovative thinking and ability to develop practical solutions to real-world engineering challenges. With 17 years of academic and research experience, Dr. Boopathi has enriched the engineering community through his teaching and mentorship roles. He has served in various engineering colleges in Tamilnadu, India, where he has imparted knowledge, guided students, and contributed to the overall academic development of the institutions. Dr. Sampath Boopathi's diverse background, ranging from mechanical engineering to computer-aided design, along with his specialization in manufacturing and optimization, positions him as a valuable asset in the field of engineering. His research contributions, patents, and extensive teaching experience exemplify his expertise and dedication to advancing engineering knowledge and fostering innovation.

Pankaj Dadheech is currently working as a Professor & Deputy Head in the Department of Computer Science & Engineering (NBA Accredited), Swami Keshvanand Institute of Technology, Management & Gramothan (SKIT), Jaipur, Rajasthan, India (Accredited by NAAC A++ Grade). He has more than 18 years of experience in teaching. He is currently working a Professor & Dy. HOD in the Department of Computer Science & Engineering (NBA Accredited), Swami Keshvanand Institute of Technology, Management & Gramothan (SKIT), Jaipur, Rajasthan, India. He has published 25 Patents at Intellectual Property India, Office of the Controller General of Patents, Design and Trade Marks, Department of Industrial Policy and Promotion, Ministry of Commerce and Industry, Government of India. He has published 8 International Patents (USA, South African, Australian, Germany) & 2 Copyrights. He has 73 publications in various International & National Journals, 63 papers in various National & International conferences. He has published 9 Books & 35 Book Chapters.

Shilpi Dubey is working as an Assistant Professor in the department of computer application in the the school of engineering and technology (UIET), CSJM University, Kanpur, UP. He has more than 22 year of experience in teaching UG and PG courses as well as the industrial experience. His research area is Marketing and General Management.

Prabjot Kaur did her Ph.D. in Operations Research: Decision Sciences from Birla Institute of Technology, Mesra, Ranchi. She is presently working as an Assistant Professor in Department of Mathematics, BIT, Mesra, Ranchi. She has a total of 14+years of experience including both research and teaching. Her area of research include Multiple Criteria Decision Making (MCDM) & Fuzzy MCDM, Intuitionistic fuzzy sets, optimization, inventory management and medical diagnosis. She has successfully completed a major UGC research project titles" A Decision support system for vendor selection problem under intuitionistic fuzzy environment". She has guided and guiding Ph.D. thesis work. she has guided around 40 master's thesis. She has total 40+ publications both in reputed national and international journals. She has presented/attended conferences and workshops in countries like France, Turkey, Maldives, Greece, etc. She has written a book titled" A fuzzy approach to vendor selection problem". She has also been reviewer in several good journals. She has been doctoral committee member for several departments of her institute. She has also given invited talks in several institutes around the country. She was in the

Board of Governors at BIT, Mesra from May 2014-2015 and presently in governing body of the institute run school. She is in board of studies RKDF University. She is in interview board committee of Usha Martin University. She was a Program Officer in NSS unit of BIT, Mesra, Ranchi.

George Williams Kennedy is a lecturer at the Faculty of Law, Topfaith University, Mkpatak Akwa Ibom State Nigeria. He is a researcher and has published several articles in international journals.

Sunil Kumar is an Assistant Professor in the Department of Information Technology at School of Engineering & Technology (UIET), CSJM University, Kanpur, India. He has more than twelve years of experience teaching computer science and engineering subjects and have rich number of publications in his research domain. He is a doctoral candidate at J.C. Bose University of Science and Technology, YMCA, Faridabad, Haryana, India. His research focuses on the identification of pulmonary diseases using machine learning and imaging techniques. He passed his Bachelor of Technology degree from the Institute of Engineering and Technology (IET), CSJM University, Kanpur, India, and his Master of Technology degree from the YMCA Institute of Engineering, Faridabad, India.

Rashmi Mahajan is a triple post graduate and is a Masters of Computer Management, Post Graduate Diploma in Business Management [Marketing] & Masters of Business Studies [Marketing]. She has completed her PhD in Marketing Management and a Diploma in Training & Development from Indian Society for Training & Development, Pune Chapter. She has around 19+ years of experience teaching undergraduate as well as post graduate students and has 3 PhD scholars pursuing their PhD under her. She has published various papers in National as well as International journals and has 2 patents and 1 copyright credited to her name. She alswo has 1 Chapter Published. She is a Professor, Head of Department of International Business & Dy. Director of BIIB in Sri Balaji University Pune (SBUP).

Abhishek Kumar Mishra, MCA, M.Tech., Ph.D, works as the Associate Professor, Department of Computer Science & Engineering, School of Computing Science & Applications in IFTM University, Moradabad, U.P., India. He has been nearly two decades of experience in teaching and his areas of specializations are Cryptography, Artificial Intelligence, Image Processing, Network security, big data. He has published eight patents and 25+ papers in International journals/ Conference proceedings. He has book Machine Learning Concepts by AGPH Books. He has participated in several National Workshop, International Conferences and Technical Events. He is regularly invited to deliver lectures in various programmes for imparting skills in research methodology to students and research scholars. He is also member of board of studies, Academic council in several universities.

Balakumar Muniandi is an Associate Professor of Practice in the Department of Electrical and Computer Engineering. He worked as a Postdoctoral research associate in Electrical and Computer science Engineering (ECE), University of Massachusetts, where he developed an energy-efficient Cellular Neuromorphic Computing (CNN) chip in deep sub-micron process. He was also worked as an R&D Engineer in Hsinchu Science Park (Silicon Valley of Taiwan), Taiwan. During his PhD, he is a key person in Indo-Taiwan bilateral project for developing "MPPT based solar battery charger system". His research interest mainly focuses on power management circuits, battery chargers, mixed signal IC designs, GaN gate driver, Smart battery management system for electric vehicles and Neuromorphic computing.

Binay Kumar Pandey is currently working as an Assistant Professor in Department of Information Technology of Govind Ballabh Pant University of Agriculture and Technology Pantnagar Uttrakhand, India. He obtained his M. Tech with Specialization in Bioinformatics from Maulana Azad National Institute of Technology Bhopal M. P. India, in 2008 . He obtained his First Degree B. Tech at the IET Lucknow (Uttar Pradesh Technical University, Uttar Pradesh and Lucknow) India, in 2005. In 2010, he joined Department of Information Technology of College of Technology in Govind Ballabh Pant University of Agriculture and Technology Pantnagar as an Assistant Professor and worked for various UG and PG projects till date. He has more than ten years of experience in the field of teaching and research. He has more than 40 publications in reputed peer journal reputed journal Springer, Inderscience (sci and socopus indexed journal and others) and 3 patent. He has many awards such PM Scholarship etc . He session chair in IEEE International Conference on Advent Trends in Multidisciplinary Research and Innovation (ICATMRI-2020) on December 30, 2020 organized by Pankaj Laddhad Institute of Technology and Management Studies; Buldhana, Maharashtra, India.

Ankush Sharma is an engineer, MBA and PhD in management with 20 + years of experience in the field of teaching and research.

Mehmet Ali Silgu has completed his PhD from Istanbul Technical University. He is currently working as an Assistant Professor in the Department of Civil Engineering at Bartin University, Turkey. He has more than 30 papers in reputed journals. His areas of research include traffic modelling, autonomous vehicles, intelligent transportation systems and public transportation.

Index

I

K

L

M

N

O

P

R

S

T

V

X

www.ingramcontent.com/pod-product-compliance
Lightning Source LLC
LaVergne TN
LVHW062142300926
849161LV00010B/2602

* 9 7 9 8 3 6 9 3 1 3 4 7 3 *